AUTOMECHANICS

Herbert E. Ellinger

Associate Professor,
Transportation Technology Department
Western Michigan University

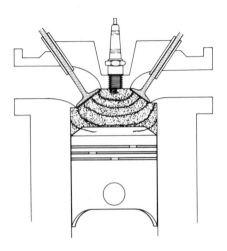

AUTOMECHANICS

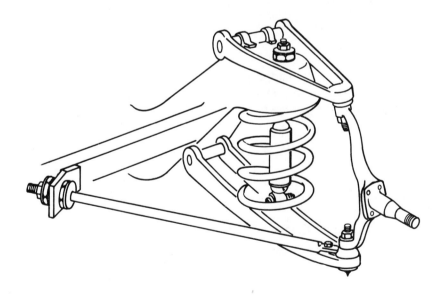

Prentice-Hall, Inc.
Englewood Cliffs, N.J.

10   9   8   7

ISBN: 0–13–055152–X

Library of Congress Catalog Card Number: 79–179623
Printed in the United States of America

PRENTICE-HALL INTERNATIONAL, INC., *London*
PRENTICE-HALL OF AUSTRALIA, PTY. LTD., *Sydney*
PRENTICE-HALL OF CANADA, LTD., *Toronto*
PRENTICE-HALL OF INDIA PRIVATE LIMITED, *New Delhi*
PRENTICE-HALL OF JAPAN, INC., *Tokyo*

Contents

Preface   ix

Acknowledgments   xi

1 Introduction to the Automobile   1

    1-1 Vehicle Design   3
    1-2 Vehicle Service   5

2 Automobile Engine Operation   7

    2-1 Basic Engine Construction   8
    2-2 Engine Cycles   8
    2-3 Engine Classification   9
    2-4 Basic Engine Specifications   14
    2-5 Engine Efficiency   16

3 Intake and Exhaust Manifolds   19

    3-1 Intake Manifold Criteria   20
    3-2 Intake Manifold Features   21
    3-3 Intake Manifold Configuration   26
    3-4 Exhaust Manifold Criteria   28
    3-5 Exhaust Manifold Compromises   28
    3-6 Mufflers   29

Contents

4 Cylinder Head and Valve Train   32

    4-1 Combustion Chamber Types   33
    4-2 Intake and Exhaust Ports   35
    4-3 Coolant Passages   36
    4-4 Lubricating Passages   38
    4-5 Intake and Exhaust Valve Mechanisms   38

5 Piston, Ring and Rod Assemblies   49

    5-1 Piston Criteria   50
    5-2 Piston Pins   56
    5-3 Piston Rings   58
    5-4 Compression Rings   58
    5-5 Oil Control Rings   61
    5-6 Connecting Rods   62

6 Shafts, Bearings and Oil Seals   66

    6-1 Crankshaft   67
    6-2 Camshaft   70
    6-3 Dynamic Oil Seals   75
    6-4 Engine Bearings   76

7 Engine Block and Gaskets   83

    7-1 Block Design   84
    7-2 Block Manufacturing   87
    7-3 Gaskets and Static Seals   90
    7-4 Block Attachments   92

8 Cooling System Operation   95

    8-1 Cooling System Requirements   96
    8-2 Cooling System Types   97
    8-3 Liquid Cooling System Design   99
    8-4 Cooling System Maintenance   104

9 Engine Lubricants and Systems   107

    9-1 Lubrication Principles   108
    9-2 Engine Lubrication Requirements   109
    9-3 Properties of Motor Oil   110
    9-4 Motor Oil Deterioration   113
    9-5 Motor Oil Additives   113
    9-6 Engine Lubrication System   114
    9-7 Crankcase Ventilation   119
    9-8 Lubrication System Maintenance   119

10 Engine Service Procedures   123

    10-1 Engine Disassembly   124
    10-2 Cleaning   127

    10-3 General Inspection   128
    10-4 Valve Condition   133
    10-5 Valve Train Condition   136
    10-6 Valve System Service   137
    10-7 Piston Condition   141
    10-8 Piston Service   144
    10-9 Shafts and Bearing Condition   148
    10-10 Shaft and Bearing Service   153
    10-11 Block Condition   153
    10-12 Block Service   154
    10-13 Engine Assembly   157

11 Mechanical Characteristics   161

    11-1 Piston Motion   162
    11-2 Engine Balance   164
    11-3 Inertia Torque   166
    11-4 Rocking Couples   167
    11-5 Multi-Cylinder Engine Balance   167
    11-6 Bearing Loads   168
    11-7 Torsional Vibration   168
    11-8 Valve Train Characteristics   169
    11-9 Valve Spring   171
    11-10 Cam Lobe Features   171
    11-11 Valve Train Flexibility   172
    11-12 Overhead Cam   173
    11-13 Lifters   173

12 Normal and Abnormal Combusiton   176

    12-1 Thermodynamic Laws   177
    12-2 Ideal Cycle   178
    12-3 Actual Cycle   178
    12-4 Normal Combustion   180
    12-5 Abnormal Combustion   181
    12-6 Gasoline Requirements   183

13 Automotive Engine Carburetors   187

    13-1 Carburetion Requirements   188
    13-2 Carburetion Principles   191
    13-3 Carburetor Circuit Details   197
    13-4 Carburetor Service   213

14 Automotive Batteries   223

    14-1 Nature of Electricity   224
    14-2 Battery Cell Operation   225
    14-3 Cell Failure   227
    14-4 Automotive Storage Battery Features   228
    14-5 Battery Maintenance   229
    14-6 Battery Testing   230
    14-7 Battery Charging   232

15 Starters and Starting Systems   234

    15-1 Series Electrical Circuit   235

15-2 Series Starter Circuit 236
15-3 Parallel Electrical Circuits 236
15-4 Electromagnetism 237
15-5 Starter Motor Principles 239
15-6 Electromagnetic Induction 239
15-7 Starter Drives 240
15-8 Starter Motor Construction 241
15-9 Starting System Testing 243

16 Charging Systems and Regulation 246

16-1 Generator Principles 247
16-2 Semiconductors-Diodes 250
16-3 Alternator Rectification 253
16-4 Testing Charging Circuits 256
16-5 Charging System Regulation 263
16-6 Transistors 266

17 Ignition System Operation 272

17-1 Ignition Timing and Engine Speed 273
17-2 Ignition Timing and Engine Load 273
17-3 Required Voltage 273
17-4 Ignition System Operation 275
17-5 Oscilloscope Measuring Instrument 276
17-6 Coil Operation 277
17-7 Primary Condenser 280
17-8 Leakage 281
17-9 Ignition Resistor 281
17-10 Transistor and C-D Ignition 282
17-11 Distributor Operation 282
17-12 Spark Plugs 286
17-13 Spark Plug Cables 288
17-14 Ignition System Testing 288
17-15 Ignition Timing 291
17-16 Distributor Testing 292
17-17 Ignition System Service 294

18 Automotive Engine Testing 298

18-1 Dynamometer in Testing 299
18-2 Dynamometer Types 300
18-3 Dynamometer Application 302
18-4 Dynamometer Limits 302
18-5 Dynamometers for Automotive Service 302
18-6 Dynamometer Function 303
18-7 Tune-Up Procedures 303
18-8 Service Requirements 305
18-9 Trouble Shooting 305

19 Control of Automotive Emissions 307

19-1 Smog 308
19-2 Vehicle Emissions 309
19-3 Emission Regulations 313

19-4 Exhaust Emission Reduction 313
19-5 Measurement of Emissions 315
19-6 Emission Control 316
19-7 Maintaining Safe Emission Levels 320

20 Automotive Clutch Operation 324

20-1 Clutch Requirements 325
20-2 Clutch Design 327
20-3 Clutch Service 332

21 Standard Transmissions 335

21-1 Transmission Requirements 335
21-2 Transmission Design 338
21-3 Transmission Operation 341
21-4 Parts Details 343
21-5 General Disassembly Procedures 344
21-6 Transmission Service 345

22 Automatic Transmissions 347

22-1 Torque Converter 348
22-2 Planetary Gears 351
22-3 Transmission Gear Trains 353
22-4 Driving and Holding Devices 355
22-5 Drive Line Features 359
22-6 Transmission Shift Requirements 362
22-7 Oil Pressure 363
22-8 Control System 365
22-9 Automatic Transmission Service 369
22-10 Automatic Transmission Fluid 372

23 Propeller Shaft and Rear Axle 375

23-1 Propeller Shaft 376
23-2 Propeller Shaft Service 380
23-3 Rear Axle Requirements 383
23-4 Differential Design Features 386
23-5 Limited Slip Differential 393
23-6 Rear Axle Service 394

24 Automotive Brake Systems 404

24-1 Brake Types 404
24-2 Braking Requirements 405
24-3 Dual Servo Drum Brake Details 409
24-4 Disc Brake Details 413
24-5 Brake Actuation Principles 414
24-6 Details of Brake Actuation Components 416
24-7 Power Brakes 424
24-8 Brake System Service 425

Contents

25 Tire Design and Operation   433

25-1 Tire Construction   434
25-2 Tire Design Features   436
25-3 Tire Operation   440
25-4 Tire Selection   442
25-5 Tire Service   444

26 Vehicle Handling and Suspension   448

26-1 Handling Requirements   449
26-2 Suspension Requirements   449
26-3 Rear Suspension Design   450
26-4 Vehicle Dynamics   452
26-5 Front Suspension Design   454
26-6 Suspension Control Devices   458
26-7 Suspension Service   461

27 Steering and Wheel Alignment   464

27-1 Camber   465
27-2 Steering Axis Inclination   465
27-3 Caster   467
27-4 Toe   469
27-5 Steering Linkages   469
27-6 Slip Angle   470
27-7 Wheel Alignment   471

27-8 Alignment Adjustment   476

28 Steering Gear and Columns   480

28-1 Standard Steering Gear   481
28-2 Power Steering Gear   483
28-3 Power Steering Pumps   487
28-4 Power Steering Service   490
28-5 Steering Column   491
28-6 Steering Column Service   495

29 Instruments and Accessories   497

29-1 Electrical Circuits   498
29-2 Lights   503
29-3 Instruments   506
29-4 Accessories   508

30 Automotive Air Conditioning   513

30-1 Air Distribution System   514
30-2 Refrigeration System   515
30-3 Air Conditioning Requirements   515
30-4 Refrigeration Controls   516
30-5 Compressor   517
30-6 Service   518

Glossary   521

Index   535

Preface

Automobiles are rapidly changing as a result of different buyer markets, rising production costs, and the passage of new state and Federal regulations. These changes continually cause an increase in the knowledge required by an automechanic. To keep abreast of these changes, the automechanic student, as well as the professional, must continue to study to update himself. Obsolete items and methods must be given up in order to allow efficient work on new and revised automotive units.

The author found that current textbooks were either too elementary or too highly engineering-oriented for the needs of his classes. With encouragement from his friends and associates, this textbook has developed from class lecture notes and from reference materials collected over a ten-year period. Much of the material has been successfully used in the author's classes and by many of his students who have become successful automechanics teachers.

This book is written as a text for advanced high

school and post high school students as well as for individuals who are interested in obtaining a more thorough understanding of automobile component operation and service. The general approach in the text is to show the operating requirements, then describe typical design features that are used to meet these requirements. This is followed by a discussion of normal service requirements and service procedures. An attempt is made to use features that are common to the majority of domestic automobiles. This is followed by discussion of variations from these basic features.

At many places within the text, it is useful to place numerical values on items described to show relationships—for example, the valve and port size relationship to cylinder bore size. The numerical value and percentages given in the text are average values used in passenger cars. Actual values for any specific component may be quite different from numerical values presented because the part's design objective may have been quite different from the average part design objective.

This text is limited to domestic passenger cars in use when the manuscript was written. Obsolete features are purposely avoided unless they are required to show the development of a current feature. Experimental and limited production designs have also been avoided, except where a high interest level dictates a need for a short discussion. The text deals specifically with automotive products that the student will most likely work with when he finishes his training.

The author has avoided discussion of specific make or model vehicle component disassembly and reassembly. The discussion is directed to the reason a part must function in a particular manner and how a malfunction of that part can be recognized. This is followed by a brief discussion of procedures that may be used to correct these malfunctions. The text is intended to be used along with detailed applicable service manual instructions.

The order in which the material is presented in the text has been successfully used in the author's classes. The text discussion parallels normal automotive component disassembly, examination, reassembly, and adjustment procedures. This gives the student an opportunity to use the text to study the component's details as he works through his shop or laboratory project. In general, the individual chapters are complete so they are useful in nearly any order. Where needed, references are given to preceding chapters for specific details not covered in that chapter.

In preparing the manuscript, all current domestic automobile shop service manuals were consulted to be sure that features covered were up-to-date. This source was backed up by detailed discussions of these features as found in papers presented to the Society of Automotive Engineers. Service information prepared by supplier companies and reference to a number of engineering textbooks was used to supplement these sources.

The author wishes to express sincere thanks to the large number of individuals who have given encouragement, provided material and criticized manuscript drafts. Special thanks is given to Mr. James VanDePolder, a colleague of the author, who supplied many very useful recommendations and to Dr. Harley Behm, the author's Department Chairman, who limited special work assignments to allow time to compile the manuscript. The unrestricted use of the automotive laboratories, automotive equipment and training aids at Western Michigan University to take many of the photographs is especially appreciated. Many thanks are given to Helen Pressey for manuscript typing. Linda, the Author's daughter-in-law, was especially helpful in reading galley proofs. Final recognition must be given to the Author's wife. Without her encouragement this book would not have been written.

Herbert E. Ellinger

Acknowledgments

A great number of individuals and organizations have cooperated in providing reference material and illustrations used in this text. The author wishes to express sincere thanks to the following organizations for their special contributions:

American Motors Corporation
American Society for Testing and Materials
A. P. Parts
The Association of American Battery
    Manufacturing, Inc.
Beckman Instruments, Incorporated
The Bendix Corporation
Bohn Aluminum and Brass Company
Borg and Beck Division, Borg Warner
    Corporation
Champion Spark Plug Company
Chrysler Motors Corporation
Chrysler-Plymouth Division of Chrysler
    Corporation
Cleveland Graphite Bronze Division, Clevite
    Corporation

Acknowledgments

Curtiss-Wright Corporation
Dana Corporation
The Dow Chemical Company
Eaton Valve Division, Eaton, Yale and Towne,
    Incorporated
Federal-Mogul Corporation
The Firestone Tire and Rubber Company
Ford Motor Company
Ford Division of Ford Marketing Corporation
Autolite-Ford Parts Division, Ford Motor
    Company
General Motors Corporation:
  AC Spark Plug Division
  Buick Motor Division
  Cadillac Motor Car Division
  Central Foundry Division
  Chevrolet Motor Division
  Delco Morane Division
  Delco-Remy Division
  Oldsmobile Division
  Saginaw Steering Gear Division

B. F. Goodrich Tire Company
The Goodyear Tire and Rubber Company
Gould-National Batteries, Inc.
Greenlee Brothers and Company
Independent Battery Manufacturers Association,
    Inc.
Johnson Products, Inc.
Kelsey-Hays Company
Modine Manufacturing Company
Monroe Auto Equipment Company
Moog Industries, Inc.
Muskegon Piston Ring Company
The Prestolite Company
Raybestos-Manhattan
Sealed Power Corporation
Society of Automotive Engineers
Sunnen Products Company
TRW, Michigan Division
TRW, Replacement Division
Union Carbide Corporation
UniRoyal, Incorporated
Walker Manufacturing Company

AUTOMECHANICS

AUTOMOBILES

chapter 1

Introduction to the Automobile

"Why did they build a car **that** way?" is a common question asked by many students.

To understand the reasons why a vehicle is built in a certain way, it is necessary to know some of the questions a manufacturer must answer before he has his engineers design a car. Each major domestic automobile manufacturer produces a number of body styles, body sizes, engine sizes, transmission types, colors, optional equipment, etc. Vehicles are obviously built to meet differing owner needs. What is best for one owner may be entirely inadequate for another. For instance, the vehicle requirements of a single man are quite different from the requirements of a married man with four children.

The first thing a manufacturer must consider is the specific job the vehicle, that is to be designed, should be capable of doing. This is called the *design objective*. For example, is the vehicle going to be required to carry a heavy load at low speeds or a light load at high speeds. Each of these operations obviously requires a different type of vehicle. The design objective may be more vivid if the reader considers a race car. It is not driven to the track, but towed or transported on a trailer or truck. A race car is not designed to operate on the highway and would be very difficult to drive in city traffic. The tow car, on the other hand, will operate satisfactorily in traffic, but would be a very poor race car. When discussing which car is best, a person must always state what type of operation the vehicle is designed for.

When designing a vehicle, the engineer must consider maximum required acceleration, speed, economy, load to be carried, ride and handling characteristics, size, etc., that will be expected from the vehicle. The finished vehicle is a blend of these components, one feature traded off against another, to produce the final product. The maximum limits of these features are called the *design parameters*.

The next step to be considered is durability. How many miles should the vehicle operate before service is required? For example, a passenger car is designed to operate over 100,000 highway miles before major service is required. An Indianapolis

race car needs to complete only 500 racing miles. A dragster can make 100 quarter mile runs in 25 miles of driving. Each part of the vehicle has a specific design life, which takes into account its operating load, speed, temperature, lubrication, etc. For example, ball bearing manufacturers provide tables which list the ball bearing life expectancy based on operating speed and load. Overloading reduces bearing life expectancy and underloading increases life expectancy.

Once the design requirements are known, the manufacturer must consider cost. With the exception of special purpose vehicles, such as factory racing team cars, vehicles are designed to be sold to the general public in competition with vehicles made by other manufacturers. One of the best selling points is low price. Therefore, one of the major design objectives is to lower the price without compromising the design parameters. In some cases, a large reduction in cost can be accomplished with only a slight compromise in a design objective and still keep the vehicle competitive.

Sometimes, a manufacturer does not update his products as rapidly as his customers would like. This often happens with engines that are mass produced by automatic machines in a plant designed especially for that engine. Minor changes can be

Fig. 1-1 Automatic engine production machinery (Greenlee Brothers & Company).

done by readjusting the tooling. In some cases, it is more economical to build a new plant than to revise an existing one when a completely new engine is to be built.

One method of reducing cost is to change the manufacturing method. A forged part may be replaced by a cast part and a cast part is often replaced by a stamping or sintered metal part. In this way, the cost of part is reduced by reducing the number of manufacturing operations that are required to be done on the part before it can be used in the vehicle. This type of process change is illustrated throughout this text.

Plastics are replacing metal for non-structural parts having complex shapes. In some cases, entire vehicles are made from fiberglass and plastic. Plastic parts generally reduce manufacturing costs when made in quantity, as well as reducing weight.

Many product features are the result of the engineer's preference. These preferences are usually based upon previous satisfactory performance of the design. There is a tendency to continue those features until they becomes uneconomical or unpopular, or until new engineering management takes over. An example of this was Ford's use of a transverse spring for a number of years after other manufacturers dropped it. Engineering preference has generally been pushed into the background by the other design requirements that the vehicle must meet.

1-1 VEHICLE DESIGN

Vehicle design must start with occupant seating. No matter what the designer wishes, the vehicle must have room for the driver, passengers and load. The vehicle must have enough engine power to move the load at the desired speed and enough braking power to safely stop the vehicle. While moving, the vehicle must be controllable, so it can be driven to follow changes in the roadway and traffic conditions.

Body and Frame. The occupants should be provided with a comfortable ride to minimize fatigue. The seats must be firm with adequate support. Driver visibility must be excellent in all directions. Noise level and vibration should be as low as possible.

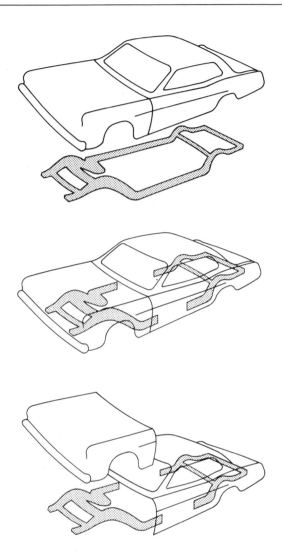

Fig. 1-2 Body and frame construction methods. (a) Separate body and frame, (b) unitized construction, (c) unitized body with stub front frame.

Different construction methods are used among the manufacturers and their vehicle models. Separate body and frame construction has been used for the longest time. In this type of construction, the engine, drive line, and running gear are firmly fastened to the frame; then the body is mounted to the frame with insulators to minimize noise and vibration transfer.

A second type of construction is the unitized body, in which the frame is part of the body structure. Body panels add strength to the frame pieces

3

that form part of the structure. The running gear and drive line are attached with large soft insulators to minimize noise and vibration. If the insulators are too soft they tend to give the vehicle a spongy ride, and if they are too hard they do not insulate properly. Careful insulator design and location will produce a vehicle that is satisfactory to drive and ride in.

A third type of construction combines features from both of the preceding types. It uses a stub frame from the fire wall forward and a unitized body from the fire wall back. The unitized portion is very rigid, while the stub frame provides an opportunity for good insulation. This construction method is generally applied to larger body styles.

Manufacturers select their construction method by deciding which type is most economical for them to build, while still providing the noise, vibration, and ride characteristics they want to have in their vehicle. The largest number of standard-size vehicles use separate body and frame construction. The majority of small vehicles use unitized construction.

Engine. Most automobiles use a gasoline fueled reciprocating engine mounted ahead of the passengers. This location seems to provide the most room for occupants and load, as well as being a safety factor in a head-on collision. It also allows placement of the cooling radiator at the front of the car with a minimum of ducting and hoses. Engines have been placed behind the rear axle (rear engine), and between the occupants and the rear axle (midship). Neither has extensive application in domestic automobiles.

Some specialty automobiles use a different type of engine. The diesel engine is used in some taxicab fleets, because it uses considerably less fuel than the gasoline engine when operated at low speeds. It is quite common in Europe, where fuel costs are much greater than in the United States. The rotating combustion chamber engine is gaining popularity in small European and Japanese cars. Its use will probably increase. Turbine engines show promise, especially in commercial vehicles. They are powerful, lightweight, and low on harmful emissions. They are ideally suited to replace some diesel engines in over-the-road load carrying vehicles.

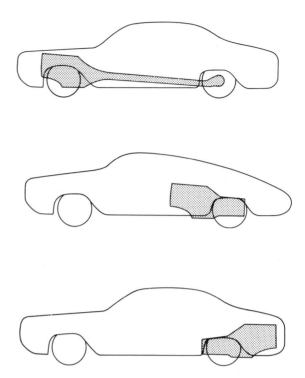

Fig. 1-3 Engine locations. (a) Front, (b) midship, (c) rear.

Drive Line. The drive line carries power to the drive wheels. A clutch or torque converter is connected to the engine crankshaft to provide a means to effectively disconnect the engine from the drive line, so the engine can idle while the vehicle is stopped. It is engaged to drive the vehicle.

A transmission is located directly behind the clutch or torque converter. Its function is to provide gear reduction for high torque to start the vehicle moving and drive it up steep grades. The transmission will also provide a reverse gear for backing the vehicle. Gear range selection may be either manual or automatic.

In front-engine vehicles, the transmission is located under the front floor pan. A propeller shaft is required to carry the engine power to the rear axle. It has universal joints on each end to provide flexibility as the suspension position changes.

A differential on the rear axle splits the incoming power to each drive wheel. This also allows the drive wheels to turn at different speeds as they go over bumps and around corners.

Vehicles with front wheel drive, or with midship or rear engines usually combine the transmission and differential, so they do not have a propeller shaft.

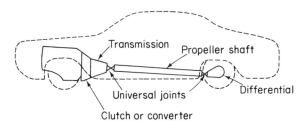

Fig. 1-4 Power drive line.

Running Gear. The four tire footprints are the only place the vehicle touches the road. All of the engine power, steering and braking forces must operate through these tire-to-road contact footprint areas. Any time the tire does not contact the road or skidding begins, vehicle control is reduced or lost. The suspension's job is to keep the tire in contact with the road as much of the time as possible, even on rough roads, while supporting the vehicle.

The suspension consists of springs, shock absorbers, and linkages or arms. The suspension system must be strong enough to resist axle twisting from high engine power and from brake reaction.

Brakes are mounted inside the wheels. Hydraulic force from the brake pedal pushes the brake shoes against a case iron surface with enough force to slow wheel rotation. This, of course, slows the vehicle. Brake designs are either drum type or disc type. Most applications using disc brakes have disc brakes on the front and drum brakes on the rear.

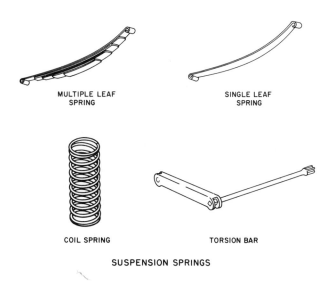

MULTIPLE LEAF SPRING

SINGLE LEAF SPRING

COIL SPRING

TORSION BAR

SUSPENSION SPRINGS

Fig. 1-5 Suspension spring types (Monroe Auto Equipment Company).

The running gear is supported with either coil, leaf, or torsion bar springs. Coil springs are most popular. They require links and arms to hold the axle in position. Leaf springs can hold the axle in position without an additional device. Torsion bars require the same type of support as coil springs.

1-2 VEHICLE SERVICE

A vehicle is only serviced when preventative maintenance is due, when the owner wants a change in performance, appearance, or comfort items, or when there is a specific problem. Preventative maintenance includes service that is done at regular intervals, so the operator will not encounter problems. This service includes oil changes, lubrication, tune up, brake adjustment, tire rotation, etc. It is routine when done according to standard operating procedures.

Change in performance, appearance and comfort items usually involve installing a manufactured item such as power brakes, air conditioners, or radios. In most cases, these items are available in a kit with all the necessary parts and detailed installation instructions. Items may need to be replaced as well as added to give a performance change. This type of service would include changing cylinder heads, manifolds, differential gears, wheels, tires, etc. Here again, the service is routine. The technician knows exactly what the customer wants. Unfortunatly technicians do not always follow the manufacturer's installation and adjustment directions. If the improperly installed part does not function correctly, the manufacturer is usually blamed and not the improper installation.

Most service work involves a repair of the part causing the customer's problem. This kind of work should start with a clear understanding of what the customer is concerned about. He wants his car repaired so it will operate correctly at a minimum cost to him.

The majority of vehicle problems can be corrected by straightforward service procedures. These involve checking the system to identify the problem, testing to pinpoint the cause, making the required repairs then rechecking for proper operation. In some cases, the cause of the problem is extremely difficult to pinpoint. Under these conditions a technician's detailed knowledge of the parts' functions and their interrelationships with the other parts, along with his ability to use test equipment, allows him to rapidly and accurately correct the problem.

The rest of this book is designed to provide the technician with a background so he understands why the vehicle parts are made as they are, what the parts are required to do, and how they accomplish their required task.

Review Questions
Chapter 1

1. Why does cost play such an important part in vehicle design?

2. What things are done to keep vehicle cost down?

3. What are the advantages and disadvantages of the three body construction methods?

4. Why is front-engine placement used in most automobile applications?

5. What is the main job of the running gear?

6. When is service done on automobiles?

7. What must a technician know before he can correct a customer's complaint?

Quiz 1

1. What is the main reason for differences that exist in passenger cars?
   a. design objectives
   b. manufacturing problems
   c. engineering preference
   d. competitive advantage.

2. The basic reason for changing the manufacturing method of a part is usually to
   a. make use of new materials
   b. modernize the design
   c. change manufacturer's tooling
   d. reduce cost.

3. When used, unitized frames are usually incorporated in
   a. small compact cars
   b. intermediate cars
   c. full size cars
   d. large luxury cars.

4. Most domestic automobiles use a front engine and rear driving wheels. A major reason that this is done is to give the
   a. best tire traction
   b. best vehicle handling characteristics
   c. most room for passengers and luggage
   d. most easily serviced arrangement.

5. Diesel engines are used in some passenger cars to
   a. increase reliability
   b. reduce fuel costs
   c. increase high torque outputs
   d. reduce maintenance.

6. The main function of the clutch is to
   a. shift gears
   b. provide smooth vehicle starts
   c. disconnect the engine and drive line
   d. allow the engine to idle.

7. The universal joint in the drive shaft is necessary to
   a. provide an easy method to disconnect the drive line
   b. carry engine torque to the drive wheels
   c. produce a smooth turning drive line
   d. allow drive wheel suspension free movement.

8. All vehicle operational control is dependent upon
   a. engine, brakes, and steering
   b. steering and suspension design
   c. driver's reaction time
   d. tire-to-road footprint friction.

9. A major objective of suspension design as applied to vehicle operation is to
   a. support the load
   b. keep the wheels on the road
   c. provide a soft ride
   d. absorb shock.

10. Vehicle problems can usually be corrected by
    a. preventative maintenance
    b. installing new parts
    c. straightforward service procedures
    d. making slight adjustments.

chapter 2

Automobile Engine Operation

Energy is required to produce power. Natural energy, such as water power, is converted to useful rotating mechanical power through mechanical devices such as water wheels and turbines. Chemical energy in fuel is converted to heat by burning the fuel at a controlled rate. This process is called *combustion*. When combustion occurs in a space separated from the power producing chamber, the engine is said to be an *external combustion* engine. If combustion occurs within the power chamber, the engine is called an *internal combustion* engine. Engines used in automobiles are internal combustion heat engines. They convert gasoline's chemical energy into heat within a power chamber that is called a *combustion chamber*. Heat energy released in the combustion chamber raises the temperature of the combustion gases within the chamber. The increase in gas temperature causes the gas pressure to increase. The pressure developed is applied to a piston head or a turbine wheel to produce a usable mechanical force that is converted into useful mechanical power.

The internal combustion engine has been used since some of the first self propelled vehicles. Its development over the years has proven it to be the most reliable engine for vehicles at a reasonable cost. Recently there has been a great deal of concern over the damage being done to our environment by the emissions (exhaust gases) of automotive engines. A great amount of engineering time has been spent to develop an external combustion engine with a very low level of harmful vehicle emissions. There are a large number of complicated problems to be solved. They include problems with the heat transfer medium, warm up time, fluid sealing, boiler, condenser, transfer pumps and engine weight.

2-1 BASIC ENGINE CONSTRUCTION

A basic automotive engine has a piston that moves up and down, or reciprocates, in a cylinder. The piston is attached to a crankshaft with a connecting rod. This arrangement allows the piston to reciprocate in the cylinder as the crankshaft rotates. The pressure developed in the combustion chamber will push the piston downward and, thereby, force the crankshaft to rotate.

The combustion chamber above the piston must be recharged with a fresh combustible mixture after each combustion, so valves are provided. The intake valve allows a fresh charge to enter for the combustion cycle. An exhaust valve releases the spent gases after the piston has moved to the bottom of the stroke. Valves are opened and closed at the correct time by a camshaft driven from the crankshaft.

Moving parts in contact with each other will wear rapidly unless they are lubricated. Every engine has a lubricating system that provides an oil film between the bearing surfaces to prevent contact.

A cooling system is required to remove excess heat from the metal surrounding the combustion chamber. If the heat were to remain, the parts would overheat, expand, and seize.

A fuel system and an ignition system are also required to supply the correct air/fuel mixture ratio and to ignite it at the proper instant.

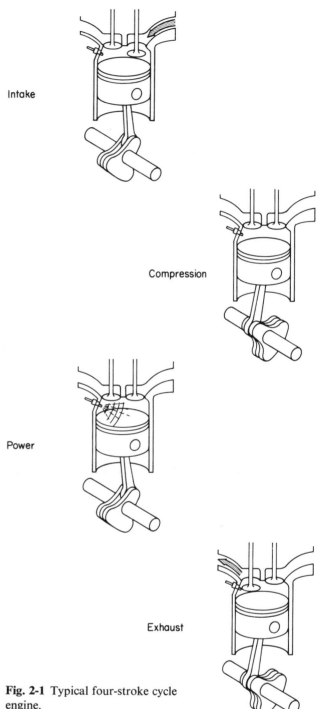

Intake

Compression

Power

Exhaust

Fig. 2-1 Typical four-stroke cycle engine.

2-2 ENGINE CYCLES

Engine cycles are identified by the number of piston strokes required to complete the cycle. A piston stroke is a one-way piston movement between top and bottom of the cylinder. Most automobile engines use a four-stroke cycle.

The four-stroke cycle starts with the piston at top of the stroke. An intake valve opens as the piston moves down on the first, or *intake stroke*, allowing the combustible charge to enter the cylinder. The intake valve closes near bottom center and the piston then moves up on the second stroke, or *compression stroke*, to squeeze the charge into a small space. Near the top of the compression stroke, the spark plug ignites the charge so the fuel will burn. The heat released raises the charge pressure and the pressure pushes the piston down on the third, or *power stroke*. Near the bottom of the stroke, the exhaust valve opens to release the spent exhaust gases as the piston moves up on the fourth, or *exhaust stroke* to complete the 720° four-stroke cycle. The piston is then in a position to start the next cycle with another intake stroke. The four-stroke cycle is repeated every other crankshaft revolution.

Some small engines use a two-stroke cycle. This cycle starts with piston at top center on the power stroke. As the piston nears the bottom of the power stroke, the exhaust opens to release the spent gases. The intake opens very shortly after the exhaust opens and a charge is forced into the cylinder. This aids in pushing the exhaust gases from the cylinder. Both valves close as the piston starts up on the compression stroke. The two-stroke cycle engine has a power stroke each crankshaft revolution.

2-3 ENGINE CLASSIFICATION

Internal combustion engines are described by referring to a number of their different design features. These can be broken down into classifications that can be readily recognized.

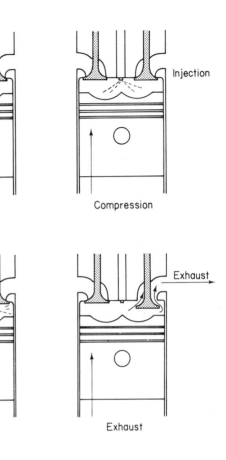

(a)

Fig. 2-2 Typical open chamber four- and two-stroke cycle diesels.

(b)

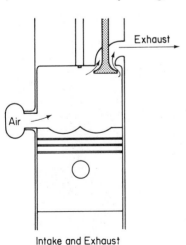

Intake and Exhaust

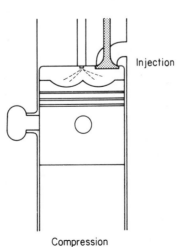

Compression

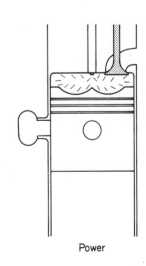

Power

Operating Cycles. Four-stroke cycles and two-stroke cycles, as previously described, are the most common engine operating cycles. A third cycle, the turbine cycle used in gas turbine engines, is beginning to appear in ground vehicles. This cycle is continuous, with a constant quantity of compressed air and fuel being supplied to the combustion chamber. A constant flow of high pressure gas from the combustion chamber is directed through a turbine to produce a usable rotating force.

Ignition Types. Engines are also classified according to their type of ignition. Most automobiles use gasoline mixed with correct proportions of air, as a fuel. This mixture is then ignited with a spark plug at the correct instant in the cycle. It is, therefore, called a spark ignited, or SI engine. Heavy-duty vehicles may use less expensive distillate as a fuel. In these engines, the air is compressed considerably more than in spark ignited engines. It, therefore, becomes quite hot. Near the end of the compression stroke, distillate fuel is injected under high pressure into this hot compressed air. The fuel ignites spontaneously, releasing heat which further increases the combustion chamber pressure. An engine with this type of ignition is called a compression ignition, or CI engine.

Cooling Methods. Most automobile engines use a liquid, usually water, plus an antifreeze, to maintain the engine at a constant operating temperature. This is done by transferring heat from the metal surrounding the combustion chamber to the liquid. The cooling liquid flows to a radiator where the heat is removed by running the liquid through thin-walled tubes that are exposed to a flow of atmospheric air. This system is called a *liquid cooling* system.

Some automobile engines maintain a constant operating temperature by transferring heat from the metal around the combustion chamber directly to the air without an intermediate liquid cooling

Fig. 2-3 Cooling system types (a) Liquid, (b) air. (Chevrolet Motor Division, General Motors Corporation).

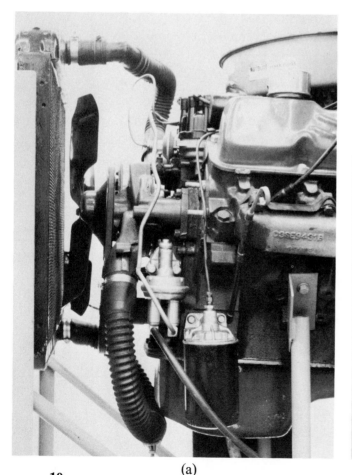

(a)

(b)

medium. This is done by ducting air across fins that surround the combustion chamber. Cooling the engine by this method is called *air cooling*.

Engine Configuration. The power that an engine produces is in direct proportion to the volume of air that it uses. Engine designers may change this volume by altering the piston displacement in each cylinder, by changing the number of cycles per minute, by better air flow design or by the number of cylinders used. Materials, manufacturing processes, and performance requirements are used to adjust the engine design and operating characteristics for each application requirement.

The modern automobile uses four, six, or eight cylinders. Generally speaking, as more power is required from the engine, more cylinders are used. In the evolution of the internal combustion spark ignited engine, the four- and six-cylinder engines most often use an inline cylinder arrangement; that is, the cylinder centerlines are parallel, one next to the other. They are usually located within a single casting, called a block, and the connecting rods are connected to a common crankshaft.

Eight-cylinder engines are usually made in a form that might be considered two four-cylinder blocks set at a 90° angle to each other, using a common crankshaft. The two blocks are in one casting in this engine, forming a V-8 arrangement.

Several rear engine drive automobiles use a four- or six-cylinder engine with half of the cylinders at 180° to the other half. The cylinder centerlines are usually in a horizontal plane and they are, therefore, called horizontally opposed engines.

Notable examples of still different combinations in production are V-4, V-6, V-12, V-16, and inline straight eight. These are usually limited production engines and are built to serve special operational requirements.

Valve Arrangement. Engines may be classified according to the location and type of the valve system employed. Valves may be placed in the block adjacent to the cylinder. This allows the inlet and outlet passages, called ports, to be short and surrounded by coolant. The head is a simple top for the cylinder. It includes a passage for coolant, an opening for a spark plug and a cast impression that forms the top of the combustion chamber. With both valves located on one side of the cylinder, a

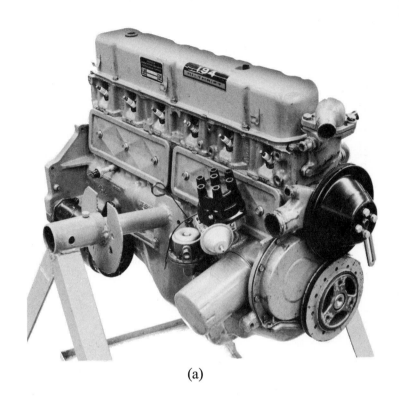

(a)

Fig. 2-4 Cylinder arrangements (a) inline, (b) 90° V.

(b)

cross-section view would be an L-shape. This type of valve arrangement is, therefore, called an L-head or flat-head engine.

A modification of this type of engine has one valve on each side of the cylinder. It is called a T-head engine because of its appearance in a cross-sectional view.

Most current automotive engines have both valves in the cylinder head. This reduces the cost of the engine block and allows better engine breathing by providing a large inlet port on one side of the head and a large exhaust port on the other side. The head is a large complex casting that provides openings for valve ports, coolant, valve actuating devices and lubricant. The added cost and complexity of this type of cylinder head is offset by the reduced cost of the block and by the added performance produced by better engine breathing. This type of engine may either be called an *overhead-valve* engine or an *I-head* engine.

An engine combining the features of both the L-head and the I-head engines has been produced. One valve is in the head and the other valve is in the block. This is called an *F-head* engine. It has many of the advantages of both L-head and I-head engines, but it also has many of their disadvantages as well. The F-head engine has seen limited production.

Camshaft Location. In engines that have valves in the block, the valves are operated by a camshaft located directly below the valves. In an I-head engine, with valves in the head, the camshaft is usually located in the block. An alternate location in some engines places the camshaft above the valves on the head. This is called an *overhead-cam* engine.

When the camshaft is located in the block, the overhead valves are driven through a lifter, pushrod, and rocker arm assembly. When the camshaft is located on the head, the valves are actuated by some type of cam follower.

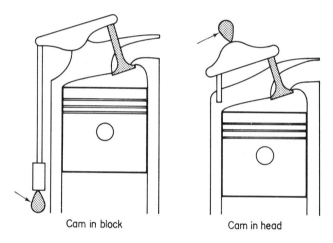

Cam in block   Cam in head

Fig. 2-6 Cam locations.

Rotating Engines. Two relatively new engine types only partly fit into the preceding classifications. One is the rotating combustion chamber engine and the other is the turbine. Both have continuously rotating members, which eliminates the stop and start reciprocating motion of the piston engine.

The rotary combustion chamber engine operates on the four cycle principle. It consists of a three-lobe rotor that turns with an eccentric motion within a two-lobe epitrochoid-shaped housing. A changing volume results as the rotor turns, sweeping around inside the housing. Valves are located in the housing, so that gases may be inducted and exhausted at the correct point in the cycle. A spark plug is properly placed in the housing so that ignition will occur at the correct instant to produce

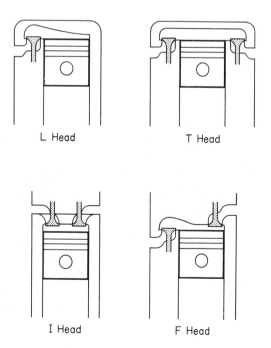

L Head   T Head

I Head   F Head

Fig. 2-5 Valve arrangements.

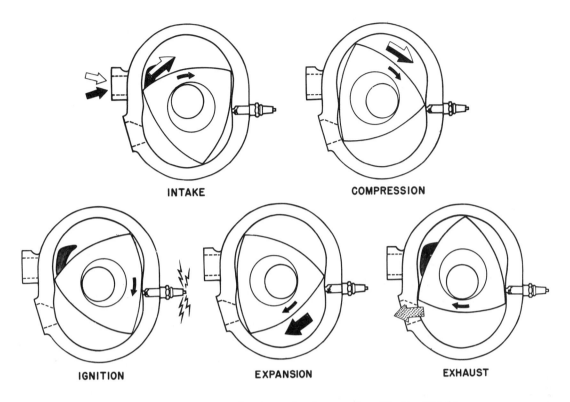

INTAKE   COMPRESSION

IGNITION   EXPANSION   EXHAUST

Fig. 2-7 Rotating combustion chamber engine (Curtiss-Wright Corporation).

Fig. 2-8 Schematic of a vehicle turbine engine (Chrysler Motors Corporation).

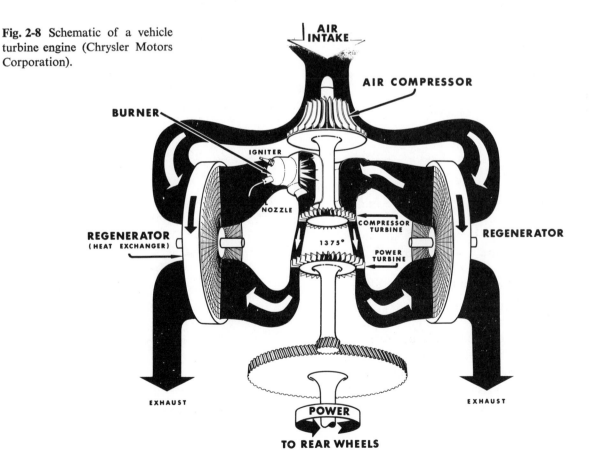

AIR INTAKE

AIR COMPRESSOR

BURNER

IGNITER

NOZZLE

COMPRESSOR TURBINE

1375°

POWER TURBINE

REGENERATOR (HEAT EXCHANGER)

REGENERATOR

EXHAUST   EXHAUST

POWER

TO REAR WHEELS

maximum effective combustion chamber pressure, forcing the rotor to turn. The rotor is connected by gears to the output shaft.

The ground turbine has four major parts: compressor, combustor, or burner, compressor-turbine, and power-turbine. The compressor and compressor-turbine are mounted on a single shaft. The compressor-turbine spins the compressor to blow air into the combustor where the fuel is added. Once ignited, the combustion flame continues as long as the correct air/fuel mixture is present. The expanding gases flow through the compressor-turbine to supply power for the compressor, and then on to the power-turbine. The power-turbine is connected to a transmission to deliver power to the drive wheels.

2-4 BASIC ENGINE SPECIFICATIONS

A number of commonly used specifications are used to describe and compare engines. They include terms such as displacement, compression ratio, torque, and horsepower.

An engine's displacement is the volume swept or displaced by the pistons in one revolution of the crankshaft. Engine displacement is calculated by multiplying the cylinder's cross-sectional area by the stroke and the number of cylinders. Use the following equation to calculate engine displacement:

Displacement (in^3)

$$= .785 \times \text{bore (in)}^2 \times \text{stroke} \times \text{no. of cylinders}$$

Example: What is the displacement of an engine that has a 4 inch bore and a 4 inch stroke?

Displacement $= .785 \times 16$ sq in $\times 4$ in $\times 8$ cyl

$$= 402 \text{ cubic inches}$$

Compression ratio is often confused with displacement because each is related to piston position and to cylinder volumes. In most engines, when the piston is at the top of its stroke, it is flush with the top of the block. The combustion chamber

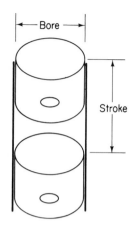

Fig. 2-9 Cylinder dimensions.

volume above the piston at the top of the stroke is the cavity in the head modified by the shape of the piston head. This volume, added to the displacement of one cylinder, will give the volume above the piston at the bottom of the stroke. The compression ratio is the ratio of the volume in the cylinder above the piston when the piston is at the bottom of the stroke to the volume in the cylinder above the piston when the piston is at the top of the stroke.

Compression Ratio

$$= \frac{\text{Volume in cylinder at the bottom of the stroke}}{\text{Volume in cylinder at the top of the stroke}}$$

Example: What is the compression ratio of an engine with 50.3 cubic inches displacement in one cylinder and a combustion chamber cavity of 6.7 cubic inches?

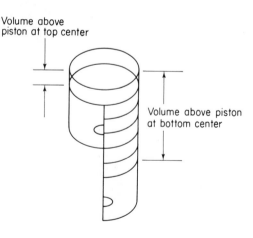

Fig. 2-10 Compression ratio.

$$\text{Compression ratio} = \frac{(50.3 + 6.7) \text{ cubic inches}}{6.7 \text{ cubic inches}}$$

$$= \frac{57.0}{6.7} = 8.5$$

An increase in compression ratio increases the compression pressure and temperature of the charge. When the charge ignites, it produces higher combustion pressure that gives the engine more turning effort or torque. High compression ratios are limited by rapid fuel decomposition (knock or detonation). High octane rating fuels are able to operate knock free, because they do not decompose at these high pressures and temperatures.

Torque is the work produced by an engine resulting from the pressure on the top of all of the pistons which push on the crankshaft through their connecting rods. The actual torque of the crankshaft varies as the cylinders move to different cycle positions. Engine torque is the average torque produced by all of the cylinders throughout the cycle, and it is measured in pound-feet. It is the number of pounds at the end of a one-foot lever arm that would be required to balance the engine's twisting effort. This twisting effort goes through the vehicle drive line to turn the drive wheels. When the twisting force or torque is greater than the tire's friction on the road, the wheels will spin as the vehicle is accelerated. If the torque is not great enough to drive the vehicle up a steep incline, the transmission can be shifted into a different gear ratio to multiply torque. When torque is doubled by the transmission, the output speed is halved. To maintain constant speed, the torque must balance the load. With a constant torque, an increase in load will slow the engine, while a decrease in load will allow the engine to speed up.

Power is work done in a given period of time. The quicker a given amount of work is accomplished, the more power required. One *horse-power* is the amount of energy required to do 33,000 foot-pounds of work in one minute. If this same work were done in fifteen seconds, it would require four horsepower.

Engine horsepower is measured in two ways. One is to use electronic equipment to indicate average combustion pressures within the cylinder, then apply these pressures to the piston on each power stroke. This is called indicated horsepower. It can be calculated by the formula:

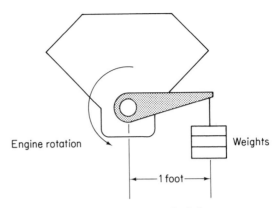

Fig. 2-11 Torque principle.

$$\text{Indicated Horsepower} = \frac{P L A N K}{33,000}$$

When:

P = Average indicated pressure
L = Length of stroke in feet
A = Area of cylinder cross section
N = Number of power strokes per min.
K = Number of cylinders

Example: If an eight cylinder engine with a 4-inch bore and 4-inch stroke produces its maximum horsepower at 4400 rpm, what is its indicated horsepower when the average indicated pressure is 131 psi?

Indicated Horsepower

$$= \frac{131 \text{ lb/in}^2 \times .33 \text{ ft} \times 12.6 \text{ in}^2 \times 2200 \times 8}{33,000 \text{ ft lb/hp}}$$

$$= 292 \text{ hp}$$

Engine horsepower relates output torque to engine speed. If torque were to remain constant, the power an engine produced would be directly proportional to speed. However, torque does not remain constant. The actual horsepower the engine produces is measured on a dynamometer and is called brake horsepower. Torque and speed readings obtained from the dynamometer are substituted in the following formula to calculate brake horsepower:

$$\text{Brake Horsepower} = \frac{\text{Torque} \times \text{RPM}}{5252}$$

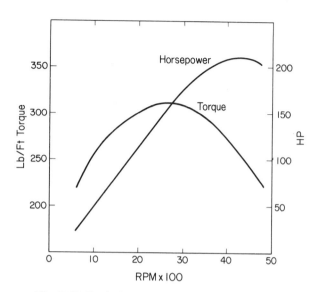

Fig. 2-12 Typical torque and horsepower curves.

Example: What horsepower is an engine developing when it is producing a torque of 310 pound-feet when running at 4400 rpm?

$$\text{Brake horsepower} = \frac{310 \times 4400}{5252}$$

$$= 260 \text{ hp}$$

The constant 5252 is developed from the angular rotation of the crankshaft and the work equivalent to one horsepower.

Indicated horsepower is greater than brake horsepower. Their difference is considered a loss to friction and is called friction horsepower.

$$\text{Friction horsepower} = \text{IHP} - \text{BHP}$$

Example: What is the friction horsepower of an engine that produces 292 indicated horsepower and 260 brake horsepower?

$$\text{Friction Horsepower} = 292 - 260 = 32 \text{ hp}$$

2-5 ENGINE EFFICIENCY

Efficiency is output divided by input. It is commonly said that one engine is more efficient than another engine. Any expression of engine efficiency must be related to some input and output values.

Horsepower values may be used to compare engines. Brake horsepower divided by indicated horsepower gives the engine's mechanical efficiency. It is expressed as:

$$\text{Mechanical efficiency} = \frac{\text{BHP (output)}}{\text{IHP (input)}}$$

Example: What is the mechanical efficiency of an engine that produces 292 indicated horsepower and 260 brake horsepower?

$$\text{Mechanical efficiency} = \frac{260}{292} = 89\%$$

Volumetric efficiency relates the actual air consumption of an engine to the maximum possible air consumption at that speed.

Volumetric efficiency

$$= \frac{\text{Actual air consumed (output)}}{\text{Maximum possible air consumption (input)}}$$

Example: What is the volumetric efficiency of an engine that will displace 510 cubic feet per min and uses 460 cubic feet per min?

$$\text{Volumetric efficiency} = \frac{460}{510} = 90\%$$

Any change in throttle position, engine speed, or engine load will change volumetric efficiency. At slow speeds and full throttle there is sufficient time to fill the combustion chamber with air at atmospheric pressure. As engine speed increases, there is less time for the air to move through the intake valve so volumetric efficiency decreases. Volumetric efficiency also drops as the throttle is closed to restrict inflowing air. The speed and torque that an engine produces is controlled by changing the engine's volumetric efficiency with the throttle.

A third type of engine efficiency is thermal efficiency. This relates the maximum available heat energy in the fuel to the brake horsepower heat equivalent that the engine produces. One horsepower is equivalent to 42.4 BTU per minute. Gasoline has approximately 110,000 BTU per gallon. Using these figures, the engine thermal efficiency can be calculated by the formula:

Thermal efficiency

$$= \frac{\text{BHP} \times 42.4 \text{ (BTU/min)}}{110,000 \text{ (BTU/gal)} \times \text{Gal used/min}}$$

Example: What is the thermal efficiency of an engine developing 40 horsepower at 60 mph using 4 gal of gas per hour (15 mi per gal or 1/15 gal per min)?

Thermal efficiency

$$= \frac{40 \text{ hp} \times 42.4 \text{ BTU/min}}{110,000 \text{ BTU/gal} \times 1/15 \text{ gal/min}}$$

$$= 23.1\%$$

Maximum gasoline engine thermal efficiency is approximately 25%. The rest of the heat energy is used to overcome friction or is expelled with the exhaust or through the cooling system.

The primary value of these formulas is to help the technician grasp an understanding of terms used to describe engines as well as being an aid to understanding engine operating principles. They can be of further use to compare engine operation characteristics between two engines.

Review Questions
Chapter 2

1. Define piston stroke.

2. Describe the four-stroke cycle.

3. Use the engine classification methods to classify two engines that you are familiar with.

4. What are the common cylinder arrangements?

5. What are the common valve arrangements?

6. Calculate the displacement of an engine with known bore and stroke.

7. How do displacement and compression ratio differ?

8. Why is a high compression ratio desirable?

9. What limits the usable compression ratio?

10. How is torque measured?

11. How much torque is required to maintain a constant speed?

12. How does power differ from torque?

13. How does indicated horsepower differ from brake horsepower?

14. What is the basic formula used to measure any type of efficiency?

Quiz 2

1. The force that causes the engine to run is
   a. an explosion in the cylinder
   b. high pressure gases pressing on the piston
   c. gasoline's chemical energy when mixed with air
   d. high compression ratio with gasoline and air.

2. During engine design the firing order is determined by the
   a. cylinder arrangement
   b. crankshaft design
   c. valve placement
   d. camshaft position.

It is unfortunate that an engine has not, as yet, been designed to meet these ideal requirements under all operating conditions. For minimum manufacturing cost, tolerances must be quite large so the valve and ignition timing between cylinders is not exactly the same. The charge flowing through the manifold passages encounter different passage sizes, angles, different temperatures and different flow rates. All of these tend to make the charge quality and quantity supplied to each cylinder somewhat different, especially at low engine speeds. Intake manifolds that are carefully designed will provide more uniform charge distribution to the cylinders and, therefore, help to make the engine run smoothly, but are costly to manufacture.

3-1 INTAKE MANIFOLD CRITERIA

The carburetor delivers finely divided droplets of liquid fuel into the incoming air in a combustible air/fuel ratio. These particles start to evaporate as they leave the carburetor. With the engine operating at the most efficient conditions, about 60% of the fuel will be vaporized by the time the charge reaches the combustion chamber. This means that there will be some liquid droplets suspended in the charge throughout the manifold. The droplets stay in suspension at high mixture velocities through the manifold. At maximum horsepower, these velocities may reach 300 feet per second. Separation of the droplets from the air occurs when the mixture

Fig. 3-1 Fuel delivered to the manifold in droplets.

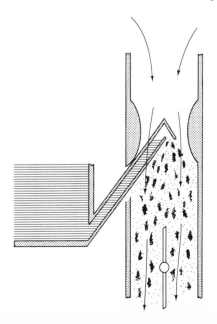

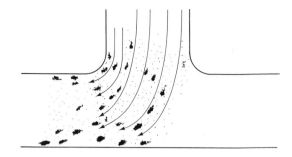

Fig. 3-2 Fuel droplets flowing around a manifold bend.

velocity drops below 50 feet per second. Intake velocities at idle speeds are usually below this value and, therefore, extra fuel must be supplied to the charge in order to deliver a combustible mixture to the combustion chamber at low engine speeds.

Manifold sizes are a compromise. They must be large enough to allow adequate flow for maximum power and small enough to maintain sufficient velocities to keep the fuel droplets in suspension as required for equal mixture distribution. Manifold size is one of the reasons that engines designed especially for racing will not run at low engine speeds. They have manifolds large enough to reach maximum horsepower, but their size allows fuel separation to occur at low speeds. Passenger car engines are primarily designed for economy at light-load, part-throttle operation. Their manifolds, therefore, have a much smaller cross-sectional area to maintain adequate mixture velocities throughout their normal operating range.

It should be noted that fuel separation problems do not exist on engines that have fuel injected into the manifold near the inlet valve. These engines can operate satisfactorily at low speeds, even with large manifold cross-sections.

In a four-stroke cycle, the inlet stroke is approximately one-fourth of the entire cycle. On a single cylinder four-cycle engine, the carburetor would be working only on the intake stroke, which is one-fourth of the time. Four cylinders could, therefore, be attached to the same carburetor with cylinders timed so that each cylinder took a different quarter of the 720° four-stroke cycle. Using this technique, one carburetor would satisfy the requirements of four cylinders just as well as it would satisfy one cylinder. This is exactly what is done in modern V-8 automotive engines. In these engines, the manifold is divided into two sections, each supplying four cylinders. When a carburetor with two large air

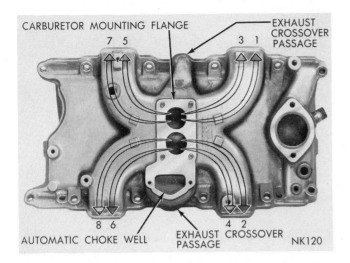

Fig. 3-3 Each side of the carburetor feeds four cylinders. (Chrysler-Plymouth Division, Chrysler Corporation)

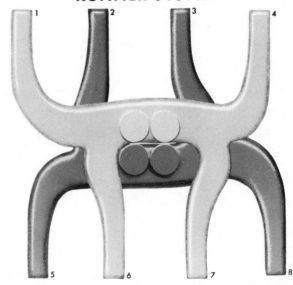

Fig. 3-4 Manifold runner core configuration (Ford Motor Company).

openings, called a two-barrel carburetor, is used on a modern V-8 engine, one opening supplies each manifold passage or *runner*. The cylinders are timed so that only one cylinder draws a charge from the carburetor air opening or barrel at a time.

Six cylinder inline engines usually have a single barrel carburetor to supply all of the cylinders. In these engines, the single carburetor barrel will be supplying two cylinders at the same time. Therefore, a carburetor used on these engines usually requires a larger barrel than the carburetor barrel used on V-8 engines, where each barrel supplies four cylinders.

3-2 INTAKE MANIFOLD FEATURES

The intake manifold's primary function is to carry the air/fuel mixture from the carburetor to the intake port in the head. As it flows, the mixture picks up heat that evaporates the liquid fuel droplets, gradually changing it into a gaseous air/fuel mixture.

Runners. On some economy engines one intake passage, or runner, between the carburetor and cylinder supplies two adjacent cylinders. Most modern engines have separate runners to each intake port. This allows the designer an opportunity to make all runners in the engine an equal length and size to aid in equal air/fuel charge distribution to each cylinder.

Fig. 3-5 Manifold runner type (Courtesy of Chevrolet Motor Division, General Motors Corporation).

Intake manifolds used on most V-8 engines are built with runners on two levels in order to fit them between the heads. Successive firing cylinders are fed alternately from the upper and lower runners so the runner design must match the cylinder firing sequence. The runners may be a *log type* that have the largest possible cross-section area for maximum air flow. Many are made in an *H* pattern that is a compromise between maximum performance and the best use of the space available. Some runners are called *tuned runners*. In the tuned runners, the length is designed to take advantage of the natural pressure wave that occurs in a gas column. When the pressure wave reaches the cylinder, the inlet valve is timed to open, allowing the charge to enter the cylinder with a super-charging or ram effect. On engines using four-barrel carburetors, the primary barrels are often centered on the runners to give good low- and mid-range performance during most operation. The secondary barrels only operate at full throttle which only occurs at a very small percentage of the operating time so unequal charge distribution is not as critical.

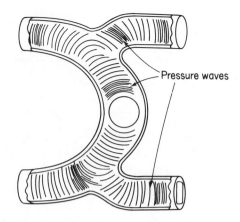

Fig. 3-6 Pressure waves in the manifold runner.

The charge flow through the intake manifold is dependent upon the number of abrupt runner bends, the smoothness of the interior wall and the cross-sectional runner shape. Sharp bends tend to increase fuel separation. The air, having less mass, is able to make turns much more quickly than the heavy fuel droplets. Rough interior runner surfaces will add a drag and turbulence to charge velocity, upsetting charge distribution. A round runner shape has the greatest cross-sectional area for its wall surface area; however, a round section is not always the most desirable. Passenger car engine manifold

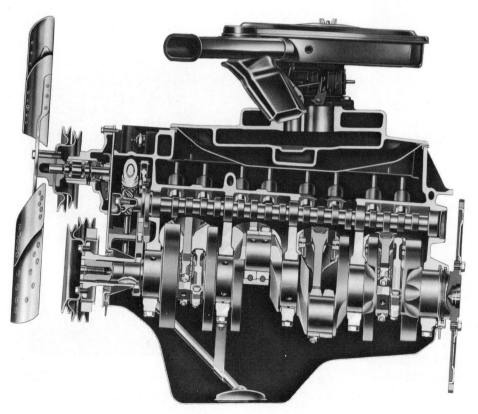

Fig. 3-7 Flat manifold floor (Cadillac Motor Car Division, General Motors Corporation).

runner floors are flat, so that any liquid fuel that drops out of the charge will spread in a thin layer over the manifold floor and rapidly evaporate. The rear of the engine is lower than the front for better drive line positioning. Manifolds are designed so that the manifold floor is level when the engine is mounted in the chassis. The flat manifold floor keeps any liquid fuel from running to a low point. Rectangular and oval shapes are used to take advantage of the available space for more cross-section area at the expense of relatively more wall surface area when compared to round runners. Main intake runners have cross-sectional areas of approximately .008 square inch per engine cubic inch displacement (CID) and branch runners have cross-sectional areas of approximately .006 square inch per CID. Ribs and guide vanes are often positioned in the floor of the manifold runners to aid in equal distribution of the intake gases to the cylinders, even though some of the fuel may still be in the liquid form. It is just as important for the fuel to have equal distribution as it is for equal air distribution.

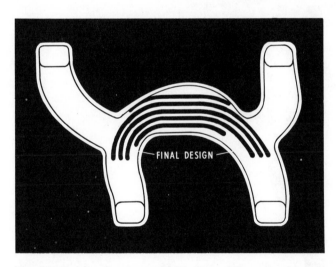

Fig. 3-8 Guide rib on manifold floor (Chevrolet Motors Division, General Motors Corporation).

Manifold Heat. Heat is required to evaporate liquid fuel between the carburetor and the combustion chamber. If heat is taken from the air, the charge temperature is lowered and less heat is available for evaporation. In current production engines additional heat must be supplied to provide satisfactory fuel evaporation for smooth engine operation when the engine is cold. A mixture temperature range from about 100°F to 130°F will

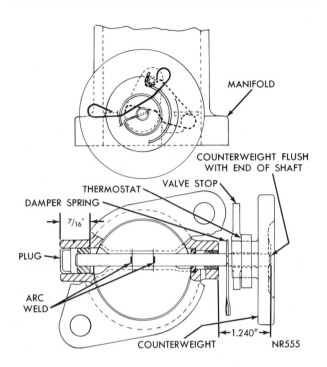

Fig. 3-9 Heat riser valve (Chrysler-Plymouth Division, Chrysler Corporation).

provide satisfactory fuel evaporation. Heat is supplied during low temperature operation in many current V-8 engines by using a thermostatic valve, called a heat riser, to route exhaust gases through a passage, called a crossover, positioned to heat the floor of the manifold directly under the carburetor. When the engine gets to full operating temperature, the heat riser valve bypasses the exhaust gas away from the intake manifold crossover, sending them directly out through the exhaust system. Excessive heating causes the charge to expand in the manifold. This will reduce the mass of the charge that is available to the cylinder, thus reducing the engine power. An overheated charge can also lead to undesirable abnormal combustion processes, two of which are called detonation and pre-ignition. It is, therefore, important that the intake manifold is not overheated.

Some engines have used engine coolant to supply heat to the mixture by providing passages for the warm coolant to flow around the intake runners. This heat is not available until the engine begins to warm up. Heat from the coolant is used

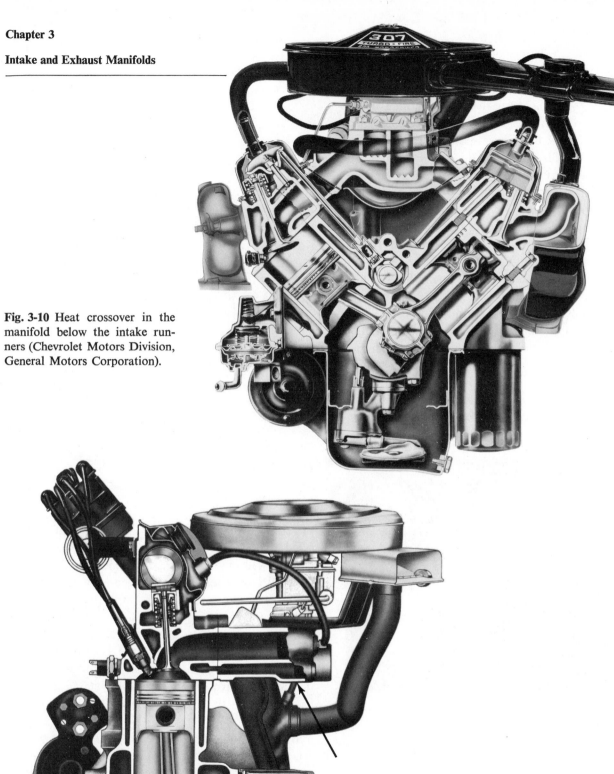

Fig. 3-10 Heat crossover in the manifold below the intake runners (Chevrolet Motors Division, General Motors Corporation).

Fig. 3-11 Engine coolant used to heat the intake runners (Chevrolet Motors Division, General Motors Corporation).

(a)

(b)

Fig. 3-12 Automatic choke heat stove. (a) In exhaust manifold, (b) in intake manifold.

where mechanical design makes it difficult to use exhaust heat and where a uniform temperature is desired. Manifolds often contain a coolant passage whose function is to connect the cooling system between the V-heads to provide a common cooling outlet for the engine cooling system.

Choke Heat. The carburetor is designed with a choke to provide an excessively rich fuel mixture for starting. This is necessary because intake gas velocity is low during cranking and no extra heat is available for fuel evaporation before the engine

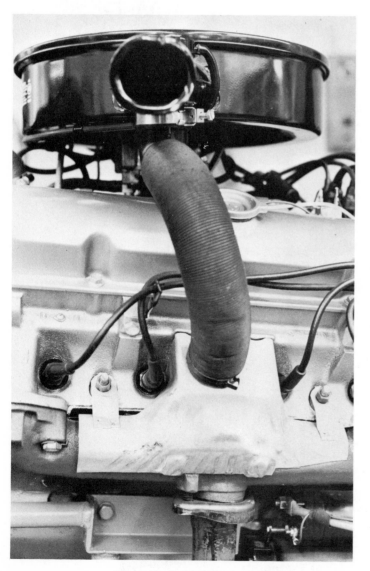

Fig. 3-13 Carburetor air preheater.

starts. Most chokes are automatic and are controlled by a temperature-sensing thermostatic coil choke closing spring. In some applications, heat is delivered to the thermostatic spring through a tube from a heat chamber called a stove that is located in the manifold where it can sense exhaust temperatures. This stove could be in the exhaust manifold or in the exhaust crossover passage of the intake manifold. An alternate method uses a pocket in the intake manifold in which the thermostatic choke coil is placed. This location allows the thermostatic coil to sense exhaust temperature at the exhaust crossover in the intake manifold. A link connects the thermostatic coil with the carburetor choke plate linkage.

Air Preheat. Excessive hydrocarbon emissions are produced by cold engines as the result of poor intake gas evaporation. To minimize these emissions, a large number of engines have been provided with air preheaters. Warmed air is picked up adjacent to the exhaust manifold and fed into the air filter. A thermostatic valve limits the maximum temperature to 100°F by gradually mixing underhood air with the preheated air. When the underhood air reaches 100°F, the thermostatic valve completely closes off the preheated air inlet.

3-3 INTAKE MANIFOLD CONFIGURATION

Two general configurations appear on modern V-8 engine intake manifolds. Some engines use an *open-type* manifold. Runners go through the open-type branches. Other branches provide for exhaust crossover and coolant flow. This design allows good control of manifold runner tuning is lightweight, and is low cost. Lifter valley covers are needed on engines using this type of manifold. In some engines, the covers are an extension of the intake manifold gasket.

A second configuration of the intake manifold is a *closed-type* manifold. This manifold has cast metal between the runners and is designed for use as a lifter valley cover as well as a manifold. It is heavier and more expensive to make than the open type. Because of the many joints involved, more care is required when installing to correctly place the gaskets and seals so they will not leak. Using the closed-type manifold, it is possible to lower the runners, the carburetor, and, consequently, the

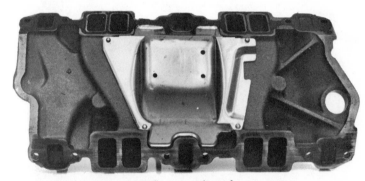

Fig. 3-14 Open-type intake manifold.

automobile hood line. The large mass of metal used in closed-type manifolds tends to retain engine noise and this results in quieting engine operation noise.

Closed-type manifolds have the exhaust crossover located adjacent to the lifter valley where engine oil could contact the surface. Hot exhaust in the crossover would heat the oil that lands on its surface to cause coking and oil burning. Therefore, shields are provided to keep the oil from contacting

Fig. 3-16 Sheet metal deflector under exhaust crossover.

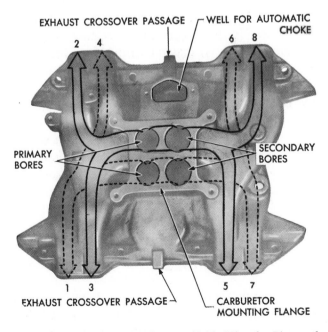

Fig. 3-15 Closed-type intake manifold (Chrysler-Plymouth Division, Chrysler Corporation).

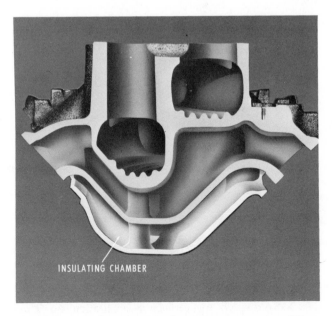

Fig. 3-17 Cast air passage under exhaust crossover (Chevrolet Motor Division, General Motors Corporation).

27

(a)

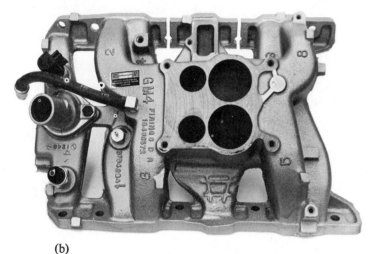

(b)

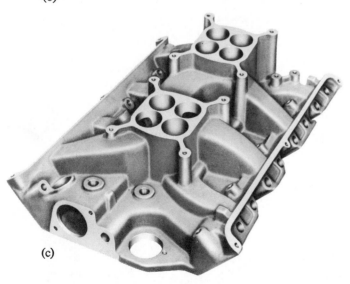

(c)

Fig. 3-18 Provision for carburetor application (a) Three two-barrel carburetors, (b) one four-barrel carburetor, (c) two four-barrel carburetors (Ford Motor Company).

these hot surfaces. A sheet metal deflector may be fastened to the lifter valley side of the intake manifold or a large single-piece manifold gasket may serve this function. Some closed-type manifolds are designed with a passage that provides an air insulating space between the exhaust crossover passage and the lifter valley. This results in good insulation and noise reduction.

Intake manifolds used on passenger car engines may be designed to use three two-barrel carburetors, one four-barrel carburetor, or two four-barrel carburetors.

3-4 EXHAUST MANIFOLD CRITERIA

The exhaust manifold is designed to collect high temperature spent gases from the cylinder exhaust ports and carry them to an exhaust pipe, exhaust silencer or muffler, and on to the tailpipe, where they are vented to the atmosphere. This must be done with the least possible restriction or back pressure while keeping the exhaust noise at a minimum.

Exhaust gas temperature will vary according to the power produced by the engine. The manifold must be designed to operate at engine idle and sustain full power. Under full power conditions the exhaust manifold will become red hot, causing expansion, while at idle it is just warm, causing little expansion. In passenger car operation, however, the engine will normally be run under light-load, part-throttle conditions, where the manifold temperatures will be between these extremes. Generally, the exhaust manifold is made from cast iron that can withstand extreme temperature thermal shock. It is bolted to the head or to the block in a way to allow expansion and contraction. Some manifolds are designed so that no parting surface gasket is required, while others require a gasket.

3-5 EXHAUST MANIFOLD COMPROMISES

The exhaust manifold is designed to minimize exhaust gas flow restriction. Some manifolds use cast-rib deflectors or dividers inside to guide the exhaust gases toward the outlet as smoothly as possible. An optimum exhaust passage cross-section must be established with well-proportioned flow areas, smooth flow paths and maximum branch separation within the limits of the chassis environment. The chassis front suspension, steering gear box and fender skirts limit the space that is available for the exhaust manifolds. In general, the chassis and engine are designed first and then the manifold is designed to fit into the remaining space. This is not as much of a compromise as it might seem, because severe bends have no measurable effect on exhaust systems as long as the required cross-section is maintained.

Some exhaust manifolds are designed to go above the spark plug, while others are designed to go below. The spark plug and the carefully routed ignition wires are often shielded from the exhaust heat with sheet metal deflectors.

Some exhaust manifolds have provision for a thermostatic heat riser valve built into the manifold to direct exhaust gases through the intake manifold crossover passage during warm-up. Often, a stove for the automatic choke is also incorporated in the exhaust manifold. Some manifolds are even designed with brackets on which are mounted such

components as generators, and air conditioning compressors.

Exhaust systems are especially designed for the engine-chassis combination. The exhaust system length, pipe size, and silencer are designed, where possible, to make use of the tuning effect of the gas column resonating within the exhaust system similar to the tuned intake runner. However, the entire system is designed so that exhaust pulses from the cylinders are emitted to the manifold when the least pressure exists, rather than during a high pressure wave as is done on intake manifolds. This helps scavenge the exhaust gas from the cylinder, allowing more useful space for the fresh charge and, consequently, more engine power can be produced. Tuning can be most effective at one engine speed or at certain harmonics of that speed. Manifolds are, therefore, tuned to the most desirable engine rpm for the particular vehicle involved. Short pipe lengths favor high-rpm power peaks, while longer lengths tend to increase torque in the mid-range speed used in passenger car applications.

3-6 MUFFLERS

When the exhaust valve opens, it rapidly releases a high-pressure gas. This sends a strong air wave through the atmosphere which produces a sound called an explosion. It is exactly the same sound produced when the high-pressure gases from burned gunpowder are released from a gun. In an engine, the pulses are released, one after another, so the explosions seem to blend together in a steady roar. The muffler is designed to change this roar to a quiet hum.

Sound is air vibration. When the vibrations are large, the sound is loud. The muffler traps the large bursts of high-pressure exhaust gas in an expansion chamber and releases them gradually before the next high-pressure burst arrives. In this way, the muffler silences engine exhaust noise.

Sometimes, resonators are used in the exhaust system. They provide additional expansion space at critical points in the exhaust system to additionally smooth out the exhaust gas flow.

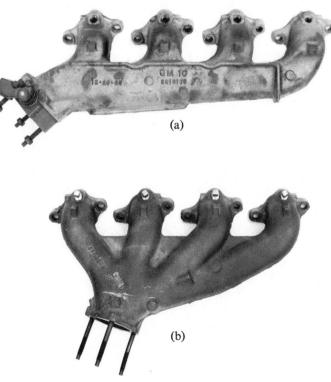

(a)

(b)

Fig. 3-19 Exhaust designs. (a) Standard engine, (b) performance engine.

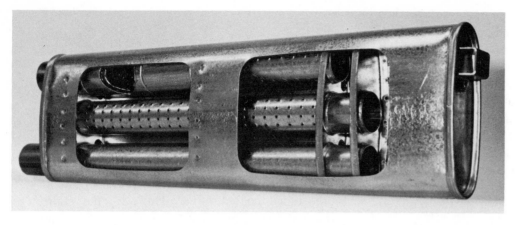

Fig. 3-20 Muffler interior.

Review Questions
Chapter 3

1. What is the basic requirement for smooth engine operation?

2. What causes fuel separation in the intake manifold?

3. Why are six-cylinder engine carburetor barrels larger than carburetor barrels used on V-8 engines?

4. What are some of the reasons for *not* using tuned intake runners?

5. Racing engines do not use manifold heat. Why is manifold heat required on passenger car engines?

6. What are the possible advantages of the crossover choke, based on the engine design considerations stated in Chapters 1 and 2?

7. Large diameter exhausts with smooth bends have the least restriction. Why, then, are exhaust manifolds used on passenger cars designed in so many different ways?

8. Under what conditions does the exhaust pipe length become critical?

9. How does a muffler silence exhaust noise?

Quiz 3

1. Which of the following will insure smooth engine operation?
a. even fuel delivery to each cylinder
b. equal power impulses in each cylinder
c. correct carburetor adjustments
d. having manifold runners the same length

2. Fuel mixture flow rates below 50 ft per sec in the intake manifold result in
a. maximum possible power which is below advertised horsepower

b. carbon buildup in the intake manifolds
c. even mixture being delivered to each cylinder
d. fuel droplets separate from the mixture.

3. Compared to the same size single cylinder engine, running at the same speed, a four cylinder engine would require a carburetor
a. the same size
b. twice as large

c. four times as large

d. eight times as large.

4. In passenger car engines, the bottom of the intake manifold is usually flat. Which of the following is the best reason for this design?
   a. make the largest cross-section possible for the manifold wall area surface
   b. improve fuel evaporation in the manifold
   c. allow space for two runner levels
   d. provide even mixture distribution to the cylinders

5. The exhaust crossover in the manifold is most helpful to engine operation during
   a. cold starts
   b. warm up
   c. acceleration
   d. legal highway speeds.

6. The primary reason for adding air preheat to engines is to
   a. improve engine startability
   b. minimize carburetor icing
   c. reduce harmful emissions
   d. prevent engine freezing at very low temperatures.

7. Closed-type intake manifolds are gaining in popularity among engine manufacturers because they
   a. reduce engine noise
   b. reduce engine weight
   c. improve mixture flow to the cylinders
   d. improve gasket positioning during assembly.

8. A shield is used between the engine interior and the base of the intake manifold casting to
   a. direct the crankcase gases to the ventilating system
   b. prevent engine oil leakage
   c. control the amount of heat that gets to the manifold
   d. minimize oil coking and burning.

9. Short length manifold tuning produces the most pronounced effect during
   a. idle speeds
   b. acceleration while passing
   c. turnpike speeds
   d. high speeds.

10. The muffler silences the exhaust by
   a. holding pressure in the exhaust system
   b. removing noise producing vibrations
   c. gradually releasing the high gas pressure
   d. reducing the explosion noise produced by the cylinder.

chapter 4

Cylinder Head and Valve Train

The passenger car engine is designed to operate smoothly at all engine loads and speeds while developing high power output and high efficiencies. *Smoothness* is defined as the lack of objectionable or disagreeable engine vibration detected inside the passenger compartment. Engine vibration can be caused by mechanical unbalance or by abnormal combustion. An unbalanced rotating crankshaft and reciprocating pistons produce undesirable vibration and roughness. Abnormal combustion produces excessive rates of pressure buildup in the combustion chamber which leads to engine roughness.

Combustion (discussed in more detail in Chapter 12) is a very complex chemical process resulting from the fuel reactions within the combustion chamber. These reactions will differ with the fuel type, combustion chamber shape, cooling system efficiency, location of the sparkplug and valves, compression ratio and the quantity of the intake charge. One of the most important of these factors is the combustion chamber shape.

The combustion chamber is shaped on the bottom by the piston head, on the side by the cylinder wall and on the top by the cylinder head. The piston is nearly at the top of the stroke when combustion takes place so that very little of the cylinder wall is exposed to combustion. The combustion chamber shape, therefore, is primarily the result of the shape of the top of the piston and the shape of the pocket formed in the cylinder head. These shapes have a great deal to do with the control of combustion smoothness.

4-1 COMBUSTION CHAMBER TYPES

Combustion chambers of modern automotive overhead valve engines have evolved from two basic types. One is the *non-turbulent hemispherical chamber* and the other is the *turbulent wedge chamber*. Each has advantages that new combustion chamber designs attempt to combine to form the best possible compromise design.

Hemispherical Combustion Chamber. In non-turbulent hemispherical combustion chambers, the charge is inducted through widely slanted valves, compressed, then ignited from a centrally located spark plug. The smallest possible distance exists between the spark plug and all edges of the combustion chamber so that combustion, which radiates out from the spark plug, will be completed in the least possible time. The end gases that cause abnormal combustion have little time to react and, therefore, knock is reduced to a minimum. The rapidly burning charge in the hemispherical combustion chamber causes a high rate of pressure rise. When the engine is run under medium and heavy loads at low engine speeds, it will produce some engine roughness and noise. If this type of operation is encountered in passenger cars, it may be objectionable to the passengers. However, laboratory and road tests have shown that the hemispherical combustion chamber is the best type for use in race car application where low speed conditions are seldom encountered.

Hemispherical combustion chambers are usually fully machined to produce the required shape. This is a necessary but expensive operation that increases engine cost.

Fig. 4-1 Hemispherical combustion chamber.

Wedge Combustion Chamber. The turbulent wedge combustion chamber is designed to produce a uniform burning rate by controlling combustion. This results in smooth power production. In turbulent wedge combustion chambers, the charge is inducted through parallel valves and compressed. As the piston nears the top of the compression stroke, the piston approaches a low or flat portion of the head. The gases are squeezed out of this area, called a *squish area*, into the larger portion of the combustion chamber. This produces turbulence within the charge. The spark plug, which is positioned in the highly turbulent part of the charge, ignites the charge. Ignition is followed by smooth and rapid burning. Combustion radiates out from the spark plug. The end gases remaining in the squish area would be subject to abnormal burning, but because this area is squeezed very thin, less than .100″ when the piston is at the top center, the end gases are cooled and do not react. This squish area is, therefore, also called a *quench area*. Required combustion rates can be controlled by changes in the combustion chamber shape. The engine designer can make seemingly unimportant modifications in the combustion chamber shape that result in large changes in the peak pressure timing and peak pressure magnitude. He can, therefore, design the combustion chamber to specific engine and fuel requirements. Turbulent combustion chambers usually remain *as cast* in the head, with no machining being done.

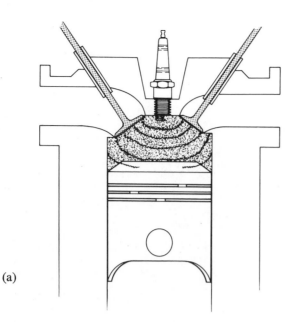

(a)

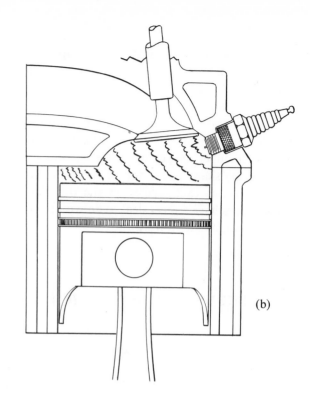

(b)

Fig. 4-2 Normal combustion. (a) hemispherical combustion chamber, (b) wedge combustion chamber (Dana Corporation).

Fig. 4-3 Wedge combustion chamber.

Unburned hydrocarbon emission from engines has become critical. The charge adjacent to the combustion chamber surface, from .002″ to .020″ thick, does not burn because the combustion chamber surface cools the surface charge to a temperature below its ignition temperature. These unburned surface hydrocarbons are expelled with the burned gases on the exhaust stroke as unburned hydrocarbon emissions. Combustion chambers with low surface area for their volume, such as the hemispherical combustion chamber, emit less unburned hydrocarbons than the wedge combustion chamber which has a relatively high surface area to volume ratio.

The trend in combustion chamber design is to take advantage of the best features of each type and, at the same time, eliminate the less desirable features. This is done by changing the valves of the wedge head to divergent angles, repositioning the spark plug, reducing the quench area and reducing the combustion chamber area-to-volume ratio. The resultant combustion chamber is very efficient and smooth burning while running on available pump grades of gasoline. They are used *as cast* rather than having expensive machined chambers. These chambers are called by names such as polyspherical, hemi-wedge and kidney shapes.

(a)

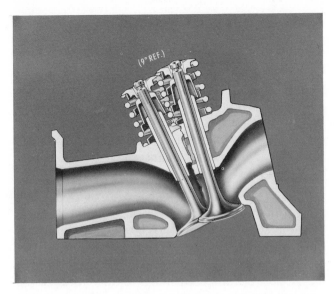

Fig. 4-4 Modified combustion chamber. (a, b) Divergent valves, (c) open combustion chamber (Chevrolet Motors Division, General Motors Corporation).

Fig. 4-5 Siamesed intake and exhaust ports.

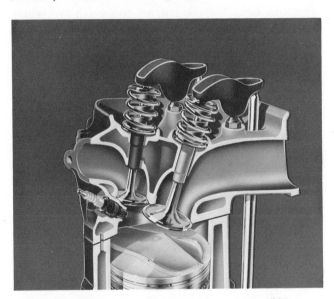

(b)

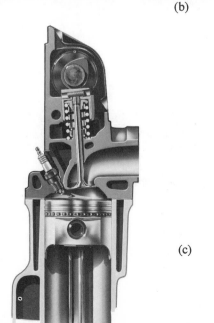

(c)

4-2 INTAKE AND EXHAUST PORTS

Intake and exhaust system passages cast in the cylinder head are called *ports*. They lead from the manifold to the valves. An optimum design is not always possible because of space requirements for head bolt bosses, valve guides, cooling passages, and pushrod opening clearances. Inline engines have both intake and exhaust valves located on the same side of the engine. Often, two of these cylinders share the same port because of the restricted space available. Such ports are called *Siamesed ports*. Larger ports and better breathing is possible in engines that have the intake port on one side of the head and the exhaust port on the opposite side. In these engines, a separate port is usually provided for each cylinder.

The design criteria aim is to provide an intake and exhaust system that will meet the engine's maximum power needs with the minimum restriction and, at the same time, provide satisfactory charge distribution in the induction system at part throttle and idle speeds. The engine designer may make use of air-flow measuring equipment to develop a satisfactory compromise that will meet these criteria.

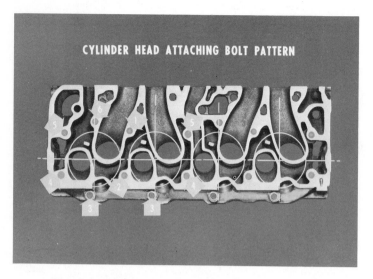

Fig. 4-6 Separate intake and exhaust ports (Chevrolet Motors Division, General Motors Corporation).

The flow of gases is often different than one might think. At times, an apparent restricting hump within a port may actually increase the air flow capacity by redirecting the flow to an area that is large enough to handle the flow. Modifications in the field, such as *porting* or *relieving*, would result in restricting the flow of such a carefully designed port.

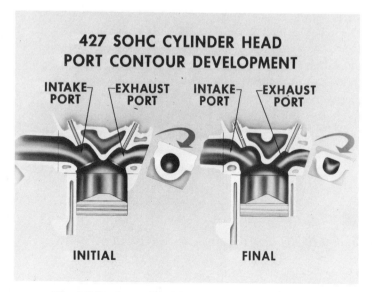

Fig. 4-7 Intake and exhaust ports for high gas flow rates (Ford Motor Company).

4-3 COOLANT PASSAGES

Coolant flow within the engine is designed to flow from the coolest portion of the engine to the warmest portion. Coolant is fed into the block where it is directed all around the cylinders. It then flows upward through the gasket to the cooling passages cast into the cylinder head. The heated coolant is collected at a common point and returned to the radiator to be cooled and recycled.

Relatively large openings are provided into the head cooling passages. They are necessary because the cooling passage core must be supported through these openings while the head is being cast. After casting, the core is broken up and removed through the support openings. Openings to the outside of the engine are closed with expansion plugs or soft plugs, either of a convex type or a cup type. The openings between the head and the block are very often too large for the correct coolant flow. When this occurs, the head gasket performs an important function by providing a calibrated restriction with punched holes so that the coolant will have the correct flow rate at each opening. Therefore, it is important that the head gasket is installed correctly for proper engine cooling.

Special cooling nozzles or deflectors may be designed into the head to direct the coolant toward

Fig. 4-8 Coolant flow control. (a) Head, (b) gasket covering left hand cooling passage opening.

Fig. 4-9 Valve gear lubrication. (a) Oil feed through hollow pushrod (Chevrolet Motors Division, General Motors Corporation).

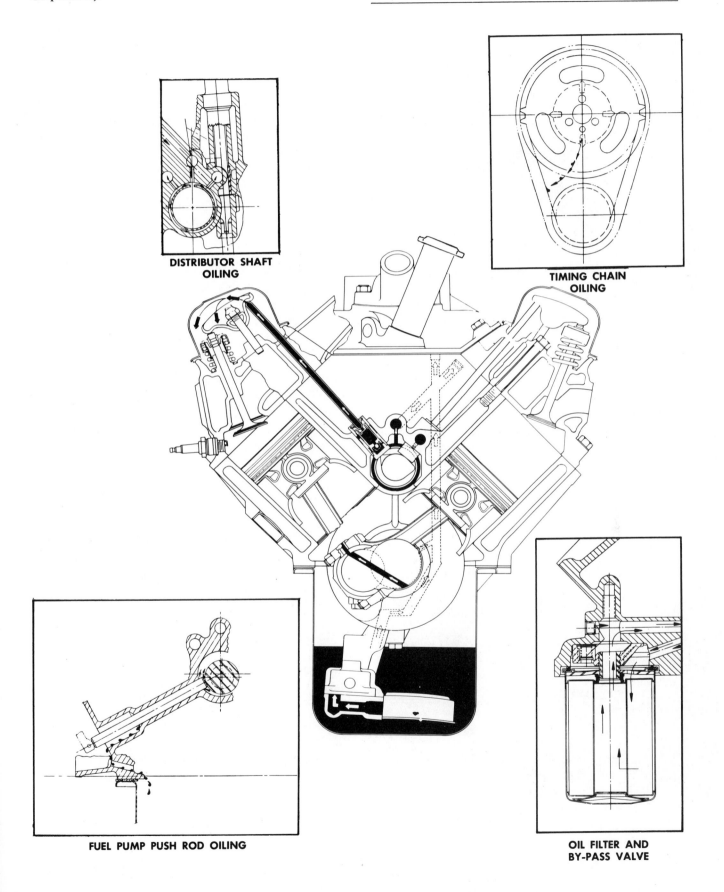

DISTRIBUTOR SHAFT
OILING

TIMING CHAIN
OILING

FUEL PUMP PUSH ROD OILING

OIL FILTER AND
BY-PASS VALVE

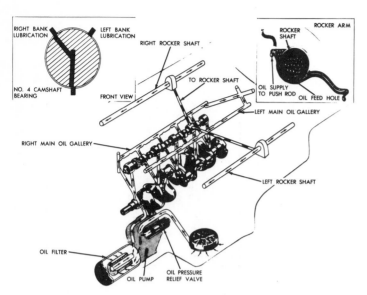

Fig. 4-9 (b) Oil feed passages drilled through head (Chrysler-Plymouth Division, Chrysler Corporation).

a portion of the head where localized heat must be removed. Usually this is in the area of the exhaust valve. Some of the deflectors are cast in the cooling passages, while others are pressed-in sheet metal nozzles. Pressed-in nozzles are replaceable in some engines.

Fig. 4-10 Typical pushrod type valve train.

4-4 LUBRICATING PASSAGES

Lubricating oil is delivered to the overhead valve mechanism, either through the valve pushrods or through drilled passages in the head and block casting. Special openings in the head gasket are provided to allow the oil to pass between the block and head without leaking. After the oil passes through the valve mechanism, it returns to the oil pan through oil return passages. Some engines have drilled oil return holes, but most of the engines are provided with relatively large cast holes that allow the oil to return freely to the engine oil pan. The cast holes are large and do not become easily plugged. They also tend to lighten the head casting, thus reducing cost and total engine weight.

4-5 INTAKE AND EXHAUST VALVE MECHANISMS

Automotive engine valves are a *poppet valve* design that operate in a reciprocating manner. The valve is opened by a cam that is timed to the piston position and crankshaft cycle. It is closed by one or more springs.

The cam is driven by timing gears, chains, or belts, located at the front of the engine. The gear or sprocket on the camshaft has twice as many teeth as the one on the crankshaft. This results in the required two crankshaft turns for each turn of the camshaft in four-stroke cycle engines.

Most valve design features are the same for all valves; however, intake valves control the inlet of cool, low-pressure charges, while the exhaust valves must handle hot, high-pressure gases. This means that exhaust valves are exposed to more severe operating conditions and, therefore, are made from much higher quality and more expensive materials than the intake valves.

Valve Design. Extensive testing has shown that there is a definite relationship between the different dimensions of valve geometry. Engines with bores of from three to eight inches should have intake valves approximately 45% of the bore size. The exhaust valves should be approximately 38% of the bore size. The intake valve needs to be larger than the exhaust valve to enable it to handle the same gas mass because the intake valve controls low velocity, low density gases.

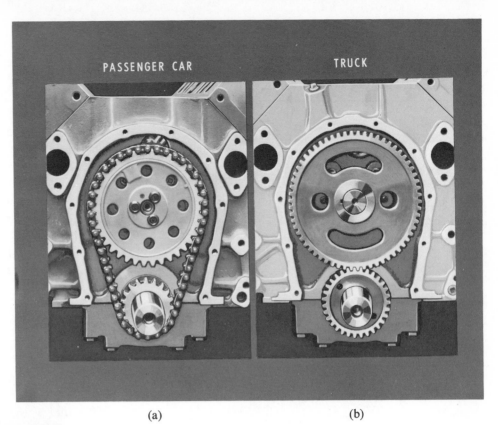

PASSENGER CAR   TRUCK

(a)   (b)

(c)

Fig. 4-11 Cam shaft drivers. (a) Chain, (b) gear, (c) belt (Chevrolet Motor Division, General Motors Corporation) (d) overhead chain (Ford Motor Company).

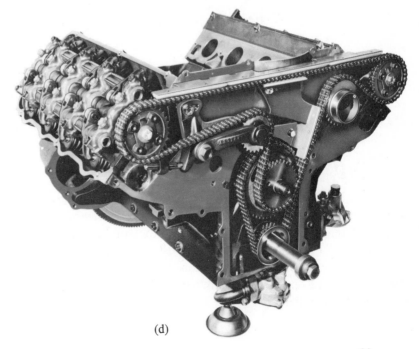

(d)

Fig. 4-12 Valve head types from rigid to elastic.

The exhaust valve, on the other hand, controls high velocity, high pressure, denser gases that can be handled by a smaller valve. Exhaust valves are, therefore, approximately 85% of the intake valve size. Valve head diameter, for satisfactory operation, is nearly 115% of the port diameter and the amount the valve opens, called valve lift, is close to 25% of the valve diameter.

Poppet valves may be designed from the extremes of a rigid valve to an elastic valve. The rigid valve is strong, holds its shape, and conducts heat readily, but is susceptible to valve leakage and burning, while the elastic valve is able to conform to valve seat shape so it seals easily but it runs hot and the flexing encourages breaking. The most popular shape is one with a small cup in the top of the valve head. It offers a reasonable weight, good strength and good heat transfer at a slight cost penalty.

The valve face angles have been carefully selected to give the best compromise. With a given small valve opening distance the opening space around the valve face increases as the face angle is reduced. This value can be calculated by using the trigonometric function, the cosine, of the valve face angle. Even though a flat valve with a face angle of 0° provides maximum valve opening for a given lift it is very difficult to seal when it is closed. Poor sealing will lead to valve burning and a short useful valve life.

The sealing force on the valve seat is increased as the valve angle is increased. Forty-five degree face angles are used on exhaust valves and on intake valves where higher seating pressures are preferred and where deposits must be either crushed or wiped off to prevent valve leakage.

Valve Materials. Valve design and gas flow considerations have been well established to provide satisfactory performance in the modern engine. Increasing durability and cost will continue to be subjects of valve development studies. These problems are most apparent in valve metallurgy and manufacturing techniques. New manufacturing techniques must be developed as new valve materials are developed to maintain valve economy. Most of the recent valve development work has been done on exhaust valves that are subjected to an increasingly severe operational environment.

Alloys used in exhaust valve materials are chromium for oxidation resistance with small amounts of nickel, manganese, and nitrogen added. Heat treating is used whenever necessary to produce desired valve properties. Some exhaust valves are manufactured from two different materials where a one-piece design cannot meet the hardness and corrosion-resistance specifications desired. The valve heads are made from special alloys that can operate

Fig. 4-13 Two piece valve (Sealed Power Corporation).

valve stem, the sodium transfers heat from the valve head and dissipates it through the valve stem and guide. In general, one-piece valve design using properly selected materials will provide satisfactory service for automotive engines.

Valve Guides and Seats. The valve face closes against a valve seat to seal the combustion chamber. The seat is integrally formed in the head casting of automotive engines. Insert seats are used in some applications where corrosion and wear resistance is critical. Insert seats are also used as a salvage procedure for integral automotive engine valve seats that have been badly damaged.

Valve seat distortion is one of the major causes of valve problems. Distortion may be transient as the result of pressure and thermal stress or it may be permanent as the result of mechanical stress.

at high temperature, have physical strength, resist lead-oxide corrosion and have indentation resistance. These heads are welded to stems that have good wear-resistance properties. In severe applications, facing alloys are welded to the valve face and valve tip.

Some heavy-duty applications use hollow stem exhaust valves that are partially filled with metallic sodium. The sodium becomes a liquid at operating temperatures. As it splashes back and forth in the

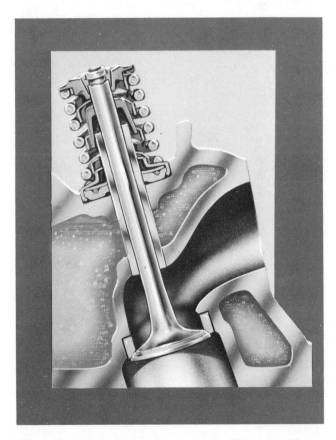

Fig. 4-15 Valve guide and seat insert (Chevrolet Motors Division General Motors Corporation).

Fig. 4-14 Hollow valve stem (Sealed Power Corporation).

Fig. 4-17 Valve spring lock types (a) and stem grooves (b).

(a)

(b)

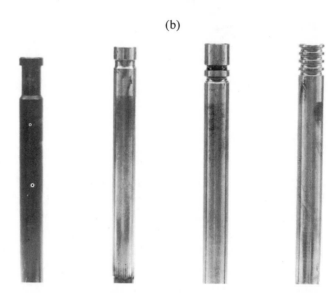

Valve seat distortion must be kept at a minimum for maximum valve service life. This means that the engine must be correctly and carefully assembled using proper parts.

A valve guide supports the valve stem so that the valve face will remain perfectly centered or concentric with the valve seat. Here again, the valve guide is generally integral with the head casting for better heat transfer and lower manufacturing costs. Insert valve guides are always used where the valve stem and head materials are not compatible.

Valve Springs and Locks. A valve spring holds the valve against the seat when the valve is not being

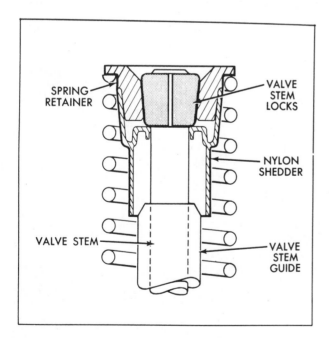

Fig. 4-16 Valve spring retaining method (Cadillac Motor Car Division, General Motors Corporation).

operated. One end of the valve spring is seated against the head. The other end of the spring is attached under compression to the valve through a valve spring retainer and a valve spring keeper or lock.

Valves usually use a single inexpensive valve spring. When this does not provide adequate control, additional devices are added. Variable rate springs provide added spring pressure when the valve is in its open position. This is accomplished by using closely spaced coils on the cylinder head end of the spring. The closely spaced coils also tend to dampen natural frequency vibrations that may exist in a uniformly wound coil spring. Some valve springs use a flat coiled damper inside the spring. This eliminates spring surge and adds some valve spring tension.

Multiple valve springs are used where large lifts are required and a single spring has insufficient strength to control the valve. Multiple valve springs generally have their coils wound in opposite directions to control surge and valve rotation.

A large number of valve locks have been used on the end of the valve stem to retain the spring. They have evolved from simple, low-cost lock pins and horseshoes to the current high-quality, split-cone lock or keeper. The inside surface of the split lock uses a variety of grooves or beads, depending upon their holding requirements. The outside of the split lock fits into a cone-shaped seat in the center of the valve spring retainer.

One-piece valve spring retainers may be machined or forged. They are made from high quality steel so they will hold their shape under the pounding they receive in operation. Some retainers have built-in devices that cause the valve to rotate in a controlled manner. These cost more than plain retainers and so they are only used where it is desirable to increase valve service life.

Valve Oil Seals. Oil consumption by leakage past the valve guides is a problem in the overhead valve engine, especially around the intake valve stem where a high vacuum exists in the port. A lot of design effort has gone into the development of deflectors and valve guide seals. Some early designers used umbrellas above the retainers that deflect the oil from the rocker arm to the area outside the valve spring. Later designs used synthetic rubber seals between the valve stem and retainer so that the retainer acted in the same manner as the umbrella. As more control was required, synthetic cups were placed on the valve stem and over the valve guide base. Some of these float and some are fastened. Plastic seals against the valve stem may be used in the synthetic cups. Some advanced designs use a full plastic seal that is heat bonded to the valve retainer under the spring to deflect the oil outside of the valve guide boss.

Care must be used when installing valve seals to be sure they are correctly installed and not damaged. Careless installation will result in oil leakage that will lead to excessive oil consumption.

Rocker Arms. Rocker arms reverse the upward push of the pushrod to a downward push on the tip of the valve. Engine designers make good use of the rocker arm to reduce the movement of the cam follower or lifter and pushrod while maintaining valve lift by using a rocker arm ratio of approxi-

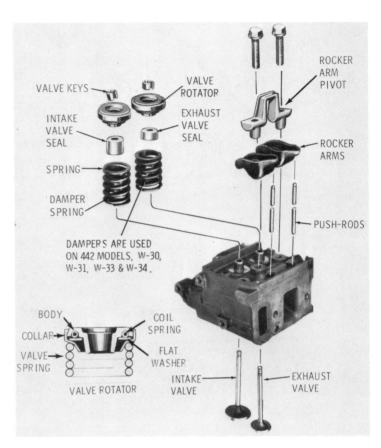

Fig. 4-18 Valve rotator location (Oldsmobile Division, General Motors Corporation).

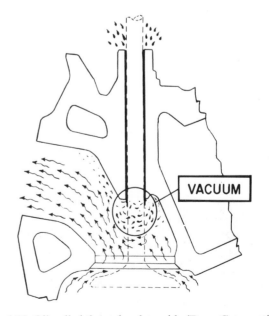

Fig. 4-19 Oil pulled through valve guide (Dana Corporation).

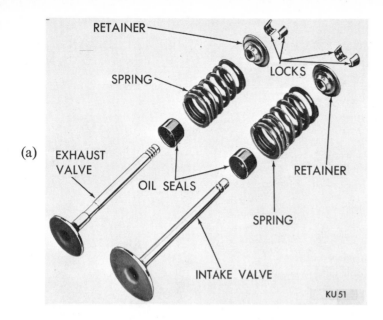

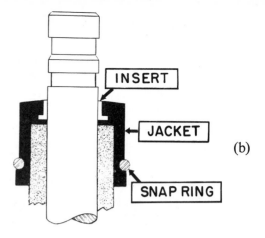

Fig. 4-20 Valve seal location. (a) (Chrysler-Plymouth Division of Chrysler Corporation), (b) (Dana Corporation).

Fig. 4-21 Cast rocker arm types.

Fig. 4-22 Stamped rocker arm types.

Fig. 4-23 Types of pushrod ends.

mately 1.5:1. For a given amount of lift on the pushrod, this ratio would open the valve 1.5 times the pushrod lift.

Rocker arm design has undergone change in new engine designs as a result of cost reduction programs and the need for divergent valve placement angle that is required in advanced combustion chamber designs. Rocker arms have been cast, forged, and stamped. Forged rocker arms are the strongest, but require expensive machining operations. They may have bushings or bearings installed to reduce friction and increase durability. Cast rocker arms cost less to make and do not usually use bushings but they do require several machining operations. They are not as strong as forged rocker arms, but are satisfactory for passenger car service.

Several types of stamped rocker arms have been developed. These are the least expensive type to manufacture. They are lightweight and very strong. Two general types are in use, those that operate on a ball stud or a pivot bar and those that operate on a shaft. The ball-stud and pivot-bar types are lubricated through hollow pushrods. The shaft type is lubricated through oil passages that come from the block, through the head and into the shaft, then to the rocker arms.

Pushrods. Pushrods are designed to be as light as possible and still maintain their strength. They may be either solid or hollow; however, they must be hollow if they are to be used as passages for oil to lubricate rocker arms. Pushrods use a convex ball end on the lower portion that seats in the lifter. The rocker arm end is also a convex ball, unless there is an adjustment screw in the pushrod end of the rocker arm. In this case, the rocker arm end of the pushrod has a concave socket and the mating adjustment screw has a convex ball end.

Lifters and Tappets. Valve lifters or tappets follow the camshaft's cam contour and convert cam geometry to a reciprocating motion in the valve train. The majority of lifters have a relatively flat surface that slides on the cam. Some lifters, however, are designed with a roller to follow the cam contour, rather than a flat surface. Because of the expense of making the roller lifters, flat lifters are used wherever possible. When the flat lifters are not able to provide satisfactory performance, roller lifters are used.

The valve train, like other manufactured parts, is made with a tolerance. This tolerance makes it necessary to have some means of clearance adjustment in the valve train system, so that the valve will positively seat. Valve train clearance must not be excessive or it will cause noise or result in failure. Two methods are commonly used to make the necessary *valve clearance or lash* adjustments. One

(a)

Fig. 4-24 Adjusting valve lash. (a) At pushrod end, (b) pivot ball.

(b)

is a solid valve lifter with a mechanical adjustment and the other is a lifter with a hydraulic adjustment built into the lifter body.

In L-head engines, the solid valve lifter usually has an adjusting screw in the lifter. Overhead valve engines have an adjustment screw at the pushrod end of the rocker arm or a nut at the pivot point of ball socket. Adjustable pushrods are available for some specific applications.

Valve trains using solid lifters require the valve train to run with some clearance to insure positive valve closure, regardless of the engine temperature. This clearance is matched by a gradual rise in the cam contour, called a ramp, to take up the clearance before the valve is opened. This ramp insures quiet operation. Valve trains using hydraulic lifters run with no clearance because the hydraulic unit is designed to take up any lash that may be present. Some models of engines have mechanical adjustments as well as hydraulic adjustment. The mechanical adjustments are used to place the hydraulic unit in its midrange position for normal operation. Because no clearance exists in valve trains using hydraulic lifters, no quieting ramp is provided on their cams.

The solid lifter is solid in the sense that it transfers motion axially from the cam to the pushrod or valve. Its physical construction is a lightweight cylinder, either hollow or with a small diameter center section and full diameter ends. In some types, the external appearance is the same as hydraulic lifters.

The major parts of a hydraulic lifter consist of a hollow cylinder enclosing a closely fit hollow plunger, a check valve, and a pushrod cup. Engine oil pressure is fed by an engine passage to the exterior lifter body. An undercut portion allows the oil under pressure to surround the lifter body. Holes in the undercut allow the oil under pressure to go into the center of the plunger and down through the check valve to a clearance space between the bottom of the plunger and interior bottom of the lifter body base, filling this space with oil at engine pressure. Slight leakage designed into the lifter allows the air to bleed out of the unit and allows the lifter to leak down if it should become over-filled as a result of *pump up* caused by excessive engine speeds.

The pushrod fits into a cup in the top open end of the lifter plunger. A hole in the pushrod cup, pushrod end, and hollow pushrod allows oil to transfer from the lifter piston center, up through the pushrods to the rocker arm, where it lubricates the rocker arm assemblies.

As the cam starts to push the lifter against the valve train, the oil below the lifter plunger is squeezed and it tries to return to the lifter plunger center; however, a lifter check valve traps the oil below the lifter plunger, hydraulically locking the operating lifter length. The lifter then opens the valve as one solid unit. When the lifter returns to the flat of the cam, engine oil pressure again replaces any oil that may have leaked out of the unit.

The hydraulic lifter's job is to take up all clearance in the valve train. Occasionally, engines are run at *excessive* speeds. This tends to throw the valve open, causing *valve float*. Under these conditions, clearance exists in the valve train. The hydraulic lifter will take up this clearance as it is designed to do. When this occurs, it will prevent the valve from seating and is called *pump up*. Pump up will not occur when the engine is operated in its designed speed range.

Fig. 4-25 Typical solid valve lifters. The external appearance of the two lifters on the right is the same as a hydraulic lifter. The one on the far right is disassembled to show the internal parts required to control oil flow to the pushrod.

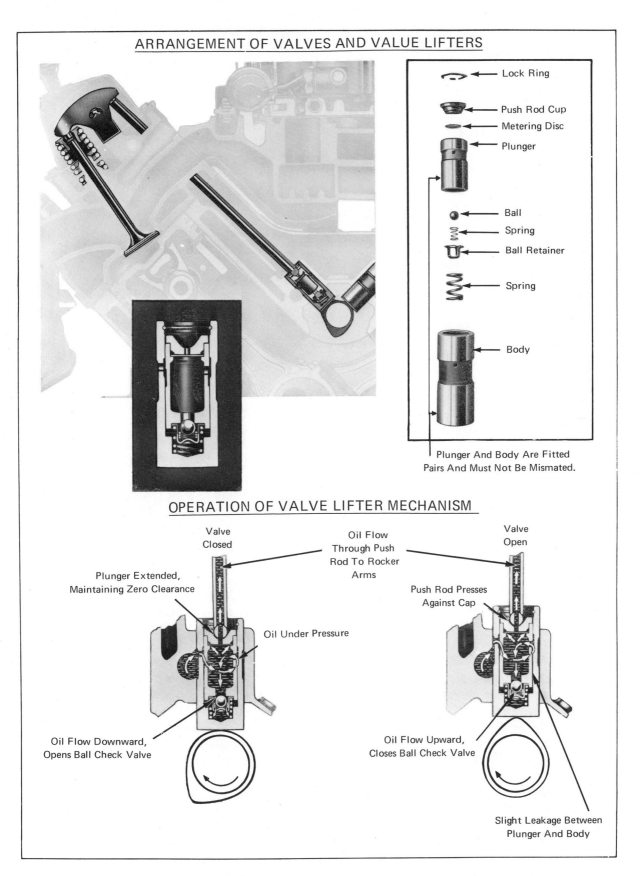

ARRANGEMENT OF VALVES AND VALUE LIFTERS

Lock Ring

Push Rod Cup

Metering Disc

Plunger

Ball

Spring

Ball Retainer

Spring

Body

Plunger And Body Are Fitted
Pairs And Must Not Be Mismated.

OPERATION OF VALVE LIFTER MECHANISM

Valve
Closed

Oil Flow
Through Push
Rod To Rocker
Arms

Valve
Open

Plunger Extended,
Maintaining Zero Clearance

Push Rod Presses
Against Cap

Oil Under Pressure

Oil Flow Downward,
Opens Ball Check Valve

Oil Flow Upward,
Closes Ball Check Valve

Slight Leakage Between
Plunger And Body

Fig. 4-26 Hydraulic valve lifters (Cadillac Motor Car Division, General Motors Corporation).

Review Questions
Chapter 4

1. What are the advantages of turbulent and non-turbulent combustion chambers?

2. What may be the reason for an obvious bump in a head port?

3. What is the reason that some head gasket holes do not match the holes in the head?

4. What methods are used to get oil to the overhead valve assemblies?

5. How is excess oil prevented from running down the valve stem into the port?

6. Why are multiple valve springs used?

7. When are valve rotators used?

8. What is the purpose of rocker arm ratio?

9. Under what conditions is it necessary to have hollow pushrods?

10. What are the advantages of flat lifters and of roller lifters?

11. When are stamped rocker arms used rather than cast rocker arms?

12. Why do solid lifters never have problems with float when hydraulic lifters may?

Quiz 4

1. In a wedge-shaped combustion chamber, the squish area is designed to
   a. cool the end gases
   b. modify the compression ratio
   c. reduce the combustion chamber volume
   d. increase the speed of combustion.

2. Reduction of the squish area in modern engines has
   a. reduced the engine's displacement
   b. reduced unburned hydrocarbon emission
   c. increased combustion chamber turbulence
   d. increased the combustion chamber area to valve ratio.

3. Siamesed ports have little effect on an engine's maximum power because
   a. they are larger than individual ports
   b. they are used for slow moving intake gases
   c. connecting cylinders have the same displacement
   d. connecting cylinders use them alternately.

4. Head gasket holes may not match the openings in the head on some engines. The most likely cause of the mismatch is
   a. a manufacturing error
   b. an incorrect gasket
   c. for coolant flow control
   d. to adjust the compression ratio.

5. Valves are closed by the
   a. cam
   b. spring
   c. rocker arm
   d. pushrod.

6. Exhaust valves can be made smaller than intake valves because
   a. intake gases are cooler
   b. intake gases take more volume
   c. exhaust gas has expanded
   d. exhaust gas moves at high speeds.

7. Sodium filling used in the exhaust valve stem
   a. keeps the gas from getting as hot
   b. transfers heat from the valve head to guide
   c. lightens the valve for high speed operation
   d. increases the valve strength.

8. Oil seals are used on valves to keep the oil from getting into the
   a. intake manifold
   b. rocker cover
   c. cylinder
   d. cooling system.

9. Rocker arm ratio is used to
   a. reduce lifter movement
   b. adjust cam lift
   c. limit pushrod length
   d. control valve timing.

10. Hydraulic lifter excess pump up occurs any time the
    a. engine runs at high speeds
    b. oil pressure peaks
    c. valves stick closed
    d. valves float.

chapter 5

Piston, Ring, and Rod Assemblies

All of an engine's power is developed by burning fuel in the presence of air in the combustion chamber. Combustion heat causes the combustion gas to increase its pressure. The force of this pressure is converted into useful work through the piston, connecting rod, and crankshaft.

The piston forms a movable bottom to the combustion chamber. It is attached to the connecting rod that forms a swivel joint at each end. The connecting rod is connected to an offset portion of the crankshaft, called a crank throw, crank pin or connecting rod bearing journal. Piston rings seal the small space between the piston and cylinder wall keeping the pressure above the piston. When the combustion pressure builds up in the combustion chamber it pushes on the piston. The piston, in turn, pushes on the piston pin or wrist pin that connects the piston to the upper end of the connecting rod. The lower end of the connecting rod pushes on the crank throw providing the force to turn the crankshaft. This turning force, called torque, turns the drive wheels through a drive train.

As the crankshaft turns it develops inertia that causes it to continue turning to bring the piston back to its initial position where it will be ready to transfer torque from the next combustion. While the engine is running this cycle continues with the piston reciprocating and the crankshaft rotating. These motions impose mechanical forces on the parts. The combustion heat and mechanical forces are a major consideration in the part design.

5-1 PISTON CRITERIA

When the engine is running, the piston starts at the top of the cylinder, accelerates downward to a maximum velocity at approximately halfway down, then comes to a stop at the bottom of the cylinder during 180° of crankshaft rotation. During the next 180° of crankshaft rotation, the piston starts to move upward, accelerates to a maximum velocity and then comes to a stop at the top of the stroke. Thus, the piston starts, accelerates, and stops twice in each crankshaft revolution. This reciprocating action of the piston produces large inertia forces. The lighter the piston can be made, the less inertia is developed. Less inertia will allow higher engine operating speeds.

The piston operates with its head exposed to the hot combustion gases while the skirt contacts the relatively cool cylinder wall. This results in a temperature gradient or temperature difference of about 275°F from the top of the piston to the bottom.

The automotive engine piston, then, is more than a cylinder plug that converts the combustion pressure to a force on the crankshaft. It is a fine compromise between strength, weight, and thermal expansion control; at the same time, it must support piston sealing rings. The piston must have satisfactory durability to *live* under these conditions while performing its function and while sliding against a cylinder wall.

As engine designs have developed over the years, aluminum alloys have proved to be the best material from which to make pistons. Aluminum provides adequate strength with light weight. It does, however, increase the thermal expansion problem because the aluminum alloys have greater expansion rates than the cast iron used in the blocks and cylinder bores in which the pistons operate.

To further complicate piston design problems, modern automobile styling limits the space available for the engine while, at the same time, the customers demand increased engine performance. The easiest way to provide more engine power is to increase the engine displacement by enlarging the cylinder bore size and lengthening the piston stroke. Each of these require more space; however, more space isn't available. The passenger car engine designer has been able to increase engine displacement while still maintaining engine size by reducing the height of

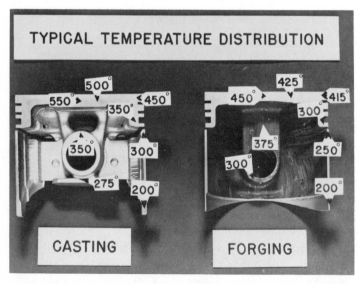

Fig. 5-1 Typical piston temperature distribution (Michigan Division of TRW).

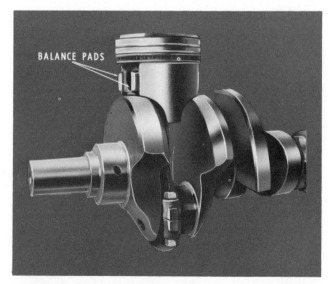

Fig. 5-2 Piston to crankshaft clearance (Chevrolet Motors Division, General Motors Corporation).

the piston to a bare minimum. The piston still must be able to have enough strength to support combustion pressures and reciprocating loads, to have enough skirt to guide the piston straight in the bore, to have expansion control for quiet, long-life operation, and to be able to hold the piston rings perpendicular to the cylinder wall.

Piston Heads. Because the piston head forms a portion of the combustion chamber, its configuration is very important to the combustion process. Generally, the low cost, low performance engines have flat-top pistons. Some of these flat-top pistons come

so close to the cylinder head that recesses are cut in the piston top to provide valve head clearance. Pistons used in high powered engines may have raised domes or a *pop-up* on the piston heads, which will increase compression pressures. Pistons used in other engines may be provided with a depression or a *dish* that may be varied in depth as a means of providing different compression pressures required by engine model specifications.

(a)

(b)

Fig. 5-3 Piston head shapes from flat (a) to dished (e) and pop-up (f, g).

(c)

(d)

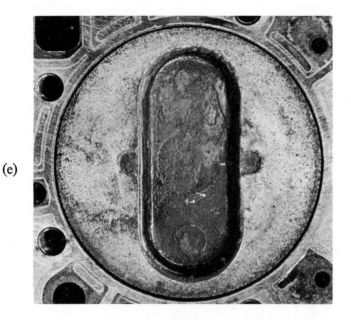

(e)

(f)

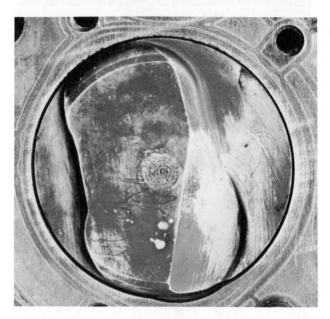

(g)

The piston head must have enough strength to support combustion pressures. Ribs are often used on the underside of the head to maintain strength while reducing material to lighten the piston. These ribs are also used as cooling fins to transfer some of the piston heat to the engine oil.

Fig. 5-4 Internal piston ribs (Sealed Power Corporation).

Piston Ring Grooves. Piston ring grooves are located between the piston head and skirt. The width of the grooves, the width of the metal between the grooves or lands, and the number of rings are critical in determining minimum piston height. Some heavy-duty pistons have oil ring grooves located on the piston skirt below the piston pin. Passenger car engines use two compression rings and one oil control ring, all located above the piston pin.

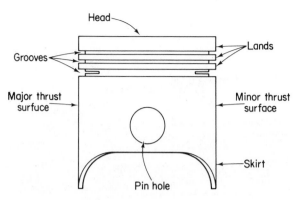

Fig. 5-5 Piston nomenclature.

The piston ring groove depth must be deep enough to prevent ring bottoming in the base of the groove. Its depth becomes critical when used with some piston ring expander designs. The groove must be true and flat so that necessary sealing can occur. Oil ring grooves must be vented so that oil scraped from the cylinder wall can flow through the piston to the crankcase. This venting is done through drilled holes, saw slots, or cast slots.

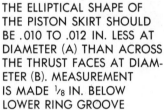

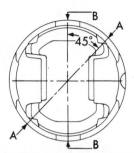

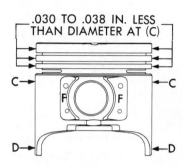

THE ELLIPTICAL SHAPE OF THE PISTON SKIRT SHOULD BE .010 TO .012 IN. LESS AT DIAMETER (A) THAN ACROSS THE THRUST FACES AT DIAMETER (B). MEASUREMENT IS MADE ⅛ IN. BELOW LOWER RING GROOVE

DIAMETERS AT (C) AND (D) CAN BE EQUAL OR DIAMETER AT (D) CAN BE .0015 IN. GREATER THAN (C)

Fig. 5-7 Piston skirt cam shape (Chrysler-Plymouth Division, Chrysler Corporation).

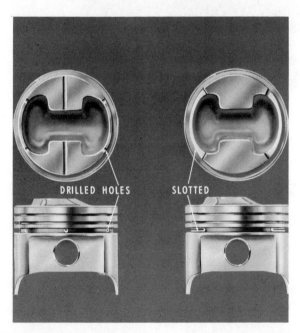

Fig. 5-6 Oil return openings (Chevrolet Motors Division, General Motors Corporation).

Piston Skirt. Piston expansion was a minor problem in older engines with cast iron pistons. Owners of these engines would tolerate piston slap noise from large piston-to-cylinder wall clearances on cold engines if the slap noise would stop when the engine warmed up. Some means of piston expan-

sion control was required as the owner demanded quiet operation and as the engine power increased.

Piston expansion was first controlled through *slotted piston skirts* that were more closely fitted in the cylinder. The piston would expand into the slot as it was heated during operation. The most popular slot types were the U slot and the T slot. The U slot design had two slots on the piston skirt that were connected together near the top of the piston skirt forming an inverted U shape. The T slot had one slot down the piston skirt with a cross slot at the upper edge of the piston skirt to form a T slot design. This method of expansion control carried over into the early aluminum pistons.

Aluminum pistons expand more than the cast iron pistons and the expansion slot piston skirt was too weak for the increased power demand required from the new engines. A better method of expansion control was devised using a *cam ground piston skirt*. The piston thrust surface closely fitted the cylinder, while the piston pin boss diameter fitted loosely. As the cam ground piston was heated, it would expand along the piston pin, so it became nearly round at normal operating temperatures.

Later model engines have modified cam ground piston skirts by adding a progressively round skirt

53

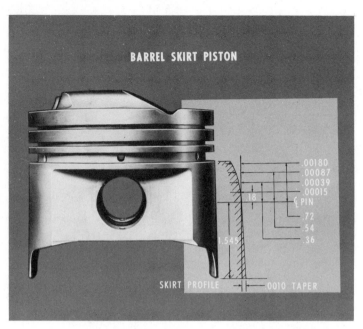

Fig. 5-8 Barrel skirt piston (Chevrolet Motors Division, General Motors Corporation).

 (a)

 (b)

Fig. 5-9 Piston oil slot and heat dams. (a) Cast slot, (b) saw slot, (c) saw slot with cast opening below piston pin.

 (c)

cam drop or barrel shape. The lowest portion of the piston is further from the combustion chamber and expands less than the upper portion. Therefore, the lower portion of the piston skirt may be made larger than the upper portion of the skirt at the thrust diameter. This allows the lower portion of the skirt to have a closer cold fit in the cylinder for quiet operation, while at the same time providing satisfactory service life.

Some pistons have horizontal separation slots that act as heat dams. These slots reduce heat transfer from the head to the lower skirt and, consequently, reduce the skirt temperature with an accompanying reduction in expansion. By placing the slot in the oil ring groove, some manufacturers use the slot for oil drain back as well as for heat control. Placing the slot below the piston pin isolates the skirt from piston pin boss deflections that occur on the power stroke.

A major development in expansion control was accomplished by casting the piston aluminum around two stiff steel struts. The struts are not chemically bonded to the aluminum nor do they add any strength to the piston. There is only a mechanical bond between the steel and aluminum. The bi-metallic action of this strut in the aluminum causes the piston to bow outward along the piston pin. This allows the thrust faces to expand at a slower rate than the cast iron cylinder in which they operate. Steel strut insert pistons allow good operation clearances while at the same time allowing cold clearance as small as .0005″, which will eliminate cold piston slap and noise.

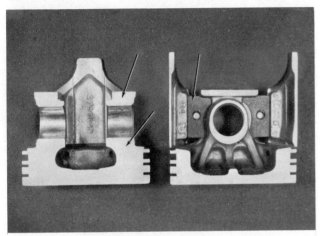

Fig. 5-10 Steel strut insert in piston.

Heavy-duty pistons are cylindrical castings with ring grooves at the top, using a trunk-type skirt. As the automotive passenger car requirements increase, the number and thickness of the piston rings has decreased and the cast aluminum piston skirt has been reduced to a minimum by using an open-type

Fig. 5-11 Open slipper skirt cast piston.

slipper skirt. High performance engines need pistons with added strength. They use impact extruded pistons whose design falls between these two extremes of heavy-duty and automotive pistons.

Fig. 5-12 Forged piston (Michigan Division of TRW).

Finish. For maximum life, piston skirt surface finish is important. Turned grooves or waves .0005″ deep on the surface of the piston skirt produce a finish that will carry oil for lubrication. A thin tin-plated surface (approximately .00005″ thick) is also used on some aluminum pistons to help reduce scuffing and scoring during boundary lubrication. The piston skirt must ride on a film of lubricating oil to operate satisfactorily. Any time oil film is lacking, metal-to-metal contact will occur, and this starts scuffing. Piston scuffing leads to poor oil control, short piston life, roughened cylinder bores, and scuffed rings.

Piston Balance. Pistons are provided with enlarged pads or skirt flanges that are used for controlling piston weight. Material is removed from these pad surfaces as the last machining operation to bring the piston within weight tolerances set by the manufacturer.

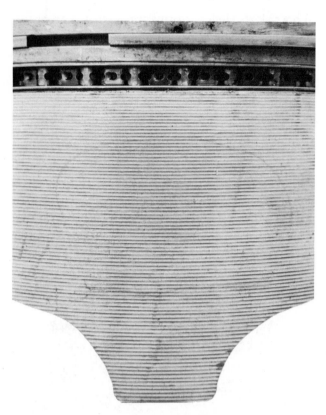

Fig. 5-13 Piston surface finishes in common use.

Fig. 5-14 Location of piston balance weight pads.

5-2 PISTON PINS

Piston pins are used to attach the piston to the connecting rod, transferring the combustion chamber pressures and piston forces to the connecting rod. The piston pin is made from high quality steel in a tubular shape to provide adequate strength at a minimum weight. Sometimes the interior hole is tapered, large at the ends and small in the middle of the pin. This gives the pin strength that is proportional to the location of the load. Of course, a double-taper hole such as this is more expensive to manufacture and is only used where its weight advantage merits the extra cost.

Piston Pin Offset. Piston pin holes located in the piston are not centered but are located toward the major thrust surface approximately .062″ from the piston center line. Pin offset is designed to reduce piston slap and noise that results from crossover action as the connecting rod swings past both upper and lower dead centers.

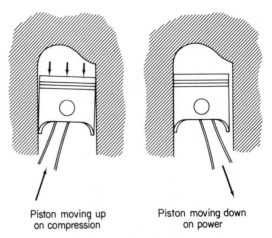

Fig. 5-16 Piston offset control as the crankshaft crosses over top center.

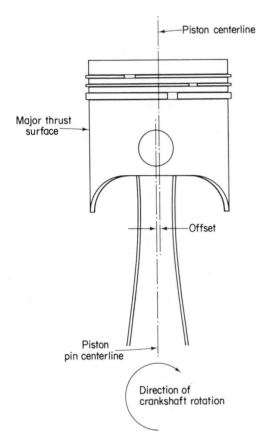

Fig. 5-15 Piston pin offset.

As the piston approaches top center in normal operation, it will be riding against the minor thrust surface. When compression pressure becomes high enough, the greater area of the piston head on the minor thrust side resulting from pin offset causes the piston to cock slightly in the cylinder. This places the top of the piston skirt on the minor thrust surface and the bottom of the piston skirt on the major thrust surface against the cylinder wall. When the crankshaft crosses over top center, the connecting rod angularly forces the piston toward the major thrust surface. The lower skirt is already in wall contact with the major thrust surface so that the rest of the piston skirt wipes into full wall contact, thereby controlling *piston slap*.

Locating the piston offset toward the minor thrust surface will provide a better mechanical advantage. This offset direction is often used in racing engines where noise and durability are not as important as maximum performance.

Piston Pin Fits. The finish and size of piston pins are very closely controlled. Piston pins have a finish nearly like a mirror. Their size is held to tenths-of-thousandths of an inch so that exact fits can be maintained. If the piston pin is loose in the piston or in the connecting rod, it will cause a rattle while the engine is running. If the piston pin is too tight in the piston, it will restrict piston expansion along the pin diameter and will, therefore, produce piston scuffing. Normal piston pin clearances range from .0005″ to .0007″, which provides adequate freedom for movement between the piston and pin.

Piston Pin Retaining Methods. It is necessary to retain piston pins so that they stay centered in the piston. If piston pins were not retained, they would move endwise and gouge the cylinder wall. Piston pins are retained by one of three general methods. The piston pin may be full floating, having some type of stop located at each end; it may be fastened to the connecting rod; or it may be fastened to the piston.

Full-floating piston pins in automotive engines are retained by lock rings located in grooves in the piston pin hole at the ends of the piston pin. Some

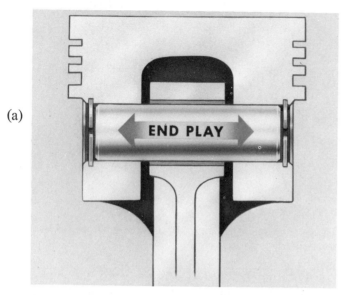

(a)

(b)

Fig. 5-17 Piston pin retaining devices. (a) Retaining ring (Ford Motor Company), (b) clamp bolt.

engines use aluminum or plastic plugs in both ends of the piston pin. These plugs may touch the cylinder wall without scoring, thus holding the piston pin centered in the piston.

Piston pins may be retained in the connecting rod by a clamp bolt located in the piston end of the connecting rod. The piston pin has an undercut which allows a portion of the clamp bolt side to locate the pin in the piston center. The bolt then clamps the rod around the pin, holding it securely. A newer method of retaining the pin in the connecting rod is to make the connecting rod hole slightly smaller than the piston pin. The pin is installed by pressing it into the rod so that it will be securely held by the press fit. With this method, care must be

exercised to insure correct hole sizes and correct centering. The press fit method is the least expensive to produce and is, therefore, found in the majority of passenger car engines.

Automobile engines do not fasten the piston pin to the piston. On heavy duty engines where this is done, a cap screw through one side of the piston boss enters a hole or contacts a flat on the piston pin, thus retaining the pin. The cap screw is only placed on one side so that clamping does not interfere with normal piston expansion along the pin.

5-3 PISTON RINGS

Piston rings must provide two major functions; first, to form a sliding combustion chamber seal that will prevent *blow-by* of high pressure gases past the piston, and second, to keep engine oil from getting into the combustion chamber. The rings also transfer some of the piston heat to the cylinder wall where it is removed from the engine by the cooling system.

Piston rings are classified as two types, compression rings, located toward the top of the piston, and oil rings, located below the compression rings. The first piston rings were made with a simple rectangular cross-section. This cross section was modified by tapers, chamfers, counterbores, slots, rails and expanders. Piston ring materials have also changed from plain cast iron to materials such as pearlitic and nodular iron as well as steel. Piston rings may be coated with chromium or molybdenum materials.

5-4 COMPRESSION RINGS

In order to obtain maximum power from the combustion pressure a compression ring must form a seal between the moving piston and cylinder wall, at the same time keeping friction at a minimum. This is done by providing sufficient static or built-in mechanical pressure to hold the ring in initial contact with the cylinder wall during the intake stroke. Combustion chamber pressure during the compression, power, and exhaust strokes is applied to the top and back of the ring to provide the added force on the ring required for combustion chamber sealing during these strokes.

Fig. 5-18 Dynamic sealing force on the compression ring (Dana Corporation).

Mechanical pressure of the ring results from the ring shape, material characteristics and expanders. Rings are manufactured with a cam shape in their free state. When the piston ring is compressed to the cylinder size, it becomes round and develops the required mechanical tension. Additional piston ring control is provided by chamfers and counterbores that cause the ring to twist when it is compressed to the size of the cylinder. Twist is used to

Fig. 5-19 Ring twist resulting from ring shape.

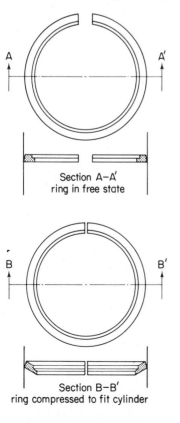

A ————— A'

Section A–A'
ring in free state

B ————— B'

Section B–B'
ring compressed to fit cylinder

provide line contact sealing on the cylinder wall and in the piston ring groove. Line contact provides a relatively high unit pressure for sealing while, at the same time, allowing low total force which results in low friction. Expanders are sometimes used under compression rings when additional static force is required. When pressure exists in the combustion chamber, it acts on the top piston ring, forcing it to flatten on the base of the piston ring groove sealing the ring and piston joint. For this sealing, it is important that the ring groove be flat and square. Pressure above and behind the ring will force it against the ring groove bottom and against the cylinder wall to produce an effective moving combustion chamber seal.

The piston ring joint will allow some leakage past the top compression ring. This leakage is useful to provide the required dynamic pressure on the second ring, so it can develop its required sealing force in the same manner as the top ring develops sealing force. Piston ring gap is critical, however. Too much gap will cause excessive blow-by that will blow oil from the cylinder wall. This oil loss would be followed by piston ring scuffing. Insufficient clearance, on the other hand, would cause the piston ring ends to butt when hot. Ring end butting increases the mechanical force against the cylinder wall, causing excessive wear and possible engine failure.

A butt-type piston ring gap is the most common type used in automotive engines. This, obviously, is the least expensive to manufacture. Some low speed industrial engine manufacturers use a more expensive tapered or seal-cut ring gap to reduce losses of the high-pressure combustion gases.

Fig. 5-20 Piston ring joint gap types.

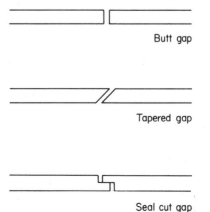

Butt gap

Tapered gap

Seal cut gap

Chapter 5

Piston Ring and Rod Assemblies

As engine speeds have increased, inertia forces on the piston rings have also increased. Engine manufacturers have found it desirable to reduce inertia forces by reducing piston ring weight. This has been done over the years by narrowing the piston ring in fractional steps from $\frac{1}{4}$ inch to as low as $\frac{1}{16}$ inch.

A discussion of piston ring cross-section must start with a rectangular shape. This was modified with a tapered face that would contact the cylinder wall at the lower edge of the piston ring. When a chamfer or counterbore relief is provided on the upper inside corner of the piston ring, the relief will cause the ring to twist in the groove in a positive direction, giving the same wall contact as the taper-face ring; at the same time it will provide a line contact seal in the groove. Sometimes the twist and taper face are used on the same ring.

Fig. 5-21 Compression ring cross sections as installed (conditions exaggerated).

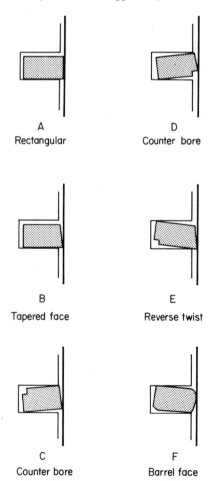

A
Rectangular

D
Counter bore

B
Tapered face

E
Reverse twist

C
Counter bore

F
Barrel face

Some second rings are notched on the outer lower corner. This, too, provides a positive ring twist. The sharp lower-outer corner becomes a scraper that helps oil control, but it has less compression control than the preceding types.

By chamfering the ring lower-inner corner, a reverse twist is provided. This seals the lower outer section of the ring and piston, thus improving oil control. Reverse twist rings require a greater taper to maintain the desired ring face to cylinder wall contact.

Some rings replace the outer ring taper with a barrel face. The barrel is .0003″ per .100″ of piston ring width. Barrel faces may be found on rectangular rings as well as on torsionally twisted rings.

Piston ring facing materials are very important to provide maximum service life. Prior to World War II, rings were made *entirely* of cast iron. This practice was modified during the war as a result of aircraft engine piston ring development. Techniques were developed to put a chromium face on the piston ring face. This hard chromium surface greatly increases piston ring life, especially where abrasive materials are present in the air. During manufacture, the chromium-plated ring is slightly chamfered at the outer corners and about .0004″ of chrome is plated on the passenger car engine compression ring face. These are pre-lapped or honed before being packaged and shipped to the customer.

Early in the 1960's, molybdenum piston ring faces were introduced. These rings also proved to have good service life, especially in high temperature applications and under scuffing conditions. Most molybdenum-faced piston rings have a .004″ to .008″ deep groove cut on the ring face that is filled with molybdenum, using a metallic spray method, so that there is a cast iron edge above and below the molybdenum. This edge may be chamfered on some applications.

Molybdenum-faced piston rings will survive under heat and scuffing conditions better than chromium-faced rings. Under abrasive wear conditions, chromium-faced rings will have a better service life. There is little measurable difference between these two facing materials with respect to blow-by, oil control, break-in, and horsepower. Piston rings with either of these two types of facings are far better than plain cast iron rings. Often, a molybdenum-faced ring will be found in the top groove and a chromium-faced ring in the second groove.

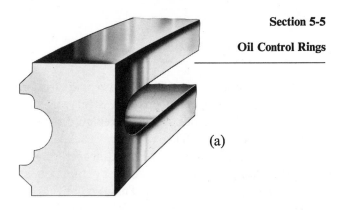

(a)

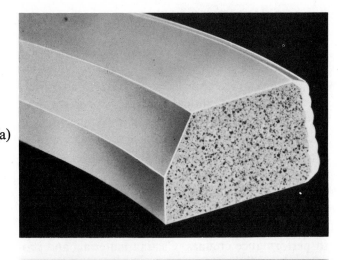

(a)

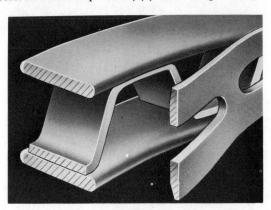

(b)

Fig. 5-23 Cast vented oil rings. (a) Cast, (b) cast with rails and expander (Dana Corporation).

(b)

Fig. 5-22 Compression ring facing. (a) Chromium, (b) molybdenum (Sealed Power Corporation).

Fig. 5-24 Steel ribbon oil ring rails, expanders and spacers [(a) Sealed Power Corporation, (b) Dana Corporation].

5-5 OIL CONTROL RINGS

Originally, piston rings were not divided into compression and oil rings, but were plain rectangular rings. The first rings to be called oil rings were tapered rings with a scraping lower edge that removed a large part of the oil from the cylinder wall on the piston down stroke. These rings were then vented by machining slots through the ring, groove and through openings in the piston. This machining produced two scraping edges that performed better than the single edge. Steel spring expanders were added to improve radial pressure that forced the ring to conform to the cylinder wall. Many expander designs are used. They may either act as a spring between the ring groove base and the ring or their force can result from radial action when the two ends of the expander butt together under a compression force as the ring is forced into the ring groove by the cylinder.

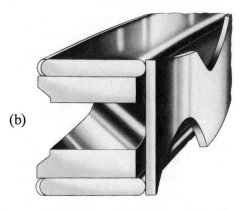

(a)

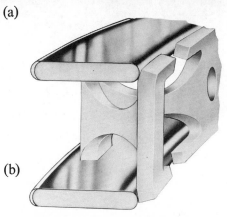

(b)

As the oil ring requirements became greater, cast iron was no longer satisfactory. Steel rails with chromium or other types of facings replaced the cast iron scraping edges. The rails are backed with expanders and separated with a spacer. Some expander designs provide the spacing function as well as the expansion function. This type of oil ring is lightweight, having desirable low inertia loads, and is well-ventilated so the oil can easily flow through it to the crankcase. It provides excellent oil control and has a long service life. All of this is provided at a low cost and is, therefore, used on volume-produced passenger car applications.

The piston ring cannot do its job unless it can seal against the cylinder wall through its entire normal service life. Cylinder wall finishes are critical. The cylinder wall is honed with a 60° included-angle cross hatch pattern. The coarseness of this finish must be compatible with the requirements of the piston ring facing materials. In general, the finish roughness should be a satin finish of about 25 micro-inches. Micro-inches are a measure of the average surface smoothness from the highest hump to the lowest depression.

Fig. 5-25 Cylinder wall finish.

5-6 CONNECTING RODS

The connecting rod transfers piston reciprocating force to crankshaft rotation. The small end of the connecting rod reciprocates and the large end follows the crank pin rotational pattern. These dynamic motions make it desirable to keep the connecting rod as light as possible and still have a rigid beam section. Lightweight rods also reduce the total connecting rod material cost.

Connecting rods are manufactured by both casting and forging processes. Forged connecting rods have been used for years and are always used in performance engines. Casting materials and processes have been improved so that many high production standard passenger car engines are able to replace forged connecting rods with less expensive cast connecting rods. Their cost is reduced both in the initial casting cost and in the machining cost. Generally speaking, the forging method produces lighter weight, but more expensive connecting rods.

The connecting rod design is basically two ring forms that encircle the piston pin and the crankshaft rod journal. From each of these ring forms a tangential fillet blends into a tapered I-beam section that makes up the rigid rod strut. The large splitting-ring form for the crankshaft end is machined after the cap is assembled on the rod so that it forms a perfect circle. Assembly bolt holes are closely reamed in both the cap and connecting rod to assure alignment. The connecting rod bolt diameters have piloting surfaces which bear in these reamed holes. The bolt heads are formed so that they have two or three sides which bear against the rod bolt bosses. The fourth side is left off so that there is sufficient cylinder skirt clearance as the crankshaft turns. Some connecting rod bolt heads are made on an angle to provide adequate clearance.

In some engines, offset connecting rods provide the most economical distribution of main bearing space and crankshaft cheeks. The amount of offset of the piston pin end and the crankshaft journal end is measured in the lengthwise direction of the engine. Usually, the offset is divided equally between each end, keeping the connecting rod column perpendicular. Offset rods do not have as good a bearing endurance quality as symmetrical rods. Bearing failure occurs in the bearing edge halves nearest the shank where the loads are greatest.

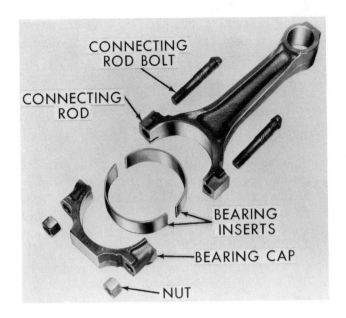

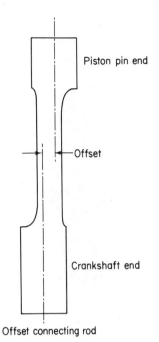

Fig. 5-27 Offset connecting rod.

Others have a balancing boss above the piston pin as well. Some manufacturers put balancing bosses on the side of the rod near the connecting rod center of gravity. Balancing is done on automatic balancing machines prior to being installed in an engine.

Fig. 5-28 Connecting rod balancing bosses.

Fig. 5-26 Connecting rod assembly. (a) Bolts (Cadillac Motor Car Division, General Motors Corporation), (b) Cap screws (Ford Motor Company).

The sweep or path of the connecting rod must clear all engine parts as the crankshaft rotates. This would require minimum bolt center line distance and minimum head and nut size. The large end, however, needs to be large enough to carry a connecting rod bearing that is designed to support the dynamic loads. The length of the bearing usually determines bearing high speed endurance capacity.

Connecting rods are made with balancing bosses, so their weight can easily be held to specifications. Some have balancing bosses only on the rod cap.

63

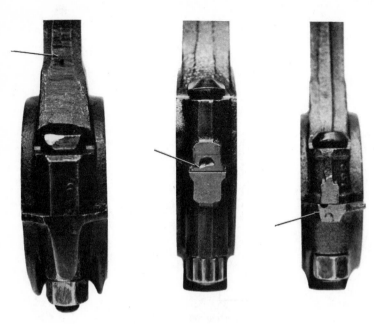

Fig. 5-29 Rod spit and bleed holes.

Most connecting rods have *spit holes* that bleed some of the oil from the connecting rod journal. The hole may be drilled or it may be a chamfer on the cap parting surface. Oil is thrown from the spit hole into the cylinder that the rod is in on inline engines and into the opposing cylinder in the opposite bank on V engines. This oil is aimed so that it will splash into the interior of the piston and lubricate the piston pin. Occasionally, adequate lubrication is obtained without a spit hole. A hole similar to the spit holes is provided as a *bleed hole* to control oil flow through the bearing. Some heavy-duty engine connecting rods are drilled lengthwise. Oil flows through the drilled passage to the piston pin. This is an expensive process and is only used where the spit-hole method will not supply adequate lubrication.

Review Questions
Chapter 5

1. How has piston design helped the engineer fit a large displacement engine into a small space?

2. How does the piston head configuration affect engine performance?

3. In a standard engine, which side of the engine does the major piston thrust surface face?

4. Why is piston thermal expansion control required on passenger car engines?

5. What is the value of *cam drop* grinding on piston skirts?

6. Illustrate the bi-metallic action of the steel strut in the aluminum piston.

7. How can reverse offset be helpful in performance engines?

8. Why is the press fit method of retaining piston pins less expensive than the other methods?

9. What are the major functions of piston rings?

10. Under what condition is combustion pressure leakage an asset?

11. What are the advantages of coated piston rings?

12. What advantage does the reverse twist ring have over the forward twist ring?

13. Under what conditions are piston ring expanders used?

14. What are the advantages of forged connecting rods? Cast connecting rods?

15. When are offset connecting rods used?

Quiz 5

1. A *dish* in the piston head is used to
   a. control compression ratio
   b. adjust engine displacement
   c. lighten the piston weight
   d. provide valve clearance.

2. Steel struts are used in some pistons to
   a. keep the piston from expanding
   b. make a stronger piston
   c. reduce piston weight
   d. control the direction of expansion.

3. Slipper skirt pistons are required with engines that have
   a. short connecting rods
   b. high power outputs
   c. require high strength pistons
   d. aluminum pistons in cast iron cylinders.

4. Piston pins are offset in high production passenger car engines to
   a. increase engine power
   b. fit the engine design configuration
   c. minimize piston slap
   d. control piston expansion.

5. The majority of piston pins are kept from touching the cylinder wall by
   a. press fit in the piston
   b. interference fit in the rod
   c. retaining rings at each end of the pin
   d. clamp bolt on the rod.

6. Expanders are used with some piston rings. Their primary purpose is to
   a. make up for cylinder wear
   b. reduce dynamic tension
   c. increase static tension
   d. compensate for piston ring wear.

7. High pressure combustion gases leak through the top ring gap. This leakage
   a. helps seal the second ring
   b. is undesirable
   c. overloads the second ring
   d. is finally controlled by the oil ring.

8. Chamfers and counterbore reliefs on piston rings are used to
   a. help the ring remain free in the groove
   b. control blow-by
   c. minimize carbon build-up
   d. twist the ring for a line contact.

9. Compression rings are often coated. The coating that withstands high temperature scuffing the best is
   a. molybdenum
   b. chromium
   c. teflon
   d. iron oxide.

10. Oil bleed holes are used in connecting rods to
    a. lubricate the piston pin
    b. control air flow through the bearing
    c. control maximum oil pressure
    d. prevent oil leakage from the engine.

chapter 6

Shafts, Bearings, and Oil Seals

Automotive engines have only two major rotating parts, the crankshaft and the camshaft. Power from expanding gases in the combustion chamber is delivered to the crankshaft through the piston, piston pin, and connecting rod. The connecting rods and their bearings are attached to a bearing journal on the off-set crank throw. Thus, the combustion force is transferred to the crank throw after the crankshaft has moved past top center to produce turning effort or torque which rotates the crankshaft. The camshaft is rotated by the crankshaft through gears, with chain driven sprockets or by belt-driven sprockets. The camshaft drive is timed so the valves open in relation to the piston position.

The crankshaft rotates in main bearings. These bearings are split in half so they can be assembled around the crankshaft bearing journals. The camshaft, in pushrod engines, rotates in sleeve bearings that are pressed into bearing bores within the engine block. Overhead camshaft bearings may be either sleeve-type or split-type bearings depending on the design of the bearing supports.

(a)

(b)

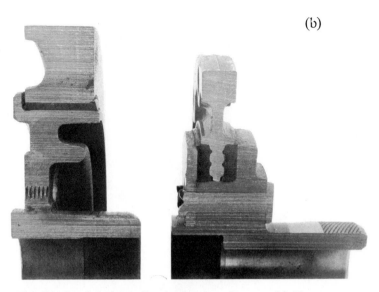

Fig. 6-1 Crankshaft torsional vibration damper. (a) Front view, (b) section view of two types.

Both shafts must be capable of supporting the intermittent variable loads impressed on them and still have the necessary properties to function as good bearing journals.

6-1 CRANKSHAFT

All of the engine power is delivered through the crankshaft. The shaft must have the necessary shape and must be made from proper materials to meet these power demands.

Crankshaft Requirements. Each time combustion occurs, the force deflects the crankshaft as it transfers torque to the output shaft. This deflection occurs in two ways, to bend the shaft sidewise and to twist the shaft in torsion. The crankshaft must be rigid enough to keep the deflection low.

Crankshaft deflections are directly related to engine roughness. When these deflections occur at the same vibrational or resonant frequency, that is vibrations per second, as another engine part, the parts will vibrate together. These vibrations may become great enough to reach the audible level, producing a "thumping" sound. If this type of vibration is allowed to continue, the part may fail.

Harmful crankshaft resonant frequencies are dampened with a torsional vibration damper. This damper usually consists of a cast iron inertia ring mounted to a cast iron hub with an elastomer sleeve. Elastomers are synthetic rubber-like materials. The inertia ring size is selected to control the amplitude of the crankshaft vibrations for each specific engine.

Crankshaft Material and Manufacturing. Crankshafts used in high production automotive engines may be either forged or cast. Forged crankshafts are stronger than the cast crankshafts, but they are more expensive. Casting materials and techniques have improved cast crankshaft quality so that they are being used in more and more engines.

Forged crankshafts are made from SAE 1045 or similar type steel. The crankshaft is formed from a hot steel billet through a series of forging dies. Each die changes the shape of the billet slightly, finally forming the crankshaft blank with the last die. These blanks are then machined to finish the crankshaft. Forging makes a very dense, tough shaft with a grain running parallel to the principle stress direction.

Two methods are used to forge crankshafts. One method is to forge the crankshaft in-place.

67

Fig. 6-2 Forged crankshaft. Forging lines indicate winding or twisting to index crankpins.

Fig. 6-3 Cast crankshaft showing overlap and fillets as well as a straight casting mold parting line.

This is followed by straightening. Forging in-place method is usually used with forged six-cylinder crankshafts. A second method is to forge the crankshaft in a single plane, then wind it to index the throws at the desired angles. Shaft blanks are straightened as part of the winding process. Forged crankshaft design is limited by the die geometry and the forging parting lines. This means that forged crankshaft design must be a compromise between crankshaft requirements and manufacturing capabilities.

Automotive crankshafts may be cast in steel, nodular iron, or malleable iron. The major advantage of the casting process is that crankshaft material and machining cost is reduced because the crankshaft may be made close to the required shape and size, including all complicated counterweights. The only machining required is grinding bearing journals and finishing front and rear drive ends. Metal grain structure is uniform and random throughout, thus the shaft is able to handle loads from all directions. Counterweights on cast crankshafts are slightly larger than counterweights on a forged crankshaft because the cast shaft metal is less dense and therefore somewhat lighter.

Crankshaft Design Features. The angle of the crankshaft throws in relation to each other are selected to provide a smooth power output. V-8 engines use 90° and 6-cylinder engines use 120° crank throws. The engine firing order is determined from the angles selected. Counterweights are used to balance static and dynamic forces that occur during engine operation.

Ample strength or torsional stiffness is one of the most important crankshaft design requirements. This can be provided by using materials with the correct physical properties, by having sufficient journal and crank cheek size, and by minimizing stress concentration through large fillets and properly placed lightening holes. Main- and rod-bearing journal overlap increases crankshaft strength because more of the load is carried through the overlap area rather than through the fillet and crankshaft web.

Stress tends to concentrate at oil holes drilled through the crankshaft journals. They are usually located where the crankshaft loads and stresses are minimal. The edges of these oil holes are carefully chamfered to relieve as much stress concentration as possible.

Fig. 6-4 Balance hole drilled in crankpin.

(a)

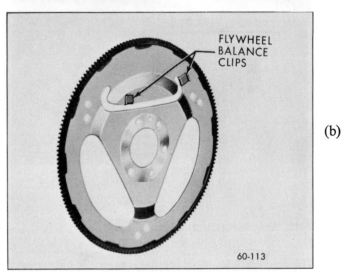

(b)

Fig. 6-5 Dynamic balancing weight. (a) Damper, (b) flywheel (Buick Motor Division, General Motors Corporation).

Lightening holes in the crank throws do not reduce their strength if the hole size is less than half of the bearing journal diameter. These holes will often increase crankshaft strength by relieving some of the crankshaft's natural stress. In some cast crankshafts, the hole in the center of the crank throw is used for balancing, by controlling the hole depth.

Most crankshaft balancing is done during manufacture. Holes for balance are often drilled in the counterweight to lighten them. Sometimes, these holes are drilled after the crankshaft is installed in the engine. Some manufacturers are able to control their casting quality so closely that counterweight machining for balancing is not necessary. Several engine manufacturers do final engine balancing with the engine running. Balance of these running engines is accomplished by adding weights to the damper hub and to the flywheel or automatic transmission drive plate.

Automatic transmission pressure and clutch release forces tend to push the crankshaft toward the front of the engine. Thrust bearings in the engine will support this thrust load as well as maintain the crankshaft position. Smooth bearing journal surfaces are ground on a small boss located on the crankshaft cheek adjacent to one of the main bearing journals. The main bearing has bearing flanges that ride against these thrust bosses. Thrust bearings may be located on any one of the main bearing journals.

It has been found through experience that journal grinding and polishing direction is very important. The bearing will last much longer when the journal is ground against the direction of normal rotation than if it is ground in the direction of normal rotation. This can be illustrated by realizing that the surface finish left by grinding has slightly bent whiskers like the teeth of a very fine file. It is smooth when the shaft turns with the direction of the

69

Fig. 6-6 Thrust bearing.

teeth, but it acts like a fine milling cutter when the direction of rotation is toward the teeth.

There are many crankshaft designs. The engineer bases his selection on previous crankshaft performance and experience, modified by cost considerations. New understandings in metallurgy and manufacturing techniques along with a better understanding of the load requirements will continue to lead to crankshaft improvements.

6-2 CAMSHAFT

The second rotating shaft is the camshaft. Its major function is to operate the valve train. Cam design is the major factor in an engine's operating characteristics.

Camshaft Requirements. The camshaft is timed to the crankshaft so that the valves are opened and closed in relation to crankshaft angle and piston

position. This allows the engine to have maximum volumetric efficiency at the engine speed selected. Cam lobe design has more control over engine performance characteristics than any other single engine part. Engines identical in every way except cam lobe design may have completely different operating characteristics and performance.

Fig. 6-7 Camshaft contour; Left, standard cam; right, performance cam.

The camshaft is driven by the crankshaft through gears, sprockets and chains, or sprockets and timing belts. The gears or sprockets are keyed to their shafts so that they can be installed in only one position. The gears and sprockets are then indexed together by marks on the gear teeth or chain links. When the crankshaft and camshaft timing marks are lined up, the cam lobes are indexed to the crankshaft throws of each cylinder, so that the valves will open and close correctly in relation to the piston position.

As the camshaft lobe pushes the lifter upward against the valve spring force, a backward torsion force is developed in the camshaft. After the lobe goes past its high point, the lifter moves down the back side of the lobe, causing a forward torsion force. This action produces an alternating torsion force at each cam lobe. These alternating torsion forces are multiplied by the number of cam lobes on the shaft. The camshaft must have sufficient strength to minimize torsion twist and to be tough enough to minimize fatigue.

Most valve trains use a spherical lifter face, 50″ to 80″ in diameter, that slides against the cam lobe. It contacts the lobe off center, because the lobe has a slight taper across its face. This produces a turning effort on the lifter to cause rotation. In operation, there is a wide line contact between the lifter and the cam lobe where the highest pressure

Fig. 6-8 Camshaft timing marks.
(a) Gear drive, (b) chain drive.

Fig. 6-9 Camshaft to lifter contact that tends to twist the cam.

Fig. 6-9 *Continued*

Fig. 6-10 Wide line cam to lifter contact.

loaded surface is produced in an engine. Therefore, a great amount of design effort has gone into the metallurgy, heat treatment, design and lubrication of the cam-to-lifter contact surface.

Camshaft Materials. Most automotive camshafts are made from hardenable alloy cast iron. It resists lifter wear and bearing wear, as well as providing the strength required. The very hardness required of camshafts makes them susceptible to chipping through edge loading or through careless handling.

Some heavy duty engine camshafts are made of steel. These must have case hardened journals and lobes to give them the required durability. Steel camshafts are also required in engines that use roller lifters.

Fig. 6-11 Cast iron and aluminum nylon timing gears.

The crankshaft gear or sprocket that drives the camshaft is made of sintered iron. The camshaft gear, when gears are used, has teeth made from a soft material to reduce noise. This whole gear is made of aluminum or fiber. When a chain and sprocket is used, the camshaft sprocket may be made of sintered iron or it may have an aluminum hub with nylon teeth for noise reduction. The timing chains are either a silent chain or roller chain.

Fig. 6-13 Oil groove around the outside of the cam bearing.

Fig. 6-12 Silent and roller timing chain.

Fig. 6-14 Indexing oil holes in a cam journal.

Camshaft Design Features. The camshaft is cast as one piece with lobes, bearing journals, drive flanges, and accessory gear blanks close to finished size. The drive end is finished first so the cam lobes will be correctly indexed. The accessory drive gear is finished with a gear cutter and the lobes and journals are ground. The remaining portion of the camshaft surface is not machined.

Camshaft bearing journals must be larger than the cam lobes so that the camshaft can be installed in the engine through the cam bearings. Some engines have each cam bearing progressively smaller from the front journal to the rear, while other engines use the same size camshaft bearing journals on all journals.

Some engines make use of the camshaft journal or camshaft bearing to transfer lubrication oil from the main oil gallery to the crankshaft. Cam bearing clearance is critical in these engines. Other engines use drilled holes in the camshaft bearing journals to meter lubricating oil to the overhead rocker arm each time the holes index between the bearing inlet and the outlet to the rocker arm.

Each camshaft must have some means to control the shaft end thrust. Two methods are in common usage. One method is to use a thrust plate between the camshaft drive gear or sprocket and a flange on the camshaft. This thrust plate is attached to the engine block with cap screws. A second method is to allow the natural thrust developed by the oil pump and distributor turning effort to hold the camshaft into the block. A flange on the back of the camshaft drive rides against the front of the block, preventing the camshaft from moving backward into the engine. Some camshafts also add a button, spring or retainer on the timing cover to limit forward motion of the camshaft.

73

Camshaft materials and manufacturing methods follow standard industrial practices. Cam lobe contour features greatly affect an engine's performance. These contours are the most critical camshaft design features and require very careful machining.

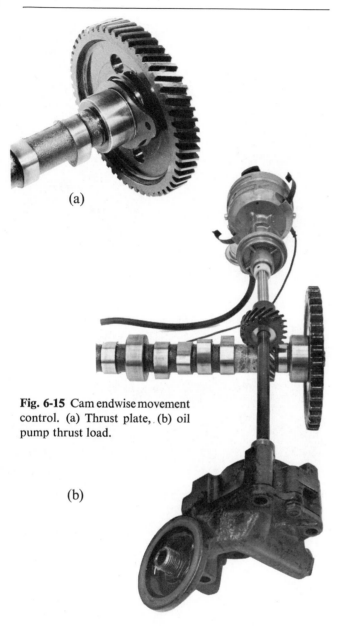

Fig. 6-15 Cam endwise movement control. (a) Thrust plate, (b) oil pump thrust load.

Fig. 6-16 Fuel pump eccentric locations on camshafts.

An eccentric cam lobe for the fuel pump is often cast as part of the camshaft. The pump is driven from this eccentric by a long pump linkage or pushrod. Some engines drive the fuel pump with a steel cup type eccentric that is bolted to the front of the cam drive gear. This allows a damaged fuel pump eccentric to be replaced without replacing an entire camshaft. It also allows the fuel pump to be mounted well forward on the engine, away from the exhaust, where it will be near the cool air coming into the front of the vehicle. This helps reduce the chance of vapor lock in the fuel pump and lines.

Dynamic oil seals are used between two surfaces that have relative motion between them, such as a shaft and a housing.

Dynamic Seal Operational Requirements. In engines, the seals keep liquids and gases in and keep contaminants out. They must do this with a minimum drag or friction. Oil seals must not press against the moving part so tightly that they wear a groove in the moving parts.

Some dynamic seals are designed to withstand a lot of pressure, such as piston rings, while others seal against little pressure, such as front and rear crankshaft oil seals. Seals in an engine that seal around rotating shafts are classified as radial positive-contact seals.

Seal selection is dependent upon the rubbing speed, fluid pressure, operating temperature, shaft surface requirements, and space available. When these factors are known for a specific application, the oil seal type can be selected.

Dynamic Seal Materials. Dynamic seals used in automotive engines are most frequently made from a rope packing or from synthetic rubber.

Rope packing is the least expensive type of dynamic seal and is often used as a rear main bearing seal. It provides close contact between the seal and shaft without undue pressure. It, therefore, has very low friction and wear characteristics.

Lip-type dynamic oil seals are also used in engines. Some lip-type oil seals are made from leather, while others are made from synthetic rubber. Synthetic rubber is generally used for the lip-type seals in automotive engines. They can stand more shaft eccentricity and run-out than the rope-type seals. They can operate at higher shaft speeds, but they require a finer shaft finish to provide long life sealing. Lip seals place more load on the shaft than the rope-type seal and, therefore, they seal better.

Dynamic Seal Design Features. Sealing is the result of an interference fit between the shaft and the seal. Rope-type seals must be packed into the seal groove, then trimmed to length. They do not function properly if they are stretched into the groove because this leaves gaps behind the seal for the oil to seep through. To help the rope packing to seal, the shaft surface under the packing may have a

(a)

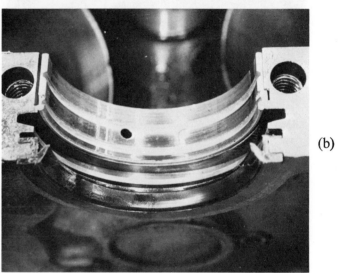

(b)

Fig. 6-17 Rear main oil seals. (a) Rope packing, (b) lip seal.

Fig. 6-18 Compressing rope seal in place (Chrysler-Plymouth Division of Chrysler Corporation).

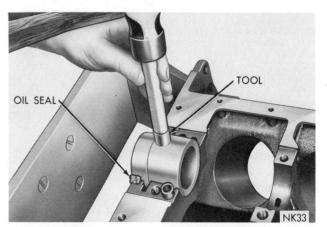

Fig. 6-19 Knurl finish on crankshaft under the rope-type seal.

Fig. 6-20 Lip seal with spring tension.

Fig. 6-21 Oil slinger ring.

special finish grind or knurl that tends to pump the oil back into the engine.

The lip-type seal is designed so that an increase in pressure to be sealed will increase the lip pressure against the shaft for better sealing. A spring tension element is used to augment normal lip pressure in high speed applications, where excessive run-out occurs or where the fluid viscosity is low.

The seals must run with a very thin flow of lubrication. Ideal seal operation allows an oil meniscus to form on the outside of the seal with no leakage. If the seal had no lubrication, it would wear the shaft very quickly.

Lip seals are usually held in a steel case or are supported by bonding on to a steel support member. This makes the seal become a one-piece seal, as the type installed on the front of the timing cover, or as a split seal type installed on a rear main.

The oil seal is aided by an oil slinger on both front and rear ends of the crankshaft. The rear slinger may be a flange on the crankshaft. The front slinger is usually a stamped steel ring or cup located between the damper hub and the crankshaft timing gear. The majority of oil that comes along the shaft is thrown clear of the shaft by the slinger. The seal is then able to handle any oil that remains on the shaft.

6-4 ENGINE BEARINGS

Engine durability relies on bearing life. Bearing failure usually results in immediate engine failure.

Bearing Requirements. Engine bearings are designed to support the operating loads and, with the lubricant, provide minimum friction. This must be done at any designed engine speed. The bearings must be able to continue to function for long periods, even when small foreign particles are present in the lubricant.

Most engine bearings are plain or sleeve bearing types, as contrasted to roller, ball, and needle bearings, which are called anti-friction bearings, that are used where minimum lubrication is available. Properly lubricated plain bearings cause no more friction than the so-called anti-friction bearings because the shaft is actually rolling on a film of lubricant. In automotive engines, the lubricating system continuously supplies lubricant to each bearing. Only residual oil will be present during engine starting before the pressure builds up. During this period, the oil film will be borderline; that is, the oil film is so thin that the high spots of the shaft and bearing will actually contact each other. This will result in high friction and wear. After the oil film is established, friction drops and metal-to-metal contact is eliminated, thus stopping wear. Bearing and journal wear will only occur when the parts come in contact with each other or when foreign particles are present between them.

It is important that the engine designer provide bearings large enough so that the bearing unit load is within strength limits. Bearing load capacity is calculated by dividing the bearing load in pounds by the bearing projected area. The projected area is the bearing length multiplied by bearing diameter. The load on engine bearings is determined by developing a polar bearing load diagram which shows the magnitude and direction of the instantaneous bearing loads.

Here again, opposing objectives are at work. The automobile designer wants the engine to develop the greatest power and, at the same time, he wants to make the smallest engine size possible. This would dictate the use of small bearings with high bearing loads. As greater bearing loads are applied, bearing life is reduced, unless a higher quality, more expensive bearing is installed. To keep cost down, one of the major design objectives of bearing engineers is to select the lowest cost bearing that will adequately meet the engine's operational requirements.

Bearing Performance Characteristics. Bearings tend to flex under intermittent loads. This is especially noticeable in reciprocating engine bearings. Bearing metals, like other metals, tend to fatigue and break after being flexed for a period of time. Flexing starts fatigue that shows up as fine cracks in the bearing surface. These cracks gradually deepen almost to the bond, then cross over and intersect with each other. This eventually allows a piece of bearing material to fall out. The length of time before failure is called the fatigue life of the bearing.

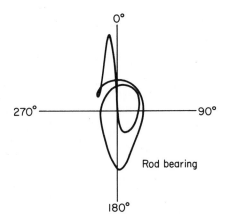

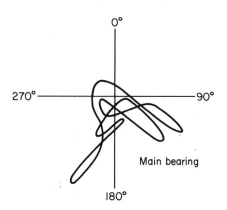

Fig. 6-22 Typical rod and main bearing load diagrams.

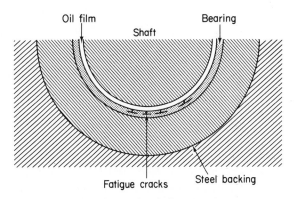

Fig. 6-23 Bearing fatigue cracks.

Bearings must have a long fatigue life for normal engine service. The harder the bearing material, the longer is its fatigue life. Soft bearings have a low fatigue life and a low bearing load strength; however, they are generally less expensive and are used in applications where the bearing requirements are low.

Manufacturing costs increase as the manufacturing tolerances decrease. To enable manufacturers to build engines with economical manufacturing tolerances, the bearing must have the ability to conform to small variations in the shaft position. This ability of bearing materials to creep or flow slightly to match shaft variations is called *conformability*. The bearing conforms to the shaft during the engine break-in period. In modern automobile engines, there is little need for bearing conformability or break-in, because automatic processing has held machining tolerances very close to the nominal size.

Engine manufacturers have designed engines to produce minimum crankcase deposits by providing them with oil filters, air filters and closed crankcase ventilation systems that minimize contaminants. Still, some small foreign particles get into the bearings. The bearings must be capable of allowing these particles to embed in the bearing surface so they will not score the shaft. To embed the particle, the bearing material gradually works across the particle, completely covering it. This bearing property is called *embedability*.

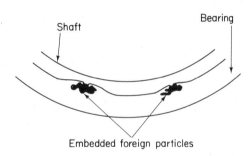

Fig. 6-24 Foreign particles embedded in a bearing.

Under some operating conditions causing temporary bearing overload, the oil film will break down, allowing the shaft to come in contact with the bearing. As the rotating crankshaft contacts bearing high spots, the spots become hot from friction. This could cause localized hot spots of bearing material that would seize or weld to the crankshaft. The crankshaft would then pull the particles around with it, scratching or scoring the bearing surface. Bearings have a characteristic called *score resistance* that prevents the bearing materials from seizing to the shaft during oil film break down. It is usually the result of the relatively low melting temperature of the bearing material.

Modern motor oils contain a number of additives that provide the oil with characteristics needed to satisfy engine requirements. In time, under high engine temperatures and high bearing loads, the additives break down, combine with moisture and form acids. The bearing's ability to resist attack from these acids is called *corrosion resistance*. Corrosion can occur over the entire surface of the bearing, removing material to produce excess oil clearance. It can also leach or eat into the bearing material, dissolving some of the bearing material alloys. Either type of corrosion will reduce bearing life.

Bearing Materials. Three bearing materials are used for automobile engine bearings: babbitt, copper-lead, and aluminum. A .010″ to .020″ thick layer of these bearing materials is applied over a low carbon steel backing. The steel provides adequate support for the shaft load. The bearing material meets the rest of the bearing requirements.

Babbitt is the oldest automotive bearing material. Its base is either lead or tin, which is alloyed with small quantities of copper and antimony. Babbitt is still used in applications where soft material is required for soft shafts running under moderate loads and speeds. It will tolerate occasional borderline lubrication and oil starvation without failure.

Copper-lead is a stronger and more expensive bearing material than babbitt. It is used for intermediate and high speed applications. Tin, in small quantities, is often alloyed with the copper-lead bearings. This bearing material is most readily damaged by corrosion from acid accumulation in the engine oil. Corrosion results in bearing journal wear as the bearing is eroded by the acids.

Aluminum is the newest material to be used for automobile bearings. Automotive-bearing aluminum has small quantities of tin and copper alloyed with it. This makes a stronger but more expensive bearing than either babbitt or copper-lead.

Aluminum, with a small percentage of lead, is used for high quality intermediate strength bearings. Most of its bearing characteristics are equal to or surpass babbitt and copper-lead. Aluminum bearings are well suited to high speed, high load conditions.

Because of its expense, aluminum is often used along with bearings made from other bearing materials. For example, aluminum bearings may be used for the highly loaded lower main bearing shell with babbitt being used for the lightly loaded upper bearing shell on a single bearing journal.

Bearing Manufacturing. Modern automotive engines use precision insert-type bearings. The bearing is manufactured to very close tolerances so that it will fit correctly in each application. The bearing, therefore, must be made from accurate materials under closely controlled manufacturing processes.

Most of the precision insert bearings are manufactured in a continuous strip process. The low carbon steel backing is delivered to the bearing manufacturer in a roll. This steel must be within .001″ of the thickness required. In processing, it must be cleaned, flattened, and heated to the required bonding temperature.

The bearing material is applied to the steel strip in either of two ways, casting or sintering. In the casting process, molten bearing alloy is poured on the backing strip where it bonds as it cools. The sintering process is similar. Small particles of the bearing materials are mixed in a powdered state. The powdered bearing material is spread evenly on the continuous steel backing strip. It is then pressed and heated until it fuses together and bonds to the steel. Bonds of both processes are chemical, rather than mechanical. The finished strip is sheared into bearing blanks as it leaves this production line. The blanks are formed and coined to size in presses, then punched and machined to the final bearing configuration.

Many of the copper-lead and aluminum bearings have an overlay or third layer of metal. This overlay is usually babbitt. Babbitt overlay gives the bearing properties of high fatigue strength, good conformity, good embedability, and low corrosion. Obviously, the overplated bearing is a premium bearing. It is also the most expensive because the over-plating layer, from .0005″ to .001″ thick, is put on the bearing with an electroplating process.

Overplate reduces bearing distress by cushioning the journal during the first few break-in hours of running. Once the bearing has adapted itself to the bearing journal, it will have a satisfactory life even when the overplate is gone.

Bearing Design. The physical design of the bearing must consider the loads being applied to the

Fig. 6-25 Layers of bearing material (Sealed Power Corporation).

journal. In automotive engines, the load varies in magnitude and direction. Maximum bearing areas must be located where the forces or loads are the greatest. Oil holes and grooves are located on the lightly loaded areas of the bearing.

Oil enters the bearing through the oil holes and grooves. It spreads into a smooth wedge-shaped film that supports the bearing load by hydrodynamic action of the oil as is described in Chapter 9. Under high journal speeds, during high rpm operation, the oil film may no longer be able to maintain its laminar or smooth layer flow. When laminar flow breaks down, turbulent flow occurs and disrupts the bearing oil film. This ineffective lubrication may result in bearing failure.

Many bearings are provided with oil bleed holes so that the bearing will continue to be supplied with a fresh oil supply as described in Section 5-6. This flow keeps an adequate quantity of oil supplied to the bearing for hydrodynamic lubrication and provides a means of bearing cooling. Often, this oil bleed hole is made to aim oil at the cylinder wall for lubrication. When it does, the hole is called a *spit hole*.

A bearing design has been developed that does not require oil bleed holes. The bearing is of an eccentric design that has close clearances on the highly loaded bearing areas. This provides several spaces for the oil film to develop and, at the same time, provides adequate oil flow from the bearing edges for proper cooling.

The bearing to journal clearance may be from .0005″ to .0025″, depending on the engine. Doubling the journal clearance will allow more than four times

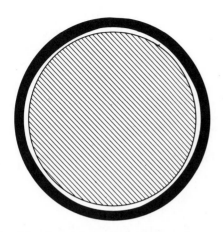

Fig. 6-26 Eccentric bearing design (exaggerated).

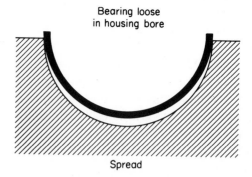

Fig. 6-27 Bearing spread and crush.

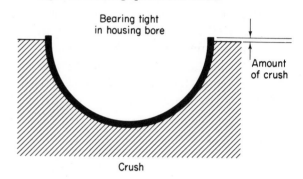

as much oil to flow from the edges of the bearing. The oil clearance must be large enough to allow an oil film to build up, but small enough to prevent excess oil flow that would cause loss of oil pressure. A large oil flow at one of the bearings would starve other bearings further along in the oil system. This would result in failure of the oil-starved bearing.

The bearing design also includes bearing spread and crush. The bearing has a slightly larger arc than the bearing housing. This is called *bearing spread* and is from .005″ to .020″ wider than the housing bore. A lip or tang allows the bearing to be located endwise in the housing and spread holds the bearing in the housing while the engine is being assembled. When installed, the bearing half protrudes slightly above the parting surface. When the cap is assembled, the ends of the two half bearing shells touch and are forced together. This force is called *bearing crush*. Crush holds the bearing in place and keeps the

bearing from turning when the engine runs. Crush must exert a force of at least 12,000 psi stress at 250°F to hold the bearing in place. Forty thousand psi stress is considered maximum without damaging the bearing or housing.

The engineer will select a bearing that is the least expensive bearing that will perform satisfactorily in operation. Replacement bearings should be at least as good a quality bearing as the original bearings, using the same oil holes and grooves. Modified engines have different bearing requirements and, therefore, they may require a higher quality bearing to provide satisfactory service.

Review Questions
Chapter 6

1. What are the major rotating engine parts?

2. What deflection occurs in the crankshaft?

3. What does excessive crankshaft deflection cause?

4. Compare forged and cast crankshafts.

5. What is internal and external engine balancing?

6. Why is a thrust bearing necessary on a crankshaft?

7. How does journal grinding and polishing affect bearing life?

8. How does the cam lobe affect engine operation?

9. What causes torsion forces in a camshaft?

10. What design features are used to reduce the timing gear and chain noise?

11. Why are large bearing journals used on camshafts?

12. How can cam bearing clearance affect connecting rod bearing lubrication?

13. What causes cam end thrust?

14. What is the advantage of having the fuel pump eccentric near the front of the engine?

15. What are the advantages of each type of oil seal?

16. What might happen if the knurl under the shaft seal were machined in the wrong direction?

17. What is the difference in friction characteristics between plain bearings and roller bearings?

18. What is the basic cause of bearing wear?

19. Why is bearing conformability important?

20. What is the basis for selecting engine bearing quality?

21. How does a plain bearing handle foreign particles that get between it and the shaft?

22. What causes corrosion of engine bearings that are running in motor oil?

23. What are three materials used for automotive engine bearings?

24. Why are bearing shells, using different materials, sometimes mixed on a single bearing journal?

25. What is the value of a bearing overlay?

26. What are two purposes of a spit hole?

27. Why is bearing spread necessary in a bearing shell?

28. What holds the bearing in place during engine operation?

Quiz 6

1. A crankshaft damper ring is used to reduce the effects of
   a. connecting rod bearing loads
   b. crankshaft bending moments
   c. flywheel loads
   d. torsional vibration.

2. One of the most important crankshaft design requirements is that the crankshaft have
   a. the correct throw angle
   b. ample strength and torsional stiffness
   c. the lightening holes properly spaced
   d. overlapping main and connecting rod journals.

3. The engine part that has the greatest effect on a specific engine power output characteristic is the
   a. crankshaft throw angle
   b. engine's displacement
   c. cam lobe design
   d. bore-to-stroke ratio.

4. Continuous camshaft end thrust results from
   a. the eccentric fuel pump drive cam lobe
   b. spherical lifter face designs
   c. oil pump driving forces
   d. timing chain driving forces.

5. Lip-type oil seals perform better in some installations because they
   a. can stand more shaft eccentricity
   b. will operate on a rougher shaft finish
   c. cost less
   d. have lower friction properties.

6. An oil slinger is used to throw oil
   a. away from the oil seals
   b. onto the timing chain at the front of the engine
   c. away from the clutch at the rear of the engine
   d. onto the camshaft to provide lubrication.

7. Engine bearings are selected on the basis of the
   a. least expensive that will meet the requirements
   b. bearing which will last longest
   c. operation under marginal lubrication
   d. best available bearing.

8. Bearing conformability property is most important
   a. for maximum bearing service life
   b. if operated with a slightly bent shaft
   c. when crankshaft journals become scored
   d. during the first few minutes of operation.

9. Bearing material that is most susceptible to corrosion is
   a. babbitt
   b. copper-lead
   c. aluminum
   d. aluminum-babbitt.

10. Engine bearings are held secure in their housing bore during operation by the bearing
    a. tang
    b. spread
    c. crush
    d. cap torque.

chapter 7

Engine Block and Gaskets

The engine block, which is the supporting structure for the entire engine, is made of cast iron, or from cast or die cast aluminum alloy. All other engine parts are mounted on it or in it. This large casting supports the crankshaft and camshaft and holds all of the parts in alignment. Large diameter holes in the block casting form the cylinder bores to guide the pistons. The holes are called bores because they are made by a machining process called boring. Combustion pressure loads are carried from the head to the crankshaft bearings through the block structure. The block is provided with webs, walls, and drilled passages to contain the coolant and lubricating oil, and to keep them seperated from each other. Mounting pads or lugs on the block transfer the reaction loads caused by engine torque to the vehicle frame through attached engine mounts. A large mounting surface at the rear of the engine block is used to fasten a bell housing and transmission. The modern engine block meets all of these requirements and has a longer service life than any other part of the engine.

The head, pan, and timing cover attach to the block. They need to have their attaching joint sealed so they do not leak. Gaskets are used in the joint to take up machining irregularities and changes from pressure and temperature extremes.

7-1 BLOCK DESIGN

Most domestic production automobile engines under 250 cubic inch displacement are inline overhead-valve six-cylinder engines. There was a time when the inline eight-cylinder engine was popular. However, as casting technology developed, production of a one-piece V block was possible, and this design gradually replaced the inline eight.

Inline engine cylinders are numbered from the front to the rear, number one being at the front. The V engines present a different problem because, in a sense, they are two four-cylinder engines with their bases together and sharing the same crankshaft. Two approaches have been used to number the cylinders of V engine blocks. One manufacturer (Ford) numbers the right block from one to four and the left block from five to eight. In general, the other manufacturers number their cylinders in the order in which the connecting rods are attached to the crankshaft, starting with number one at the front of the crankshaft and going back to number eight at the rear. Some of these engines have the first cylinder at the right front. Most of the V-8 engines, however, use a numbering system having number one cylinder at the left front. As with all parts of the automobile, right and left are viewed from the driver's position.

The four-stroke cycle and crankshaft angles must be considered in the V-block design. For an even firing engine, the V-8 must have its block at 90° (720° ÷ 8 cylinders). A V-6 or V-12 engine could use 120° or 60° blocks and have even firing impulses. One manufacturer once made a 90° V-6 engine as a production engine. This did not have even firing and required the use of carefully tuned engine mounts for satisfactory vehicle service.

The engine block primarily consists of the cylinders with a web or bulkhead to support the

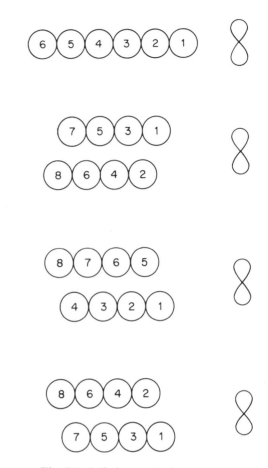

Fig. 7-1 Cylinder numbering systems.

crankshaft and head attachments. The rest of the block consists of a water jacket, a lifter chamber and mounting flanges. In most engine designs, each main bearing bulkhead supports both a cam bearing and a main bearing. The bulkhead is well-ribbed to support and distribute loads applied to it. This gives the block structural rigidity and beam stiffness throughout its useful life.

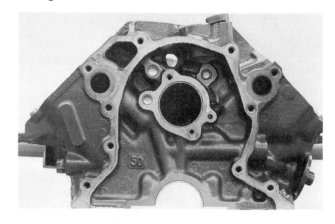

Fig. 7-2 V-block engine.

Two types of lower block designs are in use. One is called a V block. The base of this block is close to the crankshaft centerline. The second type of block is called a Y or deep block. In this type, the deep skirt extends the oil pan rail well below the crankshaft centerline.

Fig. 7-3 Y-block engine.

The V block is the smallest and lightest of the two engine block types. The amount of cast iron used in it is kept at a minimum, making it a small compact lightweight block. Covers, such as the oil pan and timing cover, are largely lightweight aluminum die castings or steel stampings.

The deep skirt block improves the stiffness of the entire engine. It provides a wider surface on which to attach the bell housing. This greater rigidity assures smooth, quiet engine operation and durability. The deep skirt must be wide enough to clear the connecting rods as they swing through the block and, therefore, large oil capacity is provided with its use.

The cylinder head is fastened to the top surface of the block, called the block *deck*. The deck has a smooth surface to seal against the head gasket. Bolt holes, with National Course (NC) threads are positioned around the cylinders to form an even holding pattern; using four, five or six head bolts around each cylinder in automobile engines. These bolt holes go into reinforced areas within the block that carry the load to the main bearing bulkheads. Additional holes in the block are used to transfer coolant and oil.

The cylinders may be of a skirtless design, flush with the top of the crankcase, or they may have a skirt that extends into the crankcase. Extended

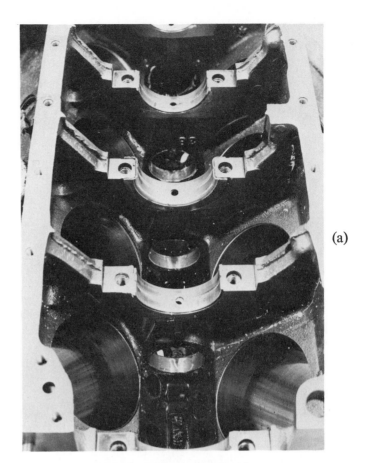

(a)

Fig. 7-4 Cylinder lower end. (a) Skirtless, (b) extended skirt.

(b)

Fig. 7-5 Small clearance between crankshaft counterweight, cylinder skirt and piston.

skirt cylinders are used on engines with short connecting rods. In these engines, the pistons move very close to the crankshaft and require the cylinder skirt to go as low as possible to support the piston when it is at the lowest point in its stroke. This allows the engine to be designed with a low overall engine height since it has a small block size for its displacement size.

Cylinders are surrounded by cooling passages. In most skirtless cylinder designs, the cooling passages extend nearly to the bottom of the cylinder. In skirted cylinder designs, the cooling passages are limited to the upper portion of the cylinder.

During casting, the molds and cores are supported from outside. The core supports and casting vents will leave holes in the casting. Core holes in the block deck are closed with the gasket and head. Core holes left in the external block wall are machined to be sealed with soft plugs.

Soft plugs are of two designs. One is a convex design. For its use, the core hole is counterbored

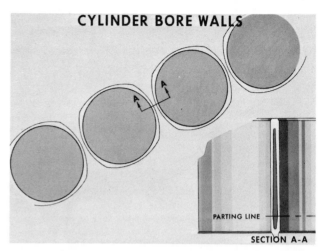

Fig. 7-6 Cylinder wall cooling passages (Ford Motor Company).

with a shoulder. The convex soft plug is placed in counterbore, convex side out. It is driven in and upset with a fitted seating tool. This causes the edge to enlarge to hold it in place. The second type of hole plug is a cup type. This type is fit into a smooth, straight hole. The cup is slightly bell-mouthed, so that it tightens in place when it is driven in to the correct depth with a seating tool.

Fig. 7-7 Convex-type soft plug.

An engine block has many oil holes that carry lubricating oil to the required locations. During manufacture, all of the oil holes are drilled from the outside of the block. Oil holes are rarely cast in engine blocks. When a curved passage is needed, intersecting drilled holes are used. In some engines,

Fig. 7-8 Cup-type soft plug and pipe plugged oil passages.

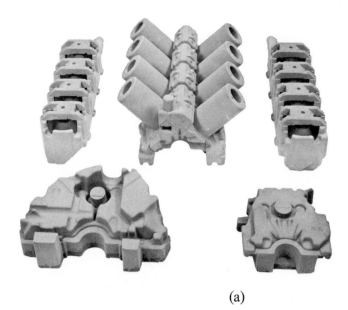

(a)

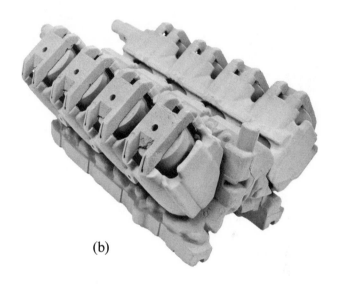

(b)

plugs are placed in the oil holes to divert oil to another point before coming back to the original hole, on the opposite side of the plug. After oil holes are drilled, the unneeded open ends may be capped by pipe plugs, steel balls or cup-type soft plugs. End plugs are a source of possible oil leakage in operating engines.

7-2 BLOCK MANUFACTURING

Cast iron cylinder block casting technology has come through a period of rapid development. The trend is to make blocks with larger cores, using fewer individual pieces. Oil-sand cores are forms that shape the internal openings and passages in the engine block. Prior to casting, the cores are supported within a core box. The core box also has the exterior

Fig. 7-9 Casting cores. (a) Separate cores, (b) assembled cores, (c) core box (Central Foundry Division, General Motors Corporation).

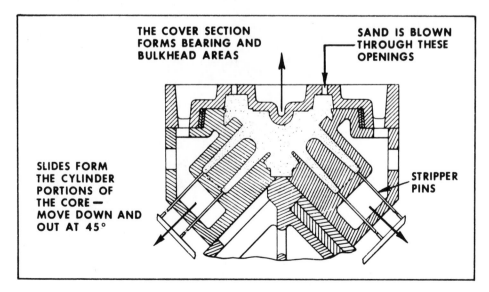

THE COVER SECTION FORMS BEARING AND BULKHEAD AREAS

SAND IS BLOWN THROUGH THESE OPENINGS

SLIDES FORM THE CYLINDER PORTIONS OF THE CORE — MOVE DOWN AND OUT AT 45°

STRIPPER PINS

(c)

Fig. 7-10 Die cast aluminum cylinder and case (Chevrolet Motor Division, General Motors Corporation).

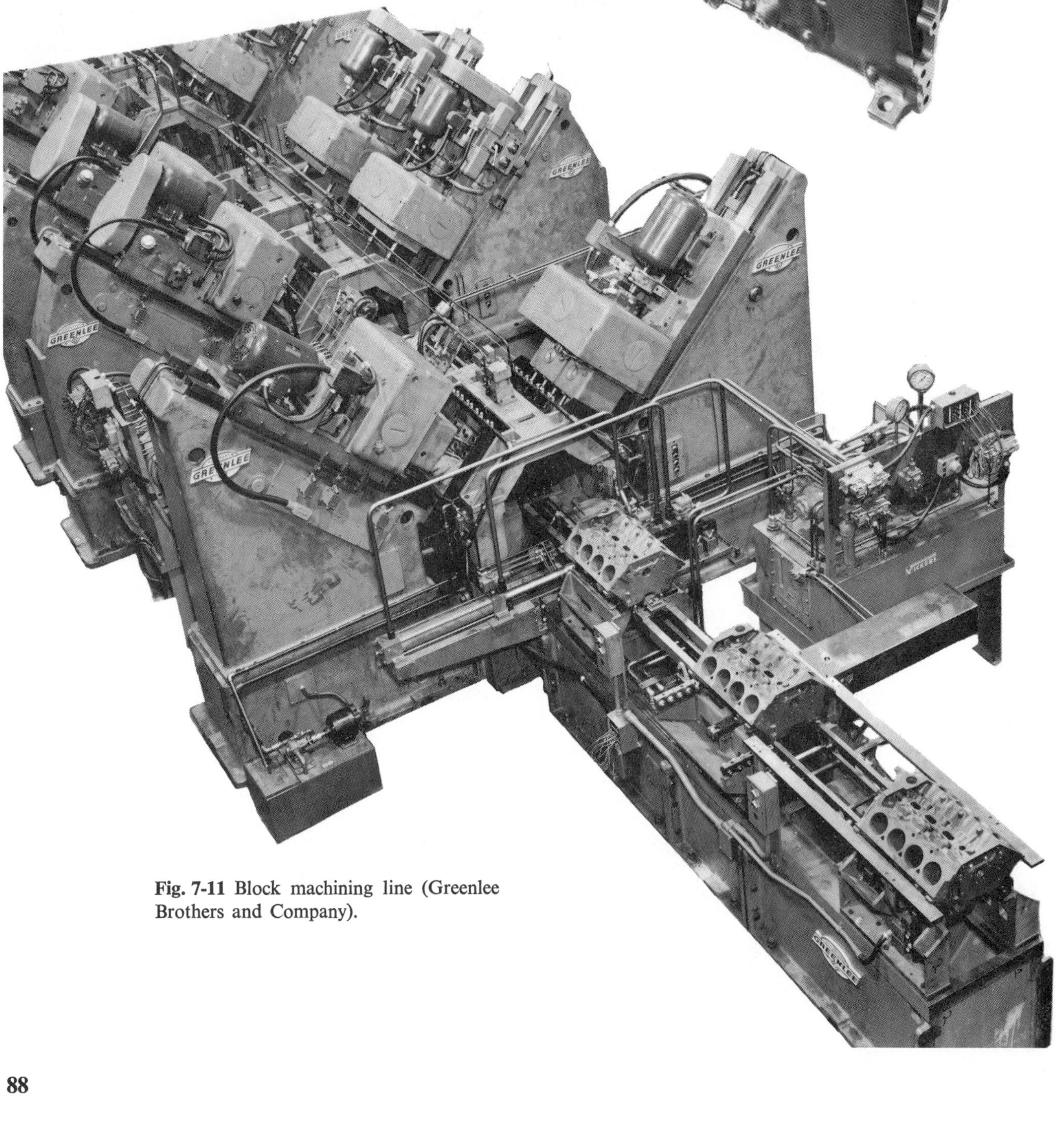

Fig. 7-11 Block machining line (Greenlee Brothers and Company).

block form liner. Special alloy cast iron is poured into the box. It flows between the cores and core box liner. As the cast iron cools, the core breaks up. When the cast iron has hardened, it is removed from the core box and the pieces of sand core are removed from the casting by vigorous shaking.

One way to keep the engine weight as low as possible is to make the block with minimum wall thickness. Engine designers and foundry techniques have made lightweight engines by making the cast iron block walls and bulkheads only as heavy as necessary to support their required loads. Much of the ability to do this is the result of cores made of a minimum number of pieces that are secured firmly in place during casting. If they should shift or float in the molten cast iron, the block wall would either be too thick or too thin in places.

Aluminum is used for some cylinder blocks. Early aluminum blocks were cast in a manner similar to cast iron blocks. They were equipped with a mechanically bonded cast iron liner for each cylinder. A more recent fabrication technique is to die cast the block from silicon-aluminum alloy without using cylinder liners. Pistons with zinc-copper-hard iron coating are required for use in the aluminum bores.

After thorough cooling and cleaning, the block casting goes to the machining line. The top, bottom and end surfaces are cleaned and semi-finished with a broach. A broach is a large slab with a number of cutting teeth. Each tooth cuts a little more than the preceding tooth, somewhat like a large coarse contoured file. One pass of the broach will smooth both the cylinder decks and the lifter valley cover rail. A second pass will smooth the upper main bearing bores and the oil pan rail. Some of these surfaces are completed with the broach operation, while others need to be finished with a mill, a final broach, or a boring operation. The ends of the block may be finished with a third broach.

The cylinders are bored and honed in a number of step operations until they have the required size and finish. A slight notch or scallop is cut into the edge of the cylinder on some engines using very large valves. All drilling and thread tapping is accomplished on the block line.

The main bearing caps, which are cast separately from the block, are machined and installed on the block for a final bore finishing operation. With caps

(a)

Fig. 7-12 Main bearing cap attachments. (a) Two bolt, (b) four bolt, (c) cross bolted (Chrysler-Plymouth Division, Chrysler Corporation).

(b)

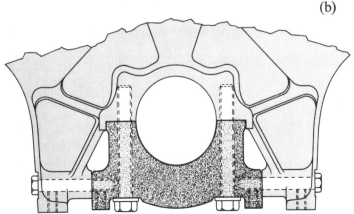

(c)

installed, the main bearing bores and cam bearing bores are machined to the correct size and alignment. On some engines, these bores are honed to a very fine finish and size. Therefore, main bearing caps are not interchangeable or reversible. They may have cast numbers indicating their position.

Standard production engines use two bolts to hold the main bearing cap in place. Heavy duty and performance engines often use additional main bearing support bolts. These could be a cross bolt design in a deep skirt block or a four-bolt main cap in the V-block design. Remember that combustion chamber gases expansion force will try to push the cylinder head off the top and the crankshaft off the bottom of the block. The engine is held together with the head bolts and main bearing cap bolts screwed into bolt bosses and ribs that are cast in the block. The extra bolt on the main bearing cap helps to support the crankshaft when high combustion pressures and machanical loads exist.

7-3 GASKETS AND STATIC SEALS

Oil, coolant, and gases flow through passages in the engine block. These are usually kept separate by cast iron walls, plugs, covers and caps. They must not leak either internally or externally. Gaskets or static seals are used between attaching engine parts to seal the joint, thus preventing leakage.

Requirements. Gasket requirements become greater as engine pressures and temperatures become greater. Four gasket properties must be considered by the engineer when selecting gaskets for each specific application. The gasket must be impermeable, comformable, resilient, and resistant.

Each gasket must be *impermeable* to the fluids it is designed to seal. If the fluid could penetrate the gasket, it would leak and the gasket would be of no value.

Gaskets must *conform* to any existing surface imperfections. This includes machining surface roughness and slight parting surface warpage.

A *resilient* gasket property will allow the gasket to maintain sealing pressure, even when the joint

is slightly loosened as a result of temperature changes or vibration.

The environment of the gasket will change with variations in temperature, pressure, and age. The gasket must be *resistant* to all expected changes in its environment for the engine service life.

Gasket Materials. Many materials are used for gaskets, depending upon the sealing requirements and the cost. One of the oldest gasket materials is cork, a natural material from the bark of mediterranean oak and cork pine trees. For gaskets, the bark chips are held together in sheets with bonding materials, often rubber compounds. This makes a highly impermeable gasket that conforms easily. Cork's use is limited to lightly loaded joints, having uneven surfaces, such as rocker covers and oil pans. Aluminum coatings on cork gaskets help reduce heat deterioration. In some cases, the cork gaskets are rubber coated.

Fig. 7-13 Cork, paper and composite gasket materials.

Cork is often replaced by gaskets made of fibers. These fibers may be cellulose, asbestos or a mixture of the two. Gasket fibers are bonded together with a binder. The binder material used determines the gasket's properties. Some gaskets use binders that are impermeable to oil, while other gaskets swell on contact with oil. Gaskets that are designed to swell are used where the joint to be sealed cannot be tightened. The gasket's swelling will seal the joint. Gaskets that swell are not used where high pressures are present. Generally, fiber-base gaskets rather than cork are used under high pressures. Fiber gaskets require a better parting surface smoothness than is needed for cork gaskets.

Molded oil-resistant synthetic rubber is often

used where the sealing requirements dictate special seal designs. These are often used in oil pan corner joints and on intake manifold ends.

One of the most difficult sealing jobs in the engine is to seal the cylinder head to the block parting surface. The earliest head gaskets were copper coated asbestos. The copper sealed into the machining marks of the head and block while the asbestos provided resilience and conformability. As engine designs were improved, copper on the gaskets was replaced by steel to withstand the higher pressures and temperatures. Steel rings, called *fire rings*, were applied to the gaskets around the cylinder openings to seal the combustion chambers. Similar rings were added around some of the other gasket holes as well.

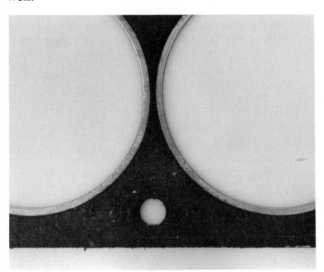

Fig. 7-14 Head gasket with a fire ring.

Continued development of the engine manufacturing techniques provided smoother and flatter parting surfaces, and increased engine power brought on the embossed steel head gasket. A raised rib or embossed portion gives steel gaskets the required resiliency. A soft aluminum coating placed on steel gaskets will seal into the parting surface machining marks.

A later head gasket development uses a thin steel core with a thin coating of asbestos rolled on the outside to give the gasket the desirable resilient properties needed as the head and block change temperature and as the pressure varies within each cycle. Most head gaskets must be installed in a specified direction because the gasket is often used to help control engine coolant flow. When this is

required, the gasket is marked *top* or *front*. When it isn't marked, the gasket should be installed with the stamped identification numbers toward the head.

Timing cover gaskets are usually thin fiber or paper. Cork, fiber and synthetic rubber are used in different parts of the oil pan. The intake manifold uses embossed steel or reinforced fiber gaskets. Cork or synthetic rubber sections are used on the lifter valley cover portion of the intake manifold.

It is a common practice to use a new gasket each time a part is assembled. The price of a new gasket is small compared to the labor cost of installing it. After use, a gasket will have lost most of its sealing properties. To avoid leaks, always use new gaskets.

Fig. 7-15 Steel embossed head gasket.

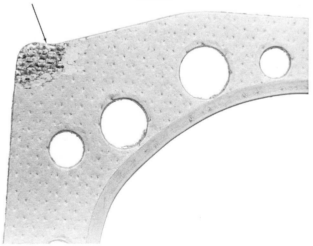

Fig. 7-16 Head gasket with a steel core and a thin asbestos outside coating.

91

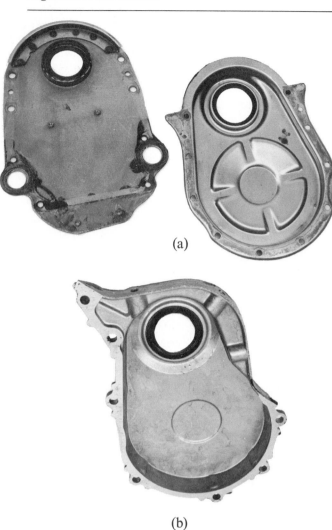

(a)

(b)

(c)

Fig. 7-17 Timing covers. (a) Stamped steel, (b) cast, (c) cast with fuel pump pad, (d) cast with fuel pump, water pump, oil pump and distributor attachments included.

7-4 BLOCK ATTACHMENTS

A number of parts are attached to the engine to enclose it and to adapt it to the vehicle. These include covers, housings and mounts.

Bell Housing. A bell housing enclosing the flywheel and clutch or torque converter is attached to the rear of the engine. It is positioned with dowel pins for alignment. Offset dowels and shims between the block and bell housing may be used to align the bell housing in standard transmission applications, so the clutch shaft matches the pilot bearing. In original production, some bell housings are attached to the block before assembly. The bell housing's transmission hole is then machined to match the main bearing bore alignment. This minimizes drive-line misalignment. Alignment of the automatic transmission is simplified by using a flex plate transmission drive. Most automatic transmission cases form the bell housing, while standard transmissions have a separate bell housing with clutch lever attachments. Aluminum bell housings are usually used in passenger car applications to keep the weight as low as possible.

Timing Covers. Manufacturers use a variety of timing covers. The simplest consists of a stamped sheet metal cover attached with cap screws. Its only purpose is to cover the gears to keep foreign objects out and to keep the engine oil in. Some engines use a cast cover in the same way. A cast cover also tends to muffle the timing drive noise.

(d)

Fig. 7-18 Typical insulating rubber engine mount.

Some timing covers are die cast. These covers work in the same way as the cast covers. The die cast process produces a finished cover with little or no additional work. Die cast tooling is much more expensive than cast tooling; however, a saving is made in machining costs when using die cast parts.

Some manufacturers have made the timing cover more complicated by including the oil pump and distributor drive along with the fuel pump and water pump. The die cast process is used so that there is a minimum of machining operations. With these covers, the engine block contains no accessory drives.

Engine Mounts. Engines are mounted to the vehicle through rubber insulators. The engine vibrational characteristics are checked in the engineering laboratories and the engine mounts positioned close to vibration *nodes*, which are points of minimum vibration. The rubber used in engine mounts is especially compounded to absorb vibrations characteristic to each specific engine model. The mounts are usually located about halfway back on each side of the block. The rear engine mount is located at the rear of the transmission, so the engine-transmission combination is supported at three points.

Review Questions
Chapter 7

1. How are cylinders numbered in V-8 engines?

2. How are right and left banks of an engine identified?

3. What is the purpose of the block bulkhead?

4. What are the advantages of a deep skirt block?

5. What are the advantages of a V-block?

6. What are the advantages of having a cylinder skirt extend into the crankcase?

7. How does the cylinder skirt design affect the cooling passages?

8. What is the purpose of soft plugs used in engine blocks?

9. How are oil holes made in engine blocks?

10. What is the purpose of using casting cores that have a minimum number of pieces?

11. What makes broaching a desirable machining operation?

12. Why is it imperative to replace the main bearing caps in their original position?

13. Why are four bolt main bearing caps used on some engines?

14. What is the primary purpose of gaskets or static seals?

15. What different types of gasket materials are used for engine gaskets?

16. What is the requirement for fire rings on head gaskets?

17. Why is it a good practice to use new gaskets?

18. What are the uses of front engine covers or timing covers?

Quiz 7

1. Most of the new automotive engine designs use a V-block. As compared to the Y-block, the V-block is
   a. adaptable to high production machining
   b. quieter and smoother running
   c. smaller and lighter
   d. more rigid.

2. Soft plugs are required in engine blocks to
   a. allow for expansion if the coolant freezes
   b. seal core support openings
   c. provide a place for cleaning the block
   d. give some flexibility to the block design.

3. Main bearing caps should always be replaced in their original position because
   a. they were machined in place
   b. they will not fit any other bearing
   c. it is the way they were numbered
   d. it is a good servicing practice.

4. Oil passages in an engine block are
   a. cast openings
   b. seldom required
   c. also useful to lighten the block weight
   d. drilled holes.

5. What engine characteristic usually requires the use of cylinder skirts that extend into the crankcase?
   a. low overall engine height
   b. long connecting rods
   c. rigid block structure
   d. maximum cylinder block cooling

6. The most critical gasket sealing problem occurs at the
   a. intake manifold
   b. rocker cover
   c. oil pan
   d. head.

7. What gasket property is required to maintain a sealed joint during temperature changes and vibration?
   a. impermeability
   b. conformability
   c. resiliency
   d. resistance

8. What type of gasket material is usually used on timing covers?
   a. cork
   b. fiber
   c. molded synthetic rubber
   d. copper coated asbestos

9. After disassembly it is recommended to replace
   a. cork gaskets
   b. cork and fiber gaskets
   c. all but metal gaskets
   d. all gaskets.

10. Engine mounts are attached to the side of the block and are located
    a. to balance the engine
    b. to support the rear of the engine
    c. at vibration nodes
    d. at the most convenient point.

chapter 8

Cooling System Operation

The automotive engine cooling system's primary function is to maintain the normal operating temperature of the block and head. Coolant flow is held at a minimum during warm up until the normal engine temperature is reached, then the coolant flow is gradually increased as required to maintain the normal temperature. If the engine operating temperature is too low, scuffing and wear rates will increase. If temperature is too high, hard deposits which can cause part sticking and passage clogging form. Operating the engine at normal temperatures will minimize these problems and provide maximum engine service life.

Two types of cooling systems are used in passenger cars, air and liquid. Some imported passenger cars use air cooling. Current domestic passenger cars use liquid cooling systems. The coolant removes the excess heat from the engine and carries it to a radiator where it releases the heat to the air.

Satisfactory cooling system operation depends upon the system's component design and the operating conditions. The design is based on the engine's heat output, radiator size, type of coolant, size of coolant pump, fan type, thermostat, and system pressure. Operating conditions change; for example: driving in traffic, changing engine speeds and engine loads by driving up and down hills, and towing a trailer. Correct functioning of all cooling system parts is critical when the engine is operated under heavy loads in a hot climate. Unfortunately the cooling system is usually neglected until a problem occurs, when correct routine maintenance could have prevented the problem and the inconvenience the problem caused.

8-1 COOLING SYSTEM REQUIREMENTS

The cooling system must allow the engine to warm up to the required operating temperature as rapidly as possible, then maintain that temperature. It must be able to do this when the outside air temperature is as low as $-30°F$ and as high as $110°$. This will allow proper carburetion, provide satisfactory oil viscosity, and give the correct part fits and clearances within the engine.

Peak combustion temperatures in the engine cycle run from 4000 to 6000°F. They will average from 1200 to 1700°F throughout the operating cycle. Continued temperatures as high as this would weaken engine parts, so heat must be removed from the engine. The cooling system keeps the head and cylinder wall at a temperature within their physical strength limits.

Low Temperature Requirements. Minimum engine operating temperatures are critical for proper engine operation. When the temperature is too low, there is insufficient heat to properly vaporize the fuel mixture so that extra fuel is necessary to provide satisfactory engine performance. The heavy portion of the gasoline does not vaporize and remains as unburned fuel. Cool engine surfaces quench part of the combustion, leaving partially burned fuel as soot. It also cools the burned by-products, condensing moisture that is produced during combustion. The unburned fuel, soot and moisture go past the piston rings as blow-by gases, washing oil from the

cylinder wall and diluting the oil in the pan. This exposes the cylinder wall and piston rings to excessive scuffing and wear.

Gasoline is a hydrocarbon with additives to reduce detonation, surface ignition, corrosion, gum formation and ice formation. Some of the anti-knock additives contain chlorine and bromine. Gasoline combustion is a rapid oxidation process in which heat is released as the hydrocarbon fuel chemically combines with oxygen from the air. For each gallon of fuel used, a moisture equivalent of a gallon of water is produced. It is a part of this moisture that condenses and gets into the oil pan, along with unburned fuel and soot, and causes sludge formation.

The condensed moisture combines with unburned hydrocarbons and additive constituents to form carbonic acid, surfuric acid, nitric acid, hydrobromic acid and hydrochloric acid. These acids are chiefly responsible for engine wear by causing corrosion and rust within the engine. Rust occurs rapidly when the coolant temperature is below 130°F. Below 110°F, water from the combustion process will actually accumulate in the oil. High cylinder wall wear rates occur anytime the coolant temperature is below 150°F.

High Temperature Requirements. Maximum temperature limits are also required to protect the engine. High temperatures oxidize the engine oil. This breaks the oil down, producing hard carbon and varnish. If high temperatures are allowed to continue, they will lead to plugged piston rings and stuck hydraulic valve lifters. High temperatures reduce the oil's viscosity, that is, they thin the oil. This may allow metal-to-metal contact within the engine, which will cause high friction, loss of power, and rapid wear. Reduced oil viscosity allows the oil to get past the piston rings and through valve guides into the combustion chamber to cause excessive oil consumption.

The combustion process is very sensitive to temperature. High coolant temperatures raise the combustion temperatures to a point that detonation and pre-ignition may occur and, if allowed to continue for any period of time, will lead to engine damage.

Normal Temperatures. Between low temperature and high temperature extremes, there is a normal operating temperature range. The minimum normal temperature, controlled by a thermostat, has been gradually increased from 160°F to 180–190°F. Some engines run with a minimum temperature as high as 200°F. The maximum possible temperature on liquid cooled engines is limited by the coolant's boiling point and radiator's capacity. On air cooled engines, it is limited by the air temperature and flow rate. Engine operating temperature should be kept between these extremes, usually at the minimum temperature, for proper engine operation and maximum service life.

8-2 COOLING SYSTEM TYPES

All of the heat passed to the cooling system is eventually transferred to the *ambient*, or surrounding air. Direct transfer from the cylinder to air is used by air cooled engines. The liquid cooled engines are indirectly cooled. The coolant serves as a heat conveyor to carry heat from the cylinder to the radiator where it is dissipated into the air.

Air Cooling. Air cooling is used on a few low horsepower automobile engines. It is usually used where weight or simplicity are important. They require air baffles or shrouds and a high volume fan to direct the cooling air across fins on the surface of the head and cylinders. Any cracks or leaks in the baffles or shrouds will misdirect the cooling air flow, resulting in overheating a part of the engine.

Liquid Cooling. The majority of automobiles use liquid cooled systems. Coolant flows through the engine, where it picks up heat. It then flows to the radiator where the heat is given up to the outside air. The coolant continually recirculates, its temperature rising as much as 15° as it goes through the engine, then cooling back down as it goes through the radiator. The coolant flow rate may be as high as 1 gallon per minute for each horsepower the engine produces.

Coolant Types. For a given volume, water is able to absorb more heat than any other liquid coolant used in automobiles. Water, however, has both a high and a low usable temperature limit. It boils at 212°F and freezes at 32°F. There are very few places in the United States where the temperature does not at sometime drop below the freezing point of water. Antifreeze protection is required when these low temperatures are anticipated. Low temperature protection is also required on some factory installed air conditioned cars to keep the heater core from freezing. All manufacturers recommend the use of *ethylene-glycol-based* antifreeze mixtures for this protection. This type of antifreeze is sometimes called *permanent* type, even though manufacturers recommend its replacement each year or two,

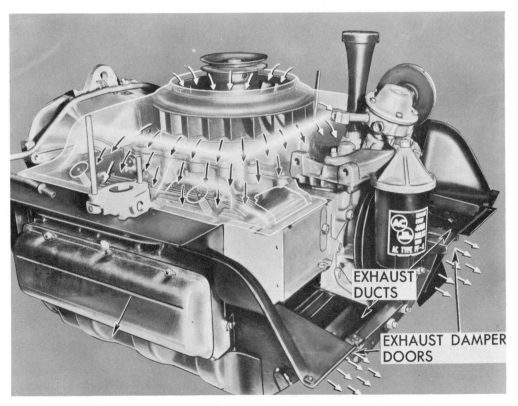

Fig. 8-1 Air cooled engine (Chevrolet Motor Division, General Motors Corporation).

EXHAUST DUCTS

EXHAUST DAMPER DOORS

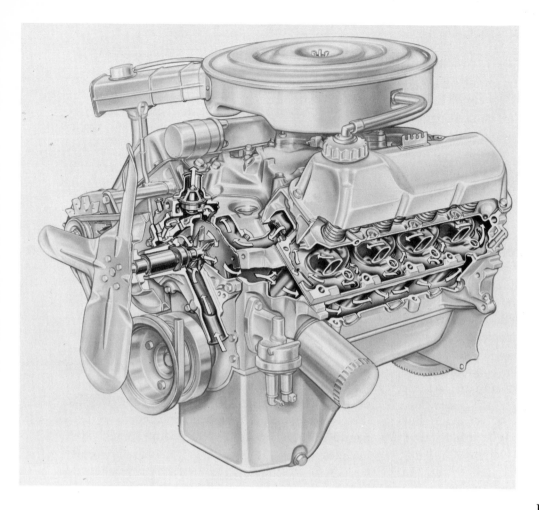

Fig. 8-2 Liquid cooled engine (Ford Motor Company).

depending on the specific vehicle manufacturer. Ethylene-glycol antifreezes have anti-corrosion additives and water pump lubricants blended into them. When antifreezes are not used, these required additives may be purchased separately and added to the cooling system water by the operator.

Only the minimum required amount of ethylene-glycol-based antifreeze should be used. It is expensive and, therefore, it is economical to use the minimum required amount. At the maximum protection, an ethylene-glycol concentration of 60% will absorb less than 90% as much heat as water. An added advantage in using ethylene-glycol-based antifreeze is the fact that its boiling point is higher than water's boiling point. Its use will allow the cooling system to run at a higher temperature level, so that a smaller radiator may be used on the vehicle. It is also helpful to increase the boiling point of the coolant on cars equipped with air conditioning.

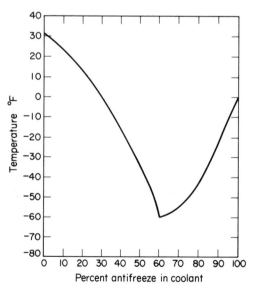

Fig. 8-3 Ethylene glycol–water freezing curve.

98

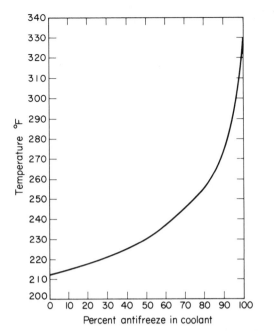

Fig. 8-4 Ethylene glycol–water boiling curve.

8-3 LIQUID COOLING SYSTEM DESIGN

Coolant enters the engine at the center of the inlet side of the pump. The coolant pump is a centrifugal pump, pulling coolant in at the impeller center and discharging it at the impeller tips. The pump is sized and the impeller designed to absorb no more power than necessary to provide adequate coolant flow. It is driven by a belt from the crankshaft. The belt is tightened with an idler. On most engines, the alternator serves as the belt tightening idler. As engine speeds increase, more heat is developed and more cooling capacity is required. The belt driven pump increases the impeller speed as the engine speed increases to provide extra coolant flow when it is needed.

Fig. 8-5 Coolant pump impeller and scroll.

Coolant leaving the pump impeller is fed through a *scroll*, a smoothly curved passage that changes the fluid flow direction with minimum loss in velocity. The scroll is connected to the front of the engine to direct the coolant into the block. On V engines, two outlets are used, one for each cylinder bank. Occasionally, diverters are necessary in the coolant pump scroll to equalize coolant flow between the cylinder banks for equal engine bank cooling.

Coolant Flow in the Engine. Coolant may flow through the engine in two ways, parallel and series.

(a)

(b)

Fig. 8-6 Coolant flow types. (a) Parallel, (b) series.

In the parallel system, coolant flows into the block under pressure, then crosses the gasket to the head through holes adjacent to each cylinder. In the series flow system, the coolant flows around all of the cylinders on each bank to the rear of the block where large passages allow the coolant to flow across the gasket to the rear of the heads. The coolant flows forward through the heads to an outlet at the highest point in the engine cooling passage located at the front of the engine. Some engines use a combination of these two systems and call it a series-parallel coolant flow.

The cooling passages inside the engine must be designed so that the whole system can be drained. It must also be designed so that there are no pockets in which steam can form. In series flow systems, bleed holes or steam slits in the gasket, block and head provide this function by short circuiting a very small amount of coolant. Often, this short-circuited coolant is directed to flow coolant on hot areas in the head, such as exhaust valves, spark plugs and the exhaust crossover.

By-pass. A thermostat is located at the engine outlet to restrict coolant flow until the engine reaches the thermostat-set operating temperature. The cooling system is provided with a *by-pass* that allows a small part of the coolant to circulate within the engine during warm-up while the thermostat is closed. The by-pass is a small passage that leads from the engine side of the thermostat to the inlet side of the coolant pump. Coolant will flow through the by-pass, short circuiting the radiator anytime there is a pressure difference on the ends of the by-pass, even if the thermostat is open. The by-pass may be cast or drilled into the engine and pump parts. This is called an internal by-pass. It may be an external by-pass visible as a hose on the front of many engines that connects the engine coolant outlet to the coolant pump. The by-pass aids in uniform warm-up, eliminates hot spots and prevents excessive coolant pressure in the engine when the thermostat is closed.

Thermostat. The thermostat is a temperature controlled valve placed at the engine coolant outlet. An encapsulated wax-based plastic pellet positioned on the engine side of the thermostatic valve is linked to the valve. As the engine warms, heat swells the pellet, opening the thermostat through a mechanical link. As the thermostat opens, it allows some coolant to flow to the radiator to be cooled while the remaining portion of the coolant continues to go through the by-pass. This partial opening varies according to the engine cooling requirements needed to maintain normal temperatures. The coolant pump provides the force that causes coolant to flow. This flow is restricted by a closed thermostat and, therefore, the flow rate is low. The thermostat restriction causes system pressure to rise. As the thermostat gradually opens, coolant flow rate increases and

(a)

Fig. 8-7 Cooling system bypass. (a) Internal, (b) external.

(b)

Fig. 8-8 Typical thermostats (The Dow Chemical Company).

pressure lowers. The thermostat will be wide open with maximum coolant flow only under extreme heating conditions, such as idling in traffic or pulling up a long steep grade in warm weather.

Radiator. The engine coolant outlet is connected to the top of the radiator by hoses and clamps. Coolant moves from the top to the bottom of the radiator as it cools. It leaves the lower radiator through an outlet and hose, going into the inlet side of the pump where it is recirculated through the engine.

Much of the cooling system's capacity is based on the function of the radiator. Radiators are designed to obtain the maximum rate of heat transfer using minimum material and size to keep cost as low as possible. Vehicle designs also dictate available radiator space and, consequently, affect their designs.

Two types of radiator cores are in common use in domestic automobiles, the *serpentine* fin core and the *plate* fin core. In each of these types, coolant flows through oval shaped tubes. Heat transfers through the tube wall and soldered joint to fins. The fins are exposed to an air flow which removes heat and carries it away from the radiator.

Most automobile radiators are made from

yellow brass or copper. These materials are corrosion resistant, have good heat transfer ability, are easily formed, have the required strength characteristics and are easily repaired by soldering. Some applications have used corrosion protected steel; however, steel is seldom used in automobile radiators. Aluminum is used for radiators in special applications where weight is critical.

Core tubes are made from .0045″ to .012″ sheet brass, using the thinnest possible materials for each application. They are rolled into round tubes and the joints sealed with a locking seam. The tubes are then coated with solder, compressed into an oval shape and cut to length. Fins are formed from .003″ to .005″ copper or brass, again using the thinnest possible material to save weight and cost.

Serpentine fins are formed, stacked between the tubes, and held in a fixture. These assemblies are heated in an oven to fuse the joints and then the assembly is submerged in liquid solder. Capillary action pulls solder into the joints, assuring a tight joint that will readily transfer heat. The serpentine type is usually used in passenger cars. It is the least

(a)

Fig. 8-9 Radiator core types. (a) Serpentine, (b) plate type (Modine Manufacturing Company).

(b)

expensive of the two types and cools as well as the plate type. The serpentine type is held together with the soldered joint alone, while the plate type is mechanically held by the plate fins as well as solder. Plate-type cores are, therefore, stronger than the serpentine cores.

The main limitation to heat transfer in a radiator is on the air side. Heat transfers from the water to the fins as much as seven times faster than the heat transfers from the fins to the air, assuming equal surface exposure. The radiator's heat transfer capacity is the result of the number of fins per inch, the radiator height, width, and thickness, and the number of coolant tubes. The core must be capable of dissipating heat energy approximately equal to the power produced by the engine. Each horsepower is equivalent to 42.4 BTU per minute. As the engine power is increased, the heat dissipation requirement is also increased.

Coolant tubes are straight, free flowing tubes. The fins are often given a pattern to break up any smooth laminar air flow that would insulate their surface. This turbulent flow will increase heat transfer rate, but will also add air resistance. Care is taken to design a radiator that will provide maximum cooling with minimum air resistance. With a given face area, radiator capacity may be increased by increasing the core thickness, packing more material into the same volume or both. Its capacity may also be increased by placing a shroud around the fan so more air will be pulled through the radiator.

Radiator headers and tanks that close off the ends of the core are made of sheet brass .020″ to .050″ thick. These are fitted with tubular brass hose necks. The supporting sides are usually steel. The filler neck and the drain boss are brass. When a transmission oil cooler is used in the radiator, it is placed in the outlet tank where the coolant has the lowest temperature.

Radiators may be of the down flow or cross flow designs. In down flow designs, hot coolant from the engine is delivered to the top radiator tank and cool coolant removed from the bottom. In cross flow designs, hot coolant goes to a tank on one side of the radiator and flows across the radiator through the coolant tubes to the tank on the other side. In the

Fig. 8-10 Down flow radiator (The Dow Chemical Company).

down flow designs, the coolant reserve tank is located on the top, or inlet side. In the cross flow design, the reserve tank is placed on the outlet side. Neither type is more or less efficient than the other. Available space generally dictates the choice of the two designs. In some vehicle designs, where radiator space is small, a separate expansion, or surge tank, is used. This is usually positioned at the highest part of the cooling system so that it can act as a vapor separator as well as a filler neck.

Fig. 8-11 Cross flow radiator (Modine Manufacturing Company).

Pressure Cap. The filler neck is fitted with a pressure cap. The cap has a spring loaded valve that will allow cooling system pressure to build up to

Fig. 8-12 Separate expansion tank.

Fig. 8-13 Pressure cap with the vacuum valve held open.

the cap pressure setting, and then release the excess pressure to prevent system damage. The cap is also fitted with a vacuum valve that allows air to re-enter the system as the system cools, rather than collapsing radiator parts with a vacuum. SAE standard latching notches on the cap and neck are sized so that a high pressure cap will not fit a low pressure system.

Automobile engines are pressurized to raise the boiling point of the coolant. The boiling point will increase approximately 3°F for each pound increase in pressure. Under standard atmospheric pressure, water will boil at 212°F. With a 15-pound pressure cap, water would boil at 257°F, which is a maximum temperature even for the lubricating system. This high pressure serves two functions. First, it allows the engine to run close to 200°F with no danger of boiling coolant. Second, the higher the coolant temperature, the more heat it can transfer. The heat transferred by the cooling system is

proportional to the temperature difference between the coolant and the outside air. This characteristic has lead to small high pressure radiator designs that are capable of handling large quantities of heat. It can be seen that for proper cooling, it is imperative to have the right pressure cap correctly installed.

A problem that sometimes occurs under these conditions involves the coolant pump. To function, the inlet side of the pump has a lower pressure than its outlet side. If inlet pressure is lowered too much, the coolant at the pump inlet could boil, producing vapor. The pump will then spin the coolant vapors and not pump coolant. This condition is called *pump cavitation.*

Fan. Air is forced across the radiator core by a cooling fan, usually attached to a hub on the coolant pump shaft. It is designed to do its job at the lowest fan speed with the engine at its highest coolant temperature. The fan is sometimes shrouded to increase the cooling system efficiency. The horsepower required to drive the fan increases much faster than the fan speed increases. Higher speed increases the fan noise level as well. Thermo-regulating and viscous-drive fans have been developed to drive the fan only as fast as required and to limit maximum fan speed. This reduces the fan power

Fig. 8-14 Thermo regulating fan and shroud.

Radiator core performance

Water flow per foot of core width:
  A - 10.2 GPM (0.69 ft/sec through tubes)
  B - 20.3 GPM (1.39 ft/sec through tubes)
  C - 30.5 GPM (2.08 ft/sec through tubes)
  D - 50.8 GPM (3.47 ft/sec through tubes)
  D - Above 50.8 GPM

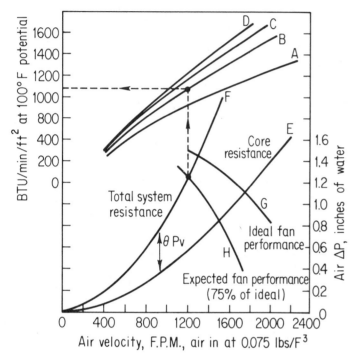

Fig. 8-15 Radiator and fan performance curves (Modine Manufacturing Company).

requirements and the fan noise. Fans with flexible plastic or flexible steel blades have also been developed. These fans have high blade angles that will pull a high air volume when turning at low speeds. As the fan speed increases, the blade angle flattens, reducing the horsepower required to drive it at high speeds.

Extra Heat Loads. Cooling systems have an added heat load when air conditioning is used. The high temperature air conditioning condenser is usually located ahead of the radiator and this raises the incoming air temperature 10 to 20°F. Air conditioned cars usually are equipped with a larger capacity radiator and a higher capacity fan than cars

without air conditioning. High capacity cooling systems are also used on cars equipped for trailer towing.

Retarded spark emission controls increase heat rejection to the cooling system. There may be as much as 25% additional rejection heat at idle. In traffic, the additional heat may become critical. To help relieve this critical situation, many engines are equipped with a temperature sensing vacuum valve. When the coolant reaches a critical temperature, engine vacuum is used to advance distributor timing. This improves combustion, but reduces emission control; however, it lowers the heat rejection rate, so the engine does not overheat.

Most of the heat absorbed from the engine by the cooling system is wasted. Some of this heat, however, is recovered by the vehicle heater. Heated coolant is by-passed through core tubes of a small heater. Air is passed through the heater fins, then sent to the passenger compartment. In some vehicles, the heater and air conditioner work in series to maintain vehicle compartment temperature.

8-4 COOLING SYSTEM MAINTENANCE

The cooling system is one of the most maintenance free systems in the engine. Normal maintenance involves an occasional check on the coolant level when the engine is cool. Removing a pressure cap from a hot engine will relieve the cooling system pressure while the coolant temperature is above its atmospheric boiling point. When the cap is removed, the pressure will drop to atmospheric pressure, causing the coolant to immediately boil. Coolant will be lost and someone may be injured or burned by the high temperature coolant boiling out of the filler opening.

Manufacturers recommend that a cooling system be flushed and the antifreeze be replaced at specific time intervals. Some recommend a change each year, while others recommend a change every other year. The antifreeze should be drained to remove rust and scale from inside the engine cooling passages, as well as to remove depleted antifreeze additives. After flushing with clear water, fresh antifreeze coolant mixture with new additives should be installed.

This would also be a good time to check the

condition of the coolant and heater hoses. Do not overlook the thermostat by-pass hose. Hoses should be replaced if there is any sign of deterioration. A broken hose will cause the coolant to be lost and allow the engine to overheat.

If there is no temperature gauge on the vehicle, it is desirable to remove the thermostat and check its opening temperature in a heated water bath with a thermometer.

Fig. 8-17 Checking a pressure cap.

Fig. 8-16 Checking a thermostat opening temperature.

The pressure cap should be checked to see that it maintains the correct pressure. A low setting will reduce the cooling system efficiency and it may allow a loss of coolant.

Both the coolant pump and the fan depend upon the drive belt. This should be checked periodically to see that it is in good condition. It should be replaced if it has any indication of deterioration. Care should be exercised to see that the belt is installed on the correct pulley. Many engines use a

number of belts and it is easy to mix the belts and pulley positions.

One thing that is often overlooked in cooling system maintenance is plugged radiator fins. Bugs often jam into the fins, blocking the air flow. The bugs should be blown out with high pressure air from the back of the radiator to the front. High pressure water may also be helpful in dislodging the bugs.

Sometimes, routine maintenance does not "cure" an overheating problem. If it is due to poor coolant circulation, the system can be *back flushed*. This procedure involves removing the hoses from the engine and radiator. A mixture of water and air is forced through the outlet side of the radiator and through the engine outlet with the thermostat removed. If this does not provide free coolant flow, the radiator will have to be sent to a radiator shop for an acid treatment or disassembled for cleaning the tubes. If the engine block is plugged, the engine will have to be disassembled, the core plugs removed and the cooling system scraped out.

In most cases, proper maintenance will keep the engine cooling system functioning satisfactorily for the life of the vehicle with no major repairs required.

Review Questions
Chapter 8

1. What are the functions of a cooling system?

2. What problems are caused by low temperature engine operation? High temperature operation?

3. What type of engines would probably use air cooling?

4. Why is antifreeze needed in some factory installed air conditioned cars?

5. What protection is required in the coolant when ethylene-glycol-based antifreezes are *not* used?

6. Why is the minimum antifreeze recommended?

7. Why does the coolant always enter the pump at the center of the impeller?

8. What is meant by parallel and series cooling systems?

9. How does a cooling system thermostat work?

10. When would a thermostat be wide open?

11. What is the value of a shrouded fan?

12. What is the purpose of a surge tank?

13. What conditions have allowed small radiators to be used with high powered engines?

14. How do emission controls affect the cooling system?

15. What routine maintenance is done on a cooling system?

Quiz 8

1. The use of more than the minimum required quantity of glycol-based antifreeze will cause the coolant to
   a. transfer more heat
   b. boil at a low temperature
   c. freeze at high temperatures
   d. cool the engine too much.

2. When the thermostat is closed, coolant will always flow through the
   a. radiator
   b. heater core
   c. by-pass
   d. atmospheric valve.

3. The thermostat on an emission-controlled engine would most likely be wide open after prolonged
   a. idling in traffic
   b. driving at sustained highway speeds
   c. engine operation at high rpm
   d. use of the same coolant.

4. Radiators are down flow or cross flow design. The cross flow design
   a. is more efficient
   b. is less efficient
   c. does not affect efficiency
   d. increases efficiency in some designs.

5. The primary purpose of the pressure cap is to
   a. prevent coolant leaks
   b. prevent air leaks
   c. reduce the cooling system pressure
   d. increase the coolant boiling point.

6. Water pump cavitation can occur on engines using a pressure cap when no air leak exists. This could result from
   a. boiling coolant at the pump inlet
   b. centrifugal force producing pressure at the pump
   c. poor pump seals
   d. a loose pump impeller.

7. Some of the heat rejected to the cooling system may be recovered and used by
   a. recirculating the hot coolant
   b. increasing the radiator capacity
   c. crankcase emission control devices
   d. the heater core.

8. The most critical heat transfer limiting point of a liquid cooling system is between the
   a. block and the coolant
   b. head and the coolant
   c. coolant and the radiator
   d. radiator and the air.

9. Removing the radiator cap on a hot engine will usually result in a loss of coolant. This occurs because
   a. coolant pressure pushes the coolant out
   b. reduced pressure allows the coolant to boil
   c. the hot coolant has expanded and will push out of the radiator neck
   d. the pump has caused rapid coolant circulation.

10. Engine overheating may be caused by
    a. a thermostat stuck open
    b. a pressure cap stuck closed
    c. an overfilled coolant system
    d. plugged radiator fins.

chapter 9

Engine Lubricants and Systems

Lubricating oil is often called the life blood of an engine. It circulates through passages in the engine that carry it to all of the engine's rubbing surfaces. Its main job is to form a film between these surfaces and keep them from touching. This action minimizes friction and wear within the engine. The lubricant has useful secondary functions. Cool lubricant picks up heat from the hot engine parts and takes it to the oil pan where it is cooled as air moves past the pan. The oil flow also carries wear particles from the rubbing surfaces to the pan so the particles will cause no further damage within the engine. Oil between the engine parts cushions the parts from shock as the combustion charge fires.

The lubricant used for motor oil must have properties that will allow it to meet the engine requirements. The motor oil's most important property is its thickness at its normal operating temperature. If it is too light the oil rapidly leaks from the clearances, thus allowing the parts to contact, resulting in scoring to the parts. When the thickness is too heavy the oil will require excessive power to overcome drag between the rubbing surfaces. This characteristic is noticeable when comparing the cranking speed of the engine, cold and warm.

Secondary properties, usually in the form of additives, are put in the oil by the motor oil producers to provide the oil with an ability to clean the engine, minimize scuffing, reduce rusting, resist oxidation and maintain the oil's viscosity characteristics. The oil should be replaced when its properties no longer protect the engine.

9-1 LUBRICATION PRINCIPLES

Lubrication between two moving surfaces results from an oil film that builds up to separate the surfaces and support the load. To understand this principle, consider how slippery a floor seems to be when a liquid is spilled on it. The liquid, either water or oil, supports a person's weight until it is squeezed out from under his feet. If oil were put on a flat surface and a heavy block pushed across this surface, the block would slide more easily than if it were pushed across a dry surface. The reason for for this is that a wedge-shaped oil film is built up between the moving block and the surface. This wedge-shaped film is thicker at the front or leading edge than at the rear. If the block were to be held still, the oil would be gradually squeezed out from under the block and the block would settle down on the surface. As soon as the block starts to move again, the wedge-shaped oil film will be re-established.

The force required to push the block across a surface is dependent upon the block weight, how fast it moves, and the thickness or viscosity of the oil. If the block is heavy, it will quickly squeeze the oil from under the surface. The faster the block is

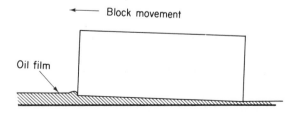

Fig. 9-1 Wedge shaped hydrodynamic oil film.

moved, the less time is available for oil to be squeezed out, so a heavier load can be supported as speed is increased. This principle is used in water skiing.

The other factor in an oil film's ability to support a load is the oil's thickness. Thin oil would squeeze out faster than thick oil; therefore, the thick oil can support a much greater load. The oil can be too thick. If the oil becomes too thick it becomes sluggish, so that it will require great effort to move the block over the oil. If the oil is too thin, the block is not supported completely and the block will drag slightly on the surface. For any given block weight and moving speed, there is one oil thickness which requires the least effort to move the block. The force required to move the block divided by the pressure caused by the block weight is called the *coefficient of friction*.

The principle just described is called *hydrodynamic* lubrication. Hydro refers to liquids, as in hydraulics, and dynamic refers to moving materials.

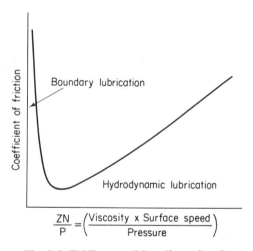

Fig. 9-2 ZN/P curve (Non-dimensional).

Hydrodynamic lubrication occurs when a wedge-shaped film develops in a liquid between two moving surfaces. When this film becomes so thin that the surface high spots touch, it is called boundary lubrication.

As the coefficient of friction increases, it takes more effort to move the block. The least effort is required when the correct wedge-shaped oil film exists. The coefficient of friction will increase during boundary lubrication or when the oil is too thick. This can be shown on the dimensionless graph in Figure 9-2, where the oil thickness or *viscosity* is expressed as Z, the speed at which the block moves across the surface is expressed as N and the pressure caused by the block weight is expressed as P. The coefficient of friction is minimum for one value of ZN/P. If the load P is increased, the value of ZN/P is reduced and the film moves left toward boundary conditions. Any increase in speed will increase ZN/P and move the expression to the right. It takes more effort to increase the speed while using the same viscosity and load. For any constant speed and load, the oil film is dependent upon the oil viscosity. Viscosity is oil's most important property.

Flat surface lubrication only exists in a few places in automotive engines. Some of these are thrust bearings, valve tips and lifter bases on the cam. Most moving surfaces are similar to flat bearing surfaces, but they are somewhat curved. They still use the same hydrodynamic lubrication principles just described. These surfaces may be curved in one way to form a cylinder wall, lifter bore, or valve guide. When curved in the other direction, they are used as main, connecting rod and camshaft bearings.

The engine oil pressure system delivers a continuous supply of oil to the lightly loaded portion of bearing surfaces. Hydrodynamic lubrication takes over as the shaft rotates in the bearing to produce a wedge-shaped hydrodynamic oil film that is curved around the bearing. This film supports the bearing and, where using oil of the correct viscosity, will reduce the turning effort to a minimum. Changes in viscosity, speed, or load affect the bearing lubrication in the same way they do with a block moving on a flat surface just described.

A crankshaft main bearing will be used to describe typical bearing lubrication. When the engine is not running, the crankshaft pushes much of the oil from around it as it settles to the bottom of the bearing. As the starter is cranked, the crankshaft tries to roll up the bearing side wall. If some surface oil remains on the bearing, the shaft will slide back to the bottom of the bearing when it hits this oil. Continued turning will repeat this sequence of climbing and sliding back. The sequence continues until the oil pump supplies fresh oil to the bearing journal. The shaft continues to try to climb up the bearing wall; however, it now grabs oil instead of the bearing surface. This pulls oil around the shaft, forming a curved wedge-shaped oil film that supports the crankshaft in the bearing.

Most bearing wear occurs during the initial start and continues until a hydrodynamic film is established.

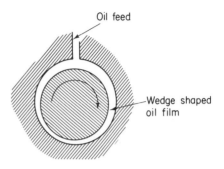

Fig. 9-3 Wedge shaped film around a journal bearing.

A continuous new oil supply is required to maintain the oil film because oil will leak from the side of the bearing. This oil leakage flushes contaminants from the bearing as well as removes heat that is generated in the bearing.

One of the engine lubrication system's functions is to maintain a positive and continuous oil supply to the bearings. Engine oil pressure is high enough to get the oil to bearings with sufficient force to produce adequate oil flow for proper cooling. Normal engine oil pressure range is from 30 to 60 psi while the hydrodynamic film pressures developed in the high pressure areas of the engine bearings may be over 1000 psi. The relatively low engine oil pressures, obviously, couldn't support these engine loads without hydrodynamic lubrication.

9-2 ENGINE LUBRICATION REQUIREMENTS

The greatest lubrication demand in engines is usually considered to be the bearings. Their lubrication is necessary for maximum service life of the engine; however, their lubrication is quite simple and is easily met with properly designed bearings using oil with the correct viscosity.

The highest unit pressures actually occur between the cam lobes and valve lifters. Much of modern motor oil formulation is based on the oil's ability to minimize lifter scuffing and wear. Cam lobes are not lubricated with positive pressure, but rely on oil thrown from the connecting rods and on oil that drains back from the rocker and lifter chambers.

Valve assemblies, pistons, piston pins, oil pump-distributor drive, and cam drives only require a surface film of oil. The loads are relatively light, so that oil received from splash is usually adequate. Oil under slight pressure is usually directed to the rocker arms. The amount of pressure is not important, only that the oil is positively delivered to the moving surface needing lubrication. Some engines direct an oil flow to the cam drive. This oil helps to cushion the drive and reduce noise.

Automobile engines also use engine oil to operate hydraulic valve lifters. This places another and different kind of requirement on the engine oil. Hydraulic lifters are manufactured with extremely close fitting parts, to minimize leakage. Small foreign particles that get into these clearances could cause the lifter to malfunction. The engine oil must keep the lifter clean, limiting deposit formation that would cause lifter sticking.

9-3 PROPERTIES OF MOTOR OIL

The most important motor oil property is its thickness or viscosity. As an oil cools, it thickens and as it heats up, it gets thinner; therefore, its viscosity changes with temperature. The oil must have a low enough viscosity at low temperatures to allow the engine to start. Thick oil at low temperatures causes a very high coefficient of friction as can be seen on the right side of the ZN/P curve in Figure 9-2. If this coefficient of friction becomes too great, the cold engine will not have enough energy to carry over from one firing impulse to the next. When this happens, the engine will not start. There is a maximum oil viscosity that will allow an engine to start at any specific temperature. On the other end of the scale, with the engine hot, the oil thins and the viscosity lowers. If the viscosity becomes too low, boundary lubrication will occur and the coefficient of friction will increase, as is shown on the left end of the ZN/P curve. Motor oil must have

its viscosity between these two extremes. It must be thin enough to allow the engine to start when cold and it must still have enough body or viscosity to develop the correct hydrodynamic lubrication film when it gets to its normal operating temperature. An index of the change in viscosity between the cold and hot viscosity is called *viscosity index*. All oils thin as they get hot; however, oils with a high viscosity index thin less than oils with a low viscosity index.

The viscosity of an oil is determined by one of several types of viscosimeters. The oldest and most familiar viscosity measurement device is the Saybolt viscosimeter. It consists of an accurately machined brass tube with a calibrated opening in its bottom called a Universal orifice. The tube is surrounded by a bath that is maintained at the test temperature. In operation, the tube is fitted with a stopper at its lower end, then filled with the sample oil. It is given time to stabilize at the test temperature. When the test temperature is reached, the stopper is pulled from the tube, allowing the sample to flow through the Universal orifice. The viscosity from this test is reported as *Saybolt Universal Seconds* (SUS). Minimum wear occurs when the viscosity is from 30 to 40 SUS at the operating temperature.

Two test temperatures are used to classify motor oils, 0°F and 210°F. The 0° test indicates the oil's viscosity at low temperatures and the 210° test indicates the oil viscosity at normal engine operating temperatures.

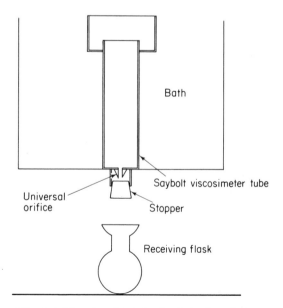

Fig. 9-4 Line drawing of a Saybolt viscosimeter.

Viscosity testing by the Saybolt viscosimeter is quite time consuming and is being replaced by alternate viscosity test methods. The 210° high temperature test is done using a test procedure for opaque liquids and the results are reported in *centistokes*, the designation for kinematic viscosity. In this test, a measured amount of oil sample is drawn into a glass viscosimeter tube, then placed in a 210° bath. The top of the sample is drawn slightly above two test lines. The time it takes the sample to drain from one test line to the next is measured in seconds. The seconds are multiplied by the viscosimeter correction factor to get the viscosity value in centistokes. This test may be repeated a number of times for accuracy without draining the viscosimeter tube. It is easy and faster to use than a Saybolt viscosimeter.

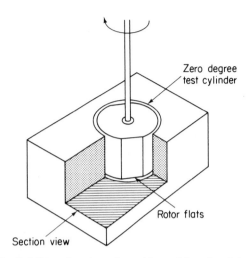

Fig. 9-6 Line drawing of a cold cranking simulator.

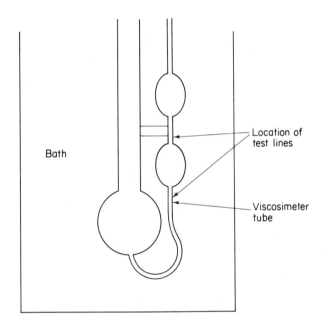

Fig. 9-5 Line drawing of a glass kinematic viscosimeter tube.

Another test procedure uses a Cold Cranking Simulator that is replacing the Saybolt viscosimeter for 0° tests. The Cold Cranking Simulator has a rotor, with two flats, that is placed in a cylinder. The cylinder is then filled with the sample and the whole unit cooled to 0°. At this test temperature, the rotor is turned by a constant speed motor. The effort required to turn the rotor is reported in *centipoise*, a measurement of absolute viscosity. Here again, the test is quicker and simpler than the Saybolt viscosity test.

Motor oils are sold with an SAE number stamped on the top of the oil can. This number indicates the viscosity range in which the oil fits. These numbers are taken from a range of viscosities. Oils tested at 0° are given an SAE number, followed by the letter "W". This "W" at one time indicated a winter grade of oil. Oils that are tested at 210° have a number without a following letter. For example, SAE 30 indicates that the oil has only been checked at 210 degrees and falls within this grade classification *when hot*. SAE 20W-20

SAE Viscosity Number	Viscosity Units	At 0°		At 210°	
		min	max	min	max
5 W	Centipoises	–	1,200	–	–
	SUS	–	6,000	–	–
10 W	Centipoises	1,200	2,400	–	–
	SUS	6,000	12,000	–	–
20 W	Centipoises	2,400	9,600	–	–
	SUS	12,000	48,000	–	–
20	Centistokes	–	–	5.7	9.6
	SUS	–	–	45	58
30	Centistokes	–	–	9.6	12.9
	SUS	–	–	58	70
40	Centistokes	–	–	12.9	16.8
	SUS	–	–	70	85
50	Centistokes	–	–	16.8	22.7
	SUS	–	–	85	110

Fig. 9-7 Table comparing viscosity to SAE number (Courtesy of the Society of Automotive Engineers).

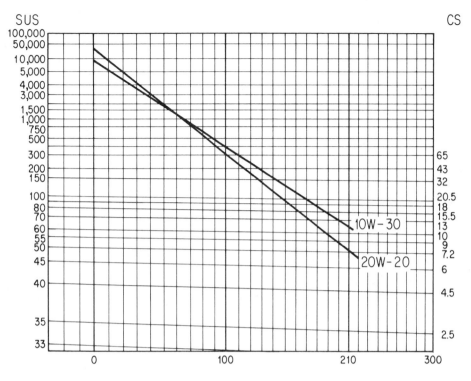

Fig. 9-8 Viscosity plotted on a standard viscosity-temperature chart (Courtesy of the American Society for Testing and Materials).

indicates that the oil has been tested at both zero and 210° and falls into the respective classifications. An SAE 10W-30 multigrade oil is one that meets the SAE 10W specification when cooled to zero degrees and meets the SAE 30 classification when heated to 210°. Multigrade oils must have a higher viscosity index than straight grade oils.

Even though viscosity is the most important oil property motor oil has additional properties that are important. The lowest temperature at which oil will pour is called its *pour point*. Below this temperature, the oil will not be liquid, so it will not be able to produce hydrodynamic lubrication and, therefore, could not be used below this temperature.

As oil is heated, the volatile portions will boil off. When the volatile vapors can be ignited with a small flame, the oil is at its *flash point*. The temperature at which the vapor continues to burn is called the *fire point*. Oil cannot function above the flash point temperature because of its changing characteristics. The maximum useful range of a motor oil is between the pour point and the flash point temperatures. The flash point test is also used to determine if used motor oil contains gasoline contaminants. These are more volatile than the motor oil and will evaporate and burn at a much lower temperature than the oil itself.

Motor oil must also resist oxidation, a form of oil breakdown. It must not bubble or foam,

which would upset the hydrodynamic film. Neither the oil or additives should break down and form acids that will corrode and cause scuffing or rusting engine parts. They must disperse contaminants to keep the engine clean.

The American Petroleum Institute (API), working with engine manufacturers and oil companies, has set an engine oil performance classification. Oils are tested and the oil can is marked (usually printed) with the API classification as well as the SAE viscosity number. The API classification is the only way a customer can identify the oil properties for use in his engine.

Oil classifications available in the service stations have the prefix "S". Straight mineral oil is type SA classification. It was formerly called ML and should only be used in engines that operate under mild conditions requiring no additional protection. Oil for mild engine operation requiring some protection by compounding is called type SB classification; it was formerly called MM. Engines requiring protection from high and low temperature deposits, wear, rust, and corrosion require oil classification SC, which was formerly the 1964 MS oil. The SD classification, the former 1968 MS oil, is designed for the most severe type of engine service, such as low deposit buildup developed during stop and go service, as well as oxidation from high speed, high temperature operation. Only SD oil is recommended for use in automobiles built after 1968 by automobile manufacturers.

Oils with the SA engine oil performance classification do not have to pass any operational tests. Oils classified as SB must pass both the single cylinder engine bearing weight loss test L-38 and the Chrysler Corporation developed cam-lifter scuffing test sequence IV. The SC oil classification uses all of the SB tests and adds the General Motors Corporation developed test sequences IIA and IIIA for scuffing, sludge and varnish; the sequence V, developed by Ford, to measure sludge build-up, piston varnish, valve tip wear, ring sticking and oil screen clogging; and the single cylinder L-1 test for piston ring groove plugging. The most severe tests are placed on SD classified oils. They have the same basic tests as the SC oils but they use updated sequence II B, III B and V B tests. In addition the SD oils must pass the Falcon rust test developed by Ford that simulates the worst possible engine operating conditions with a plugged crankcase breather system running at low temperatures. Oils that can pass all of these tests meet the SD performance classification and are satisfactory for use in current passenger car engines.

Additional service classifications are used for diesel engines. These are CA, CB, CC, and CD. Oils may be rated for several service classifications at the same time. If they are, the oil may be used for any one of the types of service.

9-4 MOTOR OIL DETERIORATION

As oil is used, it deteriorates and requires changing. Two general types of oil deterioration exist—contamination and breakdown.

Oil may be contaminated with dirt or coolant. The most common type of contamination, however, is from the blow-by gases that work their way past the piston and rings. If crankcase ventilation is poor and the engine is cool, blow-by gases remain in the crankcase and mix with the oil. The undesirable blow-by constituants primarily consist of partially burned fuel and water vapor. Unburned fuel dilutes the oil. The highly acidic water from combustion causes rusting and corrosion. Both combine with polymerized and oxidized hydrocarbons, produced during combustion, undergoing further change in the oil to form sludge "binders" that hold organic

solids, inorganic salts, wear particles, and fuel soot together. When these particles get large enough, they drop out of the oil and deposit in the engine as a cold-engine sludge of mayonnaise consistency.

When an engine is run at normal operating temperatures for some time, the oil gets hot and breaks down. Oil breakdown is the result of hot oil combining with oxygen, and is called oxidation. This will eventually form hard carbon and varnish deposits on engine parts when it is allowed to build up over a long period of time. Two hundred and fifty degrees is the normal maximum engine oil temperature.

Engine oil additives tend to deteriorate and be used up as the oil is used. When they can no longer do their designed job, the oil loses some of its necessary properties. Engine oils should be changed before sludge develops, before oxidized deposits form, and before the additives lose their effectiveness.

9-5 MOTOR OIL ADDITIVES

Additives are used in motor oils for three different reasons: (1) to replace some properties removed during refining, (2) to reinforce some of the oil's natural properties, and (3) to provide the oil with new properties it did not originally have. Oils from some petroleum oil fields require more and different additives than oils from other fields. Additives are usually classified according to the property they add to the oil.

Anti-oxidants reduce the high temperature contaminants. They prevent the formation of varnish, reduce bearing corrosion, and particle formation.

Corrosion preventatives reduce acid formation that would cause bearing corrosion.

Detergents and dispersants prevent low temperature sludge binders from forming and break the sludge particles into a finely divided state. The particles will stay in suspension in the oil to be removed from the engine with the oil at the drain period.

Extreme pressure and anti-wear additives form a chemical film that prevents metal to metal seizure anytime boundary lubrication exists.

Viscosity index improvers are used to reduce viscosity change as the oil temperature changes.

Pour point depressants coat the wax crystals in the oil so they will not stick together and the oil will then be able to flow at lower temperatures.

A number of other oil additives may be used to modify the oil. These include rust preventatives, metal deactivators, water repellents, emulsifiers, dyes, color stabilizers, odor control agents, and foam inhibitors.

The oil producer must be careful to check the compatibility of the oil additives he uses. A number of chemicals that will help each other can be used for each of the additive requirements. However, with improper additive selection, the additives may oppose each other and lose their benefit to the oil. Each oil producer balances the additives in his oil to provide an oil with desirable properties that meet the engine's needs.

Additives available at service stations, or *proprietary* additives, generally cannot add any needed desirable property to the oil that it does not already possess. It is even possible that these additives may neutralize some of the additives already in the oil, thus degrading the oil instead of improving it. The procedure usually recommended by the engine manufacturer is to use only SD or MS oil without additional proprietary additives. When adding oil between changes, it is a good practice to add the same brand and grade of oil that is already in the engine, thus minimizing the chance of having conflicting additives.

9-6 ENGINE LUBRICATION SYSTEM

Automobile engines use a *wet sump* in their lubrication system. The sump is the lowest part of the system and in automobile engines, this is the oil pan. It is called a wet sump because it holds the oil supply. Some racing and industrial engines use a dry sump. A scavenger pump in these engines draws the oil out of a relatively small sump and returns it to a separate oil supply tank. The engine oil pump draws oil from this tank to feed the engine lubrication system.

All production automobile engines have a *full pressure* oil system. The pressure is maintained by an oil pump that picks up the motor oil through a passage from an inlet screen in the oil pan and forces it into the lubrication system under pressure. The inlet screen may be supplied with a *brake stop baffle* that keeps the inlet screen covered during sudden stops.

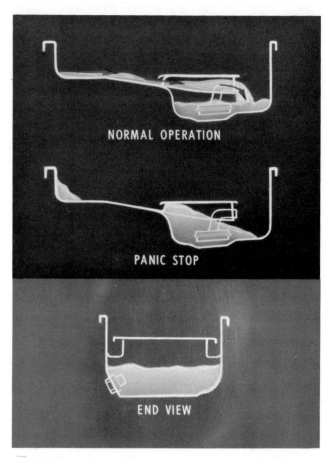

Fig. 9-9 Oil movement in the pan during vehicle maneuvers (Chevrolet Motor Division, General Motors Corporation).

Oil Pressure. The oil pump is driven from a gear on the camshaft. In most engines, the distributor drive gear meshes with the camshaft gear. The oil pump is driven from the end of the distributor shaft. Some engines have a short shaft-gear that meshes with the cam gear to drive both the distributor and oil pump. Occasionally, an engine is built that uses separate gears on the distributor and on the oil pump. Both mate with the same cam gear. With these drive methods, the pump turns at one half engine speed. In one engine type the oil pump is driven by the front of the crankshaft.

Automotive oil pumps are of two types, gear and rotor. The gear-type oil pump consists of two spur gears, in a close fitting housing. One gear is driven and the other idles. When pumping, oil is carried around the outside of each gear in the space between the gear teeth and the case. As the teeth mesh in the center, oil is forced out, thus producing oil pressure. The rotor type oil pump is essentially a special lobe-shaped gear meshing with the inside of a lobed rotor. The center lobed section is driven and the outer section idles. As the pump rotates, it carries oil around between the lobes. As the lobes mesh, they force the oil out under pressure in the same manner as the gear-type pump. The pump is sized so that it will maintain at least 15 psi in the oil gallery when the engine is hot and idling. Pressure will increase as the engine speed increases, because the engine driven pump also rotates faster.

In engines with full pressure lubricating systems, maximum pressure is limited with a *pressure regulator or relief valve*. If a pressure regulator valve was not used, the engine oil pressure would continue to increase as the engine speed increased. Maximum pressure is usually limited to the pressure that will deliver an adequate quantity of lubricating oil to engine locations required. Three to six gallons per minute are required. After the oil leaves the pump, oil films are maintained by hydrodynamic forces. Excessive oil pressure requires more horsepower and provides no better lubrication. High oil pressure and resulting high rates of oil flow may, in some cases, tend to erode engine bearings.

Oil pressure is produced when the oil pump has a larger capacity than all of the "leaks" in the engine. The "leaks" are the clearances at end points of the lubrication system, such as the edges of bearings, the rocker arms, the connecting rod spit holes, etc. These clearances are designed into the engine and are necessary for its proper operation. As parts wear and clearance becomes greater, they will leak more. The oil pump's capacity results from its size, rotating speed, and physical condition. If the pump is rotating slowly as the engine is idling, oil pump capacity is low. If the "leaks" are greater than the pump capacity, engine oil pressure is low. As the engine speeds up, the pump capacity increases and tries to force more oil out of the "leaks". This causes the pressure to rise until the pressure reaches the regulated pressure.

A third consideration, engine oil viscosity, is

Fig. 9-10 Typical oil pump drive method.

Fig. 9-11 Gear-type oil pump.

Fig. 9-12 Rotor-type oil pump.

involved in both the pump capacity and the oil leakage. Very low viscosity or thin oil slips past the edges of the pump and flows freely from the "leaks". Hot oil has a low viscosity and, therefore, is often accompanied by low oil pressure. Cold oil is more viscous and usually results in high pressures, even with the engine idling. Putting higher viscosity oil in an engine will raise the engine oil pressure to the regulated setting at a lower engine speed.

The pressure regulator is located downstream from the pressure side of the oil pump. It generally consists of a spring-loaded piston and, in a few cases, a spring-loaded ball. When oil pressure reaches the regulated pressure, it will force the regulator valve back against the calibrated spring, compressing it as the valve is forced back. This allows a controlled "leak" from the pressure system at a rate that will maintain the set regulated pressure. Any change in the regulator valve spring pressure will change the regulated oil pressure; higher spring pressures will cause higher maximum oil pressures. In most engines, the oil that is released by the regulator valve is routed to the inlet side of the oil pump to be recirculated through the pump. The regulator valve is, therefore, usually located in the oil pump housing or pump cover. This method of oil flow

from the regulator valve prevents foaming and excessive oil agitation so a solid stream of lubricating oil will be delivered by the pump.

Oil Filter. Oil leaving the pump flows to the oil filter where large particles are trapped, allowing only clean oil to flow into the engine. Filters are designed to trap large particles that could damage engine bearings. Very fine particles flow through the filter. These particles are so fine that they can get between engine clearances and do no damage. As the filter traps particles, the holes in the filter become partly plugged. As they plug, the filter traps even smaller particles, thus doing a better filtering job. This better filtering, however, restricts oil flow and this could result in bearing oil starvation. All filters or filter adapters have a bypass check valve so that if the filter plugs, oil can bypass the plugged filter and go directly into the engine. The bypass valve is set at from five to fifteen psi, depending on the engine and normal pressure drop across the filter element.

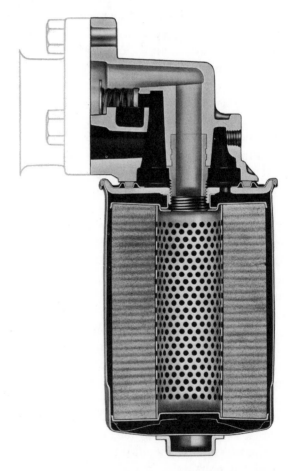

Fig. 9-14 Cross section of a typical oil filter (AC Division, General Motors Corporation).

Fig. 9-13 Oil pressure relief valve releases excess oil to the pump inlet.

Filters or filter adapters are also supplied with a check valve that keeps the filter full when the engine is stopped. It keeps the oil from leaking back through the oil pump into the pan, so the oil pump remains primed and provides rapid oil pressure buildup when the engine starts.

Oil Passages. From the filter, oil goes through a drilled hole that intersects with a drilled main oil gallery or longitudinal header. Inline engines use one oil gallery. V engines may use two main galleries or one main gallery and two valve lifter galleries. Drilled passages through the bulkheads allow the oil to go from the main oil gallery to the main and cam bearings. In some engines, oil goes to the cam bearings first, then to the main bearings, while other engines direct the oil to the main bearings first, then to the cam bearings. Hydrodynamic films will build up to lubricate the bearings and journals. It is important that the bearing oil holes align with the drilled passages in the bearing saddles, so that proper lubrication will be provided. Excessive bearing wear will cause excessive oil throw off from the side of the bearing and, thus, starve a bearing located further downstream in the lubricating system. This is a major cause of bearing failure. If a new bearing were installed in place of the starved bearing, it, too, would fail unless the bearing with excessive throw off were also replaced. For proper operation, the lubrication system must be balanced so that each bearing uses only the designed amount of oil and leaves enough oil in the system for the remaining bearings.

The crankshaft is drilled to allow oil from the main bearing oil groove to be directed to the connecting rod bearings. This oil forms a hydrodynamic oil film on the connecting rod bearing to support bearing loads. From here, some of the oil may be sprayed through a spit or bleed hole. The rest of the oil leaks from the edges of the bearing and is thrown against the inside surfaces of the engine. Some of the throw-off oil lands on the camshaft to lubricate the lobes. Some of the oil splashes on the cylinder wall to lubricate the piston and rings. Some splashes onto the piston pin. Oil that lands on the interior wall drains back into the oil pan for recirculation through the lubricating system.

The oil gallery may intersect or have drilled passages to the valve lifter bores to lubricate the lifters. When hydraulic lifters are used, the gallery

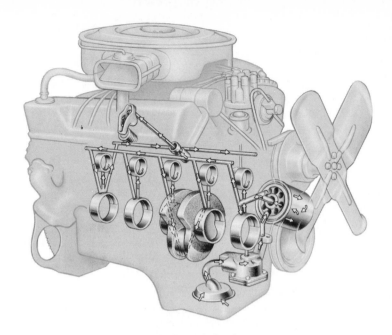

Fig. 9-15 Typical engine lubrication system (Ford Motor Company).

Fig. 9-16 Oil cross hole drilled in a crankshaft.

Fig. 9-17 Piston pin lubricated from the spit hole.

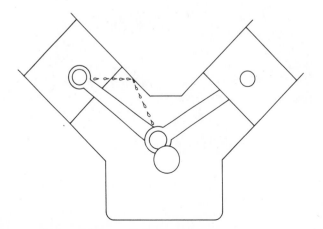

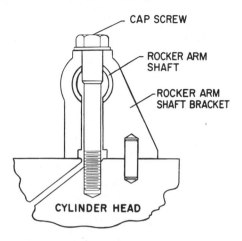

Fig. 9-18 Oil passages around a rocker support bolt (Dana Corporation).

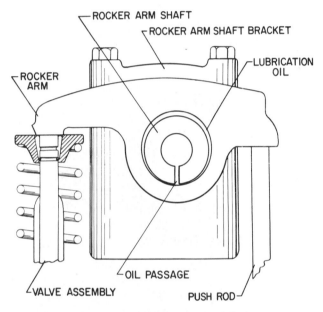

Fig. 9-19 Rocker arm lubricated from a shaft (Dana Corporation).

oil pressure keeps refilling them. On some engines, oil from the lifters goes up the center of a hollow pushrod to lubricate the pushrod ends, the rocker arm pivot and the valve stem tip. In other engines, an oil passage is drilled from the gallery or from a cam bearing to the block deck, where it matches with a gasket hole and a hole drilled in the head to carry the oil to a rocker arm shaft. Some engines use an enlarged head bolt hole to carry lubricating oil around the head bolt to the rocker arm shaft. Holes in the bottom of the rocker arm shaft lubricate the rocker arm pivot. Often, holes are drilled in cast rocker arms to carry oil to the pushrod end and to the valve tip. Rocker arm assemblies only need a surface coating of oil so the oil passage to rocker assembly is reduced using restrictions or metered openings.

Oil that seeps from the rocker assemblies is returned to the oil pan through drain holes. These oil drain holes are often placed so that the oil drains on the camshaft or on cam drive gears to lubricate them.

Some engines have a positive oil flow directed to the cam drive gears or chain. This may be a nozzle or a chamfer on a bearing parting surface that allows oil to spray on the loaded portion of the cam drive.

Oil Pan. Oil in the oil pan is subjected to a number of forces. As the car accelerates, brakes, or is turned rapidly, the oil tends to slosh around in the pan. Pan baffles and oil pan shapes are often used to resist oil sloshing to keep the oil inlet under the oil at all times. As the crankshaft rotates, it acts like a fan and causes air within the crankcase to rotate with it. This can cause a strong draft on the oil, churning it to entrap air bubbles. A baffle or windage tray is sometimes installed in engines to eliminate this problem. Windage trays have a good

Fig. 9-20 Windage tray.

side effect by reducing the amount of air disturbed by the crankshaft so less power is robbed from the engine at high crankshaft speeds.

9-7 CRANKCASE VENTILATION

Crankcase ventilation systems are installed on all engines to remove blow-by gases from the engine. Some older engines had a screened inlet and a *draft tube* outlet that would draw vapors from the crankcase while the car was in motion. Vehicle emission studies have shown that these blow-by gases contribute to air pollution. Vehicle emission laws were passed to equip engines with positive crankcase ventilation (PCV) systems. The draft tube was replaced with a PCV valve and connecting hoses to pull the crankcase vapors into the intake manifold where they are sent to the cylinder to be burned in the combustion chamber. Under some operating conditions, the gases would be forced back through the inlet filter. A line connecting the inlet to the carburetor air filter allows back-up vapors to be inducted through the carburetor with the incoming air. This effectively eliminates all crankcase emissions and, at the same time, provides adequate crankcase ventilation that will reduce oil contamination and deposit buildup.

9-8 LUBRICATION SYSTEM MAINTENANCE

During the service life of an engine, most of the lubrication system service involves oil and filter changes. Oil selection is based on the manufacturer's or petroleum companies' recommendations. These recommendations are based on extensive laboratory and fleet testing to check the compatibility of the oil to the engine. One consideration that the oil recommendation must include is the lowest expected temperature. A viscosity grade is recommended that will allow easy engine starting. A minimum starting viscosity is 5000 centipoise. Most automobile engine manufacturers recommend a multigrade oil which will allow easy cold starts and provide adequate protection when warm. A second consideration is the type of service that is to be en-

countered. Automobile manufacturers recommend SD or MS service classification oil.

All automobile companies recommend using an original equipment oil filter. These are tailored to the engine requirements. High quality replacement filters are available and do an acceptable job of filtering the lubricating oil. They must, however, be designed for the specific engine application.

There is much debate about the most desirable oil change period. The automobile manufacturer's recommendations usually differ from the petroleum company's recommendations. An oil drain period is established by considering the oil's contamination, the additive's continued effectiveness, and the original oil service classification. Running a laboratory analysis on the engine oil is the only way to determine the actual condition of the used oil. This, of course, is only possible in research and engineering laboratories. Manufacturers use this method, along with extensive service tests by both the engine manufacturers and the petroleum companies to determine safe drain periods. The results of these tests are passed along to their respective service organizations as the recommended oil change period.

Low speed stop-and-go traffic driving causes the engine to run cool so sludge will start to build up. This type of vehicle operation puts a very few miles on the vehicle each month; however, the contamination continues to build up rapidly for each mile traveled. A time period recommendation is usually provided to take care of vehicles that are operated in this manner.

High speed, high temperature engine operation builds up varnish and carbon-type deposits. This type of operation builds mileage rapidly over a short period of time. An oil change period based on mileage is recommended to take care of this type of vehicle operation.

Most automobiles are operated with a mixture of low speed and high speed driving. The usual oil change recommendations are made on both a time and mileage basis to take care of any "normal" operation. It is further recommended that if the vehicle is operated under abnormal conditions, such as dusty roads, the oil should be changed more frequently.

If the oil change periods are extended beyond the manufacturer's recommendations, contaminants may become so large and heavy that they will fall out of the oil and deposit in the engine. When this happens, they cannot be removed from the engine when draining used oil. These deposits continue to build until the engine is disassembled and cleaned.

Engine designs have reduced contamination buildup and have increased the oil change interval. Some of these engine design features are: splash pans under the intake manifold heat riser to keep the oil away from this hot surface so the oil won't be oxidized; rocker assembly oil return passages are enlarged to allow the oil to rapidly return from hot areas to the oil pan to keep it from oxidizing; high temperature thermostats quickly warm the oil to reduce cold sludge buildup. Extended oil drain periods will not satisfactorily protect older engines that do not include the features designed for long drain periods. The drain period should not extend beyond the manufacturer's recommendation for each specific engine model.

Super premium engine oils have been developed to operate during extended oil drain periods. These oils are made from selected grades of lubricating oil stock. Improved additives are blended with it to give the oil the required long life properties.

Extended oil drain periods are only recommended on engines with the proper design features when using super premium oils. Other engines and oil combinations require more frequent oil drain periods.

The difference between the automobile engine manufacturer and the petroleum company recommended oil drain period is the result of different philosophies. The automobile manufacturer's recommendations are to the original automobile owner. If these recommendations are followed, the average original owner will have minimum maintenance expense. The petroleum company recommendations, on the other hand, are based on conservative views that would provide the longest service period between overhauls. This would give minimum lifetime costs if one drove enough miles to "use up" the engine's useful life. In general, it can be stated that the petroleum companies recommend oil changes twice as often as the automobile manufacturers.

Engine oil consumption is another maintenance requirement. The average automobile owner has no idea how much oil is being consumed by the engine until he finds that it is necessary to add oil between oil changes. He seldom concerns himself about oil consumption until it becomes excessive. The only way he can tell if the consumption is excessive is by the amount of oil he adds to the engine between oil changes.

Motor oil can get out of the engine through the combustion chamber or through leaks. Leaks generally result from loose, poor fitting, or damaged gaskets, or from damaged oil seals. In some cases, leaks may result from cracked engine parts. Leaks are usually repairable without requiring an engine overhaul.

Oil can get into the combustion chamber past the piston rings, through the valve guides, through some intake gasket leaks, and through the PCV system. Of these leaks, the most expensive one to repair is the oil leak past the piston rings.

Unless excessive oil consumption affects engine operation, as evidenced by hard starting or sluggish performance, its correction will be based on economics, pride, or law. Most automobile manufacturers do not consider oil consumption to be excessive and requiring repair on new engines unless the engine uses more than one quart to each 500 to 700 miles. Fortunately the mileage is seldom this low. As the engine mileage builds up, its oil mileage will decrease.

The economic consideration in oil consumption relates the cost of the oil to the cost of the repair job. If oil consumption is a result of a gasket, seal, or cracked part, the repair cost is generally low. If it requires overhaul, such as reringing, the repair cost will far exceed the cost of the additional oil consumed.

Many people have enough pride in their automobiles that they are willing to pay the possible high cost to have all leaks repaired, to eliminate exhaust smoke, and have minimum oil consumption. They will have it repaired without considering economics. Some states have pollution laws that will not allow vehicles to be operated with visible exhaust emissions. In these cases, the oil consumption will have to be maintained at a low level, regardless of cost.

Excessive oil consumption, then, is a compromise between the value of the car, the cost of repair, the cost of the extra oil, the owner's pride, and the operating laws.

In addition to motor oil, many oil and chemical companies package proprietary additives that the customer may add to his motor oil. Some of these materials are solvents that dissolve deposits, some are detergents and depressants, and others are oil thickeners. These products are similar to the products the oil manufacturers have already blended into the oil to give it the required properties at a minimum cost to the consumer. The proprietary products are high priced additives that increase the cost of the oil when they are used and they are of doubtful value in a "normal" engine that is using recommended oils. Solvents and detergents added to the oil may be useful for freeing sticking hydraulic lifters and valves. When they free up, the oil should be

drained and replaced with a fresh change of the proper engine oil. If a thickener is desired, purchasing a heavier grade for a refill is less expensive than using a lighter grade with an oil thickener. As the engine runs, the additive thickener breaks down and the oil thins out, thus losing the desired characteristics.

When one considers the great amount of money spent by the automobile manufacturer and petroleum companies to match the engine and the oil, it seems wise to follow their recommendations. The manufacturer's warranty is based on these recommendations and, therefore, this will provide satisfactory lubrication for a normal service life of the engine lubrication system.

Review Questions
Chapter 9

1. What are the purposes of lubricating oil in an engine?

2. Define hydrodynamic lubrication.

3. How does the coefficient of friction change as changes are made in oil viscosity, surface speed and load?

4. How does engine oil pressure affect hydrodynamic lubrication?

5. Why does most of the bearing wear occur during engine starts?

6. What engine parts have the most severe lubrication requirements?

7. What determines the high and low viscosity limits of a motor oil?

8. Why is the Saybolt Viscosity Test method being replaced?

9. How does a multigrade oil differ from its API engine oil performance classification?

10. How do low temperature oil contaminants differ from high temperature oil contaminants?

11. How does an oil's SAE viscosity number differ from its API engine oil performance classification?

12. Why is it often recommended that added oil should be the same kind as the oil already in the engine?

13. Describe the oil flow through a gear and a rotor oil pump.

14. How does oil viscosity affect oil pressure?

15. What determines the lowest oil pressure the engine will produce? What determines the highest oil pressure?

16. What is the purpose of an oil filter?

17. Why are bypass and check valves incorporated in the oil filter system?

18. Through what different parts does the oil flow to lubricate a connecting rod bearing? Name these parts in order, starting with the oil pump.

19. How is the piston pin lubricated?

20. How can excessive clearance on one bearing cause a different bearing to fail?

21. How does oil get to the rocker arm assemblies?

22. What is the purpose of the oil pan baffles?

23. What is the purpose of the positive crankcase ventilation (PCV) system?

24. What is the basis of oil selection for an engine?

25. Upon what considerations does the manufacturer base the oil change period?

26. How can an operator determine excessive oil consumption?

Quiz 9

1. Engine bearing lubrication depends upon hydrodynamic lubrication. This results from
   a. a wedge of oil between moving parts
   b. the oil pump forcing oil between the bearing and journal
   c. oil splash as the connecting rods hit the oil in the pan
   d. centrifugal force as the oil is thrown from the shafts.

2. Oil feed holes are placed in bearing journals at the
   a. highly loaded portion
   b. lightly loaded portion
   c. most convenient location
   d. end of each oil passage.

3. An engine maintains regulated oil pressure at 45 psi with the oil that is in it. If the oil viscosity were to be increased, one would expect the oil pressure gauge to read
   a. 35 psi
   b. 40 psi
   c. 45 psi
   d. 50 psi.

4. Engine oil's maximum viscosity is limited by
   a. a low coefficient of friction
   b. the engine's ability to crank when cold
   c. the oil's thin fluid body
   d. the engine's maximum operating temperature.

5. Engine oil contamination occurs in the least number of miles during
   a. short trip stop-and-go driving
   b. city traffic driving
   c. turnpike driving
   d. pulling a loaded trailer.

6. When selecting suitable engine oil, one must consider viscosity and
   a. thickness
   b. oil additives
   c. API service classification
   d. cold cranking characteristics.

7. The primary basis for selecting oil drain periods is
   a. mileage since last oil change
   b. time since an oil change
   c. additives used in the oil
   d. the oil's cold cranking characteristics.

8. In most oil pumps, the pressure regulator valve directs the excess oil to the
   a. oil filter
   b. oil pan
   c. pump outlet
   d. pump inlet.

9. The PCV system's primary job is to remove
   a. water vapor
   b. oil vapor
   c. unburned hydrocarbons
   d. blow-by gases.

10. If engine maintenance is neglected and the oil filter plugs, the
    a. engine has oil starvation
    b. oil flows through a bypass
    c. pressure builds up and ruptures the filter
    d. oil consumption increases rapidly.

chapter 10

Engine Service Procedures

A well designed engine is reliable and durable when it is properly assembled, properly maintained, and properly operated. With the exception of an occasional malfunction, engines are correctly assembled to production tolerances when they are manufactured. The owner is responsible for proper maintenance. This consists of periodic oil, coolant, filter, and ignition parts replacement. Abuse occurs when the engine is run for extended periods at low as well as at excessively high temperatures. Either running at full power at low speeds (lugging), or running at very high engine speeds will abuse the engine.

Engine maintenance is done at routine intervals. Additional service is required between these routine intervals when an engine problem develops. An engine problem may show up as it affects engine operation, such as loss of power, rough running, overheating, or improper instrument indications. It may show up as a loss of oil, coolant, or fuel. Visible emissions and broken parts are further indications of an engine problem.

The driver or mechanic must first recognize that a problem exists. He will then have to determine the cause of the problem. This is done by *observing the symptoms* that the problem produces. The symptoms show up in instrument checks, visual indications, sounds produced by the engine, and the smell of engine emissions. The problem can be identified through an analysis of the symptoms when one understands how the parts operate in relation to each other. Trouble shooting charts are often helpful in problem analysis for specific vehicle applications.

When it has been determined that the engine has an internal problem, it is desirable to analytically check the engine as it is being disassembled to identify the exact cause of the problem.

10-1 ENGINE DISASSEMBLY

The engine exterior should be given a thorough visual inspection before any work is done. Special attention must be given to any physical damage, leaks at gaskets, exterior contamination, or deposits in the manifold and coolant hoses. This should be followed by an external cleaning using steam or water soluble cleaners to remove surface grime.

Fig. 10-1 Cylinder bore wear (Dana Corporation).

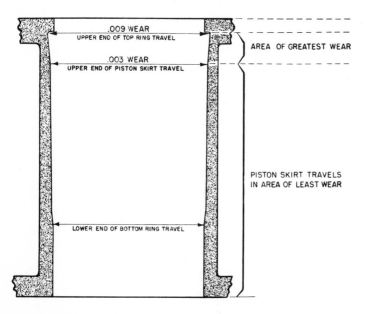

This makes the engine easier to work on and helps to keep dirt out of the engine. All fluids should be drained from the engine.

Engines are usually disassembled by first removing the engine accessories and spark plugs. This is followed by removal of the rocker covers to first expose a part of the engine interior. The rocker chamber condition indicates the general condition of the rest of the engine. A careful examination of the engine and parts as they are removed will allow the technician to find the cause of a specific problem. This can be immediately related to the associated parts as they have been operating in the engine. The location of each engine part should be identified in the engine, so that when an abnormal condition is encountered, the associated parts can also be checked for their contribution to the abnormality.

Manifolds. The manifolds are removed. If the gaskets are stuck, a flat blade, such as a putty knife, can be worked beside the gasket to loosen it, taking special care to avoid damaging the parting surfaces. The parting surfaces are checked for signs of leakage. If a lifter valley cover is used, it should also be removed. This exposes more of the engine interior, allowing further inspection. Heavy pasty deposits indicate low temperature operation. Hard deposits indicate high temperature operation. If the engine has been operated normally, with frequent oil changes of SD service classification oil, the lifter valley will be almost free from deposits.

Rocker arm pivots or shafts are loosened and the pushrods removed. They should be kept in order so abnormalities can be pinpointed. The lifters are then removed and kept in order.

Heads. Cylinder head bolts are removed and the head lifted from the block deck. If the head gasket is stuck, careful prying will loosen it. Take special precautions not to pry on edges that will break. Do not scratch the parting surfaces, because that may cause a leak when the engine is reassembled. The combustion chamber is now exposed. A visual inspection will show indications of oil consumption, overheating, or engine damage. Normal combustion chambers will be coated with a layer of hard, light colored carbon. If the combustion chambers have been running too hot, the carbon will be thin and lighter colored. If they have been running cold, the carbon will be thick, dry, and black.

Heavy wet carbon deposits result from oil that is entering the combustion chamber. Careful examination may indicate the exact oil entry point.

Pre-ignition or detonation damage can usually be seen from the block deck view. Badly burned or poor seating valves are evident in the head. These are all of the parts that need to be removed for a "valve job". Valve and rocker disassembly will still be required.

The engine crankshaft can be turned to lower the pistons, one at a time, to the bottom of their stroke. In this position, the cylinder bore should be measured just above the piston and just below the ridge in a direction crosswise to the engine. This will indicate the amount of cylinder wear that exists. If this wear is excessive, the cylinders will have to be bored to an oversize. Boring requires engine removal from the vehicle and complete disassembly.

Pan. When the engine is out of the vehicle, it is inverted to remove the oil pan. If it is still in the vehicle, the engine may have to be loosened from its mounts and jacked up high enough to allow the oil pan to be removed. Universal joint socket wrenches allow easy pan bolt removal while the engine remains in the chassis.

Deposits in the bottom of the pan are another clue to engine condition. Heavy mayonnaise consistency deposits come from low temperature operation. Particles that have worn from contacting metal parts fall to the bottom of the pan. These may be seen in a close examination of the pan deposits.

Piston and Rod Assembly. The ridge above the top ring travel must be removed *before* the piston and connecting rod assembly is removed. This is necessary to avoid catching a ring on the ridge and breaking the piston. Failure to remove the ridge will probably result in breaking the second piston land when the engine is run after reassembly with new rings. The ridge is removed with a cutting tool that is fed into the metal ridge. A guide on the tool prevents accidental cutting below the ridge. This job should be done carefully with frequent checks of the work so that no more material than necessary is removed.

Before removal, the connecting rods are checked for numbers beside the parting surfaces. If not numbered, they should be numbered in some manner so they can be reassembled in exactly the same

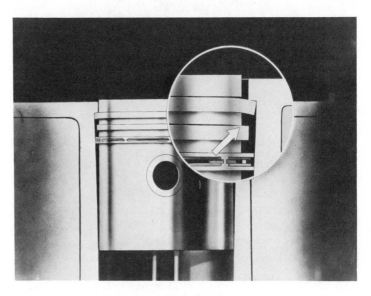

Fig. 10-2 Usual failure of second land if the cylinder ridge is not removed (Sealed Power Corporation).

Fig. 10-3 Ridge removal.

Fig. 10-4 Rod and main bearing numbers.

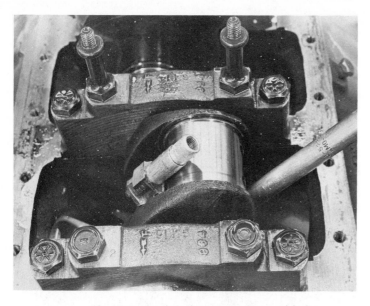

Fig. 10-5 Crankshaft protectors on rod bolts.

Fig. 10-6 Crank journal nicked by a rod bolt.

Fig. 10-7 Pulling crankshaft damper (Chrysler-Plymouth Division, Chrysler Corporation).

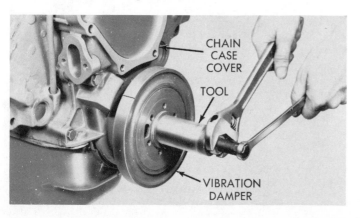

position. Connecting rod nuts are taken off the rod to be removed so the rod cap with its bearing half can be removed. The rod bolts are fitted with protectors made of aluminum or short pieces of rubber hose. These keep the rod bolts from touching the bearing journal surfaces on the crankshaft. If they did touch, the sharp threads of the bolts could easily nick the surface in such a way that a new bearing would be damaged. The connecting rod is carefully pushed up until the piston rings are free of the block deck. This must be done carefully because the piston ring drag stops when the rings are free of the cylinder bore. Excessive force on the rod will allow the piston to jump out of the bore when the ring moves out past the block deck. If the piston is not caught, it will fall to the floor and be damaged. When removed, the rod cap and bearing should be placed back on the rod to keep them together. This procedure should be followed with all of the other pistons. No further parts need to be removed from the block when the so-called "ring and valve job" is to be done.

Shaft removal. If the camshaft is to be removed with the engine in the chassis, it is usually necessary to remove the radiator and grill. It is necessary to pull the engine from the chassis if the crankshaft is to be removed.

The next step in disassembly is to remove the water pump and crankshaft damper. The damper should only be removed with a threaded puller. If a hook-type puller is used around the edge of the damper, it will probably pull the damper ring from the hub. If this happens, the damper assembly will have to be replaced with a new unit. With the damper off, the timing cover can be removed, exposing the timing gear or timing chain. Examine these parts for excessive wear and looseness. Bolted cam sprockets can be loosened and removed to free the timing chain. Pressed-on sprockets are removed by pulling the camshaft from the block. This may require removal of the crankshaft gear at the same time. It is necessary to remove thrust plate retaining screws when they are used.

The camshaft must be carefully eased from the engine to avoid damaging the cam bearing or cam lobes. Bearing surfaces are soft and scratch easily while the cam lobes are hard and chip easily.

The main bearing caps should be checked for position markings before removal. They have been

Fig. 10-8 Removing a valve lock.

machined in place and will not perfectly fit in another location. After marking, they can be removed to free the crankshaft. After the crankshaft is removed, re-install the main bearing caps and bearings to reduce the chance of damage.

Sub Assemblies. At this point, the engine is disassembled into its major sub assemblies. Valve springs are compressed to remove valve split lock retainers. Valves can be removed from the cylinder head. Carefully remove any burrs at the valve lock groove that keep the valve from sliding freely through the guide using a file or hand stone. Keep rocker arms, springs, retainers, locks or keepers, and valves in order so they can be carefully examined as related parts. Piston rings may be removed from the pistons.

Fig. 10-9 Removing a piston ring.

The piston pin is removed from the piston and rod. Retaining rings are removed from full floating pins while press fit pins must be pushed from the connecting rod using special pressing tools to avoid breaking the piston. Removal of all passage and core opening plugs will facilitate a thorough block and head cleaning.

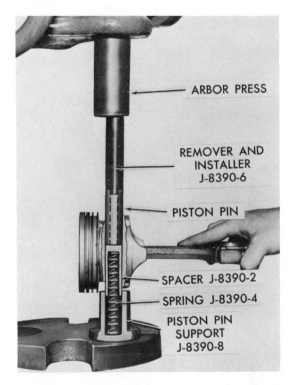

Fig. 10-10 Pressing a piston pin from a piston and rod (Cadillac Motor Car Division, General Motors Corporation).

Part abnormalities that are noted during disassembly should be rechecked along with associated parts. Parts that are obviously damaged beyond reconditioning will have to be replaced. They should be set aside until inspection is complete; then they should be discarded.

10-2 CLEANING

Parts that are not obviously damaged or worn beyond use should be cleaned. Cleaning parts is usually relegated to the "flunkey". However if the technician cleans the parts, he will be able to make a detailed observation of the part's condition that indicates the kind of service and operation the engine has had. This type of detailed observation is useful in analyzing malfunctions noted during parts inspection.

Two basic types of cleaning are done on an engine, degreasing and decarbonizing. Degreasing is usually done with petroleum spirits that only remove grease and oil. Some degreasing cleaners can be

(a)

Fig. 10-11 Cleaning a piston. (a) Head, (b) ring groove.

(b)

mixed with petroleum spirits or kerosene, sprayed on the parts, then hosed off with water. This will remove dirt as well as grease and oil.

Decarbonizing chemicals are available as a bath in which the parts to be cleaned are submerged. Heating the decarbonizing bath will speed cleaning action. After a soak period, parts are removed and hosed off with water. Decarbonizing materials are very irritating to the skin. They should be immediately rinsed off if they contact the skin.

Vapor degreasers do a very effective job of cleaning parts. Parts come from the tank with a powdery surface that is easily brushed off.

Some heavy carbon on cylinder heads and valves can be removed with a wire brush. Special brushes are made to be used in an electric drill motor. Wire brushes should not be used on pistons.

Piston heads and grooves are cleaned by scraping. Special care should be taken to avoid rounding off the corners or removing metal.

Frequently, automotive shops use abrasive blasting equipment to clean parts. The abrasive is usually a glass or plastic bead. These beads have a tendency to lodge in corners of the parts so they must be thoroughly cleaned from parts before the engine is assembled.

When all of the parts are thoroughly cleaned, they are ready for inspection.

10-3 GENERAL INSPECTION

As with each preceding step, inspection should start with a good visual inspection. When either premature or high mileage failure has occurred, a visual inspection will aid in evaluation of the parts' interrelationship so that corrective measures may prevent recurring failures. Parts are examined for wear patterns, scoring and pitting, foreign materials, and contamination. When abnormalities are found, the mating parts should be thoroughly examined to determine the specific cause of failure.

The visual inspection is followed by a dimensional inspection. All parts are measured and their dimensions compared to the manufacturer's specifications for the specific engine being worked on. Specifications give sizes and clearances. Parts must either be within specification tolerances or be reconditioned so they fall within the specification tolerances before being used again. Parts that cannot

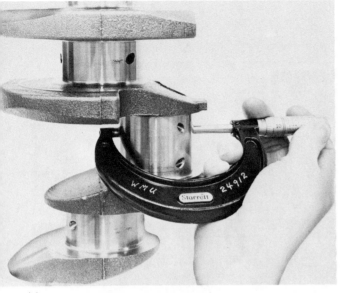

(a)

(a)

Fig. 10-12 (a) Measuring a crankshaft journal with a 2″–3″ micrometer. (b) Micrometer shows a reading of 2.113 inches.

(b)

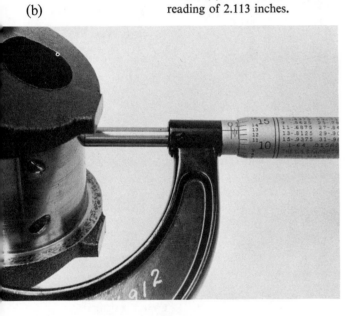

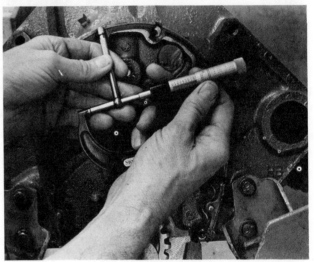

(b)

Fig. 10-13 Using a telescopic gauge to measure a hole (a), then measuring the gauge with a micrometer (b).

Fig. 10-14 Measuring a hole with a small hole gauge (a), then measuring the small hole gauge with a micrometer (b).

(a)   (b)

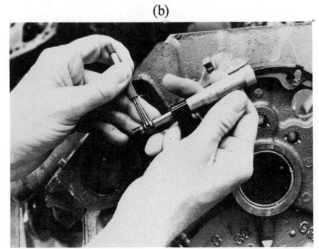

Fig. 10-15 Checking crankshaft runout with a dial gauge with only the end main bearing shells installed.

Fig. 10-16 Measuring with special dial gauges. (a) Cylinder bore, (b) valve seat runout.

(a)

(b)

be made to meet the specifications should be replaced.

External diameters and out-of-round conditions are measured with micrometers. Micrometers should be checked with a reference gauge before using to assure accuracy. Inside diameters are transferred to a telescopic gauge or small hole gauge. These gauges are then checked with an outside micrometer to obtain the measurement. Inside micrometers are available for large diameter hole measurement; however, they are seldom used for engine service.

A bend in a cylindrical object is checked by supporting the object in vee blocks or bearings at each end with a dial gauge tip placed against the center. Bend is indicated by the dial gauge movement as the object is turned. This type of bend measurement is called *run-out*. Some small parts, such as pushrods, may be rolled on a flat surface to observe run-out as the part rolls.

Dial gauges on a special fixture are used to measure cylinder bore out-of-round and taper. Measurement of valve seat out-of-round requires another special dial gauge application. A standard dial gauge with a support may be used to measure shaft end play, gear backlash, valve in guide looseness, valve opening travel, and flange run-out.

(a)

(b)

Fig. 10-17 Typical methods to use a dial gauge. (a) Crankshaft end play (American Motors Corporation), (b) valve guide clearance (American Motors Corporation), (c) camshaft end play, (d) flywheel runout.

(c)

(d)

Thickness or feeler gauges are used to measure clearance between two flat surfaces, such as crankshaft thrust clearances, gear backlash, piston ring side clearance and gap clearance.

A square is used to check the squareness of parts, such as valve springs. Parting surface flatness can be checked with a straightedge placed across a part in several directions. The amount of warpage or bend can be determined by trying to slide various thickness gauges under the straightedge.

(a)

(b)

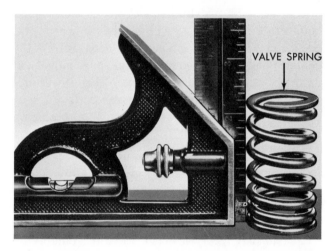

Fig. 10-19 A square being used to check valve spring straightness (Chrysler-Plymouth Division, Chrysler Corporation).

Fig. 10-20 Measuring the amount of Plastigauge crush to check bearing clearance (Dana Corporation).

Fig. 10-18 Typical thickness gauge measurements. (a) Cam end play, (b) oil pump gear end clearance, (c) oil pump radial clearance.

(c)

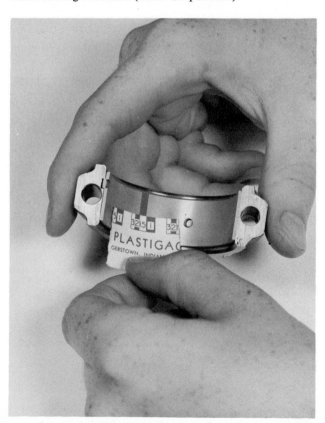

Clearances between closely fitting assembled parts, such as bearing clearances can be accurately measured with Plastigauge strips. A strip of Plastigauge is laid across the area being measured. The parts are assembled correctly, tightened to the correct torque, then disassembled. The width of the Plastigauge crush indicates the amount of clearance. The smaller the clearance, the more crush exists, making the Plastigauge pattern wider.

Highly stressed parts used in performance engines are checked for cracks with specialized nondestructive testing procedures. A magnetic particle inspection called Magnaflux, is used to check iron and steel parts. In this process, the part is magnetized and covered with iron particles. These particles are attracted to any magnetic pole that forms adjacent to a weak area or on cracks.

Fig. 10-21 Magnetic particle inspection showing a crack in a gear.

Parts made from non-magnetic materials are checked with a fluorescent penetrant called Zyglo. The clean part is dipped in the penetrant, rinsed, and dipped into a developer. The part then is inspected under an ultraviolet light. Any place that penetrant soaks into a surface crack will show up as a white line.

10-4 VALVE CONDITION

A careful examination of the valves removed from the engine will indicate causes of valve failure. Valves fail because their operating limits have been

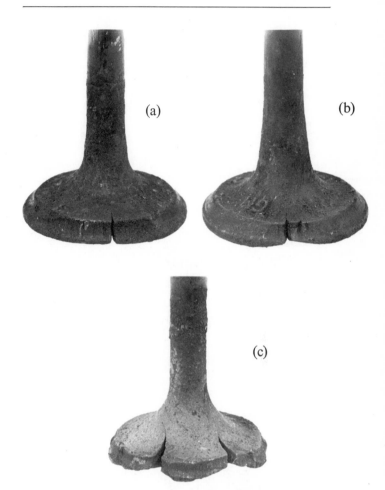

Fig. 10-22 Stages of valve face guttering.

exceeded. The cause of the failure must be corrected to enable new or reconditioned valves to perform satisfactorily. Valve failure results from misaligned valve seating, excessive temperature, high velocity seating, and high mileage. These conditions are usually interrelated.

Valve Seating. Valve burning or guttering is one of the common types of valve failure. It results from poor seating that allows the high temperature and high pressure gases to leak between the valve and seat. Poor seating may result from insufficient valve lash, hard carbon deposits, valve stem deposits, excessive valve stem-to-guide clearances, or out-of-squareness between the valve guide and seat.

Insufficient valve lash may result from improper valve lash adjustment on solid lifter systems. The

133

Fig. 10-23 Cupped valves. Right valve is severely cupped.

Fig. 10-24 Valve face peening.

Fig. 10-25 Heavy carbon buildup on a valve.

build up on the valve stem. These deposits cause the valve to stick in the guide so the valve does not seat properly and the valve face burns.

If the valve stem has excess clearance, too much oil will go down the stem to increase deposits. In addition, wide valve guide clearance will allow the valve to cock, especially with rocker arm action. This keeps the valve from seating properly and leakage occurs, burning the valve face.

Sometimes, the cylinder head will warp as the head is tightened during assembly. Other times, heating and cooling will cause warpage. When head warpage causes valve guide and seat misalignment, the valve cannot seat properly.

clearance will also be reduced in operation from valve head cupping or valve face seating wear.

Hard carbon deposits may loosen from the combustion chamber and become caught between the valve face and seat, holding the valve slightly off its seat. This reduces valve cooling through the seat and allows some of the combustion gases to escape. Continued pounding on hard particles gives the valve face a peened appearance. Positive valve rotors help to combat the effects of deposits on the valve burning.

Fuel and oil on the hot valve will break down to become hard carbon and varnish deposits that

Fig. 10-26 Valves broken by thermal shock.

Excessive Temperatures. High valve temperature occurs when the valve does not seat properly; however, it can occur even when the valve is seating properly. Cooling system passages in the head may be partially blocked by casting imperfections or by deposits built up from the coolant. Extremely high temperatures are also produced by pre-ignition and by detonation. Both of these cause a very rapid increase in temperature that can cause uneven heating, giving a thermal shock to the valve. The shock can cause radial cracks in the valve which, in turn, will allow the combustion gases to escape and gutter the valve face. If the radial cracks intersect, a pie-shaped piece will break from the valve head. A thermal shock can also be produced by rapid cycling from full throttle to closed throttle and back again.

High speeds require high gas velocities. The high velocity exhaust gas impinges on the valve stem and tends to erode the metal. The gases are also corrosive so the valve stem will tend to corrode. The corrosion rate doubles for each 25°F increase in temperature. Erosion and corrosion of the valve stem cause *necking* that weakens the stem and leads to breakage.

Misaligned Valve Seats. Each time the valve closes when the valve-to-seat alignment is improper, the valve head must twist to seat. If twisting or bending becomes excessive, it fatigues the stem and the valve head will break from the stem. The break appears as lines arcing around a starting point.

High Velocity Seating. High velocity seating is indicated by excessive valve face wear, valve seat recessing, and impact failure. It can be caused by excessive lash in mechanical lifters and by collapsed hydraulic lifters so the valve hits the seat without the effect of the cam ramp to ease it onto its seat. Excessive lash may also be caused by wear of parts such as the cam, lifter base, pushrod ends, rocker arms, and valve tip. Weak or broken valve springs allow the valves to float away from the cam lobes so the valves are uncontrolled as they hit the seat. The normal tendency of hydraulic lifters is to pump-up under these float conditions and this reduces valve impact damage.

Impact breakage may occur under the valve head or at the valve lock grooves. The break lines radiate from the starting point. The valve head usually falls into the combustion chamber and is

Fig. 10-27 Valve stem necking.

Fig. 10-28 Valve stem breakage from misaligned seat.

Fig. 10-29 Valve broken from high velocity seating that turned over and punctured the piston.

jammed between the piston and head. In most cases, it will ruin the piston before the engine can be stopped.

High Mileage. High mileage indications show excessive wear of the valve stem, guide, valve face, and seat. They are usually accompanied by considerable deposits. The valves will, however, still be seating and will show no indication of cracks or burning.

10-5 VALVE TRAIN CONDITION

Valve failure may be the result of the valve train condition. This is usually evident as wear. Valve train wear can result from exceeding operating limits and from loss of lubrication.

(a)

Fig. 10-30 Cam wear. (a) Cam lobe worn round, (b) tappet face worn concave.

(b)

Camshaft. Camshaft failure shows up as cam lobe failure. Lobe failure starts as small pits caused by heavy edge wear. The lobe will gradually break down as the engine is operated until it looks like a round journal. A badly worn cam will cause badly worn lifters. Occasionally, the lobe will chip as the result of impact damage, usually from careless handling.

Fig. 10-31 Chipped cam lobe.

Lifters. Camshaft lobe failure will damage the lifter face. Face failure may start with pits or with smooth wear. The face gradually becomes concave. Pitted or concave faces are not repairable, but should be replaced. For maximum service life, it is recommended to install new lifters with a new cam. A worn cam may rapidly damage new lifter faces and thus give a short lifter service life.

Hydraulic lifter parts are selective fit and cannot be interchanged between each other. Lifters that show no abnormal wear should be disassembled and cleaned, one at a time, to avoid intermixing parts. After reassembly, they should be checked for leak down rate. If the rate is excessive, the lifter should be replaced.

Rocker Arms. Rocker assemblies should be disassembled and thoroughly cleaned to remove sludge and varnish. When worn, rocker shafts and matching rocker arms should be replaced. A worn face on a stamped rocker arm requires replacement of the rocker arm. Some of the older cast rocker arms could have their faces ground, but this practice has been discontinued. Replace worn stamped rocker arms, pivot balls, or shafts.

Pushrods. Pushrod failure results from lack of lubrication or from overstressing. Lack of lubrication results in excessive pushrod end wear. Overstressing will cause bent pushrods. Rod bend can be detected by rolling the pushrod across a flat surface. Any wobble indicates a bent rod. Pushrods that are bent or worn must be replaced.

Valve Springs. Valve springs may rotate in use and become shiny on the end. They may develop pits or take a set. Wear and pits are checked visually. Valve spring set may result in warping the spring or loss in tension. Spring tension is checked in a valve spring gauge. The spring tension is checked at the installed length and at the valve open length. Pressure loss up to 10% is serviceable. Any valve spring abnormality is cause for replacement. Because valve springs are inexpensive, they are often replaced each time the valve system is reconditioned.

Fig. 10-32 Checking valve spring pressure.

Valve Retainers and Locks. Inspection of valve retainers and locks is limited to a visual inspection. Cracks and wear or questionable serviceability are reasons for replacement. If they should fail, the valve could fall into the combustion chamber and do extensive damage.

10-6 VALVE SYSTEM SERVICE

Inspection of the valve system parts will enable the technician to find the cause of valve failure. Parts that are obviously beyond repair are put aside. The remaining parts are serviced for continued use.

Cylinder Head. Most of the service work on a cylinder head involves work on the valve guides and seats. The clean head gasket surface is draw-filed flat to remove any raised portions and then checked for bend and warpage with a straightedge. The head surface must be ground or milled flat if a thickness gauge more than .006 inch will fit between

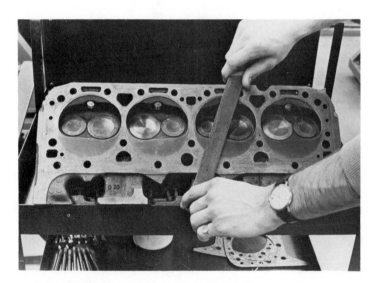

Fig. 10-33 Draw filing head parting surface.

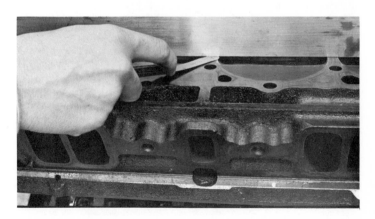

Fig. 10-34 Checking head flatness.

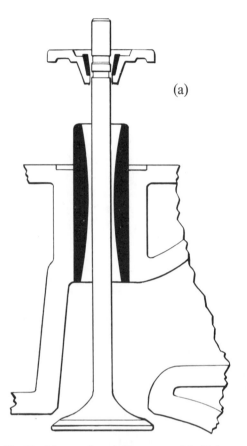

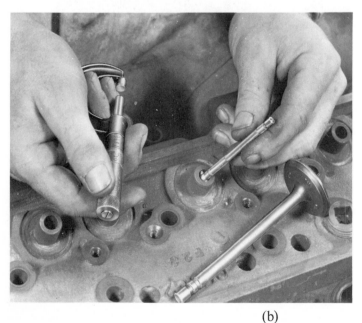

Fig. 10-35 Checking valve guide wear. (a) Valve guide wear, (Dana Corporation) (b) checking the wear with a telescopic gauge (Dana Corporation).

the straightedge and head. If warpage is not corrected, it will misalign the seats and guides when the head is torqued on the block deck. Equal amounts should be removed from both heads on V engines to maintain the equal match between the intake manifold and head. Additional material will have to be removed from both intake manifold gasket surfaces of the heads to keep the manifold and head openings aligned. Tables are available in automotive machine shops to calculate the required amount.

After the head surfaces have been conditioned, the valve guides are checked. Normal service limit is 50% greater than new limits. The guide is checked on each end and in the middle with a small hole gauge and micrometer. Guides with excess clearance may be reamed to take an oversize valve stem or they may be knurled.

Knurling provides a satisfactory valve guide repair when correctly done. The knurling process produces a spiral groove on the interior of the guide with a sharp edged wheel supported by a special tool. Metal is displaced inward adjacent to the groove, making the hole smaller. Successively larger wheels are used until the valve will no longer enter the guide. The guide is then reamed to provide the correct valve stem-to-guide clearance.

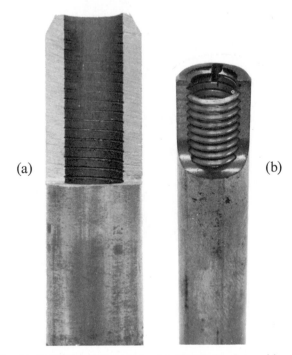

Fig. 10-36 Valve guide repair. (a) Knurled valve guide, (b) brass spring valve guide insert.

Another valve guide repair method is to tap a thread in the valve guide, then insert a special spiral brass spring in these threads. This is followed by a burnishing tool that firmly presses the brass into the threads. The final step is to ream the brass insert to the correct size.

The valve seat must be concentric with the valve guide. Seat faces are ground with a stone driven through a holder that is supported by a pilot placed in the guide. The stone must be dressed or cleaned with a diamond tool on a dressing fixture to correctly align the stone face with the holder center to ensure the correct seat face angle and to clean the stone grinding surface. Light grinding cuts are made to clean and align the seat surface while removing minimum material.

The valve and seat are ground with a 1/2 to 2° *interference angle*. This produces high contact pressure at the large edge of the seat which rapidly seal the valves and prevents leakage. Seat run-out must not exceed .002″.

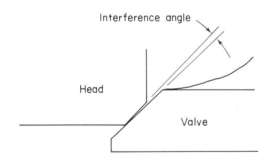

Fig. 10-37 Valve seat interference angle.

Valve seat grinding widens the valve seat. Normal seat widths range from 1/16″ to 3/32″, depending on the engine. The top of the seat can be adjusted downward by *topping* the seat with a 15° grinding stone. The lower edge can be raised by throating with a 70° grinding stone. Seat location must be checked with a new or reconditioned valve. The valve is coated with *prussian blue* or *mechanics blue*, then inserted in the guide and lightly bounced on the seat to transfer the blue to the seat. The valve is removed, wiped clean and re-installed. A second light bouncing should transfer the blue back onto the valve to show a full circle contact pattern at the position about 1/4 of the valve face below the valve margin.

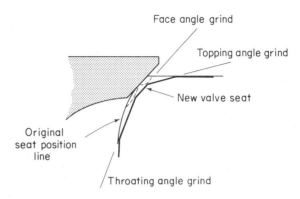

Fig. 10-38 Method of adjusting valve seat position.

Valve Service. Valve faces are ground on a valve grinder. The grinder head is set at the correct valve angle to provide the recommended interference fit and the grinding stone dressed to remove any stone roughness. The valve is clamped in the work head as far down as possible to prevent vibrations. The rotating grinding wheel is fed slowly to the rotating valve face. Light grinding is done as the valve is moved back and forth across the grinding wheel face, keeping the valve from going off the edge of the wheel. The valve is ground only enough to clean the face. Aluminized valves will loose their corrosion resistance properties when ground, so for

Fig. 10-39 Valve face grinding.

139

Fig. 10-40 Valve tip grinding.

satisfactory service, they must always be replaced.

Slight imperfections on valve tips can be removed by grinding in a special fixture. A maximum of .020″ may be ground from the tip. If more is required, the valve must be replaced.

Reconditioned valves are installed in reconditioned guides to check the final valve length. The valve will not close if the valve tip extends too far from the valve guide on engines with hydraulic lifters and nonadjustable rocker arms. If the valve is too long, the tip may be ground as much as .020″ to reduce its length. If it is too short, the valve face or seat may be reground, within limits, to allow the valve to seat deeper. Where excessive grinding has been done, shims can be placed under the rocker shaft to provide correct hydraulic lifter plunger centering. These shims must have the required lubrication holes to allow oil to enter the shaft.

Valve retainers and locks are installed on valves without the spring. The distance from the retainer to the head is measured to check the installed spring length. If it is too long, shims up to 1/16″ may be

Fig. 10-41 Measuring installed valve stem length.

Fig. 10-42 Measuring installed valve spring length.

installed at the head end of the spring to shorten the spring length within limits. If the valve requires more than 1/16″ shim, the valve and possibly the seat will have to be replaced.

Any sharp edge produced during servicing should be removed with a hand stone. This reduces the chance of damaging seals or wear on the sharp edges.

Head Assembly. The head and valve parts should be thoroughly cleaned to remove all traces of grinding grit and dirt that may have accumulated while the parts were disassembled. Each valve is lubricated with clean motor oil as it is installed. New valve seals are used. Springs and valve locks must seat squarely and securely. The valve tip should never be struck in an attempt to seat the valve or lock. Striking won't help seating, but it may initiate a fracture that would break the valve. If only a valve job is being done, the head can be installed with new gaskets and the cap screws tightened to correct torque values. Manifold and accessory installation follow.

10-7 PISTON CONDITION

Normal piston wear shows up as even vertical wear on the thrust surfaces and slight looseness of the top ring in the groove. This type of piston can usually be reconditioned for additional useful service.

Fig. 10-43 Normal piston skirt wear.

(a)

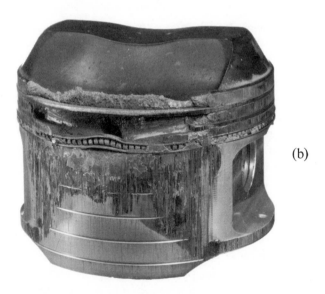

(b)

Fig. 10-44 Piston damage from detonation. (a) Moderate damage (Dana Corporation), (b) severe damage (Dana Corporation).

Heat Damage. Holes in pistons, burned areas, severely damaged ring lands, and scoring are obviously abnormal conditions. The exact nature of the abnormalities should be determined so that the cause can be corrected and the driver given advice that will minimize the possibility of the damage recurring.

141

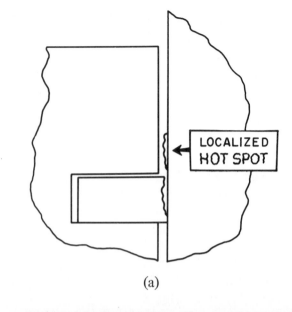

Fig. 10-45 Piston damage from pre-ignition (Champion Spark Plug Company).

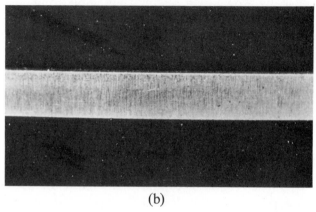

(a)

(b)

(c)

Combustion knock or detonation will burn the edge of the piston from the head down in behind the rings. This burning usually occurs at a point furthest from the spark plug where the hot end gases rapidly release their heat energy through detonation. Pre-ignition results from multiple flame fronts that build temperature and pressure early in the combustion cycle. High temperature softens the piston, allowing combustion pressure to break-through, usually near the middle of the piston head.

Another form of heat damage is scuffing. This usually occurs when excessive heat causes the piston to expand until it becomes tight in the cylinder bore. This squeezes the lubricant from the cylinder wall and allows metal-to-metal contact. Excessive heat can come from a malfunctioning cooling system as well as abnormal combustion.

Piston rings may get hot spots from a lack of lubrication, from high combustion temperatures or from ineffective cooling systems. Metal from the ring hot spots will transfer to the cylinder wall, scuffing the ring and piston.

Fig. 10-46 Piston ring scuffing. (a) Exaggerated drawing of ring metal transfer (Dana Corporation), (b) scuffed piston ring face (Dana Corporation), (c) scuffed cylinder wall (Dana Corporation).

142

Fig. 10-47 Piston rings stuck in their grooves (Dana Corporation).

Worn piston rings allow hot combustion gases to blow by the piston as well as allowing oil to come up from the crankcase to the combustion chamber. Hot combustion gases meet the oil in the area of the rings where the heat partially burns the oil. This produces hard carbon around the rings, causing them to stick in the grooves. If this is the only piston problem, it can be corrected by a thorough cleaning and installing new piston rings.

Fig. 10-48 Skirt wear caused by a misaligned connecting rod.

Corrosion Damage. Lowering operating temperatures will produce a corrosive mixture in the oil. This would be aggravated by coolant leakage into the combustion chamber. Corrosion will produce mottled gray pits on the aluminum piston.

Mechanical Damage. Piston damage can result from mechanical problems. Connecting rod misalignment will show up as a diagonal thrust surface wear pattern across the piston skirt which indicates that the piston is not operating straight in the cylinder. This, in turn, means that the rings are not running perpendicular to the wall, so they cannot seal properly.

Piston damage can come from the loss of a piston pin lock ring. The lock will come out if the lock grooves are damaged, if the lock ring is weak or if the rod is bent so a side load is placed on the piston pin forcing it against the lock ring. The piston and possibly the cylinder will be badly damaged as the lock ring slides between them. A new piston is required when this type of damage occurs.

Fig. 10-49 Damage caused by a loose piston pin lock ring (Sealed Power Corporation).

143

Piston skirts crack, usually near the piston pin boss. Cracks generally occur at high mileage, because of overloading or improperly designed pistons. Any crack in a piston is cause for rejection.

Dirt entering the engine greatly increases the wear rate. Dirt will scratch and wear the face of the piston rings and wear the side of the ring and groove. The top piston ring side clearance must not exceed .006″. Dirt may be airborn and come in through an ineffective air filter element or through an air leak between the filter and the carburetor air horn. Dirt in the oil will affect piston skirt and oil ring wear. Worn piston rings must be replaced. Piston ring groove side wear is usually uneven. This causes the ring to only hit the high spots that result in high localized side loads on the ring when the ring inertia is greatest. These loads may break the ring which, in turn, may excessively damage the piston.

10-8 PISTON SERVICE

Pistons may be reconditioned if they have no obvious defect that would be cause for rejection. Piston reconditioning is usually done with specialized service equipment in an automotive machine shop. The operations are listed here to help provide an understanding of the reasons for each operation.

Ring Grooves. The top ring grooves with excessive side clearance are machined about .025″ wider than the standard groove. A steel groove spacer is placed above the new ring in the machined groove to return the side clearance to standard dimensions.

Skirt. Piston fit in the bore is checked by placing the piston in the cylinder, together with a long strip feeler gauge on the piston thrust side. A force of five to ten pounds on the feeler gauge indicates correct clearance. A pull of less than five pounds requires the use of a thicker gauge strip. A pull of more than ten pounds requires the use of a thinner gauge. If the clearance is greater than is specified, the piston will have to be expanded.

Fig. 10-50 Cracked piston.

(a)

Fig. 10-51 Piston groove wear. (a) Cross section of a worn groove (Dana Corporation), (b) side view of a worn upper groove (Dana Corporation).

(b)

Fig. 10-52 Damage caused by a broken ring (Dana Corporation).

Fig. 10-54 Measuring piston to cylinder clearance.

Fig. 10-53 Piston groove reconditioning. (a) Groove machining (Dana Corporation) (b) groove spacer in place (Dana Corporation).

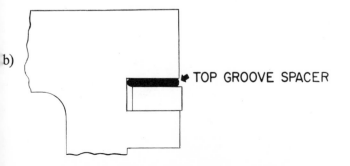

TOP GROOVE SPACER

Fig. 10-55 Piston resizing. (a) Knurling tool (Dana Corporation), (b) appearance of a knurled piston (Dana Corporation).

(a)

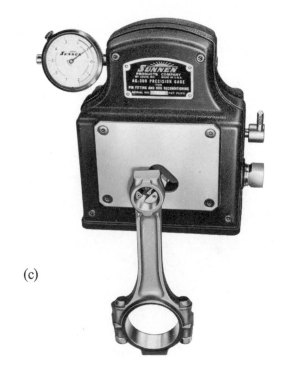

(c)

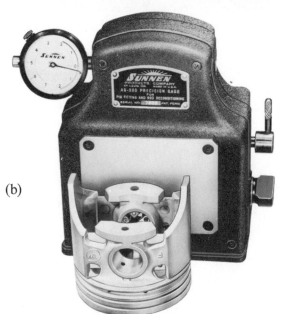

(b)

Fig. 10-56 Piston pin fitting. (a) Honing a piston pin hole, (b) and (c) checking a piston pin hole size (Sunnen Products Company).

Fig. 10-57 Checking connecting rod alignment.

In operation, the piston skirt will wear or collapse. Wear also occurs on the cylinder wall. The combination of wear and collapse will produce excess piston-to-cylinder clearance. Piston skirts are expanded by producing an interrupted surface on them that displaces metal upward between the teeth of the knurling tool. This effectively increases piston skirt size. Skirt size can be controlled by the amount of pressure placed on the knurling tool. The knurled piston surface carries lubricating oil to help maintain an oil film while providing a close fitting clearance to reduce noise.

Pins. Piston pins may be replaced with new oversize pins. The holes in the piston and connecting rod are accurately sized with a pin hone. Tight fitting piston pins may cause the piston to seize on the pin in its expanded position, producing piston skirt scuff near the piston pin boss. If the pin is too loose, it will produce a knock or rattle when the engine is in operation.

The automobile machine shop usually services the connecting rod and piston as an assembly. In addition to fitting a new piston pin, the connecting rod is checked for alignment. It will be straightened as part of normal piston assembly service.

Cylinder Wall Service. The cylinder wall is usually serviced before the pistons are replaced. The upper cylinder ridge was removed as the engine was disassembled. Smooth glazed cylinder walls provide good anti-scuff surfaces and need no further service. Cylinder walls that are wavy or scuffed should be smoothed by honing as described in Section 10–12.

Piston Assembly. The new piston rings are fitted into the lower portion of the cylinder, pressed down with a piston head, and the end gap measured with a feeler gauge. Minimum gap should never be less than specified. If it is, the ends could touch during operation. This would cause severe ring scuffing and possibly ring breakage. Excess clearance is not critical unless it is more than .040″ greater than specifications.

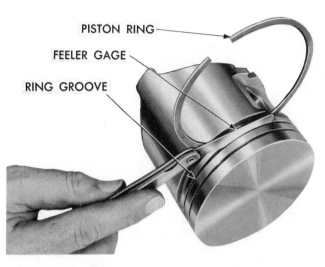

Fig. 10-59 Measuring piston ring side clearance (Chrysler-Plymouth Division, Chrysler Corporation).

Rings are carefully installed on the piston. This can best be done by using the same tool that was used to remove the ring. Cast iron rings break easily if twisted or stretched too much. Extreme care must be exercised when installing rings when special tools are not available.

The side clearance should be checked on each ring before the rings are installed. If any clearance is too small, the ring groove should be checked to correct the fault. Small clearance is most likely the result of some hard carbon overlooked during cleaning or from handling damage that has nicked the ring land. All rings must move freely in the ring grooves.

Before assembly, the piston and cylinder wall are given one last cleaning, then coated with fresh motor oil. Protectors are put over the rod bolts to avoid crank journal damage. A ring compressor is used to hold the piston rings all the way into their grooves as the piston is eased into the cylinder. Piston binding as it is pushed into the bore is usually caused by a ring slipping from the compressor and catching on the block deck. Forcing the piston into the cylinder will break the ring and possibly the piston land. Pistons must go into their original cylinder and they must face in the correct direction to avoid valve interference.

Fig. 10-58 Measuring piston ring gap (Dana Corporation).

(a)

(b)

Fig. 10-60 Installing pistons. (a) Using an adjustable steel ring compressor, (b) using a cast iron ring compressor.

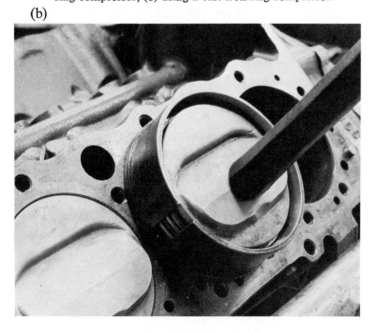

New connecting rod bearings are usually installed at the same time as new rings are being installed. The crankshaft is usually in serviceable condition if the only problem was a "ring job". Standard or undersize bearings will produce rod bearing clearances within specifications. Bearing backs must be clean and dry. The bearing surface should be lubricated with fresh motor oil. Bearing

caps should be tightened to the correct torque using the correct size socket that won't cause the cap to shift as it is tightened. Standard engine assembly procedures are followed, using new gaskets and seals.

10-9 SHAFT AND BEARING CONDITION

Shaft damage includes damaged bearing journals, bends or warpage, and cracks. Shafts with abnormalities must be reconditioned or replaced.

Crankshaft. The crankshaft is one of the most highly stressed engine parts. The stress increases four times every time the engine speed doubles. Any sign of a crack is a cause to reject the crankshaft. Cracks in high production passenger car engines can be detected with a close visual inspection. High rpm racing crankshafts should be checked with Magnaflux to show up any minute crack that would lead to failure.

Bearing journal scoring is one of the most common crankshaft defects. Scoring appears as scratches around the journal circumference, generally near the center of the journal. Dirt and grit carried in the oil enter between the journal and bearing. If the particles are too large to get through the oil clearance, they will partially embed in the bearing and scratch the journal. Dirt can also be left on the journal during assembly. Maximum journal life depends upon the continuous supply of clean lubricating oil.

Fig. 10-61 Crankshaft scoring at the oil hole from dirt and grit.

(a)

Crankshaft journals can have nicks or pits in them. Nicks are caused by carelessness when the journal is bumped with another part while exposed. Pits can be caused by corrosion.

A bent crankshaft can be detected by supporting the end main bearing journals in vee blocks. A dial gauge on the middle bearing journal will show run-out as the crankshaft is turned. If vee blocks are not available, the crankshaft can be supported by the two upper half end bearings in the block as described in Section 10-3. The other bearing shells must be removed. A dial gauge is used in the same manner to indicate the shaft bend or run-out.

Journals will wear out-of-round and become tapered. Out-of-round and taper are measured with a micrometer, taking measurements at a number of different locations on each journal.

Rough journals and slight bends can be corrected by grinding the journals on true centers. Shafts with excess bend should be straightened before grinding.

If the relatively inexpensive standard production crankshaft is damaged beyond grinding limits, it should be replaced. More expensive racing crankshafts, or crankshafts that are to be modified, can have the journals built up by welding or by special metal spray techniques. They are then straightened and reground. This process is expensive and, therefore, is only done when it is less costly than purchasing a new special crankshaft.

Fig. 10-62 Careless handling caused the crankshaft nick (a) which, in turn, scored the bearing (b).

Fig. 10-63 Grinding a crankshaft.

(b)

Camshaft. Cam lobe damage is the most usual type of camshaft failure. Lobe surface breakdown usually starts at the highly loaded cam nose where extreme pressures exist. Wear becomes rapid once the damage breaks through the cam's hard surface, causing pitting, grooves, scoring or flaking. The most critical period for cam wear is the first fifteen minutes of operation after the engine is assembled. Cam lubrication is critical during this time when engine lubrication is marginal. Manufacturers recommend specific cam surface lubricants to be used during assembly. They run all the way from SD motor oil to especially prepared lubricants available at their own dealer parts department.

Cam lobes are designed with a slight taper across the surface and the tappet or lifter has a slight crown. This leaves the contact point slightly away from the geometrical center. The offset causes lifter rotation that produces a nearly even wear pattern. A flat based lifter or a used lifter on a new camshaft will contact the high edge of the cam lobe, producing edge wear that could lead to surface breakdown.

Fig. 10-64 Cam lobe wear. (a) Normal, (b) edge wear.

Abnormal passenger car camshafts, like crankshafts, are replaced. Camshafts can be reground on special profile cam grinders. This can be done as a repair procedure or as a means of modifying the cam contour. It is generally more expensive to grind a camshaft than to purchase a new standard production camshaft. Grinding is, therefore, only done on special camshafts and on some low production heavy-duty camshafts.

Grinding a camshaft increases the distance between the top of the lifter and the rocker arm. Adjustable rocker arms can be changed to compensate for this distance. Non-adjustable rocker arms with hydraulic lifters would require a longer pushrod. The new pushrod adds to the expense of camshaft grinding.

Bearings. Bearing distress or failure will result from foreign particles, from lubrication breakdown, from overloading, and from corrosion. Any bearing failure is cause for replacement; however, a close visual examination of bearing distress will indicate the cause of failure. The cause must be corrected before the engine is reassembled.

The best procedure to examine bearings is to remove the bearing shells from the block, rods, and caps. They should be placed on a table in the location used in the engine, bearing face up. Abnormalities can then be related to each other and to the shaft journals.

Foreign particles are dirt, metal chips, or abrasives. Dirt may have been left in the engine when it was assembled, even between the bearing and cap. It may enter through breather openings or through faulty filters. The dirt is carried in the oil to the bearings. Metal chips may have lodged in the engine during machining operations. They are also produced as internal parts wear. Normally, the small metal particles from wear will settle to the bottom of the oil pan, get trapped in the oil filter or be drained from the engine with the used oil. When rapid breakdown and wear occurs, the particles may move through the lubrication system to the bearing. The most likely causes of small metal particles are oil pump gear wear, cam and lifter wear, and timing gear wear. Aluminum particles may come from piston skirt wear. Abrasives are left in the engine after reconditioning parts anytime the parts are not thoroughly cleaned using proper cleaning methods. Abrasives tend to embed in soft

Fig. 10-65 Bearings laid out for inspection.

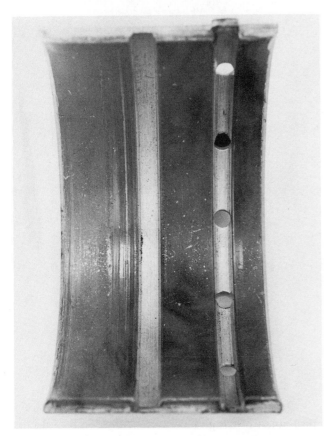

Fig. 10-66 Foreign particles embedded in a bearing.

particle can be determined by scraping some of the embedded material from the bearing surface near the parting surface where most material will collect. Steel particles can be picked up with a magnet. Aluminum particles will dissolve in a drop of 10% solution of sodium hydroxide, producing bubbles. Other particles, such as dirt, brass and copper can best be identified by their color.

Lubrication breakdown may result from the motor oil not getting to the bearing, from heat that excessively thins the motor oil, and from overloading the bearing so oil is squeezed from the bearing surface. These problems are interrelated and may occur at the same time. Oil starvation wipes or extrudes low melting temperature bearing material

Fig. 10-67 Bearing damage resulting from lack of lubrication. On the left is a partially damaged bearing and on the right is an excessively damaged bearing.

bearing metals, like aluminum, brass, copper, and babbitt. When this happens, the abrasives rapidly cut into the hard bearing journal that is running against them. Soft metals should never be reconditioned by using an abrasive.

Foreign particles embed in bearings and are checked to determine their source. Bearing materials tend to cover them so they will not damage the shaft. Large particles will not embed, but will score the bearing and shaft. The specific type of embedded from the steel backing. Temperatures may increase enough to even cause the steel bearing backing to turn to a blue color from overheating.

The main reason oil does not get to a bearing is excessive oil leakage or throwoff from other bearings that are closer to the oil pump. When leakage from bearing clearances becomes greater than the oil pump's capacity, at the speed the pump is running, oil starvation will occur. Worn cam bearings often cause this oil leakage. The valve train holds the camshaft down on the bottom of the bearing all of the time so that all of the wear occurs on the lower side of the bearing. The excess bearing clearance above the cam does not knock because the load is always in the downward direction. Oil delivery to the upper side of the worn cam bearing can freely escape to the pan, thus reducing the amount of oil available to the main and rod bearings where oil starvation may occur. Blocked oil passages are usually the result of misaligned oil holes in a bearing shell. The mismatch is readily visible on the outer surface of the bearing shell.

Oil starvation may occur at very high engine speeds in some engine designs. High crankshaft rotational speed may cause centrifugal forces in the oil holes that are greater than oil pump pressure. The oil must have a laminar or smooth flow to provide a hydrodynamic oil film. At excessive speeds, the film can no longer flow smoothly and turbulence will develop. This causes voids in the oil surface and oil starvation occurs in these voids.

As the lubrication film breaks down, friction and heat increase. Heat thins the oil which, in turn, reduces the lubrication film. This process is unstable and increases rapidly until bearing failure occurs.

Full throttle, low speed operation or *lugging*, puts very high loads on the bearings. High loads tend to squeeze oil from the bearing. Thin oil will squeeze out faster than a more viscous oil. Engine and engine parts manufacturers caution against lugging because it causes rapid damage to engine parts. Lugging can only occur with vehicles equipped with a solid drive line. Automatic transmissions allow enough slippage at low speed, full throttle operation so that lugging cannot occur.

Each time a load is applied on a bearing, the bearing surface slightly flexes. Flexing occurs during all engine operation. Its effects increase as the engine loads increase. Gradually, the flexing will cause bearing fatigue, which will be indicated by fine cracks in the bearing surface. In time, the cracks will join at the backing bond to loosen pieces of the bearing material from their backing. The loosened piece overheats, then melts, which increases the rate of bearing failure.

Fig. 10-68 Bearing fatigue failure.

Bearing overloading may occur on a part of a misaligned bearing. This may be the result of a bent rod or shaft, or a warped engine block. Journal taper usually results from journal wear; however, it is always possible to have faulty grinding.

Lightly loaded short trip driving does not produce sufficient heat to drive off condensed water and gases. These collect in the oil, causing acid and sludge. The acid attacks the bearings and the bearings corrode.

Faulty bearing installation can lead to premature failure. Bearings that fit too tightly will not leave enough oil clearance so oil starvation occurs. Bearing shells with insufficient crush may rotate with the shaft. Dirt that becomes trapped behind the bearing shell causes a tight spot in the bearing which will fail.

Careful interpretation of bearing distress will pinpoint the cause of the distress. The cause can be corrected so that the reconditioned engine will have a normal service life.

10-10 SHAFT AND BEARING SERVICE

Inspection of the crankshaft shows abnormalities. A shaft in good condition only needs to have the bearing journals polished with fine polishing cloth. Polishing should be done in the direction opposite that of rotation to minimize the effects of microscopic "teeth" that result from polishing.

If crankshaft wear, bend, or scoring is beyond limits, it should be reground to a standard undersize. Crankshaft grinding is done on special grinding equipment by a highly skilled operator.

Camshaft repair is limited to regrinding when it is more economical or expedient than purchasing a new camshaft.

Bearings are replaced as a normal reconditioning procedure. The correct size bearing should be selected to provide proper bearing clearances.

Dynamic oil seals are replaced each time the engine is disassembled to the point the seals are accessible. Seals are inexpensive, compared to the work required to get at them if they leak later on. Replacement is a good preventative maintenance procedure.

10-11 BLOCK CONDITION

Block abnormalities occur in the cylinder wall, cooling system, shaft bore alignment, and broken parts. All of the other engine parts depend upon the block for support, alignment and operating climate.

Cylinder wall wear is one of the most noticeable block conditions. Cylinder walls, in normal use, have a smooth glaze from the burnishing effects of the piston and rings during operation even when taper, out-of-round, and wavy wall conditions exist. Dirt and broken rings will cause scratches on the wall. If the scratches are allowed to remain, they will allow oil to go into the combustion chamber on the

Fig. 10-69 Cylinder wall scratch caused by a broken piston ring.

intake stroke and combustion gases to blow into the crankcase during the power stroke.

Occasionally, the connecting rod is allowed to strike the bottom edge of the cylinder wall as the piston and rod assembly are removed or installed. This will nick the bottom edge of the cylinder and raise sharp points. If these points are not removed, they will scratch the piston skirt.

Fig. 10-70 Piston skirt damage caused by a damaged lower edge of the cylinder wall.

153

Piston pin locks that come out of the piston will usually score the cylinder wall. If the piston pin drifts out of its bore, it, too, will score the wall. Occasionally, they produce such deep scores that they break into the coolant jacket. When this happens, a thin walled cast iron sleeve may be installed. The cylinder is bored oversize to a diameter to accept the sleeve. The sleeve is pressed in, then bored to the required cylinder diameter.

The cooling system may be plugged with deposits or, in unusual cases, may be miscast when a casting core was damaged. The water jacket should be thoroughly checked. Core plug openings should be checked for evidence of leakage.

In operation, the block is stressed mechanically and thermally. Mechanical stress comes from assembly bolt torques, combustion pressures, and dynamic loads. Thermal stress from combustion heat may cause the block to warp and take a set. The block must be checked for parting surface flatness, especially the head deck, and for shaft bore alignment. Misalignment of shaft bores can be recognized by the bearing distress difference between the bearing shells. Bearing bore alignment can be checked with a properly ground test arbor .001″ smaller than the bearing bore that is bolted in place

of the crankshaft. The block is aligned if the test arbor can be turned with a 12″ handle. Alignment may also be checked with a straightedge placed across three or more bearing saddles. A feeler gauge one half the bearing clearance should *not* go between the straightedge and saddle. If it does, warpage exists.

Cracks in the block will allow leaks or will not support engine loads. Some cracks are repairable and others are not. The location of the crack and cost of repair is the basis upon which the technician makes his decision to repair or replace the block. Cracks on the exterior portion of the coolant jacket are usually repairable. Cracks in main bearing webs are not repairable.

10-12 BLOCK SERVICE

Blocks that have normal wear within specification limits may require no reconditioning. Many piston ring manufacturers recommend installing their rings on the worn glazed cylinder walls.

Fig. 10-72 Honing a cylinder.

Fig. 10-71 Checking main bearing saddle alignment with a straightedge.

Cylinder Walls. Some ring manufacturers recommend breaking the cylinder wall glaze with a hone before installing new rings. When honing is not required, it eliminates the time needed for honing and for cleanup, and so reduces reconditioning cost.

The cylinder wall should be honed to straighten the cylinder if the wall is wavy or scuffed. If honing is being done with the crankshaft in the block, the crankshaft should be protected to keep honing chips from getting on the shaft.

Honing should be done with a clean lubricated cylinder hone, using 180 to 280 grit stones. The hone must be stroked fast enough to produce the proper crosshatch finish.

(a)

Fig. 10-73 Appearance of a cylinder wall after honing (Dana Corporation).

(b)

It is extremely important to thoroughly clean the cylinder wall after honing to remove all abrasive grit. If the crankshaft is in the block, cleaning is accomplished by thoroughly oiling the wall and wiping with a clean rag, repeating this operation a number of times until a clean rag is not discolored by abrasives. If the block is bare, cleaning should be done by scrubbing the wall with a brush using soap and water. Gasoline, kerosene, or commercial cleaners will remove the oil, but will allow abrasives to remain on the cylinder wall; therefore, they should not be used to clean the cylinder after honing.

Cylinder walls that are worn or scored beyond honing limits should be bored to the smallest standard oversize that will clean the cylinder walls. New oversize pistons are required to fit oversized cylinders.

Fig. 10-74 Appearance of the cylinder wall after boring. (a) Rough boring (Dana Corporation), (b) Finish boring (Dana Corporation).

Cylinders are bored perpendicular to the block deck. If there is any deck warpage, it must be ground or milled flat before boring cylinders. This usually is done on a large table with a grinder or cutter work head that rotates in the center nearly flush with the surface. Passing the block back and forth across the work head takes small cuts until the surface is clean and smooth.

Cylinder boring is done with a piece of equipment especially designed for this process, usually called a *boring bar*. It consists of a power-driven

155

cutting tool in a rigid arbor. The arbor is aligned on the cylinder center, near the bottom of the cylinder bore where the least wear has occurred. When centered, the boring machine is clamped in position, often on the block deck surface. The arbor is raised and fitted with a cutting tool. The cutting tool is adjusted to the diameter desired and the cylinder is then bored from the top down. Several passes, rough and fine, may be required to enlarge the cylinder to the required size. The size is determined by the new piston that is to be used. Pistons should be available before boring begins so the cylinder can be bored to an exact size required. The cylinder is bored to .0005 to .002″ less than required. Cylinder size and required wall finish are completed by honing. This is followed by the thorough cleaning that is normally done after honing.

Cam Bearings. Cam bearings are replaced when servicing the block. The cam bearings are sleeve-bushing steel-backed precision bearings. They are removed and installed using the same tool, either with a slide hammer or a long screw. Some cam bearing tools use adapters installed in three bearings with an adapter shaft inserted in the adapters. A lock is placed on the shaft adjacent to the adapter

in the bearing to be removed. The other two adapters act as guides to maintain alignment. The shaft is forced endwise, sliding the bearing from its bore. The new correct size and type bearing is installed on the adapter and turned so the oil holes will index. The bearing is carefully started into the bore, then pulled to its normal position. This process is repeated on each camshaft bearing. An expansion plug is placed behind the rear cam bearing to seal the opening. Other cam bearing tools remove and install the cam bearing without the guide adapters.

If oil pump drive bushings are used, they can be replaced at this time when new bearings are needed. This usually requires pulling and installing equipment especially designed for this specific job.

Main Bearings. Main bearing bores in the block require no service if there is no sign of warpage. When warpage exists, the main bearing bores must be *line bored*. Before boring, .015″ is removed from the main bearing cap parting surfaces, then the caps are installed on the block. The block is centered in a line boring machine. The cutting tool is set to the original bore diameter, then each crankcase bearing housing is bored on the same center.

Line boring may be done on the bearings rather than in the crankcase bearing housing. The block is fitted with .060″ undersize bearings; these are bored to provide proper crankshaft main bearing oil clearance.

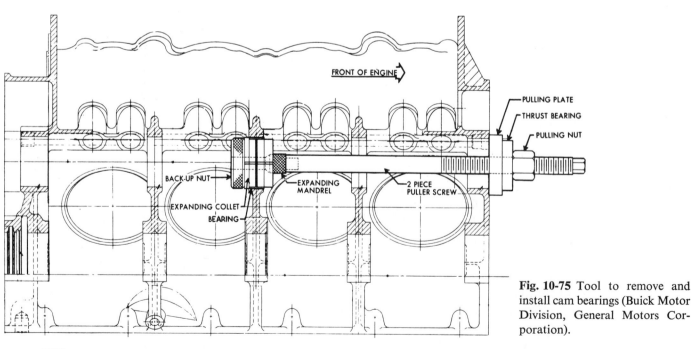

Fig. 10-75 Tool to remove and install cam bearings (Buick Motor Division, General Motors Corporation).

Fig. 10-76 Badly worn oil pump.

include cleaning and chamfering all threaded and oil hole openings, removing casting burrs with a hand grinder, honing lifter bores, priming the interior of the block with special paint, modifying the main bearing oil passages, balancing crankshaft and rod assemblies, hand grinding the combustion chambers to make their volumes equal, checking the valve to piston clearance, and many other fine details that reflect the individual engine rebuilder's touch.

10-13 ENGINE ASSEMBLY

The first step in engine reassembly is a final, thorough cleaning to remove any dust or dirt from the parts. Gasket sealing compound is put on the edges of the core plugs and they are seated in the block. All screw plugs are installed. The camshaft is liberally coated with the recommended lubricant, and carefully slipped into place, care being maintained not to knock the plug from the rear of the camshaft bore. Some manufacturers have a special cam holding tool to keep this from happening and others depend on a thrust plate.

The rear main oil seal is installed before the crankshaft is replaced. The crankshaft and new main bearings are lubricated with SD motor oil. The crankshaft, and bearing caps are installed and the caps are torqued. It is helpful to check crankshaft turning effort with a torque wrench after each cap is tightened. If the turning effort increases appreciably after one cap is tightened, remove that cap and determine the cause of binding. Use this procedure of measuring turning effort throughout engine assembly. Any tight spots or binding that exists will show up immediately, so it can be repaired before any further assembly is done. Care must be exercised to make sure all gaskets and seals around the rear main bearing cap are correctly installed, following any special instructions for that specific engine type.

Cam gears, sprockets and chains are aligned and installed. Gear or chain backlash should be rechecked to see that it is within limits. A new oil seal is installed in the timing cover. If a slinger ring is used, it is installed on the crankshaft, followed by the timing cover with a new gasket. The gasket

Oil Pump. Oil pumps are cleaned and inspected. They are checked for clearance between the gear and housing. The gears are checked for backlash. If the pump parts are worn or scored, the pump should be replaced. There is no recommended oil pump repair procedure.

Water Pump. Water pump problems usually result from rough bearings, leaking seals, or a damaged impeller. Present day pumps are serviced as a unit. When a problem does exist, the pump is replaced with a new or factory rebuilt assembly. The pump is often replaced on an overhauled engine as a preventative maintenance item.

Covers. All parting surfaces should be flat and free from nicks or scratches. Cast covers can be smoothed by attaching abrasive paper to a flat surface, then passing the cover over the abrasive surface until the entire surface is clean. Stamped metal covers and pans can be straightened by placing the edge on a flat surface and tapping the high spots to flatten them.

Special Considerations. Engines that are to be used to provide maximum service life are reconditioned to provide minimum service clearances. Engines that are to be used for maximum performance, on the other hand, are reconditioned to provide maximum service clearances and minimum combustion chamber volumes. This technique is called *blue printing* the engine. It requires very careful fitting and balance of all components. Blue printing takes special equipment and a lot of time, so it is a costly procedure. Special techniques will

Fig. 10-77 Measuring the assembled engine turning torque.

is usually coated with a non-hardening gasket compound. The crankshaft damper is installed before the timing cover is tightened. This allows the oil seal and timing cover to center itself on the damper hub. The cover is then tightened to the correct torque.

Piston assemblies are installed in the manner previously described.

Oil pump gears are given a light coating of heavy oil or light grease to provide initial lubrication that will allow the pump to prime itself. The pump is installed with new gaskets and seals. Windage trays or baffles are installed where they are used.

Oil pan seals are carefully placed in position so they will seal properly. The pan is installed and the retaining bolts snugged up, then torqued.

Heads are assembled and installed as previously described. Lifters are installed in their original locations, and the pushrods installed, taking care to get them in the correct location and the correct end up. These are followed by the rocker arms. If

the rocker arms are adjustable, this is a good time to adjust them, because the lifters and possibly the camshaft are visible. Engine manufacturer's adjustment procedures should be followed; however, this visibility gives a chance to doublecheck to see that the lifters are on the cam base circle when lash is being adjusted. Where used, the lifter cover is installed over the lifter valley, using a new gasket.

Intake manifold gaskets are carefully placed in the correct location and the manifold eased into position. Gasket placement is rechecked, then the manifold bolts are tightened. Where recommended, the correct torquing sequence should be used. This is followed by installing rocker covers with new gaskets. The water pump and outlet neck are installed with new gaskets.

If the engine is to be painted, all of the openings should be covered or old parts installed to mask the openings. The surface oil that accumulated during assembly must be removed before painting.

If the engine is going directly into a chassis, it should be dressed by installing a flywheel, bell housing or transmission, fuel pump, carburetor, distributor, alternator, power accessories, and drive belts. Ideally, the engine should be pre-oiled before starting. This is done by forcing oil into the engine through the oil pressure opening. If this is not possible, the engine should be cranked with the spark plugs removed until the oil pressure builds up.

If the engine is going to be stored, the engine openings should be sealed and the entire engine sealed in a plastic cover.

A well-designed engine that has been correctly reconditioned and assembled using the techniques described should give reliable and durable service for many miles. Premature failure will result from overlooked problems or from operational abuse.

Review Questions
Chapter 10

1. What type of service is required for maximum engine reliability?

2. What is the basis for determining that a problem exists in an engine?

3. Why is it important to make a careful detailed study during disassembly of an engine?

4. What conditions should be checked in the lifter chamber?

5. How is the cylinder checked for cylinder wear while the pistons are still installed?

6. Why should the oil pan deposits be examined in an engine?

7. Why is it important to remove the cylinder ridge before removing pistons?

8. Why is it important to check rod and main cap numbers before removal?

9. Why are protectors put on rod bolts before removing the piston-rod assembly?

10. What kind of damper puller should be used?

11. What precautions should be observed when removing the camshaft and crankshaft?

12. When is it necessary to remove burrs on valve stems?

13. What should be done with parts that are damaged too badly for reconditioning?

14. What are two basic types of cleaning methods for engine parts?

15. How should hard carbon be removed from pistons?

16. Is there any advantage in the technician spending his time cleaning engine parts?

17. Why is it desirable to make a visual inspection before a dimensional inspection?

18. How are inside diameters usually measured in automotive engines?

19. What methods are used to check shaft run out?

20. Where can a dial gauge be used for a dimensional inspection?

21. What methods can be used to measure closely fitting parts?

22. List the parts that can be inspected with Zyglo.

23. List the parts that can be inspected with Magnaflux.

24. What causes valve burning?

25. What causes a valve to break?

26. What valve problem does a sudden change in temperature cause?

27. Why is it recommended to replace the lifters and camshaft at the same time?

28. How are valve springs checked for further service?

29. Why is it extremely important to be sure the valve keepers are in good condition?

30. What may be the result of a warped cylinder head?

31. What can be done when valve stem-to-guide clearance is excessive?

32. What is an interference angle between the valve face and seat?

33. How is valve seating determined?

34. Why is it necessary to check valve stem length?

35. How is valve spring installed length checked?

36. What types of piston failure may occur?

37. Name the piston servicing operations.

38. What precautions should be observed when installing piston rings?

39. How should a crankshaft be checked to see if it is satisfactory for continued service?

40. What repair procedures are done on a crankshaft?

41. What malfunctions should be checked on a camshaft?

42. Why are the crankshafts and camshafts used in high production engines replaced rather than repaired when abnormal conditions exist?

43. Name the causes of bearing failure.

44. What items should be checked on a bare block to determine their condition?

45. When should a cylinder be honed?

46. How should a honed cylinder be cleaned?

47. When is it necessary to line bore the block?

48. What service is done on the water pump?

49. What is meant by *blue printing* an engine?

50. Describe the engine assembly techniques.

Quiz 10

1. A cylinder-wear check to determine the need for reboring should be done when the
   a. heads are removed
   b. pan is removed
   c. ridge is removed
   d. pistons are removed.

2. If the cylinder ridge is not removed when new rings are installed, it will most likely cause trouble after reassembly by
   a. allowing blow-by
   b. breaking the second piston land
   c. causing pre-ignition
   d. allowing the piston to hit the valve.

3. The crankshaft should be protected from damage *during* engine disassembly by
   a. coating with Lubriplate
   b. keeping it in the block until the rest of the engine is disassembled
   c. marking the postion of the main bearing caps
   d. installing rod bolt thread protectors.

4. Before the valves are pushed out of the guide, they should be checked for
   a. burrs at the valve lock grooves
   b. burned valve faces
   c. broken valve springs
   d. damaged valve locks.

5. How do valve seating failures usually show up in disassembly?

   a. excessive deposits
   b. radial cracks in the valve head
   c. broken valve stem
   d. valve face burning.

6. A valve stem would most likely break from
   a. low valve spring tension
   b. high valve spring tension
   c. lugging-type engine operation
   d. rapid changes in engine speeds.

7. A scuffed piston skirt is usually the result of
   a. low temperature operation
   b. excessive clearance
   c. lubrication breakdown
   d. a large amount of hard carbon buildup.

8. The need for early engine overhaul is usually due to
   a. heavy duty operation
   b. operation in a warm climate
   c. infrequent engine tuneups
   d. dirt in the engine.

9. Low speed, full throttle operation will lead to early engine bearing failure. This type of bearing distress is called
   a. embedded failure
   b. wiping failure
   c. fatigue failure
   d. scoring failure.

10. The most noticeable abnormal block condition is
    a. block deck warpage
    b. bearing bore misalignment
    c. cylinder wall wear
    d. cooling jacket deposits.

chapter 11

Mechanical Characteristics

An engine can be designed to meet all of the engine breathing, combustion and performance objectives at the same time disregarding all of the vibration, reliability and durability objectives. Such an engine, however, would be of little value in the modern passenger car. A major objective of passenger car engines is to have an engine that will run smoothly throughout a reasonable service life. The engine must be carefully designed so that the parts are strong enough to support the imposed loads and still be as light as possible.

While studying engines, many students think in terms of engine modifications that will allow an engine to provide more performance. This is often done with little regard to increased loads that more performance would impose on the engine parts. A study of engine dynamics is important in helping the student appreciate what can and often does happen, when these additional loads are placed on engine parts.

Parts are in balance when their center of gravity remains fixed. Any cyclic change in the parts' center of gravity will cause vibration. If cyclic vibration occurs at the parts' natural frequency, the amplitude or size of the vibration will increase and the part may fail.

Engine vibration results from parts that change their center of gravity while moving. Rotating shafts, such as a crankshaft and a camshaft, may be balanced to maintain a fixed center of gravity that will produce no vibration. Turbine and rotating combustion chamber engines run smoothly because their center of gravity moves very little. While some engine vibration is due to rotating masses, most of the standard internal combustion engine vibration results from reciprocating motion of the pistons with their connecting rods and from the reciprocating motion of the valve train. To eliminate vibration resulting from piston motion requires the greatest design care to provide satisfactory engine balance. A finely balanced engine will allow high engine speeds and will give the engine greater reliability and durability.

In order to understand engine balance, one must first understand the motions of the engine parts and the loads imposed on them throughout the engine cycle.

Fig. i1-1 Crankshaft arcs. A, B, and C are equal, but piston movements X_A, X_B, and X_C are unequal.

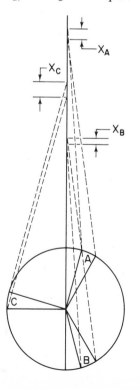

As the reciprocating mass, which may be considered the weight in pounds, of each piston goes from top to bottom center, it shakes the engine in a direction parallel to the cylinder. Engine shaft masses are twisted or jerked forward and backward as *torsional vibration* when loaded valve lifters go over the cam and when pistons are accelerated and decelerated. Balancing complications increase with complex connecting rod motions. The connecting rod's upper end reciprocates while its lower end rotates during operation. This results in a continually changing connecting rod angle that causes the piston to move further while the crankshaft is turning in the upper half of the cycle than it does when the crankshaft is turning in the bottom half of the cycle. On multi-cylinder engines, the forces between cylinders may operate together to cause a greater unbalance or the forces may oppose and balance out each other to increase the natural engine balance.

11-1 PISTON MOTION

It is important for an engine designer to know the exact position of the piston at each crankshaft angle to calculate engine balance, as well as to know engine ignition timing, engine breathing, and the combustion process. All of these depend upon piston position and piston movement. An easy way to express piston movement is to use percentage of the stroke compared to the angle of the crankshaft. This can be measured where the crankshaft extends outside of the engine. The crank angle can be measured directly on the crankshaft when the engine is not running and indirectly using a stroboscopic light, such as a timing light, while the engine is running.

Piston Position. Piston position in relation to the crankshaft angle can be calculated mathematically or developed graphically. The graphical method will be presented here to help the reader visualize engine dynamics. These methods can be applied to any engine being studied.

Piston position, in relation to the crankshaft angle, may be determined graphically by making a scale line drawing of the piston pin, crank pin and main bearing journal centers at each crank angle (θ) being investigated. All angles being studied can be superimposed on the same drawing if light lines are used.

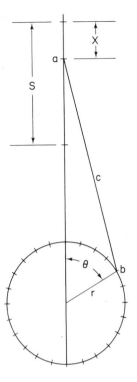

Fig. 11-2 Scale drawing of crankshaft and rod position. Length r is proportional to 1/2 the stroke and C is proportional to the connecting rod length.

Assume that a half-scale drawing is to be used. The first step is to draw a circle whose diameter is one-half the engine stroke, with a long center line extending upward. The circle should be marked off in the degree increments being investigated (for example, every fifteen degrees, as in Figure 11-2). The next step is to make an independent straight edge proportional to the actual engine connecting rod length (c). In this example, using one-half scale, it would be one-half the length of the connecting rod's bearing and piston pin center-to-center distance. The independent straight edge may be a measured length on a straight edge, a compass length or a divider length. Place one end of the independent straight edge on the circle (b) at the angle being investigated (θ). The other end of the independent straight edge should be placed on the upward extending center line (a). Mark this point on the center line. Move the independent straight edge to each of the other crank angles being investigated and repeat the marking process. The half-scale position of the piston (x) at each crank angle may be measured on the vertical center line from the top mark downward. This distance multiplied by inverse scale (in this example, the inverse

of the scale one-half is two) will give the actual piston position. The piston position divided by the full stroke (x/s) will give the percentage of the stroke that the piston has traveled at each crank angle. The return stroke from 180 to 360 degrees is a reverse duplicate of the piston position during the first 180 degrees of crankshaft rotation.

This graphical procedure relates the piston position to the crankshaft angle. The crankshaft angle can be measured in degrees on the vibration damper so the crankshaft angle may be used to locate the piston position in further studies of engine balance, volumetric efficiency, and combustion.

Piston Velocity. Bearing surfaces, including the piston sliding in the cylinder, have limiting surface speeds that cannot be exceeded. If exceeded, they will cause abnormal wear. These speeds are limited by the design and finish of the parts, by materials from which they are made, by loads impressed upon them and by the lubrication provided.

The piston reaches its maximum speed at 50% of the stroke. This speed, or *velocity*, of the piston increases in direct proportion to the engine speed. If the crankshaft rpm were doubled, the velocity of the piston would be doubled.

Many times, engines are compared by using the distance their pistons travel each minute, called piston speed, rather than any instantaneous piston speed. The piston speed in feet per minute is the distance the piston slides in a cylinder each minute. Remembering that the piston makes two strokes for each revolution, the equation for the piston speed is:

$$\text{Piston speed} = \frac{2sN}{12 \text{ in/ft}} \text{ ft/min}$$

where:

s = stroke in inches

N = engine rpm

A short discussion of acceleration and velocity may be helpful for those who are not acquainted with these terms. They are easily understood if they are related to vehicle performance.

A speed of 60 miles per hour is *velocity*. Each mile is 5,280 feet and so, with simple arithmetic, miles per hour can be changed to 316,800 feet-per-hour. This is a large number. If it is divided by 3600 seconds per hour, the 60 miles per hour velocity could be expressed equally as well as a velocity of 88 feet per second. A velocity of 44 feet per second is 30 miles per hour and a velocity of 132 feet per second is 90 miles per hour.

$$\text{Velocity (ft/sec)} = \frac{\text{speed (mi/hr)} \times 5280 \text{ (ft/mi)}}{3600 \text{ (sec/hr)}}$$

$$= \text{speed} \times 1.466 \text{ ft/sec}$$

Vehicle *acceleration* is necessary to go from a standstill to a velocity such as 88 feet per second (60 miles per hour). If this is done quickly, acceleration must be high; if it is done slowly, acceleration is low. If it takes 8.8 seconds to reach 88 ft/sec velocity, the acceleration would be 10 feet per second for each second (10 ft/sec²), assuming constant acceleration. If it would have taken 11 seconds to reach the velocity of 88 feet per second, the acceleration would have been only 8 feet per second for each second (8 ft/sec²). Acceleration is the *amount of change* in velocity each second. It can be expressed as:

$$\text{Acceleration (ft/sec}^2) = \frac{\text{Velocity (ft/sec)}}{\text{Seconds}}$$

Piston Acceleration. As the piston moves from top center down to bottom center of the stroke, it will accelerate to a maximum velocity, then decelerate back to zero at the bottom center.

Acceleration increases as the square of the engine speed. If the engine speed is doubled, acceleration is four times as great. Acceleration will also increase in direct proportion to any increase in length of the engine stroke at the same crankshaft rpm.

11-2 ENGINE BALANCE

A single engine cylinder will be used to describe basic engine balance. This will be followed by applying these same concepts to a multi-cylinder engine.

Unbalance is the result of both rotating and reciprocating masses. For the purpose of this discussion, *mass* will be equal to weight in pounds. The rotating mass consists of the crank pin and lower one third of the connecting rod. The reciprocating mass consists of the piston, piston pin, piston rings and the upper two thirds of the connecting rod. The actual rotating and reciprocating weight of the connecting rod and piston assembly is weighed when it is in a horizontal position.

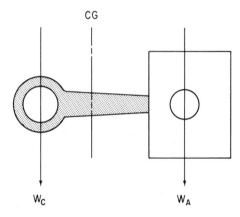

Fig. 11-3 Connecting rod–piston assembly weight. Weight W_C is the centrifugal weight and weight W_a is the reciprocating weight.

Rotating Mass. The rotating mass of the crank pin portion of the crankshaft can be balanced with an equal counterweight mass. By selecting a larger counterweight, the rotating mass of the lower third of the connecting rod can also be balanced. Any force that tries to move the center of gravity of the rotating mass is called a *centrifugal force*.

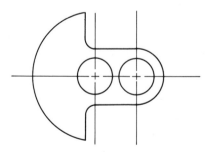

Fig. 11-4 Counterweight balances the crank pin.

Properly sized counterweights are capable of balancing the centrifugal force of the crank pin and lower connecting rod.

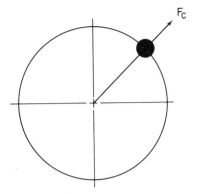

Fig. 11-5 Counterweight force is always radial from the main bearing center.

When the rotating parts are perfectly balanced, no centrifugal force is applied to the main bearings at any speed. Therefore, they would produce no shaking effect on the engine or on its mounting. Unfortunately, perfect balance is impossible.

Reciprocating Mass. The reciprocating mass is not as easily balanced as the rotating mass. The piston moving up and down in the cylinder induces a shake parallel to the cylinder center line. This shake is accompanied by harmonic vibrations that are multiples of the initial or primary vibration.

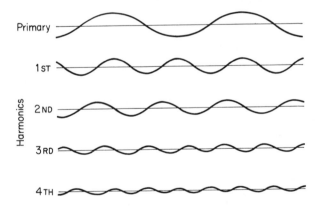

Fig. 11-6 Primary unbalance shake with its harmonics. Harmonics may add to or minimize total vibration.

Higher harmonic vibrations have smaller amplitudes. Harmonics above the sixth harmonic are negligible in automotive engines. An additional balance factor results because the piston moves more than halfway down the cylinder as the crankshaft turns 90° from top center. This increases engine balance complexity.

Primary Vibrations. As the piston goes to the bottom of the cylinder, its inertia tends to continue to move it downward, but it is stopped by the connecting rod, crankshaft and engine block. This results in a downward movement or vibration of the entire engine. As the piston returns to the top of the cylinder on the upward stroke, its inertia tends to keep going up, but it is again restrained by the connecting rod, crankshaft and engine block. This puts an upward motion or vibration on the entire engine. The up-and-down movement, or shake, of the engine caused by piston movement is called the *primary vibration*. One heavy up-and-down vibration cycle is produced for each engine revolution. The primary vibration has the same number of cycles per minute, called *frequency*, as the engine rpm.

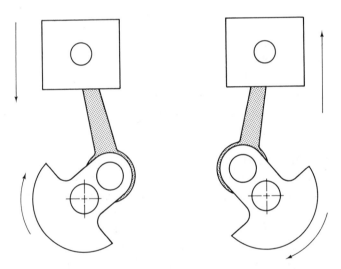

Fig. 11-7 Counterweight balancing the piston in the up-and-down direction.

The counterweight could be enlarged to balance the entire primary vibration because the counterweight is always moving in a direction opposite the piston. The counterweight goes up as the piston goes down and when the counterweight goes down, the piston goes up. However, if this large a weight were to be added to the crankshaft, it would cause a side shake as great as the original up-and-down shake, because there is nothing to counteract the weight's centrifugal force in the horizontal direction. Therefore, the crankshaft counterweight size must be a compromise between the vertical and

165

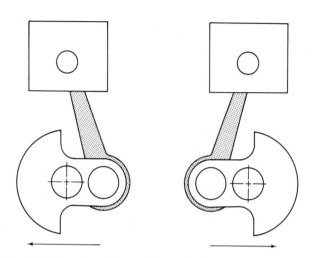

Fig. 11-8 Counterweight unbalance in the horizontal position.

horizontal unbalance conditions. The usual practice is to make the primary crankshaft counterweight size somewhere between the vertical and horizontal shake conditions so that unbalance is reduced in the most objectionable direction. This weight balance proportion will differ with the engine and type of vehicle in which it is used.

Secondary Vibrations. Secondary vibrations occur at the same time as primary vibrations, but they make two complete up-and-down cycles during one crankshaft revolution. At top center, both primary and secondary vibration forces are upward. This adds to the total unbalance force. At 90°, the primary force is zero while the secondary force

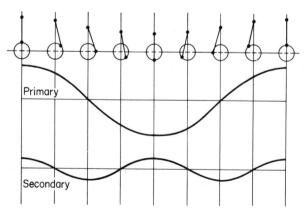

Fig. 11-9 Primary and secondary vibrations in relation to piston pin position.

is downward. At bottom center, the primary force is downward, but the secondary force is again in an upward direction, so that the forces oppose each other and tend to reduce the total unbalance force. When the crankshaft arrives at 270°, the primary force is again zero and the secondary force is again downward. The amplitude of the secondary vibration forces are from one-third to one-fourth that of the primary force.

It can be seen that for the complex motion of the engine's moving masses to be satisfactorily balanced requires a great deal of care. The higher the engine's running speed, the more critical engine balancing becomes, because the vibrations at high speeds could become very large and damage the engine or car.

The only way that secondary shaking forces can be balanced is to have two counterweights of the correct size geared to rotate at twice the engine speed and in opposite directions. In practice, secondary counterweights are only used in some large diesel engines that produce excessive vertical vibration resulting from secondary shaking forces.

11-3 INERTIA TORQUE

Inertia is the property of an object that is at rest, to remain at rest, or, if in motion, to stay in motion. Inertia must be overcome on the drag strip to get the car going. It must again be overcome by the brakes to get the car stopped after going through the traps.

The inertia force of the reciprocating mass is transmitted to the crankshaft through the connecting rod. This causes a complex turning or twisting effect on the crankshaft, either forward or backward, that is called *inertia torque*. The inertia torque,

Fig. 11-10 Inertia torque vibrations are always zero at top and bottom center.

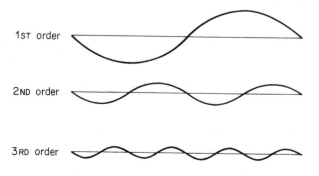

like engine vibration, can be divided into a first, second, and higher order vibrations. The first-order inertia torque makes one revolution for each engine revolution and the second-order inertia torque makes two. All orders of inertia torque are zero at top and bottom of the stroke, because piston motion stops at these points.

11-4 ROCKING COUPLES

During engine design, some consideration is given to the problem of *rocking couples* in engines. Rocking couples occur when the vibrations at each end of the engine move in opposite directions, causing the engine to rock endwise. This occurs on some four-stroke cycle engine designs and on most two-stroke cycle designs, when the piston on one end goes up and the piston on the other end goes down. The characteristics of the rocking couple in any engine are a function of the engine's crankshaft design and engine firing order.

11-5 MULTI-CYLINDER ENGINE BALANCE

Multi-cylinder engines are made as an assembly of single cylinders, each having the previously analyzed vibrational characteristics. The crankshaft is designed so that, in as far as possible, the forces of one cylinder oppose and thus balance the forces from the other cylinders. This *natural balancing* is best accomplished in inline six and V-8 designs.

The six-cylinder engine has three pairs of crankshaft connecting rod journals spaced at 120°. To avoid a rocking couple balance problem, the end two cylinders are paired, the middle two cylinders are paired, and the remaining two cylinders are paired. Forces on these three journal pairs balance each other so that a six-cylinder engine has natural primary and secondary balance. To complete engine balance, the crankshaft has balance weights that statically balance the rotating masses.

The V-8 engine is also a completely balanced engine when the crankpins are in two planes at 90° to each other. Most automotive V-8 engines have the crankshaft rod bearing journals designed so that when looking at the front of the engine, No. 1 is at 0°, No. 2 is at 270°, No. 3 is at 90°, and No. 4 is at 180°.

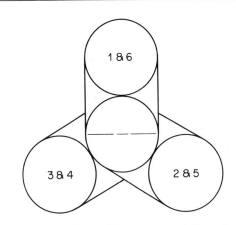

Fig. 11-11 Crank pin positions on an inline six-cylinder engine.

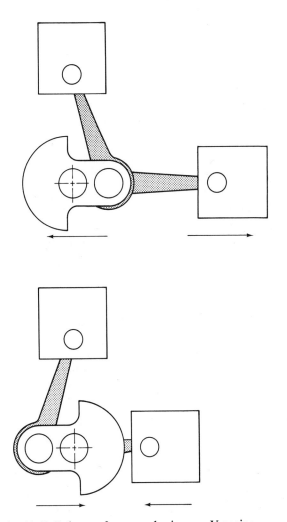

Fig. 11-12 Balance of one crank pin on a V engine.

167

Consider the two connecting rods that are mounted on the first crankshaft rod bearing journal of a V-engine. The center lines of these two cylinders are at 90° to each other. Side shake caused by a fully balanced counterweight of one cylinder is offset by the second cylinder that is connected to the same connecting rod journal. What would have been side shake on a single-cylinder engine becomes the balance weight for the paired cylinder.

The V-8 engine with a two-plane crankshaft in current use has no rocking couple. Each of the vibrational forces is balanced with opposing forces from the other paired cylinders.

Different cylinder combinations have been used and will continue to be used in automobiles; however, these two arrangements presented are, by far, the most common types.

11-6 BEARING LOADS

The foregoing discussion shows how centrifugal and inertia loads in an engine are balanced in the inline six and V-8 engines. This balance means that the engine will run smoothly in a vehicle. Loads, however, do still exist in an engine. They must be absorbed by the engine bearings and structure. An engine designer usually develops a *bearing load diagram* to illustrate the loads that will be applied to the bearing, as previously shown in Figure 6-22. From this, he is able to develop sufficient engine structural strength and to select bearings that will adequately carry these engine loads.

Loads on a connecting rod journal are the result of combustion pressure, inertia loads, and centrifugal loads. The combined connecting rod loads are balanced to provide minimum unbalanced loads on the main bearings and, thus, have the minimum engine vibration.

The pressure on top of the piston at any point in the cycle can be determined by using a pressure-volume diagram. The development of this diagram is described in Section 12-3. Pressure at any combustion chamber volume, multiplied by the cross-sectional area of the cylinder, will give the force on the piston at that specific cycle position.

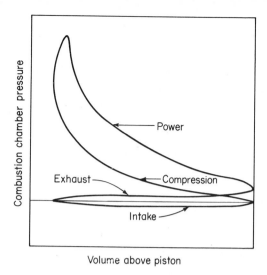

Fig. 11-13 Typical pressure–volume diagram of one cycle of a running engine (not to scale).

Combustion pressure, inertia and centrifugal forces combine to provide the bearing load. They do not add directly. The combustion chamber forces and inertia forces act up-and-down, but are modified by the connecting rod angle. Centrifugal force always acts in a radial direction, straight out from the crankshaft center. A bearing load diagram showing the summation of the loads on the connecting rod may be developed by mathematical or graphical means. Total crankpin loads of a V-8 engine are the sum of the loads applied by the pair of connecting rods attached to them. Loads on the main bearings are half the sum of the loads of the crankpin on each side of the main bearing. Each engine has its own bearing load diagram. The diagram is altered by any change in speed, load, weight, or engine design.

11-7 TORSIONAL VIBRATION

Each time a cylinder fires, the expanding gases push the piston downward. This force is transmitted through the piston pin, connecting rod, the bearing to the crankshaft crankpin. The force on the crankpin produces a twist or torque in the crankshaft. This torque is directed through the drive line to the rear wheels to move the vehicle.

Pulses are produced by the combustion chambers. The *frequency* of the pulses, or how fast they are produced, is based on the engine speed and number of cylinders. The *amplitude*, or size of the force, is determined by throttle position and engine load. Any rigid part, such as a crankshaft, will vibrate at a natural frequency. If the engine pulses have enough amplitude and the pulse frequency matches the crankshaft natural frequency, the crankshaft will torsionally vibrate. *Torsional vibration* or twist is the same type of vibration a driver feels in the steering wheel when the car's front wheels shake or shimmy.

Torsional vibration puts no load on the main bearings because torsional vibration twists around the main bearing centerline and does not bend the crankshaft. If excess torsional vibration is allowed to continue, the crankshaft will eventually break. Dampers are placed on the front of the crankshaft to oppose, and thus reduce, the torsional vibration amplitude. The damper size and construction must match the crankshaft vibrational frequency and amplitude requirements. If a damper from one engine is used on a different model engine, it could increase, rather than reduce torsional vibration amplitude. This would result in a rough running engine and early engine failure.

Torsional vibration dampers are made by placing a heavy cast iron inertia ring around a damper hub, as shown in Chapter 6. It is held in place with a flexible coupling, usually an oil resistant rubber or elastomer sleeve having the required flexible properties. The inertia ring size and weight movement opposes the engine torsional vibrations, thus providing a relatively smooth engine power output. This, in turn, helps to provide a long useful engine service life.

11-8 VALVE TRAIN CHARACTERISTICS

Lobes on the camshaft and the valve gear are designed to help provide smooth engine operation and power output through a wide operating speed range. Engine operation is affected by valve opening and closing points, by amount of valve lift, by the rate at which valves open and by valve duration. A compromise is made from the ideal cam lobe design because of the weight of the valve train parts, by their flexibility and by valve spring characteristics. In general, valve trains are designed to provide good engine performance and to operate quietly for a long service period.

Valve Timing. Valve timing may be defined as the crankshaft angle at which the valve leaves its seat during opening and arrives back at its

seat during closing. Sometimes, they are specified starting at five thousandths of an inch lift. These points are further identified by indicating if they occur before or after the piston reaches upper or lower dead center. *Dead center* is the point at which the piston is at its upper or lower extreme.

The four-stroke cycle is usually described by starting at the beginning of the intake stroke with the minimum volume above the piston. For the example here, however, the description will start with the piston at the start of the power stroke.

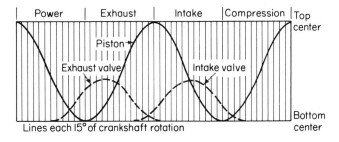

Fig. 11-14 Valve opening in relation to piston position.

The intake charge trapped in the combustion chamber is ignited and burned gases expand on the piston downstroke. As the piston approaches the bottom center, the exhaust valve leaves its seat, allowing the spent combustion gases to *blow down* to atmospheric pressure. The exhaust valve becomes fully open as the piston reaches maximum velocity on the upstroke. It reaches its seat after the crankshaft rotates past top center on the upstroke.

The intake valve starts to open slightly before top center (BTC) and continues to open as the crankshaft turns. Both intake and exhaust valves are open at the end of the exhaust stroke and at the beginning of the intake stroke. This period is called *valve overlap*.

During this part of the crankshaft rotation, the piston moves very little and the valve moves rapidly. When the piston velocity becomes fast enough to allow the charge to be inducted, the intake valve has already reached its wide open position.

Toward the bottom of the intake stroke, the valve begins to close and the piston slows down as it approaches bottom center. The valve touches the

169

seat soon after the piston starts to move up to compress the charge.

Valve timing is often diagrammed as a valve timing spiral, showing the number of degrees and the part of the cycle that the valves are off their seats. This is called valve duration. High speed engine operation requires high valve duration. Smooth, low speed operation uses short valve duration and small valve overlap. High production domestic automobile engines compromise these two conditions to provide reasonable high performance with adequate part throttle and idle smoothness.

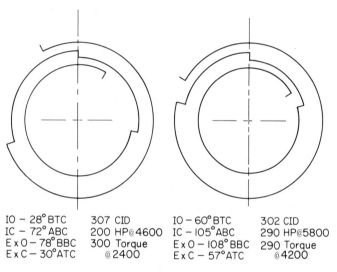

IO – 28° BTC	307 CID	IO – 60° BTC	302 CID
IC – 72° ABC	200 HP@4600	IC – 105° ABC	290 HP@5800
ExO – 78° BBC	300 Torque	ExO – 108° BBC	290 Torque
ExC – 30° ATC	@2400	ExC – 57° ATC	@4200

Fig. 11-15 Comparison of cam timing between a standard passenger car engine and a similar engine with a performance cam.

Valve Motion. There is much more to valve train dynamics than timing and duration. Lift is another factor that must be considered. The valve needs to be opened far enough to allow the gases to flow freely. The greater the valve lift, the easier the gases can flow, especially at high speeds. Valve lifts greater than 25% of the valve head diameter show very small power gains compared to the mechanical forces required to operate valve trains with higher lifts. Engine power results from the amount of mixture charge that the engine consumes. This fact can be recognized when you see engine power increasing as the throttle is opened to allow a large amount of mixture charge to enter the

combustion chamber. It would seem that maximum lift would be ideal; however, as with any mechanism, the valve train has mass and mass has inertia.

In order to achieve the desired valve lift, the valve mass must be *accelerated* to a maximum *velocity* or speed, then slowed down or decelerated until it stops at maximum valve lift position with the valve wide open. As the engine continues to turn, the valve train will be accelerated to maximum velocity in the closing direction, then brought to a smooth, easy stop on the valve seat. Typical valve lift, velocity and acceleration curves are shown in Figure 11-16.

In a valve train, the valve moves at its highest velocity when it is about halfway open. It is accelerated up to this velocity by the cam lobe pushing on the lifter. If acceleration is too rapid, it would be like hitting it with a hammer, causing excessive loads to be placed on the cam and valve mechanism. This could result in *valve train* failure. Modern pushrod engine valve trains are accelerated from .0003 to .0005 inches per degree[2]. (Remember that degree equals time for known engine speeds.) Maximum valve train velocities are between .006 to .009 inches per degree.

The valve begins to decelerate or slow down right after it reaches maximum velocity. The cam is not designed to hold the lifter so that valve train deceleration or negative acceleration control depends upon the valve spring to hold the lifter against the cam lobe. After reaching its wide open position, the cam falls away from the lifter and the valve spring must accelerate the valve train to keep the lifter in contact with the cam lobe until maximum closing velocity is reached.

The cam lobe decelerates the valve train from the maximum closing velocities until the valve is eased onto its valve seat.

Fig. 11-16 Typical cam motion curve.

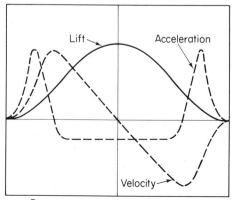

Degrees

Fig. 11-17 Valve bent by the piston when the valve was floating at high engine speed.

11-9 VALVE SPRING

The desired valve motion is designed into the cam lobe shape. The valve train is held together and is held against the cam lobe by the valve spring. If the valve spring is not strong enough to decelerate the valve train, the lifter will be tossed from the cam and *float* so that control of valve motion will be lost. This often occurs when an engine is run at speeds higher than the normal valve train maximum design speed. In extreme cases, the valve could still be open as the piston comes to the top of its stroke so that the piston would hit and damage the valve. Standard valve springs exceed the normal maximum design requirements by 30%. Installing high pressure valve springs would allow higher valve train speeds, but would also overload the valve train and cause excessive and costly cam and valve train wear.

11-10 CAM LOBE FEATURES

Cam lobe shape is developed from a base circle that is blended to a nose circle with two flank circles. A lifter slides on the cam lobes to produce valve opening and closing characteristics. The valve is closed while the lifter contacts the base circle. The flank circle configuration produces acceleration and velocity characteristics while the nose circle

affects lift and the time that the valve is nearly wide open. This action was shown in Figure 6-9.

The cam lobe size is limited by the lifter diameter. The lifter diameter, in turn, is limited by the space available in the engine. Lifter edges must be outside the cam nose, so that the cam lobe contacts the bottom of the lifter and not the lifter edge. Generally, lifters are slightly off-center from the lobe, so the asymmetrical force causes the lifters to rotate in operation to give a long service life.

The valve cannot immediately go from being at rest to full speed. This kind of action would produce severe shock. Instead, the valve is gradually lifted from the seat, then accelerates to maximum velocity. During closing, the valve is decelerated by the cam lobe as it is smoothly eased onto the valve seat. A *ramp* takes up any clearances in the valve train as the lobe starts to open the valve and a ramp eases the valve onto its seat during the last portion of the flank curve. Valve train stress during valve opening is kept below 150,000 psi for maximum durability.

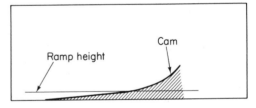

Fig. 11-18 Cam ramp.

The ramps on the cam lobe raise at a constant velocity of .001″ movement at the valve for each two degrees of cam rotation. The ramp is long enough and high enough to take up any looseness or lash in the valve train before increasing opening velocity. *Lash* is provided in the valve train to accommodate changes in temperature, wear, deflection and hydraulic lifter leak down. The cam lobe is designed to allow the valve to open and close while on the ramp. The closing ramp is most critical of the two. If the valve is allowed to hit the seat hard as it closes, it will bounce and, in a short time, the valve or seat will be damaged.

Hydraulic lifters have no lash, but they do have a short ramp. Their opening ramp rises much faster than the solid lifter cam ramp. The closing ramp is large enough to compensate for a slight hydraulic lifter leakage that occurs while the valve is held off its seat. Any change in lifter type must be accompanied by a change in the camshaft to produce maximum performance with satisfactory durability.

11-11 VALVE TRAIN FLEXIBILITY

It would be ideal if actual valve action followed the design, but it doesn't because of the valve train's elastic characteristics. As the valve is accelerated to open, the valve train is pushed together causing the pushrod to bend slightly. When the valve train reaches maximum velocity and begins to decelerate, the valve train tension is relaxed, causing the valve train to overshoot the design curve. It trails the cam during negative acceleration in the closing direction until it reaches maximum velocity. As the cam decelerates, the valve train will again compress and close more rapidly than the design closing speed. The wear pattern produced by this action can be seen in Figure 10-64.

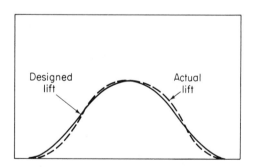

Fig. 11-19 Actual cam lift compared to design lift (exaggerated).

Valve Spring Surge. Another factor that affects valve train operation is valve spring surge. When compressed slowly, a spring compresses evenly. When compressed rapidly, the first coils are compressed sooner than the last coils. This high initial compression rebounds, sending a *surge* throughout the spring. If the spring were improperly designed,

spring surge could cause the valve train to lose contact with the cam, thus losing control and possibly causing engine damage.

Valve surge usually occurs at a harmonic velocity. To counteract this effect, valve springs often have closely spaced coils at one end of the spring that change the spring harmonic frequency and, thus, dampen the spring harmonic surge. Closely spaced coils are placed at the stationary end of the valve spring, against the head, to minimize the mass of the reciprocating portion of the valve train. When the valve spring harmonic occurs at a lower harmonic number, friction valve spring dampers, as described in Chapter 4, are used to eliminate valve spring surge.

Gas Pressure. Exhaust valve opening is further modified by combustion pressure. The valve train must push the exhaust valve against the combustion pressure until the valve opens. If a 1.5″ exhaust valve were to be opened into 100 psi combustion chamber pressure, it would require approximately 175 pounds force plus the force of valve spring pressure to move the exhaust valve off its seat. As soon as it came off the seat, it would no longer require the extra 175 pounds, and so the valve would start to surge open.

Valve train deflections can be reduced by increasing the valve train stiffness without increasing its weight or the valve train could be designed so that vibrations do not excite its natural frequencies. Generally, the valve train is designed so its natural frequency is above normal operating speeds. These frequencies could, however, be reached at abnormal engine speeds.

If more engine speed is required, the valve train stiffness can be increased with a stronger camshaft, stronger rocker arms and stronger rocker arm supports. Weight can be reduced with hollow

Fig. 11-20 Pressures on the exhaust valve prior to valve opening.

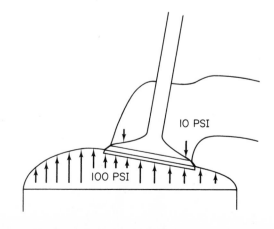

pushrods, hollow lifters, hollow valve stems and thinning the valve head. Reducing weight often reduces durability. It is interesting to note that many hollow pushrods and "solid" lifters are used to carry oil to the rocker arms. The oil in these parts must be included in calculating the weight of parts and, therefore, they will have a relatively large operating weight, even though they are hollow.

Critical Valve Train Speeds. The design of the valve train establishes the critical speed at which natural vibrations are excited. The design or shape of the cam lobe determines how close to this critical speed the valve train will operate. Rapid valve train acceleration reduces the critical speed, thus lowering the useful maximum engine speed, even though rapid valve train acceleration would improve high speed engine breathing. Here again, the engine designer must compromise opposing factors.

11-12 OVERHEAD CAM

Overhead cam engines have a stiff valve train and, therefore, they have a high natural frequency. High natural frequencies allow higher acceleration rates while still keeping the valve train below its critical speed. This makes a low valve overlap possible, allowing good idle operation while, at the same time, providing good high speed breathing because the valves can be opened rapidly without valve toss. The overhead cam design reduces the cost of the engine block and makes an easy air cooled design. No pushrods go through the head, so large intake and exhaust ports for engine breathing are possible. The overhead cam engine has some disadvantages, however. The camshaft drive is costly and often noisy, especially on V engines using two cylinder heads. The overhead camshaft placement usually increases engine height and this affects styling. The added cost compared to the added performance limits its use to small passenger car and racing car applications.

11-13 LIFTERS

Hydraulic lifters have largely replaced solid lifters in passenger car engines. They reduce the noise level and require no periodic adjustment. Their design eliminates valve lash by filling the lash space

with oil. If an engine with hydraulic lifters is oversped, the valve train will be tossed from the cam and the valves will float. Oil pressure in the lifter will attempt to remove this extra lash caused by toss, resulting in hydraulic lifter *pump-up*. When too much hydraulic lifter leakage occurs, or loose plunger fit is present, lifters will leak down and cause clatter.

Automobile camshafts are made from hardenable alloy cast iron, while lifters are made from hardenable high carbon steel. Lifters have a slightly convex bottom that slides on the cam lobe. It always contacts the highest part of the cam lobe. Contacting surfaces are hardened, so they will operate for thousands of miles with proper lubrication. If the surface starts to break down, it goes rapidly, completely ruining the cam and lifter.

Some heavy duty and performance engines use roller lifters on a steel camshaft. The camshaft must have a completely different shape with a roller lifter because the contact point is near the center of the lifter and not at the highest point of the cam, as on the convex face lifters. It is necessary to key roller lifters in their guide, so the roller will always run parallel to the cam lobe.

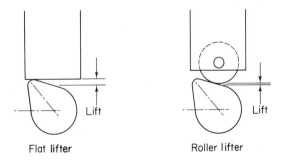

Fig. 11-21 The amount of lift compared between a standard and roller lifter at the same cam angle.

Roller lifters are used in heavy duty engine applications to provide durability when the valve train loads are high and there is a high surface speed between the camshaft and lifter. Roller lifters increase the weight of the valve train along with the associated problems previously discussed. The major disadvantage, however, is the added cost of the roller lifters for engines that can operate satisfactorily with convex lifters.

Properly designed valve trains operated within their design speed range will provide satisfactory engine idle, high power and long durability. Modifications from the original design may lead to poor performance and short valve life.

Engine dynamics are primarily concerned with the engine's two rotating shafts and the reciprocating action of the pistons and valve with their connecting linkages. Other moving parts such as the distributor, oil pump, fuel pump, water pump and generator cause very little vibration because their mass is small compared to the rest of the engine. They may be individually balanced, especially the generator. These items will usually produce undesirable noise rather than a vibration complaint when they are out of balance.

Review Questions
Chapter 11

1. Why is it important that a technician understand the mechanical characteristics of an engine?

2. How does the shift of center of gravity cause vibration?

3. Describe the motion of the connecting rod during engine operation.

4. What happens to the piston speed, maximum velocity and acceleration, as the engine speed is changed from 2000 rpm to 4000 rpm?

5. For a smooth running engine, what forces need to be balanced?

6. What problem is introduced when a counterweight is designed to balance the entire reciprocating mass on a single-cylinder engine?

7. How does a balanced engine affect the main bearings?

8. What are harmonic vibrations?

9. What are the primary and secondary vibration frequencies of an engine running at 3000 rpm? How do their amplitudes differ?

10. How do unbalance forces differ from inertia torque forces?

11. What causes a rocking couple in engines?

12. How does a 90° vee engine design help the balance problem?

13. Does balancing reduce the loads within an operating engine?

14. What factors cause bearing loads?

15. What is the value of a bearing load diagram?

16. Draw a graph similar to Figure 11-14 for an engine being worked on.

17. Make a valve timing spiral for two different engines.

18. What causes valve float?

19. What causes lifter pump-up?

20. When does the valve spring cause valve movement?

21. What is the purpose of a cam ramp?

22. What is meant by critical valve train speed?

Quiz 11

1. Engine vibration results from
   a. cylinder firing impulses
   b. crankshaft rotation
   c. a moving center of gravity
   d. counterweight motion.

2. Valve timing and engine breathing are based on
   a. piston position
   b. crankshaft rotation angle
   c. connecting rod motion
   d. combustion rates.

3. Maximum piston velocity occurs when the crankshaft is
   a. close to top center
   b. slightly less than 90° after top center
   c. slightly greater than 90° after top center
   d. close to bottom center.

4. What is the average ft/min piston speed of an engine with a 4" stroke running at 2000 rpm?
   a. 1749 ft/min
   b. 1333 ft/min
   c. 666 ft/min
   d. 269 ft/min

5. Movement of the recprocating parts of a V-8 engine are balanced by the crankshaft counterweight and
   a. counter shaft
   b. flywheel
   c. crankshaft damper
   d. mating piston.

6. Engine output characteristics can be changed by
   a. modifying the cam lobe shape
   b. increasing the cylinder bore
   c. revising the crank angles
   d. reducing the flywheel weight.

7. The valves are fully open when the piston is
   a. near upper center
   b. near lower center
   c. moving near maximum velocity
   d. approaching maximum acceleration.

8. After initial valve acceleration, the valve train is forced to move by the
   a. height of the cam lobe
   b. ramp on the cam
   c. high velocity gas flow
   d. valve spring.

9. Hydraulic lifter valve float is the result of
   a. high engine speeds
   b. sticking lifter check valves
   c. valve toss
   d. high oil pressure.

10. The main advantage of an overhead cam is its ability to allow
    a. high valve acceleration rates
    b. the engine to be manufactured more economically
    c. quiet engine operation
    d. an increase in engine rigidity.

chapter 12

Normal & Abnormal Combustion

The ignition timing and carburetor used on an engine are not arbitrarily selected, but rather their selection is based on the engine's requirements. When an engine is designed or redesigned, final engine requirements are measured using a dynamometer where the required engine timing and air/fuel mixture ratios are determined for each speed and power setting. Distributors and carburetors are selected and calibrated to meet engine requirements for both power and economy as indicated in dynamometer tests.

The power produced by an engine is the result of a series of individual combustions within the cylinders. When the best air/fuel ratio and best timing are used, each individual combustion chamber will produce its maximum effective pressure for the engine conditions existing at that moment.

Much is known about the combustion process, with variations that result from changes in engine design, changes in operating conditions, and changes in the use of different fuels. In spite of this, continual basic research is being carried on to better understand and control combustion so that engines may convert more of the fuel energy into useful work and produce longer engine service life. These objectives must often be modified to meet vehicle emission regulations.

The internal combustion engine is one of a number of heat engine types. Heat engines operate on thermodynamic principles, which are the processes involved in transformation of various forms of energy within gases. In the internal combustion engine, the fuel energy is converted to heat during combustion. This heat is transformed to useful work by expansion of the heated combustion gases that are trapped in the combustion chamber. Transformation processes involving heat can be expressed in terms of thermodynamic laws. They are presented here to provide the reader with a general introduction to the physical principles used in engine operation.

12-1 THERMODYNAMIC LAWS

The first law of thermodynamics states that the total amount of energy in the world is constant. It may change from one "state" to another, but the energy is never lost. This is followed immediately by a second law that states that energy continually decreases in its ability to perform useful work. Heat energy in a gas always flows from a higher temperature to a lower temperature while doing work. This process is irreversible unless the work is done on a gas.

Keeping the first two laws in mind, Boyle's and Charles' laws are used to calculate the amount of change that occurs in the pressure, volume, and temperature of a gas as it does work or as work is done upon the gas. When using thermodynamic equations the pressure and temperature values must be in "absolute" scales. The absolute pressure (PSIA) is gauge pressure (PSIG) plus atmospheric pressure. The absolute temperature is the number of Fahrenheit degrees plus 459.6. This gives the absolute temperature value in degrees Rankin or °R.

Boyle's law states that as a given mass of gas expands, its pressure decreases. If no heat is added to or taken from the gas mass during this process, the initial volume multiplied by the initial pressure will be equal to the new volume times the new pressure, when using absolute unit values ($P_1V_1 = P_2V_2 = $ Constant) with no heat gained or lost. The

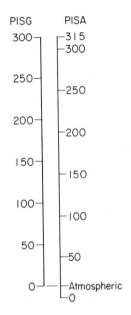

Fig. 12-1 Gauge pressure compared to atmospheric pressure.

mass of gas is usually expressed as its weight in pounds.

Charles' law is given in two parts. It relates temperature to either volume or pressure, with the other remaining constant. If the volume of a gas is held constant and heated, its pressure will increase. The ratio of initial temperature to final temperature, in degrees Rankin, will equal the ratio of initial pressure to final pressure when using absolute pressure values ($T_1/T_2 = P_1/P_2$). The pressure of a quantity of gas may be held constant by allowing the gas to expand while it is heated.

Fig. 12-2 Fahrenheit, Rankin and Centigrade temperature scales compared.

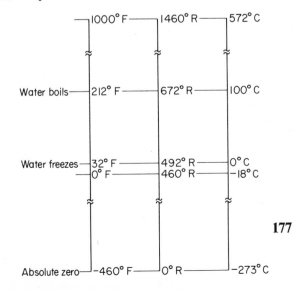

177

The ratio of the initial temperature of the gas to the final temperature in degrees Rankin will equal the ratio of the initial volume of the gas to the final volume ($T_1/T_2 = V_1/V_2$).

Boyle's and Charles' laws can be combined and are useful in the study of internal combustion engine operating processes. The combined law states that the initial pressure times the initial volume divided by the initial temperature is equal to the final pressure times the final volume divided by the final temperature ($P_1V_1/T_1 = P_2V_2/T_2 = $ Constant) when no heat is added to or removed from the system. This relationship always holds true for any gas and always equals the same value for a specific gas. This value is called the universal gas constant (R). It can be expressed for all gases in the formula $PV = wRt$, where w is the weight of one mole of the gas (1 mole = 379 cu ft under standard conditions). For air, the gas constant R is 53.37 ft-lb/lb-degree Rankin.

12-2 IDEAL CYCLE

The overall performance of the four-stroke cycle internal combustion engine is primarily determined by the events that occur in the cycle between intake valve closing and exhaust valve opening, while both valves are closed. The working gases become trapped in the cylinder, and are compressed, burned, and expanded. During this time, useful work is produced within the cylinder in sufficient amounts to carry the engine through the other strokes and still have power available for the output shaft.

When the intake valve closes, the gas charge is trapped in the combustion chamber, then compressed. The volume of this gas gets smaller as the piston moves up on the compression stroke, causing its pressure and temperature to increase according to thermodynamic laws. Toward the end of the compression stroke, ignition occurs. This starts as a flame front that burns across the trapped gases, converting the fuel energy to heat energy. Combustion is completed rapidly, with the piston slightly beyond top center, during the part of the cycle when there is very little change in the combustion chamber volume. Combustion releases heat from the

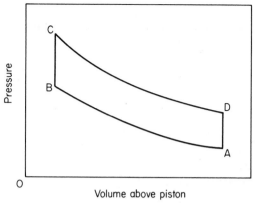

Fig. 12-3 Ideal cycle.

fuel which, in turn, increases the gas temperature. The high temperature gases increase combustion chamber pressure according to thermodynamic laws. This resulting high pressure is impressed on the top of the piston, forcing it downward against crankshaft resistance, to produce useful work.

The numerical value of the temperature, pressure and volume may be calculated for any instantaneous piston position using thermodynamic laws, if one assumes an ideal thermodynamic cycle condition where no heat is lost from the gases. In the ideal cycle, as shown in Figure 12-3, the air is compressed with no change in total heat (A–B). At the end of the compression stroke, combustion would take place with no change in volume, increasing the total heat in the gases and raising the temperature, resulting in a pressure rise (B–C). The piston would move downward, without a change in the new total heat within the gases, expanding the combustion chamber volume which, in turn, reduces the pressure and temperature of the gases (C–D). At the end of the power stroke, the spent gases are released, dropping cylinder pressure (D–A).

12-3 ACTUAL CYCLE

The actual cycle is somewhat different from the ideal cycle as a result of a number of modifying factors. Mechanical action of the valve mechanism makes it impossible to have instantaneous valve opening and closing. Combustion takes time and the piston cannot be stopped while combustion is allowed to occur; therefore, the fuel energy is released gradually. Another modifying factor is that the cylinder walls, which have a temperature higher than the gases at the beginning of the compression stroke, transfer heat from the walls to the gases at this time. During the combustion stroke, the cylinder walls are cooler than the gases and heat will then transfer from these gases to the cylinder walls. The working gas within the combustion chamber is not air, as assumed in the ideal cycle, but is a mixture of air, evaporated gasoline, water vapor, and some exhaust gases remaining from the previous cycle. During compression, and immediately after ignition, chemical reactions take place in the charge, thus the composition of the combustion gases is constantly changing during the cycle. All of these factors modify the ideal cycle so that the final result is the actual cycle.

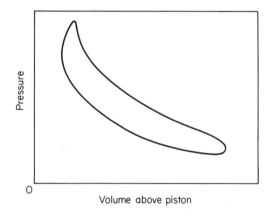

Fig. 12-4 Actual cycle pressure–volume curve.

Even with these many modifications of the ideal cycle, negligible error is involved in the assumption that the working medium approaches perfect gas conditions. This assumption is used to study the actual cycle of internal combustion engines.

Power produced by the engine crankshaft is approximately one-fourth of the total heat energy in the fuel. The rest of the fuel energy is used to operate the engine or is rejected through the cooling system and through the exhaust system. Operating losses result from engine friction, power required to operate the fuel, oil, and coolant pumps, as well as from intake and exhaust system pumping losses.

A brief description of the equipment required to measure cylinder pressure will help the reader to be aware of the components required to study combustion.

The actual pressure within a combustion chamber can be measured using a quartz piezoelectric crystal pickup mounted in a spark plug. The piezoelectric crystal signal is proportional to the pressure

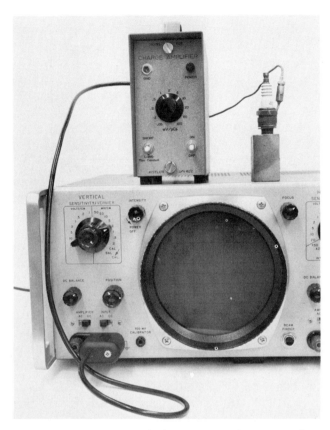

Fig. 12-5 Equipment required to measure the pressure in a running engine.

imposed upon it. This signal is amplified and fed into an oscilloscope. The oscilloscope line, called a trace, is triggered to start at a known point in the cycle, usually at the beginning of the compression stroke. The scope trace has a time base and its height is proportional to pressure. With proper equipment calibration, the exact pressure value may be observed on the oscilloscope grid. If the oscilloscope time base is synchronized with the engine rpm, the base becomes equivalent to crankshaft rotation degrees as well as time. A photograph of the resulting pressure-crank angle scope trace of a running engine may be used to determine actual combustion chamber pressure at any crank angle or point in the thermodynamic cycle. This trace is very useful in understanding what happens in the combustion chamber during normal and abnormal combustion.

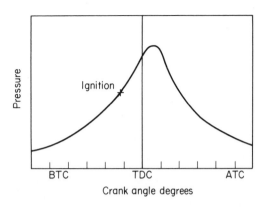

Fig. 12-6 Typical pressure-time diagram.

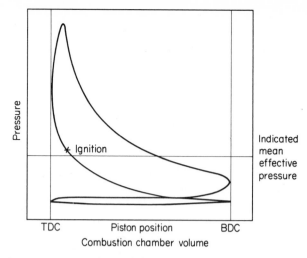

Fig. 12-7 Mean effective pressure of a typical combustion cycle.

The pressure-time or pressure-crank angle oscilloscope trace of an entire cycle can be replotted to form the frequently used pressure-volume diagram of the actual engine cycle. Consideration must be given to the piston position at each crank angle plot point when replotting the P-T curve to form the P-V curve. The detailed method of determining piston position has been described in Chapter 11.

It has been proven that the area under the trace is equivalent to work the gas force exerts on the piston during the stroke.

The actual pressure-volume trace can be placed on the oscilloscope face if the scope x-axis has a signal that is proportional to piston position. This usually requires an electro-mechanical device to indicate the piston position. Its electrical signal is then fed into the oscilloscope x-axis to show combustion chamber volume.

Pumping-loss work is required to pull the gases into the combustion chamber on the intake stroke and to force the spent gases out through the exhaust system. This negative work or operating loss is subtracted from the total positive work produced during the power stroke, to determine the net engine output. Under wide open throttle conditions, the *indicated mean effective pressure* (IMEP) is a pressure, that when applied to the piston area during one stroke, will do the work which is the net output of the positive combustion chamber pressure for one cycle. This can be determined through the use of the pressure-volume indicator diagram of the cycle from which it received its name. Brake mean effective pressure (BMEP) is derived from the brake

horsepower the engine delivers on a dynamometer. It is the net pressure that would be applied to the piston area to produce the brake horsepower actually being developed.

12-4 NORMAL COMBUSTION

A spark plug ignites the charge near the end of the compression stroke. The spark produced across the plug electrodes must have sufficient energy to raise the gas temperature between them to a temperature at which the charge burning becomes self-sustaining. From this point, a flame front moves smoothly across the combustion chamber during normal combustion. Charge burning will take place during approximately fifty degrees of crankshaft rotation. Actual combustion is much more complex than it first appears from this simplified description. In reality, the combustion gases go through many steps or phases during the combustion process. These processes may be divided into two types, *preflame reactions* and *combustion*.

A simple example is helpful in understanding preflame reactions. If one were to light a piece of paper with a match, the paper would first turn brown, then ignite, producing a flame. The charge in the combustion chamber reacts in a similar way. As the gases are compressed and the temperature rises, chemical reactions take place that change the character of the charge. These preflame reactions prepare the charge for burning.

After ignition takes place, the flame front moves out in a modified spherical fashion, depending upon combustion chamber turbulence. The heat energy

180

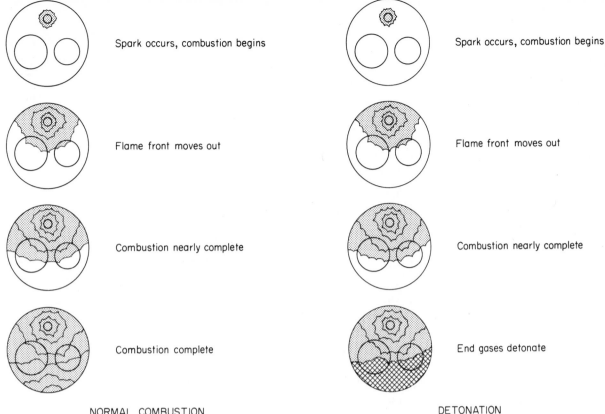

Spark occurs, combustion begins

Flame front moves out

Combustion nearly complete

Combustion complete

NORMAL COMBUSTION

Fig. 12-8 Flame front movement during normal combustion.

Spark occurs, combustion begins

Flame front moves out

Combustion nearly complete

End gases detonate

DETONATION

Fig. 12-9 Flame front movement during detonation.

released behind the flame front increases combustion chamber pressure and temperature. Higher combustion chamber pressure and temperature increase the preflame reactions in the charge, called the *end gases*, that remain ahead of the flame front. These reactions become more rapid at higher engine compression ratios. If the reactions increase too rapidly, abnormal combustion will result.

12-5 ABNORMAL COMBUSTION

Abnormal combustion may be divided into two main types—*knock* and *surface ignition*. Each of these types result in loss of power and in excessive temperature. Continued operation under either of these abnormal conditions will result in physical damage to the engine, as shown in Chapter 10.

Detonation. Engine knock or detonation is the result of rapid preflame reactions within the combustion chamber's highly-stressed end gases. The reactions become so rapid that spontaneous ignition of the end gases occurs. This results in very rapid combustion rates within the end gases that are accompanied by high-frequency pressure waves.

These waves impinge or hit on the combustion chamber walls and cause a vibration noise that is called knock.

The knock shows up on the pressure-degree scope trace, which is modified during knock conditions. Large and rapid cylinder pressure fluctuations are observed immediately after the normal peak pressure. The trace shows that knock takes place near the end of combustion just after maximum cylinder pressures have occurred. This causes a change in the crank angle where pressure occurs, thereby reducing engine power.

Fig. 12-10 Pressure-time diagram of detonation.

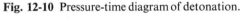
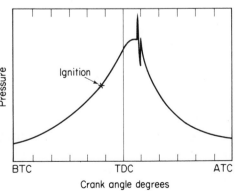

Reducing Detonation. The tendency for an engine to knock with any given fuel can be reduced by any method that will lower either or both combustion pressure and temperature, or one that will reduce the time the end gases are subjected to high pressures and temperatures. In addition, a change to a fuel that is less susceptible to rapid preflame reactions will reduce the engine's tendency to knock.

Compression ratio has a major effect on compression pressure. As the compression ratio is raised, the power that an engine is able to develope increases as the result of higher combustion pressures produced. These high pressures, however, cause a greater knock tendency. Fuels with high anti-knock properties will operate in higher compression ratio engines, thus allowing the engine to run knock free while developing high power. Lower compression ratios are required in low emission engines to run knock free on low octane unleaded gasoline.

Combustion chamber design also affects engine knock. Combustion chambers whose end gases are in a squash or quench area tend to have low knocking tendencies. This is because the end gases are thin and close to a cool metal surface. Cooling the gases causes a reduction and slowing of end gas preflame reactions and, thus, reduces the engine's tendency to knock. Combustion chamber turbulence is also useful in reducing an engine's knocking tendency by mixing cool and hot gases, thereby preventing a concentration of static end gases in which preflame reactions can take place rapidly.

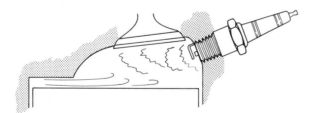

Fig. 12-11 End gases cooled in the quench area.

Surface Ignition. Abnormal combustion, called surface ignition, is a broad term that indicates any source of ignition other than the spark plug. The effect of surface ignition, because it produces a

secondary ignition source, is to complete the combustion process faster than normal. Here again, the result is to have maximum pressure occur at the wrong time in the cycle, causing the engine to develop less power.

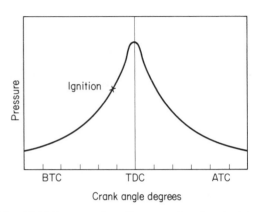

Fig. 12-12 Pressure-time diagram of surface ignition.

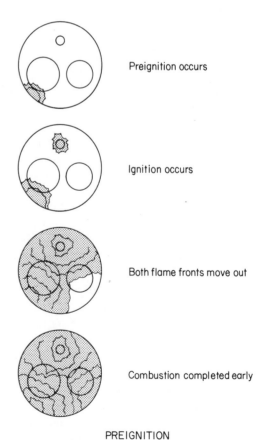

Preignition occurs

Ignition occurs

Both flame fronts move out

Combustion completed early

PREIGNITION

Fig. 12-13 Flame front movement during pre-ignition.

One source of secondary ignition is hot spots, such as spark plug electrodes, protruding gaskets, sharp valve edges, etc. These can become so hot during engine operation that they have enough heat energy to form a second source of ignition. These sources seldom occur in modern engine designs as long as the engines have proper maintenance.

Another source of secondary ignition is combustion chamber deposits. These deposits result from the type of fuel and oil used in the engine and from the type of engine operation. Fuel and lubricant suppliers have been doing extensive research to produce products that minimize deposit ignition. A deposit ignition source may be a hot loose deposit flake that ignites one charge and is then exhausted from the engine with the spent exhaust gases. This is called a *wild ping*. Sometimes, the flake will remain attached to the combustion chamber wall. When this happens, it will ignite successive charges until the deposit is consumed or engine operating conditions are changed. This type of ignition is called *deposit ignition*.

Names are given to many specific abnormal combustion conditions that are caused by surface ignition. If surface ignition occurs before the spark plug fires, it is called *pre-ignition*. It may be audible or inaudible. It may be a wild ping or it may be continuous runaway surface ignition. If it occurs after the ignition is turned off, it is called *run-on*.

Continuous pre-ignition can result in rapid engine damage, usually holes through the piston. Another phenomena resulting from pre-ignition is engine *rumble*. Rumble is a low frequency vibration of the lower part of the engine that occurs when the maximum pressure is reached in the cycle earlier than normal. Rumble first became evident as a problem when engine manufacturers were able to greatly increase engine compression ratios when high octane rating fuels became available. This allowed the manufacturer to improve engine power with minor engine changes and with little thought to increase the strength of the engine crankshaft and block. Corrective measures were taken in succeeding engine models; therefore, rumble has been nearly eliminated from modern engines.

It is interesting to note that knock-resistant fuels and anti-knock additives tend to increase combustion chamber deposits and, therefore, to increase the tendency to cause surface ignition. Fuel manufacturers have had to put additional additives in their fuel which will modify combustion chamber deposits in an attempt to reduce the deposit ignition tendency resulting from the anti-knock additive deposits.

Abnormal combustion seldom occurs in modern production automotive engines using the recommended grade of fuels and motor oils, with good engine maintenance. Some problems may exist in engines that are used exclusively for low-speed, short trip driving. Abnormal combustion frequently occurs in engines that are modified for maximum performance.

12-6 GASOLINE REQUIREMENTS

Gasoline for automobile engines must meet the engine's needs. It must be clean and non-corrosive to the fuel system parts. It must be light or volatile enough to allow vaporization at low temperatures,

Fig. 12-14 Apparatus used to check gasoline volatility by distillation.

so that the engine may be started, but not so volatile that it will vaporize in the fuel lines, causing vapor lock and thus preventing fuel flow. It also must not be so heavy that it will not be burned in the combustion chamber. If this happens, the unburned fuel will run down the cylinder wall, washing the lubricating oil from the wall and diluting the motor oil. The fuel's volatility property is measured by a standard distillation test. In the distillation test, a 100 milliliter (ml) sample is heated in a distillation flask. The vapors are led through a condenser and the condensate is collected in a 100 ml graduated cylinder. The temperatures of the vapors in the flask are recorded as each 10 ml is collected in the cylinder. The temperature-recovery curve is plotted on a distillation graph. The most volatile parts of the gasoline will evaporate at the lowest temperature, while the less volatile parts evaporate at higher temperatures. Motor fuel distillation range falls approximately between 90°F and 400°F. The distillation curve is nearly the same for all motor gasolines, regardless of the grade or brand. The volatility of all gasoline grades is adjusted several times a year, as the weather and temperature are expected to change. Volatility is increased as the minimum expected temperature decreases during winter months and decreased as the minimum expected temperature increases in the summer.

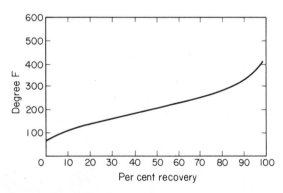

Fig. 12-15 Typical distillation graph.

Octane Number. The primary difference between grades of gasoline is their anti-knock quality. Premium brands are made from selected refinery stock and often contain additional anti-knock additives.

Test	Premium	Regular
Api°	63.2	62.6
Sulfur	0.025	0.041
Gum mg/100 ml	1	1
Lead 9/gal	2.72	2.20
Research octane	99.9	94.8
Motor octane	92.0	86.4
RVP	12.4	12.2
Initial boiling pt.	81	84
5	91	95
10	107	106
20	131	125
30	158	149
50	211	200
70	251	258
90	322	337
95	356	368
End	405	408

Fig. 12-16 Specifications for premium and regular motor gasoline.

They have a higher octane rating than regular grades. The octane rating is a scale that indicates the gasoline's resistance to knock or detonation.

The fuel octane number is determined in a standardized, single-cylinder, variable compression fuel research engine. The engine is first adjusted to standard conditions while operating on a reference fuel. Under these standard conditions, the knock meter (peak pressure measurement meter) is adjusted to mid-scale. The sample fuel to be tested is then run in the engine under the same standard conditions as the reference fuel. The fuel mixture is adjusted to produce maximum knock and the compression ratio is adjusted to produce the standard knock meter reading. While keeping all conditions constant, the engine is then run on *reference fuel* blends, one blend with slightly higher knock and one blend with slightly lower knock than the sample being tested. The sample fuel is assigned an octane number between the two reference blends that bracket the sample's knock meter reading. One primary reference fuel (PRF), *iso-octane*, has been assigned 100 as an octane number and the other primary reference fuel, *n-heptane*, has been assigned 0 as an octane number. A blend of these primary reference fuels is given as the percentage of iso-octane in n-heptane of that blend. For example, if the PRF blend contained 95% iso-octane and 5% n-heptane, the blend will have a 95 octane rating. Octane numbers above 100 octane can be tested by adding tetraethyl lead to iso-octane to make reference fuel blends above 100 octane. Different reference fuel blends necessary to "bracket" the sample fuel can be easily selected by referring to a table based on compression ratio that shows the approximate octane number.

Two different fuel research engines and test procedures are used to test motor fuels. One is called the Research Method and the other is called the Motor Method. The Research Method engine ' is run at 600 rpm with the inlet air temperature adjusted to compensate for barometric pressures. The Motor Method engine is run at 900 rpm while holding the mixture temperature at 300°F. Gasoline will produce a different octane number by each test method, as shown in Figure 12-16. The Research Method usually gives a higher octane number than the Motor Method. The difference between these two octane numbers is called the fuel's "sensitivity." The sensitivity of the fuel is the result of the type of petroleum stock from which the gasoline was made.

Octane Number Requirements. Gasoline has an octane number rating and each engine has a minimum *octane requirement* below which it will not run knock-free. The octane number requirement of the engine is the result of the engine's combustion chamber design, the operating mean effective pressure, the humidity, the temperature, and the deposits present in the combustion chamber.

Two types of tests are used to measure engine octane number requirement. The Modified Uniontown procedure is a test to check the engine for best customer satisfaction. This is done by determining the minimum octane required under the most severe operating conditions of the fuel and engine combination. The Modified Borderline procedure tests the engine throughout its operating range and can be duplicated on a number of fuel samples. The Cooperative Research Council (CRC) selects samples of automobiles each year to determine their octane requirements. CRC uses both test procedures to report engine octane requirements.

Details of these two tests are different; however, they do have a common technique. In both tests, the engine is operated on the sample fuel at specified speeds, using specified ignition timing. The knock intensity is determined by ear and is reported as borderline, trace, moderate, or heavy knock.

In these road tests, the engine is operated on a primary reference fuel blend (iso-octane and

Fig. 12-17 Engine and instruments used to check the octane rating of gasoline.

Knock Test

Condition	Research	Motor
* Engine speed	600	900
Oil temperature	135	135
Coolant temperature	212	212
Intake humidity 9r/lb air	25–50	25–50
* Intake air temperature	125	100
* Mixture temperature	—	300
* Spark advance	13	varies with CR
Fuel/air ratio	adj for max knock	adj for max knock

Fig. 12-18 Engine operation specifications for rating gasoline octane number.

n-heptane) that is close to the octane number requirement expected. If the engine knocks more than required by the test procedure, the octane number of the reference fuel blend is raised. If it knocks less than required, the reference fuel blend is lowered. The engine's octane number requirement is equivalent to the primary reference fuel blend that gives specified knock intensity required by the test procedure.

Review Questions
Chapter 12

1. What are the first and second laws of thermodynamics?

2. What is meant by absolute pressure and temperature?

3. What is the universal gas constant for air?

4. Describe normal combustion.

5. What modifications convert the ideal cycle to the actual cycle?

6. The crank angle is not directly proportional to piston position. Why is this so in spark-ignited engines?

7. How does time affect the end gas preflame reactions?

8. How can turbulence reduce knocking tendency?

9. What might be the result of putting too many anti-knock additives in the gasoline?

10. How does proper maintenance prevent abnormal combustion?

11. What is the greatest difference in motor gasoline grades?

12. How is 90 octane primary reference fuel made?

13. How can fuel be tested above 100 octane?

14. How does octane requirement differ from octane number?

Quiz 12

1. Thermodynamics is a study of the
   a. action of a thermometer
   b. moving heat
   c. action of the pistons moving after combustion
   d. transfer of heat energy.

2. Engine power is produced in the combustion chamber by
   a. expanding gases
   b. an explosion of the induction charge
   c. high temperatures
   d. the air/fuel ratio and ignition.

3. How much of the gasoline's total heat energy is transferred into useful work by the engine?
   a. 25%   b. 50%   c. 75%   d. 100%

4. An oscilloscope is used in combustion studies to show
   a. secondary ignition output
   b. combustion chamber pressure
   c. actual combustion temperatures
   d. instantaneous air/fuel ratios.

5. A P–V curve shows the
   a. positive value of the gasoline
   b. partial vacuum in the manifold
   c. actual engine cycle
   d. engine power produced.

6. Excessive preflame reactions result in
   a. pre-ignition   c. rumble
   b. detonation   d. wild ping.

7. Detonation occurs
   a. during the early part of combustion
   b. just before the middle of combustion
   c. just after the middle of combustion
   d. near the end of combustion.

8. Engine starting ability and fuel distribution are based on the fuel's
   a. octane number
   b. octane requirement
   c. volatility
   d. vapor pressure.

9. The primary difference between motor gasoline grades is
   a. octane number
   b. octane requirements
   c. volatility
   d. vapor pressure.

10. The motor octane number of gasoline is checked by
    a. distillation
    b. operation on a road test
    c. a fuel research engine
    d. using the modified borderline procedure.

chapter 13

Automotive Engine Carburetors

The automobile engine carburetor is only a part of the automobile's fuel system. The rest of the fuel system consists of a fuel storage tank, and a fuel transfer system combining a fuel pump, fuel filter, and connecting lines. The fuel system is required to keep an adequate fuel supply at the carburetor inlet at all times. An air filter is used to admit only clean air and an evaporative emission system is designed to keep gasoline vapors contained within the vehicle.

The carburetor is designed to mix the air and fuel in proper proportions to provide the correct air/fuel mixture for the operating conditions. It does this by sensing the operator's demands and the engine needs through differences in pressure at various points within the carburetor. The sensing pressure at these points is called a pressure *signal*. It is used to control the proper amount of fuel that is fed into the incoming air flow.

The air/fuel mixture leaves the carburetor as a mixture of air full of extremely small liquid fuel droplets, similar to liquid paint coming from a paint spray gun. These extremely small droplets are called *atomized fuel*. Most of the atomized fuel evaporates as it flows through the manifold from the carburetor to the combustion chamber to provide a combustible air/fuel mixture vapor.

The carburetor is equipped with a number of specialized circuits to cover the wide range of air flow and air/fuel mixture demands. An idling engine needs a low air flow with a rich air/fuel mixture. At cruising the engine requires a moderate air flow and lean air/fuel mixture. During high speed conditions the engine uses a large air flow with a rich air/fuel mixture. The carburetor meets these requirements and the additional requirement of providing short periods of rich air/fuel mixtures for starting and acceleration.

13-1 CARBURETION REQUIREMENTS

Engine fuel needs are first determined at idle, cruise, and full power, then a carburetor is designed to meet them. The carburetor must supply the correct quality air/fuel mixture to the engine in a quantity that will meet the operator's demands between idle speeds and full throttle. It must match the engine's needs to the operator's demands so that the engine will develop the power that the operator requires. It must do this as economically as possible. These basic engine fuel requirements are modified to help the engine meet emission regulations.

Fuel Ratio Requirements. In most spark-ignited engines, the air and fuel are mixed and delivered to the combustion chamber as a combustible mixture. Combustible air/fuel mixtures range from 8:1 to 20:1 by weight. The ideal mixture is 14.8:1 in which the oxygen contained in the air is the correct amount to burn the entire quantity of fuel. This is a *stoichiometric* mixture. Internal combustion engines normally operate on air/fuel ratios between 11.5:1 (rich) and 15:1 (lean), except at idle where mixtures may go as rich as 9.5:1 for cars built before 1968. For later models this figure is 14:1.

Engine power results from expansion of the combustion chamber gases. In order to insure maximum expansion that will produce maximum

power, it is necessary to have enough fuel to use all of the oxygen from the air. Fuel mixture ratios of approximately 12:1 provide this rich mixture at high power settings.

To get maximum economy from an engine, all of the fuel must be burned so that the maximum amount of energy is released. In this case, an air/fuel ratio of 14.8:1 or leaner is used.

Fuel distribution in the manifolds at idle is poor because low gas velocities allow fuel dropout. Rich mixtures are delivered by the carburetor so the leanest cylinders will still receive a combustible mixture. Other cylinders, of course, receive an excessively rich mixture under idle conditions. Uneven mixture between cylinders will cause rough engine idle. Engines that are designed for minimum exhaust emissions run on leaner air/fuel ratios and higher engine idle speeds than engines without emission controls.

It makes no difference if an engine is carbureted or fuel-injected, the engine still needs the same fuel mixture ratios. Fuel-injected engines that discharge their fuel close to the intake valve have more even mixture ratios between cylinders than carbureted engines because fuel injection does not depend upon air velocity and air/fuel mixing in the manifold to deliver the fuel to the cylinder.

The carburetor or fuel injector supplies a rich mixture for idle, a lean mixture for cruising conditions, and a rich mixture for power and high speed operation. The air/fuel ratio compared to the air

Fig. 13-1 Typical air/fuel ratio graph. Line A is cruising, line B is full throttle and line C is engine vacuum.

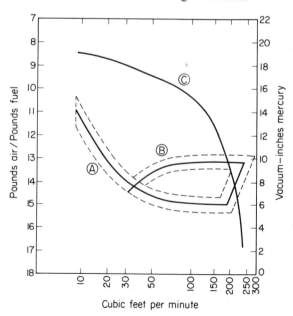

flow into the engine would be plotted as Curve A in Figure 13-1. A full throttle air/fuel ratio would appear as Curve B.

The actual carburetor or fuel injection system is built to a tolerance so mixture ratios will fall near the ideal, within a flow band, as shown by the dotted lines. Emission carburetors are held to very close tolerance. After assembly, production carburetors are checked on a flow bench that will measure air and fuel flow at a number of vacuum settings. These are checked against a master graph that looks similar to Figure 13-1.

If a carburetor were to run *rich* beyond the tolerance, power would fall off and the engine would use excessive fuel. The unburned fuel may foul spark plugs and, in extreme cases, dilute the oil on the cylinder walls which, in turn, would cause excessive cylinder and ring wear. If the carburetor were to run *lean* beyond the tolerance, power would also fall off. Lean mixtures cause misfiring, along with high localized temperatures that often cause pre-ignition and detonation. Eventually, excessively lean mixtures produce burned spark plugs and valves.

Additional Considerations. The foregoing discussion assumes the engine is operating at a constant speed under a constant load. This is called a *steady state*. Additional devices are required to provide correct mixtures for driveable engine operation in a passenger car. While cranking, air flow in the engine is very slow and the fuel is not broken into the desirable small droplets. Therefore, it will evaporate slowly. A *choke* is installed to provide a very rich mixture so that enough of the volatile portion of gasoline will evaporate to produce a combustible mixture to ignite for starting.

The carburetor or fuel injection system is required to supply small droplets of finely divided fuel to the intake air in the correct proportions to meet the engine's requirements. The liquid fuel evaporates from the surface of the atomized droplets. Smaller or finer droplets increase the evaporation rate. For maximum volumetric efficiency, about sixty per cent of the fuel should be evaporated between the fuel discharge nozzle and the cylinder.

When the engine is cold, manifold evaporation is slow and the engine oil is thick; therefore, more energy is required to keep the engine running. To keep the engine running until it becomes warm, the throttle is held slightly open with a device called

a *fast idle cam*. This fast idle cam is usually controlled by a linkage from the choke, so the cam will be released as the choke opens.

The throttle is opened suddenly to produce rapid acceleration. Air, with its low mass per unit volume, will start to flow much more quickly than the heavier fuel, leaning the mixture. Carburetors are equipped with a device called an *accelerator pump* which provides extra fuel for a few seconds after the throttle is opened until fuel can start to flow in the normal carburetor systems.

Fuel injection systems are not standard on passenger car engines and are, therefore, beyond the scope of this discussion. It should be remembered, however, that fuel injection systems still must provide an air/fuel mixture ratio that the engine needs, just as a carburetor is required to do.

Carburetor Pressures. The air/fuel mixture delivered by a carburetor is controlled by differential pressures and different sized or metered openings for fuel and for air. To operate a carburetor correctly, it is necessary to establish base line fuel and air pressures. The base line fuel pressure is established by the fuel level in the carburetor float bowl and the base line air pressure is atmospheric pressure. As the pistons go down on their intake stroke, manifold pressure is lowered or depressed. To say it another way, vacuum is increased. Any increase in engine speed while keeping a set throttle position will increase the engine manifold vacuum. It should be noted that under these conditions, the engine manifold vacuum is an indication of the engine's efficiency. With a fixed throttle and load, any change in ignition timing or fuel mixture that results in an increase in engine speed indicates more efficient combustion. Conversely, any decrease in vacuum indicates a decrease in engine efficiency. This difference in pressure between atmospheric and manifold is the driving force that causes the air/fuel mixture to flow into the carburetor.

Air velocity through the large carburetor opening called a barrel is the result of atmospheric pressure forcing air into the partial vacuum that is within the manifold. The greater the difference between atmospheric pressure and manifold vacuum,

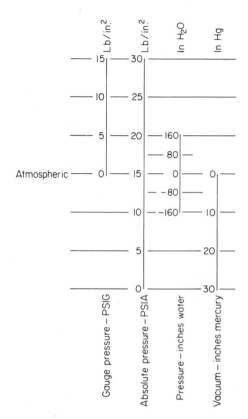

Fig. 13-2 A table relating gauge pressure, absolute pressure, vacuum, and water pressure.

the greater the air flow and the pressure forces within the carburetor.

Differential pressures create the *signals* within a carburetor that are used to control fuel flow into the air stream which, in turn, will create the air/fuel mixture needed. The quantity of fuel that flows through the sized carburetor fuel openings, called jets, is the direct result of jet size, jet shape, and difference in pressure between the upstream and downstream side of the jet.

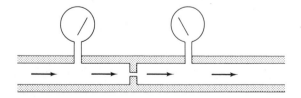

Fig. 13-3 Pressure drops as fluid flows through an orifice.

A throttle plate is placed in the base of the barrel between the carburetor and the manifold so that the passage may be effectively closed. With the throttle nearly closed, atmospheric pressure cannot fill the manifold as rapidly as the pistons evacuate it, so the engine has a high vacuum that may also be called a *pressure depression*. As the throttle is opened, air enters the manifold, increasing velocity and decreasing vacuum. At wide open throttle, vacuum is very low and air velocity through the carburetor is very high. Air, moving at high velocity, causes pressure reduction within the air flow.

Fuel Pump. Fuel is delivered from the fuel tank to the carburetor by a fuel pump. The inlet stroke of the fuel pump diaphragm is operated by a cam through a spring-loaded linkage. Fuel comes in from the tank through a one-way inlet check valve. It is forced out toward the carburetor through an outlet check valve by a spring-loaded diaphragm. The amount of fuel pressure impressed on the carburetor is controlled by fuel pump spring calibration.

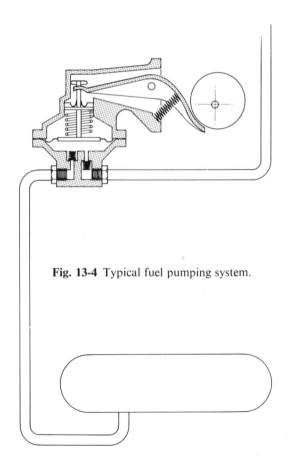

Fig. 13-4 Typical fuel pumping system.

13-2 CARBURETION PRINCIPLES

The following discussion will describe carburetor operation, adding units as a need for them is shown. Carburetor system designs to be presented apply to high-volume domestic production automotive carburetors.

Simple Carburetor-Main System. Air flowing through the carburetor must pass a restriction in the barrel called a *venturi* which increases inlet air velocity at the narrow portion or throat. This high velocity is accompanied by a lower pressure within the air stream. The change in pressure which results from the high velocity air flow is used as one of the signals to help meter the fuel flow.

The simplest carburetor consists of a float and valve system, a float bowl to hold the gasoline, an air horn with a venturi, a throttle plate to control the air flow to the carburetor, a fuel passage between the float bowl (fuel reservoir) and the venturi, and a metering jet for controlling fuel flow. In this simple carburetor, the discharge nozzle and venturi must be located *above* the fuel level, so the fuel will not drop out of the nozzle when the engine is not running.

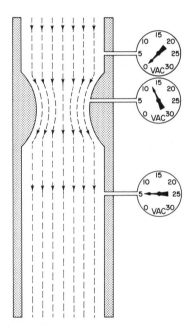

Fig. 13-5 Changes in pressure as air flows through the venturi.

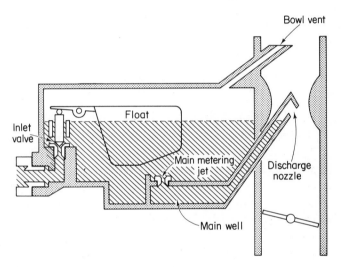

Fig. 13-6 A simple carburetor.

The amount of fuel allowed to enter the carburetor is controlled by a float inlet valve and seat. It maintains a constant fuel level in the carburetor float bowl by opening or closing the inlet valve. This specified fuel level establishes the base line fuel height or pressure head within the carburetor used for fuel flow control. Differential pressure that results from engine vacuum and high velocity air flow through the barrel air horn and venturi provides the signal required to force the correct quantity of fuel through metering devices within the carburetor.

In simple carburetor operation, air flows into the manifold as the throttle plate is opened. The air flow reduces pressure in the venturi. Atmospheric pressure, acting on the fuel through a vent in the float bowl forces some of the fuel through the metering jet into the main well and out the discharge nozzle that is within the narrow portion of the venturi. This fuel mixes with the air as it is carried into the manifold.

The main metering jet is sized so that the air/fuel ratio delivered to the manifold is within a combustible range. As the throttle plate is opened still further, more air flows through the venturi, lowering pressure further. This causes more fuel to flow, thus maintaining a combustible air/fuel mixture ratio.

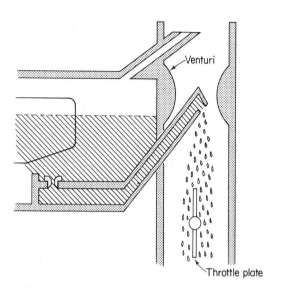

Fig. 13-7 Fuel flow from the carburetor nozzle.

This simple carburetor would have limited use, because it has a narrow range of operation. The air/fuel ratios do not remain constant, as has been suggested, because fuel, like other liquids, has mass, surface tension, and adhesion. Surface tension causes the fuel to hold together in large droplets, rather than breaking up into fine droplets that are necessary for rapid evaporation. Adhesion, which is the tendency of a liquid to cling to a surface, causes the fuel to break away from the discharging nozzle in large droplets. The viscosity of the fuel tends to restrict its flow.

In a simple carburetor, the pressure drops faster in the venturi than the increase in air volume,

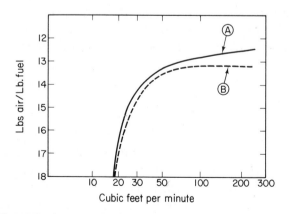

Fig. 13-8 Simple carburetor air/fuel curve A modified by a compensating air bleed to curve B.

so that the mixture gradually becomes richer as air flow increases. All automotive carburetors have some type of compensating device to correct for this enriching tendency. The most common of these devices is an air bleed.

An air bleed is a metered hole in the air horn above a passage leading to the main well. When low pressure exists at the discharge nozzle, air enters the main well through the air bleed. Here, air and fuel mix as they go from the main well to the discharge nozzle. This mixture of air and fuel causes the fuel to be broken into a sudsy air/fuel emulsion and reduces adhesion of the fuel to the passage walls. This occurs because the surface tension and viscosity of the mixture are less than fuel alone. Air coming in the air bleed will also reduce the enriching effect of a plain discharge nozzle as shown as line B in Figure 13-8. The effect of surface tension and adhesion is reduced when using an air bleed so the air/fuel ratio will remain constant when correct size air bleeds are selected.

Many carburetors add a perforated tube in the main well or a perforated air well adjacent to the main well. Air may bleed through the perforated tube either from the outside inward or from the inside outward, depending on the particular carburetor design. The amount of fuel flow into the main well is determined by the main jet size and design, and by the fuel level in the well. When the discharge nozzle rapidly draws fuel, the fuel level in the main well is lowered because the main jet cannot supply it fast enough. Holes in the main well tube compensator are gradually uncovered as fuel is drawn from the main well. This will let more air into the main well as fuel flow discharge increases. This compensates for the plain discharge nozzle normal enrichment as well as helping to atomize the fuel being discharged into the air stream.

Air bleeds are sometimes designed to act as an anti-percolator. When a hot engine is turned off, the engine heat will warm the carburetor. This causes the volatile portion of the fuel to boil or percolate, vaporizing that part of the gasoline within the carburetor. It is vented through the anti-percolator rather than building up pressure that would force raw fuel out of the discharge nozzle, flooding the manifold. A properly placed air bleed will allow these vapors to be vented into the air horn, thus minimizing flooding and hot-start problems. Bowl vents, often mechanically opened when the throttle

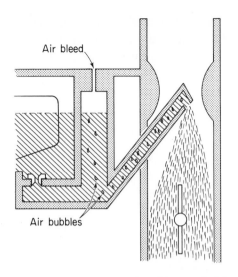

Fig. 13-9 Fuel flow from a nozzle with an air bleed compensator.

Fig. 13-10 Fuel level change in the main well as air flow increases through the venturi.

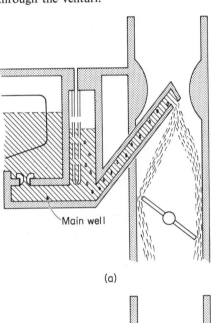

(a)

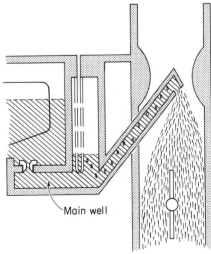

(b)

is closed, will allow bowl vapors to vent outside the carburetor rather than pushing fuel out of the discharge nozzle. This helps to reduce hot-start problems, but it does add to overall vehicle emissions. Evaporative emission control carburetors have the float bowl vented to a vapor absorption system which will trap evaporative emissions.

Idle System. The carburetor main system previously described will allow an engine to run with correct mixtures at cruising speeds. When the engine is slowed, air velocity through the venturi will reduce. At some point, fuel delivery will decrease rapidly, the mixture will lean beyond a combustible mixture and the engine will stop. To maintain engine operation at low speeds, an idle and low speed system must be included in the carburetor.

Fuel for the idle system is usually taken from the main well up a passage to a point above the fuel level. The passage is often an *idle tube* that extends into the main well passage. In some carburetors, this idle tube has a metered orifice at its lower end. Usually, an idle air bleed is provided at the upper point.

Fig. 13-11 Typical mechanically opened float bowl vents.

The *idle air bleed* serves two functions. The first is similar to the main air bleed because it adds air to the fuel to reduce its viscosity and helps to atomize it. Its second function is that of a "syphon breaker". With the idle discharge nozzle located below the fuel level, fuel would continue to flow when it wasn't needed if a syphon breaker was not used. The air bleed at the highest point in the idle system serves this syphon breaking function. In some model carburetors, the idle air bleed will also help as an anti-percolator device when the engine is stopped, by providing a means to allow vapors to vent into the air horn.

From the idle air bleed, fuel is led down a passage past an idle restriction to a port or opening just below the throttle plate, where high vacuum exists as the engine is idling. Atmospheric pressure in the carburetor bowl pushes idle fuel through the main jet into the main well, up the idle tube where it picks up additional air at the air bleed, then down the passage through the idle restriction and out into the vacuum below the throttle plate.

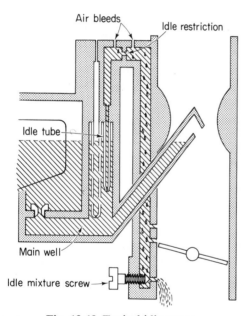

Fig. 13-12 Typical idle system.

The engine requires a correct air/fuel mixture in sufficient volume to operate at its normal idle speed. The required air volume is supplied by the amount of the air passage opening around the throttle plate. The fuel quantity is controlled by a manually adjusted tapered idle needle fuel screw. This screw is usually located in an opening or idle port below the throttle plate. As the needle is screwed into the port, fuel is restricted and the mixture leans. As the

needle is backed out of the port, the effective port size is enlarged and the mixture enriched. The fuel control screw adjusts engine idle smoothness.

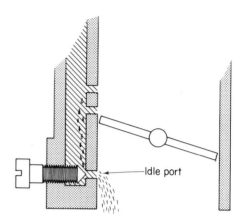

Fig. 13-13 Air and fuel flow at idle.

As the throttle moves off idle, vacuum acting on the idle port is reduced so that less fuel is supplied. This would result in a lean mixture. To eliminate this leaning problem, additional ports, called *transfer ports*, are placed between the idle passage and the carburetor throat in the barrel just above the throttle plate. At idle, these transfer ports act as additional air bleeds because they are exposed to atmospheric pressure above the throttle plate. As the throttle is opened, the transfer ports are exposed to high air velocity that flows around the throttle plate and to the vacuum below it. The vacuum and velocity will draw fuel from these transfer ports as well as from the idle port, providing the necessary additional mixture for transition from the idle system to the main system.

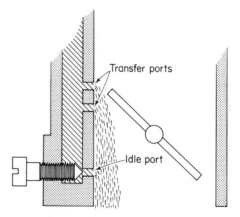

Fig. 13-14 Air and fuel flow during transition.

Power System. More mixture volume is required to produce more power. Maximum power also requires a rich air/fuel mixture. Carburetors can be designed to provide main system air/fuel ratios for economy cruise conditions or for maximum power, by correctly sizing fuel jets and air bleeds. Most carburetor main system air/fuel ratios are designed for economical cruising conditions, so they need a *power system* to provide the air/fuel ratio required at full throttle. Some carburetor main systems, however, are designed to provide air/fuel ratios for full power. These carburetors need an *economizer system* to lean the fuel ratio at cruising conditions. Whether the system is called a power system or an economizer, it will provide lean mixtures for cruising speeds and rich mixtures for high power, as shown by the curve in Figure 13-1.

Power systems have a metering device that allows additional fuel to flow into the main well. The additional fuel raises the fuel level in the main well so that the venturi vacuum won't have to lift the fuel as high. A higher fuel level allows more fuel to be discharged, thus producing a richer air/fuel mixture.

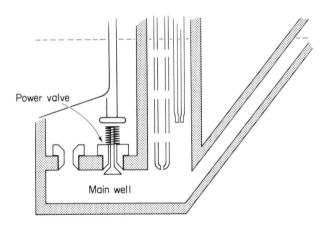

Fig. 13-15 Typical power valve.

The power system is put into operation as the engine vacuum drops to a specified value, about five inches of mercury, or as the throttle is opened to a pre-determined position, about sixty degrees. Some carburetors combine both vacuum and mechanical sensing systems to operate the power jet. Most current model automotive carburetors, however, use vacuum sensing alone.

Carburetors that have four barrels use two primary barrels during idle, transfer, and cruising conditions. Under power conditions, the secondary barrels are also opened to provide additional air/fuel mixture volume. These work along with the power system of the primary barrels to deliver an adequate quantity of air/fuel mixture for high power engine operation.

Acceleration Systems. At cruising speeds, fuel entering the cylinder is composed of vapors, atomized fuel, and liquid fuel. During low speed cruising operation, the engine runs with a high manifold vacuum and a reduced air flow. This running condition allows the manifold to become warm. The high vacuum and high temperature causes liquid fuel to completely evaporate, so that the manifold runners become dry.

When the throttle is suddenly opened, the first liquid fuel delivered will wet the manifold runner walls. Only the vapors and atomized fuel reach the cylinder. Since the fuel mass does not start to move as rapidly as air, the main system is slow to operate during sudden acceleration. These conditions produce a temporary leanness that will cause a misfiring often called *stumble*. Automotive carburetors are provided with an accelerating pump to inject additional fuel into the manifold to compensate for this initial lean mixture.

An engine, represented by Figure 13-17, is to be accelerated from A to D. While running at point A, the accelerator is opened to provide wide open throttle (WOT). The acceleration pump supplies

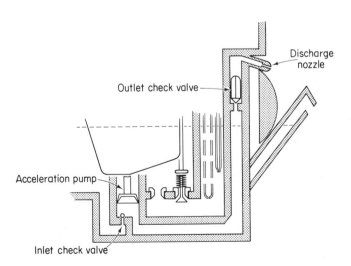

Fig. 13-16 Typical acceleration pump system.

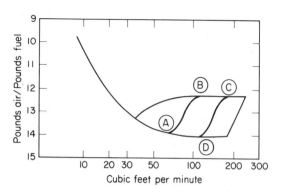

Fig. 13-17 Air/fuel ratio during acceleration from point A to point D.

added fuel to bring the mixture up to point B. The power system carries the engine to point C, at which time the accelerator is reduced to road load. The air/fuel curve returns to point D, which is the desired new road load condition.

The acceleration pump consists of an expanding and contracting chamber. The chamber is connected to the float bowl through an inlet check valve device. Its outlet is connected to an acceleration pump discharge nozzle through an outlet check valve and passage. When the throttle is closed, the chamber expands. This pulls the outlet check valve onto its seat and pulls the inlet valve off its seat, allowing fuel to enter the chamber from the float bowl. When the throttle is opened, the inlet check valve is forced against its seat and the outlet check is forced off its seat, allowing fuel to be injected into the air stream through the acceleration pump discharge nozzle. Under steady state engine operating conditions, the acceleration pump chamber is at rest and no fuel will flow. This requires a firm seating outlet check valve so that fuel is not pulled through the system by manifold vacuum or high velocity air flow.

Choke Circuit. Because of the low rate of fuel vaporization at low temperatures, the carburetor must deliver a very rich fuel mixture during a cold start so that there is sufficient fuel vapor available to produce a combustible mixture at the cylinders. The choke circuit in the carburetor provides this enrichment.

A choke plate is installed on a shaft in the air horn above the venturi. During cold starts, the choke is closed so that engine vacuum is impressed on the main discharge nozzle as well as on the idle ports. This pulls fuel from both systems until the mixture is rich enough to allow the engine to start. Two different methods may be used to close the choke prior to starting, a manual method and an automatic method. Most automotive carburetors use automatic chokes.

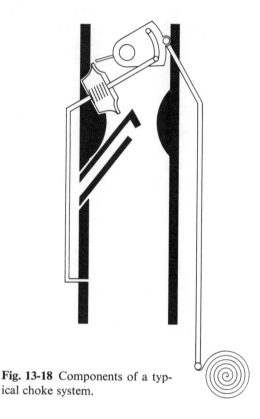

Fig. 13-18 Components of a typical choke system.

An automatic choke has a heat-sensing bimetallic spring that places a closing force on the choke linkages as the spring cools. When the driver is ready to start a cold engine, he depresses the accelerator, then removes his foot from the pedal. This releases the choke linkages and the choke immediately closes. The linkage is designed to keep the choke plate nearly closed until the engine starts. If some problem other than lack of fuel prevents the engine from starting, the engine will flood. To correct a flooded engine, the throttle linkage is provided with a device called an *unloader*, which slightly opens the choke when the throttle is opened wide.

As soon as the engine starts, it requires additional air and less fuel. This air is provided by a partial choke plate opening. Two forces are used to open the choke plate against the bi-metal spring force. First, the choke shaft is off-centered on the choke plate. This results in a velocity-sensing unbalanced force in the opening direction. The second force opposing the bi-metal spring is a vacuum sensing variable displacement chamber that connects to the choke shaft through a linkage. Under light engine loads, high manifold vacuum provides a choke opening force through the vacuum chamber. Under heavy engine loads, manifold vacuum is low and the velocity high, so the offset choke plate forces the choke open. As the engine warms up, the bi-metallic spring force gradually weakens, allowing the choke to be progressively opened while still maintaining a combustible air/fuel ratio.

In a cold engine, the lubricating oil's viscosity is high. More energy is required to keep a cold engine running, so the carburetor throttle plate must be opened more than is normally required by warm engines at idle. Automotive carburetors are equipped with a *fast idle cam* that serves to hold the throttle partially open during warmup. The fast idle cam is operated by the choke through linkages. When the throttle is slightly depressed on a cold engine, the choke closes and this, in turn, pulls the fast idle cam into position. The cam will remain in the fast idle position as long as the throttle is not touched, even if the engine becomes warm and the choke opens completely. While driving during warmup, the fast idle cam will move to the required position for satisfactory idle speeds each time the throttle is opened. When the choke becomes fully open, the fast idle cam will completely release when the throttle is opened from its idle stop.

Return Check. Sudden throttle closing in some carburetor applications results in an abnormally high manifold vacuum. The light air quickly stops while the heavy fuel continues on toward the cylinder. This may cause a rich mixture and engine stalling. A device called a return check or anti-stall dashpot is used to eliminate this stalling problem. The return check is usually an air-vented diaphragm chamber or a fuel diaphragm that will catch the throttle linkage as it approaches its closed position. A vent in the diaphragm will dampen the throttle

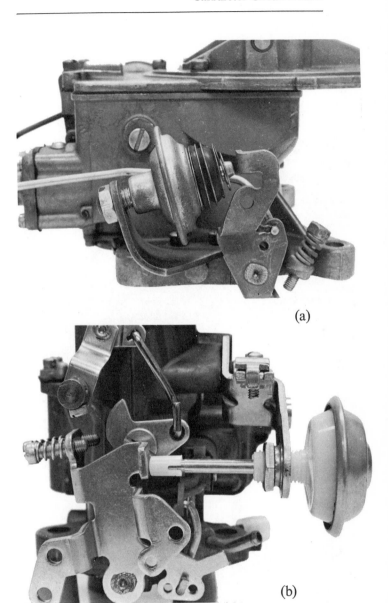

(a)

(b)

Fig. 13-19 Typical anti-stall dashpot or return checks.

end-closings by gradually allowing the throttle to close against the stop under controlled conditions. The return check is only used where carburetor-engine-vehicle combinations require its use.

13-3 CARBURETOR CIRCUIT DETAILS

Any make of carburetor used on one type of engine must supply the same air/fuel mixtures to meet the

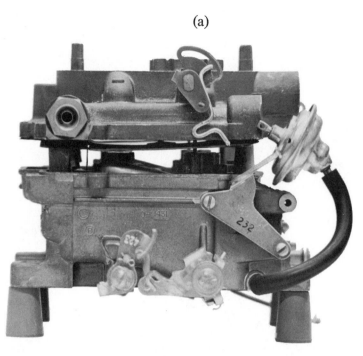

(a)

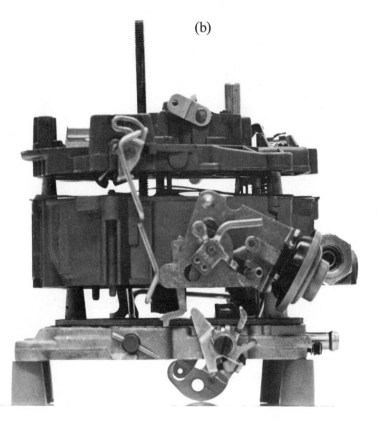

(b)

Fig. 13-20 Carburetor sections separated. (a) Two section carburetor, (b) three section carburetor.

engine's needs. Carburetor manufacturers use different construction methods and details in the carburetor circuits to provide the correct mixture.

Carburetor Materials. Carburetor parts are made from a number of types of materials. Generally, zinc alloys are used for the main float bowl body and the air horn cover. Lower throttle bodies are made of aluminum or cast iron. Mineral-filled phenolic resin has been used for a heat-insulating float bowl. Carburetor jets and internal rods are most often made of brass. Gaskets and seals are made from fuel-resistant fiber and synthetic rubber. Floats have historically been hollow sheet brass; however, lightweight fuel resistant plastic is gradually replacing brass as float material. Carburetor linkages and cams have been made of steel rods and stampings. Here again, some plastic parts are replacing metal parts.

There are a minimum number of standard carburetor body parts in each carburetor model. Different size drilling and jetting can make these standard parts into carburetors that are adaptable to different individual engine requirements. This is why many carburetors look alike, but are not inter-changeable between engine applications. Setting number tags attached to most carburetors are the key to the specific jetting and engine application.

Float and Needle Valve. Carburetors use a float to establish the operating fuel level, called *wet fuel level*, by opening and closing a needle-type inlet valve on a valve seat. The inlet valve tip is commonly made of a synthetic rubber-like elastomer material called Viton. The float must provide a force sufficient to close the valve against fuel pump pressure. Increases in fuel pump pressure will require a higher closing force to maintain the same wet fuel level. This can only be accomplished by sub-merging the float somewhat deeper by bending the float arms slightly. If the float mechanical position or *float level* is set without checking wet fuel level, it could actually lead to a high wet fuel level when fuel pump pressure is high or to a low wet fuel level when fuel pump pressure is low. A small spring pull clip often connects the float arm and float valve to aid in opening the float valve as the fuel level lowers.

Some carburetors have small float bowls and, consequently, small floats. The required float force

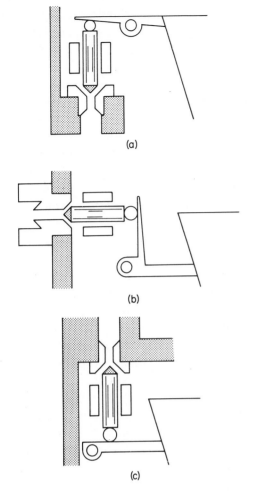

(a)

(b)

(c)

Fig. 13-21 Float bowl inlet valve types.

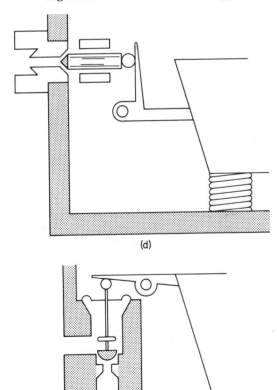

(d)

(e)

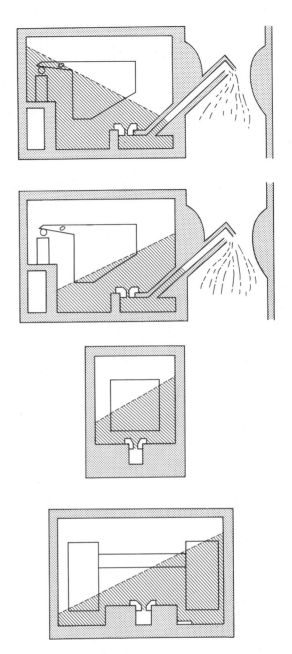

Fig. 13-22 Fuel action in the bowl as the vehicle is stopped quickly, accelerated rapidly, or turned violently.

alone is insufficient for adequate control so the float is aided by a spring, as shown in Figure 13-21d. Another type uses a partially balanced inlet valve. In each of these systems, the float adds the small additional force required to close the valve on its seat against fuel pump pressure.

The foregoing discussion has ignored vehicle dynamics. During operation, an automobile will be accelerated, decelerated and turned rapidly. It will also go up and down hills, tilting the engine.

199

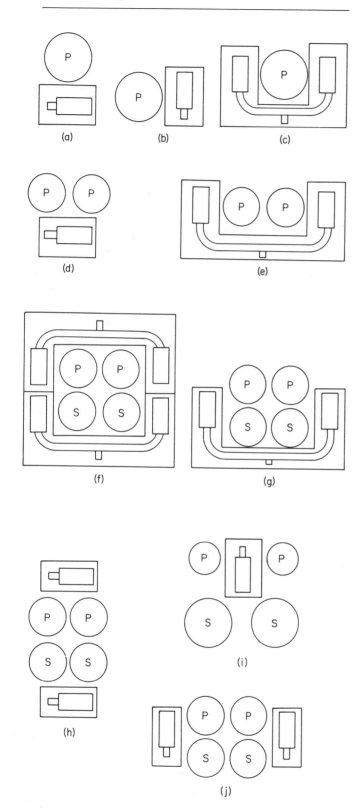

Fig. 13-23 Common carburetor barrel, float pontoon assembly and float bowl arrangements.

Fuel in the float bowl acts as any liquid in an enclosed container. During rapid acceleration, fuel will go to the back of the bowl. On braking, it goes to the front. On turns, it flows to the outside. The more violent the maneuver, the more the gasoline moves. The carburetor is designed so that the main jets are not uncovered during these maneuvers. It is also designed so the maneuvers do not flood the engine manifold by overflow from the main discharge nozzle. Floats and bowls are designed to minimize these effects by centering the metering units and by providing multiple small metering units.

Four-barrel carburetors may have one float and float bowl for the primary and another for the secondary barrels. Some carburetors use one float assembly to feed the primary and secondary pair on one side and another float assembly to feed the pair on the other side. Both single-pontoon and two-pontoon float assemblies are used. These may be located on the side of the carburetor or at front and rear. Another design uses a single centrally located float bowl with a single-pontoon float assembly for both primary and secondary barrels. A small float bowl will allow fuel to be controlled with less chance of fuel uncovering jets during violent maneuvers. The small bowl will also produce less percolation vapors when the engine is turned off. This, in turn, reduces hot start problems. A disadvantage for this small float bowl type occurs when the warm engine is stopped and fuel in the pump vaporizes. Upon attempted restart, the fuel in the bowl is exhausted before fuel pressure can be re-established while cranking.

Idle System. The idle fuel delivery system is called the *idle system*. As previously mentioned, the idle system takes fuel up a passage, usually through an idle tube with a restricting orifice or small metered opening at its lower end, to a passage above the fuel level where it meets an idle air bleed. Some carburetors have two idle air bleeds with a restriction between them to help meter idle fuel. The fuel is led down a passage past transfer ports to the mixture screws and idle ports. Two-barrel carburetors have a complete separate idle system for each barrel. All four-barrel carburetors have idle systems in each of the primary barrels. Some four-barrel carburetors also have a secondary idle system to aid in transition as the secondary throttle plates open.

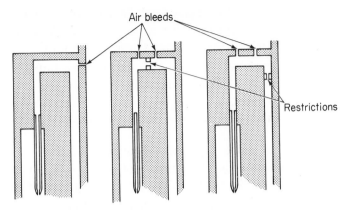

Fig. 13-24 Typical idle air bleed arrangements.

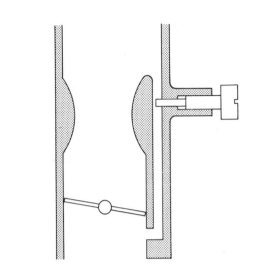

Fig. 13-26 Air bypass type idle speed adjustment.

Idle air control is often neglected when discussing the idle system. Most carburetors feed idle air around slightly open throttle plates. An idle stop screw holds the throttle plate open sufficiently to allow the required air flow which will maintain correct idle speed. The idle stop screw is manually adjusted.

Some models of carburetors use an air bypass system to supply idle air. In these carburetors, the carburetor throttle plate is tightly closed. All of the air must enter the manifold through an air passage that is controlled with a large diameter adjusting screw. As the screw is loosened, more air is allowed to enter the manifold, thus increasing engine speed. Air adjustment must be synchronized with the idle mixture screw for correct idle speed and smooth operation. Carburetors designed for emission control have a sealed device that limits the maximum rich idle mixture settings to prevent over-richening the idle mixture.

Fig. 13-25 Idle mixture control types.

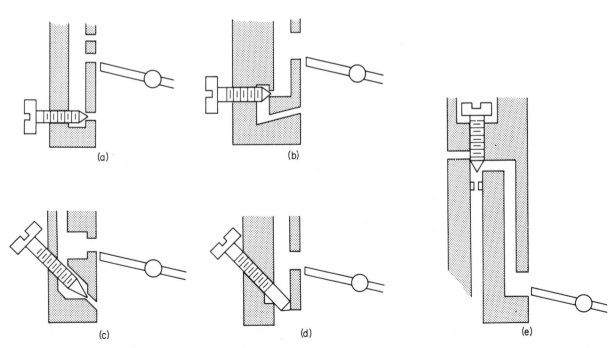

Engines with a high idle load, such as air conditioning and power steering, become hot while idling. Engine heat soaks into the carburetor body and vaporizes some of the fuel from the float bowl. These vapors are led into the air horn through bowl vents where incoming air draws them back through the carburetor barrel with the incoming air, producing an over-rich mixture that is delivered to the manifold. To compensate for this condition, some carburetors are equipped with a *hot idle compensator*. It consists of a valve on a bi-metallic spring. When the carburetor gets hot, the bi-metallic spring opens an air passage, allowing air to bypass the throttle plate to go into the manifold. This will lean the over-richened mixture and increase engine speed to compensate for the extra fuel vapors

(a)

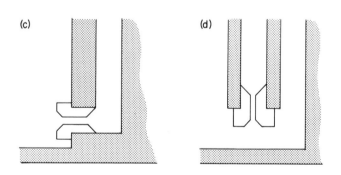

Fig. 13-27 Hot idle bypass arrangements.

(b)

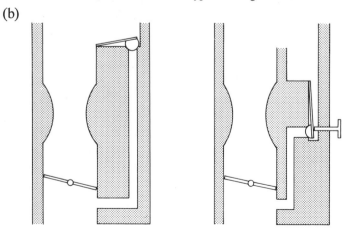

and for the added engine loads. When the carburetor cools, the bi-metal valve closes the port and the carburetor returns to normal idle conditions.

Care should be taken to see that the hot idle compensator is closed when setting the engine idle. In some cases, a small pin is provided to seat the idle compensator while adjusting engine idle.

Main and Compensation System. The main and compensation system consists of a main jet, main well, discharge nozzle, and a compensating system.

The main jet is a threaded bushing with a carefully-sized hole in it. The holes in the jets are so critical in some models that they are individually checked on a flow calibrator before the jet number is stamped on them. They should *never* be prodded with a wire or drilled. This will upset their carefully controlled calibration.

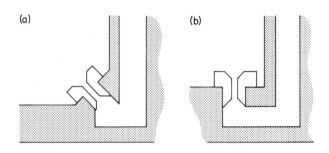

Fig. 13-28 Main jet arrangements.

The *main well* is a passage that is either diecast or drilled in the carburetor body. It is on the downstream end of the main jet and encloses the main well vent tube. The discharge nozzle is on the extreme end of the main well, and may be a part of the body casting or it may be an added attachment part.

Many carburetors have a discharge cluster in which the discharge nozzle; much of the carburetor metering calibration, such as the air bleeds; the

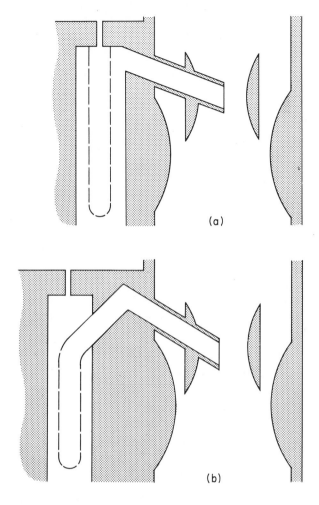

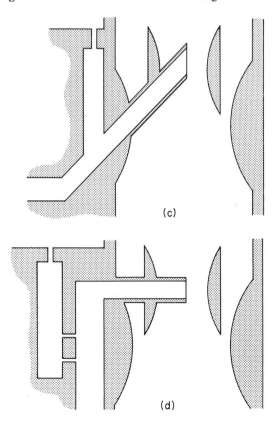

Fig. 13-29 Main air bleed vent tube arrangements.

Fig. 13-30 Typical discharge clusters.

main well tube; and the idle tube are located. This discharge cluster fits on top of the main well, allowing the tubes to go into the main well.

Some carburetors use multiple venturis, one inside of another, around the discharge nozzle to provide the required vacuum signal strength for use in air/fuel mixture control. Each small venturi's lower edge is located in the narrowest portion of the next larger venturi so that vacuum force is multiplied and they are therefore called boost venturis. This arrangement also provides a complete air curtain around the fuel being discharged, so that it will thoroughly mix with the air.

Power Circuit. The power circuit comes into operation near full throttle. It consists of an engine power sensing device and a method of adding about 15% more fuel to the main well than is possible through the main jet alone. This system is supplemented on four-barrel carburetors by providing an

203

Single venturi

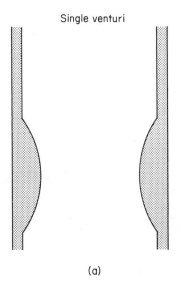

(a)

Double venturi

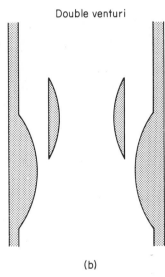

(b)

Triple venturi

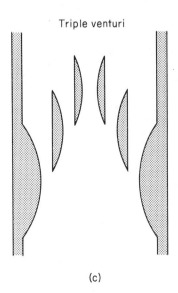

(c)

Fig. 13-31 Common venturi arrangements.

additional quantity of rich air/fuel mixture to enter the manifold through secondary carburetor bores.

Throttle position was one of the first methods used to control the power circuit. It requires a *mechanical link* between the throttle and power mechanism. This link's setting is critical for correct enrichment. As the throttle approaches a predetermined position, approximately 75% of full throttle, the linkage would start to mechanically open the fuel enrichening device. The power device rapidly reaches full activation through link and bell crank geometry as the throttle is opened fully.

Under some operating conditions, *engine vacuum* will more accurately sense engine power requirements than throttle position. Engine manifold vacuum is a function of engine speed and throttle position. At high engine speed and part throttle, as at turnpike speeds, the manifold has a relatively high vacuum, from 14 to 16 inches of mercury (Hg). As the throttle is opened, engine vacuum drops. The vacuum will be about 1″ Hg when the throttle is fully open. Experience has shown that the power system should begin to enrich the mixture when manifold vacuum drops to 4″ to 6″ Hg.

A spring-loaded expanding chamber, either a piston in a cylinder or a diaphragm chamber, is used to sense engine vacuum and open the enriching device. Vacuum contracts the chamber against a calibrated spring. The calibrated spring expands the chamber when vacuum becomes too low to hold it compressed, activating the enriching device.

The calibrated spring controls power jet timing. There are no adjustments. Some carburetors used for different applications have different calibrated spring strengths. Other carburetors use shims on the spring seat to change spring tension and, thus, the power valve timing may be set. There are no linkages to be accidentally bent out of alignment or adjusted. Most carburetors use the vacuum sensing method of power jet operation. Some carburetors use a combination of both mechanical and vacuum methods to more fully cover engine requirements. This combined system generally does not provide enough performance advantage to compensate for its complexity and extra cost.

Two types of mixture enriching devices are used; *metering* or *step-up rods*, and *valves*. They are activated by one of the power sensing devices. Both types allow more fuel to flow from the float bowl into the main well than can be supplied by

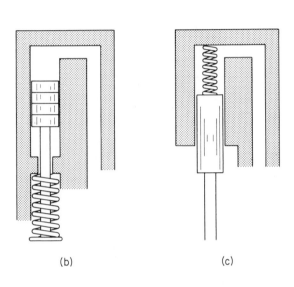

(a)

(b)   (c)

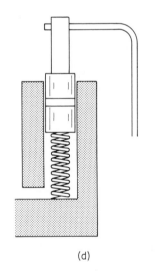

(d)

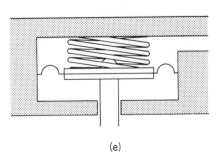

(e)

Fig. 13-32 Power system operating methods. (a) Mechanical operation, (b), (c), (d), and (e) vacuum operation.

the main jet alone, thus raising the fuel level in the main well. This reduces the distance the fuel must be raised to the discharge nozzles and, consequently, more fuel will be delivered. Added fuel will result in a richer air/fuel mixture as previously explained.

Metering rods or step-up rods extend through the main metering jet, one in each primary main jet. In lean cruise, fuel goes through the annulus space formed between the jet hole and the rod. The rod has two or more different diameters, or it may have a taper. When the power sensing device calls for a rich mixture, the rod is pulled upward so that the smaller diameter portion of the rod is in the main jet. This means that there is, in effect, a large main jet through which the fuel can flow, thereby enriching the mixture. Some emission control carburetors use a sealed calibration screw that limits the movement of the tapered metering rod to avoid excessive enrichment.

A single-barrel carburetor, using the metering rod enriching device, has one main jet, one metering rod and one actuating device. Two-barrel carburetors using metering rods use two main jets and two metering rods. They may be used with either

Automotive Engine Carburetors

one sensing device for both metering rods or used with a separate sensing device for each metering rod. Four-barrel carburetors have power systems on the primary barrels and these operate in the same manner as those in two-barrel carburetors.

Power valves are used in many carburetors. The valve may be either a *poppet* valve or a *ball check* valve. These types are always operated by a vacuum sensing device. The valve remains closed under cruise conditions at high vacuum. When vacuum falls, a spring on the sensing control opens

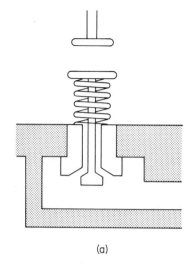

(a)

Poppet valve

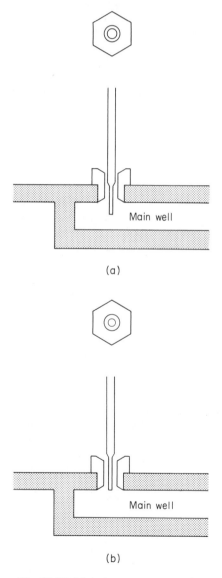

(a)

(b)

Fig. 13-33 Metering or step-up rods.

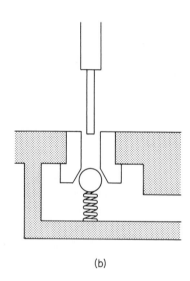

(b)

Ball check valve

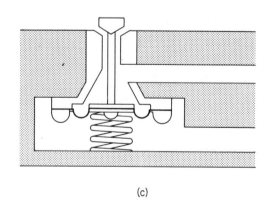

(c)

Poppet valve
diaphragm actuated

Fig. 13-34 Power system valves.

the power valve, either directly or through an actuating rod. This opens a passage that allows fuel to bypass the main jet to help fill the main well. A single bypass valve is all that is required for single-two- or four-barrel carburetors.

The secondary barrels in four-barrel carburetors come into operation near wide open throttle conditions when a large volume rich air/fuel mixture is required and, therefore, the secondary barrels have normally rich carburetor jetting. They also use the same sensing signals that are used by the power system; that is, throttle position and manifold vacuum. Secondary barrels may also use air velocity flowing through the primary barrels to sense engine requirements.

Some four-barrel carburetors have a mechanical linkage between the primary and secondary throttle shafts. The secondary throttle plates start to open after the primary throttle plates have opened approximately 60 degrees. Both primary and secondary throttle plates reach wide open at the same time to allow maximum air flow at full throttle.

Mechanically controlled secondary barrels can be opened at full throttle and low engine rpm. A sudden opening will momentarily reduce air velocity

(b)

(c)

(d)

Fig. 13-35 Mechanically operated secondary throttle valves. (a) Both throttles closed, (b) primary nearly open and secondary closed, (c) secondary starts to open as primary is opened further, (d) secondary fully open as primary becomes fully open.

(a)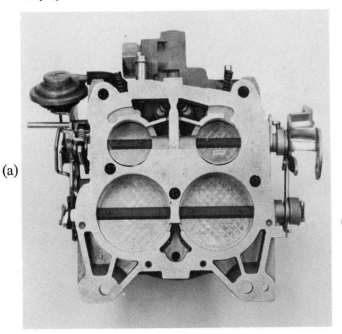

(a)

(b)

Fig. 13-36 Velocity valve. (a) Closed, (b) open.

Fig. 13-37 Secondary throttle opening linkages. (a) Mechanical linkage, (b) vacuum linkage.

(a)

(b)

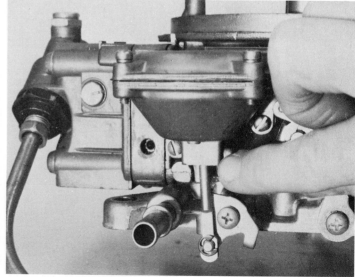

through all the carburetor bores by allowing air to flow through the secondary bores. In many carburetors, this low velocity reduces primary venturi vacuum to the point that fuel will not flow from the primary main nozzle. When this happens, the engine gets a large quantity of lean mixture which causes the engine to misfire. An air valve or velocity valve in the secondary air horn is used to eliminate this type of lean mixture problem. The air valve shaft is offset to provide an unbalanced condition that will sense air flow. In static position, the unbalanced valve may be counter-balanced by a weight or torsion spring. When the secondary throttle is suddenly opened, the air valve stays closed until engine speed increases carburetor air velocity. Then, dynamic unbalance of the offset air valve allows the air valve to open gradually, while maintaining a pressure depression equivalent to about three inches of water (Inches of water is a more sensitive measurement than inches of mercury). This keeps the engine from getting a large amount of lean mixture at low engine speeds. As engine speed continues to increase, the air valve gradually opens, keeping the air/fuel mixture at a combustible ratio. Air valve opening may be dampened with a calibrated air-bleed, controlled-vacuum diaphragm chamber or with a fuel damper chamber to eliminate the *bog* or *sag* that results from the air valve opening too quickly.

Some four-barrel carburetors open the secondary throttle plates with a spring-loaded vacuum diaphragm that is linked to the secondary throttle shaft. While manifold vacuum is high, the diaphragm is held by a calibrated spring to keep the secondary throttle plates closed. As the primary throttle is opened, air velocity increases primary venturi vacuum. This vacuum pulls the diaphragm against the calibrated spring. The secondary throttles are opened with a linkage from this diaphragm movement. This system of operation is very sensitive to the actual engine requirements without the need to use a secondary air valve system.

Secondary throttle shafts are provided with a locking device that keeps the secondary throttle plates closed when the choke is being applied. Only the primary barrels are equipped with a choke to provide rich mixtures during warmup. The engine would stall as a result of a lean mixture if the secondary throttles were opened while the engine still required partial choking.

Acceleration Circuit. The acceleration circuit consists of a variable displacement chamber that senses fuel requirements working with an inlet and an outlet check valve to supply fuel to a discharge nozzle. When the throttle is closed, fuel is drawn into the chamber. through the inlet check valve. When the throttle is opened, the fuel is forced out of the chamber through the outlet check valve and discharge nozzle.

The variable displacement chamber or pump may be either a piston in a cylinder or a diaphragm sided chamber. When the throttle is closed, the

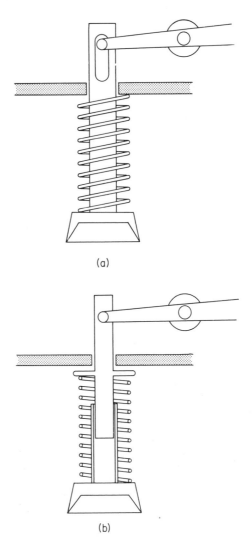

(a)

(b)

Fig. 13-38 Energy stored in an accelerator spring during closing and during opening.

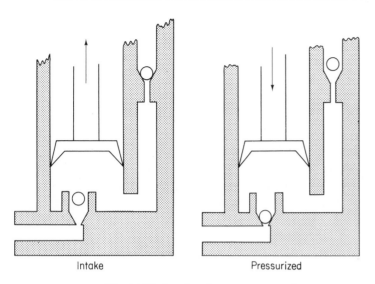

Fig. 13-39 Acceleration pump operation.

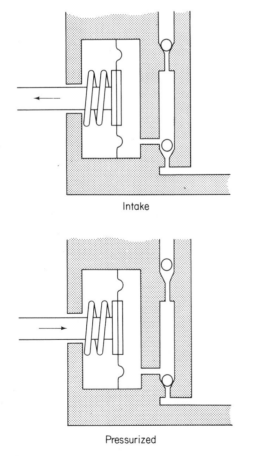

Fig. 13-40 Acceleration diaphragm operation.

chamber is expanded to draw fuel into the chamber. This expansion may be controlled by a mechanical link from the throttle shaft or by high engine vacuum that is normal any time the engine is running at part throttle. When the linkage or engine vacuum releases the pump, the pump spring forces the chamber to contract and force fuel out. Pump spring action against the fuel provides sufficient fuel injection duration as fuel is forced from the discharge nozzle to wet the manifold and allow the main system time to begin to function. Pump energy may be stored in the acceleration pump spring as the throttle is closed by the linkage or by vacuum. An alternate method used on some mechanical linkages is to store the energy in the spring as the throttle is opened.

The acceleration pump inlet is located in a passage between the float bowl and the acceleration pump chamber. Sometimes, the valve is an inexpensive free floating ball. In other carburetors, the ball check valve is spring-loaded to insure positive seating. Another popular inlet check valve is an elastomer or fuel resistant synthetic rubber disc over the inlet passage. The disc is lifted on the inlet stroke and compressed against the opening on the outlet stroke. Some acceleration pumps have an inlet check valve in the pump plunger shaft. This system works well because the entire pump is submerged within the fuel of the float bowl. A simple pump inlet valve method is to fit the pump plunger with a flexible loose fitting seal. On the upstroke, fuel enters the pump well around the seal. On the downstroke, the seal is forced out against the pump chamber wall to seal the acceleration pump well.

The outlet check serves two functions. It keeps air from entering the pump chamber on the intake stroke and it keeps the outlet pump passage full of fuel, ready to be used at any instant. Here again, a ball check is popular. The ball check may be free floating, spring-loaded or weighted. Because the acceleration pump discharge nozzle is often in high velocity air, there may be sufficient suction to cause the outlet check to leak. To prevent this in some carburetors, the outlet check valve is weighted to prevent leakage. Some carburetors use a heavy outlet needle valve rather than the lightweight ball type check valve.

The acceleration pump discharge nozzle sprays its charge into the air stream at each primary barrel. The quantity must be correct for each specific

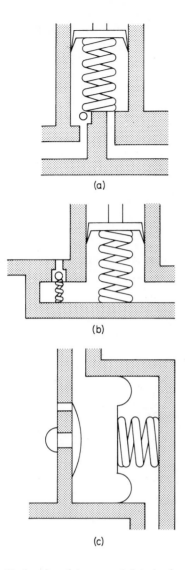

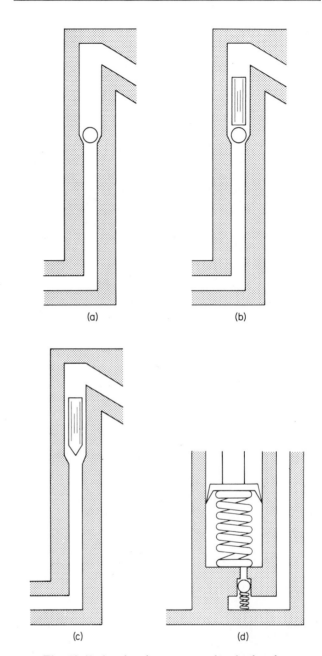

Fig. 13-41 Acceleration pump inlet check valve types.

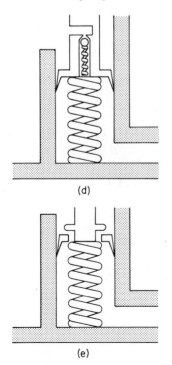

Fig. 13-42 Acceleration pump outlet check valve.

engine application. Discharge quantity is controlled by the acceleration pump spring calibration, the linkage adjustment, and the discharge nozzle opening size. Because standard carburetor castings and linkages are used for a number of engine applications, some acceleration pumps will provide more fuel than the engine requires so these carburetors are

211

provided with an opening, leading from the passage between the outlet check and the discharge nozzle, to the top of the float bowl that will allow excess fuel and vapors to return to the bowl.

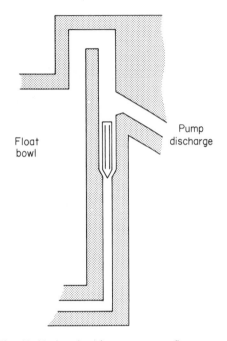

Float
bowl

Pump
discharge

Fig. 13-43 Acceleration pump overflow return.

Automatic Choke Circuit. Two forces balance to produce the correct choke opening. A temperature sensing bi-metal spring provides a closing force. Engine vacuum, along with an unbalanced choke plate, provides an opening force.

The bi-metallic heat sensing spring may be located integrally with the choke shaft on the carburetor air horn. Heat is piped to this type of bi-metal spring from a choke stove located where it is exposed to exhaust heat, such as the exhaust manifold or the exhaust crossover in the intake manifold. Many later engine designs place the bi-metal spring in a pocket or well cast on the outside of the manifold where it can be exposed to exhaust heat. The spring is connected to the choke shaft by a crossover link.

Engine vacuum sensing force is applied to the choke shaft through a link between the shaft and a vacuum piston or a vacuum diaphragm. This vacuum force tends to pull the choke open against the bi-metal spring force. The tendency of choke vacuum pistons to gum up and stick in their bores has led to the popular use of the vacuum diaphragm opening method.

Carburetor Icing. Heat is required to evaporate fuel as it flows through the carburetor. Much of the heat is removed from the air itself, thus lowering the air temperature. If the air is cooled below the

Fig. 13-44 Carburetor choke spring. (a) On choke shaft, (b) in manifold well.

(a)

(b)

temperature at which the moisture in the air condenses, called the *dew point*, moisture from the air will collect on the throttle plate and surrounding carburetor area. If this temperature is below 32°, the moisture will freeze, causing ice to form in the throttle plate area of the carburetor. Ice blocks the transfer passages, as well as effectively changing the shape of the carburetor bore. This upsets carburetor calibration, enriching the mixture and stalling the engine.

Icing will most likely occur when there is high humidity and the temperatures are between 30° and 50°F. When the engine first starts, no problem will be noticed because the ice hasn't had time to build up. When the engine is warmed up, the carburetor parts are above the freezing temperature so ice will not form. Carburetor icing occurs during the warmup period after the engine has run at light loads for about five minutes. It occurs quicker with slight throttle openings than with higher throttle openings. Engines that are sensitive to carburetor icing often have their idle mixture adjusted to the lean side and have idle speed set at maximum.

Modern emission control systems pre-heat the air before it enters the carburetor, effectively eliminating this type of icing problem. Many manifolds direct exhaust gas on the carburetor base by making a bypass in the manifold crossover to minimize icing.

13-4 CARBURETOR SERVICE

Other than routine idle adjustments, carburetors should not be rebuilt until the engine operation problem can be positively identified as a carburetor problem. This means that all other engine systems should be checked for correct functioning before condemning the carburetor. Carburetor problems usually show up as a flooding condition, malfunctioning choke, severe backfiring, sticking throttle, inability to set idle, and no acceleration pump action.

Many carburetor problems occur when a technician improperly services the carburetor. They are usually a result of incorrect cleaning methods, improper torques on assembly screws, incorrect part assembly or installing wrong parts. All carburetor parts must be handled with care and kept clean. Jets should only be cleaned with solvents and

Fig. 13-45 Choke opening piston (left) and choke opening diaphragm (right).

air pressure. Pushing wires through carburetor holes will scratch their inner surface and change their calibration so the carburetor cannot meter fuel correctly, causing the engine to operate improperly.

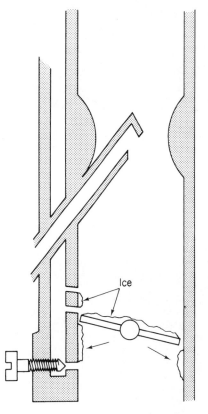

Fig. 13-46 Carburetor icing location.

213

Fig. 13-47a

Fig. 13-47b

Fig. 13-47c

Fig. 13-47d

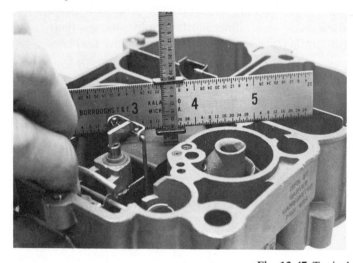

Fig. 13-47 Typical methods used to measure float levels.

Fig. 13-47e

Fig. 13-47f

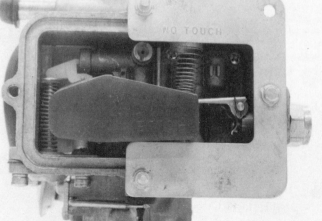

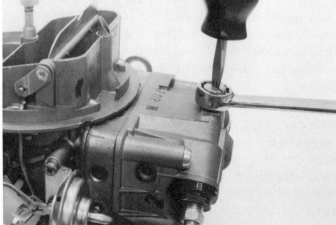

Fig. 13-49a

Fig. 13-48 Typical method used to measure bowl vent clearance.

Fig. 13-49c

Fig. 13-49b

Fig. 13-49 Typical acceleration pump adjustment.

Fig. 13-49d

Fig. 13-49e

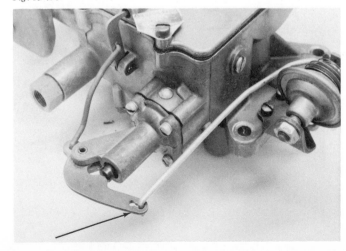

Fig. 13-50a

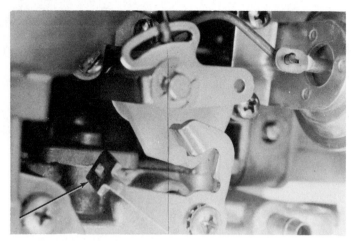

Fig. 13-50b

Fig. 13-50c

Fig. 13-50 Typical choke unloader adjustments.

Fig. 13-50e

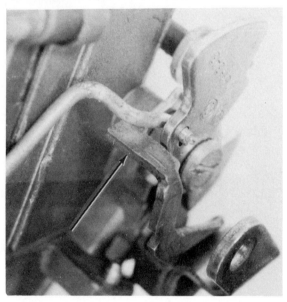

Fig. 13-50d

Carburetor service usually involves a complete disassembly, cleaning metal parts in a good carburetor solvent, rinsing with hot water, and drying them with compressed air. Parts are inspected to see that they are in normal condition. The carburetor is reassembled with required replacement parts. New gaskets and seals are always used. During assembly, carburetor settings must be checked.

Fig. 13-51a

Fig. 13-51b

Fig. 13-51c

Fig. 13-51 Fast idle cam adjustments.

Fig. 13-51d

A number of specific settings should be checked on all carburetors. These settings must be adjusted if they are not within specifications. The specifications and specific checking methods, as well as adjustment procedures, may be found in the service manual that covers the specific carburetor.

The items that are commonly checked and set on carburetors are the:

1. Float level
2. Bowl vent valve clearance
3. Acceleration pump adjustment
4. Choke unloader adjustment
5. Fast idle cam position
6. Secondary throttle adjustment
7. Wet fuel level (Some carburetors)
8. Engine idle speed and mixture

Additional settings may be required on some carburetors. The applicable service manual should be checked for specific setting details when setting carburetor adjustments.

Idle settings are made by first adjusting the idle speed. This is followed by adjusting the idle mixture to provide smooth idle at a specified air/fuel ratio. The speed is readjusted. This is followed by a recheck of the idle mixture for a final setting. Where used, idle limit stops must be in place. If they have been removed for adjustment, they must be replaced with new limiters.

Automotive Engine Carburetors

Fig. 13-52a

Fig. 13-52b

Fig. 13-52 Secondary throttle adjustments.

Fig. 13-53a   *Fig. 13-53b*

Fig. 13-53 Methods used to measure and adjust wet fuel level.

Fig. 13-54a

Fig. 13-54b

Fig. 13-54c

Fig. 13-54d

Fig. 13-54e

Fig. 13-54f

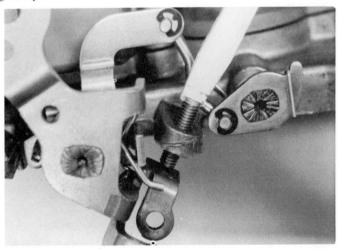

Fig. 13-54 Idle speed adjustments.

Fig. 13-54g

Fig. 13-54h

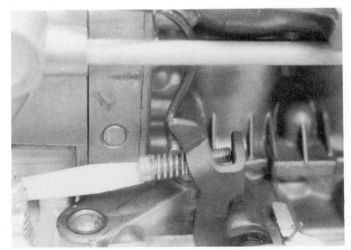

Fig. 13-55a

Fig. 13-55b

Fig. 13-55c

Fig. 13-55d

Fig. 13-55e

Fig. 13-55 Idle mixture adjustments.

Review Questions
Chapter 13

1. What is the ideal air/fuel ratio?

2. Why is a rich mixture used for power and a lean mixture used for economy?

3. How does the air/fuel ratio delivered by fuel injection differ from fuel ratio delivered by a carburetor?

4. Draw a typical air consumption to air/fuel ratio curve.

5. What physical condition of engine components results from too rich or too lean air/fuel mixtures?

6. What establishes the base line fuel and air pressures in a carburetor?

7. What does manifold vacuum indicate?

8. What is the purpose of signal pressures in a carburetor?

9. What produces the force in the fuel pump to push fuel to the carburetor?

10. What causes fuel to flow in a carburetor?

11. Why is compensation necessary in a main system?

12. Why is an anti-percolator necessary?

13. How does the idle air bleed act as a syphon breaker?

14. How is idle speed adjusted?

15. How is idle smoothness adjusted?

16. What is the purpose of the transfer ports?

17. Why is a power system needed in a carburetor?

18. When does the power system operate?

19. How does an inlet and outlet check valve operate in an acceleration pump circuit?

20. When does the acceleration pump operate?

21. What closes and what opens an automatic choke?

22. When does the fast idle cam operate?

23. When is a throttle return check used?

24. What materials are used for carburetors?

25. What determines the force necessary to close the inlet needle valve?

26. Define wet fuel level and float level.

27. Why are the jets located near the center of a carburetor?

28. Why does the idle circuit rise above the float level before discharging below the throttle plate?

29. Why are secondary idle systems sometimes used?

30. What is the purpose of a hot idle compensation system?

31. Why is jet hole size and shape critical?

32. What is an advantage of a discharge cluster?

33. What is the advantage of multiple venturis?

34. When does a power circuit operate? What is its purpose?

35. What actuates the power circuit?

36. What controls power-circuit timing?

37. How do step-up rods differ from power valves?

38. When do secondary barrels open?

39. Why are air valves used in secondary barrels along with secondary throttle plates?

40. What causes the diaphragm-controlled secondary throttle plate to open?

41. What controls the acceleration pump intake?

Quiz 13

1. Air/fuel ratios that a given carburetor delivers are controlled by
   a. engine speed
   b. carburetor size
   c. grade of gasoline used
   d. differential pressures.

2. The force that provides fuel pump pressure is provided by the
   a. return spring
   b. diaphragm
   c. cam eccentric
   d. check valves.

3. The normal enriching tendency of the main fuel system is corrected by the
   a. main metering jet
   b. venturi shape
   c. compensation system
   d. float level.

4. Highest engine vacuum occurs during
   a. idling
   b. acceleration
   c. cruising speeds
   d. maximum speeds.

5. When accelerating from cruising speeds, the first liquid fuel delivered by the carburetor
   a. gives the engine added power
   b. wets the intake manifold wall
   c. is wasted until the engine picks up speed
   d. increases fuel velocity.

42. What forces the acceleration pump to contract?

43. What type of valves are used on the acceleration pump inlet and outlet?

44. What provides the choke opening force? Closing force?

45. When is carburetor icing most likely to occur?

46. How does carburetor icing affect engine operation?

47. Look up the specific service instructions for one model carburetor. List the service operations.

6. The fast idle cam operates any time the
   a. engine idles
   b. choke is not open
   c. engine is started
   d. engine floods during a hot start.

7. The hot idle compensation will usually operate during
   a. long idle periods
   b. the return to cruise after acceleration
   c. deceleration from turnpike speeds
   d. just after the choke opens during warm-up.

8. A boost venturi is used to increase
   a. engine power
   b. fuel pressure
   c. the rate of acceleration
   d. carburetor vacuum.

9. Vacuum operated secondary barrels open whenever
   a. the throttle is fully opened
   b. the driver wants to accelerate
   c. there is very little vacuum
   d. there is a high vacuum.

10. Carburetors should be serviced
   a. whenever the engine does not perform correctly
   b. only after everything else has been checked
   c. any time fuel is not delivered to the engine
   d. on a periodic mileage basis

chapter 14

Automotive Batteries

After electrical phenomena was first recognized, scientists gradually pieced together enough information to allow them to successfuly use electricity, even though they did not understand the nature of electricity. Early useful sources of electricity were the dry cell and the battery. When the science of electronics developed it was found that electricity was actually the movement of electrons through conducting materials.

The lead-acid type battery is the primary source of automotive electricity for starting today's engines. It also serves as a reserve source of electricity for the vehicle's electrical running load. The battery size that is installed in a vehicle is selected for the kind of use to which it will be subjected. Vehicles with large engines require a greater cranking force so a large battery is used. Large batteries are also used in vehicles with a number of electrically operated accessories. Small batteries are found in vehicles with small engines and light electrical loads.

A properly maintained lead-acid battery of the type used in automobiles will give from three to four years of trouble free service. Proper maintenance involves keeping the battery clean, charged, full of water, and well supported in the battery case. When a battery fails to start the engine the technician must be able to check the battery and the rest of the electrical system to determine the cause of failure in order to properly repair the problem. It could be the battery that has failed or it could be that the other electrical system parts have failed.

14-1 NATURE OF ELECTRICITY

All matter is composed of atoms, which are made up of particles called *protons*, *electrons* and *neutrons*. The structure of the atom is often compared to the solar system. The center of the atom, called the *nucleus*, is made of neutrons and protons. Neutrons have a *neutral* electrical charge and protons have a *positive* electrical charge. The nucleus is surrounded with rapidly spinning electrons that are *negatively* charged particles. These lightweight electrons weigh only 1/1800 as much as a proton or a neutron.

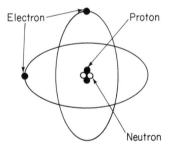

Fig. 14-1 Particles of an atom.

It is difficult to comprehend the fact that atoms, even in solid matter, are mostly space, like the solar system. To rationalize this, it might be helpful to consider a simile using an airplane propeller consisting of two blades. When the propeller is spinning it appears to be a flat disc, even though there is mostly space between the blades. This spinning disc would act more like a solid than empty space if one tossed a rubber ball at it. If this spinning disc could be tumbled fast enough, it would look and behave like a solid ball. The atom appears much the same. A number of electrons rapidly

spinning around a nucleus at velocities as high as 4000 miles/second may produce an object that is called solid.

When the number of electrons in an atom equals the number of protons, the atom has a neutral charge. The negative charge of each electron will balance the positive charge of each proton. The electrons spinning about the nucleus rotate at different distances away from the nucleus. As they rotate, they form shells at different energy levels. The electrons rotate in a fashion similar to a satellite rotating around the earth. Satellite orbits may be close to the earth or they may extend into space, depending upon the energy or velocity of the satellite. Electrons in the lower orbits are bound tightly to the nucleus, while electrons in the outer orbits of many materials are loosely bound. Electrons may be removed from or added to the loosely bound outer orbit of these material types.

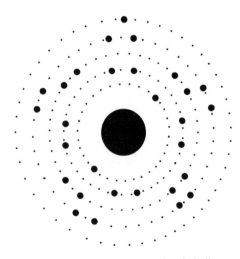

Fig. 14-2 Electron energy level shells.

An atom is an extremely small particle. Usable matter is made up of large groups of atoms or combinations of atoms. For instance, water is made from hydrogen and oxygen atoms, petroleum is made from atoms of hydrogen and carbon, steel is made from iron, carbon, manganese, phosphorus and sulfur atoms.

The electrons from the outer shell of the atoms in conducting matter may detach from their orbit and enter the orbit of another atom or become a free electron. The electrons move through materials in a random fashion or *drift* so that the net change is zero. That is, every electron that leaves an atom's orbit is replaced by an electron from another atom. Metals have many free drifting electrons. These materials are called *conductors*. It is interesting to note that they have three or less electrons in their outer orbits. Materials with five or more electrons in the outer orbit have a tighter bond to the nucleus with few drifting electrons. These materials are called *insulators*.

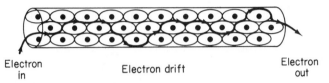

Electron in   Electron drift   Electron out

Fig. 14-3 Electron drift.

Atoms that pick up an extra electron in their outer shell have more electrons than protons, and, therefore, the atom is said to have a negative charge. If an atom were to give up one of its electrons to a neighboring atom, it would have one more proton than electron. It would then have a positive charge. Atoms with either extra or missing electrons are called *ions*. If they have an excess of electrons, they are *negative ions*. When they are missing some electrons, they are *positive ions*.

Copper is a good conductor with many free electrons drifting within it. If the conductor has one end connected to a source of extra electrons and the other end connected to an object that lacks electrons, the general drift of electrons in the conductor will be away from the excess electrons and toward the object that lacks electrons. This drift occurs because like charges repel and unlike charges attract each other. This forced drift from the collision of the electrons will produce an *energy wave* that moves through the conductor at a speed approaching the speed of light. This wave proceeds like a series of rear end collisions on a crowded highway, where the collision rate proceeds much faster than the movement of any one of the vehicles involved in the collision.

Fig. 14-4 Electron drift in one direction.

EMF forcing electron into conductor

Repeling force moves electrons along conductor

The net drift of electrons through a conductor in one direction is *electricity*. The rate of drift is called *current* and expressed in *amperes* (A). The electrical force that causes directional electron drift is called *electromotive force* (EMF). In automobiles, the initial EMF is produced by a battery or charging system. The EMF or amount of electrical pressure is expressed as *voltage* (V). The higher the voltage, the greater the electrical force capable of moving electrons within the conductor.

14-2 BATTERY CELL OPERATION

Chemical reactions between different materials involve the movement of electrons in the outer shell of some of their atoms. Electron movement is an electrical reaction. If it results from chemical reactions, it is called an *electro-chemical* process. Movement of electrons resulting from a chemical reaction may be controlled by controlling the chemical process producing the electrical current. This process can be reversed so that electrical currents cause a chemical reaction.

A storage battery is an electro-chemical device. It has a voltage and can produce a current as the result of chemical reactions that deplete battery materials. A reverse current forced through the battery can cause chemical reactions that restore battery materials.

Cell Construction. A simple storage battery *element* is made of two dissimilar metal plates that are kept from touching each other by a *separator*. This element is submerged in a liquid sulphuric acid solution called *electrolyte*. Electrolyte is a liquid material whose atoms become ionized in solution. These ionized atoms are free to move about in the solution. The acidity of the electrolyte weakens the electron bonds of the plate materials so the electrons can drift, causing positive and negative ions to be formed in the plate material. The active material on one of the plates is lead dioxide, usually called *lead peroxide* (PbO_2). It is a dark brown, small grain crystalline material. The crystalline type of structure is very porous so the electrolyte can freely penetrate the plate. Electrons leave the lead peroxide

225

plate and enter the electrolyte, leaving positive ions in the lead peroxide plate.

The active material on the other plate is porous or *sponge lead* that is easily penetrated by electrolyte. Electrons leave the electrolyte and enter the lead, giving them excess electrons that produce negative ions in the sponge-lead plate.

The electromotive force between the lead peroxide plate and sponge-lead plate is 2.13 V. Cell voltage results from the type of materials used in the plates and not the plate size, shape, or number of plates.

If a conductor connects the plates outside the cell, electrons can leave the negative plate and flow through the conductor to the positive plate. This process may continue as long as the chemical action within the cell transfers electrons to the negative plate. This process is said to be *discharging* the cell.

Fig. 14-5 Battery construction showing the connector going through the partition (Chevrolet Motor Division, General Motors Corporation).

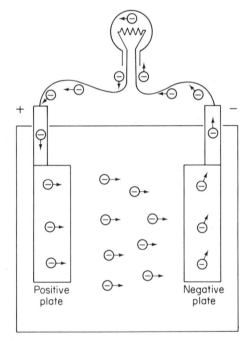

Fig. 14-7 Electron movement in a complete circuit.

Cell Chemical Reaction. During discharge, excess electrons are allowed to leave the sponge-lead plate through the exterior conductor, leaving positive lead ions (Pb^{++}) on the plate. Negative sulphate ions (SO_4^{--}) from the electrolyte are attracted by the positive lead ions. They combine to form neutral lead sulphate ($PbSO_4$) on the negative plate. During this time, the lead peroxide (PbO_2) of the positive

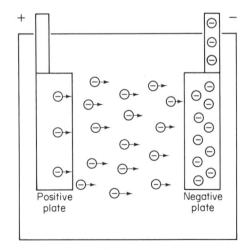

Fig. 14-6 Electron movement within a cell.

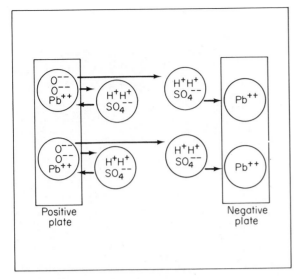

Fig. 14-8 Chemical ion movement in a cell during discharge.

plate combines with hydrogen and oxygen ($4H_2$) from the electrolyte to release electrons as a positive lead ion (Pb^{++}) and water (H_2O) is formed. The positive lead ion from this reaction combines with a negative sulphate ion (SO_4^{--}) of the electrolyte to form neutral lead sulphate ($PbSO_4$) on the positive plate.

During discharge, this reaction will continue as long as active material remains. In an ideal cell that is completely discharged, the plates will both become lead sulphate and the electrolyte will become water. Fully charged electrolyte has a *specific gravity* 1.26 times as heavy as pure water. The specific gravity of water is 1.00. The specific gravity of the electrolyte indicates the amount of electrical activity remaining in the cell. A measurement of the cell's specific gravity is called the cell's *state of charge*.

The electrochemical process is reversible. It is only reversible because the lead sulphate stays on the plates. If a cell is connected to a voltage higher than the cell voltage, electrons will flow backward through the cell. This reverse electrical current causes a reverse chemical action. Sulphate ions leave the plates and re-enter the electrolyte. The plates again become lead and lead peroxide. The cell can only be charged or discharged as fast as the ions will form and the electrons move to the negative plate.

In operation, battery cells are continually being slightly charged and discharged. They are seldom fully discharged, but are usually kept near full charge.

As the cell reaches the fully charged state, hydrogen gas is formed at the negative plate and oxygen gas is formed at the positive plate. This process is called gassing. Because of this, care must be exercised to avoid a spark at the cell opening. In the presence of a spark, these gases combine with a sudden explosion that can ruin the cell and throw acid out of the cell.

14-3 CELL FAILURE

After repeated charging cycles, the active plate materials loosen, bit by bit, from the plate and fall into a space in the bottom of the cell. This material forms an inactive sludge. Reduction in the useful portion of the plates may reach a stage at which the cell is called *worn out*.

Another form of cell failure is called *sulphation*. Sulphate from the acid combines with the lead plate as the cell discharges. If a battery is allowed to stand in a discharged condition, the lead sulphate hardens into permanent coarse white crystalline structure. The sulphate part of the plate becomes inactive. In effect, sulphation reduces the useful surface area of the plate.

Bridging or *treeing* is a form of cell failure. This is the result of cracks in the separator through which crystalline bridges form. These bridges connect the positive and negative plates, causing a short circuit within the cell that discharges the cell. Bridging usually results from buckled plates, vibration or mechanical damage.

Overcharging can result in cell failure. Continued charging after the battery reaches the fully charged condition will cause an increase in temperature and buckled plates. In advanced stages of failure, the plate may develop chunky shedding.

Excessive shock and vibration can cause slight plate and separator movement. If this movement is continued, the surfaces of these parts wear so they become loose in the case. In time, they will either break or short circuit.

14-4 AUTOMOTIVE STORAGE BATTERY FEATURES

The automotive battery is made of six cells. Each cell produces slightly over two volts. The cells are connected end to end, with the negative terminal of one cell attached to the positive terminal of the next cell. This type of connection is called a *series* connection. Each cell increases the voltage two volts more than the preceding cell so that a six-cell battery is a twelve-volt battery.

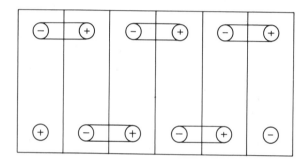

Fig. 14-9 Cell connections in a 12-volt lead acid battery.

Fig. 14-10 Cell construction.

Within each cell, there are a number of plates with separators between them. The plates are made from a finely cast lead–antimony alloy grid that is filled with active plate material. In each cell, there is always one more negative plate than positive plate. An eleven-plate battery has five positive plates and six negative plates in each cell. There is a negative plate on each side of the positive plates to provide maximum battery performance. The plates are connected together within each cell to form a *positive group* and a *negative group*. They are interleaved with separators to keep them from touching. This assembly of plates and separators is called an *element*.

The separators are made from resin impregnated cellulose fiber, microporous rubber, and plastic. They are flat on one side and ribbed on the other. The ribbed side is placed against the positive plate to allow free electrolyte flow along the positive plate. Some batteries use a fiberglass mat over the positive plates to help hold the material in place on the grid, thereby reducing loss of active material into the

bottom of the case, a phenomenon called *shedding*.

The element is placed in a snug-fitting case. When electrolyte is added, it is called a *cell*. Four bridges in the bottom of the case support the plates. Sub feet on the positive plates rest on bridges 1 and 3, while sub feet on the negative plate rest on bridges 2 and 4. This supports the plates, at the same time reducing the tendency for them to short circuit within the cell.

Six cells are connected together to form a twelve-volt automobile battery. The battery case with six compartments is made from hard rubber, plastic or bituminous composition. It must withstand the acid electrolyte, shock, and vibration, as well as temperature extremes.

The element connecting post in older batteries came above the case cover where a connector strap was used to connect the element of one cell to the element in the next cell. Current automobile cell connections are below the cell cover. Two methods are used in this type, over-the-partition and through-the-partition. In over-the-partition types, the cell

Fig. 14-11 Battery with cell connectors going over the partition (The Prestolite Company).

connector goes up to the underside of the cover where it crosses the cell partition. The connector extends down in the next cell to connect to the plates. This types of connector keeps acid from seeping through the cover, provides a shorter electrical path than the above-the-cover connector, and uses less material. This results in increased battery efficiency at a reduced cost and lower weight. Through-the-partition type connectors further reduce the amount of material to further reduce the cost. It shortens the electrical path to reduce electrical loss to a minimum. Sealing the connector at the partition is critical with the cell connector going through the partition.

The cover is sealed to the case and partitions with bituminous or resin materials. These materials form an acid tight joint that remains sealed during vibrations and temperature changes. Automotive batteries with one-piece covers are not repairable and must be replaced when they no longer function properly.

Each cell must have sufficient electrolyte to cover the plates. As the cell gases, hydrogen and oxygen separated from the electrolyte by hydrolysis will escape from the cell. This must be replaced with water before the plates are exposed to the air and dry out. Openings over the cell are usually designed to show the full electrolyte level. Vent plugs or caps designed to allow gases to escape while retaining liquid electrolyte are fitted in the openings. If the battery is overfilled with water so that the vent hole is plugged, electrolyte will be forced from the cell ahead of the gases. The loss of acid reduces the battery's ability to function. Spilled acid will corrode parts surrounding the battery as well as providing a potential leak between the battery posts.

14-5 BATTERY MAINTENANCE

Ideal battery maintenance is so simple that it is usually ignored. The battery must be kept clean, it must be kept full of electrolyte and it must be properly recharged after it has been used. If these three things are done, old age, accident, or carelessness are the only reasons for battery problems.

The battery is usually neglected until it fails to function properly. When this happens, the battery may be in such poor condition that it requires replacement. Battery failure is by far the most common source of road service calls.

The battery should be properly installed in the vehicle's battery carrier. Hold-down brackets are tightened to hold the battery firmly, but not so tight they will crack the battery case. Battery cables should be cleaned and securely attached to the battery posts.

Occasionally, the battery should be removed and thoroughly cleaned. If acid is present on the outside of the battery or the carrier, it may be neutralized with ammonia or baking soda. The battery and the cable clamps should then be thoroughly washed with hot water and a soft brush. When it has dried, petroleum jelly is often put on the posts and cable clamps to retard corrosion and oxidation.

The electrolyte level should be checked frequently. In many service stations, the electrolyte is checked each time the engine oil level is checked. Only distilled water is recommended for addition to the electrolyte. In some areas, however, drinking water has been satisfactorily used for battery water, but it is not recommended by battery manufacturers.

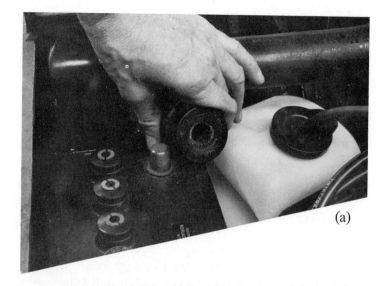

(a)

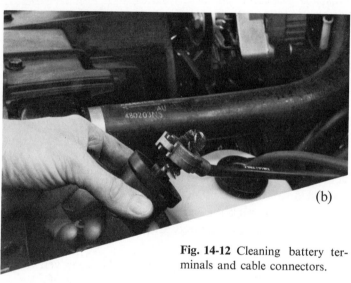

(b)

Fig. 14-12 Cleaning battery terminals and cable connectors.

The amount of current flow in an electrical circuit is expressed as *amperes*. While charging, the current forced through a battery is called the charging rate. A 3- to 5-A charging rate is required to bring the battery up to full charge. The voltage impressed on the battery by the vehicle charging system controls the charging rate. The automobile voltage regulator should be adjusted to limit the voltage to a value that will produce this charging rate. If the regulator is set too low, there will not be enough EMF to force current flow to charge the battery. If it is set too high, the EMF will force a

high current flow which will cause excessive gassing and cause the battery to overheat. This will make the battery use too much water, corrode or oxidize the positive plate grids, and cause the plates to buckle.

A battery may be charged at higher rates when it is partly discharged. This is called the charge *acceptance rate*. The acceptance rate is controlled by the rate at which the ions can form and the electrons transfer in the battery active material. A battery with a low state of charge can accept a higher charging current than a battery that is near a full state of charge. The actual state of charge may be determined by the battery's specific gravity.

14-6 BATTERY TESTING

Batteries should be tested to prevent vehicle problems that result from battery failure. The battery is tested to determine its per cent of charge and how well it either produces or accepts current. The voltage is tested while a known current flows. If the voltage of a fully charged battery is low while discharging or if it is either too high or too low while charging, the battery is faulty.

State of Charge. A fully charged standard automobile battery in temperate climates has an electrolyte specific gravity of 1.26. This is called 1260. At 75% charge, it is 1230; at 50% charge, it is 1170; at 25% charge, it is 1120; and discharged, it is 1070. Batteries used in arctic climates have a slightly stronger acid electrolyte while batteries used in the tropics use a slightly weaker acid electrolyte. Current practice is to use the same battery in all temperate climates. Using an acid concentration higher than necessary will shorten battery life. Acid concentration is measured with a calibrated float called a *hydrometer*. The hydrometer floats higher as the acid concentration increases. Temperature affects the hydrometer reading. Standard readings are taken at 80°. If the electrolyte is cooled, it thickens and gives false high readings. When the electrolyte is above 80°, it thins and gives a false low reading. The hydrometer reading must be corrected to determine the battery's actual *state of charge*. For each ten degrees below 80°, four (4) hydrometer points must be subtracted from the hydrometer reading to get the actual state of charge. For each ten degrees above 80°, four (4) hydrometer

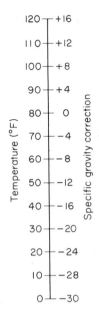

Fig. 14-13 Specific gravity correction for temperature.

points must be added to the hydrometer reading to get the actual state of charge.

Cell voltage changes slightly with the charge on the plate's surface. A fully charged cell, open circuited with no current flow, will have 2.13 V. At lower states of charge, the open cell voltage drops to 2.09 V at 75%, to 2.0 V at 50%, to 1.99 V at 25% and to 1.94 V when completely discharged. Some battery test methods use the open-circuit cell test with an expanded scale voltmeter to replace the hydrometer method. In use, voltmeter prods must contact the cell connectors. This is not possible with over-the-partition and through-the-partition type cell connectors. With these batteries, an alternate method is to use a cadmium tip voltage tester. The tips are placed into the electrolyte of two adjacent cells to measure their voltage difference. This indicates the state of charge by comparing to specifications for standard voltages.

Battery Capacity. The voltage between the positive and negative plates in a fully charged lead-acid battery is always the same, no matter how the battery is designed or built. Its ability to produce current, however, is the result of its construction. A number of different battery rating tests have been devised by the battery manufacturers. These are standardized by the Society of Automotive Engineers (SAE) and appear in the *SAE Handbook*.

A *twenty-hour rate test* has been applied to

batteries for years. It is the steady current draw in amperes that will reduce the cell voltage to 1.75 V in 20 hours while holding the battery at 80°. This capacity is expressed in ampere-hours. Battery manufacturers use this rating to indicate battery size. The twenty-hour rate measures the amount of available reserve electrical power remaining in the battery to handle light accessory loads.

The *150- and 300-ampere rate tests* are run at 0° after a 24-hour cold soak. Terminal voltage is recorded at the end of a specific time period (5 to 15 seconds). The time period differs with different type batteries. This test is designed to indicate the battery's ability to crank a cold engine.

Batteries have a number of other rating tests that depend upon battery capacity and design. These tests include a *charging rate acceptance*, *cycling life*, and *vibration tests*.

Maximum current that can be drawn from a battery is proportional to the plate surface area exposed to the electrolyte. The length of time the current can be drawn from a battery is proportional to the amount of active material available in the battery. A battery with a large number of thin plates can produce high current for a short period of time. If a few thick heavy plates were used, the battery could not produce a high current, but could produce a low current for a long period of time. Batteries are designed to produce the type of current that is required by each application.

The automobile battery's main function is to provide electrical energy to crank the engine and, at the same time, to supply current to the ignition system. After the engine has started, the charging system provides the required electrical energy for most of the vehicle's running requirements, so the battery supplies no current. Automotive batteries are designed to have the high discharge rates required for starting. Batteries with high ampere-hour rates will usually have a higher service life than batteries that just barely meet the vehicle needs.

The capacity of a 75% to 100% charged battery may be measured by placing an open carbon-pile resistor across the terminals. With a voltmeter also attached to the battery terminals, the carbon pile is adjusted to a current flow three times the ampere-hour rating of the battery for fifteen seconds. At the end of this time period, a healthy 12 V automotive battery will have a terminal voltage above 9.5 V.

Newer test methods have been devised for testing battery capacity, regardless of the battery state of charge. The method will vary between equipment manufacturers. In general, they charge and discharge a battery through a series of cycles, both at low and high rates. The voltage at the end of the cycle indicates battery capacity. Specific test procedure and specifications are supplied by the equipment manufacturer. With this test procedure, it is obvious from the previous discussion that the battery state of charge must also be considered in comparing final voltage readings to specifications.

As the battery is charged, its voltage increases, causing a restriction of the incoming charge. This restriction is called a *counter electromotive force* (CEMF) and is measured in volts.

14-7 BATTERY CHARGING

Batteries may be charged by the vehicle charging system or by an outside source. The amperage charging rate is the result of the battery state of charge, battery condition, electrolyte temperature, and the voltage provided by the charger. A battery that is worn out will accept a high charging rate without becoming charged, because it has low CEMF and will accept a higher charging rate than a fully charged healthy battery. A sulphated battery will not accept a high charging rate, because there is little active plate surface.

Warm electrolyte is more active than cold electrolyte so it will transfer ions rapidly and, therefore, will accept a high charging rate. These all must be considered when charging a battery. The vehicle charging system senses CEMF and temperature to provide the correct charging rate to rapidly and fully charge the battery.

When a battery is less than half charged, it may be *fast charged*. Fast charging rates may be as high as 50 to 60 amperes. Fast chargers are to be used only long enough to recharge a battery to start the engine. The vehicle charging system should be used to finish charging the battery. While fast charging, battery temperature should be kept below 110° to avoid battery damage.

If the battery is to be completely charged outside the vehicle it must be charged at a low amperage rate, one ampere per positive plate per cell or less. On an eleven-plate, 12-volt automobile battery, this rate would be 5 amperes. This is about 7% of the battery's 20 ampere-hour rating. Specific gravity of the electrolyte should be checked each hour. It is fully charged when the specific gravity does not change in three successive hourly checks.

A healthy battery's voltage increases at a known rate while charging at a fixed amperage rate. It will approach 15 V when it becomes fully charged. If the voltage rises too slowly, the battery is partly shorted. If it rises too rapidly, it is sulphated. In some cases, the sulphation can be broken down by *cycling* the battery; that is, to charge, discharge and recharge the battery. If the battery is shorted or if the sulphation cannot be broken down, the battery should be replaced.

Replacement batteries are manufactured both wet and dry. Most batteries in the replacement market are dry charged. The battery plates are charged during manufacture, then dried in the absence of air. The battery is sealed to keep moisture out. In this sealed condition, the battery will remain fresh during long storage periods when kept in a cool dry location.

The dry-charged battery is activated by breaking the seals and filling the cells with electrolyte. This should be followed by a boost charge at 30 to 40 amperes until the specific gravity reaches 1250. The battery is then ready for service.

Review Questions Chapter 14

1. What is electricity?

2. What is the weight difference between a proton and an electron?

3. Which electron shells have loosely bound electrons?

4. How does the outer electron shell differ between a conductor and an insulator?

5. Describe a neutral electron drift. What happens when the drift is not neutral?

6. What happens when one electron is pushed toward a second electron?

7. What is an electro-chemical reaction?

8. Describe ion movement in a cell during discharge.

9. What precautions will prevent cell failure?

10. Describe battery construction.

11. Describe the correct battery maintenance.

12. What is battery acceptance rate?

13. What is the actual state of charge of a battery whose hydrometer reading is 1240 at 20°?

14. Compare open circuit cell voltage to the specific gravity at full charge, 75% charge, 50% charge and at 25% charge.

15. What is the basis for selecting a battery to fit the needs of a specific vehicle?

16. What happens to the battery voltage as the battery is charged?

17. How is the battery fully charged?

18. What does the state of charge test tell about the battery?

19. What are the indications of a serviceable battery?

20. What indicates that a new battery is required?

Quiz 14

1. Electricity is
   a. a chemical action on a conductor
   b. an EMF produced by a battery or generator
   c. a movement of electrons between energy levels
   d. net drift of free electrons in one direction.

2. The ampere rate at which a given automobile battery can be charged or discharged depends upon
   a. how rapidly ions can form
   b. how much cell gassing occurs
   c. the number of cells in the battery
   d. the kind of active material used on the plates.

3. The plates of a completely discharged automobile battery will be
   a. spongy lead
   b. lead peroxide
   c. lead sulfate
   d. crystalline peroxide lead.

4. A battery at 0°F has a hydrometer reading of 1225. When loaded to three times its ampere-hour rating, the battery voltage is 9.3 volts. The most likely condition of the battery is that it is
   a. sulphated
   b. worn out
   c. discharged
   d. satisfactory.

5. Battery cells are vented to allow
   a. water vapors to escape
   b. oxygen and hydrogen to escape
   c. electrolyte to get out if overfilled
   d. air to flow through the cell.

6. To fully charge a 12-V battery with a total of 66 plates the charging rate should not exceed
   a. 3 amperes
   b. 5 amperes
   c. 11 amperes
   d. 66 amperes.

7. If the battery voltage climbs too rapidly during charging, the battery is
   a. worn out
   b. shorted
   c. sulphated
   d. bridged.

8. Electrolyte coming out of the cells and wetting the cover during charging is usually the result of
   a. not removing the caps
   b. overfilling
   c. improper design
   d. overcharging.

9. In some cases, mild sulphation can be corrected by
   a. charging with a fast charger
   b. a long charge with a slow charger
   c. completely discharging the battery before charging it
   d. cycling the battery.

10. An increase in battery voltage while being charged is due to
    a. acid concentration
    b. counter electromotive force
    c. plate size
    d. battery capacity.

chapter 15

Starters and Starting Systems

The battery provides electrical energy to crank the engine and to fire the spark plugs. The positive terminal of the battery is connected to the starter through heavy insulated cables and switches. The negative terminal is connected to the engine block with another heavy cable or flexible strap. A heavy duty starter switch is operated from the driver's control.

The starter switch is used to complete the battery circuit by sending current from the battery terminals through the starter, engine block and cables. When the starter switch is open, no current will flow through the open circuit and the starter will not operate.

While cranking, the starter is mechanically connected to the engine ring gear by the starter drive mechanism. The drive mechanism is capable of engaging a stationary ring gear and protects the starter from overspeed when the engine starts.

The starter cranking speed results from the starter design, the voltage supplied by the battery through cables, and the engine cranking load. The technician can do nothing about the starter design or the engine load but he is able to make sure the starter gets maximum possible voltage. This is done by connecting a fully charged battery to the starter with proper sized cables using clean tight junctions.

15-1 SERIES ELECTRICAL CIRCUIT

If voltage is applied to an *open* conductor, free electrons will fill the conductor, but they will *not* flow. A complete circuit is required in order to have an electron flow. With a complete circuit, electrons will flow and cause an electrical current whenever voltage is applied to the circuit. The number of electrons in a current that flow past a given point in one second is expressed as *amperes*. In a given sized conductor, as the voltage decreases, amperage will decrease. Current cannot flow unless there is an electromotive force or voltage to cause the electrons to move in a closed circuit.

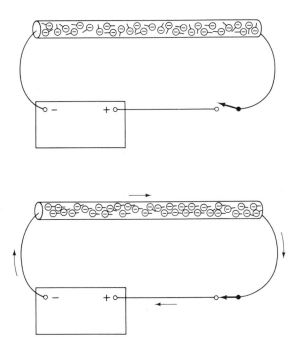

Fig. 15-1 Current flow in a series circuit when the switch is closed.

As the current flows in a conductor, the forced drift of the free electrons is hindered by collisions with atoms in the conductor. This produces heat which, in turn, increases free electron activity. In addition, some force is required to dislodge an electron from its shell around an atom. This force is provided by the free electrons. Dislodging the shell electron absorbs some of the free electron's energy. These two conditions are responsible for resistance

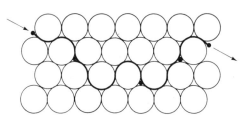

Fig. 15-2 An added electron repels electrons within the conductor.

to the electron drift or flow. Resistance to electron movement is measured in units called *ohms*.

There is a fixed relationship between the electrical pressure, *volts;* the electrical current, *amperes;* and the electrical resistance, *ohms*. This relationship is expressed in an algebraic expression: ohms = volts/amperes, and is called *Ohm's Law*. If two of these values are known, the third may be calculated. If resistance in ohms is constant, the ampere flow in a conductor is directly proportional to the voltage.

The total resistance of a conductor increases as the conductor's length increases, as its cross-section decreases, and as the conductor temperature increases. Wires normally used in automobile applications are selected to be as small as possible without causing excessive resistance, in order to minimize cost.

The resistance of a conductor or wire can be determined by measuring volts and amperes that it is carrying, and then using Ohm's Law (ohms = volts/amperes) to calculate resistance. In automotive service, specification for maximum resistance is usually given in terms of *voltage drop*. A known current is passed through the circuit in question. The voltage across that part of the circuit is measured. Using this method, the "voltage drop" can be used as a measure of circuit resistance any time the current passing through a conductor is known.

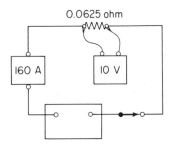

Fig. 15-3 Voltage drop across a resistance.

For example, the starter circuit resistance is .0625 ohms, while the starter has a cranking voltage of 10 V and a starter draw of 160 A.

$$\text{ohms} = \frac{\text{volts}}{\text{amperes}} = \frac{10}{160} = .0625$$

It should be noted that battery terminal voltage in this example is only 10 V while a 160-A current is flowing. The battery is only acting fast enough to maintain 10 V at this current draw. When the circuit is opened, ion activity will immediately catch up to bring the battery EMF back to 12 V.

15-2 SERIES STARTER CIRCUIT

The *SAE Handbook* specifies that automobile batteries will have negative grounds. It further states that the maximum allowable voltage drop is .2 V per 100 A for cables between the battery and starter. Switches will add some circuit resistance. Resistance in most starter circuits is well below this value. Voltage drop in the starter circuit is the result of the cable terminal condition, cable length and size, and number of wire strands in the cable.

The starter circuit voltage drop can be measured by placing one of the terminals of an expanded scale (1–4 V full scale) voltmeter *at each end terminal* of the conductor being checked while the starter *is cranking*. Any voltage reading on the voltmeter indicates resistance. The greater the voltage reading, the greater the resistance, assuming constant ampere flow to the starter.

Each conductor, switch and connector causes some resistance to current flow. When these current carrying units are connected, one after the other, as they are in the starter circuit, they form a *series* electrical circuit. Resistances in series add directly in ohm units. Voltage drops across the conductor, switches, and operating units in a circuit will add up to equal the measured battery voltage while current is flowing. No voltage drop exists when current does not flow. Full battery voltage will be measured across an open switch. It should be noted that the voltmeter is used without disconnecting any circuit connections.

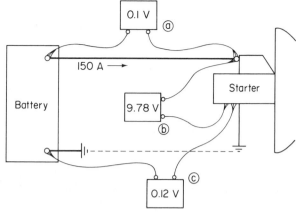

$$R_a = \frac{0.1\,V}{150\,A} = 0.00066 \text{ ohm}$$

$$R_b = \frac{9.78\,V}{150\,A} = 0.065 \text{ ohm}$$

$$R_c = \frac{0.12\,V}{150\,A} = 0.0008 \text{ ohm}$$

$$R_T = R_a + R_b + R_c$$
$$R_T = 0.00066 + 0.065 + 0.0008$$
$$R_T = 0.06646 \text{ ohm}$$

Fig. 15-4 Measuring voltage drop in a series starter circuit.

Series resistance is similar to a line of traffic going into a raceway. The restrictions are the drive-in gate, the ticket salesman, and the ticket collector. Each car that goes through the gate also goes through each of these restrictions in series, one after the other.

It should be noted that the grounded portion of the starter circuit is just as important as the insulated side. All of the current that flows through the insulated and switch side of a series circuit also flows through the grounded side. The grounded side of the circuit is often overlooked when testing automotive electrical circuits.

15-3 PARALLEL ELECTRICAL CIRCUITS

The remote starter switching circuit is in operation along with the cranking circuit while the engine is being cranked to start. Current that flows through the switching circuit is not the same current that flows through the starter circuit. Current from the battery splits, some going through the switching circuit and some going through the starter circuit. Systems that split the current are called *parallel* circuits. It is obvious that as more circuits are connected in parallel, more current will be able to flow. The only way more current is able to flow with a fixed battery voltage is to lower the circuit resistance. The parallel circuit does this.

Here again, think of the raceway entrance. If a walk-in gate is opened in addition to the drive-in gate, more people can get into the raceway than by the drive-in gate alone, even though the walk-in people are restricted by ticket sales and ticket collectors.

Each restriction or resistance to current flow may be measured in ohms. Resistances added to parallel circuits make more paths for current to flow. The formula for adding these resistances is

$$R = \frac{1}{1/R_1 + 1/R_2 + 1/R_3}$$

For example, if the starter circuit resistance is .0625 ohms and the starter switch circuit resistance is 2 ohms the total resistance of the parallel circuits would be:

$$R = \frac{1}{1/.0625 + 1/2} = \frac{1}{16/1 + 1/2} = \frac{1}{32 + 1/2}$$

$$= \frac{2}{33} = .0606 \text{ ohms}$$

As more resistances are added, the total circuit resistance will decrease. Resistances used in parallel are called a *load*.

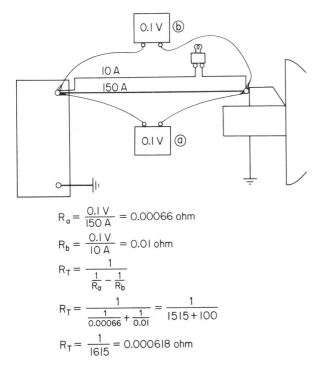

$$R_a = \frac{0.1 \text{ V}}{150 \text{ A}} = 0.00066 \text{ ohm}$$

$$R_b = \frac{0.1 \text{ V}}{10 \text{ A}} = 0.01 \text{ ohm}$$

$$R_T = \frac{1}{\frac{1}{R_a} - \frac{1}{R_b}}$$

$$R_T = \frac{1}{\frac{1}{0.00066} + \frac{1}{0.01}} = \frac{1}{1515 + 100}$$

$$R_T = \frac{1}{1615} = 0.000618 \text{ ohm}$$

Fig. 15-5 Measuring voltage drop in the starter circuit and switch circuit.

If a resistor is used to restrict current flow, it is called *resistance*. If it is used to allow more current to flow by connecting in parallel, it is called a *load*.

15-4 ELECTROMAGNETISM

Each electron acts like a very small magnet, having north and south magnetic poles. Current flowing through a conductor will tend to polarize the electrons around the atoms so their magnetic poles are generally headed in the same direction. This produces a *magnetic field* that surrounds all current carrying conductors. The magnetic field is considered to be directed from the north pole toward the south pole. If one places his left thumb pointing in the direction of electron movement, the fingers will be pointing in the direction that the magnetic field surrounds the conductor. This is called the *left hand rule*.

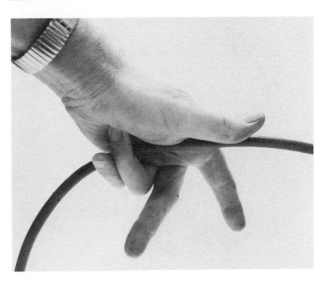

Fig. 15-6 Left hand rule with the thumb pointing in the direction of current flow and fingers pointing in the direction of magnetic flow.

The strength of the magnetic field surrounding a current carrying conductor is proportional to the current strength flowing in the conductor. If more current flows, the magnetic field becomes stronger and produces more magnetic *lines of force*. These lines are often called magnetic flux lines. Magnetic flux can be visualized as lines if iron filings are

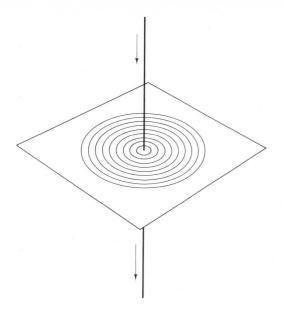

Fig. 15-7 Magnetic field built up around a current carrying conductor.

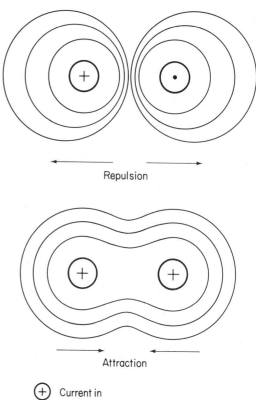

Repulsion

Attraction

⊕ Current in

⊙ Current out

Fig. 15-8 Forces resulting from magnetic fields around adjacent current carrying conductors.

sprinkled on a flat surface surrounding a current carrying conductor. Flux lines actually stretch along the conductor in the third dimension to form magnetic flux shells.

Magnetic flux lines will not cross each other. When moving in the same direction, the flux lines tend to repel each other. As the flux becomes stronger, the flux lines separate. When two magnetic fields that surround adjacent conductors run in the *same* direction *between* the conductors, their fields are displaced. The force of the displaced fields tends

Fig. 15-9 Major starter parts.

to force the conductors to separate or repel the conductors. This occurs when current flows in opposite directions in each of the adjacent conductors.

When the flux lines that surround current carrying conductors move in *opposite* directions *between* the conductors, the flux lines join up. This forms a large displaced field that produces a force which will tend to pull the conductors together or *attract* the conductors. This force occurs when the current flow in the two conductors is in the same direction. All forces try to move the conductor to the center of the magnetic field.

Starter motor operation makes use of attracting and repelling magnetic forces that surround current carrying conductors.

15-5 STARTER MOTOR PRINCIPLES

The starter consists of two major parts—a stationary electromagnet *field* and a rotating *armature*. They are often connected in series so that all of the current that enters the starter will go through both field and armature.

The field is made of a number of conductor turns or windings around a soft iron core. Wrapping the conductor around the core is one method of increasing the magnetic field strength. Magnetic field strength may be measured in *ampere turns*, that is, the amperes flowing in the conductor times the number of turns the conductor makes around the core. Increasing either amperes or number of turns will increase the strength of the magnetic field flux. Magnetic lines of force move more easily through iron than through air. The laminated soft iron core will concentrate the magnetic field so they are more effective. Core laminations are insulated from each other to reduce electrical eddy currents that resist current flow and produce heat.

The armature is made from a number of conductor loops or windings wrapped on a laminated soft iron core which is, in turn, mounted on a shaft and bearings that support it within the field. The conductor ends are soldered to copper *commutator bars*. Carbon-copper compound *brushes* are held against the commutator bars to make electrical contact between the frame and the rotating armature.

In operation, current flows through the field and through the commutator bars into the armature

windings, to develop a magnetic field around the conductors in each. The windings are designed so that the magnetic fields will attract one side of an armature winding while repelling the other side. This produces a turning effort on the armature shaft. Before the armature winding can reach its neutral point, the following set of commutator bars move into contact with the brushes. This produces the same electromagnetic force on this following armature conductor. As the armature turns, the brushes keep changing commutator bars to keep the armature rotating. The rotating force of the armature is transferred through the starter drive mechanism to crank the engine.

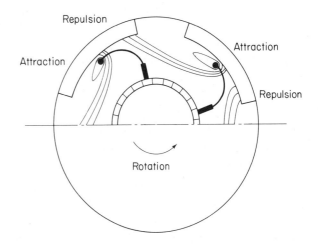

Fig. 15-10 Starter winding and field attraction and repulsion.

15-6 ELECTROMAGNETIC INDUCTION

The maximum torque or turning force developed by a starter results from the strength of its magnetic fields. This is due to the design of the starter, winding size and conductor size. In general, the more current the starter draws, the more torque will be produced by the attracting and repelling magnetic fields.

If the flux lines of a magnetic field are forced to cut across a conductor against their normal action, they will cause the electrons in the conductor to attempt to drift in one direction. The more flux

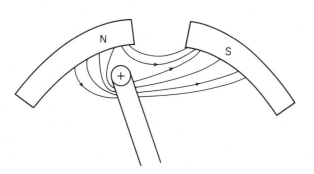

Fig. 15-11 Counter EMF induced in the conductor while rotating in a magnetic field.

lines that cut the conductor, the stronger the force to move the conductor's free electrons will become. This electromagnetic force is measured in volts, as it is in batteries. Producing an EMF through relative motion between a conductor and magnetic field is called *electromagnetic induction*. The EMF strength results from the number of flux lines cutting across the conductor each second.

Electromagnetic induction occurs in starter motors. As the starter operates, the armature is rotating within the field's magnetic flux. This produces an EMF that is in a direction opposite to the EMF imposed on the starter by the battery. It is, therefore, called a *counter electromotive force* (CEMF). Counter electromotive force strength is proportional to armature speed. As starter speed increases, its CEMF increases. When the starter mechanical load plus CEMF equals battery force or voltage, the starter will not rotate faster and its speed stabilizes. Maximum starter torque is limited by current flow and maximum speed is limited by CEMF. As a starter rotates faster, CEMF *reduces* battery amperage draw. Slowly turning starters will draw more current than rapidly turning starters because slowly turning starters develop less CEMF.

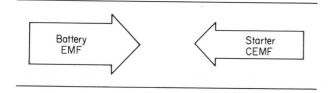

Fig. 15-12 CEMF reducing the effect of EMF.

15-7 STARTER DRIVES

Starter armatures are designed to turn at relatively high speeds to minimize amperage draw. To do this, they are geared down to the crankshaft. Starter drive ratios run from 15:1 to 20:1. Some starters have a built-in 3.5:1 reduction gear between the armature and the starter drive gear. This allows these starters to be built somewhat lighter and use a smaller crankshaft ring gear. The small starter drive gear meshes with a large ring gear mounted on the flywheel or torque converter drive plate to give the required torque multiplication ratio to crank the engine.

The starter drive must be able to engage the gears while the ring gear is not turning and be able to release the armature from the ring gear when the engine starts. Modern starters use a *solenoid* to push the starter drive gear into mesh with the ring gear. An *overrunning clutch* is used to disengage the armature when the engine starts.

The solenoid consists of two coils of wire around a movable core. Current flows through these coils when the driver turns the ignition switch to the starter switch position. Current in the solenoid coil produces a strong magnetic field that pulls the movable core toward the center of the coil. The movable core is linked to the starter drive gear, pushing it into engagement with the ring gear.

When the drive gear reaches full engagement, a set of heavy contacts on the end of the movable core connects the battery to the starter motor,

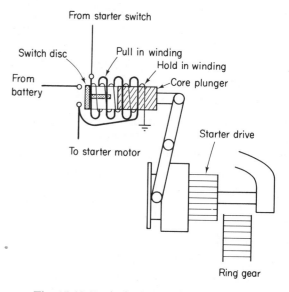

Fig. 15-13 Typical starter solenoid circuit.

bypassing the heavy solenoid coil that is called a *pull-in winding*. A second winding, called the *hold-in winding*, remains energized, while starter cranking continues. When the engine starts and the driver releases the ignition switch from the crank position, current to the solenoid is cut off. A spring pushes the movable core back out of the coil. This, in turn, pulls the starter gear from the ring gear.

The overrunning clutch is an assembly made of rollers or balls that wedge between a hub and outer race when turned in one direction and release when they turn in the opposite direction. The entire overrunning clutch assembly is splined to the armature shaft. The solenoid pushes the entire overrunning clutch assembly toward the ring gear until the drive gear is in full mesh with the ring gear. As the armature turns, armature shaft splines drive the overrunning clutch hub. Hub rotation forces the rollers up a ramp, jamming them between the hub and outer race. This pulls the outer race along, turning the starter drive gear. When the engine starts, the ring gear spins the drive gear faster than the starter will turn, the outer clutch race moves ahead of the drive rollers, rolling them down the hub ramp to release the clutch hub. The starter drive gear will run with the ring gear, causing no damage to the armature. This continues until the driver releases the starter switch, allowing the solenoid return spring to pull the starter gear from the ring gear.

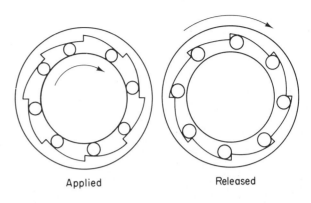

Applied   Released

Overrunning clutch

Fig. 15-14 Overrunning clutch operation.

Fig. 15-15 Brushes and fields in a starter frame.

15-8 STARTER MOTOR CONSTRUCTION

Starter fields are mounted in a starter housing called a *field frame*. Fields are held in the frame by the core that is screwed to the frame. Automotive starters have two or four field coils. Field coils are usually connected in series, one after the other. Some starters use parallel windings on some of the fields to control starter motor torque and free speed characteristics.

The armature is supported in plain bearings in the *end frames*. There is a small clearance between the armature and field to maximize the effects of the magnetic forces. Bearing wear can allow the armature to rub against the field core to cause drag that will reduce armature speed, increase the amperage draw, and reduce the available starting torque.

Four brushes are held in *brush holders* in the end frame, two opposite brushes are insulated and the remaining two are grounded. Springs and levers hold the brushes under tension against the armature's commutator. This provides good electrical contact for high starter amperage loads. If a brush spring becomes weak or the brushes wear down over half their original length, the brushes will not apply adequate pressure against the commutator. This

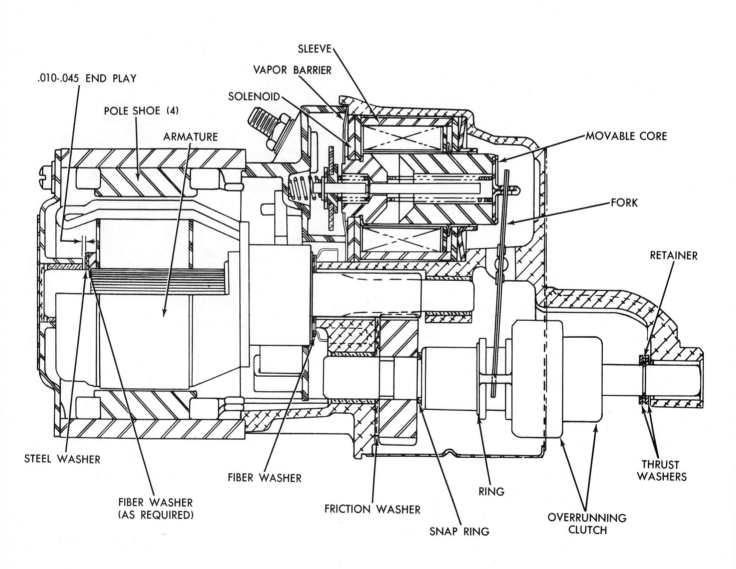

Fig. 15-16 Starter part nomenclature. (a) (Delco-Remy Division, General Motors Corporation), (b) section view (Chrysler-Plymouth Division, Chrysler Corporation).

CONTACT FINGER
SOLENOID
RETURN SPRING
PLUNGER
GROMMET
SHIFT LEVER
CONNECTORS
BUSHING
BUSHING
PINION STOP
ARMATURE
OVERRUNNING CLUTCH
FIELD COIL
SPIRAL SPLINES
ASSIST SPRING
INSULATED BRUSH HOLDER
BRUSH
BRUSH SPRING
GROUNDED BRUSH HOLDER

.010-.045 END PLAY
POLE SHOE (4)
ARMATURE
SLEEVE
VAPOR BARRIER
SOLENOID
MOVABLE CORE
FORK
RETAINER
STEEL WASHER
FIBER WASHER
FIBER WASHER (AS REQUIRED)
FRICTION WASHER
SNAP RING
RING
OVERRUNNING CLUTCH
THRUST WASHERS

Fig. 15-17 Starter brushes on the commutator.

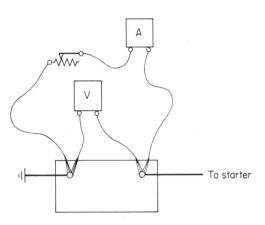

A

V

To starter

Fig. 15-18 Starter draw test.

allows the brushes to bounce which will result in arcing and burning commutator bars.

Current flows in series through the fields, insulated brushes, armature, and grounded brushes. Poor connections in any of these parts can cause high resistance and loss of cranking ability. Most of the starter resistances occur at the brush-to-commutator contacts. Armature winding to commutator solder joints will give problems if the starter has been overheated, allowing the solder to melt.

15-9 STARTING SYSTEM TESTING

An improperly cranking starter can result from a defective battery, circuit resistances, malfunctioning switches, problems in the starting motor, starter drive problems, or engine resistance. The battery should always be the first item checked when an electrical problem exists. The battery must be at least 75% charged to satisfactorily perform its required function in starter system testing.

If the engine will crank, a voltage drop test of all of the starter cables, switches and grounds should follow the battery test. If the engine does not crank, a voltage drop test across the starter switch will show if it is operating. When checking automotive switches, voltmeter terminals are placed across switch connections. Battery voltage will show with a switch open and less than .1 V will show when the switch is closed and carrying current. If the circuit is open at some other point, the voltmeter will not register. Starter switches should be checked in this manner.

A *starter draw test* is the first test made on the starter after the battery and circuit test satisfactorily. This test can be remotely done by placing voltmeter connections across the battery terminals. The battery voltage is checked while the starter cranks the engine. A carbon-pile rheostat with an ammeter is placed across the battery and adjusted so the rheostat draws enough current to cause the voltmeter to read the same voltage that it did when the starter was cranking the engine. Starter amperage draw on medium-sized V-8 engines will be from 160 to 200 A.

The starter draw test will be high when the starter cranks slowly. If the amperage is too high, the problem may be in the starter and the starter will have to be removed for further checks. Low starter draw results from a weak battery or resistance in the starter circuit.

Two tests are run on starters that have been removed from the engine. The first measures armature free speed and amperage draw at a specified voltage. This requires the use of a tachometer that can measure armature speed. A hand held tachometer with a friction attachment works well. Voltage is supplied by a battery through a carbon-pile rheostat which is used to control the voltage. One end of the carbon pile is attached to the positive battery post and the other end is attached to the starter post. A ground cable is attached from the battery negative post to the starter frame. Speed and amperage at the specified voltage can be compared to specifications. Low readings indicate starter problems.

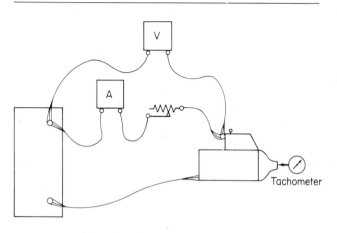

Fig. 15-19 Starter free speed test.

The second test is a *stall test* run with the armature locked so it cannot turn. Using the same connections used in the free speed test, the voltage is adjusted to specifications and the amperage read. This value is compared to the starter specifications. Low amperage readings indicate a resistance in the starter while high readings indicate a short circuit that bypasses some of the normal circuit resistance.

If the starter is found to be faulty, it should be disassembled and each component checked for correct operation. This is called *bench checking* the starter. Many shops exhange starters for rebuilt units when tests show that malfunctions exist within the starter. It is a good practice to run the free speed and stall test on any replacement starter to see that it functions correctly before installing it on the vehicle.

Review Questions
Chapter 15

1. What is an ampere?

2. What causes resistance in a closed circuit conductor?

3. What is the starter circuit resistance if the cranking voltage is 9 V with a 180 A starter draw?

4. A starter circuit has a starter amperage draw of 200 amperes. What is the resistance of a cable if it has a .1 V drop? A .15 V drop? A .3 V drop?

5. What is the individual resistance and the total resistance of the circuit in Figure 15-4 if there was a 180 A starter draw with the same voltage drops?

6. How does a resistance differ from a load?

7. Calculate the total resistance on the circuit in Figure 15-5 if the current flow at A is 150 A and at B is 10 A, while the battery supplies 10 V.

8. How does electromagnetic induction affect two adjacent wires with current running in opposite directions?

9. Name two methods that can be used to increase electromagnetic field strength.

10. What causes the starter armature to rotate when current flows through the field and armature?

11. How is starter speed limited?

12. If a starter with a 20:1 reduction did not release from the starter when the engine idles at 500 rpm, how fast would the armature be turned?

13. What causes the starter solenoid pull-in windings to cease functioning when the starter is engaged?

14. What is the purpose of an overrunning clutch in the starter drive?

15. What is the purpose of close clearances between the armature and field coils?

16. What causes commutator bar burning?

17. What is the starter system test sequence when the starter does not crank the engine properly?

18. How is the function of a switch checked?

Quiz 15

1. In most automotive application, electrical resistance is expressed in terms of
   a. ohms
   b. wire size
   c. current flow
   d. voltage drop.

2. Resistances connected in series will
   a. increase current flow at the same voltage
   b. reduce current flow at the same voltage
   c. have no effect on current flow
   d. stop all current flow.

3. Resistances connected in parallel will
   a. increase current flow at the same voltage
   b. reduce current flow at the same voltage
   c. have no effect on current flow
   d. stop all current flow.

4. Electromagnetic induction depends on
   a. magnetic field strength
   b. number of conductor windings
   c. number of flux lines cut per second
   d. speed of armature rotation.

5. An electromagnet's strength in automotive applications is expressed in terms of
   a. ampere-turns
   b. lines of force
   c. magnetic flux
   d. attraction pull measured in grams.

6. Maximum starter speed is limited by
   a. battery capacity
   b. counter electromotive force
   c. engine temperature while cranking
   d. starter current drop.

7. In domestic passenger cars, the starter is disengaged with
   a. a solenoid
   b. an over running clutch
   c. the starter crank switch
   d. a cut out winding.

8. Burned starter commutator bars result from
   a. high cranking voltage
   b. worn armature bearings
   c. high brush spring strength
   d. low brush spring strength.

9. Low starter amperage draw results from
   a. cranking a cold engine
   b. armature dragging on the field
   c. high brush spring tension
   d. a weak battery.

10. High amperage draw results from
    a. high cranking speeds
    b. tight armature bearings
    c. loose battery terminals
    d. excessive battery voltage.

chapter 16

Charging Systems & Regulation

With the engine running, the charging system is designed to supply all of the current required by the vehicle electrical load and charge the battery. The battery supplies the occasional extra electrical demand that exceeds charging system capacity. This may occur at idle speed when a large number of accessories and lights are turned on.

The charging system consists of a belt-driven generator, a regulator to limit maximum output, and electrical wiring with switches to connect it into the automobile electrical system.

In 1960 alternators rather than generators were installed on some domestic automobiles as standard equipment. By the mid 60's all domestic automobiles were using alternators. The alternator did not change the rest of the electrical system. It produced the same type of pulsing direct current that the older generator had produced. The alternator would, however, produce current at lower engine speeds, had lighter construction, would safely operate at higher speeds and was less expensive. All of these were good reasons to use the alternator.

16-1 GENERATOR PRINCIPLES

The generator makes use of electromagnetic induction principles described in Chapter 15. Relative motion between magnetic flux lines and a conductor forces the electrons to drift in one direction. This forced drift produces an EMF or voltage in the conductor. The strength of this voltage is based on the number of flux lines cutting the conductor each second.

More flux lines can be made to cut a conductor in three ways. First, by increasing the *rate* at which the flux lines cut the conductor. Second, by increasing the *number of windings* in the conductor. Third, by increasing the *magnetic flux strength*. The generator is belt-driven so its speed is dependent on the engine speed; consequently, rate has no control value. The number of generator conductor windings is part of the generator design so it cannot be used to control output. Generator output is very effectively controlled by changing the magnetic flux strength of the generator field. Generators are designed so they will produce maximum output when maximum electrical system voltage is placed across the generator field. This causes maximum field current. Maximum field strength will produce far more output than is normally required by the electrical system so the regulator is de-signed to reduce field strength to the level that allows the generator to produce the output needed by the electrical system under each operating condition.

Modern automotive generators are rectified with a diode, an electronic device that passes current in only one direction, and are usually called *alternators*. The main conductor is wound in a frame and is called a *stator*. A field winding is wound around a hub that is supported on a shaft and bearings. Pole shoes, to concentrate the flux lines, are placed over the field windings. This field assembly is called a *rotor*. The rotor turns inside the stator, forcing the flux lines to cut the stator windings.

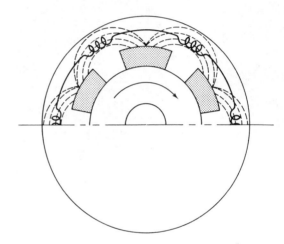

Fig. 16-2 Rotating pole shoes forcing the magnetic flux through stationary conductors.

Each end of the rotating field coil is brought to a copper ring that is insulated from the shaft. Carbon brushes ride against and slip on these rings to connect the field windings to the regulator circuit.

In operation, the regulator allows current to flow through the field windings in the rotor. This current produces a magnetic field that will magnetize the pole shoes, half north pole and half south pole. As the rotor turns, the magnetism that surrounds the pole shoes will cut the stator conductor windings. This induces voltage in the stator windings. Current will flow in the stator if it is connected into a completed electrical circuit whenever stator voltage is greater than system voltage.

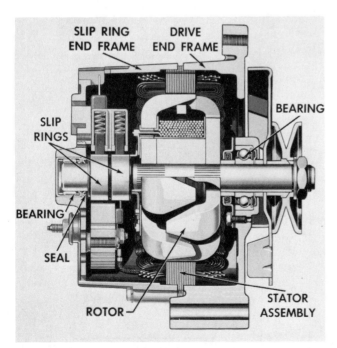

Fig. 16-1 Section view of a typical alternator (Delco-Remy Division, General Motors Corporation).

Fig. 16-3 Typical alternator rotors and pole shoes.

Fig. 16-4 Typical alternator stators and frames.

Fig. 16-5 Delta and Y alternator stator connections (The Prestolite Company).

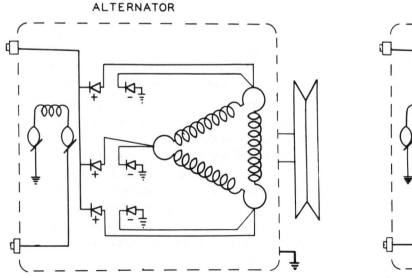

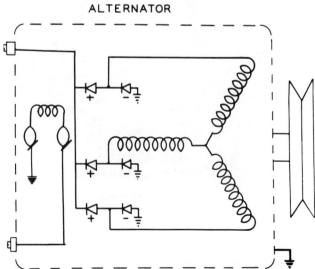

Stator. Alternator stators are made with three separate windings. Within these windings are a number of separate coils wound in series. They are spaced so the magnetic flux polarity is the same on each of the winding coils at the same time. Each coil adds to the voltage of the preceding coil so that stator windings are able to produce the designed voltage.

All three windings are connected together. The most common connection used in automobile alternators is a Y connection; however, some applications use a delta connection. Both operate in a similar manner. The following discussion of alternators will follow the Y connection type.

The three windings in a Y connection are connected together at the Y junction. The other end of each winding goes to a diode and then to the charging system.

Older type generators had a stationary field and a rotating armature, similar to the starter. The conductor in the rotating armature cut the magnetic flux lines of the stationary field. Current from the armature flowed through commutator segments and brushes to the automotive electrical system.

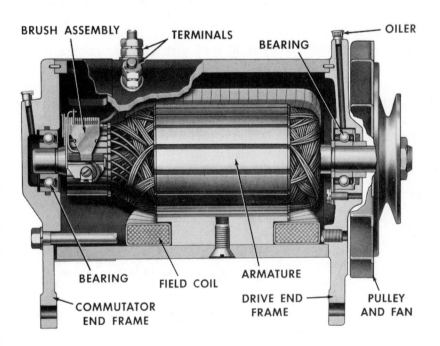

Fig. 16-6 Section view of a generator (Delco-Remy Division, General Motors Corporation).

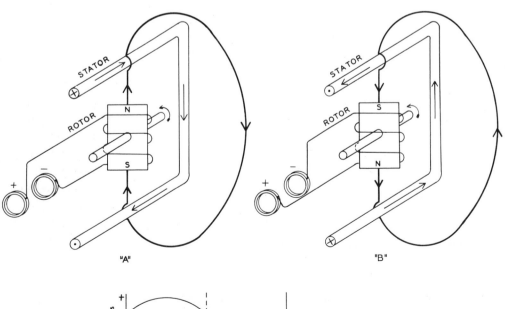

Fig. 16-7 Current reversal in the stator as the rotor turns (The Prestolite Company).

The field pole shoe fingers of the alternator rotor are alternately spaced, n-s-n-s-n-s, etc., around the rotor. Alternate magnetic fields from the rotor pole shoes cut the stator windings as the rotor turns. This causes the electrons in the stator windings to be forced one way, then back the other way as the fields alternate across the stator winding. This produces an alternating voltage in the stator. If the stator were connected directly to an outside circuit, the alternating voltage would produce an *alternating current* (AC). Automotive electrical systems, however, require the voltage and current to be in one direction. This is called *direct current* (DC). Alternating current needs to be *rectified* to become direct current.

The voltage produced by each winding is proportional to the number of flux lines cutting the winding. Flux lines start from zero at a point equidistant between pole shoes. As the rotor turns, the number of flux lines cutting the winding increases to a maximum as the pole shoe passes the winding. It again drops to zero at the next neutral point. The following pole shoe has the opposite polarity so, in effect, the flux line direction changes. This changes the winding's voltage direction. The continual buildup, first in one direction and then in another, produces a *sine wave* voltage. The name comes from the trigonometric function called sine. If a single conductor and a single two-pole magnet were used, the voltage would be proportional to the trigonometric sine of the magnet's angle in relation to the conductor. Three stationary windings are equally spaced and their voltages produce three sine waves as the rotor turns. The current produced by these voltages is called a *three-phase current*.

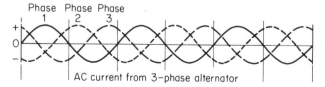

Fig. 16-8 Alternating current from three phase windings (The Prestolite Company).

Alternating current produced in the stator conductors is converted to direct current by a principle called rectification. Alternators are rectified using diodes and generators are rectified with the commutator.

16-2 SEMICONDUCTORS—DIODES

It is necessary to understand the operation of diodes if one is to understand rectification of alternator current in the automobile charging system. Diode operation is based upon semiconductor principles.

It has been previously stated that metallic atoms with less than four electrons in the outer shell are good conductors and atoms with more than four electrons are good insulators. Atoms with exactly four electrons in the outer shell are neither good conductors nor good insulators. Silicon and germanium represent materials of this type. In pure crystalline form, the electrons from adjacent atoms share the electrons of their outer shells and, in effect, they each have eight electrons in their outer shell. This makes them a good insulator.

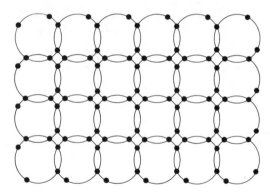

Fig. 16-9 Atom with four electrons in a structure.

If silicon, for example, is slightly contaminated or "doped" at a rate of 1:10,000,000 with impurity material that has five electrons in the outer shell, such as phosphorus, arsenic, or antimony in its crystalline form, there would not be enough space in the outer shell for nine electrons. This would leave a free electron. This type of doped material would be called a negative or *N-type* material because it already has excess electrons and would *repel* a negative charge or an electron.

If, on the other hand, the silicon were contaminated or doped with impurities such as small

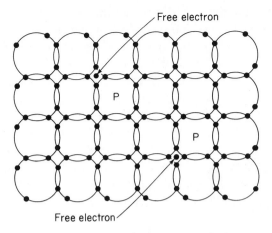

Fig. 16-10 Two atoms with five electrons within a structure made of atoms with four electrons leaving two free electrons.

particles of boron or indium crystals which have only three electrons on their outer shell, a gap without an electron would remain in the outer shell. The gap, called a *hole*, would attract an electron or negative charge. Doped material with holes is called positive or *P-type* material because it would *attract* a negative charge or electrons.

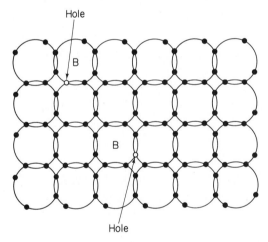

Fig. 16-11 Two atoms with three electrons within a structure made of atoms with four electrons leaving two holes.

Movement of electrons and holes can be compared to heavy slow moving traffic. Assume the cars are in a line of traffic and the first car moves up one space. This is progressively followed as each car moves into the space ahead. The cars would be progressing forward and the space would move backward. Electrons can be compared to the car and holes can be compared to the space. Electrons

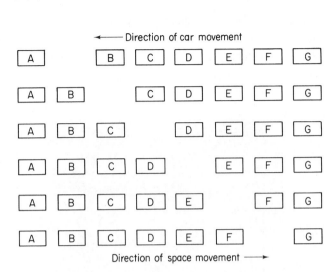

Fig. 16-12 Electron and hole movement compared to vehicle movement in traffic.

and holes move in opposite directions. A hole is the absence of an electron needed to complete an atom's outer shell.

The *P*-type and *N*-type materials are called *semiconductors*. In certain combinations of materials and of circuits, semiconductors will conduct current. In other applications, they will act as insulators. In automotive applications, semiconductors are used in diodes and in transistors.

The diode semiconductor is made under very closely controlled conditions from a thin wafer of crystal silicon. Boron is painted on one side and phosphorus on the other side of the crystal to make a junction of *P*-type and *N*-type semiconductor materials. The doped wafer is put into a high temperature furnace until the doping materials are fused into the silicon. This is followed by plating

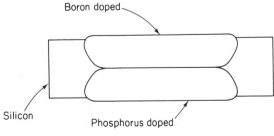

Fig. 16-13 Diode wafer.

251

the wafer for good electrical contact. It is then broken into chips 3/16″ × 3/16″ square and .007″ thick, that can be encapsuled for easy assembly into electrical circuits.

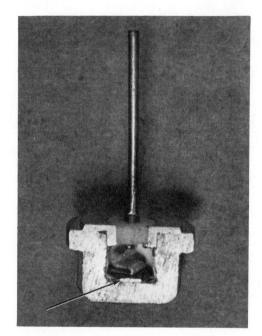

Fig. 16-14 Encapsuled diode wafer.

Within the diode, the holes in the *P*-type material attract electrons toward the *junction*, that is, a thin region between the *P*-type and *N*-type materials in the crystal. As the electrons move toward the junction, they leave positive ions behind them that hold the electrons from crossing the junction into the *P*-type material. Some electrons do drift across the junction. However, this is an insignificant amount of electron flow and does not affect diode operation.

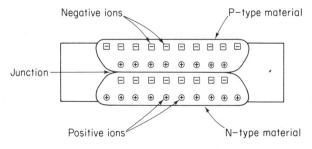

Fig. 16-15 Electron and hole movement in a diode.

If the diode is connected into a circuit with the negative side of the circuit connected to the *N*-type material and the positive side of the circuit connected to the *P*-type material, a current will flow across the diode. This is called a *forward bias*. Electrons from the circuit put additional electrons on the *N*-type material. These electrons will satisfy the positive ions that had been holding electrons from crossing the junction. With this restraining force satisfied by new electrons, the electrons at the junction move across the junction and on through the circuit, resulting in a current flow.

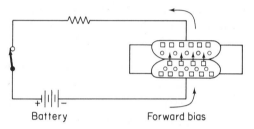

Electrons flow across junction

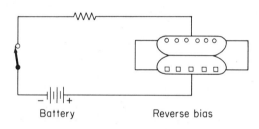

No electrons flow across junction

Fig. 16-16 Electron and hole movement with a forward bias and a reverse bias.

If the polarity of the diode is reversed, forming a *reverse bias*, the electrons in the negative side of the circuit are attracted by the holes in the *P*-type material. The *N*-type material's electrons are attracted to the positive side of the circuit. This results in moving both the electrons of the *N*-type material and the holes of the *P*-type material away from the junction. The tendency to move in opposing directions allows an insignificant current flow across the junction. In effect, there is no reverse current flow through a diode.

The diode is used as a one-way electrical check. It will allow current to flow in one direction (forward bias) by acting as a conductor and will stop the current back flow (reverse bias) by acting as an insulator.

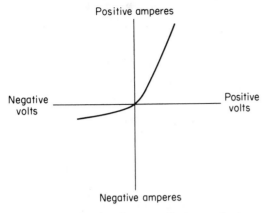

Fig. 16-17 Curve showing how a diode conducts current with voltage.

Excessive reverse voltage will force a current to flow across the diode junction, rapidly heating the diode. If the reverse voltage forces a sufficiently large current across the junction, the diode will be damaged by overheating. Some special diodes are heavily doped so they will withstand relatively large reverse currents without damage. When made in this way, they are called *Zener diodes* and are used in systems where voltage control is required. At less than the designed reverse bias voltage, they act as a normal diode. Above this designed voltage, they will conduct a reverse bias current.

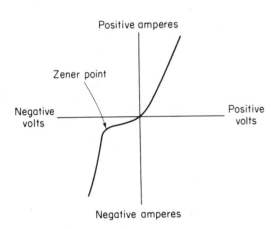

Fig. 16-18 Curve showing how a Zener diode conducts current with voltage.

Diodes used in alternators are designated as positive or as negative diodes. Their exterior case looks similar; only the actual diode chip is reversed within the case. In the negative diode, the *P*-type material is connected to the case and the *N*-type material to the diode lead. In the positive diode, the

N-type material is connected to the case and the *P*-type material is connected to the diode lead. Positive diodes have their part number printed in red and the negative diodes have their part number printed in black.

16-3 ALTERNATOR RECTIFICATION

If the current from each of the three-phase alternating voltages produced by the stator were fed through one-way electrical check valves or diodes, it would stop the reverse half of the current, while leaving the forward half to flow in the circuit. This is called *half-wave rectification*. In alternators, this would reduce the electrical output by half, so full-wave rectification is used. Full-wave rectification reverses the effective polarity of one half of the sine wave, so that the whole wave is in one direction. The electrical circuit only senses maximum voltage which is a direct current ripple. The alternating current in a generator armature is rectified by commutator bars, while the alternator current produced in the alternator stator is rectified by diodes.

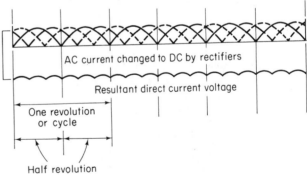

Fig. 16-19 Full wave rectification (The Prestolite Company).

In operation, the voltage in each coil builds in the positive direction, then collapses. This is immediately followed by building in the negative direction and again collapsing, operating in a continuous cycle. Each of the phases' windings are equally spaced and take turns building and collapsing. To help understand diode rectification in each of the following illustrations, the action will be stopped instantaneously when one of the phases is at zero as it is reversing its polarity.

Figure 16-20 shows the first rectifying stage as current flows from phase winding 1 to phase winding 2 (phase winding 3 is momentarily at zero). Electrons flow from the phase 1 winding, out the grounded diode and into the grounded side of the battery. This reverses the electron flow through the battery to cause the battery charging. Electrons then flow to phase winding 2 through its positive diode, through the Y connections and on to the phase winding 1 to complete the circuit.

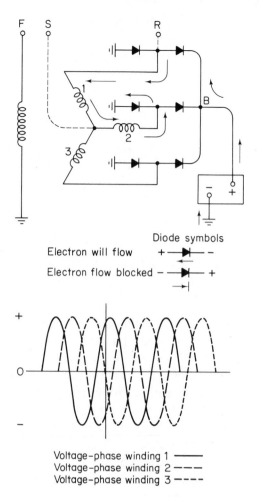

Diode symbols

Electron will flow   + ▷|– –

Electron flow blocked   – ▶|– +

Voltage-phase winding 1 ———
Voltage-phase winding 2 – – –
Voltage-phase winding 3 – – – –

Fig. 16-21 Phase 2 to Phase 1 rectification.

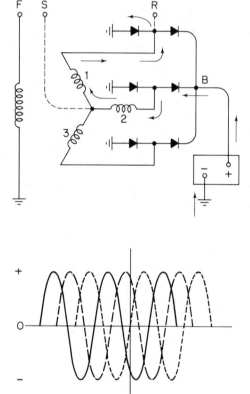

Fig. 16-20 Phase 1 to Phase 2 rectification.

The second rectifying stage is shown in Figure 16-21. With phase winding 3 neutral, the electrons flow from phase winding 2 through the grounded diode, then on to the negative battery post. Electrons move from the positive battery post through the positive diode of the phase winding 1. The circuit is completed through the Y connection.

Phase winding 2 is momentarily at zero during the rectifying stage three in Figure 16-22. Electrons

Fig. 16-22 Phase 1 to Phase 3 rectification.

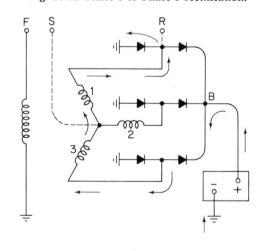

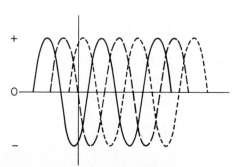

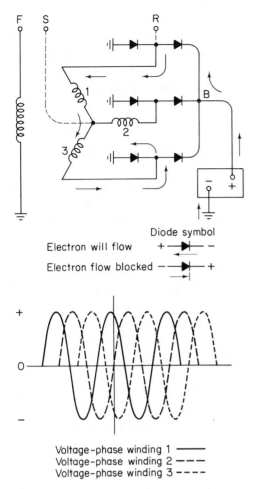

Diode symbol

Electron will flow   + ▶|— —

Electron flow blocked —|▶— +

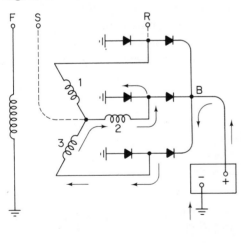

Voltage-phase winding 1 ——————
Voltage-phase winding 2 — — —
Voltage-phase winding 3 - - - -

Fig. 16-23 Phase 3 to Phase 1 rectification.

Fig. 16-24 Phase 2 to Phase 3 rectification.

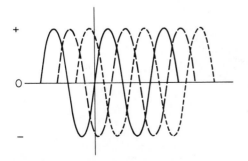

flow from phase winding 1 through the grounded diode to the grounded battery post. The flow continues to the positive diode of phase winding 3 and the Y connection to complete the circuit.

During rectifying stage four, phase winding 2 is neutral. Electrons leave phase winding 3 through its negative diode to flow to the battery. The phase winding 1 positive diode carries the electrons from the positive battery post through the winding and Y connection.

Rectifying stage five is timed to show the electron flow while phase winding 1 is at zero as it is changing polarity. Electrons flow from phase winding 2 through the grounded diode and the battery, then on into phase winding 3 through its positive diode. The circuit is completed through the Y connection.

The sixth rectifying stage is the reverse of stage five. Electrons from phase winding 3 go to the battery through the grounded diode. From the positive battery post, the electrons flow through the positive diode and into phase winding 2. The Y connection completes the circuit to phase winding 3.

It should be noted that as the electron flow reverses within the phase windings, the outside circuit from the alternator ground and from the alternator battery (BAT) terminal is always in the same direction. The entire external voltage of an alternator is a pulsating voltage in one direction, just as the voltage from the generator is pulsating in one direction. This one-way voltage is the force that moves a direct current when the circuit is completed.

Each free end of the three stator windings is connected to the leads of one negative diode and one positive diode. The three negative diodes are pressed into the alternator case or into a diode plate where they can make a good electrical connection through the engine and ground wire to the battery. The three positive diodes are pressed into a block of aluminum or heavy sheet metal called a *heat sink*. It is insulated from the alternator frame and is exposed to an air flow to keep the diodes cool. The insulated heat sink is connected to the insulated or positive side of the battery.

Battery current will not flow through the diodes because they are connected in a manner in which the battery puts a reverse bias voltage on

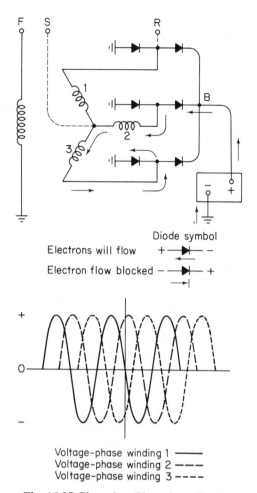

Diode symbol

Electrons will flow $+ \longrightarrow -$

Electron flow blocked $- \longrightarrow +$

Voltage-phase winding 1 ——
Voltage-phase winding 2 – – –
Voltage-phase winding 3 – – – –

Fig. 16-25 Phase 3 to Phase 2 rectification.

each of the diodes. When the operating alternator voltage increases above battery voltage, a forward bias is placed on the diodes and they conduct current to charge the battery and to supply current to operate accessories.

16-4 TESTING CHARGING CIRCUITS

Many service men do not understand charging systems. When these men have a charging system problem, they will most likely change parts until the system operates. This method is time consuming and the parts are expensive for the customer. Modern test equipment allows charging system testing to be quick and simple. Test equipment used along with a thorough understanding of charging system operating principles will lead to quick, accurate diagnosis. Only the malfunctioning part will need to be repaired, thus saving time, parts cost, and come-back.

As in any electrical test work, the first thing to check is the battery. It should be tested to see that it is healthy and charged. If it is faulty, it should be replaced with a good battery before any further tests are run.

Alternator Tests. The battery test is followed by an alternator output test. In this test, a test ammeter is connected in the charging circuit, either at the alternator or at the battery. The alternator field wire is removed and a jumper wire connected between the field terminal and battery terminal on internally grounded types or to ground on externally grounded types. A heavy carbon-pile rheostat is

Fig. 16-26 Typical diode installations in alternators.

placed across the battery and adjusted as necessary to hold the system voltage at the voltage given in the applicable specification, approximately 14 to 15 V. The engine is started, and adjusted to the required speed, about 1500 rpm. The carbon-pile rheostat is tightened to reduce charging voltage or loosened to raise voltage to specifications. Alternator output is read on the ammeter while the engine speed and voltage are operating at specification settings.

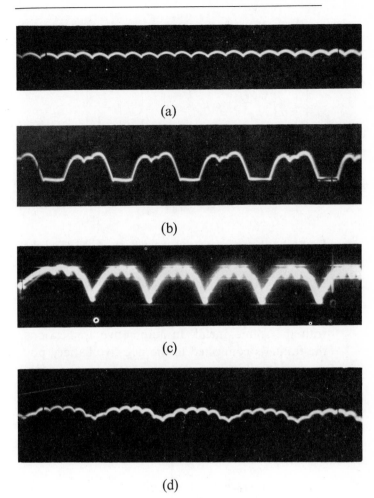

(a)

(b)

(c)

(d)

Fig. 16-28 Alternator scope patterns. (a) Normal, (b) one shorted diode, (c) open diode, (d) partially shorted diode.

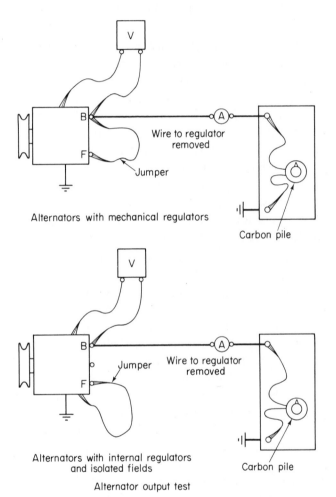

Alternators with mechanical regulators

Carbon pile

Alternators with internal regulators and isolated fields

Carbon pile

Alternator output test

Fig. 16-27 Alternator output test connections.

If the alternator output is low, further alternator tests are required. One of the best test instruments for alternator problem analysis is the oscilloscope. Many engine scopes have connections and circuits so that they can be used for alternator testing. The pattern displayed on the scope will show a normal pattern, open diode, shorted diode, open stator, or shorted stator. If several of these malfunctions occur at the same time, they will produce an unusual abnormal pattern. Serious malfunctions will show up on meters. Another means to trouble shoot the alternator is to disassemble it and check each part for malfunction so that it can be repaired.

Failure of electrical components may be classified under three causes: *shorts*, *grounds*, and *opens*. Any one of these will result in a malfunctioning electrical unit.

Shorts occur when two adjacent conductors make an electrical contact. The electrical current can go from one conductor to the next, bypassing a portion of the circuit. This part of the circuit gets no current. The short reduces circuit resistance so the conductors can carry more current and, therefore, become warmer.

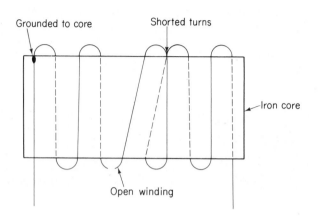

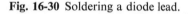

Fig. 16-29 Shorts, opens and grounds on a coil (The Pre-stolite Company).

Grounds are a special form of a short in which the insulated conductor makes electrical contact with the frame metal. In automotive applications, the frame is connected to the negative battery post so current follows the conductor to the ground point, completing the circuit in the shortest possible way, bypassing the rest of the circuit. This failure also has low resistance so more current will flow and the conductors get warm.

Fig. 16-30 Soldering a diode lead.

Shorts are usually checked by measuring the circuit resistance. An ohmmeter can be used on high resistance inoperative circuits and a voltage drop method on low resistance operating circuits. No method is in common use for circuits with very low resistance.

Grounds are checked with a continuity light. It uses a light bulb with two leads in series with a power source. One lead terminal is connected to the conductor and the other to the frame ground. The test bulb will light if a ground exists. If there is no ground, the bulb will not light.

Opens may also be checked with a continuity light. The test lead terminals are placed at each end of the conductor suspected to be faulty. An open exists if the bulb does not light. There is a complete circuit if the bulb lights. Another means of checking an open is to use a voltmeter. One voltmeter lead is attached to the ground and the other lead is touched to junctions along the conductor circuit while the battery is connected into the circuit. An open exists when the voltmeter no longer indicates battery voltage as the leads are moved from junction to junction.

The same methods used to find shorts, grounds, and opens can be used to check individual alternator components. Stators are disconnected from the diodes for checking both continuity and grounds with a 110-V test light. When necessary, unsolder and re-solder diode connections. This is done while holding the diode lead with a long nose pliers between the soldered joint and diode. The pliers act as a heat sink to draw the soldering heat into the pliers. Heat can damage a diode. To test stator winding continuity, the test bulb should light when one test lead is connected to the Y connection and the other test lead touched to the stator free ends. The stator is not grounded when one test lead is connected to the Y connection and the other test lead touched to the stator core. Stator shorts are not easily detected because they normally have low resistance. Generally, stator shorts will be evident by an overheated discolored insulation around the location of the short.

Field coil continuity in the rotor is checked by placing one 110-V test lead on each slip ring. The bulb should light. Field coil grounds are checked by placing one test lead on one of the slip rings and the other test lead on the rotor end piece. The bulb should not light.

Fig. 16-31 Testing a stator for grounding (The Prestolite Company).

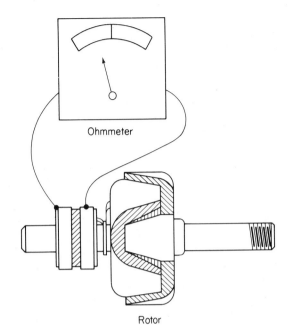

Fig. 16-33 Testing a rotor field for continuity (The Prestolite Company).

Any stators or field coils that are shorted, grounded or open, will have to be replaced. They are normally repaired only in specialized rebuilding facilities.

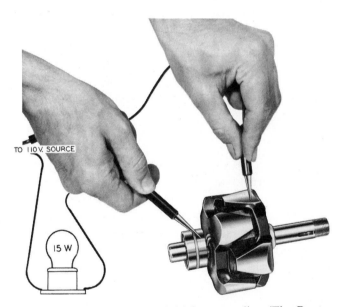

Fig. 16-32 Testing a rotor field for grounding (The Prestolite Company).

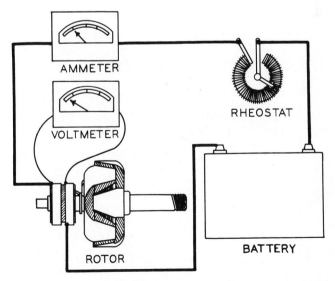

Fig. 16-34 Measuring field current draw (The Prestolite Company).

A field coil short may be tested with an ohmmeter because the field coil is a high resistance unit. Ohmmeter leads are placed on the slip rings. It can also be checked by measuring the current flow or current draw through the field at a specified voltage. If excessive current flows, the field coil is shorted.

A disconnected diode can be checked with a 12-V DC test light. The test bulb should light when one test lead is connected to the diode case and the other test lead is connected to the diode lead wire. The bulb should not light when the test leads are reversed. The diode is faulty if the bulb is either on or off with both connections. Faulty diodes are not repairable and must be replaced.

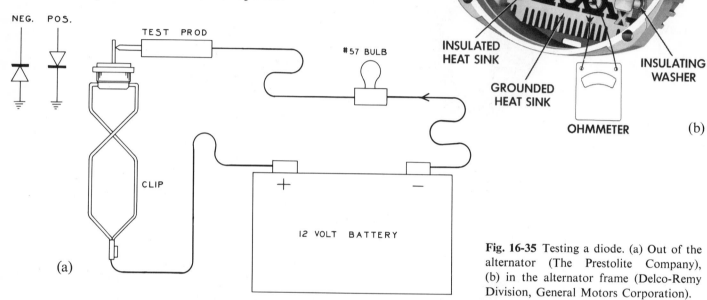

(a)

Fig. 16-35 Testing a diode. (a) Out of the alternator (The Prestolite Company), (b) in the alternator frame (Delco-Remy Division, General Motors Corporation).

Fig. 16-36 Holding the brushes with a wire for easy alternator assembly.

Some diodes can be replaced individually using the correct removing and installing tools. In other alternators, a positive or negative diode plate containing three diodes is replaced if any one of the diodes is faulty. Still other alternators are designed so the entire diode rectifier bridge is replaced when one diode is faulty. Detailed replacement procedures may be found in the applicable vehicle service manual.

Occasionally, the brush holders become grounded. These are checked with a 110-V test light from the brush to the alternator frame. Most brush holders are provided with a cross hole. A pin is inserted in the hole to hold the brush, after the brush is compressed against its spring, so the alternator may be easily assembled. After assembly, the pin is removed to allow the brushes to contact the slip rings.

Voltage Drop Tests. All conductors must be free of abnormal resistances if the charging system is to function correctly. Voltage drops throughout the charging circuit are checked while the alternator is producing 20 A in the circuit, using the same test connections as used to check alternator output. The insulated charging circuit should have a voltage drop of less than .7 V while the grounded side of the circuit should have a voltage drop of less than .1 V.

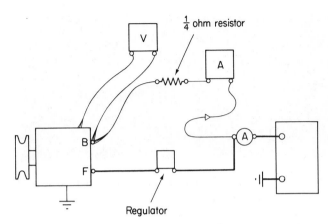

Fig. 16-38 Connections for testing voltage regulator settings.

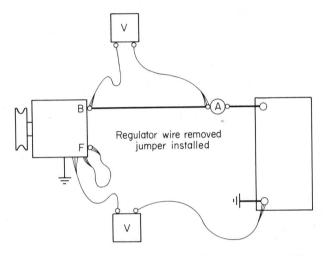

Fig. 16-37 Connections for testing charging system voltage drop. The field jumper connection is shown as it would be connected on an externally grounded type field.

Checking the Regulator Setting. The voltage regulator limits maximum voltage in the charging system. If the regulator setting is too low, the battery will not fully charge. A setting too high will shorten the service life of the ignition points, battery, electric motors, radio, lights, etc., by forcing excessive current through them. High voltage regulator settings may be first recognized as an unusual amount of headlight flare when the engine accelerates from idle. The battery will also use excessive water as a result of excessive gassing.

Charging system *voltage* increases when there is no place for the current to flow and decreases when there is a demand for electrical current. A regulator being tested must have the system placed under loads that will produce a system voltage which is in the regulator controlling range. Some manufacturers do this by using engine speed, lights, and a carbon-pile rheostat across a fully charged battery. Other manufacturers install a 1/4-ohm series

resistor in the charging circuit to add sufficient circuit resistance to increase system voltage into the regulating range. Specific test settings and specification procedures are provided by each vehicle manufacturer. These should be followed to obtain correct voltage regulator settings. Usually, the specified range is between 14 and 15 V. Test procedures vary from manufacturer to manufacturer, from model to model, and from year to year. Generally, speaking, mechanical regulators have internal field grounds, while solid-state regulators have external field grounds. It is important to use the correct applicable procedure and test specifications for the vehicle and for the test equipment being used to obtain satisfactory regulator settings.

Mechanical voltage regulators have two sets of points, normally-closed and normally-open. The normally-closed points regulate at approximately .5 V lower than the normally-open points. At set engine speeds and charging current flow (see specific applicable procedures) the regulated voltage can be read with a voltmeter. It is helpful if an oscilloscope or engine scope is connected to the regulator field while making this check.

A scope shows that regulation is accomplished by controlling the length of time a voltage surge takes place in the field coil. As the voltage increases, the full voltage surges are shorter and shorter until the normally-closed points float. As alternator speed increases, the normally-open field-shorting points

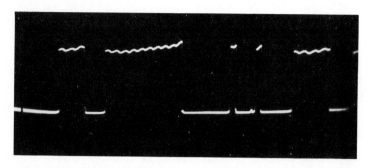

Fig. 16-39 Scope pattern of a mechanical regulator's field voltage while regulating.

make contact, reducing the voltage surges to the field coil.

Mechanical regulator voltage settings are made by adjusting the spring hanger position to increase spring pressure as higher voltage is needed. Solid-state regulators are adjusted by changing the setting of a variable resistor. If the regulator cannot be adjusted when required, it is replaced.

Field Relays. Field relays are often placed in the voltage regulator box. Their purpose is to supply current to the alternator field through the voltage regulator points when the relay points are closed. The field relay will close at approximately 8 V, fully energizing the alternator field.

Charging systems use ammeters and indicating lights to show if the battery is being charged or discharged. Some of the indicator lights parallel a resistance. Field current is fed through the resistor

Fig. 16-40 Typical voltage regulator adjustment locations.

Fig. 16-41 Voltage regulators. Regulator on the right also has a field relay on the same frame.

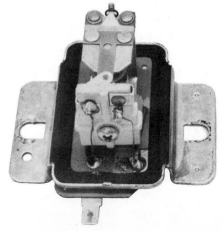

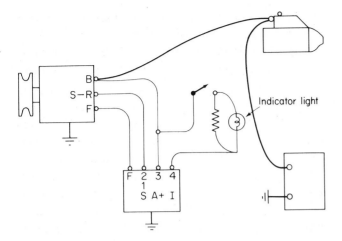

Fig. 16-42 Typical alternator-regulator circuit using an indicator light.

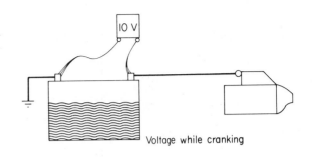

Voltage while cranking

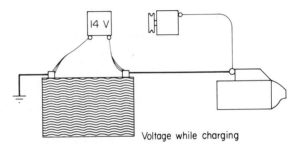

Voltage while charging

Fig. 16-43 Voltage while cranking and while charging.

and light until the field relay closes. When the relay closes, battery voltage is impressed across the regulator end of the light. With battery voltage on both sides of the light, no current will flow and the light will go out.

Many other variations are used in the charging circuit. Each should be checked with manufacturer's tests and procedures using the correct specifications.

16-5 CHARGING SYSTEM REGULATION

The battery regulates voltage in the charging system up to a maximum voltage that is limited by the voltage regulator. The maximum amount of current produced by the alternator is limited by the alternator design. Maximum current in a commutator-rectified generator is limited by a current regulator.

Battery Regulation. The battery supplies electrical power to crank and start the engine. If the start is slow, quite a bit of electrical energy is withdrawn from the battery and this results in a slightly lower battery voltage. As soon as the engine starts, the charging system comes into operation to supply the vehicle electrical load and recharge the battery. The charging system voltage increases as the battery CEMF voltage increases. While the battery CEMF is low, the charging system supplies high current to the battery. As the battery becomes charged, battery CEMF increases, decreasing the charging amperage rate. This change is accompanied by an increase in the voltage of the entire charging system. When battery CEMF reaches the regulator voltage

setting, the regulator begins to take control to limit the voltage level.

Mechanical Voltage Regulator Operation. The voltage regulator consists of breaker points mounted on an armature above a voltage sensitive coil with associated supporting mechanical and electrical components. The voltage regulator points are connected in series with the alternator or generator field. The points are *normally-closed* to allow full current flow in the field to provide maximum magnetic field flux. When charging system voltage reaches setting voltage, the regulator points open, breaking the field circuit. This stops field current and the magnetic field flux decays, reducing alternator or generator output voltage. When voltage drops, the points close, re-establishing field current and field magnetic flux. This cycle happens very rapidly, as shown on the oscilloscope, in Figure 16-39, keeping the voltage essentially constant as shown on a voltmeter.

The voltage regulator points are held closed with an adjustable calibrated spring. An electro-

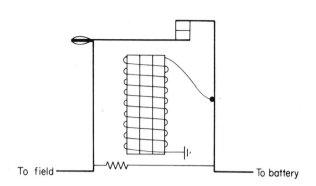

Fig. 16-44 Circuit of a typical single point mechanical voltage regulator.

magnetic force pulls the regulator armature down to open the points when system voltage reaches the setting voltage.

The electromagnet of a voltage regulator is made from a great number of fine wire turns wrapped around a soft iron core. This wire has high resistance because it is long and has a small diameter. Its high resistance will only allow a very small current to flow when charging because it is connected across the charging system from the insulated side to ground. The amount of current flowing in the regulator coil is determined by charging system voltage. As the charging system voltage increases, the current flow through the coil increases which, in turn, increases the coil's magnetic field strength.

The magnetic strength of a coil may be measured in *ampere turns*. The voltage regulator coil has a low amperage and a high number of turns. When amperage or current flow in the coil circuit is strong at a high charging system voltage, the magnetism of the coil pulls on the spring-held armature with the movable contact point attached. This separates the points to break field current flow, reducing the system voltage. The reduced voltage weakens the coil's magnetism so the armature spring closes the points. This cycle continues all the time the regulator is controlling system voltage.

A resistor is used across the regulator points to form a by-pass for some of the field current. This keeps the field flux from decaying completely when the points are open, but will weaken it to a voltage level close to nominal battery voltage. This

results in a rapid field response that will provide smooth voltage control. Other resistors may be used in the voltage regulator to reduce point burning and to aid in maintaining smooth voltage control.

In some charging systems, the resistor across the points allows somewhat more current to flow through the field while the points are open. With field current being fed through the resistor and the charging system running under light electrical loads at moderate speeds, the generator voltage matches the electrical load. When this happens, the points float and do not touch. Any increase in speed or any reduction in electrical load would result in excess system voltage.

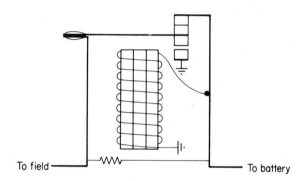

Fig. 16-45 Circuit of a typical dual point mechanical voltage regulator.

To prevent excessive voltage at higher speeds on alternators and on some high output generators, a second *normally-open* contact point is added to their voltage regulators. This second point is grounded. As system voltage increases, more current flows through the voltage regulator coil winding, pulling the armature further and causing the second set of voltage regulator points to contact the grounded point. All of the current flowing through the resistor is then directed to ground so no current flows through the field. This causes alternator field flux to decay, dropping system voltage which, in turn, reduces the voltage regulator coil magnetic field strength. When the system voltage lowers, the spring opens the normally-open grounding points, allowing current to again flow through the resistor to the field coil, building up the magnetic field flux and increasing system voltage. This action recycles, causing the points to vibrate on the normally-open grounded point.

Magnetism attracts the regulator armature

through an air gap. The effectiveness of a magnet reduces as the square of the distance through which it must act. The magnetism would be only 1/4 as effective at twice the air gap. The air gaps between the coil core and armature are critical for correct regulator operation and must be within specifications. Mechanical regulator voltage settings are adjusted by changing the armature return spring tension. Increasing spring tension increases the regulator coil strength required to move the armature. The coil magnetic strength increases as system voltage increases.

Current Regulation. The current flowing in the alternator reverses itself, increasing and decreasing as it alternates in the same manner as the voltage. As the current flow increases in a stator, it forms a magnetic field around the winding. This newly-formed field cuts across adjacent conductors within the stator coil winding. This produces a counter voltage in the adjacent conductors which opposes the initial voltage induced by the rotor field flux. This principle of inducing a counter voltage in a coil wire that is carrying an increasing or a decreasing current is called *inductance*. Maximum alternator current output is limited by the induced counter voltage. As counter voltage approaches the output voltage, amperage output stabilizes at a maximum safe value.

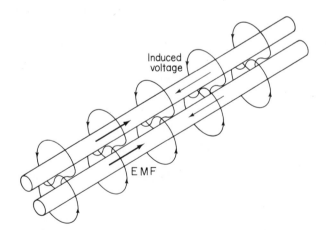

Fig. 16-46 Inductance by voltage induced from the magnetic field of current flowing in an adjacent conductor.

Current regulation of commutator rectified generators is similar to voltage regulation except the current regulator coil design is different. Normally-closed single contact current regulator points are connected in series with the voltage regulator points and field. Any time the current regulator points open, field current is lowered to the amount of current that will flow through a resistor. The current regulator coil is made of a few turns of heavy wire which carries all of the current produced by the generator. When the generator is producing maximum regulated current, the current regulator coil has enough ampere-turns to open the current regulator points. This drops field current, reducing field flux strength which, in turn, lowers generator output. The current regulator coil strength decreases as generator output current drops and this allows the armature spring to close the points, re-establishing field current in the generator. The current regulator points vibrate to limit current output.

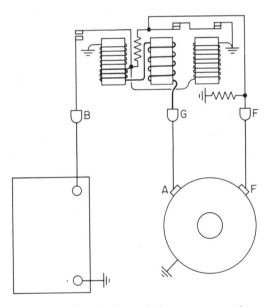

Fig. 16-47 Circuit of a typical generator regulator.

The voltage regulator and current regulator do not control the generator output at the same time. When there is a large amperage flow, electrical pressure cannot build up. When current flow is restricted, voltage will increase.

Voltage limitation is required to protect the battery and accessories. If too much voltage were to be impressed on them, it would force them to carry excess current. This, in turn, would result in overheating and short service life. Current limitation protects the alternator or generator. If they were allowed to produce more than their design current, they, too, would overheat and fail.

Reverse Current. Commutator rectified generators are provided with a *cut-out* that disconnects the battery from the charging system when the generator is not charging. The cut-out is located in the same box with the voltage and current regulators. When the engine starts, generator voltage builds up and current flows through the cut-out coil's series and shunt windings. When the ampere-turns of this circuit become strong enough, coil magnetism will pull the *normally-open* points into closed position, completing the battery to generator connection.

Current flows backward between the battery and generator as the engine is stopped. This reverse current splits at the cut-out coil, part going through the shunt winding in its normal direction and part going through the series winding in a reverse direction. The magnetic fluxes of the two cut-out windings neutralize each other, releasing the cut-out armature so the points open to disconnect the battery from the generator.

Reverse current requires no switching in diode rectified generators (alternators). It was shown in Section 16-3 how diodes prevent battery current leaking through the alternator.

Solid-State Regulation. Mechanical regulators are being replaced by solid-state regulators. They are constructed with no moving parts, making use of semiconductors, resistors, capacitors and conductors. In some regulators, these parts are assembled from individual parts. This fabrication technique is called *discrete*. Some of the units may be encapsuled into groups. These groups are assembled into an operating unit and the fabricating method is called *hybrid*. A more advanced fabrication method used to produce a single integrated circuit is called *monolithic*. Discrete and hybrid fabricating techniques are used in applications where the regulator is separate from the alternator. Monolithic techniques are used in applications that have the regulator built into the alternator case. The solid-state regulator parts work in the same manner regardless of the fabricating technique that is used.

The advantage of the solid-state regulators over the mechanical regulator is their ability to control higher field currents with improved durability and reliability. They approach a foolproof regulator system. This is done using smaller size and lower cost units when manufactured at high production rates.

The solid-state regulator must control the alternator field current just as the mechanical regulator does. On-off switching is done with a solid-state semiconductor switch called a *transistor*, rather than with breaker points that are used on the mechanical regulators.

16-6 TRANSISTORS

The transistor is another of the many uses for semiconductor material. Diodes used in automotive applications are usually made of doped silicon crystals. Transistors are usually made from germanium crystals using indium to dope *P*-type material and antimony to dope *N*-type material. A diode is made of two materials, *P*-type junctioned to *N*-type. Transistors add another junction to the diode, forming either *PNP* or *NPN* transistors with two junctions. Most automobile applications use *PNP*-type transistors in discrete and hybrid construction. The *NPN*-type is used in monolithic regulators.

Transistor Construction. Using a *PNP*-type transistor, a simplified description of the transistor manufacturing procedure starts with a germanium crystal that has been doped with antimony. It is cut into thin slices to make a wafer of *N*-type material. Pure germanium crystals are applied to each side of the *N*-type wafer. Indium is then placed on each side of this wafer and it is heated to fuse the indium into the surface germanium crystals that are on each side of the *N*-type wafer. When this is complete, it forms a single crystal wafer consisting of three regions, *N*-type material in the center and *P*-type material on each side, forming a *PNP* transistor. The *P*-type materials are close together with a very thin layer of *N*-type material between them.

PNP transistor schematic

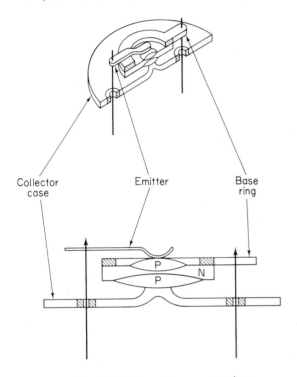

PNP power transistor construction

Fig. 16-48 Transistor construction.

The outer edge of the *N*-type material of the thin wafer is attached to a metal ring with the wafer fitting in the hole of the ring. An extension from the ring is used to attach the electrical conductor. This center *N*-type material of the transistor is called the *base*. The transistor with its base connection is placed in a copper container with the larger *P*-type area against the container inner surface. The container serves as an electrical connection called the *collector* as well as a heat sink to keep the transistor cool. A strip of metal connected to the smaller *P*-type material area serves as an electrical connection called an *emitter*. This unit is brazed together and sealed into a case. The wire from the emitter is run through the insulator from the transistor case for an electrical connection. Some transistors will also use a wire-type connector for the collector.

The actual transistor is only the small wafer crystal. Connections and case make up the bulk of the transistor assembly.

Some transistors are integrated in a complete monolithic circuit. These circuits start with a silicon wafer. The wafer is coated with a ceramic insulation and an emulsion that masks some of the insulation material. Where it is not masked, the ceramic insulation is removed by etching to expose silicon. Doping material is fused into the silicon, the wafer again is ceramic coated, masked and etched in other places, and then another doping agent is used. In some places conductors are developed, other places resistors. This process gradually builds up a complete circuit with transistors, conductors, and resistors within the wafer. The wafer is scribed and broken into chips. Each chip is a complete circuit with all operating parts required for alternator regulation. These complete circuit chips are encapsuled with electrical leads for charging circuit connections.

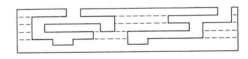

Integrated circuit buildup
(side view)

Fig. 16-49 Typical integrated circuit buildup.

Transistor Operations. A *PNP*-type transistor will be used to describe transistor operation. The *N*-type material in the central region is the base. It is made as thin as possible. The *P*-type material in the outer regions forms the emitter and collector. The emitter is connected through the operating unit to the positive or insulated side of the battery. The collector is connected to the grounded or negative side of the battery. The transistor base circuit is used to control transistor operation.

Electricity is movement of electrons. It has been previously shown that as the electrons move in one direction, holes will move in the opposite direction, holes being the lack of electrons. It is easier to understand *PNP*-type transistor operation if a simplified explanation is given in terms of hole movement rather than electron movement.

Assume that the emitter is connected through the operating unit to the positive battery terminal. The collector is connected through ground to the negative battery post, with the base circuit switch open. Whenever possible, electrons fill holes to make neutral atoms. Excess holes supplied by the battery collect along the junction between the emitter and base. Holes in the collector are attracted toward the negative side of the battery. As the holes move toward the battery, free electrons are left behind and these hold the holes in position.

When the base circuit switch is closed (having the same polarity as the collector) holes will move

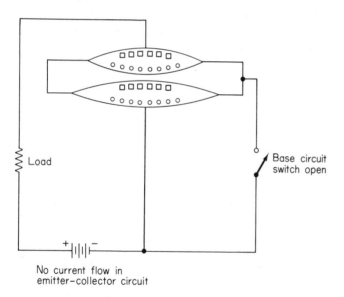

Fig. 16-50 Transistor circuit with open base circuit.

from the emitter to the base and back to the battery ground. As the holes from the emitter cross the base junction, their energy carries most of them across the second junction into the collector. This produces a current in the operating circuit. The base current is about 2.0% of the total emitter current. When the base circuit is reopened, hole movement stops, the transistor charges become neutralized, and hole movement to the collector stops, stopping the current flow from the emitter to the collector.

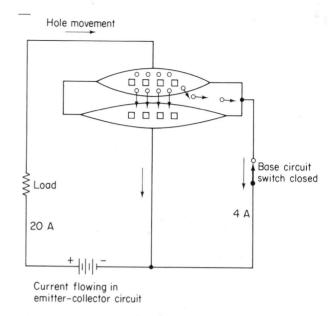

Fig. 16-51 Transistor circuit with a conducting base circuit.

Transistor Regulation. Transistor regulators are based on the same basic principle as mechanical regulators. They control alternator voltage by controlling the alternator field strength. Instead of breaker points, the transistor regulator uses a power transistor to do the required field circuit switching. The power transistor's operation is controlled by other transistors, diodes and resistors. Regulators built in a discrete or hybrid form can be repaired in some cases, but monolithic regulators cannot be repaired. It is important to understand the operation of transistor regulation in order to understand proper transistor regulator testing.

A simplified transistor regulator circuit is shown in Figure 16-53. Using the hole movement explanation method, holes come from the battery to transistor T_1 emitter. The base is connected to the ground through R_1 so it conducts. With the base conducting, current can go from the emitter to the collector and on to the alternator field to supply full alternator field current.

Battery voltage is also impressed on the emitter of transistor T_2. The base of T_2 is connected to the Zener diode D_Z which is reverse biased so no base current will flow and transistor T_2 is turned off so it will not conduct. Voltage also is impressed on resistors R_2, variable resistor R_3, R_4, and thermal resistor R_t, allowing a very small current to flow to ground. A voltage drop exists across each resistor as current flows.

Fig. 16-52 Typical transistor regulators.

The Zener diode is the sensing device in the solid-state regulator. It is used to control maximum circuit voltage. When the reverse bias voltage across the Zener diode reaches its breakdown point, it will conduct current in the reverse direction. The reverse bias voltage is equal to the voltage drop across R_2 and part of R_3. Changing the connection point of the Zener diode on variable resistance R_3 is used to adjust regulator settings.

When the Zener diode conducts, the base of transistor T_2, is turned on and T_2 conducts from the collector to ground through R_4. The collector of T_2 then places the same voltage on the T_1 base as the emitter of T_1. With the voltage the same on the emitter and on the base, transistor T_1 is effectively turned off, stopping field current to the alternator. The alternator voltage falls off when the field current stops, the Zener diode stops conduction in reverse bias which, in turn, stops the base current of T_2, turning it off. This allows the base current of T_1 to restart conduction through R_1 and begin to supply field current to the alternator. This cycle is repeated at a very high rate, controlling the alternator voltage.

The resistor R_t is sensitive to temperature. At low temperatures, it has high resistance. This reduces current flow through the series resistances. A higher circuit voltage is required at low temperatures to force the Zener diode to conduct in a reverse bias. This causes the charging system to operate at higher voltages when cold and at lower voltages when warm to be compatible with battery operation characteristics.

The basic transistor operating circuit is smoothed out and speeded up using resistors and capacitors. Transient voltages and leakage are controlled with additional diodes, resistors, and capacitors.

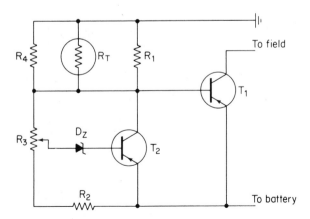

Fig. 16-53 Basic transistor regulator circuit.

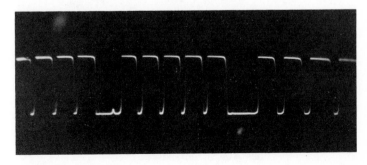

Fig. 16-54 Scope pattern of a transistor regulator's field voltage while regulating.

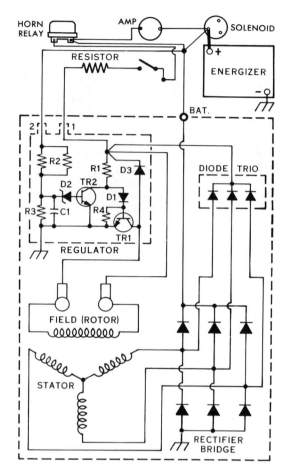

Fig. 16-55 Complete alternator-transistor regulator circuit (Delco-Remy Division, General Motors Corporation).

Review Questions
Chapter 16

1. How is generator output controlled?

2. How are the coils spaced in the stator?

3. How does the alternator differ from the older type generator?

4. In what part of an operating alternator does AC current exist?

5. Make a drawing to show how a two-pole magnet's field cuts a loop conductor.

6. What is meant by rectification?

7. What makes a material become a positive or negative semiconductor?

8. What is meant by a forward and reverse bias?

9. How does a positive diode differ from a negative diode?

10. How does half-wave rectification differ from full-wave rectification?

11. How is a grounded circuit detected?

12. How is an open circuit detected?

13. What means are used to locate a short?

14. Why is it important to use a pliers to hold the diode lead between the diode and the soldered joint when soldering?

15. Describe the stator tests to check its condition.

16. How do rotor tests differ from stator tests?

17. How should the test light act on a diode as the test leads are reversed?

18. What is the purpose of the small cross hole in the brush holder?

19. What is the purpose of a voltage regulator in the charging system?

20. What is the first indication that a voltage regulator setting is too high and too low?

21. What happens to the charging system voltage as the system resistance increases?

22. How is generator output controlled?

23. Describe the voltage regulator setting test procedure.

24. How is voltage regulator setting changed?

25. What is the purpose of a field relay in an alternator circuit?

26. How does a charging circuit indicator light operate?

27. When does a battery control charging system voltage?

28. What does a voltage regulator do to enable it to control alternator output?

29. What is the reason alternator mechanical regulators have two contact point sets?

30. How does the regulator air gap affect the magnetic pull of the voltage sensing coil on the regulator armature?

31. What limits maximum alternator current output?

32. How does the limitation of current output from a commutator-rectified generator differ from the diode-rectified alternator?

33. Why do generators need a cut-out and alternators do not?

34. What is the purpose of the Zener diode in a solid state regulator?

35. Describe the operation of a transistor in terms of the emitter, collector, and base.

36. What is the value of having a temperature-compensated voltage regulator?

Quiz 16

1. Alternator current output is controlled by the
   a. battery capacity
   b. stator resistance
   c. diode type and size
   d. rotor current.

2. Alternator output is
   a. an alternating current
   b. a three-phase current
   c. a direct current ripple
   d. either alternating or direct current, depending on the rectifier.

3. Diodes can be considered solid-state
   a. switches
   b. check valves
   c. conductors
   d. current limiters.

4. In order to have maximum alternator output the alternator must be run
   a. at high speed
   b. with a series 1/4-ohm resistance
   c. full-field current
   d. with the regulator controlling.

5. The voltage regulator controls when the alternator is turning rapidly and
   a. the battery has a low state of charge
   b. there is resistance in the charging circuit
   c. all of the electrical accessories are turned on
   d. the rotor has full-field current

6. If the voltage regulator were set too low, one might expect to encounter
   a. hard starting
   b. excessive battery water consumption
   c. flaring headlights
   d. short ignition point life.

7. What controls the charging system voltage between 12.8 V and 13.8 V?
   a. the voltage regulator
   b. partial field current
   c. stator resistance
   d. the battery

8. Maximum alternator current output is limited by
   a. induced counter voltage
   b. induced counter current
   c. the regulator
   d. diode action.

9. The voltage sensing unit in a transistor regulator is a
   a. resistor
   b. capacitor
   c. transistor
   d. Zener diode.

10. The current switching unit in a transistor regulator is a
    a. resistor
    b. capacitor
    c. transistor
    d. Zener diode.

chapter 17

Ignition System Operation

The ignition system forces an electrical arc across the spark plug electrodes to ignite the combustion chamber charge. This arc must have enough energy to increase the surrounding charge temperature to the kindling point at which the combustion becomes self-sustaining. The voltage necessary to overcome the spark plug gap resistance and cause the spark to reach the charge kindling temperature is called *required voltage*.

It makes no difference what type of ignition system is used. It may be a conventional design, it may use transistor switching or it may use a capacitive discharge system. The spark must be delivered to the spark plug with enough energy to ignite the charge.

It is not only important for the charge to ignite, but it must ignite at the correct instant so that the charge will produce maximum useful energy as the hot gases expand within the combustion chamber. The spark arc is timed so that maximum combustion chamber pressure occurs when the crank pin is 5 to 10° after top center. The ignition

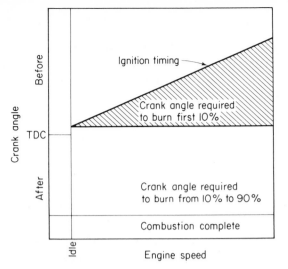

Fig. 17-1 Combustion burning rate in terms of engine speed and degrees of crankshaft rotation.

firing or timing point needs to be adjusted for charge changes that affect burning rates so that maximum pressure will always occur at 5 to 10° after top center under all operating conditions requiring power.

17-1 IGNITION TIMING AND ENGINE SPEED

The first 10% of the combustion charge burns at a constant rate, that is, it takes a specific length of time to burn, no matter what the engine speed happens to be. To compensate for this, a *mechanical timing advance* mechanism is used to advance the ignition firing point as engine speed increases.

From 10% on, combustion rate increase is proportional to engine speed, primarily because of increased turbulence created by a high velocity intake charge, combustion chamber squash area, and flame turbulence. At some high rpm, depending on the engine design, the first 10% becomes insignificant so that no further advance is required. Without this characteristic, engines could not run at high speeds.

17-2 IGNITION TIMING AND ENGINE LOAD

The mass or weight of the charge that is taken into the combustion chamber as the result of throttle position and engine load also affects timing requirements. Under light throttle conditions, high mani-

fold vacuum occurs and a small quantity of charge is drawn into the combustion chamber. Pressure resulting from compression of this charge is low and its burning rate is slow. This low pressure type of charge requires high advance to be able to complete combustion at 5 to 10° after top center. At these low compression pressures, the spark plug will arc at a low required voltage.

At low speed and full throttle, a large charge enters the combustion chamber because the open throttle provides minimum intake restriction. When compressed, this charge is dense and has high pressure. More gas molecules are present between the electrodes. Once kindled, combustion occurs quite rapidly so timing is retarded to have combustion complete at 5 to 10° after top center.

This could be compared to going to a drag race. If the race began at six o'clock, one would plan to start early enough to arrive on time. His starting time would depend on the road type, the traffic anticipated, and the weather. The ignition system anticipates the expected length of time to complete combustion, then it must start early enough in the cycle so that combustion is completed at the correct time.

A vacuum timing advance mechanism is used to change ignition timing to compensate for throttle position and engine load. Timing is advanced under high vacuum, light load operation when the burning rate is slow. It is retarded under low vacuum, heavy load operation when fast burning rates occur. The vacuum advance fully retards at full throttle because it is not required for maximum engine power. Its primary function is to provide fuel economy during part throttle operation by igniting the charge at an advance which will give maximum mean effective pressure at the operating conditions.

17-3 REQUIRED VOLTAGE

Required voltage is the actual voltage produced in the secondary ignition circuit to overcome ignition resistance and fire the spark plug. If required voltage exceeds the maximum voltage available, misfiring will occur. Voltage required to arc across the spark plug is based upon a number of operating variables and physical conditions existing in the ignition system.

Operating variables that affect required voltage are based on the compression pressure and the air/fuel mixture ratio of the charge in the cylinder. Compression pressure changes as the throttle is opened and closed, being highest when the throttle is wide open and lowest when the throttle is closed. When engine speeds increase, compression pressure lowers as a result of lower volumetric efficiency. Required voltage is low when the compression pressure is low and high when the compression pressure is high.

The air/fuel ratio effect on required voltage is lowest when the ratio is adjusted to produce best power, approximately 12:1. Any change from this air/fuel ratio, either rich or lean, will increase

required voltage. To ignite, the charge must be between the spark plug electrodes and the spark arc must have enough thermal energy to start a self-propogating flame in the mixture.

The spark plug gap is the "voltage regulator" that controls required voltage. It is located in the combustion chamber so its gap senses compression pressure and charge air/fuel mixture. Required voltage is sensitive to the gap spacing between the spark plug electrodes. A larger gap requires increased voltage. Too small a gap reduces the required voltage but also reduces the opportunity for a combustible mixture to get into the electrode gap. Small gaps also reduce the air/fuel mixture igniting range. The largest spark plug gap is required at idle speeds when the least amount turbulence exists in the combustion chamber.

At idle speeds, the charge turbulence is low and, therefore, the chance of having the correct mixture move into the spark plug electrode gap is also low. The minimum spark plug gap that will produce satisfactory engine idle is .025″. Most ignition systems use gap specification over .030″. As engine speed increases, combustion chamber turbulence will also increase and this reduces the gap requirement. In engines operating above half-load, a gap of .005″ would actually provide satisfactory operation. Combustion chamber turbulence must not, however, be so great as to blow the initial flame from between the spark plug electrodes until it becomes hot enough to maintain combustion.

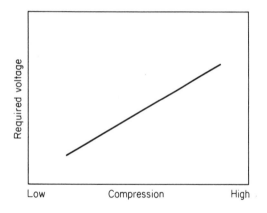

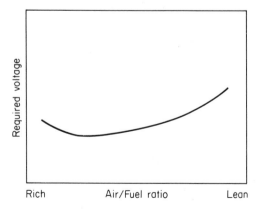

Fig. 17-2 Required voltage modified by compression and air/fuel ratio.

Fig. 17-3 Inducted charge gases reaching the spark plug electrodes (Champion Spark Plug Company).

The shape of spark plug electrodes, as well as the gap, affects required voltage. New spark plug electrodes have the lowest required voltage. The electrode becomes eroded after a number of arcs, rounding off the original sharp edges. This erosion increases the voltage requirement.

Fig. 17-4 Eroded spark plug electrodes (AC Spark Plug Division, General Motors Corporation).

Any increase in secondary circuit resistance increases the voltage requirement. Secondary wiring with loose connections increases resistance. Wide rotor gap to cap electrodes will increase resistance. Damaged secondary wires increase resistance. The difference between the voltage available from the ignition system and the required voltage is called *ignition reserve*. Misfiring occurs when no ignition reserve remains.

Fig. 17-5 Available and required voltage compared to engine speed.

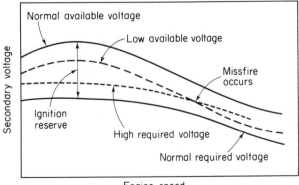

17-4 IGNITION SYSTEM OPERATION

The ignition system uses the battery as a primary source of electrical energy until the engine is started. After the engine is running, the charging system provides the primary electrical energy. Electrical power is carried through wires, switches and resistors to an ignition coil. The coil transforms low primary voltage to high secondary voltage which is delivered through a distributor to the spark plug in the cylinder, where it ignites the combustion charge.

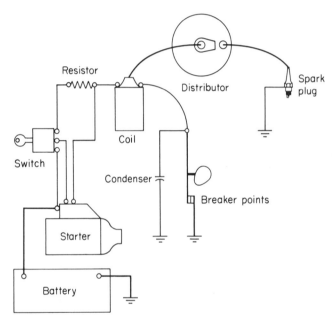

Fig. 17-6 Typical ignition system circuit.

The *ignition coil* is the *source* of the energy used to produce a spark or arc across the spark plug electrodes. It consists of two windings, primary and secondary, around a soft iron core and placed within a case using connections and insulators. The primary winding is connected in series with the battery breaker points, resistor, and ignition switch. The secondary is connected in series with the distributor rotor, distributor cap, and spark plug.

In operation, battery voltage pushes current through the coil primary. This current flow builds up a magnetic flux around the primary winding and in the soft iron core. When the breaker points open,

275

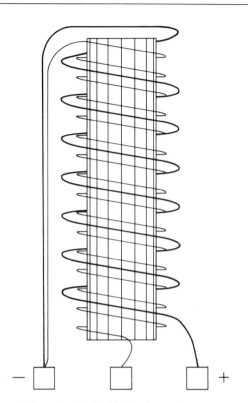

Fig. 17-7 Typical induction coil circuit.

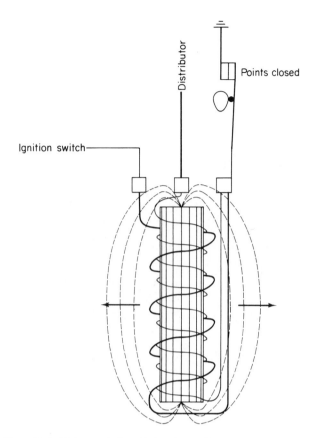

Fig. 17-8 Voltage induced in the coil secondary by the changing primary magnetic field as the ignition points open and close.

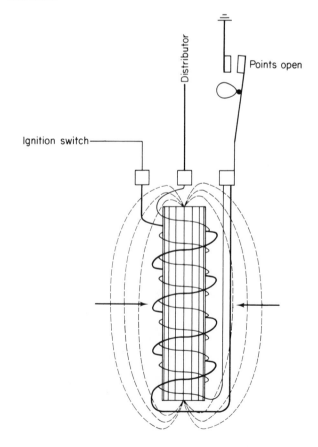

the circuit's current flow stops, causing the magnetic flux to collapse. During collapse, the flux lines rapidly cut through the secondary windings as they collapse. This rapid relative motion between the flux lines and conductor induces a high voltage in the secondary with sufficient energy to force an arc to flash across the spark plug electrodes. This entire sequence of events must occur each time a spark plug fires. In an eight-cylinder engine running at 4000 rpm, there are 266 spark plug firings each second. It is impossible to follow this action with a meter, because the meter cannot move fast enough, so a cathode ray oscilloscope is used to show this constantly changing voltage.

17-5 OSCILLOSCOPE MEASURING INSTRUMENT

A cathode ray oscilloscope display appears on the face of an electron tube that is similar to a television picture tube. The oscilloscope is powered by electrical and electronic circuits sensitive to voltage and time.

The gun in the base of the picture tube emits a stream of electrons, called a beam, that is directed toward the face of the tube between electrically charged plates. The electric charge on these plates deflects or sweeps the beam up and down or sideways. The sideways or horizontal sweep of an oscilloscope is based on time. Sweep speeds are based on centimeters per decimal part of a second, such as: .1, .01, .001, etc., of a second.

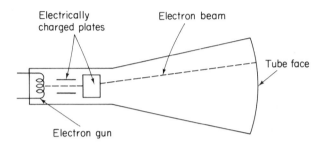

Fig. 17-9 Simplified cross section of an oscilloscope display tube.

The electron beam is focused to hit the tube screen. The screen has a coating so that it momentarily holds the light, allowing slow decay. As the beam sweeps, it leaves a light beam line on the scope face. The start of the beam movement must be initiated or triggered. When an electrical signal triggers the start of the horizontal beam sweep (x-axis), it will sweep the entire screen, then stop until it is triggered again. Each trigger impulse restarts the beam on the left side of the scope pattern, even if the beam has not completed its sweep across the screen.

Scope controls are provided to adjust voltage sensing (y-axis) and sweep rate (x-axis) as well as vertical and horizontal positioning of the sweep pattern. Using these controls, the operator can measure or look at the characteristics of any portion of the oscilloscope pattern displayed.

The ignition system has its own characteristic oscilloscope pattern. It will be used to describe the details of the ignition system operation. When the details of this pattern are known, they can be applied to ignition scopes as an aid to engine analysis and diagnosis.

17-6 COIL OPERATION

The typical standard automotive ignition coil has from 100 to 180 primary windings using #20 copper wire. The primary winding carries a high current so it becomes warm. It is, therefore, wrapped on the outside of the secondary winding to aid in its cooling. The secondary coil has 18,000 winding turns of #38 wire. Both wires are coated with insulating varnish and the winding layers are separated with oiled paper. A laminated soft iron core is placed in the center of the coils and a laminated soft iron shield is wrapped around the outside. The laminations of the core and shield limit magnetic eddy currents that would reduce coil efficiency. This assembly is placed in a can with a ceramic insulator, filled with insulating transformer oil, then sealed. Coils are not repairable. If tests show them to be faulty, they must be replaced.

Battery voltage forces a current to flow through the primary coil when the breaker points are closed. The amount of current that flows through the primary circuit is limited by the resistance of the long copper primary wire and by other resistances in the circuit. As current flow increases, the magnetic flux around the primary coil wire expands across adjacent wires which induces a counter voltage that opposes the input current flow. The counter

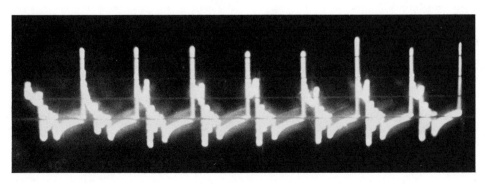

Fig. 17-10 Typical ignition scope pattern.

277

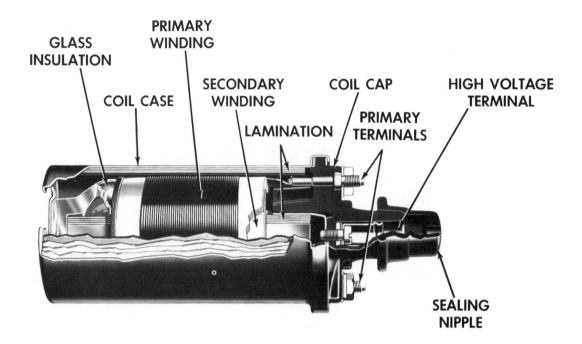

GLASS INSULATION

PRIMARY WINDING

COIL CASE

SECONDARY WINDING

LAMINATION

COIL CAP

PRIMARY TERMINALS

HIGH VOLTAGE TERMINAL

SEALING NIPPLE

Fig. 17-11 Coil nomenclature (Delco-Remy Division, General Motors Corporation).

Fig. 17-12 Primary current flow in relation to time as the points close and open to induce a secondary voltage.

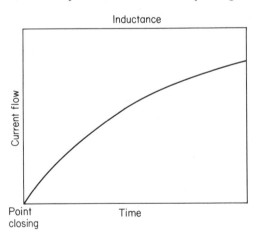

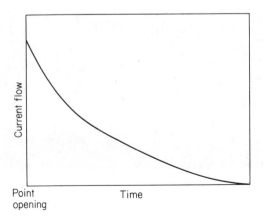

voltage slows full current buildup causing it to occur over a period of time. This characteristic is called *inductance*, as previously described in Section 16-5. The primary magnetic field buildup induces a voltage in the secondary, but it is not strong enough to form an arc across the spark plug electrodes.

Capacitance is another electrical property that affects the ignition system. When two conductors are close together but insulated from each other, the negative charges in one conductor will attract the positive charges in the adjacent conductor somewhat like electron attraction in diodes. These charges will remain as long as the conductors remain insulated from each other. In this way, they are able to store electrical energy. The capacity of the secondary ignition circuit is based on the design of the secondary coil and on the length and routing of the secondary wiring.

As current flows through the primary coil, its field flux builds up until full current flows, at which

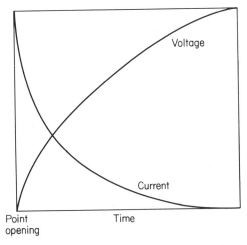

Fig. 17-13 Current and voltage in relation to time as the system capacitance becomes charged.

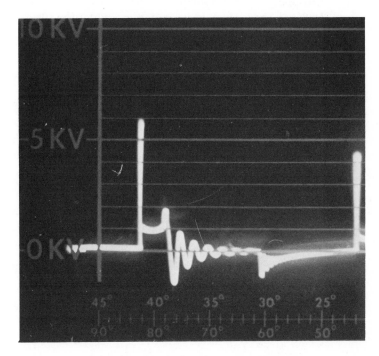

Fig. 17-14 Typical single cylinder scope pattern.

time the coil has reached magnetic saturation. This stores electrical energy in the coil by induction.

When the breaker points open, primary current flow stops, with the aid of the primary condenser. As the primary current stops, the magnetic field flux quickly collapses, cutting the coil windings.

Rapid collapse of the coil magnetic field flux produces voltage in the primary and secondary windings, charging their capacitances. The capacitive portion of the electrical energy builds up in the secondary until it has sufficient voltage to ionize gases between the spark plug electrodes. This voltage produces the familiar *spike* on ignition scope patterns. Ionization breaks down spark plug gap resistance and the required voltage falls to about one-fourth of the spike peak voltage as the arc is established. Duration of the arc is fed by inductance as the flux lines continue to collapse through the secondary windings. This portion of the ignition scope pattern is called the *spark firing line*. Ignition takes place during capacitive discharge and during the first part of inductive discharge.

The total energy that can be stored in the coil is based on primary current and on the length of time the current can flow before the breaker points reopen. Primary current is limited by the current carrying ability of the breaker points. Normally, the primary current is limited to a 4.2 A flow, which allows the breaker points to last thousands of miles. If primary current flow were increased to 5.4 A, the breaker points would burn in a very few miles. The ability to operate with high primary

currents is one of the main advantages of transistor ignition systems. A power transistor can carry twice as much current as breaker points without being damaged. The length of time the primary current can flow to build up the magnetic field is limited by the number of degrees the crankshaft turns while the breaker points are closed and by the engine's speed. The longer the current can flow, the more energy will be stored in the coil. At low engine speeds, more energy can be stored in the coil than at high engine speeds, as a result of greater coil saturation by the primary current. The primary circuit is responsible to produce *available voltage* in the secondary circuit.

The total stored coil energy is dissipated as voltage and current in the arc that forms across the spark plug electrodes. This energy can be released in a very short period of time with high voltage and high current flow or it can be released slowly at a low voltage and low current flow. Energy release from the coil could be compared to electrical energy release through light bulbs. A given amount of electrical energy from a battery could be released

279

through an instantaneous brilliant flash of a flash bulb or through a sustained dim light of a flashlight. For ignition systems, a fast energy release across the spark plug electrodes provides the best ignition of the charge. It is called a fast rise time because the capacitive portion of the energy releases rapidly, producing the ignition scope pattern spike. Fast rise time will force the arc to jump across the electrode gap on a partly fouled spark plug; however, this type of operation is demanding on secondary insulation because high voltage will try to flash over the secondary insulation, too.

Fast rise time reduces the problem of slight electrical drains. Energy discharge occurs so rapidly that slight drains, such as fouled spark plugs, do not allow time for a significant amount of energy to leak away.

17-7 PRIMARY CONDENSER

A condenser is installed electrically across the breaker points in the ignition system. It is made from two long strips of electrical conductor foil *plates* separated by insulating paper. The number of electrons that can accumulate on one side of a plate is limited by the plate's size and the distance between plates. The larger and closer together the plates are, the more electrons they can store. This electron storage ability is called *capacity*. The measurement of capacity is a farad. It is a very large unit, so the smaller unit, *microfarad* (mfd = 10^{-6} farad) is used to describe the capacity of automotive ignition system condensers.

The condenser foil strip plates and insulation are rolled together, then placed in a container and

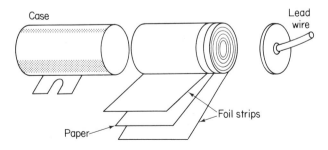

Fig. 17-15 Condenser construction.

sealed. A lead wire contacts one foil strip and the container case contacts the other. The strips of foil are close together so there is electrical attraction between electrons and holes across the insulation paper. The insulation paper keeps the circuit open so the electrons cannot cross to the other plate.

When the breaker points are closed, the primary circuit is complete and a current flows through the primary coil windings. When the breaker points open, the primary current is interrupted causing the coil magnetic field flux to start to collapse. This collapse produces an induced voltage that tends to keep the primary current flowing. This induced voltage may reach 250 V which is high enough to force the electrons across the breaker point gap as they are beginning to open. An arc across the breaker point gap would absorb electrical energy. The condenser provides a place for the electrons in the primary current to go during initial breaker point opening. The attraction of the positive condenser plate is so great that the electrons move freely into the negative plate, producing a high voltage charge on the negative plate. As the electrons pack into the condenser, they bring the primary current to a quick controlled stop which, in turn, causes a rapid collapse of the primary field flux. During this time, the breaker points have opened far enough so the voltage will not cause flashover across the breaker point gap.

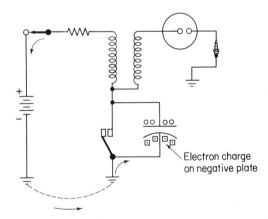

Fig. 17-16 Positive and negative charges on the condenser plates when the points open.

The high electron charge on the negative plate attempts to fill the holes in the positive plate. With the breaker points open, the only way for the electrons to get to the positive plate is back through the battery and primary circuit. As they flow, they cause a reverse current flow through the coil primary that forces a complete magnetic field flux collapse from its original direction and produces a flux buildup in the opposite direction. Electrons flow in this direction until they pack into the other side of the condenser plate, leaving holes behind them. This high charge in the reverse direction causes a second reversal and a current again flows forward through the primary circuit producing an oscillation of the primary current. Each cycle has less intensity, until the electrical energy is expended. The entire cycle is repeated when the breaker points close to again store energy in the coil by allowing a current to flow from the battery.

This rapid collapse of the primary magnetic field flux produces the high voltage (up to 25,000 V) required to ionize the spark plug electrode gap and force the arc across. The primary current flow, the rate of collapse of the coil primary magnetic field flux and the coil winding ratio between the primary and secondary windings is responsible for the maximum available voltage in the ignition system. The system seldom operates at this maximum voltage. It will only produce the amount of voltage that is required to fire the spark plug at the operating conditions.

17-8 LEAKAGE

Available voltage is produced from the total energy stored in the coil by the primary current. This energy can be reduced by secondary leakage. Leakage erodes useful available voltage by shunting some of the energy around the spark plug electrodes. One of the main causes of ignition leakage is spark plug fouling. Spark plug fouling occurs when conducting deposits build up on the nose of the spark plug insulator within the combustion chamber. If this leakage is small, the spark plug will fire. As the leakage increases, it drains away electrical energy, so that there is not enough energy remaining to produce the required arc across the spark plug gap.

The ignition system is designed for a very rapid energy release, or high rise time, so the energy is released faster than it can leak away and, therefore, will be able to flash across the spark plug electrode gap before appreciable leakage occurs.

Secondary leakage also occurs through weak

or cracked secondary insulation, especially at wire supporting brackets; across dirty coil tops; across dirty spark plug insulators and across dirty distributor caps. Moisture and carbon tracks inside the distributor may be other paths for electrical leakage.

Corona accompanies high secondary voltages. It is an external leakage along ignition wires that is sometimes visible in the dark. Corona increases as the conductor becomes wet and dirty. Eventually, corona will lead to insulation failure.

From the foregoing discussion, it would seem desirable to increase ignition system energy to overcome all required voltage and leakage. An over-capacity ignition system, however, rapidly erodes the spark plug electrodes and insulators to give short spark plug life. It also overloads the secondary insulation so that it would fail prematurely.

In summary, ignition systems are designed to supply enough energy to the spark plug electrode arc to raise the charge located between the electrodes to kindling temperature. This must be hot enough that the small flame is not quenched by the cool spark plug parts and the cool cylinder head. The ignition system energy must be large enough to meet ignition requirements and still be able to give maximum service life without overloading the ignition system.

17-9 IGNITION RESISTOR

Twelve-volt automotive ignition systems use a resistor or ballast in the primary circuit to control available voltage and total energy stored in the coil. This may be a separate resistor or a resistor wire between the bulkhead connection on the fire wall and coil. The resistor increases its resistance as its temperature increases. During low speed operation, the ignition breaker points are closed for a longer period of time than at high speeds, so more current will flow. The current reduction resulting from increased resistor temperature reduces breaker point burning during low speed operation, but does not provide full current at high speeds.

The ballast type of resistor is designed to maintain constant resistance regardless of its temperature. It limits primary current at low temperature while still providing an adequate current at high temperatures.

The ignition resistor provides about one-half of the total resistance in the primary circuit and is the only part of the ignition system that is temperature compensated.

During cranking, the ignition resistor is bypassed so that the entire electrical system voltage is placed across the coil, as shown in Figure 17-6. This provides a momentary overload for a few cycles until the engine starts. The voltage in the electrical system during cranking is lowered to about 10 V by the heavy starter draw and, therefore, it is not excessive for the coil. When the engine starts, the electrical voltage increases to the regulator voltage setting, about 14 V. The resistor then becomes effective to limit coil running voltage to approximately 7–8 V.

17-10 TRANSISTOR AND C-D IGNITION

In many applications, transistor or capacitator-discharge ignition will be superior to the standard ignition system. They provide higher available voltage with little reduction at high speeds, so their use is a special advantage at high engine rpm's. The primary field flux in these systems breaks down very rapidly to provide a very fast secondary rise time that is affected little by spark plug fouling. Spark plugs operating with these systems last longer, because the spark arc duration is not as long as on standard ignition systems.

A transistor requires that an electrical current flow through the transistor base in order to have current flow from the emitter to the collector. Some transistor ignition systems use ignition breaker points to provide controlled timing of the transistor base current. Others use a timed magnetic pulse as a rotating magnetic coil within the distributor passes a sensing coil to induce a current in the coil. The sensing coil is connected to the transistor base to provide a momentary transistor base current. Magnetic pulse distributors eliminate distributor maintenance.

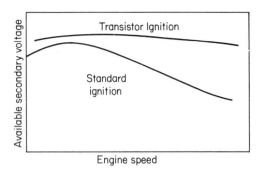

Fig. 17-17 Available voltage compared between standard ignition and transistor ignition.

Even with the transistor and capacitor-discharge system's advantages, extra cost has limited their use to applications that would misfire with standard ignition systems and to installations providing minimum maintenance.

17-11 DISTRIBUTOR OPERATION

The ignition distributor is driven from the engine camshaft at one-half crankshaft speed. The breaker points, condenser, rotor, cap, and timing advance mechanisms are located in the distributor. This arrangement puts all of the ignition system's moving parts into a single unit.

The distributor gets its name from the portion that directs the secondary output to the spark plugs in the correct order to match the engine firing order. Coil secondary output is fed to the center distributor cap tower. It flows through the tower to a button inside the cap. A spring clip on the rotor contacts the center button. The rotor has a conductor plate from the spring clip to an extended tip that comes close to the distributor cap electrodes as the rotor turns. It lines up with each distributor cap electrode in sequence as the breaker points open. This allows the secondary impulse to be directed through each spark plug lead to the spark plug in the correct firing order.

It is convenient to locate the breaker point cam on the same shaft as the rotor because these two parts must always maintain their relative position for rotor and electrode alignment. A breaker point contact set is attached to the breaker plate within the distributor. Adjustments are provided to allow the points to be positioned closer to the cam for a larger point gap or away from the cam for a smaller point gap.

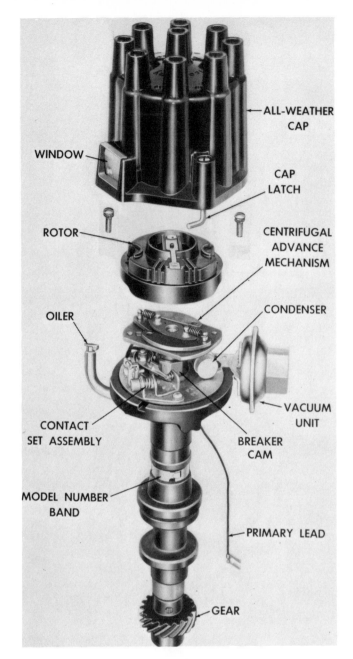

Fig. 17-18 Typical distributor nomenclature (Delco-Remy Division, General Motors Corporation).

(a)

Fig. 17-19 Breaker point position in distributor.

(b)

(c)

One cam lobe is provided for each cylinder. Six-cylinder cam lobes are spaced at 60° and eight-cylinder cam lobes are spaced at 45°. Within each of these degree angles, the points must be closed long enough to store energy in the coil and must be open far enough to minimize point arcing. The points are normally closed from 65 to 70% of the cam angle to provide coil saturation. This is known as the *dwell* angle. Any change in the breaker point gap will change the dwell approximately one degree for each .001″ change in point gap.

283

The distributor cam opens the breaker points and a breaker point spring closes the points. A weak breaker point spring will allow the points to be thrown clear of the cam so they will float. When this happens, the points will not be able to close fast enough so the dwell period with the points closed will be shortened and, consequently, the available voltage reduced. Excessively high breaker point spring tension will cause rapid rubbing block wear and point bounce as they close, which will also reduce available voltage.

Original equipment distributor points are designed to maintain constant breaker point gap and dwell. Normal breaker points gradually burn, which tends to enlarge the gap. This is countered by slight breaker point rubbing block wearing on the cam that tends to close the gap. These two service wear conditions counteract each other to keep the breaker point gap nearly constant. If wear caused the breaker point gap to decrease, the engine's basic timing angle would be retarded. If wear caused the gap to increase, the timing would advance.

The point cam is driven by the distributor shaft through a mechanical advance mechanism. The advance mechanism consists of centrifugal flyweights that are retained by springs. As the distributor shaft rotates faster, the flyweights swing outward against spring pressure. Cam surfaces on the flyweights will advance or move the breaker point cam position forward in the direction of rotation in relation to the distributor shaft position. The distributor shaft drive is timed to the engine crankshaft position when the advance mechanisms are in full retard. The distributor shaft always maintains this position in relation to the crankshaft and the advance mechanism moves from this timing base which is called basic timing. The *mechanical advance* is sensitive to engine speed, advancing as the engine speed increases to compensate for constant combustion rate that occurs during the first 10% of the combustion chamber charge burn. Flyweights and springs control the amount of timing change at each rpm. In service, the amount of advance is checked on a distributor machine. The actual advance is compared against advance specifications. Corrections in advance rate are usually made by

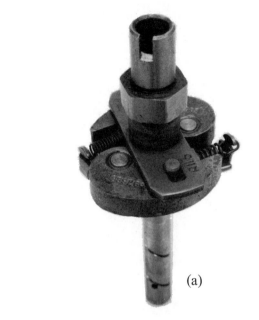

(a)

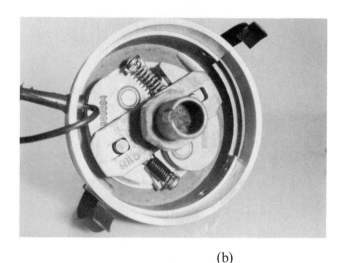

(b)

(c)

Fig. 17-20 Typical mechanical advance mechanism.

(a)

(b)

(c)

Fig. 17-21 Typical vacuum advance diaphragm assemblies.

changing the counter weight springs or the spring hanger position.

The breaker plate upon which the breaker points mount is movable within the distributor housing and is held in position by a link from a vacuum diaphragm. The outside portion of the vacuum diaphragm is connected by tubing to sense intake manifold vacuum, usually at a port within the carburetor. High engine vacuum pulls the diaphragm which, in turn, pulls the breaker plate in an advance direction (against the direction of rotation). During high vacuum operation, the engine runs with a thin lean mixture that burns slowly and, therefore, requires a high advance to complete combustion at the correct 5-10° after top center. As the throttle is opened, manifold vacuum drops, allowing the breaker plate to retard the breaker points. The charge mixture is more dense and usually richer as the manifold vacuum drops. This requires less advance to complete combustion at 5-10° after top center. The *vacuum advance* mechanism is sensitive to manifold vacuum which, in turn, is sensitive to engine load and throttle position.

In most carburetors, the vacuum sensing port is located just above the high portion of a closed throttle plate. At full idle, with the throttle closed, no vacuum is applied to the diaphragm. As the throttle is opened, the port will sense engine vacuum to advance the distributor.

Mechanical and vacuum advance mechanisms work together to provide the engine with the required advance to give the most efficient combustion at

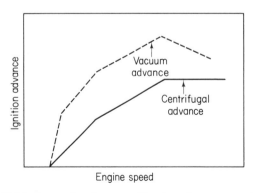

Fig. 17-22 Curve showing centrifugal and vacuum advance in relation to engine speed.

each operating condition. A change in the basic timing or advance mechanisms will depreciate normal performance. If, on the other hand, the engine is modified from the original manufacturer's configuration, timing and advance curves would also have to be modified to produce the most efficient performance.

17-12 SPARK PLUGS

The entire ignition system culminates in an arc between the spark plug electrodes. If the correct spark plug is not used, ignition will malfunction, resulting in a misfire. The spark plug must concentrate the conversion of the electrical energy to thermal energy at a location in the combustion chamber which will ignite enough of the charge so that combustion of the remaining charge will proceed in a normal manner.

The spark plug consists of three major parts, the shell, the insulator, and the electrodes. The shell supports the insulator and has threads that screw into the head. The thread portion must be long enough to allow the electrodes to enter the combustion chamber. This length is called the spark plug *reach*. If the reach were too long, it could damage the valves or piston. Threads on the spark plug are metric 14 and 18 mm threads. The shell seals the combustion chamber spark plug hole. Some shells seal with a tapered spark plug seat. Others seal with a metal spark plug gasket.

The ceramic spark plug insulator is sealed inside the shell, so that it makes a pressure and thermal seal. Much of the spark plug development work has been concentrated on the insulator. It must withstand high thermal and mechanical stress as well as insulate the high secondary voltage. During manufacturing, the insulator ingredients are formed to a putty-like consistency. The putty is formed in the insulator shape, then fired in a furnace. The finished insulator is close to diamond hardness. It is placed in the shell with sealing material, then the shell is crimped around the insulator to produce a gas-tight seal.

The center electrode is placed in a hole down

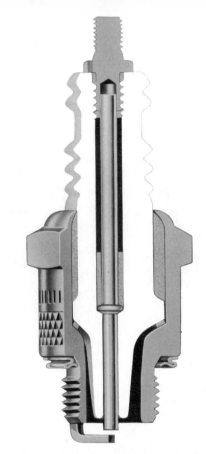

Fig. 17-23 Sectioned view of a regular spark plug (Champion Spark Plug Company).

Fig. 17-24 Resistance-type spark plug (AC Spark Plug Division, General Motors Corporation).

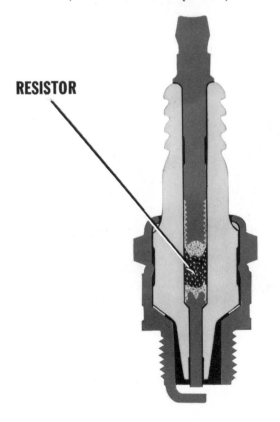

RESISTOR

through the center of the insulator. Modern electrodes are made from two pieces, one to attach the conductor and the other to extend into the hot combustion chamber. Using two pieces allows the spark plug manufacturer to select the type of metal that will best meet the requirements under which it must operate. The electrode is sealed with a gas-tight electrical conducting seal material.

Some spark plug types have a resistor installed between the two sections of the electrode. Its 10,000-ohm resistance changes the ignition secondary oscillating frequency at the instant the arc is established across the electrodes. This change in frequency moves the electrical radiation out of the television and radio frequencies to suppress interference. The resistor also provides long spark plug electrode life by cutting down peak current that flows in the arc across the electrode gap.

Spark plugs must operate within a specified temperature range. If the spark plug operates too cold, it will foul with deposits. These deposits will bleed off coil electrical energy, so the spark plug will not fire. If the spark plug operates too hot, it will erode rapidly and will cause pre-ignition. Pre-ignition will lead to physical engine damage. The minimum spark plug temperature for non-fouling operation is 650°. Above 1500°, pre-ignition will occur. Spark plugs must operate within these temperatures under all normal operating conditions.

When an engine is running under heavy loads, such as sustained high speed driving, the com-

bustion chambers become hot. During these operating conditions, a cold spark plug is usually required to prevent spark plug overheating. Engines that have a tendency to foul from oil or from light duty operation may require hot spark plugs to keep their temperature high enough to eliminate fouling. Drag racing operation is such a short time operation on each run that cold spark plugs are seldom necessary.

A cold spark plug transfers heat from the spark plug nose through the shell faster than a hot spark plug. The spark plug heat range selected for replacement spark plugs should match the manufacturer's specifications. Modified engines may require a different heat range spark plug than those specified for the original engine. Spark plugs for modified engines should be selected by working up from cold spark plugs. If fouling occurs, the next hotter heat range that does not foul should be used. In this way, it is possible to avoid pre-ignition.

It is interesting to note that the center electrode of automotive spark plugs is of negative polarity. Hot bodies are known to have increased electron activity. The center electrode is the hottest part of the spark plug and, therefore, requires the lowest voltage to force free electrons to form an arc. The hot negative center electrode helps to keep required

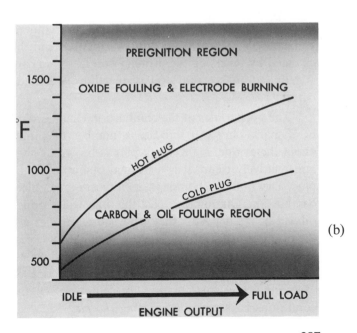

Fig. 17-25 Spark plug heat range (a) Heat flow path (The Prestolite Company), (b) temperature limits (Champion Spark Plug Company).

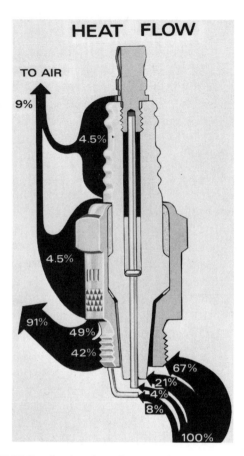

Fig. 17-26 Spark plug heat input and outflow (Champion Spark Plug Company).

Fig. 17-27 Typical spark plug tip conditions (The Prestolite Company).

voltage low. If the polarity is reversed, required voltage will increase. Secondary polarity can be changed by reversing the primary coil leads, so care is required to see that coil connections are made correctly.

The appearance of the combustion chamber end of a spark plug can indicate a number of things about the engine. If the spark plug is brown or gray and relatively clean, it is a normal operating spark plug. Dry fluffy carbon deposits indicate incomplete combustion. Oil pumping past the rings will produce oil-wet heavy deposits. Badly burned electrodes are the result of overheating. Thermal shock from excessive timing advance or from detonation will break pieces out of the insulator nose. The practice of examining the spark plugs to determine engine conditions is often called *reading the plugs*.

17-13 SPARK PLUG CABLES

Modern engines use non-metallic resistance type conductor secondary cables. As with spark plug resistors, these cables provide television and radio noise suppression (TVRS cable) of radio frequency emissions from the ignition system. Aluminum distributor cap electrode inserts are used with TVRS cable. Old model engines used metal conductor secondary cables with copper distributor cap inserts. Mixing distributor caps and cable types will produce corrosion which will add resistance to the secondary circuit.

TVRS cable should not be replaced with metal conductor cable. Ignition systems are designed to satisfactorily handle the resistance built into the cable. The use of metal conductor cables on these systems will lead to rapid spark plug electrode erosion and to radio frequency emission that causes interference in nearby radios and television sets.

17-14 IGNITION SYSTEM TESTING

The ignition system is one of the interrelated engine systems. Input voltage to the coil primary is determined by the battery or by the voltage regulator. Ignition system output is the required voltage at the spark plug. Any change in combustion chamber conditions such as compression pressure, temperature, and air/fuel mixture ratios will affect required voltage; therefore, these must be considered when testing ignition systems.

A cathode ray oscilloscope is one of the best instruments to observe overall characteristics of the complete operating ignition system. Normal or abnormal operating conditions are indicated by the scope when using information in this chapter along with applicable engine specifications.

The ignition oscilloscope displays secondary voltage on a time base. The scope sweep is usually triggered by number one spark plug cable; however, any secondary cable could be used. As the voltage raises in number one spark plug wire, a spike is produced at the right edge of the pattern. This is the trigger that immediately shifts the sweep to the left edge to begin a new pattern trace.

Anything in the primary that has an effect on available voltage is reflected in the secondary pattern. Parts which the scope pattern indication shows to be faulty, are usually rechecked with a specialized tester to verify the malfunction.

Ignition Secondary Pattern. The generator field wire is removed so there is no output and the ignition system is operated directly on battery voltage input to reduce pattern variations. This provides equal voltage input on all engines, so the pattern is standard and comparable between engines.

When the ignition points open, capacitive discharge occurs and the primary field collapses with the aid of the condenser, producing the spike

of the pattern. It only goes as high as the voltage needed to produce an arc across the spark plug electrodes. On current engines, this is from 5 to 10 kilovolts (kV). Higher readings indicate excessive resistance in the spark plug or cable. Lower readings indicate leakage or fouling. Readings on all cylinders of one engine should be within 3 kV of each other.

After the initial arc has formed, the spark continues to fire at a lower voltage level, about 25% of the required voltage that was indicated by the spike. This spark line will continue as long as there is sufficient inductive coil energy to maintain the arc. Secondary resistance causes this line to slope downward to the right. A slight slope to the right is normal for TVRS wires. A steep slope indicates excessive resistance.

When the arc across the spark plug electrodes stops, some energy remains in the ignition system. This is dissipated through a series of approximately five diminishing oscillations. Improper coil or condenser operation usually reflects in this section as less than five oscillations. When this type pattern variation occurs, the coil and condenser should be checked separately on special coil or condenser testers.

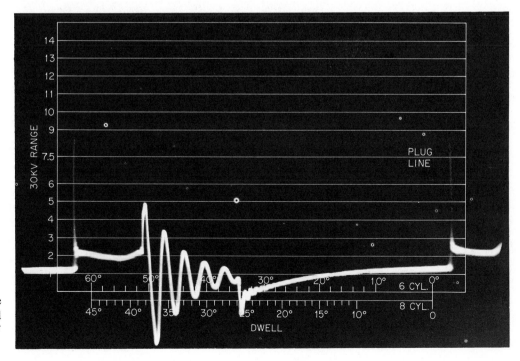

Fig. 17-28 Single cylinder scope pattern showing 8.5 kV required to form the initial arc and 2.25 kV required to maintain the arc.

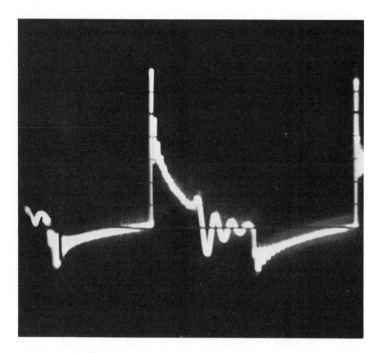

Fig. 17-29 Scope pattern showing high secondary resistance.

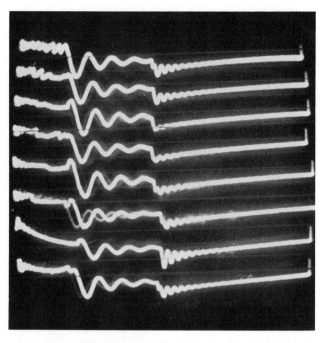

Fig. 17-30 Raster secondary scope pattern showing less than five coil-condenser oscillations.

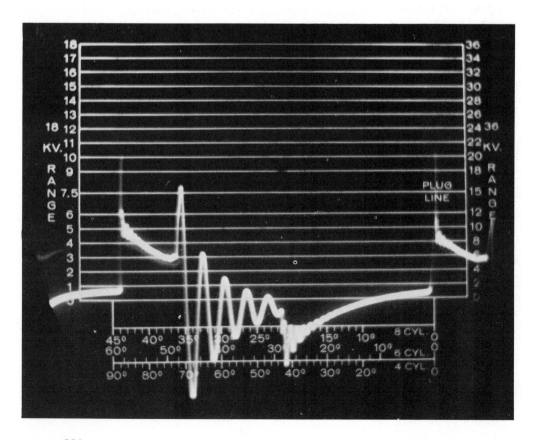

Fig. 17-31 Scope pattern showing dwell of 28 degrees on a 6-cylinder engine.

Breaker point closing allows the current to again flow into the primary windings which, in turn, induces a voltage in the secondary windings. This voltage is indicated by a sharp drop in the secondary scope pattern line followed by an oscillating recovery. The line length from this point closing signal to the next cylinder opening signal is *dwell*. It can be accurately measured on some scopes by adjusting a single pattern length to a scale on the scope face.

It is not only important to know the required voltage, but it is also important to know the available voltage to be sure sufficient *ignition reserve* is present. This is measured by removing one of the spark plug leads while the engine is running at approximately 1500 rpm with the generator field disconnected. Available voltage should be between 20 and 30 kV. Readings below 20 kV indicate problems in the primary ignition circuit. Damage can occur to the secondary insulation from the high voltage produced if the test is extended over a considerable length of time. The spark plug cable should, therefore, only be removed long enough to recognize the pattern.

The •cope pattern in the available voltage test normally has a tail half as long as the spike. If this tail is short or missing, it indicates secondary leakage.

Ignition Primary Pattern. Some ignition scopes also display a primary voltage pattern. This is useful in examining the breaker point opening and closing signal as well as checking dwell and dwell variations.

Many other items and variations may be determined with ignition scopes. Manufacturer's instructions on the scope being used should be consulted for details of the particular scope pattern indications.

17-15 IGNITION TIMING

Correct ignition timing is a basic requirement for engine operation. Power timing lights, either 110 V or 12 V, are used to check basic ignition timing. A lead connected to number one spark plug signals the timing point.

Electrical energy is stored in large condensers within the timing light. As number one cylinder fires, the signal releases this stored energy to operate the flash tube to produce a very bright flash. This flashing timing light is directed at the timing marks

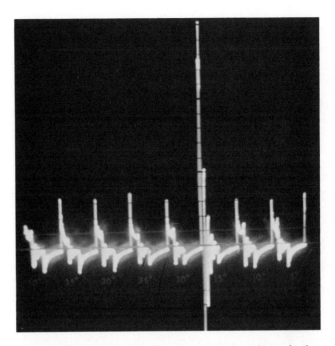

Fig. 17-32 Spark plug wire removed from the 6th spark plug to show available voltage.

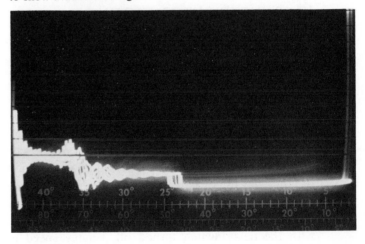

Fig. 17-33 Typical superimposed primary scope pattern of all cylinders.

on the crankshaft damper. The light flashes on and off so fast that the damper appears to be stopped. Distributor housing adjustments on the engine can be made to change the timing. Timing is checked with the vacuum hose disconnected as the engine runs at slow idle to eliminate any chance of having the distributor advance mechanisms affect the engine's basic timing.

Fig. 17-34 Typical ignition timing marks.

17-16 DISTRIBUTOR TESTING

Distributors may be tested in or out of the engine, depending upon the equipment available. Distributor advance may be checked by using a timing light that has a built-in time delay, while the engine is operated at a pre-determined rpm or degree per second. This type of timing light has an electronic circuit that will sense the signal from number one spark plug wire, then delay a known period of time before flashing the light. Time, then, is used to measure degrees of distributor advance. Engine timing advance is checked by first setting the basic timing with the delay switch turned off. Engine speed is increased to the specified test speed which will advance the timing. The timing light flash is then electronically retarded until the apparent timing mark is in its original position. The amount of timing delay is read on the instrument scale in degrees of advance.

The distributor may be removed from the engine and checked on a distributor machine. A machine electrical lead is connected to the distributor primary lead to sense point opening. A second lead may be used for a ground connection. The distributor machine has a typical ignition system built in so the

Fig. 17-35 Typical ignition advance meter used to check advance on a running engine.

Fig. 17-36 Distributor advance being checked on a distributor machine.

distributor breaker points energize a coil in the normal manner. The coil secondary flashes a neon light.

The distributor shaft is clamped to a variable speed drive mechanism. A degree wheel is a part of the drive mechanism. Secondary voltage flashes the neon light each time the breaker points are opened. This light reflects on a pointer which, in turn, lines up with the degree wheel.

The distributor is driven at speeds listed in the specifications and the actual advance is observed on the degree wheel. If the distributor is out of the specification, range, it will need further service, such as cleaning flyweight bearings, replacing flyweight springs, adjusting flyweight spring hangers, cleaning movable breaker plates or replacing the vacuum diaphragm unit.

Variations in spark timing degree and in dwell variations may indicate worn parts. See the applicable shop manual or equipment manufacturer's manual for the specific test and repair procedures.

Condensers are checked for opens, leakage, and capacity. They are so well built that they seldom fail. When failures do occur, most are the result of vibration or careless handling that breaks the leads or the ground connection.

Breaker points are checked for gap and/or dwell as well as point resistance. The breaker cam is ground with a set amount of lift. As the breaker point gap is adjusted wider, the rubbing block must

start to open the breaker points sooner in order to be wide open at the cam high point. Gap changes will, therefore, affect dwell and engine timing. If the breaker cam is not worn, point gap will be correct if dwell is correct. Breaker cams seldom wear and when they do, the wear is visible.

As breaker points operate, they develop a frosty appearance on their contact surfaces. This type of surface makes a good electrical contact. The breaker points should be checked for resistance to make sure the electrical contact is good. Resistance is checked by allowing primary current to flow with a sensitive voltmeter connected from the primary distributor lead at the coil to the distributor ground. There should be less than .1 V drop.

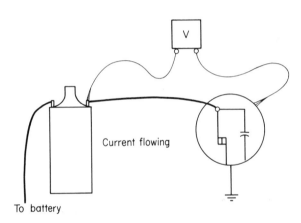

Fig. 17-38 Test connection for measuring voltage drop across the points.

To check resistance in the ignition circuit between the battery and the coil, the voltmeter should be connected between the ignition resistor switch terminal and the positive battery terminal post with the ignition switch turned on and the distributor breaker points closed. Voltage drop reading should be a maximum of .6 V. Specifications should be checked for exact values that apply to each engine or vehicle model.

Equipment manufacturers and vehicle manufacturers have devised numerous tests to quickly pinpoint malfunctions. The usual method employed is to check the entire system while it's in operation. If test indications are satisfactory, no further testing

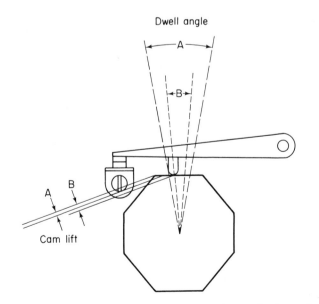

Fig. 17-37 Breaker point dwell charge as the gap is changed.

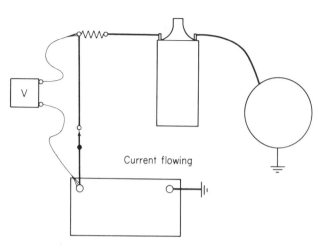

Fig. 17-39 Test connection for measuring primary ignition circuit voltage drop.

or service is necessary. If tests indicate unsatisfactory performance, the system is broken into small segments and each of them checked individually. This process is continued until the malfunction is identified. It can then be easily tested and corrected.

Coils seldom fail. When they do fail, they are often overlooked. The ignition scope pattern may suggest a coil problem. The coil must then be checked with a coil tester. These testers may use meters or an oscilloscope. Either method, when used with the correct specifications, will indicate the coil condition.

17-17 IGNITION SYSTEM SERVICE

Most routine ignition system service involves replacement of items that wear out, namely breaker points and spark plugs. Manufacturers recommend replacement of these items each 10,000 miles. If this is done on a vehicle used in normal service, the vehicle will never have malfunction involving these items. Most vehicle operators change breaker points and spark plugs at seasonal tune-ups or when they begin to cause trouble, regardless of the number of miles they have been used.

Breaker points. The recommended method of replacing breaker points is to remove the distributor

and replace the breaker points while the distributor is on a bench or fastened in a distributor machine clamp. Points must be aligned for maximum life. This is done by bending the stationary point. The gap is usually set with a flat or round thickness gauge. A dial gauge could be used to measure gap and it will give the most accurate readings, especially on used breaker points. Gap is seldom checked after the original point installation. Instead, a dwell meter is used, because it is so much more convenient to use and provides the same information.

Fig. 17-40 Method used to match the point contact after installation.

Breaker point spring tension should be checked. It should take from 17 to 20 oz to open the breaker points (see the applicable specification). Spring tension can be changed by moving the spring into the clamp nut to increase tension or moving it away from the clamp to reduce tension.

Spark Plugs. Air pressure should be used to blow any dirt and foreign material from around the used spark plug base before it is removed from the engine. A deep 6-point socket with interior insulating rubber should be used to avoid damaging the spark plug while removing and installing it. An examination of the used spark plug will indicate combustion chamber condition.

Used spark plugs may be serviced and continued in use. Spark plug service involves a thorough cleaning. Threads are wire brushed. Insulator tops are wiped clean. The electrode end is sand blasted in special cleaners designed for this cleaning. When clean, the spark plugs should be inspected for cracks and electrode wear. If any faults show up, they should be replaced. If they are to be continued in use, the gap is opened slightly and the center electrode end filed flat. The gap is reset to specifications and the spark plug re-installed.

Fig. 17-41 Checking point spring tension.

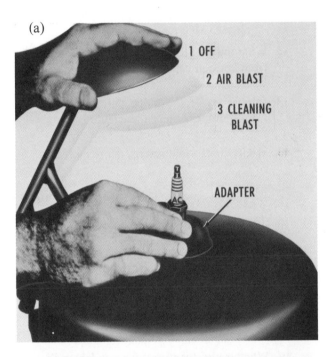

Fig. 17-42 Servicing spark plugs. (a) Cleaning (AC Spark Plug Division, General Motors Corporation), (b) filing the electrodes (AC Spark Plug Division, General Motors Corporation), (c) adjusting the electrode gap (AC Spark Plug Division, General Motors Corporation).

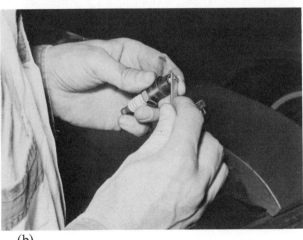

(a)

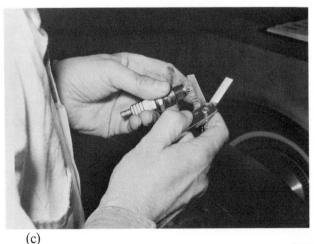

(b)

(c)

295

It is a general practice to replace spark plugs rather than spending time cleaning them, only to find they need replacing anyway. In most cases, the customer would rather have new spark plugs than spark plugs that may fail before the next normal tune-up. New spark plugs of the correct type and heat range are selected, then gapped before installation.

Other questionable or faulty ignition items indicated by the initial test should be repaired or replaced. All wiring and cables should be clean, properly supported, and all terminals secure. After service, the basic ignition timing should be set and the entire system should be retested to see that it is functioning normally.

Review Questions
Chapter 17

1. What portion of the cylinder charge burns in a given time period, regardless of engine speed?

2. What factors cause the major portion of the charge to burn at a rate proportional to crankshaft degrees?

3. Why is advance required at part throttle operation?

4. Why does the vacuum advance not affect maximum power?

5. What engine operating variables affect required voltage?

6. How does air/fuel ratio affect required voltage?

7. How does spark plug gap spacing affect required voltage?

8. How is combustion charge firing affected by spark plug electrode gap size and shape?

9. List all the ignition system items that can increase required voltage.

10. What causes the electron beam to sweep across the face of an oscilloscope picture tube and to deflect up and down?

11. How does inductance slow current flow in a coil when the circuit switch is closed?

12. What is capacitance?

13. What part of the scope pattern results from ignition capacitance?

14. What part of the scope pattern results from ignition system inductance?

15. What limits total energy stored in the coil?

16. What advantage does a transistor have over ignition breaker points?

17. What operating conditions provide maximum available voltage?

18. What are the advantages of fast rise time in ignition energy release?

19. What is the function of a condenser in the primary circuit?

20. What is the unit of the condenser capacity?

21. What factors are responsible for available voltage?

22. List the sources of secondary energy leakage.

23. What is the advantage and disadvantage of over-capacity ignition systems?

24. What are the advantages and disadvantages of transistor and capacitor-discharge ignition systems?

25. What happens to ignition timing if the breaker point gap becomes less, due to rubbing block wear?

26. What are the requirements of the spark plug insulator?

27. What is the purpose of the built-in spark plug resistor?

28. Why do spark plugs require a heat range?

29. Why is the center electrode usually negative?

30. How does the spark plug condition indicate combustion chamber condition?

31. What is the purpose of non-metallic conductor secondary cables?

32. How is the correct distributor cap to be used with TVRS cables identified?

33. Describe the important parts of the ignition scope pattern.

34. Illustrate ignition scope patterns that indicate low compression, high resistance, and spark plug fouling.

35. Why are speed and vacuum important when setting basic timing?

36. How is distributor advance tested on an operating engine?

37. Discuss ignition system service.

Quiz 17

1. Ignition timing changes with changes of engine speed and drive torque to complete combustion at
   a. 5° to 10° before top center
   b. at top center
   c. 5° to 10° after top center
   d. 15° to 20° after top center.

2. At some engine speed the distributor stops advance ignition timing. Additional advance is not used because the
   a. distributor advance mechanism is limited
   b. turbulence increases burning rate
   c. engine is seldom operated at this speed
   d. charge won't ignite fast enough.

3. The system part that determines the ignition's required voltage is the
   a. spark plug
   b. breaker points
   c. battery state of charge
   d. voltage regulator.

4. A high voltage surge is directed across the spark plugs when the
   a. ignition breaker points close
   b. ignition breaker points open
   c. coil builds up sufficient energy
   d. distributor rotor contacts the cap segments.

5. A counter voltage that retards current buildup is the result of the coil's
   a. resistance
   b. saturation
   c. capacitance
   d. inductance.

6. Increases in the ignition secondary circuit resistance
   a. increase the coil's inductance discharge
   b. increase the coil's capacitance discharge
   c. have no effect on the coil's inductance discharge
   d. have no effect on the coil's capacitance discharge.

7. Ignition available voltage is reduced by
   a. a fouled spark plug
   b. secondary leakage
   c. a cracked distributor cap
   d. primary resistance.

8. Replacing a spark plug with one of a hotter heat range may
   a. cause pre-ignition
   b. increase engine power
   c. cause spark plug fouling
   d. develop carbon deposits.

9. An oscilloscope ignition trace with the spark plug firing line sloping steeply to the right indicates
   a. low required voltage
   b. low available voltage
   c. secondary resistance
   d. primary resistance.

10. Breaker points were found to have developed a frosty appearance on their contact surfaces. This suggests
    a. normal operation
    b. misfiring
    c. high primary resistance
    d. the points were bouncing.

chapter 18

Automotive Engine Testing

Experimental automotive components are built to the automotive engineer's designs. They are then tested to see if they will meet the performance and durability objectives. The first design seldom does, so parts are redesigned to correct weaknesses and reduce costs where possible. After further testing, the parts may still require further modification, so that they can be mass produced by high volume manufacturing processes and have an adequate service life.

After the automobile is purchased by the customer it must be properly maintained so that it continues to provide satisfactory service. Proper engine maintenance includes oil changes at the recommended periods, adequate coolant protection against freezing and periodic tune-ups at scheduled intervals or whenever loss in performance is noticed. Modern tune-up methods include cleaning, replacing, diagnosing problems, adjusting components, and then retesting everything to be sure that the whole engine is functioning properly. Dynamometers have begun to find their place as useful tools for diagnosis and testing in the customer service market, especially in test lanes. Their use will continue to grow as emission control laws require the automobile owner to maintain his automobile engine at low emission levels.

18-1 THE DYNAMOMETER IN TESTING

Dynamometers are used in testing many rotating components, especially the engine, its accessories, and the chassis drive line. Many people have the misconception that a dynamometer does all the testing. In reality, a dynamometer can put a controlled load on the operating system and can measure that load. Other test equipment, such as temperature indicators, pressure indicators, accelerometers, exhaust gas analyzers, etc., are installed on the unit being tested to give readout information while operating on the dynamometer.

A dynamometer may be designed to absorb power. Mechanical energy from the driving unit must be converted into some other form of energy, usually heat or electricity. On the other hand, a dynamometer may be designed to drive the automotive unit being tested to measure driving loads. Many engineering dynamometers are able to drive as well as to absorb power.

Dynamometers are sometimes controlled by a programmed tape, so they will be able to repeat a test sequence. During the development of the Ford Indianapolis racing engine, the Ford Motor Company put a special tape recorder on an Indianapolis racing car to record the throttle position, braking, speed and load requirements used to drive around the racetrack. The tape was taken to the Dearborn Engine Dynamometer Building and connected to an engine dynamometer with a racing engine installed. The tape was used to control the engine and dynamometer cycle to follow the speed and loads used on each lap at the Indianapolis Motor Speedway. In this way, the engine could run the entire race in the laboratory. Engine failures in the laboratory showed items that needed to be improved so the engine would produce the required power and durability to compete in the Indianapolis 500 race.

Test programs are used on engines, accessories, and drive train components by all manufacturers. Sometimes, mechanical cams are used to program

the automatic test cycle and at other times tape control is used. The engine is run at a variety of speed and load conditions to simulate the typical driving condition being studied.

After the component has satisfactorily met laboratory tests, it is put into a vehicle and given road tests. Upon satisfactory completion of the road tests, it is released for production.

Most new designs are based on previous designs and on data from similar units. They are really refinements and improvements rather than completely new concepts. The final design may look altogether different than previous designs; however, they are usually the result of a number of slight modifications done step-by-step in the laboratory.

Dynamometers are used to measure *torque*. An engine output shaft is mechanically connected to the dynamometer shaft. The running engine twists the dynamometer shaft and the dynamometer applies a controlled resistance to the shaft twist. The force of the dynamometer twist, called torque,

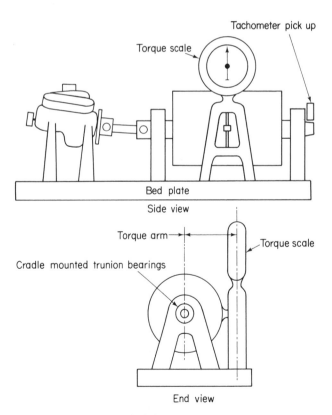

Fig. 18-1 Typical dynamometer test setup.

299

is measured in pound-feet. The only thing the dynamometer can do is to apply a controlled resistance to the turning shaft and provide a readout of the torque being produced.

Horsepower (hp) is force (lb) applied through a distance (33,000 ft) in a given period of time (1 min). In a dynamometer, the turning effort is measured by a scale reading in pounds located some distance from the center of the rotating shaft. This distance is called the *torque arm*. The arm length, in feet, multiplied by the scale reading, in pounds, will give the value in pound-feet of torque. Engine speed, in revolutions per minute, provides the time period necessary to calculate horsepower from dynamometer indications (hp = rpm × lb-ft/5252). Horsepower is usually calculated from dynamometer torque and speed readouts. Some dynamometer instrumentation uses an electric tachometer generator to energize an electrical bridge that is sensitive to the force on the arm. The resulting readout from this instrumentation is read directly in horsepower rather than in torque.

As the dynamometer braking load is increased, the engine speed decreases. If the dynamometer braking load is decreased, the engine speed will increase. At full throttle, dynamometer braking load is used to control engine speed. Used in this way, the familiar torque and horsepower curves are developed.

Only a small part of dynamometer operation time is involved in measuring maximum horsepower. Most dynamometer operation is used to determine part throttle operation and endurance of the part being tested. This is expected, because passenger cars driven by average drivers rarely, if ever, are driven under conditions that will develop maximum horsepower.

18-2 DYNAMOMETER TYPES

Dynamometers can be made in a great many ways. The most common types are electric dynamometers and water brake dynamometers. Sometimes, friction brakes and fans are used to absorb known loads and are, therefore, used as dynamometers.

Ward-Lenard Type. The cradle mounted DC dynamometer, sometimes called a Sprague dynamometer, using a Ward-Lenard absorption system, is the most flexible, as well as the most expensive type of dynamometer. The dynamometer unit is a DC motor or generator, depending upon the direction

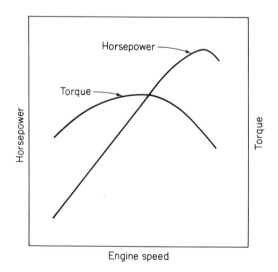

Fig. 18-2 Typical torque and horsepower curves.

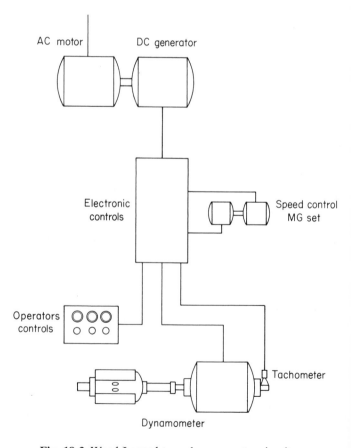

Fig. 18-3 Ward-Lenard type dynamometer circuit.

of current flow. It is connected electrically to an AC-DC motor-generator (MG) set.

The AC motor of the MG set is connected to the power line and mechanically drives the DC generator portion of the MG set. Electrical power from the DC generator portion of the MG set drives the dynamometer to mechanically crank the engine. When the engine is started, it overruns the dynamometer, causing it to generate electrical power. This DC power drives the DC portion of the MG set like a motor. It, in turn, mechanically drives the AC unit, causing it to act as an AC generator forcing AC current back into the power line to absorb engine power. Sprague dynamometers with Ward-Lenard absorption controls are often used as absorbers and drivers for engineering chassis dynamometers by mechanically connecting them to chassis rolls.

DC Dynamometers. The Ward-Lenard controlled DC dynamometers are used primarily for laboratory performance work. This same basic Sprague dynamometer may use grids for absorbing power rather than the Ward-Lenard system that absorbs power by charging back into the AC power line. A small MG set is used to produce current needed to energize the dynamometer field. The dynamometer's electric output is sent to a series of cast iron grids that convert electrical energy to heat. The grids are air cooled.

Fig. 18-4 Absorption dynamometer load bank grid.

Eddy-Current Dynamometer. Endurance running is often done with eddy-current dynamometers. This dynamometer is designed so that eddy currents will develop as the dynamometer field current is increased. Eddy currents resist rotation, absorb power, and convert the power to heat. The eddy current dynamometer is cooled with water or air. It provides good load control and is not as expensive as the Sprague dynamometer. Sometimes it is used for absorption in chassis dynamometers.

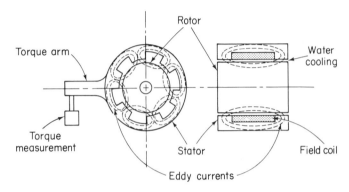

Fig. 18-5 Eddy current type dynamometers.

Water-Brake Dynamometer. Electric dynamometer absorption characteristics closely match the internal combustion engine output characteristics. Electric dynamometers must be brought up to a reasonable speed to absorb their design torque. Water-brake dynamometers, on the other hand, can absorb high torque at low speeds and, therefore, are better absorbers for some power applications. Water-brake dynamometers will function as absorbers for internal combustion engines and are used in the service market to run-in overhauled engines as well as to check engine performance against standards.

Water-brake dynamometers are basically a fluid coupling. A finned rotor turns within a stationary finned housing. The coupling is partly filled with water. The more water that is in the coupling, the more power that is required to spin the rotor within the housing. An arm keeps the housing from spinning. A scale on the end of the arm measures the force in pounds. Water within the coupling absorbs power by converting it into heat, so the

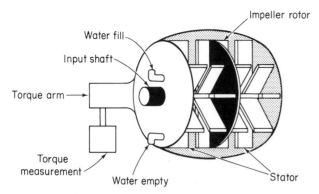

Fig. 18-6 Water brake dynamometer.

coupling water must be continually cooled. This is done by passing the water through a heat exchanger or by continually replacing part of the coupling water with fresh cool water.

Most dynamometers are used by engine and equipment manufacturers. Some are used by the large engine re-manufacturers to check their rebuilt units before sale. Engineering schools often have dynamometers as tools for research projects. Some industrial arts and vocational schools have obtained relatively inexpensive water-brake engine dynamometers for use with small engines to demonstrate internal combustion principles.

18-3 DYNAMOMETER APPLICATION

Any dynamometer type may be used as an absorber on performance or endurance tests. Large companies with many dynamometers will use the type that is the best for each individual test. Small companies and schools usually adapt presently owned dynamometers to the type of test needed, even if it is not an ideal application for the dynamometer.

All of the dynamometer types use the same principle. They absorb mechanical energy and convert it to another form of energy, usually heat or electricity. The same mathematical formula is used to calculate engine horsepower regardless of the dynamometer type used.

18-4 DYNAMOMETER LIMITS

Dynamometers have maximum and minimum limits. Their speed is limited by their mechanical strength. High speeds could throw armature windings from electric dynamometers. High speeds could overload bearing and seals, especially if a slight unbalance existed.

Maximum absorbing load is limited by heat. Overheated electric dynamomenters will cause solder to melt and insulation to break down. Overheated water-brake dynamometers will turn water into steam, which will not hold the load so control would be lost.

A fully loaded dynamometer will hold the mechanical input to a low speed, but it will not completely stop rotation without a mechanical friction brake, because of slippage. There is, therefore, a minimum speed at which the dynamometer can absorb power.

A completely unloaded dynamometer still requires power to turn the rotor or armature in the bearings and seals. As the rotational speed is increased, the rotor or armature starts to move air like a fan. This is called *windage*. Windage also requires power. There is a minimum power that any dynamometer can absorb.

Dynamometers will only operate within the envelope of mechanical strength, temperature, full load, and windage. Dynamometers must, therefore, be somewhat matched to the input power and speed to satisfactorily control torque and speed.

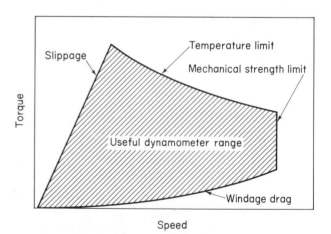

Fig. 18-7 Typical dynamometer limit curves.

18-5 DYNAMOMETERS FOR AUTOMOTIVE SERVICE

Chassis dynamometers are used in the automotive service market to check engine performance. Because of cost, their use is usually limited to high volume operators, such as fleet operators and test lane facilities. In this application, the dynamometer is used as an absorber that can *only* put a load on the

302

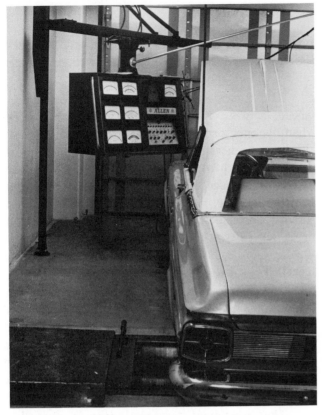

Fig. 18-8 Automotive service type chassis dynamometer.

engine and measure that load. This gives the operator an opportunity to check the engine with tune-up equipment while running under a controlled load. The dynamometer instrumentation indicates total power being delivered to the rear wheels while the tune-up equipment indicates the engine operating condition. The readings developed during a dynamometer run will have to be interpreted to determine engine condition.

18-6 DYNAMOMETER FUNCTION

Normal engine power on a dynamometer indicates satisfactory engine condition and no further detailed testing is required. Low power or rough operation indicates an abnormal condition. The cause of these conditions while running may be indicated by the tune-up instruments used with the dynamometer; if not, further detailed checks are necessary. The important point to remember is that the dynamometer's only function is to put a controlled load on the engine so that the engine performance can be tested with test instruments while the engine is running under simulated road conditions.

A dynamometer test of a vehicle may be used to check an engine to see if it needs service or it

may be used to check the engine after service to see that the engine is functioning correctly.

It should be noted that engine performance is checked as the engine is operating at that instant. It does not indicate that the engine will function as well in the future. This is like a race car that is functioning perfectly during one lap, but may not function as well on the next lap. Some part may be just about ready to fail, but this will not be indicated by the dynamometer or by tune-up instrumentation. The best method to determine continued satisfactory operation is to give the engine a good hands-on visual inspection.

18-7 TUNE-UP PROCEDURES

A preliminary visual inspection consists of checking the engine installation for cleanliness, fluid leaks, properly supported hoses and wires, physical condition of rubber and plastic parts, loose parts, chafing or worn parts, broken brackets or supports as well as the physical appearance of spark plug electrodes, breaker points, carburetor throat, throttle linkages, etc.

A good tune-up is preceded by a battery check and a survey inspection with an oscilloscope, tachometer, dwell meter, vacuum gauge, and timing light. Some test equipment units can electronically short out one spark plug at a time to measure how much its loss affects engine operation. If a weak cylinder is shorted, its loss is ineffective; however, if it is doing its share of the work, the speed will drop. These instruments indicate only satisfactory operation or that there is some weakness that requires further service. These preliminary survey tests are followed by a thorough visual inspection and a series of routine inspections or tests of items that support engine operation. The battery is always the first item to be checked for state-of-charge and capacity. This is followed by a physical check of the engine's mechanical condition.

Mechanical Condition. A tune-up cannot produce satisfactory engine operation if the combustion chamber doesn't hold compression. Most tune-up men follow the battery check by removing the spark plugs and checking each combustion chamber for its ability to compress the gases. This can be done by two methods: a compression test or a cylinder leakage test.

A compression test is run with the throttle blocked wide open and all the spark plugs removed. A compression gauge is installed in the spark plug holes, one cylinder at a time. The engine is cranked through the same number of compressions on each cylinder so cylinder pressures can be compared. Pressure in all cylinders should be within 10% of each other for standard operation. Compression pressure developed in this test is dependent upon cranking speed, and the amount and condition of lubricant on the cylinder wall. If this test shows excessive compression variation, a small quantity of oil is squirted into each cylinder through the spark plug opening and the engine cranked several revolutions. This oil will seal piston ring leakage. The compression test is again run, it is now called a wet compression test. Normal and nearly equal compression on all cylinders on this second test indicates leaking piston rings. If low or unequal compression still exists, it indicates valve leakage.

A cylinder leakage test is another method that can be used to determine combustion chamber sealing. The cylinder is turned to top center, and controlled air pressure is forced into the cylinder through a regulator. Pressure drop indicates cylinder leakage. Normal leakage may be up to 10%. When excessive leakage does exist, the exact source can be determined by listening through the carburetor for intake valve leakage, through the oil fill opening for piston ring leakage, and through the tail pipe for exhaust valve leakage.

If satisfactory combustion chamber sealing exists, it is worthwhile to proceed with the rest of the tune-up. Spark plug service is an obvious next step because the spark plugs are out of the engine for the compression test. They should be serviced or replaced with the correct spark plug.

Tune-Up Test Sequence. Several tests are run before the engine is started. In addition to the battery check, the breaker point resistance, the cranking voltage, cranking vacuum, and cranking coil output

may be checked. Instruments are attached, the engine is started and run at idle while dwell, idle speed and basic engine timing are checked.

The engine is brought up to a specified test speed, between 1500 and 2000 rpm (see equipment manufacturer's specifications for the specific speed). With the generator field disconnected, the engine scope will indicate coil polarity, required voltage, available voltage, breaker point action, ignition system leakage, and ignition system resistance. Interpretation of these readings may indicate problems that exist in the engine systems. The generator field is connected and charging system voltage is checked.

The engine is returned to idle to check idle speed and idle manifold vacuum. Some engines' specifications recommend the use of an exhaust analyzer when setting engine idle to help maintain low exhaust emission. Quick accelerations from idle will put a load on the spark plugs and the engine scope will indicate if they are functioning normally.

The instrument test may precede or follow standard tune-up service operations, such as distributor service, carburetion service, air and fuel filter service, and valve lash adjustment on solid lifter engines. Tests may show that additional tests

TYPICAL TROUBLE SHOOTING
INSTRUMENT TEST SEQUENCE

Tests Before Starting Engine

1 — Battery
2 — Point resistance
3 — Cranking voltage
4 — Cranking vacuum
5 — Cranking coil output

Tests With Engine Running

  Scope Tests (Generator Field Disconnected)

6 — Coil polarity
7 — Required voltage
8 — Breaker point action
9 — Ignition system leakage
10 — Ignition system resistance

(Field reconnected)

11 — Voltage regulation
12 — Idle speed
13 — Idle vacuum
14 — Snap acceleration

Fig. 18-9 Typical tune-up test sequence.

or adjustments are necessary. These would include battery circuit voltage drop, starter amperage draw, generator output, charging circuit voltage drop, regulator setting, ignition primary circuit voltage drop, fuel pump tests, carburetor rebuilding, and cooling system tests of the filler cap and thermostat.

The tune-up sequence may be used before or after routine service. Running the tune-up test sequence before performing routine service will point to items that require special service. This limits the service time to those items actually needing service. Running a tune-up test sequence after service insures satisfactory workmanship and customer satisfaction.

Tune-up test sequences differ for each make of test equipment. Each manufacturer provides a test sequence to be used with his equipment. He will usually supply specifications. Automotive shop manuals also show tune-up test sequences. These are often keyed to one type of test equipment, either commercial types or a type manufactured especially for the vehicle manufacturer.

Basically, all test equipment is a special application of voltmeters, oscilloscopes, ohmmeters, tachometers, dwell meters, vacuum gauges, and exhaust gas analyzers. Individual test units are packaged in cases and cabinets with interconnecting switches, shunts, rheostats, and electronic controls so that many tests can be made with few engine connections. The greatest difference in test procedures results from the different methods used to interconnect the basic test instruments. It is important to follow the procedures provided with the test equipment being used to get meaningful results.

18-8 SERVICE REQUIREMENTS

Customers only require service for routine maintenance, when they have a problem, or when appearance, comfort and performance items are needed. Tune-ups are usually classed as a routine maintenance procedure in which the preceding items are checked, tested, and serviced. Some engine problems may also be corrected by routine tune-up procedures. In this case, it would be advisable to pre-test the engine to identify the problem so that it can be definitely corrected.

Engine problems may be classified as problems that affect engine operation, such as loss of power,

rough running, overheating, excessive fuel consumption, or problems indicated by improper vehicle instrument readings. These problems are usually identified by the tune-up sequence procedure. Problems may involve leaks from the oil, fuel, and coolant systems. These are usually located visually and repaired by replacing gaskets or seals. Broken parts are located visually and repaired or replaced. Squeaking belts, seals or bearings are located by sound and sight. Some excessive emissions may be seen or smelled. These can be corrected by repairing the engine if it is causing these excess emissions.

Appearance and performance items are routine in nature, often requiring installation of a parts kit. These items, in turn, become problems if they do not operate correctly or if they do not satisfy the customer.

18-9 TROUBLE SHOOTING

Trouble shooting a customer's problem requires an understanding of how the parts of a vehicle operate, how they should normally appear and the correct use of proper test equipment and procedures. The greatest difficulty in trouble shooting is identifying the specific cause of the problem. After it has been identified, any qualified mechanic can repair it.

Trouble shooting charts are often presented to help identify the cause of problems. The best of these charts are presented in the shop manuals for each vehicle. They are more specific than a general trouble shooting chart that is designed to apply to any vehicle. In addition, most manufacturers publish service bulletins for their service men. These bulletins point out problems which frequently occur in their product line and give details on correction procedures. Keeping up-to-date on service bulletins is one of the best methods for a dealer mechanic to make quick problem diagnosis and repairs to automobiles in the product line.

An important point in trouble shooting that is frequently overlooked by the service writer or mechanic is that he does not carefully listen to the customer's complaint. The customer's description, aided by a few leading questions, will be of great help in identifying the customer's problem. Once the problem is identified, tests and inspections can be made to determine the cause of the complaint. When the cause is identified, it can be easily corrected and rechecked.

Review Questions
Chapter 18

1. What is the purpose of a dynamometer?

2. With a fixed throttle position, what effect does a change in dynamometer load have on engine speed? If the speed increased, what effect would this have on engine manifold vacuum?

3. How is horsepower determined from the dynamometer?

4. What absorption methods are used with dynamometers?

5. What part of the dynamometer is used to give force readout?

6. What limits dynamometer maximum speed, maximum absorption, minimum absorption?

7. How is a dynamometer used in tune-up?

8. Write out a tune-up sequence using a specific make of test equipment.

9. Why isn't an instrument check and adjustment sufficient for a tune-up?

Quiz 18

1. Engine dynamometers measure an engine's
   a. horsepower
   b. torque
   c. volumetric efficiency
   d. maximum speed.

2. In operation, the dynamometer
   a. measures the engines performance
   b. calculates mechanical efficiency
   c. provides information on thermodynamics
   d. converts the form of energy.

3. When the load on an engine dynamometer is reduced the engine will always
   a. increase speed
   b. reduce speed
   c. absorb more torque
   d. absorb less horsepower.

4. What would an engine's horsepower be if the engine were running at 3000 rpm and producing 175 pound feet torque?
   a. 90 hp
   b. 100 hp
   c. 150 hp
   d. 300 hp.

5. When using a dynamometer for tune-up, the dynamometer will
   a. test the ignition system
   b. measure the exhaust emissions
   c. check a high speed engine miss
   d. put a controlled load on the engine.

6. The best method to determine continued satisfactory engine operation is to
   a. give it a good visual inspection
   b. make a thorough test with an engine scope
   c. run the vehicle on a chassis dynamometer
   d. correct problems as the customer finds them.

7. The first item to be tested on a tune-up should always be the
   a. carburetor adjustments
   b. ignition timing
   c. battery condition
   d. engine compression.

8. Which of the following could be considered a survey test?
   a. oscilloscope analysis
   b. compression test
   c. alternator output
   d. idle speed.

9. To run smoothly a properly tuned-up engine must have
   a. a good distributor rotor
   b. a properly functioning fuel pump
   c. equal compression pressure
   d. correct ignition timing.

10. Customer satisfaction can be assured by
   a. checking the engine thoroughly before servicing
   b. repairing all routine service items
   c. correcting any malfunction found
   d. running a tune-up sequence after servicing.

chapter 19

Control of Automotive Emissions

Pollution has become one of the major problems in the United States. This has led to research in an attempt to stop additional pollution and to clean up presently polluted areas. Anti-pollution research indicates that the automobile is a major contributor to air pollution.

In 1952, a theory was presented suggesting that smog, a mixture of smoke and fog, was formed by the action of sunlight on hydrocarbons and nitric oxides. Additional studies confirmed this theory. The Automobile Manufacturers Association made further studies in 1954 to determine how much automobile emissions contributed to smog and air pollution. These studies led to the first vehicle emission standards, which were adopted by California, where smog and air pollution have been the greatest problem.

California's emission control standards were followed two years later by Federal standards. Later Federal regulations were adopted a year after they were put into effect by California. Federal emission control standard regulations for 1975 bring all vehicle emission control under the same standard regulations at the same time.

One problem in the control of vehicle emissions is to manufacture automobiles that will emit the low levels of harmful pollutants required by the regulations when the vehicles are new. The second problem is the control of emissions from the customer's automobile after miles of use. Emission test equipment for use in automobile service is being manufactured and technicians are being trained to test and adjust emission control devices as a part of the normal engine tune-up procedure.

19-1 SMOG

Air pollution is evident in a number of ways. It may be unsightly as smoke, soot, or dust. It may be foul-smelling as diesel odor or sewage treatment gases. The most serious type of air pollutants are those that present health hazards. Automobile emissions contribute to this last type of air pollution.

Air always has some pollution, such as fine neutral particles of dust and dirt that will settle on surfaces like the polished finish of automobiles. Other particles become concentrated and form a nucleus upon which moisture collects to form clouds, fog and rain. These small particles in the air are called *aerosols*. Natural aerosols along with industrial and vehicle emission produce one form of excessive air pollution.

Los Angeles, because of its particular location in a valley between mountains and the Pacific Ocean, has had the greatest problem with air pollution in the form of smog. The bothersome effects of smog

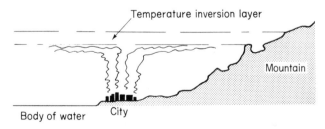

Fig. 19-1 Conditions conducive to smog formation.

have been traced to a photochemical reaction between reactive hydrocarbons and nitric oxides in the presence of sunlight. A smog atmosphere irritates the eye, damages vegetation, reduces visibility, and forms ozone, a powerful oxidizer. Smog only forms on dry, sunny days when reactive hydrocarbons and nitric oxides are present.

The principal products that precede photochemical smog formation are hydrocarbons called olefins and aromatics along with oxides of nitrogen. Olefins are especially reactive in smog formation. They are straight-chain, unsaturated hydrocarbon molecules with a double bond. The double bond is easily broken when other atoms are present to combine with the hydrocarbon molecule. In the presence of sunlight, these hydrocarbons and oxides of nitrogen are changed in a series of chemical reactions to produce smog components. The principal components of smog are: ozone, a powerful oxidizer that hardens rubber and is a health hazard in high concentrations; aldehydes, that are eye irritants; and a compound called peroxyacylnitrate (PAN), that terminates the photochemical event reaction chain. Other smog components include carbon monoxide, a toxic gas; hydrocarbons; and oxides of nitrogen.

```
    H  H  H  H  H  H
    |  |  |  |  |  |
H — C — C — C — C — C — C — H
    |  |  |  |  |  |
    H  H  H  H  H  H
```

Saturate (paraffin hexane)

```
    H  H  H  H  H  H
    |  |  |  |  |  |
H — C = C — C — C — C — C — H
    |        |  |  |
    H        H  H  H
```

Unsaturate (olefin hexene, 2)

Fig. 19-2 Saturate and unsaturate hydrocarbon molecule.

Researchers have shown that the amount of smog is reduced as atmospheric concentrations of reactive hydrocarbons are reduced. For any given concentration of reactive hydrocarbons, smog occurs at one particular concentration of oxides of nitrogen. If the oxides of nitrogen are reduced, smog will also be reduced. Therefore, reducing either hydrocarbons or oxides of nitrogen will reduce smog formation.

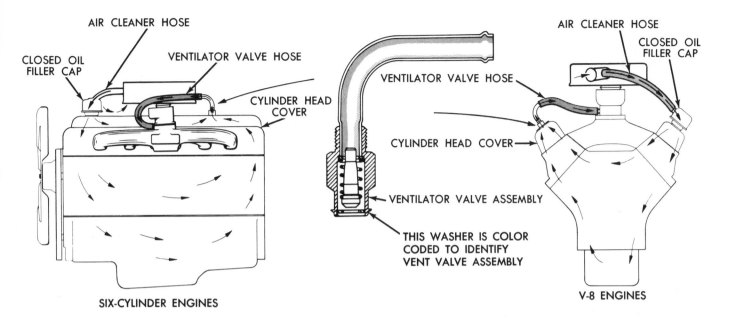

SIX-CYLINDER ENGINES

V-8 ENGINES

(a)

Fig. 19-3 Crankcase positive ventilation control. (a) Schematic of a closed system (Chrysler-Plymouth Division, Chrysler Corporation), (b) valve position with plunger closed (AC Spark Plug Division, General Motors Corporation), (c) valve position with plunger seated (AC Spark Plug Division, General Motors Corporation), (d) valve position with plunger open (AC Spark Plug Division, General Motors Corporation).

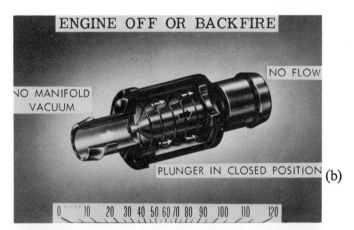

ENGINE OFF OR BACKFIRE

NO MANIFOLD VACUUM

NO FLOW

PLUNGER IN CLOSED POSITION (b)

19-2 VEHICLE EMISSIONS

Emissions come from several parts of the automobile. Of the total uncontrolled vehicle emissions, approximately 25% come from the crankcase, 60% from the engine exhaust, and 15% from the fuel tank and carburetor vents.

Crankcase Emissions. In 1961, all of the new automobiles sold in California were equipped with a crankcase breather control. This is called a positive crankcase ventilation system (PCV). It routes crankcase vapors through the intake manifold to be burned in the combustion chamber. In 1963, all new automobiles sold in the United States were equipped with PCV systems. This original open system was soon followed by a closed system that had a crankcase inlet pipe connected to the air filter. It effectively eliminated all crankcase vapor emission.

Crankcase vapors are a combination of light hydrocarbons, crankcase oil vapors and combustion

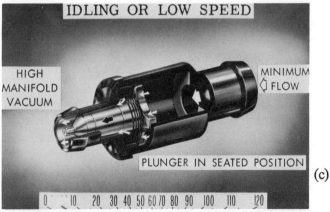

IDLING OR LOW SPEED

HIGH MANIFOLD VACUUM

MINIMUM FLOW

PLUNGER IN SEATED POSITION

(c)

HIGH SPEED

LOW MANIFOLD VACUUM

MAXIMUM FLOW

PLUNGER IN OPEN POSITION

(d)

chamber gases that have been forced past the pistons and rings during the compression and power strokes. Crankcase oil vapors are the light volatile portions of the motor oil that evaporate at operating temperatures. Combustion chamber gases that find their way into the crankcase are blow-by gases, primarily made up of gases that come from the quench area within .002″ to .020″ of the combustion chamber wall surface. These gases are cooled by the relatively low temperature wall surface until they are too cool to burn. This principle is supported by tests which show that blow-by gases have the same olefinic content as the gasoline being used. This indicates that these gases are unburned. Every time a driver opens the throttle, the blow-by rate increases, even though the throttle is not held open long enough to increase vehicle speed.

Exhaust Emissions. The exhaust emission was the next problem to be controlled. In 1966, all cars sold in California were required to have exhaust emission controls. These standards were expanded in 1968 to cover all new cars sold in the United States. In contrast to crankcase emissions that could be completely sealed, exhaust must be free to empty into the atmosphere. This means that undesirable elements in the exhaust must be reduced to safe limits. These undesirable exhaust constituants are carbon monoxide, unburned hydrocarbons, and oxides of nitrogen.

Carbon Monoxide. Complete combustion of hydrocarbons and oxygen would produce carbon dioxide (CO_2) and water (H_2O). This requires a thoroughly mixed, chemically balanced air/fuel ratio charge that has just enough oxygen in the air to combine with all of the fuel. An air/fuel mixture ratio of 14.8 : 1 by weight, which meets these balanced requirements, is said to be a stoichiometric mixture. Mixtures richer than stoichiometric will not have enough oxygen to completely burn the hydrocarbons, leaving some hydrocarbons in a partly burned condition. Carbon monoxide (CO) is one of the partly burned constituants found in the exhaust gases. Its presence indicates the percentage of combustion or air/fuel ratio. Most garage type exhaust gas analyzers measure the carbon monoxide present in the exhaust gas and display it as the air/fuel ratio on the instrument reading.

In addition to carbon monoxide, mixtures richer than stoichiometric also leave unburned hydrocarbons. These, in turn, become aerosols that can trigger photochemical smog. The obvious answer to the reduction of carbon monoxide and unburned hydrocarbon is to lean the mixtures. Experiments have shown that air/fuel ratios between 16:1 and 18:1 produce the least exhaust hydrocarbon and carbon monoxide as well as providing maximum fuel economy. Unfortunately, an engine operating on mixtures this lean would not provide satisfactory driveability. At these mixture ratios the engine will *surge*, that is, it will speed up and slow down and not hold steady speeds.

Surge is the result of poor charge ignition and poor flame front propagation through the lean mixture in the combustion chamber. Lean mixtures require higher temperatures than rich mixtures for satisfactory combustion. When these required temperatures exist, the charge will burn completely and will produce low carbon monoxide emissions. When these temperatures do not exist, the charge will not ignite, resulting in misfiring. Intermittent misfiring is evident as engine surge.

The chapter on carburetion shows that for good driveability, the engine requires a rich mixture for low speed and full power operation. Under these rich conditions, the most carbon monoxide and unburned hydrocarbon emissions are produced. High temperatures occur at full throttle operation so the majority of the combustion is complete in the combustion chamber. Low combustion temperatures exist at closed throttle using rich mixtures, resulting in high emissions. Still more carbon monoxide and hydrocarbons are emitted when the engine is decelerated from high rpm with a closed throttle. This condition is shown by a high intake manifold vacuum.

Hydrocarbons. Hydrocarbon emission at high manifold vacuum operation is the result of exhaust gases diluting the charge during valve overlap as well as poor combustion chamber scavenging during the exhaust stroke. Much of this is due to the *wall quenching* phenomenon previously described. Some of these quenched gases are blown past the piston rings to become part of the crankcase emissions.

Some are expelled through the exhaust port and become part of the exhaust emission as a result of incomplete scavenging. A large part of the quenched gases stay in the combustion chamber to burn on the next cycle. These wall quenched gases affect emissions so much that engine manufacturers have changed the engine combustion chamber design and surface to volume ratio so that the combustion chamber has more volume compared to its surface (a decrease in the surface to volume ratio).

Nitric Oxides. Nitric oxides are the other exhaust constituants that contribute to photochemical smog. They are produced by high temperature, lean mixture combustion. Stoichiometric air/fuel ratios consider only oxygen and hydrocarbons. Air contains approximately 20% oxygen. The other 80%

of air contains nitrogen and small quantities of inert and other gases. Under the high temperature lean mixture, the nitrogen and the oxygen of the air chemically combine to form nitrogen monoxide (NO), nitrogen dioxide (NO_2), nitrogen trioxide (NO_3), and so forth. These are all grouped as *oxides of nitrogen* and may be expressed as NO_x. The amount of nitrogen oxides present in engine exhaust correlates with the cycle peak combustion temperature. Under extremely lean air/fuel ratios oxides of nitrogen are reduced; however, it is difficult to operate an engine under these extremely lean conditions.

It should be noted that the lean operating mixtures which reduce carbon monoxide and unburned hydrocarbons tend to increase nitrogen oxides. Here again is a compromise that must be made to keep all of the undesirable emission constituents at a minimum level.

(a)

(b)

Fig. 19-4 Combustion chamber modified to reduce wall quenching. (a) High quench wedge head, (b) modified low quench head.

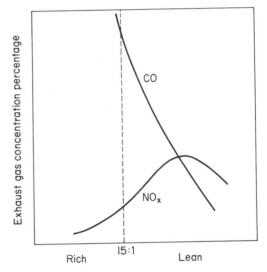

Fig. 19-5 Exhaust gas contaminant change as the air/fuel ratio changes.

Engine and Operation Factors. Other factors in addition to air/fuel ratio and manifold vacuum affect vehicle exhaust emission. One of these is ignition timing. With a given air/fuel ratio, hydrocarbon emission can be reduced by increasing exhaust temperature. This reduces the quenching effect of the exhaust manifold to more nearly complete

311

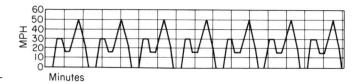

Fig. 19-7 Plot of the California 7 mode cycle emission test.

combustion and, at the same time, avoid raising the maximum combustion temperature. Retarding ignition timing is one way to raise exhaust temperature. Because the most serious hydrocarbon emission problem occurs at idle and deceleration, the distributor advance curve may be modified to provide retarded timing at high manifold vacuum while, at the same time, producing the required timing advance for all other engine operating conditions.

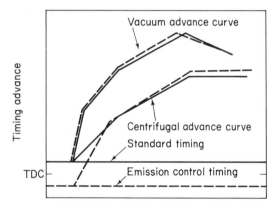

Fig. 19-6 Typical change in the distributor advance curve to reduce CO and unburned hydrocarbons at low speeds.

Combustion chamber deposits tend to increase emissions. Deposits containing lead produce higher emissions than those without lead. This is one of the factors that causes increased emission from high mileage vehicles.

Automatic transmission equipped vehicles tend to produce less emissions than standard transmission equipped vehicles. On deceleration, the standard transmission will overdrive the engine at higher speeds than the automatic transmission. Overdriving produces a higher manifold vacuum that results in high exhaust emissions.

On a given vehicle, a number of variables affect its emissions. The major variables are: individual driving habits; routes and traffic density; and car and engine performance. All of these have an effect on emissions. The effect depends upon the percentage of time the engine is operated at idle, during acceleration, during cruise and while decelerating.

Recognizing these variables, California developed a test cycle that would duplicate the average driving habits of a typical Los Angeles driver. This test cycle is called the *California Seven-Mode Cycle*. It used all four types of engine operating conditions at speeds and times that compare to the typical vehicle operation. This cycle was accepted as the standard for all new vehicles sold in the United States in 1968.

The California Cycle only measures emissions at selected vehicle speeds under thirty miles per hour. This is inadequate to measure mass standards, so the Federal government has developed a driving schedule which takes a sample of the entire exhaust mass produced on a twenty-three minute schedule. The schedule consists of a non-repetitive series of idle, accelerations, cruise and deceleration modes of various time sequences and rates. It is driven by a smooth transition through speed vs time relationships that simulate normal operating conditions.

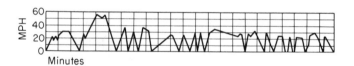

Fig. 19-8 Plot of mass sample driving schedule.

Evaporative Emissions. The last 15% of vehicle emissions to be controlled was evaporative losses from the fuel tank and from carburetor vents. California started controls of evaporative losses in 1970. The controls apply to the entire United States in 1971. Evaporative losses are the result of evaporation of light ends or highly volatile portions of the gasoline. They are entirely unburned hydrocarbons. The volatile portion of the fuel is necessary to provide vapors required for starting a cold engine. Their use in gasoline also allows the petroleum refiners to use a larger portion of the crude petroleum stock for gasoline and thus keep the gasoline price as low as possible. Petroleum producers and vehicle manufacturers work together to provide gasoline that will function satisfactorily in the engine at a minimum cost to the consumer.

Year	CO	HC	NOx	Evaporative Loss	Particulate Emission
Uncontrolled	- -	1375	- -		
1969	1.5% (34 g/mi)	275 ppm (3.3 g/mi)	350 ppm	- -	- -
Mass Standards (converted)					
1970	23 g/mi	2.2 g/mi	- -		
1971	23 g/mi	2.2 g/mi	4.0 g/mi	- -	- -
True Mass Standards					
1972	39 g/mi	3.4 g/mi	4.0 g/mi		
1974	39 g/mi	3.4 g/mi	3.0 g/mi	2 g/test	- -
1975	3.4 g/mi	.41 g/mi	3.0 g/mi	2 g/test	- -
1976	3.4 g/mi	.41 g/mi	.40 g/mi	2 g/test	1 gr/mi

Federal Standards of July 2, 1971.

Evaporative emissions from the fuel tank are the result of the fuel vapor pressure and evaporation of the volatile portion of the gasoline in the tank. These vapors, in an uncontrolled tank, are let out of the tank through a breather vent pipe. This pipe is necessary to keep the fuel tank from collapsing as fuel is used and to allow the tank to breathe as the atmospheric pressure changes or as the car is driven up and down high hills. Temperature changes also cause the air and fuel in the tank to expand and contract which requires venting.

The carburetor float bowl is in a high temperature location that allows the carburetor to hot soak when the engine is turned off. This hot soak condition, resulting from engine heat, can raise the carburetor temperature as high as 120 degrees. This high temperature will evaporate a large portion of the gasoline in the fuel bowl. These vapors are replaced with fuel in the line between the carburetor and fuel pump until all fuel pressure is dissipated. Evaporated vapors from an uncontrolled carburetor bowl will vent directly to the atmosphere and fill the air filter, then pass out of the air horn into the atmosphere as hydrocarbon emissions.

19-3 EMISSION REGULATIONS

The original limits for regulating emissions were specified in parts per million (ppm) or percentage of the emitted volume. Gasoline engines were rated as having high emissions using this standard, while diesel and turbine engines had relatively low emissions. This is because diesel and turbine engines use a very large volume of air for the amount of fuel they consume.

In 1970, a mass standard was adopted. This is a measure of the weight of the unwanted emissions in grams per mile. It put the gasoline, diesel and turbine engines on an equal footing for total pollution per mile. The maximum limits are shown in the table above.

It should be noted that as the technology to measure and control emissions developed, the allowable limits on emissions were reduced. There will continue to be much time and money spent on research to limit harmful vehicle emissions.

19-4 EXHAUST EMISSION REDUCTION

Control of exhaust emissions may take place in three ways, by controlling the charge supplied to the combustion chamber, by controlling the combustion process, or by controlling or modifying the emission after it leaves the combustion chamber. Engines may use one or several of these control methods to get the required low emission levels.

Control of the Charge. Control of the combustible charge must start with control of the fuel itself. The reactive hydrocarbon level in the exhaust will drop as olefin and aromatic hydrocarbons in the base fuel stock are reduced. This reduces the smog-forming properties of exhaust emissions.

Unfortunately, some of these unsaturated and aromatic gasoline constituents have high octane ratings. If they were eliminated from the fuel, the octane rating would be lowered, unless they were replaced with other knock-suppressing components.

Additional control of the combustion charge comes through changes in manifold size and shape and by the careful calibration of the carburetor to provide air/fuel ratios that will result in minimum emission formation. The carburetor's control is supplemented by heating devices that assist rapid engine warm-up. Rapid warm-up will cause the choke to open sooner and will help to mix the fuel charge more thoroughly. Good fuel atomization and thorough mixing in a small diameter high velocity manifold will allow the engine to operate at a lean mixture for reduced emissions and, at the same time, minimize power surging.

Lead from anti-knock additives tends to dampen oxidation of hydrocarbons in the exhaust. Removing lead from the gasoline allows additional oxidation in the exhaust to reduce hydrocarbon emission. Its removal also reduces combustion chamber deposits, oil contamination, and eliminates almost all of the particulate matter. Its major advantage, however, is to increase the life of exhaust catalytic converters. Two major problems accompany the removal of lead. The first is the loss of available power as the fuel octane number is lowered, and the second is a large increase in exhaust valve seat wear.

Control of the Combustion Process. The combustion process is controlled by combustion chamber design, amount of charge, combustion temperature, and ignition timing. For years, combustion chambers were designed to produce smooth burning, low octane requirements and high power. The chambers have been modified to reduce the surface to volume ratio to meet state and Federal emission standards. These modifications have resulted in reduced engine performance and cause a slight loss in gas mileage. The amount of charge entering the chamber depends upon throttle opening and engine speed. The only way an engine is able to increase its power is to have a larger charge enter the combustion chamber.

The amount of combustion charge affects both emissions and power. When power is needed, power becomes the dominant factor and emissions will be produced. Turbulence in the combustion will help to mix the air and fuel, thereby reducing the amount of unburned hydrocarbon emissions produced.

Combustion temperature results from the operating conditions such as the amount of charge taken into the combustion chamber, compression ratio, ignition timing, the amount of exhaust dilution and the chemistry of the fuel used. High combustion temperatures reduce hydrocarbon emissions. These same high temperatures increase the engine's octane requirement and produce oxides of nitrogen. The combustion temperature must, therefore, be kept within limits that produce minimum total emission. This, of course, is a compromise.

Ignition is timed to produce maximum mean effective pressure in the combustion chamber for the most efficient engine operation. This ignition point is called the mean best timing (MBT). Distributor advance mechanisms adjust ignition timing to ignite the charge at the MBT for all operating conditions, regardless of the speed or power at which the engine is running. Any change from MBT will reduce the engine's useful power and increase its exhaust temperature. Timing is retarded at high manifold vacuum in some engines to maintain a high exhaust temperature for a longer period of time to consume the hydrocarbons in the exhaust gases, thereby reducing hydrocarbon emission.

Modify Exhaust Gases. Control of the exhaust hydrocarbon emissions after they leave the combustion chamber is done in several ways. The first method is to add pressurized air to the high temperature exhaust gases, using a belt-driven air pump. The added air provides additional oxygen necessary to complete combustion of the unburned hydrocarbons that have come through the combustion chamber. With this system, the engine can be operated close to best power air/fuel ratios and still keep the exhaust emissions within required standards.

A second device used to control hydrocarbon emissions after they leave the combustion chamber is an afterburner or reactor. This is a chamber or series of chambers attached to the cylinder head exhaust ports or placed in the exhaust system that maintain high exhaust temperatures for a long enough time to allow the unburned hydrocarbons

Fig. 19-9 System to pump air into the exhaust gas after it leaves the combustion chamber.

to complete oxidation. Some units use a catalyst to complete oxidation. Some units use a catalyst to speed this process at a lower temperature. The afterburner takes up quite a bit of underhood space and is short-lived; however, it may eventually become a standard production item.

19-5 MEASUREMENT OF EMISSIONS

A major problem in vehicle emission control is measurement of emissions. It is a time-consuming process that involves expensive equipment. Basic gas analysis is done using a *chemical absorption process*. In this process, a sample of a mixture of gases is run through a series of chemicals, one at a time. Each chemical absorbs one of the gases from the sample, which reduces the sample volume.

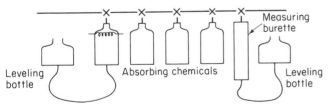

Fig. 19-10 Schematic of the chemical absorption process.

The gas component removed is reported as a percentage of the entire sample.

Obtaining a good sample for chemical absorption is an associated problem. Exhaust samples may

be trapped in a plastic bag and transferred to the laboratory for analysis. Evaporative emissions are taken from a sealed room or shed in which a vehicle has been placed. During a soak period, the vehicle and the room are kept at a specified temperature for a standard period of time prior to taking the emission sample.

A faster means of determining exhaust emission is through the use of a *non-dispersion infra-red analyzer* (NDIR). This method has become an industry standard for measuring emissions. It is calibrated with specially prepared standard gas samples. The standard gas sample quality is checked by chemical absorption.

The infra-red analyzer passes a pulsating infrared beam through each of two tubes or cells. The reference cell is filled with a non-absorbing reference gas. The sample to be analyzed flows through the sample cell. Gases in the sample cell will absorb some of the infra-red beam's energy. After passing through the gases, each of the infra-red beams hits a balanced diaphragm detector. Both sides of the detector are filled with the gas type being examined. The amount of energy remaining in each beam increases the pressure in its side of the detector diaphragm.

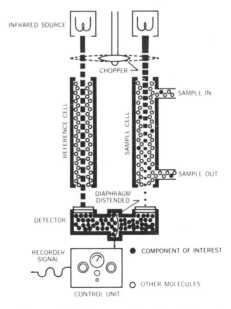

Fig. 19-11 Schematic of the non-dispersion infra-red analyzer (NDIR) sensing unit (Beckman Instruments, Inc.).

315

Unequal energy passing through the gases will cause a difference in pressure that deflects the diaphragm. Diaphragm deflection is proportional to the concentration of the gas sample being analyzed.

A separate analyzer is required for each gas component. Exhaust emissions are checked with non-dispersive infra-red analyzers for carbon monoxide and hydrocarbons (usually hexane) and nitrogen oxides.

Hydrocarbon emissions are a combination of a number of different hydrocarbon gases. Early tests only measured for hexane using a nondispersive

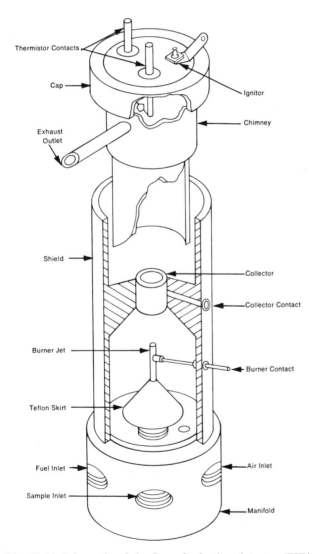

Fig. 19-12 Schematic of the flame ionization detector (FID) sensing unit (Beckman Instruments, Inc.).

infra-red analyzer. This was inadequate for mass sampling. A flame ionization detector (FID) will indicate the amount of all unburned hydrocarbons in the exhaust sample quickly and accurately.

The heart of the FID tester is a hydrogen burner that produces a negligible number of ions. Introducing a sample of the exhaust gas containing unburned hydrocarbons produces a large number of ions proportional to the amount of hydrocarbon. A voltage difference between the burner jet and collector ring attracts the ions and thus produces a small current. The current is proportional to the ions produced. Electronic equipment amplifies the current flow signal and displays the results on a meter.

Exhaust emissions testing requires the use of a $14,000 dynamometer and a minimum $25,000 instrument console in a room that has adequate ventilation and exhaust. These are usually backed up with a $75,000 computer. The California cycle sequence requires approximately fifteen minutes to run. The mass cycle takes nearly twenty-three minutes. Exhaust emission analysis is very expensive and is limited to development work and to quality control checks. It is not done as a part of tune-up procedure. A number of service level instruments that measure CO and hydrocarbons are available to help the technician do emission control maintenance.

19-6 EMISSION CONTROL

All internal combustion engines produce emissions. A number of these emissions are a hazard to health and must be controlled. Automobile manufacturers adapted several control methods to existing engines using minimum modifications until new engines and control systems could be developed and produced.

Crankcase Emissions. Crankcase emissions are completely controlled with the PCV system. It functions for a satisfactory service life with SD service classification motor oils and detergent gasolines that are in common use. PCV malfunctioning will increase engine deposits, particularly around the intake valve. The service life of the PCV valve is based on the fuel and oil quality, the oil change periods, the amount of engine blow-by, and the PCV system maintenance.

Fig. 19-13 Air pre-heater with thermostatic pellet control and vacuum override. (a) Part identification, (b) warm air supplied to a cold engine, (c) warm-cold air mix supplied to a partly warm engine, (d) cold air supplied to a warm engine (AC Spark Plug Division, General Motors Corporation).

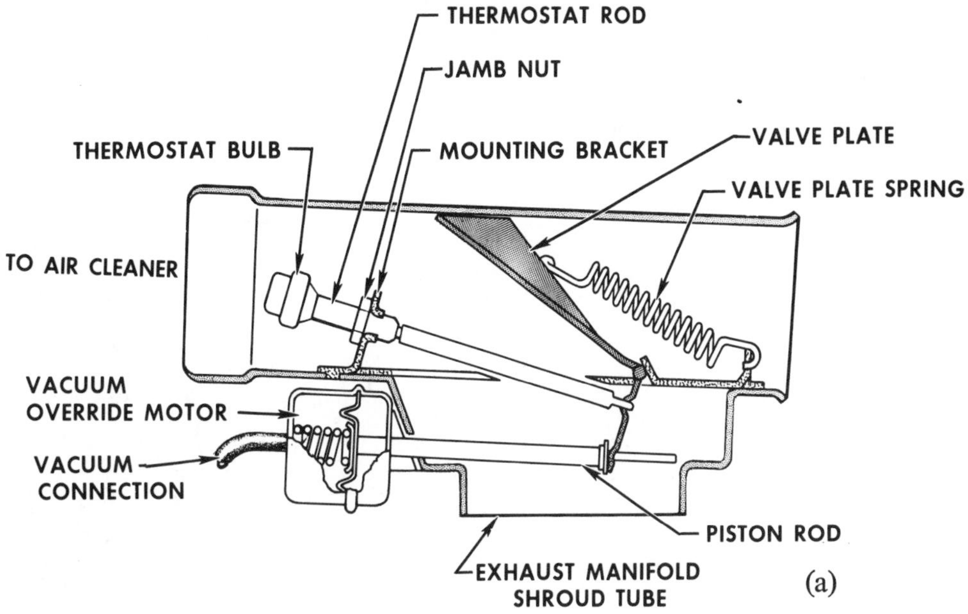

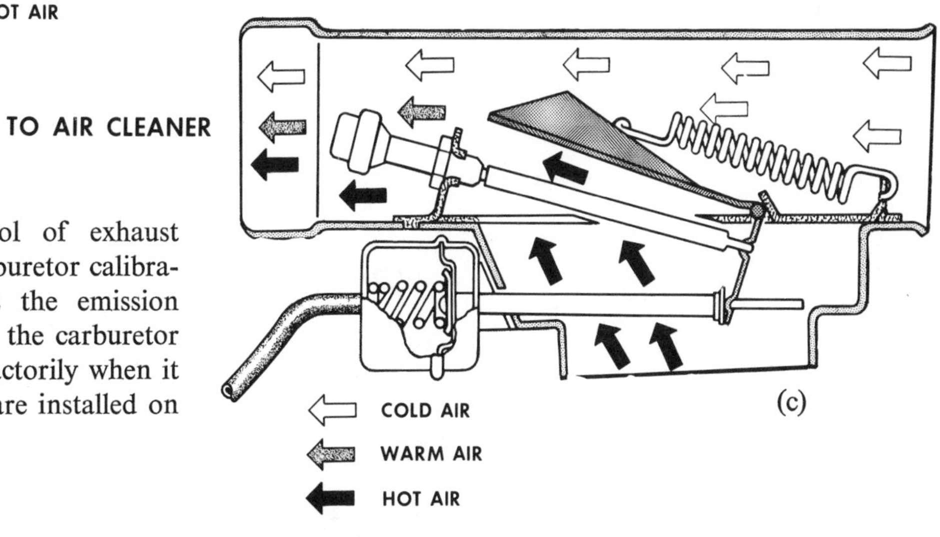

THERMOSTAT ROD

JAMB NUT

THERMOSTAT BULB

MOUNTING BRACKET

VALVE PLATE

VALVE PLATE SPRING

TO AIR CLEANER

VACUUM OVERRIDE MOTOR

VACUUM CONNECTION

PISTON ROD

EXHAUST MANIFOLD SHROUD TUBE

(a)

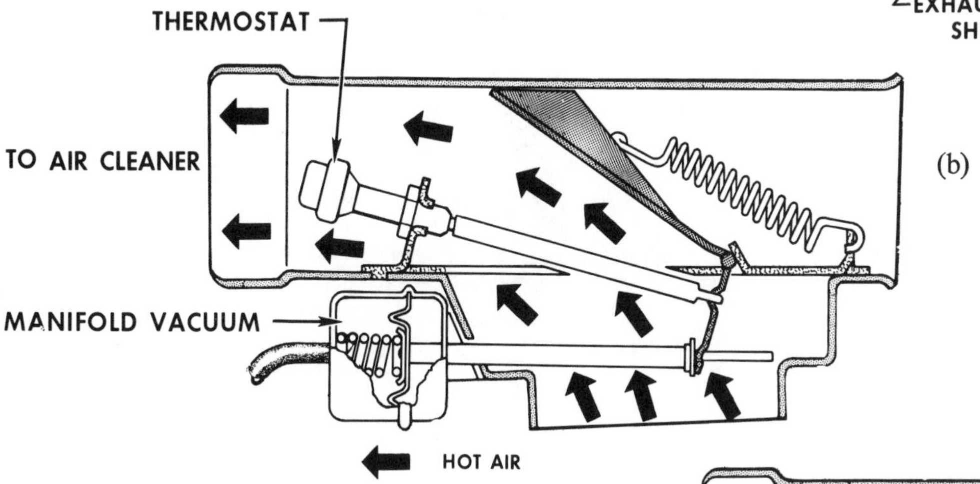

THERMOSTAT

TO AIR CLEANER

MANIFOLD VACUUM

(b)

HOT AIR

TO AIR CLEANER

COLD AIR

WARM AIR

HOT AIR

(c)

TO AIR CLEANER

(d)

COLD AIR

Exhaust Emissions. The control of exhaust emission starts with very careful carburetor calibration on the lean side. This keeps the emission forming tendencies very low. Often, the carburetor is so lean that it will not run satisfactorily when it is cold. In this case, air preheaters are installed on the engine.

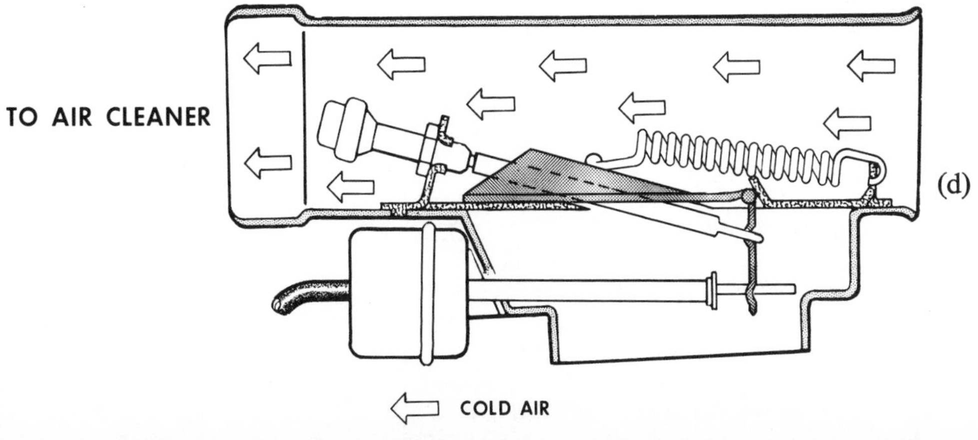

317

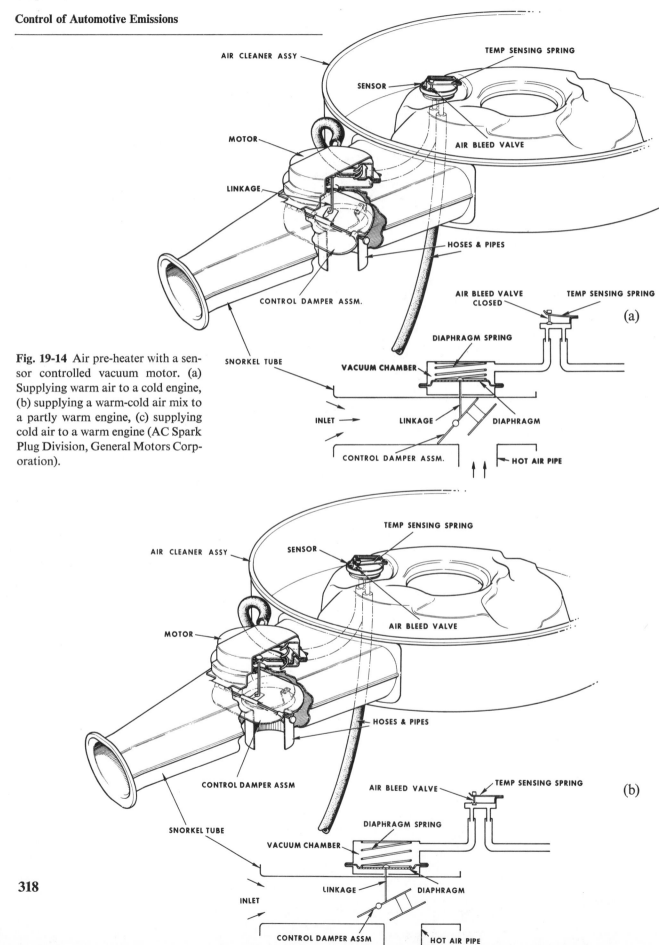

Fig. 19-14 Air pre-heater with a sensor controlled vacuum motor. (a) Supplying warm air to a cold engine, (b) supplying a warm-cold air mix to a partly warm engine, (c) supplying cold air to a warm engine (AC Spark Plug Division, General Motors Corporation).

AIR CLEANER ASSY

TEMP SENSING SPRING

SENSOR

AIR BLEED VALVE

MOTOR

LINKAGE

HOSES & PIPES

CONTROL DAMPER ASSM.

SNORKEL TUBE

AIR BLEED VALVE CLOSED

TEMP SENSING SPRING

(a)

DIAPHRAGM SPRING

VACUUM CHAMBER

INLET

LINKAGE

DIAPHRAGM

CONTROL DAMPER ASSM.

HOT AIR PIPE

AIR CLEANER ASSY

TEMP SENSING SPRING

SENSOR

AIR BLEED VALVE

MOTOR

HOSES & PIPES

CONTROL DAMPER ASSM

AIR BLEED VALVE

TEMP SENSING SPRING

(b)

DIAPHRAGM SPRING

VACUUM CHAMBER

SNORKEL TUBE

LINKAGE

DIAPHRAGM

INLET

CONTROL DAMPER ASSM

HOT AIR PIPE

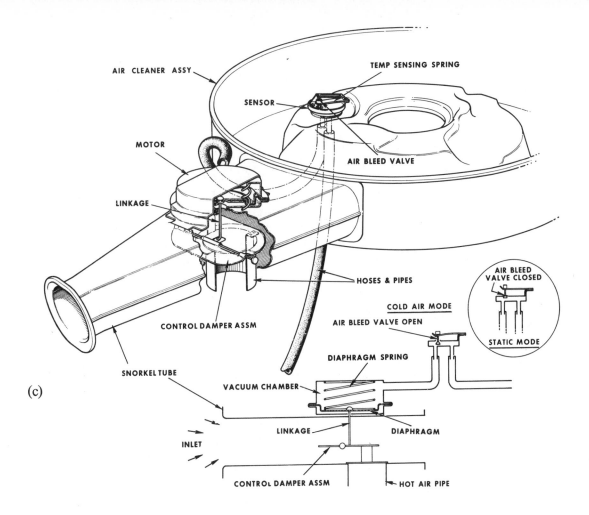

(c)

The air preheater takes air from around one of the exhaust manifolds and directs it through an air valve to the air filter or silencer. This rapidly heats the air to around 100°F. At this temperature, the choke opens rapidly to reduce emissions. A temperature control valve maintains the air silencer temperature close to 100° by adjusting the air valve with manifold vacuum. The air valve position gradually opens as the engine warms. This allows underhood air to mix with the preheated air to maintain the required minimum intake air temperature. When the underhood air temperature gets above the temperature control setting, the air valve is fully opened.

A useful side effect of the air preheater is that the rapid warm-up eliminates carburetor icing problems.

Emissions are also reduced by using a distributor advance system that allows ignition timing to be retarded during deceleration and idle for low exhaust emissions, as previously described. An engine temperature sensing valve may be installed to advance the ignition timing under conditions where prolonged engine idle causes excessive engine temperatures. This timing advance increases engine efficiency and reduces engine heat rejection to the cooling system, thereby preventing engine overheating. Emission levels during this advance period will increase.

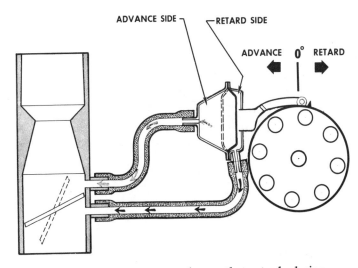

Fig. 19-15 Distributor vacuum advance that retards during deceleration (AC Spark Plug Division, General Motors Corporation).

319

A further reduction in emissions is accomplished by operating the engine at a high engine idle speed. This allows the carburetor to operate the engine with a lean air/fuel mixture and provides better charge mixing in the manifold.

Some engines depend upon exhaust gas modification for emission reduction by adding air to the exhaust after it is expelled from the combustion chamber, as described in Section 19-4. This system uses an air pump, injection nozzles and control valves. The air pump requires about one horsepower to operate. Air is drawn from the air cleaner and is blown into the exhaust ports. Check valves in the air lines are used to prevent momentary high exhaust pressures from backing into the air pump system. A valve is used to divert pump air to the atmosphere or to the intake manifold when the engine has high manifold vacuum. This will prevent backfires. During high vacuum operating conditions while decelerating, the carburetor delivers a rich fuel mixture. If the air pump continues to supply air into this rich fuel mixture, an explosion

or backfire will occur. Such an explosion could damage the vehicle exhaust system.

One of the earliest exhaust emission control methods tried was an afterburner. Two types were used, a plain afterburner and a catalytic converter. The plain afterburner maintained high exhaust temperature long enough to oxidize the hydrocarbons. The catalytic converter used a chamber with a catalyst to aid in the oxidation process of the hydrocarbons at a lower temperature than the plain afterburner. Lead from gasoline anti-knock additives contaminates the catalyst. Research continues on afterburners even though they take up valuable engine compartment and below floor pan space, along with having a short operating life. Lead has been removed from several grades of gasoline to improve catalytic converter useful life.

Nitrous oxides are formed at high combustion temperatures. Experiments have been conducted to re-cycle a portion of the exhaust gas back through the engine. Exhaust gases are, in effect, an inert gas. Inert gases mixed in the charge will lower the combustion pressure and temperature, thereby reducing formation of nitrous oxides.

Evaporative Emissions. The light end of the gasoline evaporates as the fuel temperature increases. Control of the evaporated hydrocarbons is accomplished by directing them through a separator to an absorber, while the engine is not running. When the engine is started, the vapors are drawn from the absorber through the intake manifold into the combustion chamber. The absorber may be a carbon-filled canister or it may be the engine oil in the crankcase.

19-7 MAINTAINING SAFE EMISSION LEVELS

The only method that will provide satisfactory minimum emission levels throughout the life of the vehicle is to provide proper maintenance.

Almost any engine malfunction or improper adjustment of the carburetor, engine idle speed, distributor timing, and advance, or air preheater will increase the emission level. Misfiring of one cylinder can raise the emission level to over twice its normal, controlled level.

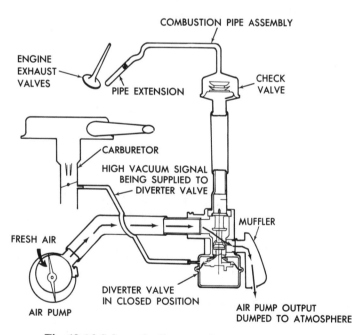

Fig. 19-16 Schematic diagram of an air pump emission control system (AC Spark Plug Division, General Motors Corporation).

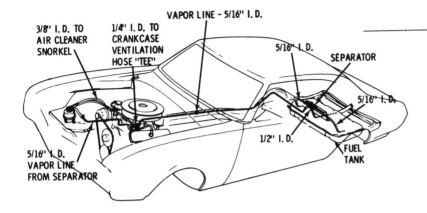

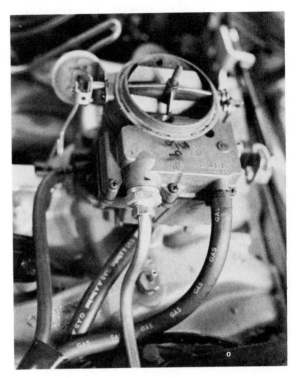

Fig. 19-17 Typical evaporative control system. (a) Vehicle layout (Oldsmobile Division, General Motors Corporation), (b) carburetor with bowl vent to the carbon canister.

Emission control systems reduce the available power from an engine and increase the fuel consumption over an identical engine without controls. In spite of this, emission controls are required by law to reduce air pollution. To get as much power from the engine as possible while keeping the emission level within standards, the vehicle must be maintained as close to manufacturer's specifications as possible.

During the development of emission standards, individual sample vehicles were checked. It was found that incorrect carburetor parts were often installed during carburetor "rebuilding". Additional examples of problems discovered while developing standards were dirty air cleaners, flooding carburetors, sticking power valves, maladjusted and sluggish chokes, as well as improper ignition timing and incorrect idle speeds.

Proper maintenance of the following items will provide a satisfactory level of emissions:

1. All air lines and tubes should be secure and in good condition.
2. The air pump belt, where used, must be in good condition and be adjusted correctly.
3. Ignition timing must be correct.
4. Ignition advance must function correctly.

5. Correct idle speed is required.
6. Idle air/fuel mixtures must be within specified limits.
7. PCV must operate freely.
8. Air cleaner must not be plugged.
9. Exhaust manifold heat valve should operate freely.
10. All components must be fully installed and installed correctly.

All settings must be made to comply with the specific vehicle manufacturer's specifications. Many of these specifications are printed on a tag mounted in the engine compartment.

The exhaust gas analyzer is available for service checks. It is used to check the idle air/fuel ratio. Proper assembly and adjustments of standard engine components is, however, the only way a service man can assure his customer that the customer's vehicle produces emission levels within approved standards.

Review Questions Chapter 19

1. What is an aerosol?

2. What is meant by a photochemical reaction?

3. What is a reactive hydrocarbon?

4. How does the PCV system eliminate crankcase vapors?

5. What forms crankcase vapors?

6. What name is given to a chemically correct mixture?

7. Why are emissions the highest during deceleration?

8. What conditions produce nitrogen oxides?

9. What engine design factors reduce emissions?

10. Where are evaporative emissions produced?

11. How did the mass standards affect the relations between gasoline and diesel engine standards?

12. How does rapid warm-up help reduce emissions?

13. What factors in the combustion chamber reduce emissions?

14. What two methods are used to modify the exhaust gas to reduce emissions?

15. What problems are encountered in measuring emissions?

16. Compare the chemical absorption and non-dispersion infra-red analyzer methods of measuring emissions.

17. What problems could result from a malfunctioning PCV valve?

18. Why does the timing advance on an engine using an emission control distributor advance when the engine is hot?

19. Why is an air diversion valve used in an air pump system?

20. How does re-cycled exhaust gas lower the combustion temperature?

21. What two methods are used to absorb evaporative emissions?

22. How can emissions be controlled at the service level?

Quiz 19

1. What physical problem usually accompanies photochemical smog?
   a. lung damage
   b. eye irritation
   c. severe headache
   d. skin rash

2. What exhaust emission is the most active in the formation of photochemical smog?
   a. CO
   b. CO_2
   c. HC
   d. NO_x

3. What noxious exhaust emission component increases as the air/fuel ratio is leaned from 15:1?
   a. CO
   b. CO_2
   c. HC
   d. NO_x

4. What exhaust emission is produced during high peak combustion temperatures?
   a. CO
   b. CO_2

c. HC

d. NO_x

5. What is the major reason for reducing the lead content of gasoline?
   a. reducing HC emission
   b. lowering the fuel cost
   c. preventing catalyst contamination
   d. minimizing engine deposits

6. Lean air/fuel mixtures are difficult to ignite. They can be made to ignite easier by increasing
   a. engine speed
   b. compression ratios
   c. charge temperature
   d. volumetric efficiency.

7. Combustion chamber surface quenching causes
   a. blow-by emission
   b. hydrocarbon emission
   c. low emission levels
   d. nitric oxide emission.

8. Hydrocarbon emission results from
   a. lean mixture
   b. high combustion temperature
   c. engine misfiring
   d. light ends in the fuel.

9. When are evaporative emissions a problem?
   a. when the vehicle is standing with the engine off
   b. when the vehicle is hot and running at turnpike speeds
   c. during deceleration and idle
   d. when high octane fuel is being used

10. Evaporative emissions are stored in an absorber. When the absorber is saturated it is
    a. replaced
    b. removed and discharged
    c. cleaned by heating to drive the vapors out
    d. cleaned with the engine running.

chapter 20

Automotive Clutch Operation

A clutch is a mechanism designed to disconnect and reconnect driving and driven members. The type of clutch discussed here is required in the drive line of a vehicle that uses a standard transmission. The engine must be disconnected from the drive line during starting to keep the vehicle from moving and to minimize engine load so the engine will start. The clutch engages the engine and drive line to power the vehicle, drive the wheels, and release the torque loads on the drive line so the transmission can be shifted from one gear ratio to another.

The automobile clutch consists of a driving pressure plate and flywheel assembly attached to the engine and a driven clutch disc attached to the transmission. When the clutch disc is clamped between the pressure plate and flywheel by springs in the pressure plate, the clutch will carry engine driving force to the transmission and drive line. Maximum driving force or driving torque occurs just before the disc slips while it is clamped between the pressure plate and flywheel. This limits the maximum amount of engine driving torque the

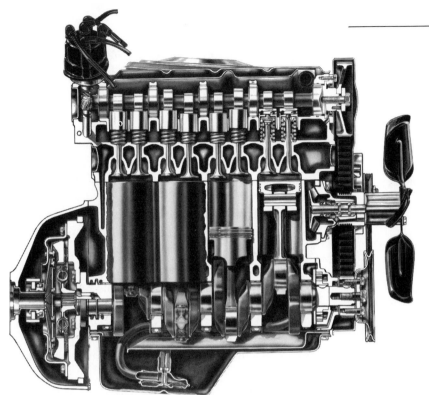

Fig. 20-1 Clutch location at the back of the crankshaft (Chevrolet Motor Division, General Motors Corporation).

clutch can deliver to the drive train. When the pressure plate is forced away from the flywheel with clutch release levers, the clutch disc is free to turn independently from the pressure plate and flywheel assembly, so no torque is transfered between the engine and the drive line.

20-1 CLUTCH REQUIREMENTS

The clutch is designed to completely disengage the drive line using relatively light pedal pressures. The highly loaded release mechanism is pivoted on rolling surfaces or knife edges to minimize friction. The release system has a mechanical leverage from 10:1 to 12:1 that will provide pedal pressures in a range of 20 to 30 pounds when using a three-inch pedal travel. The linkage is often provided with an overcenter spring that helps hold the pedal in a released position. When the pedal is slightly depressed, the overcenter spring reverses its action and helps depress the pedal.

The clutch must provide smooth engagement without grabbing or chattering. This operation depends upon the coefficient of friction of the friction surfaces, along with the cushion and damper spring action.

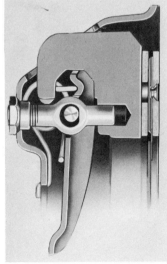

Fig. 20-2 Clutch release lever pivots (American Motors Corporation).

325

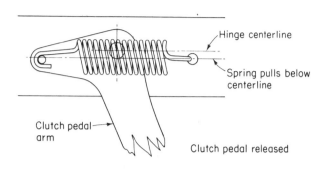

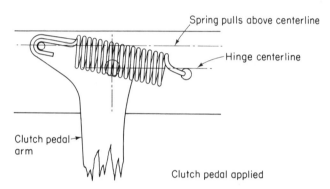

Fig. 20-3 Overcenter spring operation.

The clutch must have adequate *torque capacity* to handle the expected loads. It is usually designed to have a capacity of 125% to 150% of the maximum engine torque. Torque begins to be applied to the clutch as soon as the friction members touch. It will increase until the torque produced by the engine matches the load of the drive train. Clutch torque requirements are highest when the input member, or engine, is turning and the output member, or drive line, is stationary. Slippage occurs during engagement until the input and output members are turning at the same speed. This slippage produces heat that must be absorbed by the clutch material and then dissipated into the air that surrounds the clutch. The amount of heat absorbed by the clutch is proportional to the time required to bring the output member up to input speed. Clutch temperature is the major limiting factor in clutch capacity.

The clutch rotates with the engine and drive line. Centrifugal forces on the clutch increase as engine speed increases. The increase is at a ratio

of four times the engine speed. When centrifugal forces become greater than the strength of the parts, the clutch will fly apart or *shatter*. Race cars will often have a scatter shield to surround the clutch to protect the rest of the vehicle if the clutch should breakup at high engine speeds. Clutch "burst" speed is usually designed at twice the expected maximum engine speeds.

Inertia is another important clutch criterion. The clutch output member or disc is attached to the drive line. If the member is too heavy, its inertia will keep it spinning when the clutch is released, causing hard shifting and gear clashing. The disc should be light to allow the transmission synchronizers (described in Chapter 21) to bring the disc to the correct shifting speed.

Just as in all other automotive parts, the clutch is designed for easy manufacturing and low cost. Materials are adequate to meet their design requirements, but the clutch is not overbuilt. Larger capacity clutches are required as engine horsepower and speeds are increased. This, in turn, increases clutch torque capacity and clutch inertia.

Easy clutch maintenance is most important to

Fig. 20-4 Clutch part nomenclature (Oldsmobile Division, General Motors Corporation).

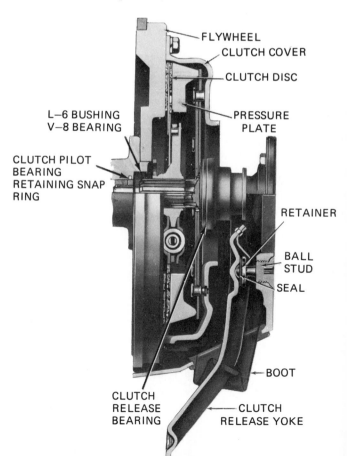

the automotive technician. The clutch linkages are easy to adjust and clutch replacement is relatively simple.

20-2 CLUTCH DESIGN

Automotive clutches operate dry. A disc with friction material on both sides is free to slide forward and backward on the splined shaft protruding from the front of the transmission. This shaft is called the transmission *clutch shaft*. The back of the clutch shaft is supported by the transmission front bearing. The front end of the clutch shaft fits into a *pilot bearing* located in the rear of the engine crankshaft. The disc is the clutch output member and always runs at output speed. The clutch input members are the engine *flywheel* and *clutch pressure plate* assembly. They always turn at engine speed. When the input speed and output speed differ, there is slippage between the pressure plate and disc. The flywheel is bolted to the engine crankshaft and the pressure plate cover is bolted to the flywheel. In operation, the disc is clamped between the pressure plate and the flywheel.

Pressure Plate Assembly. Automotive clutch engagement pressure is applied by coil or Belleville springs. The springs are wedged between a cast iron pressure plate and a stamped steel cover plate, clamping the disc between the pressure plate and flywheel. High tensile gray iron is used for both flywheel and pressure plate, because this is the best material to use with the asbestos-based friction facings used on the disc. In addition, it has sufficient mass to absorb the heat energy developed during engagement and is sufficiently rigid to prevent distortion under operating loads.

Pressure plate assemblies using coil springs have spring pockets formed in the plate and in the stamped cover. A guide projects into the spring to control the spring during high inertia loads. The assembly is held together during storage and assembly by the location of release levers.

Coil spring pressure plates are provided with three release lever tabs equally spaced around the back edge and to which the release lever struts attach. The release lever is pivoted on an eye bolt that protrudes through the cover. When assembled, the lever rests against the cover center opening and

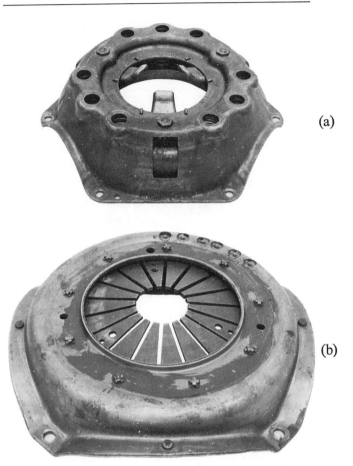

(a)

(b)

Fig. 20-5 Pressure plate. (a) Coil spring type, (b) Belleville spring type.

the lever fulcrum is pulled toward the cover with a nut on the tee pivot eye bolt. This causes the release lever strut to pull the pressure plate against the springs, holding the assembly together. Adjustment of the lever pivot eye bolt is used to correctly position the pressure plate and the release levers. When the pressure plate cover is attached to the flywheel, the pressure plate is pushed further back against the springs, compressing them still more. This relaxes the release levers. *Anti-rattle springs* are connected to the release levers to prevent undesirable noise when the clutch is engaged. Friction of the release levers causes effective clutch plate pressure to be about 85% of the value expected by measuring spring force.

A number of different torque capacity pressure plates are possible using common plates, covers and

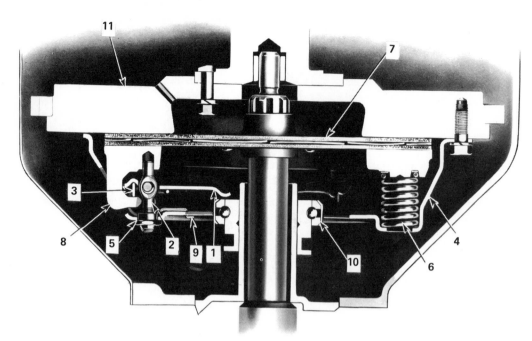

Fig. 20-6 Details of a coil spring pressure plate clutch (Chevrolet Motor Division, General Motors Corporation).

Fig. 20-7 Release levers on a coil spring type pressure plate. (a) Lever parts, (b) bolt in the plate, (c) lever attached, (d) cover installed.

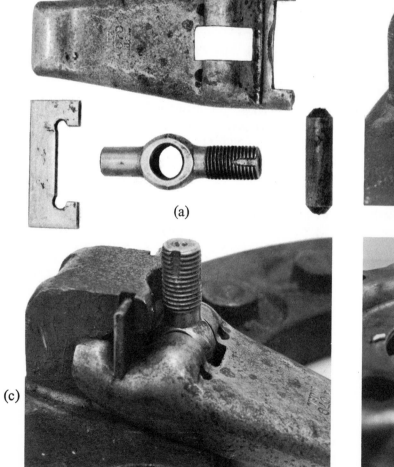

(a)

(b)

(c)

(d)

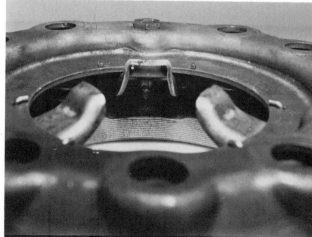

release levers. This is done by the selection of different coil spring lengths and spring rates. The springs may be long with low spring rates or short with high rates. In some cases, both types are used in the same assembly. The springs are usually color coded for identification. Springs of the same color are equally spaced around the clutch plate. In some cases, the spring seats are provided with insulators to keep clutch heat from the spring.

The *diaphragm spring* or Belleville spring pressure plate assembly has a different spring application and release operation. A Belleville spring is shaped like a nearly flat cone with an opening in the center that resists flattening. Belleville springs are used in many applications where a constant controlled load is required. With a special diaphragm configuration, a Belleville spring is used as a pressure spring in many clutches.

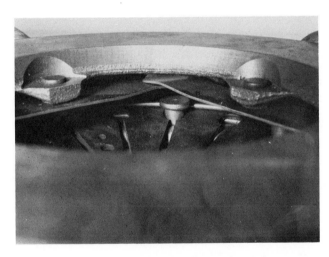

Fig. 20-8 Wire ring in a Belleville diaphragm spring pressure plate.

The Belleville diaphragm spring has a solid outer rim. The inner portion is slotted into fingers that may be straight or bent. The diaphragm spring has a wire ring ahead and behind it where it is riveted to the cover. All bending force is applied on the edges of these two wire rings. The outer rim of the diaphragm pushes evenly against the pressure plate. The Belleville's natural arc pushes between the diaphragm and the wire ring at the cover rivets. Retraction spring clips are bolted over the outer edge of the diaphragm so they hold the plate to the spring for handling and storage. Coil springs follow Hook's Law. Their force is proportional to the

amount of compression which is also called spring deflection. As the disc wears, the springs have less deflection and, therefore, will apply less force against the disc. The Belleville diaphragm spring, on the other hand, has a very interesting deflection curve. As the disc wears, pressure gradually increases, then decreases. At maximum disc wear, the spring pressure is nearly the equivalent of a new disc.

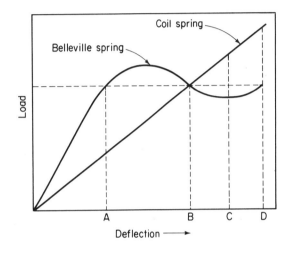

A. Engaged worn clutch
B. Engaged new clutch
C. Disengaged
D. Full pedal travel

Fig. 20-9 Deflection vs load diagram of coil and Belleville spring pressure plates.

Compared to the coil spring type, the diaphragm spring pressure plate is said to have lower weight, less pieces, less operating friction, and lower pedal pressure.

More application force may be added to the pressure plate at high engine speeds by using centrifugal weights. One means is to have weights cast on the outer ends of the release levers in a manner so their centrifugal force will apply additional loading on the plate. Another method uses centrifugal rollers that wedge between the pressure plate and cover. The use of these centrifugal systems reduces pedal effort by using weaker pressure springs that provide only a 10% torque reserve.

The Belleville diaphragm spring clutch is released by applying pressure to the ends of the

329

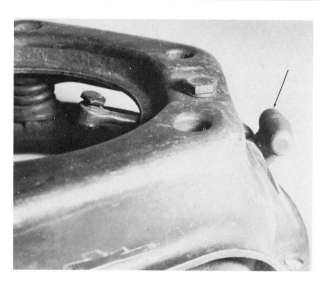

Fig. 20-10 Centrifugal weight on a clutch release lever.

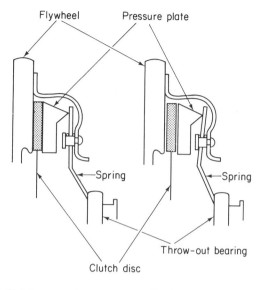

Fig. 20-11 Details of a Belleville diaphragm spring engage and release position.

diaphragm fingers. This causes the cone to flatten, pulling the pressure plate from the disc with the retracting springs.

Throw-Out Bearing. The throw-out bearing is used to transfer pedal release pressure from the stationary linkage to the rotating clutch. A release yoke is attached inside the bell housing. The yoke fingers and throw-out bearing are both attached to the release collar. The collar slides on the front transmission bearing retainer extension as the clutch linkages move the yoke.

Fig. 20-12 Throw out bearing (Number 8), on a Belleville diaphragm spring clutch (Chevrolet Motor Division, General Motors Corporation).

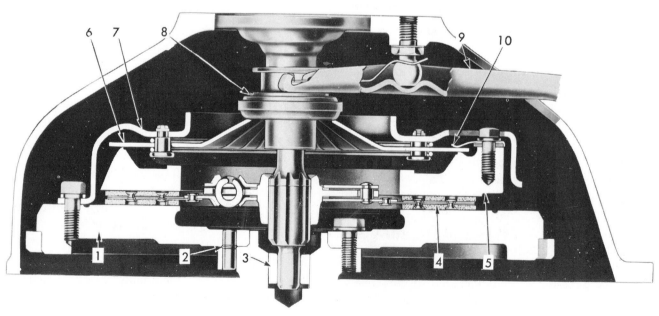

Fig. 20-13 Clutch disc showing a wavy spring steel web between the disc facings.

Disc. Clutch facings on each side of the disc transfers torque from the flywheel and pressure plate to the disc. Automotive disc linings are made from woven or random asbestos fibers that are bonded with organic resins. Sometimes, metallic chips or wire are included in the lining composition. The materials are compacted and molded to shape under high pressure and temperatures. Finished linings are riveted to the disc web.

Asbestos-based clutch facings must not operate above 450° or the binders will be driven out of the facing. This maximum temperature limits the clutch capacity. Another limit is maximum surface velocity at the time of engagement which must not exceed 6000 ft/min at the mean radius. For maximum clutch disc life, the pressure plate force should not exceed 12 lb/in² pressure against the linings. Clutch linings operating against cast iron have a coefficient of friction between .28 and .30. Coefficient of friction is the sliding force per square inch divided by the pressure applied.

Disc webs may be one piece or riveted from several pieces. The portion of the web between the facings is wavy spring steel. Each facing is riveted to the high spot with brass rivets. This assembly method provides a cushion spring between the linings so the clutch will have a smooth engagement.

The cast iron disc hub is splined to fit the transmission clutch shaft. Springs are mounted circumferentially around the hub flange, spaced between the hub and disc web. These springs act as torsion dampers to isolate engine firing pulses from the drive line. These *torsion damper springs* are held in place in stamped disc pockets. The disc is held to the hub by rivets through the disc web on one side of the hub and a doubler plate on the other side. Friction drag or addition of friction washers between the hub and disc web provide a snubbing ac-

Fig. 20-14 Damper springs in the clutch hub.

tion as the damper springs recoil following an engine pulsation.

Torque capacity of a clutch can be calculated using the formula:

$$T = NfPK \text{ lb/ft}$$

Where: T = Torque capacity
N = Number of friction surfaces = 2 in automotive clutches
f = Coefficient of friction = .3 for automotive clutches
P = Total pressure on the linings
K = disc mean radius $(r + R)/2 \ (1.02)$ ft
r = disc inner radius in ft
R = disc outer radius in ft

For an automotive single disc clutch, the formula can be simplified to equal:

$$T = .306 \ P(r + R)$$

For example, what would the torque capacity of a clutch with a pressure plate having nine springs each producing 130 lbs force pressing on a single disc clutch with a 7″ inside diameter and an 11″ outside diameter facing be? The total force (P) of the 9 springs is 1170 lbs (9 × 130). The inner clutch disc facing radius (r) is .2916 ft (3.5/12) and the outer diameter (R) is .4583 ft (5.5/12). Putting these values into the formula above to solve for torque capacity:

$$T = .306 \times 1170\ (.2916 + .4583)$$
$$= 268.48\ \text{lb-ft}$$

The torque capacity of any given clutch can be calculated by disassembling the pressure plate and measuring the spring pressures at their installed length, then measuring the inside diameter and outside diameter of the disc facing.

20-3 CLUTCH SERVICE

Service on modern clutches is limited to linkage adjustment and replacement of components. Disc lining wear is a common cause of clutch failure. A weak pressure plate will allow excessive clutch slippage that builds heat and increases wear rates. Heat will sometimes be great enough to crack or burn the cast iron flywheel and pressure plate friction surfaces. Clutch wear normally occurs during a number of vehicle starts. Automobiles used in city traffic will obviously wear out a clutch in less mileage than an automobile driven on expressways. Clutch wear rate is aggravated by "riding the clutch" as the driver rests his foot on the clutch pedal and, thus, reduces the effect of the pressure springs. This reduces clutch capacity.

Chatter or grabbing is another source of clutch failure. It results from oil on the clutch facing. Oil changes the coefficient of friction so the clutch does not apply smoothly. This problem can only be corrected by replacing the oil soaked disc and the rear crankshaft oil seal or clutch shaft seal so oil does not get on the new disc.

Maladjusted clutch linkages will cause clutch slippage if they do not completely move the throwout bearing from contacting the release levers or fingers. The usual recommendation is to adjust

(a)

(b)

Fig. 20-15 Bell housing. (a) Removable lower section, (b) one piece housing.

clutch linkages to provide a one-inch pedal free play before clutch release begins. Clutch release should be complete with the pedal at least one inch above the floor pan. Vehicle adjustment procedures should be carefully followed.

If the clutch pedal action is sluggish or the pedal does not return properly, the overcenter spring may be out of adjustment. Tightening the spring will reduce pedal effort and cause sluggish pedal return action. Loosening the overcenter spring provides a quick return, but increases pedal effort.

When proper adjustment will not correct improper clutch operation, the clutch must be disassembled. The transmission must be removed before the clutch can be disassembled because the transmission clutch shaft goes through the center of the clutch components. The drive shaft must be disconnected, the rear of the engine supported and the rear transmission mount removed. Usually, the rear mount cross member must also be removed. The transmission linkages and speedometer cable have to be disconnected, then four transmission bolts can be removed from the bell housing. The transmission is carefully moved straight back until the shaft is clear of the clutch. If the bottom half of the bell housing is not removable, the bell housing will have to be removed to get at the clutch. The pressure plate cover and flywheel should be punch marked so these balanced parts can be reassembled in the same position if they are satisfactory for re-use. Loosen the cover bolts from the flywheel and remove the clutch pressure plate and disc.

Examine the clutch for signs of wear, overheating, contamination, and broken parts. This will aid in determining the cause of failure so it can be corrected before new parts are installed.

Because of the labor expense in relation to parts cost, it is becoming a standard practice to replace all clutch parts, even if they show no signs of failure. Most shops do not have the gauging

Fig. 20-16 Clutch facing worn down to the rivets.

equipment to check spring tension and pressure plate adjustment. If one knows the history of the clutch being repaired, he may change only a few of the parts. Complete parts replacement includes a pilot bearing, disc, pressure plate and throw-out bearing. If these are correctly installed as a set, there is little chance of a comeback.

Many discs and pressure plates can be exchanged for remanufactured units that have been completely reconditioned. They are as good as new.

During assembly, the clutch must be kept clean and dry. No lubricant is used, with the exception of a very thin coat on the transmission clutch shaft and inside the throw-out bearing release collar. The disc should be checked for a free sliding fit on the transmission clutch shaft. It is then held in place against the flywheel with a clutch pilot, while the pressure plate is being fastened to the flywheel. The rest of the assembly procedures are the reverse of the disassembly procedures.

Proper clutch operation requires use of the correct parts. Discs and pressure plates may look alike, but they may have different facings, springs, lever action, etc. The incorrect application of a part will give unsatisfactory results. Follow the parts book recommendations.

If the vehicle is modified, it will most likely require a modified clutch. The information presented in this chapter will be helpful in selecting a clutch that will provide satisfactory service in a modified vehicle.

Review Questions
Chapter 20

1. What are the clutch pedal pressure and travel requirements?

2. What is clutch torque capacity?

3. Under what conditions are the highest clutch torque requirements applied?

4. What is the limiting factor in clutch torque capacity?

5. What causes clutch chatter?

6. How does clutch disc inertia affect clutch operation?

7. Why are clutches made as small as possible?

8. Name the major clutch parts.

9. Which parts of the clutch are input members and which parts are output members?

10. What materials are used for the pressure plate?

11. Describe the release lever action.

12. How are the release levers adjusted?

13. How can common parts be used for different capacity clutch pressure plates?

14. How does a Belleville spring pressure plate differ from a coil spring pressure plate?

15. What is the purpose of centrifugal weights in the clutch pressure plate?

16. How does the throw-out bearing operate?

17. Describe the clutch disc construction.

18. What is the purpose of a cushion spring between the disc linings?

19. What is the purpose of torsional damper springs?

20. Calculate clutch capacity for several disc sizes.

21. What are the common clutch problems?

22. How should clutch linkages be adjusted?

23. Why should the position of clutch parts be identified?

24. Describe the clutch replacement procedure.

Quiz 20

1. Clutch capacity is specified as its ability to
   a. engage smoothly
   b. absorb the coefficient of friction
   c. transmit torque
   d. handle the inertia loads.

2. Maximum clutch capacity is required when the vehicle is
   a. starting
   b. accelerating
   c. cruising
   d. running at full speed.

3. The major factor that limits the clutch ability to carry greater loads is
   a. operating inertia
   b. operating temperature
   c. engine speed
   d. vehicle speed.

4. The output part of the clutch assembly is called a
   a. pressure plate
   b. disc
   c. pilot shaft
   d. carrier member.

5. The clutch disc is clamped between the
   a. pressure plate and carrier member
   b. pilot and carrier member
   c. flywheel and pressure plate
   d. carrier member and flywheel.

6. A Belleville spring pressure plate is characterized by having high pressure when

   a. engaged and worn
   b. engaged and new
   c. disengaged
   d. full pedal travel is applied.

7. Centrifugal weights in a clutch pressure plate
   a. increase the force on the disc at high speeds
   b. reduce the force on the disc at high speeds
   c. increase the clutch pedal release load for starting
   d. reduce the clutch pedal release load for starting.

8. Release force is transferred to the rotating clutch assembly through the
   a. disc
   b. pressure plate
   c. throw-out bearing
   d. pilot bearing.

9. To help smooth clutch application, the disc is fitted with
   a. internal splines
   b. high coefficient of friction facings
   c. disc retracting springs
   d. torsion damper springs.

10. Oil on the clutch facings will cause the clutch to
    a. slip during application
    b. chatter or grab when fully applied
    c. change the coefficient of friction
    d. wear excessively fast.

chapter 21

Standard Transmissions

Each automobile engine produces a fixed amount of torque at any given speed and load. This torque is not great enough for low speed driving. Automobiles use transmissions to provide a means of increasing driving torque for starting, accelerating, and climbing slopes or hills. The transmission also provides a means of reversing the drive train so the vehicle may move backward. In some driving situations the transmission may be shifted into a lower gear ratio while the vehicle is coasting to force the idling engine to act as a hill retarder or brake which will slow the vehicle. This is especially useful while going down a long mountain grade because it keeps the brakes from overheating.

Standard transmissions are used in economy cars and sports cars. Generally the economy cars use two gears below direct drive and sports cars use three to provide adequate driving torque. The engine is disconnected from the drive line by the clutch whenever a gear ratio change is made. While there is no torque load being carried by the transmission, the transmission gears are allowed to synchronize at the required speed before engagement in the new gear ratio. The clutch reconnects the engine to the transmission to drive the car in the new gear ratio.

21-1 TRANSMISSION REQUIREMENTS

The gasoline engine's maximum torque occurs at an engine speed too high for starting the vehicle in motion. The transmission's first gear allows the engine to turn at high speed while the drive wheels turn at low speed, providing the torque required for starting and for acceleration. The vehicle may be accelerated whenever more torque is available than is being used. If more torque is required than is available, the vehicle will slow to a stop unless the transmission is shifted into a lower gear that will allow engine speed to increase to a higher torque speed.

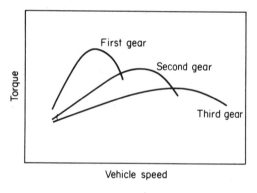

Fig. 21-1 Torque U.S. vehicle speed in each gear (not to scale).

Passenger car performance is based on acceleration, ability to go up a slope, top speed, fuel economy, noise level, and durability. Domestic passenger car engines have enough power so most of their running is in direct drive. Imported cars, on the other hand, usually have smaller engines and need to operate in reduction gears more of the time to provide adequate performance. The imports, therefore, have relatively stronger transmissions than domestic passenger cars.

Transmission gearing is designed to provide

maximum acceleration at low speed by holding the torque output to a point of impending wheel spin. Acceleration becomes less than maximum when wheel spin occurs. On the other end of the gear design, fuel economy is maximum when the engine has an 80% load with the engine speed as low as possible.

The power required to drive a vehicle increases as the cube of the speed. It takes eight times the horsepower to double the speed ($2 \times 2 \times 2$). When the power available matches the power required to push the vehicle, speed will be constant. Excess power is required for acceleration and hill climbing. Maximum speed is reached when there is no excess power remaining.

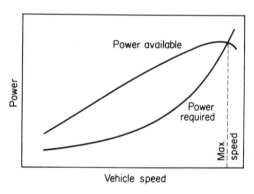

Fig. 21-2 Power available and power required curves (not to scale).

More gear ratios are required as the range of speeds from low to high increases. Trucks may have from 10 to 20 forward gear ratios. Three to four forward gear ratios are adequate for passenger cars. Three forward ratios are used in economy passenger cars. Four forward ratios give considerably better overall performance and are used for sport and performance cars.

The rear axle ratio affects vehicle performance in all transmission gear ratios. Because most of the driving is done with the transmission in direct drive, the rear axle ratio makes it possible to use the same engine-transmission combination in several different vehicle applications, thus reducing cost. Rear axle ratio used with a three-speed transmission is selected so the engine reaches maximum power before the vehicle reaches maximum speed. This provides excess power for acceleration and gradability even though it is more noisy, has poor econ-

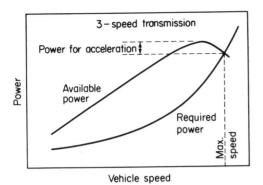

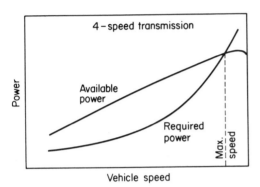

Fig. 21-3 Power available and power required curves for three-speed and four-speed transmissions.

omy, and a top speed slightly lower than would be possible with other gearing. The rear axle used with four-speed transmissions uses a ratio that will allow the vehicle to reach maximum speed at or slightly before the engine reaches maximum horsepower. The transmission's third speed can be used for acceleration and gradability. The first gear ratio

Fig. 21-4 Typical clutch shaft showing main shaft bearings and synchronizer teeth (Oldsmobile Division, General Motors Corporation).

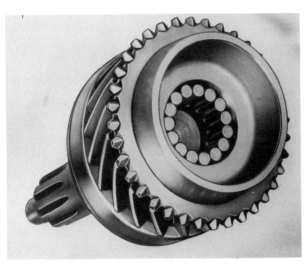

in each type of transmission is selected to provide operation up a 30% grade.

The transmission is used to reduce drive shaft speed in relation to engine speed. Full throttle engine power and torque are dependent on engine speed. Each gradually increases, peaks, and then decreases as engine speed increases from low to high speeds. Transmission gear ratios allow the engine to operate at its best speed while providing the desired drive shaft speed.

The clutch shaft, which is the transmission input shaft, turns at engine speeds any time the clutch is fully engaged. When this shaft is connected to the transmission main shaft through a synchronizer, the main shaft and drive shaft also turn at engine speed. This is direct drive.

A gear on the back of the clutch shaft engages the front gear on the counter gear cluster. The counter gear turns in a direction opposite to or counter to the clutch shaft gear. The front counter gear is usually larger and has more teeth than the clutch shaft gear. This allows the clutch gear to make *more* than one complete turn for each counter gear revolution. The torque increase is equivalent to the counter gear tooth number (driven) divided by the clutch shaft gear tooth number (driving). Small counter gears on the cluster turn larger second and first gears. The total torque increases can be determined by calculating the torque multiplication factor (TMF).

In forward gears:

$$\text{TMF} = \frac{\text{front counter gear} \times \text{last gear}}{\text{clutch shaft gear} \times \text{last counter gear in use}}$$

In reverse gears:

$$\text{TMF} = \frac{\begin{array}{c}\text{front counter gear} \times \text{reverse idler driven}\\ \times \text{ reverse gear}\end{array}}{\begin{array}{c}\text{clutch shaft gear} \times \text{reverse counter gear}\\ \times \text{ reverse idler driving}\end{array}}$$

A transmission having the following gear tooth combination is used to show how the above equations can be used to calculate torque multiplication factors.

337

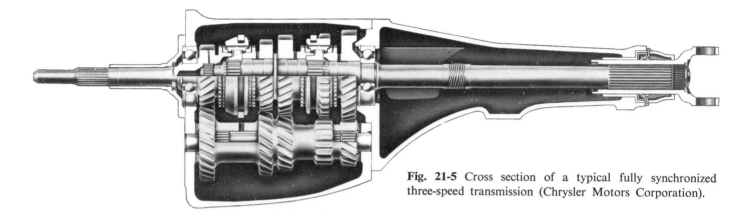

Fig. 21-5 Cross section of a typical fully synchronized three-speed transmission (Chrysler Motors Corporation).

GEAR	NUMBER OF TEETH
clutch shaft gear	20
front counter gear	28
second counter gear	20
low-reverse counter gear	15
reverse idler driven	19
reverse idler driving	17
second gear	25
low gear	32
reverse gear	38

Using the equation above the torque multiplication factor for low gear is:

$$\text{TMF} = \frac{28 \times 32}{20 \times 15} = 2.98$$

For reverse gear the torque multiplication factor is:

$$\text{TMF} = \frac{28 \times 19 \times 38}{20 \times 15 \times 17} = 3.95$$

21-2 TRANSMISSION DESIGN

Three-speed domestic transmission designs are very similar. Four-speed transmissions have more differences between them, especially in the operation of reverse gearing. The transmission has a *reverted gear train* with the input shaft and output shaft on the same centerline. An intermediate gear or

counter gear is located directly below it. Input comes from the clutch disc into the transmission through the clutch shaft. In direct drive, the clutch shaft is coupled directly to the output or main shaft so it drives the propeller shaft like a one-piece shaft. In reduction, power goes to the counter gear, then reverts back to the main shaft located on the original clutch shaft centerline.

Transmission Shifting. Old transmission designs were shifted by moving some of the gears into mesh with other gears using shifting yokes. This method has been largely replaced with synchronizing engagement. Sliding gears are used in some transmissions for first and reverse gears because the vehicle is not moving when these gears are

Fig. 21-6 Typical counter gear (Oldsmobile Division, General Motors Corporation).

COUNTERGEAR

ANTI-LASH PLATE

BEARING ROLLER

engaged. First gear may be synchronized in three-speed transmissions. It is always synchronized in four-speed transmissions. Reverse is synchronized in some late transmission designs. Speeds above first are synchronized in all current standard domestic transmissions.

Synchronizers allow the gear teeth to be in constant mesh, turning freely on their shafts. Power is connected from the gear to the shaft through a synchronizer mechanism. A shifting yoke acting on a synchronizer sleeve is used to move the synchronizer into engagement.

Synchronizer. Shifting is done with the clutch disengaged so that the only rotational drive speed comes into the transmission from the rear wheels through the main shaft as the vehicle coasts. When the transmission is in neutral, the "clutch shaft counter gear" assembly will freewheel. The synchronizer speeds or slows this assembly to match main shaft speed. This makes it possible for an inexperienced driver to rapidly shift gears without clashing them.

Two types of synchronizers are used, the *pin-type* and the *plate-* or *strut-type*. Their designs are slightly different, but they operate in a very similar manner. The majority of transmissions use a plate-type synchronizer so it will be used to describe synchronizer action.

The synchronizer consists of a hub, blocker ring, sleeve and plates. The hub with external teeth, sometimes called a drum, is splined to the main shaft. All output power is transferred from the gear to the main shaft through the hub. It is surrounded by a sleeve that has internal teeth which mesh with the external hub teeth. Three plates or inserts with a ridge running across the middle are centered in the sleeve by a groove around the inside center of

(a)

(b)

Fig. 21-8 Synchronizer block ring. (a) In blocking position and (b) in the engaging position.

the sleeve. A circular wire insert spring on each side of the hub holds the insert outward so its ridge engages the sleeve internal groove, lightly holding the sleeve centered over the hub.

Fig. 21-7 Exploded view of a typical plate type synchronizer (Buick Motor Division, General Motors Corporation).

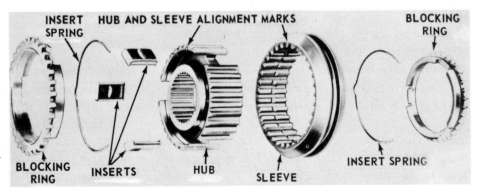

INSERT SPRING   HUB AND SLEEVE ALIGNMENT MARKS   BLOCKING RING

BLOCKING RING   INSERTS   HUB   SLEEVE   INSERT SPRING

Fig. 21-9 Synchronizer blocking ring cone clutch.

The outer edge of the synchronizer sleeve is provided with a groove in which the shifting yoke fits. Changing gears is accomplished by sliding the sleeve from its centered position on the drum until the internal sleeve teeth engage matching external teeth on the side of, and integral with, the driving gear. A brass blocking ring is fitted between the sleeve and the matching teeth to minimize coast time and to prevent engagement until speeds synchronize; then positive engagement can occur.

The internal surface of the blocking ring is the external portion of a cone-type clutch. The blocking ring surface has fine grooves that cut through the oil film. It fits on a polished tapered cone that is integral with the gear. The exterior of the blocking ring has teeth that match the hub and are chamfered on the synchronizer side. The blocking ring is driven at synchronizer hub speed by the three inserts that fit into wide slots on the synchronizer end of the blocking ring. The slots are wide enough to allow the teeth to misalign by one-half a tooth in each direction.

During a gear shift, the drive clutch disengages the engine. A shifting yoke moves the synchronizer sleeve endwise toward the gear to be engaged. The insert ridge moves the insert endwise against the blocker ring as the sleeve moves. The insert exerts a 6- to 10-pound force against the blocker ring,

engaging the cone clutch. This, in turn, pulls the blocking ring as far as the slots will allow in the direction of relative rotation, causing a mismatch of the teeth which effectively blocks engagement while a speed difference exists. When the speeds synchronize, the chamfered teeth cause a slight rotation that aligns the teeth and allows the sleeve to engage the synchronizing teeth on the side of the drive gear.

(a)

(b)

Fig. 21-10 Clutch side of blocking ring. (a) In blocking position and (b) in the engaging position.

Any time the vehicle is moving, the drive shaft rotates the transmission main shaft. The synchronizer drums are splined to the main shaft so they also rotate. The drive train between the clutch plate and main shaft, previously called the clutch shaft counter gear assembly, is the section of the transmission that must accelerate or decelerate by the synchronizer cone clutch force to allow engagement.

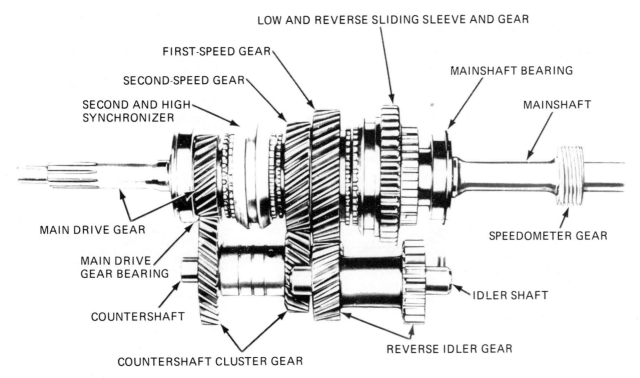

LOW AND REVERSE SLIDING SLEEVE AND GEAR

FIRST-SPEED GEAR

SECOND-SPEED GEAR

SECOND AND HIGH
SYNCHRONIZER

MAINSHAFT BEARING

MAINSHAFT

MAIN DRIVE GEAR

MAIN DRIVE
GEAR BEARING

SPEEDOMETER GEAR

COUNTERSHAFT

IDLER SHAFT

COUNTERSHAFT CLUSTER GEAR

REVERSE IDLER GEAR

Fig. 21-11 Transmission gear train with a low reverse sliding sleeve
and gear (Oldsmobile Division, General Motors Corporation).

This drive train section includes the clutch disc, clutch shaft, counter gear and all constant mesh gears. The lighter this assembly is, the quicker it will synchronize. Heavy clutch plates slow synchronization time.

Occasionally, a sliding reverse gear will have a half-synchronizer on one side. When the gear teeth are out of engagement, it can be used to synchronize first gear to the main shaft. When it is moved in the other direction, the gear teeth engage with the reverse idler to cause reverse mainshaft rotation.

Synchronizers are always located between second and third on three-speed transmissions. Four-speed transmissions have all forward speeds synchronized. Many late model three-speed transmissions also have first gear synchronized. Synchronizers on all forward speeds allow easy down shifting while the vehicle is in motion.

21-3 TRANSMISSION OPERATION

Engine power is transferred through the clutch to the transmission clutch shaft. The back of the clutch shaft has a gear that is part of the shaft. Behind

this gear and also a part of the clutch shaft are located synchronizer teeth and cone. The clutch shaft gear is always in mesh with the front gear on the counter gear cluster. The cluster gear, in turn, is always in mesh with all of the synchronized gears.

First Gear. First gear may use a sliding gear or synchronizer. When a sliding gear is used, the gear is splined on the main shaft so it can move endwise but any rotational motion of the gear turns the main shaft. A shifter collar on the gear allows the gear to be positioned by the shifter yoke. With the vehicle stopped, the shifting yoke moves the large low-reverse gear into engagement with the small low counter gear on the cluster. This connects the clutch shaft to the main shaft through the counter gear.

Synchronized first gears are always in mesh with the low counter gear. The synchronized gear has a plain bearing that allows free rotation on the main shaft. The gear is connected to the main shaft by moving the synchronizer sleeve into engagement with the gear's synchronizer teeth. Power for the gear goes through the synchronizer sleeve to the hub that is splined to the main shaft.

NEUTRAL

SECOND

FIRST

THIRD

REVERSE

Fig. 21-12 Typical three-speed gear train synchronizer position and power flow in each gear ratio (Buick Motor Division, General Motors Corporation).

Second Gear. Second speed is synchronized because the second gear is in constant engagement with the second counter gear. Like the synchronized first gear, the second gear has a plain bearing that rotates freely on the main shaft. The synchronizer sleeve connects the second gear to the main shaft for second speed operation.

A four-speed transmission's third gear operates the same as the second gear synchronized gear change.

Direct Drive. The direct drive synchronizer sleeve moves into engagement with the synchronizer teeth on the back of the clutch shaft. Engine power from the clutch shaft goes through the synchronizer sleeve to the second-direct drive synchronizer hub that is splined to the main shaft. This acts as a solid link, causing the main shaft to run

at the same speed as the engine, providing direct drive.

Gears that are not delivering power to the main shaft will idle. In first gear, the second gear idles; in second, the first gear idles. In direct drive, the counter gear, first, and second gears will idle. In all forward speeds, the reverse idler gear turns freely. Idling gears rotate, but carry no load.

Reverse Gear. Reverse action requires the use of another gear in the gear drive train. This additional gear is called a reverse idler. The reverse idler in most transmissions is in constant mesh with the counter gear, so it turns in the same direction as the clutch gear shaft. The low-reverse gear is moved into engagement with the reverse idler to reverse the drive line. The idler's forward rotation causes the main shaft to rotate backward.

Cast iron and aluminum transmission cases must be rigid enough to prevent distortion from tooth and thrust loads that tend to misalign the shafts and bearings. Gear teeth must have a tough, strong core to resist shock and a hard surface to resist pitting and abrasion. Tooth diameter and width determine the amount of torque the transmission gears can safely handle. Overloading is one of the most common causes of transmission failure.

The transmission has a mechanical efficiency above 90% in reduction gears and has an efficiency as high as 98% in direct drive. Ninety per cent of driving is done in direct drive, so the transmission produces very little drive line friction.

The clutch shaft is supported by a ball bearing in the front of the transmission and by a pilot bearing in the back of the engine crankshaft. The main shaft is supported by a ball bearing in the back of the main transmission case and by roller bearings in the back end of the clutch shaft. A sleeve-type bearing is located in the back of the

extension housing to support the loads of the propeller shaft attachment to the main shaft.

The counter gear cluster rotates on needle bearings. These, in turn, rotate on a counter shaft that is fit into reamed case holes. A short shaft supports the reverse idler gear. Clutch shaft and main shaft thrust are retained with ball bearings. Counter gear and reverse idler thrust are retained with thrust washers on each end of the gears. Washer thickness determines the thrust clearance. Drive gear teeth are cut on a helix angle, and are called helical gears. They provide quiet operation as the gears gradually mesh. This angle induces a large part of the thrust that must be retained.

Clutch shaft and main shaft ball bearings are pressed on the shaft. They are held in the case with retaining rings. The front retaining ring is fastened between the case and bearing retainer. The rear bearing may be retained in the same manner or the

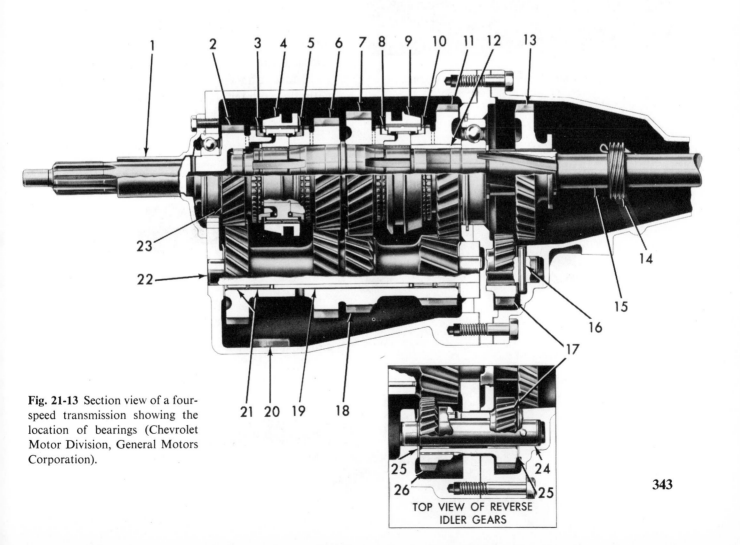

Fig. 21-13 Section view of a four-speed transmission showing the location of bearings (Chevrolet Motor Division, General Motors Corporation).

TOP VIEW OF REVERSE IDLER GEARS

343

retaining ring may snap into a groove in the transmission case bore or in the extension shaft bore.

21-5 GENERAL DISASSEMBLY PROCEDURES

The general disassembly procedures are similar for all standard transmissions. Many details, however, are quite different. An applicable service manual should be followed when disassembling a transmission.

The transmission is removed by draining the lubricant, disconnecting the drive shaft, speedometer cable, and shifting rods. With the engine supported, the rear mount and cross member is removed and the four attachment bolts removed, freeing the transmission. The transmission must be carefully pulled straight back until the clutch shaft is free of the bell housing.

Transmission disassembly starts with the removal of the cover plate. One type of cast cover plate contains the shifting fork yokes. These must be carefully removed from the yoke collars. Other transmission cover plates are stamped steel. Their only purpose is to provide access to the transmission interior. On this type, the shifting yokes must be released and slid free of the yoke collars.

Most transmissions cannot be disassembled with the counter gear in place. The counter shaft locks are removed and the shaft pushed out of the

Fig. 21-14 Clutch shaft bearing retaining ring.

(a)

Fig. 21-15 Transmission shift arms. (a) On cover plate, (b) through transmission case.

(b)

case. If available, the shaft should be pushed out with a dummy shaft of the same diameter as the counter shaft but only long enough to hold the thrust washers on both ends of the counter gear. This will help to keep all of the parts of the counter gear assembly together as a unit. The loosened counter gear is allowed to rest in the bottom of the case while the clutch shaft and main shaft are removed. These two shafts will separate at the main-shaft front roller bearings located in the back of the clutch shaft. Gears and synchronizer drums are held on the main shaft with lock rings so they will not fall off.

The extension shaft will come off from the main shaft in some transmissions and in others, the extension shaft and main shaft are removed as a unit.

When the main and clutch shafts are out, the counter gear can be lifted from the case.

Gears, synchronizers and bearings can be removed from the mainshaft by removing the retaining rings.

Generally, all needle bearings, thrust washers, gaskets and seals are replaced with new parts. Rough operating ball bearings are replaced. Any gear or synchronizer with a chipped or damaged tooth should be replaced.

Assembly is performed following a procedure that is the reverse of disassembly. All of the parts should be checked for condition and correct fit before reassembly. The parts should be thoroughly cleaned and lubricated with transmission lubricant during assembly in the case.

21-6 TRANSMISSION SERVICE

A standard transmission should last the life of the vehicle without disassembly. Failure can result from maladjusted linkages, overloading, or from forcing a gear shift.

Linkages connect from the vehicle structure to the flexibly mounted engine-transmission assembly. When the linkages are not adjusted correctly, motion of the transmission may cause the transmission to slip out of gear. Maladjustment may also cause hard shifting. The shifting linkage is provided with

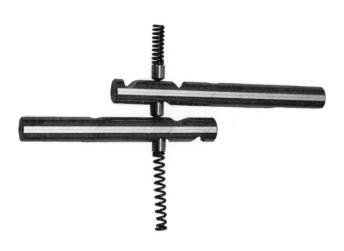

Fig. 21-16 Typical shift yoke rails with interlock.

a gate or an interlock causing the transmission to pass through neutral as shifts are made from one gear to the next. This also keeps the transmission from engaging two gears at the same time. A gate is usually located on the linkage system. An interlock is located in the transmission. It only allows shifts when all other positions are in neutral.

Transmission overloading can result from sudden clutch engagement with the engine running at high speeds and the vehicle standing. The inertia of the crankshaft, flywheel, and clutch can put very high instantaneous torque loads on the transmission gears which can break the teeth and, in some cases, the transmission case. Forced shifting can damage synchronizer blocking rings and pins. When this happens, shifting becomes difficult and the transmission may slip out of gear when it is under load. These can only be repaired by completely disassembling the transmission.

Abnormal transmission noise usually indicates a problem that requires disassembly. It may be caused by excessive counter gear end play, loose synchronizer hub, damaged or worn gears, or rough or pitted bearings. Faulty parts must be replaced to correct the problem.

Review Questions Chapter 21

1. How does the amount of torque available affect the vehicle's ability to accelerate?

2. Why are transmissions on imported cars relatively stronger than domestic passenger car transmissions?

3. How does maximum acceleration gearing differ from maximum economy gearing?

4. Why do some road racing cars use more than four transmission gear ratios?

5. How do rear axle ratios differ when used with three-speed and with four-speed transmissions?

6. What is the basis for selecting first gear ratio?

7. How does a transmission multiply torque?

8. Why is synchronizer shifting better than sliding gear shifting?

9. What part of the synchronizer transfers power to the main shaft?

10. Describe the operation of a synchronizer.

11. What is the purpose of the blocking ring?

12. What gears are synchronized in a standard transmission?

13. How does the attachment of a low gear to the mainshaft differ between a sliding gear and a synchronized gear?

14. Describe the details of the transmission drive in each gear ratio.

15. Describe the disassembly procedure of a specific transmission.

Quiz 21

1. The transmission's main purpose is to
   a. provide a means to start the car in motion
   b. run the engine while the car is stopped
   c. multiply engine torque
   d. increase the car's speed.

2. The automobile will reach maximum speed when
   a. driving power equals required power
   b. maximum engine torque is produced
   c. the engine reaches maximum hp
   d. the engine is running at maximum rpm.

3. Domestic passenger cars are geared to climb a maximum grade of
   a. 10%
   b. 20%
   c. 30%
   d. 40%.

4. Ideal shifting between gear ratios should be done when the two ratios produce
   a. equal speeds
   b. equal torque
   c. maximum speed multiplication
   d. maximum torque multiplication.

5. The transmission counter gear always turns
   a. slower and opposite the clutch shaft
   b. faster and opposite the clutch shaft
   c. slower and in the same direction as the clutch shaft
   d. faster and in the same direction as the clutch shaft.

6. The transmission synchronizer equalizes the speed of the
   a. output shaft and meshing gear
   b. counter gear and meshing gear
   c. clutch shaft and meshing gear
   d. idler gear and meshing gear.

7. One synchronizer connects the
   a. first gear to the counter gear
   b. second gear to the output shaft
   c. third gear to the clutch shaft
   d. reverse gear to the idler gear.

8. Gears that are not delivering power in a transmission will
   a. stop rotating
   b. rotate at constant speed
   c. operate at their driving speed
   d. idle.

9. The amount of torque a transmission can absorb is limited by
   a. the length of the output shaft
   b. the diameter of the input shaft
   c. gear ratios in use
   d. gear diameter and tooth width.

10. Counter gear end movement is supported by
    a. ball bearings
    b. thrust washers
    c. bushings
    d. locking pins.

chapter 22

Automatic Transmissions

The majority of domestic passenger cars are being equipped with automatic transmissions. They have become popular with the motoring public because they are efficient, convenient, easy to operate, durable, and reliable. Over the years, automatic transmissions have been built in a number of different designs. Many fine features have disappeared from new transmission designs because they were relatively expensive to manufacture and to service. Current automatic transmission designs are lighter, smaller, less expensive to manufacture, and have superior operating characteristics when compared to some of the old designs.

It would be beyond the scope of one chapter to discuss all of the automatic transmission design features. On the other hand, a detailed discussion of one type of transmission would not adequately cover the subject. Therefore, this chapter will discuss current usage by describing representative automatic transmission features. Service manuals should be followed for details that apply to any specific automatic transmission.

347

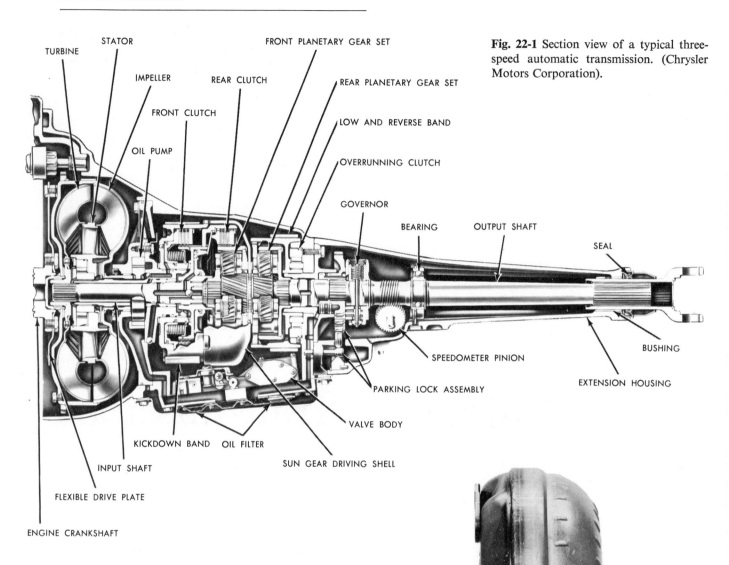

TURBINE
STATOR
FRONT PLANETARY GEAR SET
IMPELLER
REAR CLUTCH
REAR PLANETARY GEAR SET
FRONT CLUTCH
LOW AND REVERSE BAND
OIL PUMP
OVERRUNNING CLUTCH
GOVERNOR
BEARING
OUTPUT SHAFT
SEAL
BUSHING
SPEEDOMETER PINION
EXTENSION HOUSING
PARKING LOCK ASSEMBLY
VALVE BODY
KICKDOWN BAND   OIL FILTER
SUN GEAR DRIVING SHELL
INPUT SHAFT
FLEXIBLE DRIVE PLATE
ENGINE CRANKSHAFT

Fig. 22-1 Section view of a typical three-speed automatic transmission. (Chrysler Motors Corporation).

Domestic automatic transmissions have a three-member torque converter driving through a two- or three-speed automatic shifting planetary gear train. This combination provides smooth torque characteristics from starting to the designed operating speed.

22-1 TORQUE CONVERTER

The torque converter was invented by Dr. Herman Föttinger in Europe for use on marine steam turbines. Its primary function is torque multiplication through the force of hydrodynamic or fluid movement. It transmits power silently and smoothly, without shock, through speed and torque ratio

Fig. 22-2 Edge view of a typical torque converter assembly with a welded housing.

changes. Its operation is completely automatic and reliable. All of its moving parts are submerged in lubricating oil and are practically immune to wear, so the coupling will usually last the life of the transmission without service.

Torque Converter Details. The torque converter is enclosed in a stamped steel shell or housing that is connected to the engine crankshaft through a drive plate. A hub on the converter front cover fits into a counterbore in the back of the crankshaft to support the front of the converter. On the back of the converter, a converter hub is supported by a plain bearing located in the front of the transmission oil pump housing. The converter has three functional parts. The first is the driving member, or *impeller*, that is located in the back part of the converter housing and rotates at engine speed with the housing. The second part is the driven member, or *turbine*, that drives into the planetary gear train. It is mounted on the transmission input shaft. The turbine hub may be supported by and rotate in a bushing located inside the converter cover or the input shaft may be supported by a bushing mounted just inside the stator shaft. The *stator* or *reactor* is the third member of the converter. It is connected to the transmission case through a one-way clutch mounted on an extension forward from the pump cover, called the stator shaft.

The converter housing rear hub performs an additional function, that of driving the transmission front pump. The front pump produces oil pressure for the transmission controls and pressure to keep the converter full of oil. Converter charge pressure is necessary when the housing rotates. Rotation causes the oil to build up centrifugal force that throws it toward the converter's outer edge. This tends to form air pockets near the converter center. When air pockets do form, the action is called *cavitation*. Cavitation is minimized by keeping the coupling under an oil charge pressure ranging from 30 to 180 psi between different transmission models.

Oil that leaves the converter flows through a cooler and transmission lubricating passages. From there, it drains to the transmission oil pan.

Converter Operation. The converter housing is a steel stamping shaped like a tire. Its inner diameter is approximately 1/3 of its outer diameter. Stamped steel blades are fastened to the inside of the housing on the back or transmission side using unequal

Fig. 22-3 Torque converter parts, from left to right, the front of the converter housing, the turbine, the stator and on the right is the impeller made as part of the back converter housing.

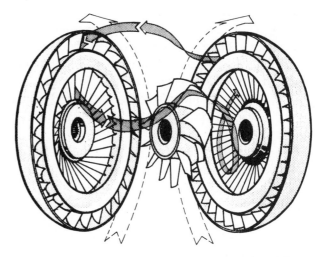

Fig. 22-4 Oil flow through the converter (American Motors Corporation).

spacing to minimize pulsation and noise. The blades, rotating at engine speed with the housing, form the impeller. When rotating, they throw converter oil outward, increasing its speed, to give the converter oil dynamic energy.

Before the vehicle starts to move, the rapidly moving oil leaving the impeller's outer edge enters the turbine outer edge. The turbine is built somewhat like the impeller. It has a curved stamped steel shell in which stamped steel blades are fastened. The high energy oil being thrown from the impeller hits the turbine blades. The turbine blades slow the oil flow rate, transferring energy from the oil to the turbine to give the turbine a turning force or torque.

The turbine blade angle is curved to severely change the oil flow direction, so most of the oil's kinetic energy is removed. As the oil's energy is removed, the oil slows down and moves toward the housing center. Its flow is changed to a direction opposite that of impeller rotation. If the oil entered the impeller flowing in this backward direction, it would take a great deal of the input power to again accelerate the oil in the forward direction. The stator is a small curved bladed wheel located at the inner portion of the converter between the turbine and impeller. It is designed to redirect the backward oil flow as it leaves the turbine outlet.

Oil leaving the turbine in a backward direction hits the face of the stator blades. A free wheeling one-way clutch prevents stator backward rotation. The stator's curved blades redirect the oil with little energy loss, so it enters the impeller in the same direction as the impeller is turning. In doing this, the stator in the torque converter-type hydrodynamic drive acts like a fulcrum in a lever system to increase torque transfer.

Some transmissions use a variable pitch stator. The blade angle can be changed from a high to a low angle. A low angle gives high torque conversion when there is a great difference between impeller and turbine speeds. A high angle gives less oil flow restriction as the turbine speed approaches impeller speed. A high angle will also be used at idle to minimize vehicle creep. The variable pitch stator is very efficient, but expensive to make.

The torque converter will have the greatest amount of torque multiplication when the turbine is stopped and the impeller is turning as fast as the engine will drive it. This is called *stall*. Maximum torque multiplication ratios at stall run from 2:1 to 2.6:1. The turbine is stopped when the vehicle is not moving because it is connected to the rear wheels through a mechanical gear train. It begins to rotate as the vehicle begins to move. Converter torque multiplication ratio gradually and smoothly reduces as the turbine speed approaches impeller

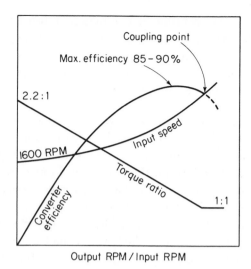

Fig. 22-5 Torque converter performance curves.

speed. The *coupling point* is reached when the turbine reaches 85% to 90% of the impeller speed. At the coupling point, the oil will leave the turbine in a forward direction, hitting the back of the stator blade. The stator rotates forward on its one-way clutch, moving with the oil flow to produce minimum oil flow resistance.

Maximum torque converter ratio at stall is built into the design by the converter size and blade angle. Stall speed of a converter is selected to prevent creep at idle and to be about 70% of the engine's maximum torque speed at *full throttle*. Operation at a high stall speed, which would provide high torque multiplication ratios, will cause excess heat to build up. A high stall speed would also produce excessive fuel consumption and noise. It would result in an excessively high coupling point that would allow the engine to race. This condition would make it impossible to fully use the engine's speed range. It is interesting to note that with the same input torque, converter stall speed is lowered at high altitude. This occurs when engine output is also lower at high altitude, so output torque is considerably lower.

During coasting, the turbine accelerates the oil, throwing it outward into the impeller. The impeller absorbs the oil's energy by trying to increase engine speed. The stator is forced to overrun. It is not efficient to operate the converter in this way, but it does help to slow the vehicle by transferring some of the vehicle's energy to the engine, forcing it to rotate faster than idle.

Cooling Oil flow through the converter must have a restricted outlet in order to maintain converter charge pressure. The transmission oil cooler and transmission gear train lubrication system provides this restriction. Two different systems are used. A series system sends all of the oil through the cooler, then on to the transmission lubrication system. The second system is a parallel system, sending part of the oil to the cooler and part to the transmission lubricating system.

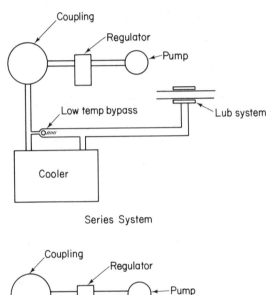

Series System

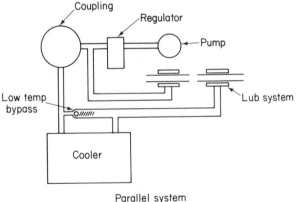

Parallel system

Fig. 22-6 Series and parallel transmission oil cooling systems.

Transmission oil is warmed as it flows across warm mechanical parts while lubricating and cooling them. Forced oil circulation in the converter also heats the oil rapidly, especially at low speeds. Serious heating problems are not encountered in turnpike driving, unless a heavy load is being pulled by the vehicle. Under severe operating conditions, oil temperatures may reach as high as 300°; however, the normal maximum limit is near 275°.

The transmission oil cooler is located in the radiator outlet tank where engine coolant temperature is lowest. This arrangement provides maximum transmission oil cooling. Some vehicles are equipped with an auxiliary, air cooled transmission oil cooler for more cooling capacity.

When transmission oil temperature is too low, the transmission will not function properly. By locating the cooler in the engine radiator, cold transmission oil is rapidly warmed to the engine operating temperature during cold weather operation. The desirable minimum operating temperature for automatic transmission oil is 190°. Temperatures lower than this produce sluggish action.

22-2 PLANETARY GEARS

The turbine shaft carries power from the torque converter to the gear train. Automatic transmission gear trains use planetary gear sets with input and output shafts located on the gear-set center line. The gear teeth are always in mesh, so gear ratio change is made by driving and holding different gear-set members. Most automatic transmissions use two planetary gear sets to obtain the required gear ratios.

Simple Planetary Gear Set The planetary gear-set cross section looks somewhat like a caged roller bearing. The roller bearing has inner and outer races separated with rollers. If the contacting surfaces of the roller bearing had teeth to prevent slippage, it would act as a planetary gear set. The inner race is called a *sun* gear, the outer race is called a *ring*, *internal*, or *annulus* gear, and the rollers are called planet *pinions*.

In the bearing, roller spacing is maintained with a cage that turns around the inner race along with the roller centers. Planet gear sets have a similar cage called a planet pinion *carrier*.

In order to have a speed or torque ratio change, the planetary gear set must have a *driving* member, an *output* member, and a *reactor* or *held* member. These members are the sun gear, ring gear and planet carrier. Any one of these members may be

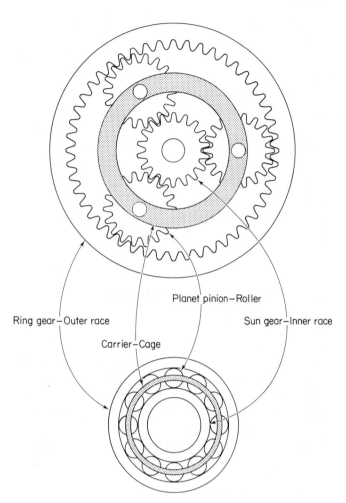

Fig. 22-7 Planetary gear set compared to parts of a roller bearing.

Ring gear—Outer race

Carrier—Cage

Planet pinion—Roller

Sun gear—Inner race

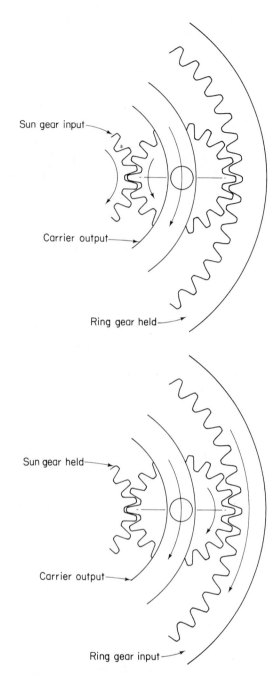

Sun gear input

Carrier output

Ring gear held

Sun gear held

Carrier output

Ring gear input

Fig. 22-8 Movement of the planetary members while transmitting torque.

held or *grounded* as power is transferred between the other two. In a simple planetary gear set, the carrier is always the output member for forward reduction. Either the sun gear is the driving member and the ring gear is held or the ring gear is the driving member and the sun gear is held. If the carrier does the driving, it will always produce an overdrive action on either the sun or ring gear, if the opposite member is held. When the carrier is held, the sun and ring gear will always turn in opposite directions to produce reverse. If the sun gear drives, it is reverse reduction and if the ring gear drives, it is reverse overdrive. When any two planet gear-set members are locked together, the complete set turns as a solid unit in direct drive. Power will not flow through

the gear set if no member is held, and the gear train would be in neutral. Any time the holding member is suddenly released while power is being transferred through the gear set, the member just released will always spin backward. Because automatic transmissions use multiple planetary gear sets, output will be either from a carrier or from a ring gear.

Calculating Planetary Gear Ratios. Simple planetary gear speed reduction ratios may be calculated if the number of teeth on each member is known. Output torque increases at the same rate as the speed decreases, so the gear ratio calculation can be used for either. In reduction, the carrier output speed reduction ratio can be calculated by the formula:

$$\text{Speed reduction} = \frac{\text{Held member}}{\text{Driving member}} + 1$$

When the ring gear is held, the ratio is always greater than 2.5. If the sun gear is held, the ratio is always less than 1.66. This leaves a large gap in the ratio obtainable from planetary gear sets. This can be shown in an example using a planetary with a held, 66 tooth ring gear and a driving, 30 tooth sun gear. The speed reduction would be:

$$\text{Speed reduction} = \frac{66}{30} + 1 = 3.20$$

If the sun gear with 30 teeth were held and the ring gear with 66 teeth were driving the speed reduction would be:

$$\text{Speed reduction} = \frac{30}{66} + 1 = 1.45$$

The gap is filled by using two planetary gear sets in the transmission.

Overdrive ratios of a simple planetary gear set with the carrier driving can be calculated with a similar formula:

$$\text{Overdrive Ratio} = \frac{\text{Output member}}{\text{Held member}} - 1$$

Using the same planetary, in overdrive the planet carrier drives, the 30 tooth sun gear is held and the 66 tooth ring gear is driven. The overdrive ratio would be:

$$\text{Overdrive ratio} = \frac{66}{30} - 1 = 1.2$$

In reverse, the carrier is held. Reverse gear ratios can be calculated by the formula:

$$\text{Reverse Ratio} = \frac{\text{Output Member}}{\text{Driving member}}$$

In reverse with the 30 tooth sun gear driving and the 66 tooth ring gear being the output member of the same planetary gear set the reverse ratio would be:

$$\text{Reverse ratio} = \frac{66}{30} = 2.2$$

These formulas can be used in calculating automatic transmission reduction ratios when all of the output of the first planetary is fed into one member of the second planetary.

22-3 TRANSMISSION GEAR TRAINS

Automatic transmission gear train members are connected together with clutches and held to the case, or grounded, for planetary reaction with either clutches or bands. These are actuated as needed by oil pressure directed to the operating units by the hydraulic control system or by overrunning free wheeling clutches.

Automotive automatic transmission designs have matured. In this process, two gear train arrangements have emerged as standards for the industry. One is the three-speed Simpson gear train and the other is the two-speed Ravingeau gear train.

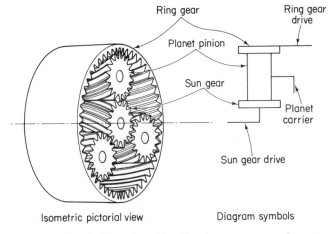

Fig. 22-9 Symbols used to identify planetary gear set parts.

Simpson Gear Train. The Simpson gear train uses two planetary gear sets each having the same size gears with the same number of gear teeth. This

353

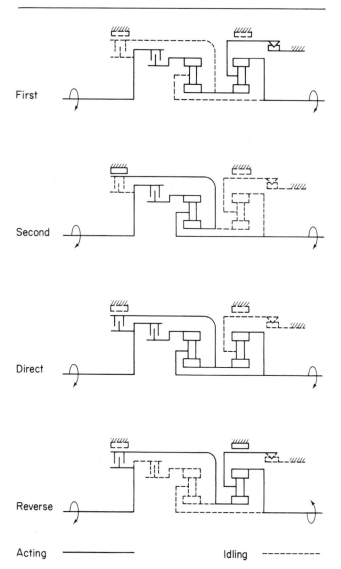

First

Second

Direct

Reverse

Acting ———————— Idling ----------

Fig. 22-10 Typical Simpson gear train operation in each gear.

reduces production costs. Three speeds provide high torque multiplication with relatively close speed ratios for smooth shifting. This gear train is used in automatic transmissions on all of the high horsepower engines and on many low horsepower engines to provide good performance with the available horsepower. A typical Simpson gear train is shown in Figure 22-10. It will be used as the reference for the following description.

In first gear, the rear clutch applies to drive the front ring gear in the same direction as the engine rotates. This direction of rotation is called forward.

The front planetary carrier is connected to the rear wheels through the output shaft so it resists movement. Forward rotation of the front ring gear causes the front planetary gears to turn on their axis, acting as idler gears, so they rotate the front sun gear backward. The sun gear becomes the front planetary output. Both planetary sun gears are made in one piece, so the rear sun gear also turns backward to drive the rear planetary. The rear ring gear as well as the front carrier is connected to the output shaft so the rear sun gear rotating in the reverse direction tries to move rear planet carrier in a reverse direction. This is prevented because the rear carrier is held to the case by the free wheeling clutch in first gear. With the rear carrier held, the reverse rotating sun gear forces the rear ring gear forward producing maximum gear reduction in the Simpson gear train.

In second gear, the front ring gear is still driven, but the sun gear is held by the front band to prevent its reverse rotation. The ring gear pulls the outer edge of the pinion forward, causing the pinions to walk around the held sun gear. This pulls the carrier forward. The carrier is connected to the output shaft so the output shaft moves forward in reduction through the front planetary. The rear carrier is released in second gear and the entire rear planetary idles forward, but does not enter into second gear reduction.

In direct drive, both clutches are applied to drive both the front planetary ring and sun gears at turbine speed. This eliminates pinion rotation and forces the carrier to rotate at turbine driving speed, along with the other planetary members.

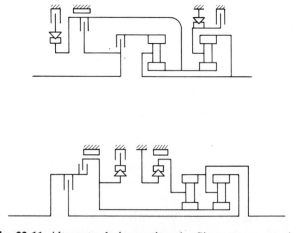

Fig. 22-11 Alternate designs using the Simpson gear train.

The carrier is connected to the output shaft so output shaft speed equals driving speed. The rear planetary also idles at driving speed.

In reverse, the front clutch is applied to drive the front sun gear. The front ring gear is disengaged and allowed to idle while the rear carrier is held to the case with the rear band. The forward rotating rear planetary sun gear turns the pinion in a backward direction. Their reverse rotation forces the rear ring gear backward to carry the output shaft in a reverse direction.

When all clutches and bands are released, input power does not reach the planetaries. This provides a neutral position for the transmission when output power is not required.

Ravingeau Gear Train. The two-speed Ravingeau gear train is at first glance somewhat more confusing than the Simpson gear train. It consists of two sun gears, two planet pinions, one carrier that carries intermeshed long and short planet pinions and one ring gear. The carrier is permanently attached to the output shaft. The large rear sun gear is splined to the input shaft.

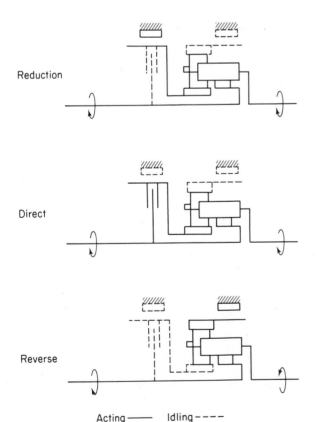

Fig. 22-12 Typical Ravingeau gear train operation in each gear.

In first gear, power comes through the turbine rotating the input shaft and the large sun gear in a forward direction. This rotates the long pinion backward. The long pinion is meshed with the short pinion so that the short pinion is turned forward. The short pinion also meshes with the small sun gear which is being held by the front band. The large forward rotating sun gear walks forward around the stationary small sun gear, pulling the carrier and output shaft forward in rotation.

In direct drive, the clutch drives the small sun gear at turbine speed so both sun gears are driven at the same speed. This carries the entire planetary assembly at turbine speed because both sun gears and planet gears are interconnected.

In reverse, the ring gear is held by the rear band. Power comes into the gear train through the large sun gear. It turns the long pinion backward. This, in turn, rotates the short pinion forward. Because the outer edge of the short pinion is engaged in the stationary ring gear, the short pinion walks around inside the ring gear in a reverse direction.

The Ravingeau gear train is in neutral when all holding devices are released.

Gear Ratios. Calculating gear ratios in planetary gear trains with two driving members is more complicated than using two simple planetaries. Solving these problems essentially involves breaking the problem into two parts. Each part is solved separately, then they are combined to calculate the total reduction. Details on these calculations are beyond the scope of this discussion.

22-4 DRIVING AND HOLDING DEVICES

Automatic transmissions use multiple disc clutches to connect driving members of the gear train. Multiple disc clutches are also used as holding devices in some transmission models. Bands and one-way clutches are only used as holding devices.

Multiple Disc Clutches. Multiple disc clutches consist of an alternating series of plates and discs. The plates are keyed on their outer edge and the discs on their inner edge. When disengaged, the discs rotate freely between the plates.

The clutch is held in the disengagement position by springs. These springs may be coil springs, wave springs or Belleville springs. The clutch is engaged with oil pressure applied to an open disc-shaped piston which has seals at both inner and outer diameters. Sufficient force is developed by the piston to compress the release spring and force the plates and discs together. Friction between their surfaces eliminates slippage.

Clutch plates have special compounded friction linings, usually paper based, and bonded on both surfaces. Grooves on the surface provide passageways for the oil to flow from the clutch as the plates come together during application.

Friction materials and fluid type affect the clutch friction. If the friction is too great, it may cause an

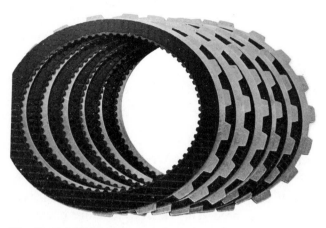

Fig. 22-13 Multiple disc clutch pack showing internal teeth on the discs and external teeth on the plates.

Fig. 22-14 Typical clutch release spring types.

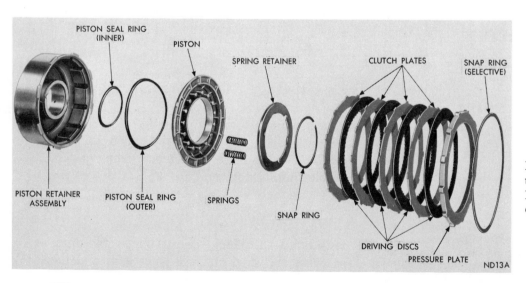

Fig. 22-15 Exploded view of a typical clutch assembly (Chrysler-Plymouth Division, Chrysler Corporation)

Fig. 22-16 A variety of clutch facing grooves designs.

Fig. 22-17 A number of different typical servo piston designs.

objectionable bump or roughness as the clutch engages. If the friction is too low, excessive slippage will occur. Slippage will allow the engine to run away and the clutch to overheat.

The coefficient of friction changes with differences in surface speed between the plates and discs. If the friction increases as they approach the same speed during engagement, they may squawk or chatter. On the other hand, some clutches require this rise in friction to minimize slippage.

Bands. Transmission bands are wrapped around the outside of a rotating drum. One end of the band is attached to an anchor. A hydraulic piston, called a *servo*, is used to tighten the band upon command from the control system to hold the drum. A spring built into the servo returns the piston to the release position when the servo is not pressurized. The

servo may act directly on one end of the band or it may act through struts and links.

The band may be a cast iron ring or a steel strap with friction lining material bonded to the inner surface. The lining may be grooved to allow the oil to escape as the band is applied.

Band adjustment is required to make sure the band does not drag on the drum in the release position and to keep the servo from bottoming as it is applied to tighten the band. Some transmissions designs have no band adjustment because the band is not used during normal driving. Bands that are used in the normal shift sequence have an adjustment either on the anchor end or on the servo end.

Band adjustment procedures usually involve tightening the band to zero clearance or against a gauging tool, then loosening the adjustment a

Fig. 22-18 Typical servo struts, links, and anchors.

357

Fig. 22-19 Typical automatic transmission band configurations.

Fig. 22-20 Typical one-way roller clutch installed in the transmission case.

specified number of turns. This is possible because the manufacturer has a known adjustment screw thread pitch. Each turn of the adjusting screw releases a specified clearance just as each turn of a micrometer opens the spacing a specified amount.

One-Way Clutches. Stators have always been mounted on one-way clutches to keep them from rotating backward during reaction and still allow them to turn freely forward when reaction was no longer required. Because of its unique properties, it has found its way into the gear train as a reaction device to hold planetary gear set members. A one-way clutch has a large torque holding capacity, fits into a small space, is completely automatic and applies no axial force when operating.

The one-way clutch is used in a fashion that causes it to be applied or to hold as the vehicle starts to move. When shifts occur, the one-way clutch very smoothly changes a reaction member to an overrunning member as the torque force direction changes.

The cam and roller type clutch is used in many applications. The cam surfaces may be on either inner or outer race surface. The rollers are usually spring loaded in a direction to aid engagement. This causes them to wedge between the two races,

Fig. 22-21 One-way clutch parts. Roller clutch on the left and Sprag clutch on the right.

jamming the races together as they try to turn in the engaging direction. When they turn in the opposite direction, the rollers move down the ramp against the spring to allow free movement between the races.

A second type of one-way clutch is a Sprag clutch. It operates between two smooth races. The engaging unit consists of a cam-shaped segment

Fig. 22-22 Edge view of the Sprag cam.

the other hand, all maximum size pieces were put together, there would be hardly enough room to get them together. This is called tolerance stack up. The correct final axial movement or end clearance is controlled by a selective fit thrust spacer somewhere in the assembly. Proper end clearance is required for correct operation. It is usually checked before transmission disassembly and again after reassembly.

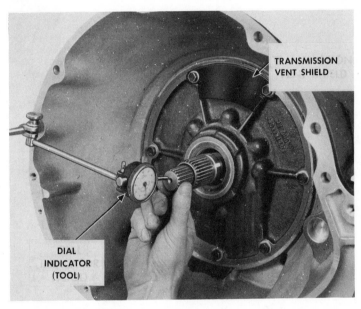

Fig. 22-23 Method of checking drive line axial clearance (Chrysler-Plymouth Division of Chrysler Corporation).

spaced in a cage between the races. Springs hold the segments against the races. The Sprag segments tip slightly to release the races so they may turn freely.

The one-way clutch cannot hold the planetary gear-set reaction member during coast because the coast force is applied in the one-way clutch release direction. Transmissions are provided with a multiple disc clutch or band that parallels the one-way clutch for use when the planetary member must be held, regardless of power flow direction. This can be seen in Figure 22-11.

In some applications, a one-way clutch is connected to the case through a multiple disc clutch. Application of this multiple disc clutch is used to bring the unit to stop for reaction while a one-way clutch releases the unit when reaction is no longer required.

22-5 DRIVE LINE FEATURES

Size and clearances in the automatic transmission are very carefully controlled during manufacture. Because of the buildup method, one part depends upon the accuracy of several other parts. For example, there are a number of shafts and thrust bearings in the transmission. Each is manufactured with its own tolerance. If a group of parts with minimum tolerance size should happen to be assembled together, excess clearance would exist. If, on

All of the rotating parts must be supported on bearings. Automatic transmissions usually use bushing-type bearings on their main rotating parts. Most of these transmission bearings are babbitt or copper-lead on a steel backing. Other materials are used where special demands require different bearing properties. All bushings are installed in bores located in either case or hub. The front of the gear train is supported on a hub extending back from the pump cover. Oil transfer rings are also located on this hub to minimize leakage as control oil transfers from the stationary hub to a rotating clutch drum. The rear of the gear train is supported by the rear of the transmission case. Shafts and drum hubs

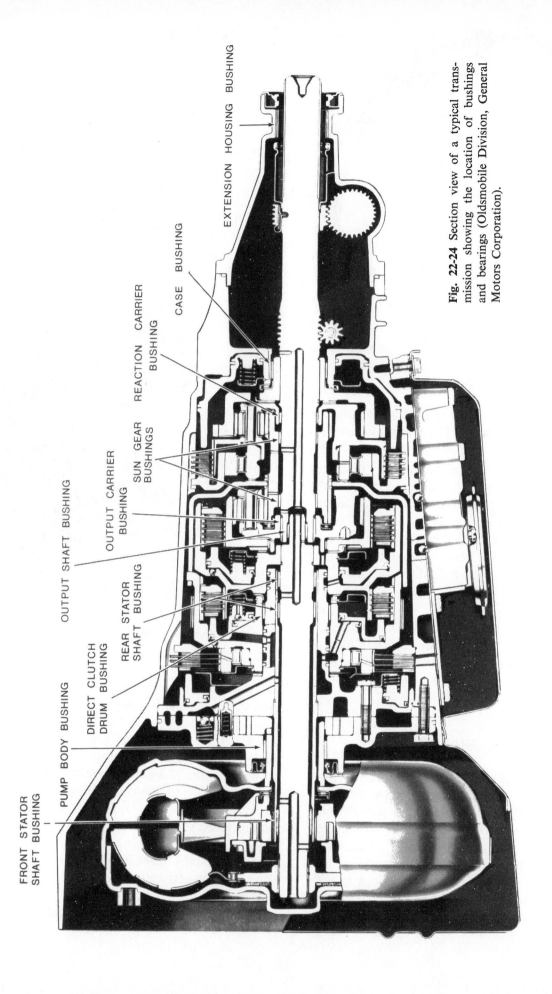

FRONT STATOR
SHAFT BUSHING

PUMP BODY BUSHING

OUTPUT SHAFT BUSHING

DIRECT CLUTCH
DRUM BUSHING

REAR STATOR
SHAFT BUSHING

OUTPUT CARRIER
BUSHING

SUN GEAR
BUSHINGS

REACTION CARRIER
BUSHING

CASE BUSHING

EXTENSION HOUSING BUSHING

Fig. 22-24 Section view of a typical transmission showing the location of bushings and bearings (Oldsmobile Division, General Motors Corporation).

support one another on these two main support locations.

The input shaft is splined between the turbine and a front clutch hub. On the front, the turbine is supported in a bearing within the torque converter cover or inside the front of the stator shaft, and the front clutch hub is mounted with a bearing on the pump cover rearward extension. The front of the output shaft rides on a bushing at the rear of the transmission case. The rear of the output shaft is supported by a bearing in the back of the transmission extension. In some transmissions, the output shaft extends almost to the input shaft while others use an intermediate shaft between them. The intermediate shaft will fit into pilot bores or bushings at the back of the input shaft and in front of the output shaft. These different details can be seen in the transmission section illustrations.

Planetary gear-set members, clutch hubs, and brake drums are splined to these shafts for driving and riding on bearings when they are required to be free turning. Non-rotating clutch and brake parts are supported by the transmission case to minimize the load that the shafts must support. In some transmissions, an oil transfer hub and seal rings are part of this non-rotating assembly.

The basic transmission disassembly procedure is to lift the torque converter from the input and stator shafts. Removal of the valve body assembly follows. The front pump assembly is removed to get to the gear train. Major gear train sub-assemblies can then be removed from the front of the transmission case.

Transmission rotating members are spaced with thrust bearings. Needle roller thrust bearings may be used where high loads are encountered. Babbitt on a steel backing is the standard thrust bearing material. Lightly loaded thrust bearings may be made of bronze, pheonolic or nylon to minimize cost.

Sub-assemblies are held together with snap rings and retaining rings. These must be removed to completely disassemble the transmission sub-assemblies. In clutches, the piston release spring is often compressed against the retaining ring. When it is, the spring must be further compressed to remove the ring. This usually requires the use of special tools.

Sub-assemblies that rotate together are often connected with drive lugs at their outer edges. This method is inexpensive to make and easy to assemble.

Fig. 22-25 Typical rear portion of pump covers with the stator shaft extending left and a clutch and bearing hub with oil transfer rings extending to the right.

Fig. 22-26 Typical thrust bearings and spacers.

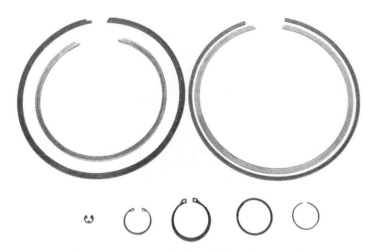

Fig. 22-27 Typical snap rings and retaining rings used to hold transmission parts in position.

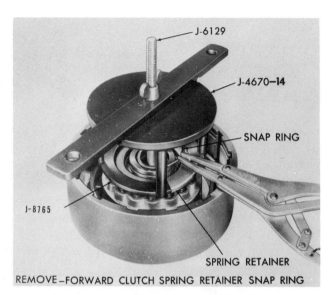

Fig. 22-28 Typical method of compressing clutch release springs so the retaining ring can be removed for clutch piston removal (Oldsmobile Division, General Motors Corporation).

Fig. 22-29 Typical drive line subassemblies.

362

22-6 TRANSMISSION SHIFT REQUIREMENTS

An automatic transmission gear ratio change is called a *shift*. Shifting requires the release of one planetary member and the application of another. Release and application must be timed so the transmission keeps engine torque under control at all times.

The reaction member of the planetary gear set always tends to turn backward while the gear set is carrying a torque load. This reaction force is proportional to the torque being carried. As the torque load transfers from one planetary member to another, the load on the reaction changes from reverse to forward direction. Ideally, the holding device should be applied or released at the instant torque reversal occurs.

During an upshift, the applied member must have a higher torque capacity than the released member. This is required because engine inertia momentarily increases torque as the engine is slowed to the new speed. This must be added to the torque being produced by the engine. When an applied holding or driving device becomes worn, it will first become apparent to the driver when it slips while it is being applied.

Shift quality or smoothness is primarily dependent upon the characteristic output torque which varies during the shift. If one member is released before the second member is applied, the transmission will momentarily be in neutral so the engine will tend to run away. On the other hand, if application occurs before release, the transmission will be momentarily locked in two gears, producing a bump. Either condition is unacceptable.

Good shift quality will transfer the load from one member to the next by allowing a slight amount of slippage to occur during application as the new member picks up the torque. This may take as long as .6 second. Excess apply time will produce smoother shifts, but these will reduce the service life of the unit. The shift that is immediate and positive will give the longest service life; however, it is unacceptable to the general motoring public.

During downshift, the engine speed must increase as the shift moves to a lower gear. Here again, the apply force must gradually come on before the holding force is released to prevent engine run away. If it occurs too soon, a bump will be noticed as it is during upshift.

The automatic transmission is dependent upon oil pressure to apply the friction units, to transfer power through the torque converter, to lubricate bearings, and to cool internal parts. Some of the fluid operating within the control valve assembly acts as a signal to start or stop a shift sequence. The oil pump is the source of transmission oil pressure.

Oil Pump. The oil pump is driven by a hub on the back of the torque converter. Its capacity must be large enough to provide required pressure at all times. This is especially critical at low speeds with full throttle operation. On the other hand, the pump capacity must not be so large as to require excessive power to operate it. At highway speeds, automatic transmission pumps are capable of pumping up to 28 gallons per minute at pressures up to 250 pounds per square inch.

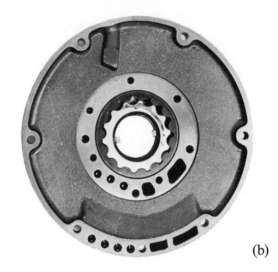

Fig. 22-31 Typical automatic transmission oil pumps. (a) Extended spur gear tooth type, (b) rotor type pump.

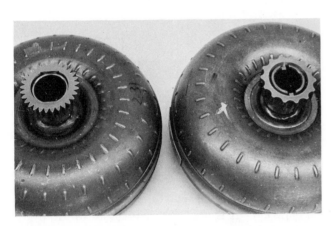

Fig. 22-30 Two typical oil pump drive methods. The small oil pump gear is driven by the torque converter housing rear hub.

The automatic transmission oil pumps are classified as a type called an *internal-external* pump, sometimes abbreviated as an IX pump. The large gear with internal teeth is in mesh at one point with the small gear which has external teeth. The small gear is driven by the torque converter hub and the large gear idles around it. One side of the pump is connected to a passage from the oil screen or filter in the bottom of the oil pan. Pump inlet occurs as the gear teeth come out of mesh as they rotate. The space between the separating gear teeth produces a partial vacuum that is filled by oil from

the pan. As the gears continue to rotate, the teeth will again begin to mesh on the other side of the pump. A pressure passage is provided to allow the oil to be squeezed from between the teeth as they mesh. This provides a continuous oil supply as long as the engine is operating.

Two tooth forms are used in automatic transmission IX pumps. One uses typical extended spur gear teeth. A crescent filler block is used between a portion of the pump where the gears are separated. This helps to separate the pump inlet from the pump outlet. The other pump is called a rotor-type pump.

Its tooth form is designed so that the high points of the tooth form almost contact at the open side of the gear set. This close operation helps to keep the inlet and outlet sides separated.

At one time, a second pump was used on the transmission output shaft. This rear pump was discontinued to reduce expense and noise when front pump designs were improved to satisfactorily provide pressure under all operating conditions. Vehicles with transmissions that have no rear pump cannot be started by pushing the vehicle. Engine operation is needed to build up the required pressure to place the transmission in gear.

Uncontrolled pump pressure varies with engine speed. Oil from the pump flows directly from the pump to a regulator valve that limits pressure to the amount required.

Two methods are used to regulate oil pressure. The standard method is to have one end of the regulator valve, called a reaction area, exposed to *pump pressure*. A spring presses against the opposite end. Pump pressure increase forces the regulator valve to move toward the spring. When the required pressure is attained, the valve opens a passage to allow excess oil to flow to the pump inlet, effectively limiting maximum pressure.

Fig. 22-32 Pressure regulator valve principles.

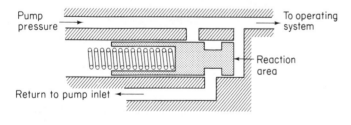

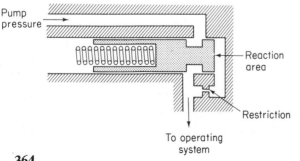

The second type of regulator valve is called a low flow valve. It is used to reduce pressures from line pressure to provide a lower regulated pressure. One application is a torque converter pressure regulator. It also operates on the principle of balancing a valve between oil pressure and a spring. The valve reaction area in this type is exposed to the valve's *outlet pressure*. When the outlet pressure reaches the required amount, the valve moves to restrict inlet flow to the valve. This effectively limits oil pressure.

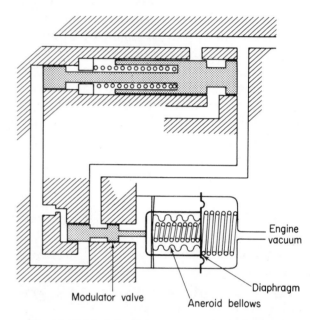

Fig. 22-33 Modulated pressure regulator principle.

Oil pressure that leaves the regulator is called *line pressure*. It is the highest pressure in the transmission. Other control pressures are reduced from it. Line pressure must be high enough to securely hold clutch pistons and band servos under the most severe loading conditions. This force may be excessive and require a lot of engine power under light loaded operating conditions. Some regulator valves are, therefore, designed to lower line pressure when less severe loads are being applied and raise them as the loads become greater. This is called modulated line pressure. Its function is to match line pressure to engine torque. This is done by allowing an oil pressure that varies with the engine power to apply pressure on the regulator valve in the same direction as the spring force acts to raise line pressure at high engine power.

22-8 CONTROL SYSTEM

The automatic transmission control system can be divided into two groups of controls. One type will cause an event to take place. This group is called *causative* controls. The second type affect shift quality and are called *smoothness* controls.

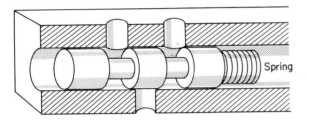

Fig. 22-34 Typical spool valve section showing pressure balance around the spool.

Sliding spool type control valves are used. Porting is accomplished through passages that surround the entire spool. This balances the side forces on the spool so it can slide freely in its bore. Most of the valves are held in one extreme position by a spring. Valving occurs when a pressure differential moves the valve toward the spring. Endwise movement aligns ports that allow oil to flow to or from

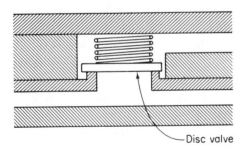

Fig. 22-35 Typical check valves.

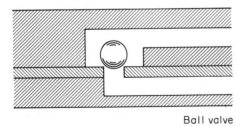

the operating unit. The spool valves are accompanied with disc- or ball-check valves to control the transmission. Check valves prevent flow until a specific pressure is reached or close passages to prevent back flow. Some check valves do both of these operations.

Valves and operating units are connected through drilled passages and through ditches cast into the case and valve body.

Fig. 22-36 Oil passages cast in a typical transmission case.

Causative Controls. Line pressure is directed to the manual valve which is connected to the driver operated selector. The manual valve directs oil pressure to operating valves used in the driving range selected. It fully applies the units required

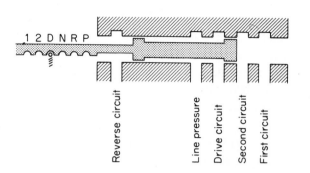

Fig. 22-37 Schematic of a typical selector valve.

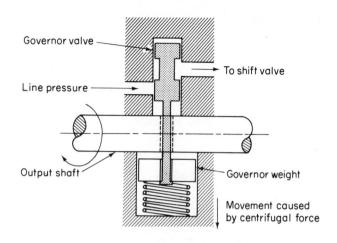

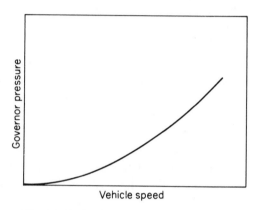

Fig. 22-39 Typical single-stage governor.

for neutral, reverse and forward range. Automatic shifting only occurs during forward range operation.

In drive range, the selector valve directs oil to a shifter valve, a governor valve, and a throttle valve. When the shifter valve moves, it opens ports to allow line pressure to flow to the required clutch piston and band servo to produce a shift in gear ratios. Oil pressure from the governor provides the force to move the shifter valve.

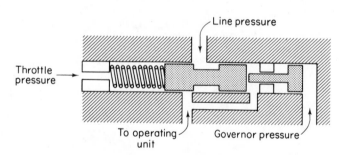

Fig. 22-38 Shift valve principles.

The *governor* is driven by the transmission output shaft and is sensitive to vehicle speed. Its pressure increases as vehicle speed increases. When the vehicle reaches the speed at which shifting should take place, the governor pressure is high enough to move the shifter valve against a spring to produce the shift. This system would be satisfactory if the loads and speeds were the same every time, but they aren't. This is why it is also necessary to have some means for the transmission to sense engine load.

The amount of power an engine produces is indicated by throttle position or by manifold vacuum.

Automatic transmissions use either of these two methods to operate valves which will produce an oil pressure signal that is proportional to engine load. It may be TV pressure (*Throttle-Valve*) or modulator pressure. This oil pressure (called TV pressure for the rest of this discussion) is proportional to the vehicle load, and is sent to the spring side of the shift valve to help the spring oppose governor pressure.

The shift valve is balanced between a spring load plus TV pressure on one end and governor pressure on the other end. Shifting occurs when the force produced by governor pressure is greater than the force created by the spring working with the TV pressure. At low throttle openings, a small amount of governor pressure is required to produce a shift, because the TV pressure is low, so the shift occurs at low vehicle speeds. At higher throttle openings, the TV pressure is higher so the governor pressure must also be higher to produce a shift. The shift will then occur at higher vehicle speeds.

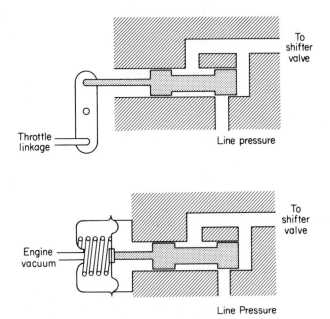

Fig. 22-40 Mechanical and vacuum operated throttle valve principles.

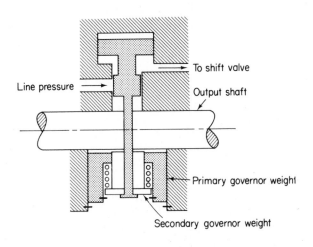

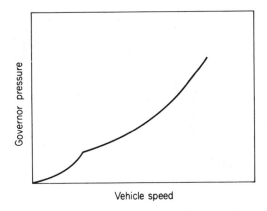

Fig. 22-41 Typical two-stage governor.

Sudden full throttle openings will raise the TV pressure much higher than governor pressure. This causes the shift valve to reverse itself, producing a transmission-forced downshift, called *kickdown*. Throttle pressure alone may not be sufficient to produce a fast downshift response. In these cases, a special valve that opens at full throttle (called a *detent*) gives detent oil pressure or boosted throttle pressure which is used in addition to TV pressure to force the shift valve back.

The shift valve is designed to move the spool to its extreme limit once movement begins. This is done by rerouting oil pressure to snap the valve to its limit. In the extreme position, either TV or governor pressure is cut off, depending upon the direction of movement.

Transmissions that use three speeds require two shift valves. Both operate in the same basic way just described. They differ in the amount of governor pressure required to make the shift. The 1-2 shift valve operates at a lower governor pressure than the 2-3 shift valve.

Two stage governor weights are used. A large weight is used to produce adequate governor pressure at low speeds. This weight is blocked and a small governor weight takes over to increase the governor pressure that is required to operate the

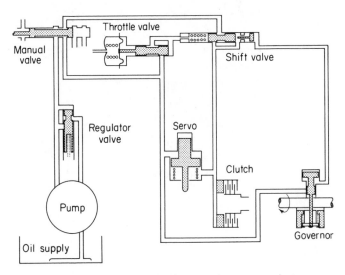

Fig. 22-42 Schematic of a basic causative automatic transmission control system.

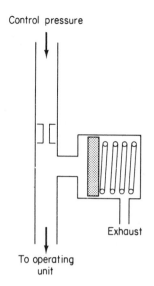

Control pressure

Exhaust

To operating
unit

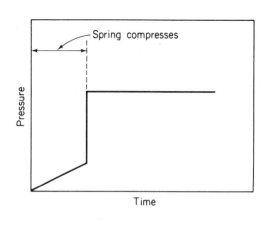

Spring compresses

Pressure

Time

Fig. 22-43 Accumulator principles.

second shifter valve. The weights set governor valve position to allow proportional oil pressure to apply against the shifter valve pressure area.

Oil pressure from the shifter valve is often used to simultaneously release one reaction member and to apply another. This direct action is usually modified to give a rapid shift that will smoothly pick up the engine torque during the shift phasing. The controls that do this are called smoothness controls.

Smoothness Controls. Smoothness controls are those control valves that help to time the application and the release of friction devices so the engine torque is always under control and prevent two gear ratios from being applied at the same time. One of the most common smoothness controls is the *accumulator*. The accumulator is basically a spring loaded piston placed parallel to the passage to be controlled. Pressure will build up rapidly in

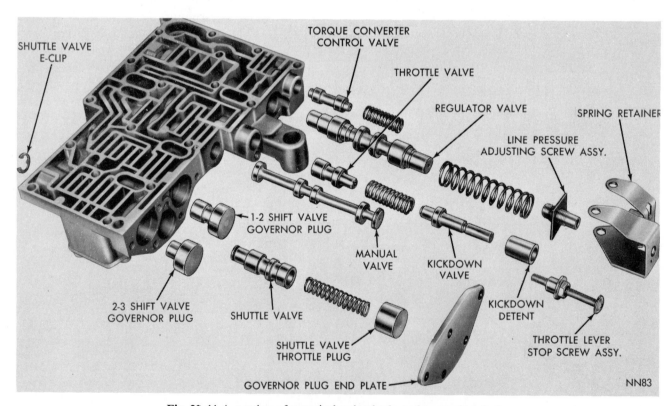

Fig. 22-44 A portion of a typical valve body, valves, and springs (Chrysler-Plymouth Division, Chrysler Corporation).

368

the passage until the accumulator piston begins to compress the spring. The pressure is relatively constant for a time as the accumulator fills. When it is full, the passage pressure again builds until it reaches full pressure. In this way, the accumulator controls the pressure for a time interval as the operating unit picks up the load, then it applies the full holding force. An accumulator may be designed into a servo or it may be a separate unit.

Other valves used to cushion the shift are called scheduling valves, shuttle valves, timing valves, etc. Even accurately drilled holes or orifices are used as an aid to cushion the shift. Their purpose is to help control the application and release of holding devices so they will have smooth shifts under any operating load and speed condition. Blocking valves are sometimes used to prevent a shift that will cause damage, if the shift were to occur at too great a speed.

Each model automatic transmission is designed to be used in a number of vehicle-engine combinations. Each engine type in these vehicles has a different torque and power curve and each vehicle has a different weight. They, therefore, require different shift patterns and shift timing. To accommodate all of these combinations, the individual shift control valves are programmed to match their vehicle-engine application. This is usually done with minor changes in the valve porting and by using different control valve springs. In some cases, the drive line is modified by changing the number of clutch plates, changing the number of pinions, or by changing some of the materials used.

22-9 AUTOMATIC TRANSMISSION SERVICE

Modern automatic transmissions require very little service unless they are abused. Abuse comes from operating at high temperatures and from forcibly changing gears with the engine operating at high rpm, especially between low and reverse. Damage may even result from towing the vehicle without removing the drive shaft because there is no lubrication when the engine is not operating the oil pump.

In nearly every case of automatic transmission failure, the failure is preceded by shift quality deterioration. This may result from maladjustment, debris in the hydraulic system, clogged screens and

filters, worn parts, or internal leakage that reduces apply pressures. When shift quality deteriorates, the wise driver will have the transmission serviced before a major and expensive failure occurs.

Inspection. The transmission should be given a thorough inspection and road test before it is removed for disassembly. This inspection includes a check for external leakage, a check of the fluid level when the transmission is thoroughly warm, a check of the manual valve, and throttle valve linkage adjustments, and a check of band adjustments. The appropriate service manual should be consulted for specific details that apply to the unit being inspected.

When a car is taken on a road test, it should be checked for shift timing and shift quality. Shift timing is determined by the vehicle speed at which the shift occurs. Shift quality refers to the smoothness of the shift and whether it is positive or delayed over an excessively long period of time. Shifts should be checked at light throttle, heavy throttle and full throttle downshift.

It is important for good transmission trouble shooting to understand the operation of the transmission driving and holding units in the drive train to know which ones are malfunctioning. This

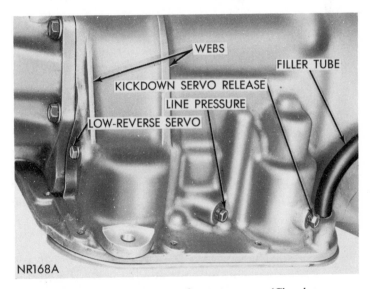

Fig. 22-45 Typical pressure taps for test gauges (Chrysler-Plymouth Division, Chrysler Corporation).

understanding must also include an understanding of the hydraulic controls system that apply and release the operating units. All manufacturers have service manuals that illustrate these systems in detail.

If the road test is inconclusive, a pressure test is advisable. Automatic transmissions are equipped with pressure taps in which pressure gauges can be fitted. The transmission is road tested or operated on a hoist while the gauges are attached. Pressure readings should be checked against specifications.

The transmission should only be removed if the problem cannot be corrected with the transmission installed. Incorrect pressure readings indicate a source of the problem. Most service manuals have detailed trouble shooting guides that are very useful in determining specific causes for abnormal operation.

Removal. When required, automatic transmission removal involves draining the transmission fluid, removing the drive shaft, starter, control linkages, speedometer cable, cooler lines, rear engine mount and cross member. The torque converter drive plate is disconnected from the converter in many transmissions, so the transmission and converter can be removed as an assembly, using a supporting jack. This procedure minimizes the chance of damage to the drive plate, pump bushing, and front oil seal. In some models, the torque converter remains attached to the drive plate when the transmission is removed, so the transmission must be pulled straight out of the torque converter.

Disassembly. Careful examination is very important when disassembling automatic transmissions. It is important to look for any abnormalities that may have caused the problem which led to disassembly. All parts should be kept clean because small particles of dirt can cause sticking control valves. Therefore, the transmission exterior should be thoroughly cleaned before disassembly and the transmission should be disassembled in a clean area.

In general terms, disassembly starts with removal of the pan, control body and the pump. Because of its close fit, pullers are usually required to remove

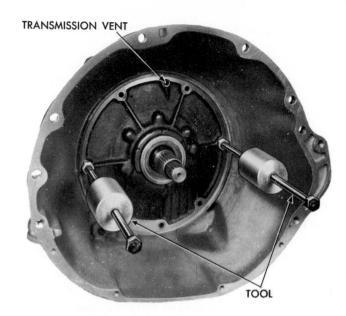

Fig. 22-46 Pullers to remove the front pump case (Chrysler Motors Corporation).

the pump. Drive train parts can be carefully slid from the case. In some cases, retaining rings must be removed to free these parts. The extension housing is removed from the back of the case. It may also require removal of a retaining ring.

The major sub-assemblies should be checked individually, cleaned, inspected and reassembled. This reduces the chance of mixing parts or improperly reassembling them. Parts are thoroughly coated with new automatic transmission fluid as they are reassembled.

Fig. 22-47 View of a typical transmission drive line with the pump removed.

Problem Areas. One of the most common items that leads to transmission failure is internal fluid leakage. Excess leakage results in reduced pressure which, in turn, reduces the holding power of clutches and bands. This allows slippage which will overheat and score the holding devices so they will have to be replaced. Internal leaks are usually not noticed until they cause faulty operation.

Internal leakage is controlled by seals between parts. These may be merely flat stamped and machined surfaces such as control valve bodies, thin transfer plates, and oil pressure trenches. These surfaces must be flat to seal. They must also be assembled and torqued correctly so that high pressures do not bend the parts which will cause leaks.

Rotating and reciprocating seals are the most likely source of excessive internal leakage. Some leakage is desirable because it allows the fluid to act as a coolant for internal parts. These seals are made of cast iron, like piston rings, or from elastomer compounds, a term that is used to describe synthetic rubber-like materials.

Fig. 22-48 Typical oil transfer passages and seal rings on the pump's rear hub.

Cast iron seals usually have butt joints with a closely controlled gap for minimum leakage. Most of them are phosphate coated to reduce wear. In some cases, they have a hook lap to hold the ends of the ring together during assembly. It is more expensive than a butt joint and is only used when necessary.

Elastomeric materials are used for front and rear seals, as well as for piston and servo seals. In some cases, they are used for gasket-type static seals. The seal material selection is based upon the maximum expected operating temperature and service life required. These materials gradually harden as they are exposed to high temperature operation over a period of time.

Fig. 22-49 Typical oil seals used in automatic transmissions. Lip seals on the left and bottom. Lathe cut seals on top and O-ring seals at the right.

Dirt is the biggest problem with reciprocating seals. It causes leak producing scratches on the seal and the bore. As seals age, they harden and do not function properly. Seals are always replaced, scratched bores may be polished. If the scratch remains after polishing, the part will have to be replaced to eliminate leakage.

Rotating seals wear on the side of the seal and in the groove as well as around the outside surface. Here again, the seal is replaced and the bore is polished if scratched. If the part still has a rough surface, it will have to be replaced for correct operation.

Elastomeric seals are made in three types, lip, O-ring, and lathe cut. The lip edge of the lip seal is deflected .030″ to .050″ when installed to seal against the bore or shaft to form the sealing surface.

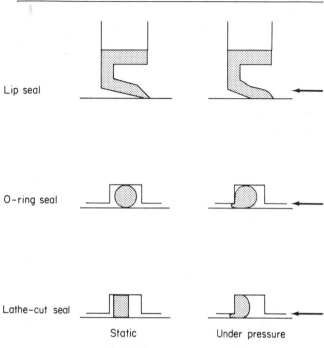

Lip seal

O-ring seal

Lathe-cut seal

Static   Under pressure

Fig. 22-50 Typical transmission seal principles.

When pressure exists against the open end of the seal, it is pushed tighter so it continues to seal. Lip seals deflect or conform as needed to take care of moderate out of round and eccentric parts.

O-ring and lathe cut seals fit loosely in a groove. The O-ring seal has a round cross section and the lathe cut seal has a rectangular cross section. They are squeezed .012″ to .025″ when installed to form a seal at their outer edge. High pressure squeezes them against the opening clearance to continue the seal under pressure. They are less expensive, but require closer tolerance than lip seals.

The transmission must be disassembled to repair a pump or gear noise. Pump noise is caused by a worn pump or by pressure variations. Gear noises result from rough or broken teeth. If any of these parts are worn, they must be replaced.

If automatic transmission bearings become worn, they allow the transmission parts to misalign. This further results in the wear of gears, clutches, and bands and may also cause seal damage. All worn bearings and bushings must be replaced. Bearing failure is usually typified by wiping, wear, and scoring.

After all sub-assemblies have been reconditioned, the transmission should be assembled, taking care to install all spacers, thrust washers, springs, etc., in their correct location and positioned properly. The service manual that applies to the transmission should be carefully followed. All new gaskets and seals should be used, and all internal parts coated with automatic transmission fluid.

During installation, the torque converter parts need to be aligned with splines and drive members. They must freely fit the stator shaft, turbine shaft, and oil pump. Forcing any of these will damage the parts. The transmission must be positioned straight against the engine to avoid putting any side load on the torque converter that would damage the shaft, bearing, or front oil seal. The rest of the installation is in the reverse order of removal.

22-10 AUTOMATIC TRANSMISSION FLUID

After the transmission is installed, it should be filled with automatic transmission fluid. The engine should be started after approximately half the fluid has been put in. Care must be taken to avoid overfilling. Oil will expand 8% from 60°F to the normal operating temperature of 240°F. This is enough to raise the level on the dipstick from the add mark to the full mark. Transmission oil level is checked when the transmission is thoroughly warm with the engine running and the selector in park or neutral, depending upon the transmission type.

Automatic transmission fluids (ATF) are compounded to meet the variety of functions to which they are subjected. Matching the fluid to the transmission is essential for good clutch plate life and band durability as well as for smooth operation and elastomer seal life. For example, if paraffinic base oil is used for the fluid, it will tend to shrink oil seals, but if naphthenic oils are used, they will act as swelling agents. ATF is made from 3/4 paraffinic- and 1/4 naphthenic-based oil.

Complex automatic transmission fluids are formulated for low temperature fluidity, oxidation resistance, anti-foaming, corrosion resistance, effect on seals, and effect on friction. Two types of fluids are used; M2C33, or *Type F*, developed by Ford for their products, and *Dexron*, developed by General Motors and used in all vehicles except Ford. The greatest difference between these two fluids is the way they affect the clutch coefficient of friction.

At the start of application, the clutch plates and discs are turning at a great difference in speed. This can be measured in feet per minute. As the clutch applies, the difference in speed reduces as it picks up the load until the driving and driven members are turning at the same speed. As the clutch sliding speeds equalize, the coefficient of friction increases with Type F fluid to give a firm aggressive shift. With Dexron fluid, the coefficient of friction reduces which results in a soft, smooth shift. The correct fluid must be used to minimize a squawk or bump as the discs and plates reach the same speed.

Red dye is added to automatic transmission fluids. This gives it an identification color that aids in determining the source of external leaks. Engine oil has a neutral color and can be differentiated from the red transmission fluid.

Automatic transmissions cause very little problem when used in standard passenger car operation. Routine service consists of an occasional oil

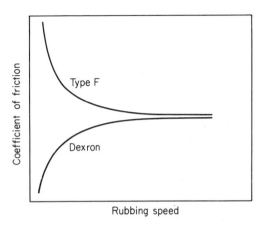

Fig. 22-51 Curve showing the coefficient of friction characteristics of two types of automatic transmission fluid.

level check. At the first sign of external leakage or abnormal shifting, they should be given a thorough inspection and the required corrections made before serious damage occurs.

Review Questions
Chapter 22

1. Describe the oil flow in a torque converter.

2. What is the meaning of torque converter stall?

3. What are the advantages and disadvantages of high stall speed?

4. What is the converter coupling point?

5. When do transmission temperatures become high?

6. How does the engine coolant help to maintain the transmission oil temperature?

7. Describe the simple planetary operation in reduction, overdrive, and reverse.

8. Describe the operation of a Simpson gear train.

9. Describe the operation of a Ravingeau gear train.

10. How does the clutch coefficient of friction affect application?

11. What is the purpose of a band anchor?

12. What are the advantages and disadvantages of a one-way clutch?

13. Why are selective fit thrust washers required?

14. Identify the shaft supporting bearings on each of the transmission section illustrations in this chapter.

15. Why is shift apply and release timing important?

16. What limits oil pump size?

17. What are the different types of regulator valves?

18. What is the advantage of modulating the oil pressure?

19. What is the difference between causative and smoothness controls?

20. Where does the oil flow from the manual valve?

21. What oil pressure makes the shifter valve move to give an upshift?

22. What delays the upshift to a higher vehicle speed?

23. What forces are used to operate the TV valve?

24. What moves the shift valve for kickdown?

25. Why is a two-stage governor used in three-speed transmissions?

26. What is the most common smoothness control?

27. How are transmissions modified to fit different vehicle engine combinations?

28. What will cause premature transmission failure?

29. What should be done before the transmission is removed for service?

30. What are the common problem areas in a transmission?

31. What might be expected to happen if the wrong type of automatic transmission fluid were used?

32. What precautions should be observed during transmission assembly?

Quiz 22

1. The torque converter stator directs the oil flow to the
   a. turbine
   b. impeller
   c. transmission pump
   d. lubricating system.

2. The torque converter provides its highest torque multiplication when the
   a. turbine is stopped
   b. impeller is stopped
   c. turbine is moving at low speed
   d. impeller is moving at low speed.

3. Operation of a torque converter at low stall speeds will produce
   a. high torque multiplication
   b. rapid heat buildup
   c. excess noise
   d. good fuel economy.

4. When the carrier is held in a planetary gear set with the sun gear driving, the gear set will provide
   a. forward reduction
   b. forward overdrive
   c. reverse reduction
   d. reverse overdrive.

5. Automatic transmission members are driven through the application of
   a. clutches
   b. bands
   c. servos
   d. synchronizers.

6. Endwise movement of automatic transmission shafts and drums may be limited by
   a. ball bearings
   b. thrust washers
   c. hydraulic pressure
   d. driving lugs.

7. An ideal holding device would release at the instant torque reversal occurs in a planetary member. A device that does this in automatic transmissions is a
   a. piston clutch
   b. Sprag clutch
   c. servo-operated band
   d. link-operated band.

8. The transmission shifter valve is moved to cause an upshift by the
   a. modulated oil pressure
   b. clutch apply oil pressure
   c. throttle controlled oil pressure
   d. governor oil pressure.

9. The transmission shifter valve movement is restricted by
   a. modulated oil pressure
   b. servo-apply oil pressure
   c. throttle controlled oil pressure
   d. governor oil pressure.

10. An accumulator is used to
    a. collect and store the oil
    b. attract all foreign materials from the oil
    c. absorb driveline shock loads
    d. act as a shock absorber.

chapter 23

Propeller Shaft and Rear Axle

Engine power flows through the transmission and is delivered to the vehicle's final drive. The final drive consists of a propeller shaft, differential assembly, and drive axle which transmits power to the drive wheels.

The propeller shaft drives a geared pinion that is meshed with a ring gear. This changes the driving force 90° from the propeller shaft to the rear axles and wheels. A differential assembly is placed between the ring gear and axles to allow the axles and wheels to turn at different speeds as they go over road irregularities and around turns.

Drive line flexibility is required to allow for suspension movement and to provide a means of dampening vibration. The propeller shaft's universal joints and slip joint allow driving torque to be delivered through drive line angle changes and relative length changes as the suspension springs compress, or jounce, and rebound. Final drive vibration is isolated with elastomer mounts, flexible torsion drives, and torsional vibration dampers.

23-1 PROPELLER SHAFT

The propeller shaft, sometimes called the drive shaft, propels the vehicle by connecting the transmission output shaft to the differential input pinion. At least one universal joint must be used to provide continuous torque driving force as suspension movement produces changes in the relative position of the propeller shaft ends. This same movement changes the distance between the ends so that the propeller shaft must include some type of slip joint.

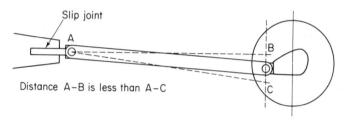

Fig. 23-1 Changes in propeller shaft length as the rear axle moves up and down.

Shaft. Driving torque and braking torque react against the chassis. At one time, the *torque tube type* propeller shaft absorbed these faces. A torque tube is a large diameter tube fastened securely to the rear axle housing and completely enclosing the propeller shaft. The torque tube is fitted into a

Fig. 23-2 Single-piece propeller shaft.

spherical ball and socket surrounding one universal joint at the transmission end. These two units carry their respective load while allowing suspension flexibility.

The torque-tube propeller shaft has been replaced by the Hotchkiss-type propeller shaft. Its essential difference is in the method used to absorb drive and braking torque. The Hotchkiss drive absorbs driving and braking torques through the front half of the rear leaf springs or through links and arms when used with coil-type springs. Details of these suspension systems are presented in Chapter 26.

The propeller shaft used with the Hotchkiss drive is essentially a steel tube having forged steel universal joints on each end. Its only function is to deliver transmission output torque to the differential input pinion. The shaft tube must be large enough to be strong enough to transfer output torque. Excess tube size increases the possibility of unbalance, is harder to straighten, tends to fan more air that may cause noise, requires more room under the floor pan, and is more expensive.

The propeller shaft, like any other rigid tube, has a natural frequency. If one end was held securely, it would vibrate at its own particular frequency when deflected and released. Its natural frequency occurs at its *critical speed*. Critical propeller shaft speed varies as the diameter of the tube changes and inversely as the square of the length. Diameters are as large as possible and shafts as short as possible to keep the critical speed frequency above the driving range. Propeller shafts over 60″ between universal joints become a source for unbalance problems. Shaft lengths are minimized by using long transmission extension housings and center universal joints with two-piece propeller shafts. When used, the center universal joint is supported by a center support bearing that must be insulated from the vehicle chassis.

Propeller shaft run-out or unbalance induces a phenomenon called *whirl*. Whirl is very similar to the action of a rope that is swung in an arc while being held at both ends. Once it has formed a bend, it keeps looping around as it rotates. Propeller shaft tubing is usually rolled from flat sheet stock, straightened within .010″ run-out and balanced within 1/4 oz-inches. This keeps the center of mass very nearly on the longitudinal axis center to minimize whirl.

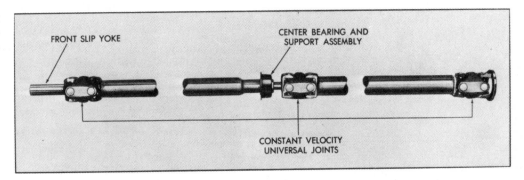

Fig. 23-3 Two-piece propeller shaft (Cadillac Motor Car Division, General Motors Corporation).

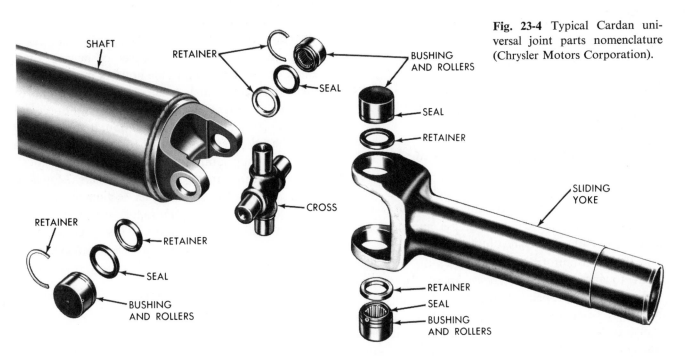

Fig. 23-4 Typical Cardan universal joint parts nomenclature (Chrysler Motors Corporation).

Universal Joint. Several types of universal joints are used in automobiles. The most common is the cross and yoke type. It is based upon principles invented independently by Cardan in Italy and Hooke in England. It is called both a *Cardan* universal joint and a *Hooke* universal joint. A second type of universal joint is formed from two cross and yoke joints and is called a *double Cardan* universal joint. Another type of universal joint was developed by Carl Weiss to give constant rotational speeds. It is built by Bendix and is called a *Bendix-Weiss* universal joint. A fourth type of universal joint used in passenger cars is a *ball and trunion* joint that acts as slip joint as well as a universal joint.

The propeller shaft in a Hotchkiss drive requires a universal joint at each end. The rear universal joint allows the shaft to drive as the rear axle housing nose twists up and down from driving and braking torque forces. The front universal joint allows the suspension to jounce and rebound while continuing to supply driving force.

The cross and yoke type universal joint operating at an angle does not transfer uniform turning motion through the joint. With the input member turning at a uniform speed, the output side speeds up and slows down during two periods each revolution. The average speed or velocity of the input and output are the same. To say it another way, the output velocity is not constant. The reason for

377

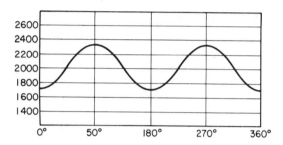

Turning radius changes as joint rotates

Fig. 23-5 Graph of a Cardan universal joint speed change with the joint operating through a 30 degree angle at 2000 rpm input.

the change in motion is that the effective lever arm length varies continually at the motion transfer point. This action is difficult to visualize in a two-dimensional illustration. It can be plotted on a graph to show the velocity increase and decrease at each portion of the revolution.

This non-uniform velocity causes the propeller shaft to increase and decrease speed. In a two universal joint propeller shaft, this is partially corrected by reversing the action at the rear universal joint. It would be completely dampened if both universal joints always operated through the same angles.

A double Cardan universal joint consists of two closely spaced cross and yoke joints with a special link yoke. The two joints work to reverse the non-uniform action and, thus, provide constant velocity. Yoke centers are maintained by a ball and socket centering device so the joint working

angle is the same in each joint half. This, then, forms a *constant velocity joint.* The output velocity is uniform when the input velocity is uniform, even though the joint center link has the typical velocity increase and decrease action.

Constant velocity universal joints are used as center joints on two-piece drive shafts. Two-piece shafts are used where drive shaft lengths would be excessive and where a low vehicle silhouette is desired. The center joint must be supported by a midship or center bearing.

Some luxury cars use constant velocity universal joints exclusively. This is much more expensive, but it produces minimum noise and vibration. These premium qualities are demanded by the buyer of luxury vehicles, even at extra cost.

The cross and yoke universal joint requires a slip joint to allow for the effect of driving shaft length change as the rear axle housing moves up and down. The slip joint is located at the front joint of the rear propeller shaft section on either a one-piece or a two-piece shaft. In this location, it is less apt to be damaged by stones thrown from the road by the tires. Most slip joints are involuted or square tooth splines on the transmission output shaft. Matching splines are located on the inner section of the front universal joint yoke. Some luxury cars use a recirculating ball-type slip joint. This operates with minimum noise and friction, but is expensive.

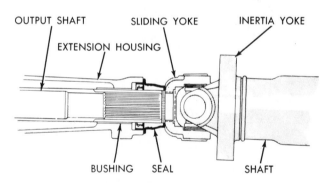

Fig. 23-7 Slip joint on the transmission output shaft (Chrysler-Plymouth Division, Chrysler Corporation).

Fig. 23-6 Double Cardan constant velocity universal joint.

378

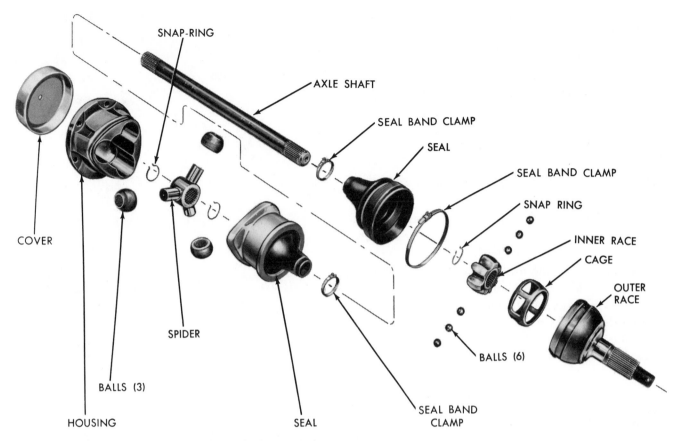

Fig. 23-8 Three ball and trunion type universal joints on the left and a Rzeppa universal joint on the right. (Cadillac Motor Car Division, General Motors Corporation).

The Bendix-Weiss universal joint is a constant velocity joint that also acts as a slip joint. It consists of two *spiders*, each having three or four arms. Each spider arm is located between the adjacent arms of the second spider. Motion of one set of spider arms is transferred to the other spider arms by steel balls wedged in grooves that are cut at an angle so the balls will always operate in a plane that bisects the joint's operating angle. Thus, it will operate as a constant velocity joint. Bendix-Weiss joints are usually used on front wheel drive vehicles, where steering is another universal joint requirement.

The ball and trunion joint allows axial movement within the joint so no separate slip joint is necessary. The balls are mounted on a spider through needle bearings. Each ball fits into a partly cylindrical housing bore that runs in the axial direction. This provides a means to drive through the joint in a radial direction and allows slip in the axial direction.

At one time a two-ball and trunion type was used. This type was replaced with the cross-and-

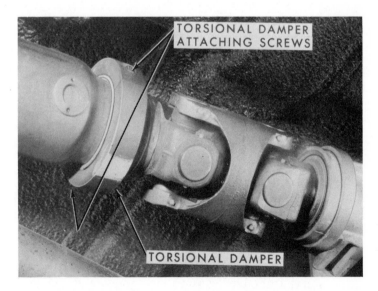

Fig. 23-9 Propeller shaft torsional damper (Cadillac Motor Car Division, General Motors Corporation).

yoke type joint because the cross-and-yoke joint transfers motion in the same way, is less expensive, and can operate through a greater joint angle.

379

A three-ball and trunion joint has been developed. The use of three equally spaced balls causes the joint to transfer constant velocity motion to the output shaft. This type of joint is an ideal joint for the inside joint on front wheel drive vehicles, because it eliminates the slip joint and transfers constant velocity motion.

Propeller shafts may use a heavy damper ring to reduce vibration. It may be located either adjacent to the front universal joint or adjacent to the rear universal joint. Some drive shafts also use an elastomer sleeve between an inner and outer drive shaft section. All torque in these shafts must be transmitted through the elastomer sleeve, thus effectively isolating the running gear vibration from the transmission.

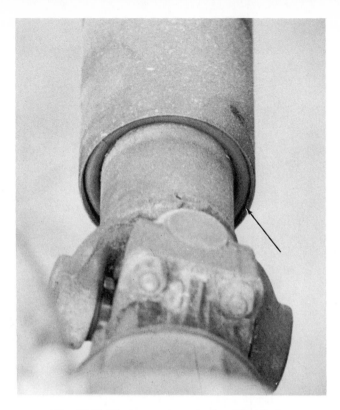

Fig. 23-10 Elastomer sleeve in the drive shaft.

23-2 PROPELLER SHAFT SERVICE

Propeller shaft problems usually show up as noise and vibration. These may result from incorrect universal joint angles, from unbalanced parts, or from loose and worn parts.

When the drive line is suspected as being the source of vibration, it should be given a good visual inspection to check the physical appearance of the propeller shaft. Problems may appear as loose universal joint parts, a damaged propeller shaft tube, or material such as undercoating stuck to the tube to cause unbalance.

After the visual inspection, universal joint angles should be checked. Special alignment checking fixtures are available as special tools for each corporation's vehicles. They use spirit levels and plumb bobs with protractors to check the joint working angles. When checking the joint angles, the vehicle must be level and resting on its axles. The front joint angle is changed by adding or removing shims from the transmission mount and the rear joint angle is changed by installing taper shims on leaf spring systems or by changing the suspension linkages on coil spring systems.

Propeller shaft run-out should also be checked. Run-out adjacent to the universal joint will give no problem if it is less than .010″; while .015″ run-out

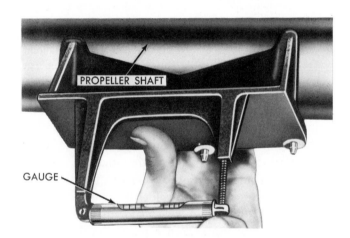

Fig. 23-11 Typical means of checking propeller shaft alignment (Chrysler Motors Corporation).

in the middle of the shaft will not produce noticeable vibration. A bent shaft is generally the result of an accident. It is usually expensive but more satisfactory to replace a bent propeller shaft than it is to try to straighten it.

Shaft unbalance causes drive line vibration. Unbalance can usually be corrected by properly positioning two worm type Wittek hose clamps adjacent to the welded balance weight at the rear of the propeller shaft. The vehicle is put on a hoist with the rear wheels removed and the lug nuts installed upside down to hold the drum in place. The drive line is run up to 60 miles per hour and vibration speed noted. (Extended operation in this manner will cause engine overheating). With the drive line turning, gradually move a chalk or crayon toward the shaft near the rear universal joint until it just touches at the high point, then quickly remove it. This effectively marks the shaft heavy spot. The shaft is then marked at each 90° adjacent to the rear universal joint. The clamps are positioned with their tightening screws together opposite the heavy spot. The vehicle test is rerun and the vibration is again noted. The clamps are then slightly rotated in opposite directions by equal amounts and the test rerun to check vibration. When the point of least vibration is found, the wheels should be reinstalled and the car road tested.

If a strobe-type wheel balancer is available, it can be used to quickly balance the propeller shaft. The pick-up is located on the carrier nose as close to the universal joint as possible. The clamps should be adjusted until the shaft falls within the normal balancing range of the balancer pick-up.

The propeller shaft must be removed to service universal joints. Before removal, each part of the shaft and companion flange should be marked so it can be reassembled in the same position. Single-piece shaft removal is accomplished by removing the rear universal joint from the differential drive pinion companion flange, being careful to keep the bearings in place. This can be done by wrapping tape around the joint bearings. The front end is removed by sliding the shaft from the slip joint. The oil seal portion of the slip joint yoke should immediately be covered to avoid damage that could cause the transmission rear seal to leak. Two-piece shafts require removal of the center or midship bearing as well as the rear universal joint companion flange before the shaft can be removed from the front slip joint.

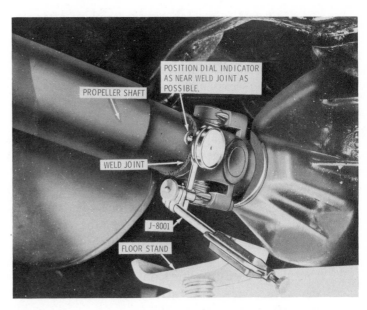

Fig. 23-12 Typical means of checking propeller shaft run out (Oldsmobile Division, General Motors Corporation).

Fig. 23-13 Wittek clamps used to balance a propeller shaft.

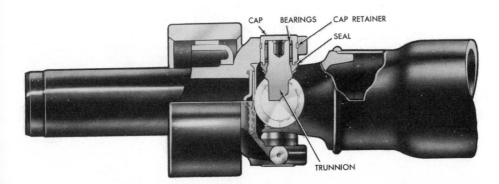

Fig. 23-14 Section view of a front Cardan universal joint showing a torsional damper ring and injected nylon ring cap retainers (Chevrolet Motor Division, General Motors Corporation).

381

Universal joints can be disassembled after the shaft is on the bench. Each manufacturer has his own special tools to speed disassembly and reassembly while avoiding damage. The basic disassembly and reassembly procedures are the same, however. Disassembly is accomplished by first removing the bearing cap retaining clips. Some original equipment joint bearing caps are held in place by an injected nylon ring. These nylon rings sheer during disassembly and are replaced with a clip type retainer. The yoke is supported around the lower bearing cap as the cross or spider is pushed down to force the lower cap from the yoke. The yoke is turned 180° to force the opposite cap from the yoke. With both bearing caps removed, the spider can be easily lifted out. Disassembled bearing caps, seals, and spacers are discarded and replaced with new parts.

Fig. 23-15 One type of tool used to disassemble a universal joint (Buick Motor Division, General Motors Corporation).

A universal joint repair kit contains new bearing cups with needle bearings, new spacers, new seals, and new retainer clips. Some kits also contain a new spider. Assembly of the joint requires

care to keep the parts in alignment so the needle rollers stay in place and no binding occurs.

The cups are filled with specified grease, usually a number 2 consistency. The spider is placed in the yoke and allowed to extend through one opening. Spacers and seals are placed on the extended spider arm. These are followed by the bearing cup. It is then pressed into the yoke. The spider is carefully moved toward the other yoke opening where the second spacer, seals, and bearing cup are installed and pressed into the yoke. Clip retainers are installed and the yoke tapped to seat the retainer clips. Each yoke section is assembled in this same manner, taking care to assemble the parts in the correct order.

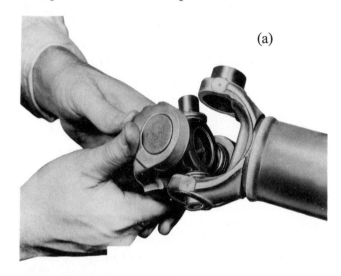

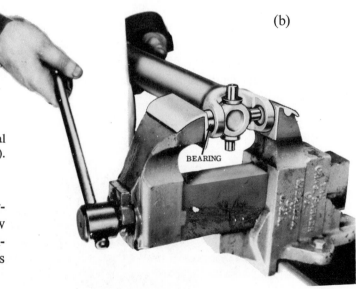

Fig. 23-16 Technique used to disassemble and reassemble a Cardan joint. (a) Removing and replacing the spider (Oldsmobile Division, General Motors Corporation), (b) pressing the bearings in the yoke (Oldsmobile Division, General Motors Corporation).

If binding occurs, it may be that a needle roller has fallen to the bottom of the cap. The cap will have to be removed to check and realign the roller.

Constant velocity universal joints are disassembled in the same manner. They also have a ball stud in the center of the joint which must be carefully disassembled and reassembled.

Two-piece propeller shafts have a slip joint just ahead of the center constant velocity joint. This slip joint is held together with a lock nut. After the shaft is on the bench, the lock nut is removed to separate the shaft in two sections. It is assembled in the reverse manner.

Center or midship bearings with their supports are usually replaced as an assembly. The assembly contains both the bearing and the insulating rubber mount. To replace this assembly, the propeller shaft will generally have to be removed from the vehicle and the two propeller shaft sections separated.

After the shaft is reassembled and installed, the universal joint angles should be rechecked for correct alignment.

23-3 REAR AXLE REQUIREMENTS

The rear axle portion of the final drive includes the differential assembly, the rear axles, and their housing. Power comes through the propeller shaft to the differential drive pinion. The pinion mates with the ring gear to change the drive rotation and torque angle 90° from the propeller shaft toward the wheels. While doing this, it provides a final speed reduction. Torque is split by the differential gears, equal torque going on each wheel in a standard differential. Drive axles carry power from the differential to the drive wheels. The axle housing supports the vehicle on axle bearings, provides reaction for driving and braking torque, and resists side loads.

Drive Pinion and Ring Gear. The side of the pinion gear meshes with teeth on the face of the ring gear to provide the final gear reduction and change the drive line rotation 90°. Modern vehicles use the *hypoid type* of gear mesh. The term hypoid is a contraction of the name of a geometrical figure called a hyperboloid of revolution. In this design, the gears have a constant velocity ratio, even though the drive pinion and ring gear axis are non-intersect-

Fig. 23-17 Lock nut holding the slip joint at the center bearing of a two-piece propeller shaft.

ing and perpendicular to each other. The pinion axis is located well below the ring gear axis. The teeth slide into mesh with at least two pair of teeth in contact at all times. This provides quiet operation and high torque carrying capacity. The low axis of the pinion allows the vehicle to have a low floor pan and propeller shaft clearance tunnel.

Drive pinion and ring gear size is largely determined by the maximum torque to be transmitted.

Fig. 23-18 Matching ring and pinion gear.

Larger sizes are required for greater torque. The gear reduction ratio is not dependent on torque capacity, but is determined by the number of teeth in the pinion and ring gears. Reduction ratio can be calculated by the formula:

$$\text{Gear ratio} = \frac{\text{Number of teeth on the ring gear (output)}}{\text{Number of teeth on the drive pinion gear (input)}}$$

For example, the reduction ratio of a differential with 47 teeth on the ring gear and 16 teeth on the drive pinion would be 2.94:1 (47/16). Passenger car rear axle ratios run from approximately 2.5:1 to 4.25:1. Lower numerical ratios help economy while high numerical ratios help torque. The ratio used for any specific vehicle is a trade-off between economy and power to provide the required vehicle performance.

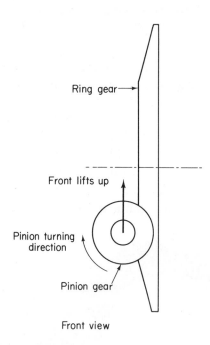

Fig. 23-19 Torque effect of the rotating pinion against a loaded ring gear.

In operation, the ring gear is mechanically connected to the drive wheels. When the vehicle is to be accelerated, the drive pinion forces the ring gear to turn forward. In doing this on rear axle type drives, the pinion tends to climb up the front of the ring gear, raising the carrier nose. Front wheel type drives would tend to move the carrier nose downward because the pinion is located behind the ring gear. Acceleration in reverse gear would cause the opposite effect. Control of carrier nose raising or lowering is accomplished by leaf springs, links, or arms. It is limited by a bumper. In independent drive suspensions, the drive torque is taken by the differential housing mount on the chassis.

Fig. 23-20 Bumper located to contact the carrier hose.

Differential. A solid connection between standard passenger car drive wheels is not desirable because the wheels seldom turn at the same speed. This difference in wheel speeds results from bumps and dips in the road surface, from slightly different tire sizes, and from different turning radii for each wheel which causes the outside wheel to turn faster than the inside wheel.

Fig. 23-21 Differential pinion gears on a differential pinion shaft.

A spur bevel side gear is splined to the inboard end of each rear axle. The teeth of at least two differential pinion gears engage these axle side gears. The differential *case* encloses the gears and supports the side gears in plain bearings. The differential pinion gears are supported and turn freely on a differential pinion shaft between the side gears. Because of this arrangement, the side gears balance on each side of the differential pinion gears. The force or torque on one axle equals the torque on the other axle.

Fig. 23-23 Differential and side gears mounted in a case. The ring gear is attached to the case and meshes with the drive pinion.

Fig. 23-22 Differential pinion gears assembled with two side gears.

Fig. 23-24 Section view of a typical unitized carrier rear axle assembly (Oldsmobile Division, General Motors Corporation).

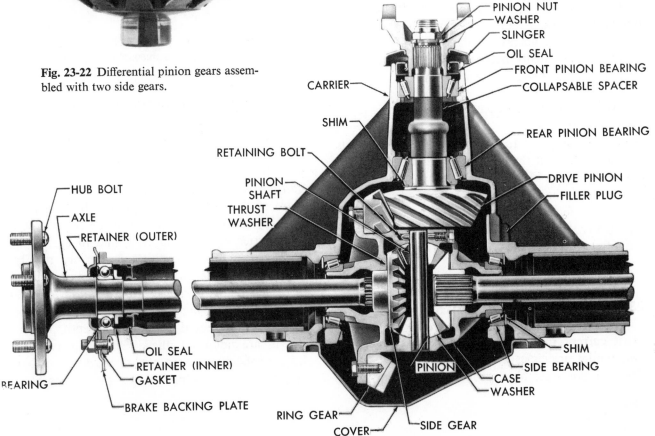

In operation, the ring gear is attached to the differential case so the case and ring gear rotate together. Because the differential pinion shaft is mounted in the case, it turns end-for-end with the case carrying the differential pinion gears around with it. The differential pinion gears, being in mesh with the axle mounted side gears, turn the axles at ring gear speed.

The differential acts as an averaging device. The case rotating speed is always equal to one half the sum of the axle speeds.

$$\text{Case speed} = \frac{\text{Right axle speed} + \text{Left axle speed}}{2}$$

For example, while making a right turn the right axle on the inside of the turn rotates 9 times and the left axle on the outside of the turn rotates 11 times. The differential case would rotate 10 times.

$$\text{Case speed} = \frac{9 + 11}{2} = 10$$

The differential also acts as a torque divider. Since the differential pinions are free to turn on their shaft, they cannot apply more force to the teeth on one side gear than they can to the other side gear. They, therefore, act as a balance by dividing the input torque equally between the axle side gears, even when their speeds are different.

Drive Axle. Current passenger cars use a semi-floating drive axle. The axle transmits driving torque from the side gears to the wheel. It also supports the vehicle weight through a bearing located at the outer end of the axle housing. The wheel mounting is overhung; that is, it is mounted outside the bearing. The outer end of the axle is subjected to bending loads from road shock and from vehicle centrifugal loads as the vehicle goes around a curve.

23-4 DIFFERENTIAL DESIGN FEATURES

Most current passenger cars use rear end drives. Differential principles are the same in all of them. The rear axle assemblies are made in different ways,

depending upon cost, torque requirements and engineering preference.

The differential drive's pinion and ring gears are fit and lapped together as a pair when they are manufactured so they will operate quietly. When installed in the carrier, they must be aligned in exactly the same relationship they had when they were lapped to provide quiet operation in the vehicle. Alignment is maintained by preloading the bearings so the parts cannot move out of their set position. Preloading involves adjusting the bearings so they have no clearance, then tightening an additional specified amount.

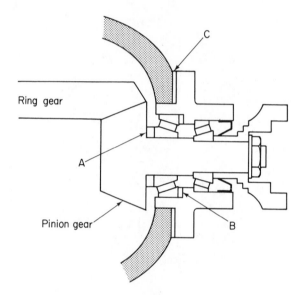

Fig. 23-25 Differential pinion composite illustration of alternate pinion depth adjustment shims.

Drive Pinion Features. The drive pinion is mounted in bearings within the carrier. The bearings are taper roller bearings with the large end of the taper toward the pinion's ends. Bearing cups are mounted in carrier bearing bores. *Pinion depth position* is adjusted by placing or removing shims between the pinion gear and rear bearing on one type, by placing shims between the pinion retainer and carrier in a second type, and in a third type, by placing shims between the carrier and rear bearing cup. Pinion setting may be marked on the pinion gear to show its correct setting depth. These marks used with special gauging tools can speed the process of setting differential drive pinion depth. When the gauges are not used, the differential may have to be assembled, checked and then disassembled to change shims to adjust proper pinion depth.

Drive pinion *bearing preload* is set in two ways. One method uses a heavy walled spacer with shims installed between the bearings. A variation of this method uses shims between the front bearing and a shoulder on the pinion shaft. Preload is set by adding or removing shims to change the effective spacing between the bearings when the pinion drive flange, or companion flange, nut is tightened to the correct torque. Preload is measured by checking pinion turning torque with an inch pound torque wrench. If the torque is too high, shims must be added. If the torque is too low, shims must be removed. The second and most popular type uses a thin wall crushable sleeve. The companion flange nut is tightened until the proper pinion turning torque is secured. The crushable sleeve keeps the front inner bearing race from turning on the pinion shaft. New crushable sleeves, sometimes called collapsible spacers, should be used each time the pinion is removed.

The drive pinion just described is a standard duty overhung drive pinion. Both bearings are on one side of the gear. Heavy duty drive pinions are straddle mounted. They have a third supporting bearing, called a pilot bearing, on the other side of the pinion gear. This reduces distortion under heavy torque loads.

Carrier bearings are lubricated by ring gear throw off. The ring gear picks up oil as it passes through the oil in the bottom of the housing. Oil is carried up and thrown forward. A cored or drilled passage in the upper carrier directs oil to pinion bearings. Oil return passages may also be provided in the carrier.

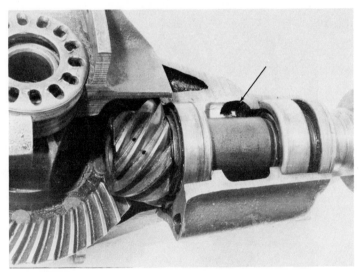

Fig. 23-27 Front bearing cast oil feed and return passages.

An axle housing breather is required to allow air to flow into and out of the housing as barometric pressures and axle temperatures change, to keep pressure equal on both sides of oil seals.

Carrier Features. The carrier supports the pinion and differential case. It is a one-piece unit cast from malleable cast iron, which is then machined. This type of construction keeps the drive pinion and ring gear in perfect alignment after they have been set. It will usually have stiffening ribs to increase its strength while still keeping it as light as possible.

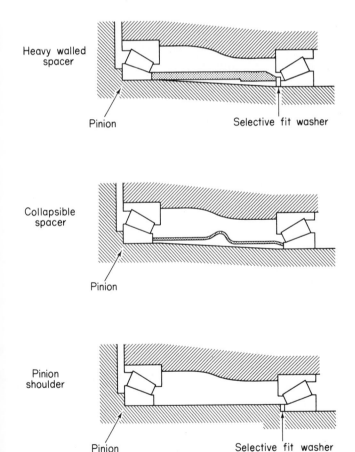

Fig. 23-26 Three types of drive pinion bearing preload adjustment methods.

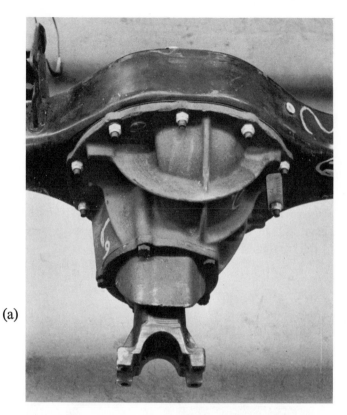

(a)

Fig. 23-28 Carrier types. (a) Separable carrier type, (b) unitized carrier type.

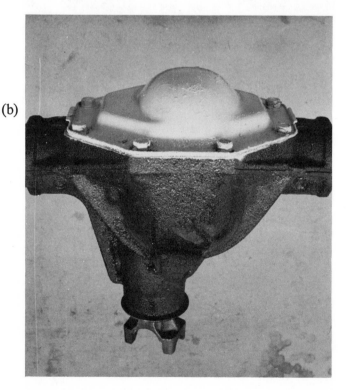

(b)

The carrier may be designed to be removed from the axle housing. When it is, the housing is often called a banjo-type housing. The SAE handbook calls it a *separable carrier* housing. If the carrier has permanent housing tubes pressed and welded in its side, it may be called a *carrier-tube* or *Salisbury-type* housing. The SAE nomenclature is a *unitized carrier* housing. Access to the differential in the unitized carrier housing is provided through a rear stamped cover. The majority of passenger cars use a unitized carrier type housing.

Tapered roller bearings, called *differential side bearings*, support the case within the carrier housing. The small end of the bearing is pointed toward the wheels. The outer bearing cup is held to the carrier bearing saddle with a bearing cap. Positioning the case in its bearing also positions the ring gear, because the ring gear is attached to the case. Ring gear position and differential side gear preload are adjusted with adjusting nuts in some carriers and in others, they are adjusted with shims.

Axle Shaft Features. Axle shafts are hot forged or extruded steel. When used, integral flanges are impact extruded on one end. After machining, they are induction hardened and shot blasted for fatigue strength. Finally, they are finished by grinding to size.

The brake drum or rotor is attached to the outer end of the axle shaft. The axle end may have a tapered end or a flange end. The flange end type is the most popular.

The outer axle bearing is located just inside the taper or flange. The bearing may be a ball bearing, a roller bearing, or a taper roller bearing. Some manufacturers use different types in different size axles.

Rear axle bearings must carry the vehicle weight which gives the bearing a radial load. It must also absorb vehicle cornering loads. These loads are called thrust loads.

Sealed and grease lubricated radial ball bearings are the most common type of rear axle bearings. They are quick and easy to assemble, needing no freeplay adjustment. They are, however, subject to early fatigue so their useful life is somewhat shorter than the other types. Differential oil lubricated straight roller bearings may roll directly on a ground surface of the axle shaft or have an inner race. This provides an inexpensive, compact bearing that

(a)

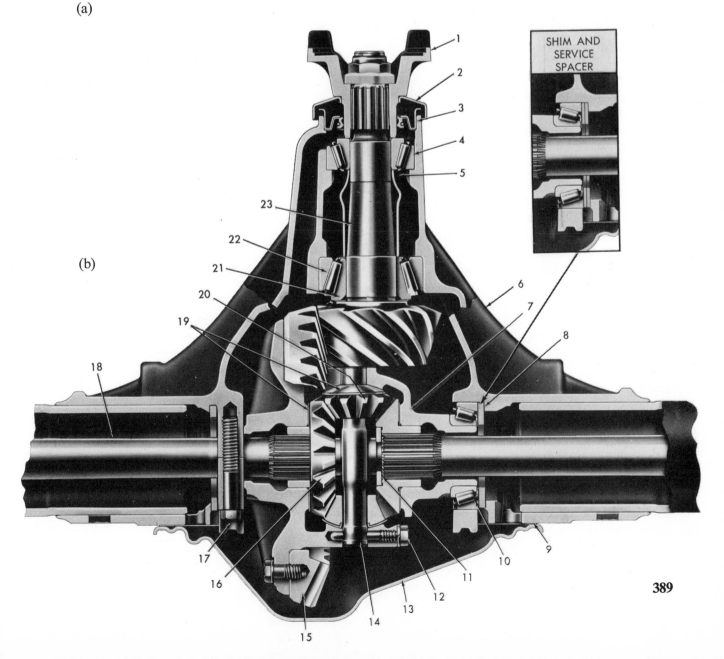

(b)

Fig. 23-29 Differential side bearing adjustment. (a) Adjuster nut type (Cadillac Motor Car Division, General Motors Corporation), (b) shim and spacer adjust (Number 8) and "C" washer axle retainer (Number 11) (Chevrolet Motor Division, General Motors Corporation).

389

is easy to assemble. Thrust loads must, however, be absorbed by the differential gears and differential pinion shaft which may cause deflecting problems. Taper roller bearings have a longer life than other types, but they are more complicated to assemble and adjust, especially when used with a flanged axle shaft.

Taper-type axle shafts usually use a taper roller bearing. The bearing cone is pressed against a shoulder on the shaft, with its small end outward. When being assembled, the axle shaft with the bearing is installed, followed by a retainer. Shims and gaskets between the retainer and bearings are used to provide correct taper roller bearing freeplay. A single unit hub and brake drum or only a hub flange may be installed on the taper shaft of the axle. A shaft key keeps the shaft from turning in the hub.

Most flange-type axles have their bearings pressed on from the inner end. The retainer is placed over the axle and is followed by the bearing. Bearings used with the flange axle may be ball, roller or taper. A collar is pressed on after the ball or taper bearing to absorb axle end thrust. The retainer is bolted to the axle housing to hold the bearing and axle in place. When taper roller bearings are used with flange shafts, one retainer may be provided with an adjusting nut for adjusting freeplay. Other axles use shims between the retainer and axle housing for freeplay adjustment. Ball bearings have built-in freeplay so they require no adjustment. Roller bearings do not absorb shaft end thrust. Shaft end thrust of axles using roller bearings without inner races is absorbed at the inner end of the axle shaft with a C washer retainer that keeps the axle from coming out of the housing. It is kept from going inward when it contacts the differential pinion shaft or a spacer block on the pinion shaft, as shown in Figure 23-29b.

Bearing retainers contain an oil seal to keep grease and oil from getting into the brake. In some units, the outer oil seal is mounted in the housing. In others, the seal is located in the retainer. Bearings that are grease lubricated have an inner seal as well as an outer seal to keep the differential oil separate from the wheel bearing grease. The inner seal is

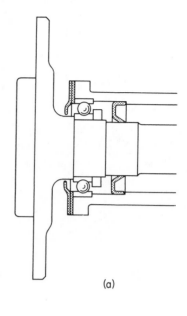

(a)

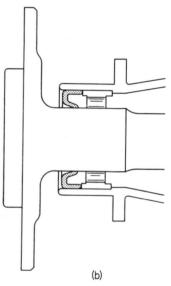

(b)

Fig. 23-30 Rear axle bearing types. (a) Ball bearings, (b) roller bearings, (c) taper roller bearings.

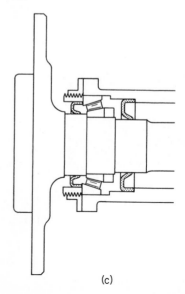

(c)

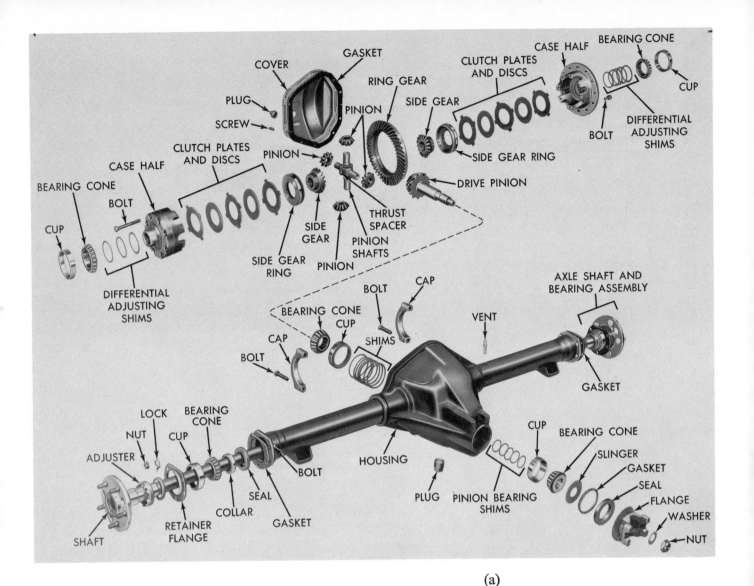

(a)

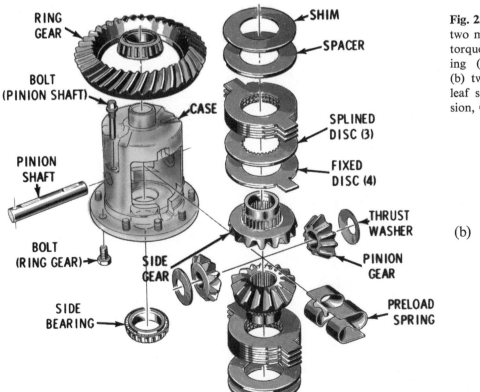

Fig. 23-31 Limited slip differential. (a) two multiple disc clutches operated by torque differences in a unitized housing (Chrysler Motors Corporation), (b) two multiple disc clutches with a leaf spring preload (Oldsmobile Division, General Motors Corporation).

(b)

391

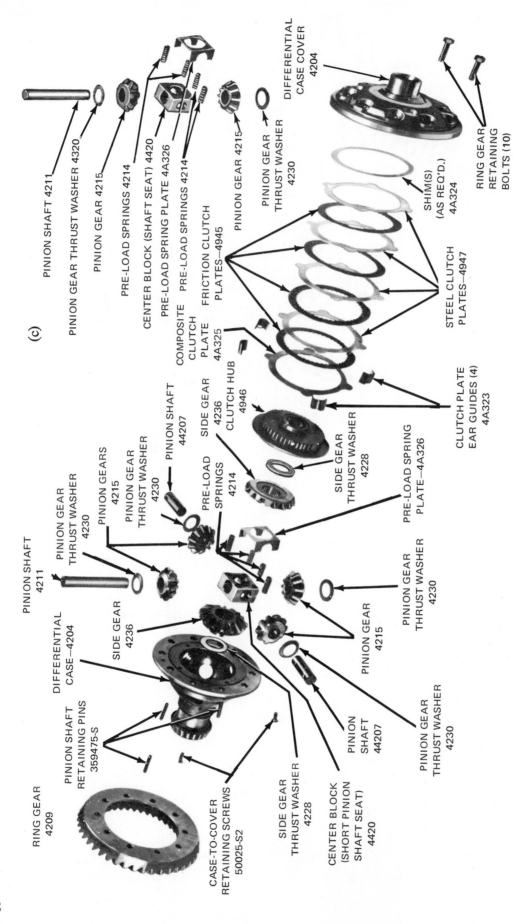

RING GEAR 4209

DIFFERENTIAL CASE—4204

SIDE GEAR 4236

PINION SHAFT 4211

PINION GEAR THRUST WASHER 4230

PINION GEARS 4215

PINION GEAR THRUST WASHER 4230

PINION SHAFT 44207

SIDE GEAR 4236

CLUTCH HUB 4946

PRE-LOAD SPRINGS 4214

PINION SHAFT RETAINING PINS 359475-S

CASE-TO-COVER RETAINING SCREWS 50025-S2

SIDE GEAR THRUST WASHER 4228

CENTER BLOCK (SHORT PINION SHAFT SEAT) 4420

PINION SHAFT 44207

PINION GEAR 4215

PINION GEAR THRUST WASHER 4230

PINION GEAR THRUST WASHER 4230

PRE-LOAD SPRING PLATE—4A326

SIDE GEAR THRUST WASHER 4228

CLUTCH PLATE EAR GUIDES (4) 4A323

COMPOSITE CLUTCH PLATE 4A325

FRICTION CLUTCH PLATES—4945

STEEL CLUTCH PLATES—4947

SHIM(S) (AS REQ'D.) 4A324

RING GEAR RETAINING BOLTS (10)

DIFFERENTIAL CASE COVER 4204

(c)

PINION SHAFT 4211

PINION GEAR THRUST WASHER 4320

PINION GEAR 4215

PRE-LOAD SPRINGS 4214

CENTER BLOCK (SHAFT SEAT) 4420

PRE-LOAD SPRING PLATE 4A326

PRE-LOAD SPRINGS 4214

PINION GEAR 4215

PINION GEAR THRUST WASHER 4230

Fig. 23-31(c) one multiple disc clutch with coil preload springs (Ford Division, Ford Marketing Corporation).

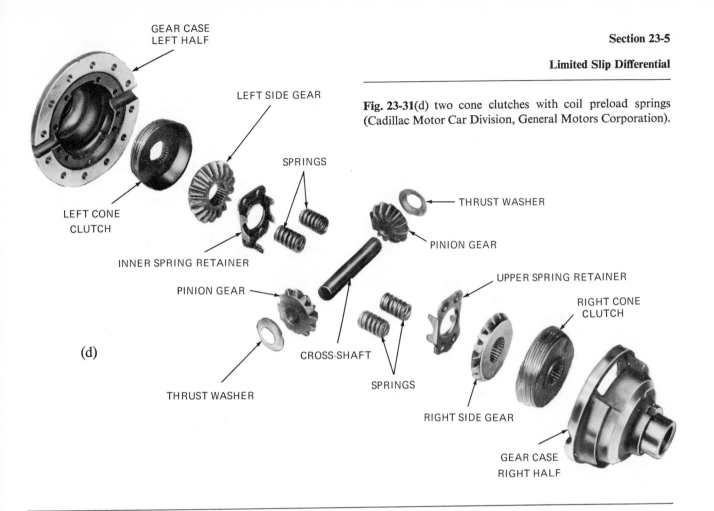

GEAR CASE
LEFT HALF

LEFT SIDE GEAR

SPRINGS

THRUST WASHER

PINION GEAR

LEFT CONE
CLUTCH

INNER SPRING RETAINER

PINION GEAR

UPPER SPRING RETAINER

RIGHT CONE
CLUTCH

(d)

CROSS-SHAFT

SPRINGS

THRUST WASHER

RIGHT SIDE GEAR

GEAR CASE
RIGHT HALF

Fig. 23-31(d) two cone clutches with coil preload springs (Cadillac Motor Car Division, General Motors Corporation).

pressed in the housing before the axle is installed. Axles using only an outer seal have the bearing lubricated with differential oil.

23-5 LIMITED SLIP DIFFERENTIAL

The torque equalizing feature of a standard differential does not adequately provide driving power when one or both drive wheels are on a slippery surface, during rapid acceleration, or when driving on rough roads. On slippery surfaces, driving torque to each wheel is no greater than the torque to the wheel with the smallest torque. On rough surfaces, the wheel would bounce free of the road and its speed would increase. When it lands on the road surface again, it will immediately have to reduce its speed to the vehicle speed. This gives the drive train a severe shock that could damage parts. Differentials have been designed to reduce or limit wheel slippage by transferring a portion of the unused

torque from the slipping wheel to the wheel with traction.

Input power comes through the pinion and ring gear to the differential case in the same manner as it does in a standard differential. The case carries the differential pinion shaft and pinions to apply torque to the side gears and axle shafts. Assume input torque remains constant when the right wheel loses traction as the vehicle starts to move. The left wheel with good traction will remain stationary holding the left side gear stationary. The differential gears will then rotate on their pinion shafts as they go around the stationary left side gear. They force the freely moving right side gear forward at twice the case speed. Loss of motion, then, occurs between the case and the free moving side gear. If these could be locked together, the wheel with traction would turn to move the vehicle.

Limited slip differentials operate on this principle. They have a clutch between the case and the

393

side gear. Clutch engagement limits movement between the case and side gear so both axles will turn with the case. The axle with traction is turned so the vehicle will move.

Two types of cluches are used in automotive limited slip differentials. One type uses a multiple disc clutch similar to the clutch plates used in automatic transmissions described in Chapter 22. Every other plate is attached to the axle shaft. The alternate plates are attached to the case. Limited slip differentials may have one large diameter clutch pack or two smaller diameter packs.

A second and more recent application uses a cone-type clutch between the case and axle shaft. A male cone connected to the axle shaft mates with a female cone in the case.

Limited slip differentials are applied by the difference in torque on the differential gears or by preload springs. Some units use both methods operating together.

Limited slip differentials using torque apply methods depend upon torque difference on each side of the differential pinion gears to cause them to bear against the side gears. This force pushes the clutch into contact, locking the axle shafts to the case, limiting slippage.

Differential clutches may be under constant spring load. Load will be limited up to the clutch capacity under any driving conditions. A Belleville-type spring is used to provide clutch loading in the constant load type.

The majority of limited slip differentials are provided with a light preload spring that statically loads the clutch. This provides limited slip traction under light tractive loads and provides a smooth transition between limiting the slippage and tractive load operation. Preload springs may be a set of coil springs, a Belleville spring or a leaf-type spring. Differential clutches of the type described will slip if overloaded, to prevent damage from high loads.

Limited slip torque transfers occur any time one wheel rotates faster than the other wheel, even in a turn. In the turn, the outside wheel must rotate faster than the inner wheel so the slip limiting characteristic transfers slightly more torque to the wheel on the inside of the turn.

23-6 REAR AXLE SERVICE

Rear axles seldom cause a problem when used in standard passenger car service. Abnormal noise or fluid leaks are usually the first signs that a problem is occurring. Problems result from damaged oil seals, bearing failure, and gear tooth wear. Limited slip differentials may also have clutch apply problems.

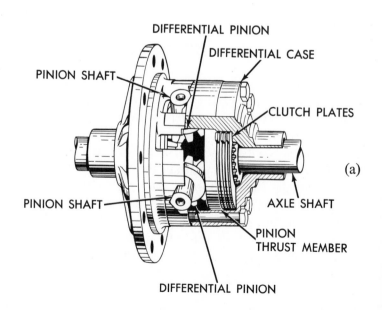

(a)

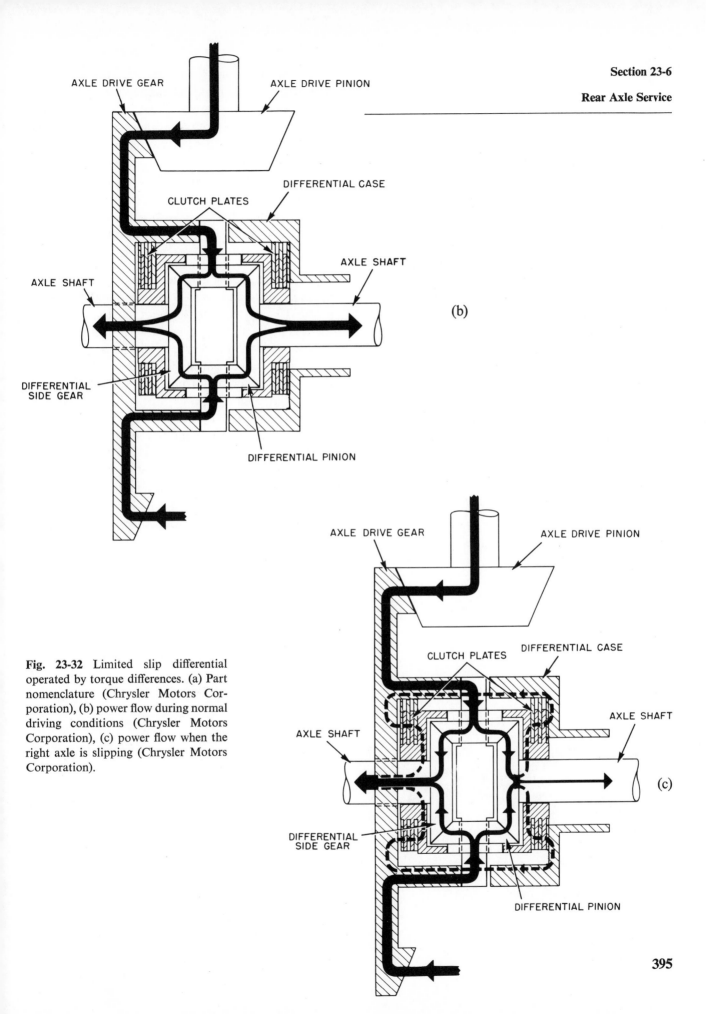

Fig. 23-32 Limited slip differential operated by torque differences. (a) Part nomenclature (Chrysler Motors Corporation), (b) power flow during normal driving conditions (Chrysler Motors Corporation), (c) power flow when the right axle is slipping (Chrysler Motors Corporation).

Seals. Drive pinion oil seals leak at the carrier nose. This seal can usually be replaced by removing the propeller shaft rear universal joint from the drive pinion companion flange after marking the nut and flange position in relation to the pinion shaft. The companion flange is removed to expose the seal. Correct seal removing and installing tools should be used to avoid damaging the seal or sealing surfaces. The parts are replaced in the reverse order, being careful to realign the marks.

Axle oil seal leakage usually allows differential oil to get into the brake, coating the brake lining with oil. A slight amount of oil will cause the brake to grab. Excess oil on the lining will cause the brake to slip. Usually, oil soaked brake linings must be replaced, as well as the axle oil seal.

The axle must be removed to replace the axle oil seal. The retainer used with ball and tapered roller bearings is bolted to the axle housing end flange so it can be removed when the brake drum has been taken off. The axle can then be carefully pulled from the housing. A puller might be necessary to slide the outer bearing race from the housing.

After the axle has been removed, the inner axle seal may be easily removed and replaced with proper tools. Outer seal replacement on flange shafts requires bearing removal. This usually damages the bearing so that a new bearing is also required.

Axles with roller bearings are removed by draining the axle oil and removing the rear cover. The differential gear pinion is removed so the axles can be pushed slightly inward to allow the C locks to be removed. Axles can then be pulled from the housing.

Bearings. Bearing failure usually shows up by a rumbling sound that is proportional to vehicle speed. The sound often becomes more distinct when the vehicle is turning a corner in a direction that puts a load on the bearing. This is especially true with taper roller bearings. In these, axle shaft end thrust is transferred through a thrust block on the differential pinion shaft between the two axles, so the thrust is taken by the bearing on the inside of the turn. This can be readily seen if one examines illustrations of the bearing installation method. Each ball bearing absorbs thrust in both directions so a thrust block is not required in axles using them.

Axle shafts using integral inner race roller bearings, taper roller bearings or ball bearings are pressed

Fig. 23-33 Installation of taper roller bearings on flanged axle shafts in a separable axle housing (Chrysler Motors Corporation).

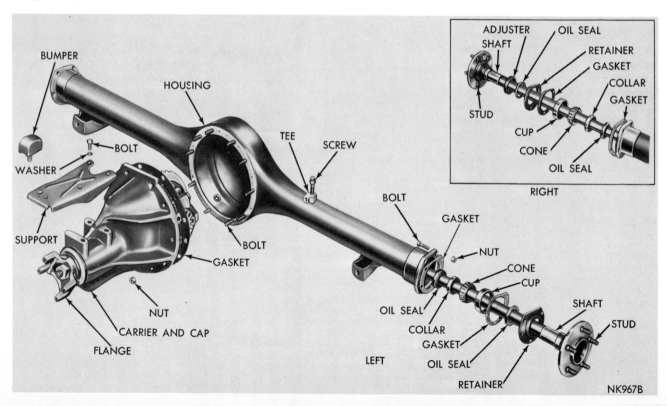

Fig. 23-34 Method used to remove the bearing retainer collar (Chrysler Motors Corporation).

Fig. 23-35 Measuring axle shaft end play.

onto the axle shaft. Special puller attachments are therefore used to remove them. The bearing retainer collar is removed first by partially cutting the collar with a chisel at 90° intervals or by drilling partly through it. This expands the collar so it can be removed easily. Some bearings have to be broken apart in order to attach pullers that will remove the inner race. While removing bearings, it is important to protect the oil seal surfaces on the axle shaft to prevent damage that could cause an oil leak.

After putting a new outer seal in the bearing retainer, the new well-lubricated bearing and bearing retainer collar are pressed on the axle shaft. They must be firmly seated against the axle shoulder so that end play can be properly adjusted.

With new seals in the housing, the axles are carefully installed through the inner oil seal and slipped into the side gear splines. When required, axle end play is adjusted with shims or adjusting nuts. A dial gauge is usually used to measure the end play.

Differential Assembly. Ring and pinion gear problems are usually evidenced by a whine under both power and coast. Driving at the float point, under neither power nor coast, is usually quiet. Noise occurring only during a turn indicates a problem between the differential and side gears. In most cases, to correct abnormal differential noise, the differential must be disassembled.

Disassembly starts by draining the differential

oil and removing axles as previously discussed. The differential carrier can then be removed from separable carrier type housings. Access to the carrier in a unitized carrier type housing that is integral with the housing is through the rear cover.

Case bearing looseness, ring gear run-out and backlash, and obvious tooth wear are checked before removing the case from the housing. This check will be of help in determining the specific cause of any differential noise.

Differential carrier side bearing caps and adjusting nuts are punch marked to assure reassembly in their same position. Adjusting nuts are loosened, when used, and the bearing caps are removed to free the case. If case adjustment is with shims, the housing must be slightly spread to release the case. This usually requires a special spreading tool. The case should be lifted from the carrier and examined for obvious defects.

Fig. 23-36 Spreading unitized axle housing to remove differential case.

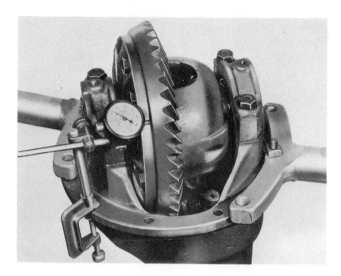

Fig. 23-37 Measuring ring gear run out (Chrysler-Plymouth Division, Chrysler Corporation).

The pinion nut is removed by holding the rear universal companion flange while loosening the drive pinion nut. The drive pinion can then be pushed out of the front bearing. Further disassembly can be accomplished by removing the ring gear, differential gears and side gears.

An inspection of the parts should show evidence of the noise problem. Only bearings that show signs of abnormal wear need to be removed for replacement. Here again, special pullers are used to protect the pinion and case.

Before assembly, parts are thoroughly cleaned. As they are assembled, they are coated with differential oil. The side gears, differential gears and ring gear are installed on the case. Bolts should be torqued to the correct specification to prevent warping the parts. Ring gear run-out must be within limits. The drive pinion is installed without an oil seal until correct pinion depth is established.

Pinion depth can be established with special tool gauges. These gauges differ greatly between manufacturers and between axle types. Service manuals give details that must be followed when using them. Setting pinion depth without special tools is a time-consuming assembly operation that

involves checking tooth contact pattern, removing to install corrective shims, then reinstalling and again checking tooth contact pattern. This has to be repeated until the correct tooth contact pattern is established.

Pinion depth can be increased by increasing shim thickness when shims are placed between the rear pinion bearing and the drive pinion gear or between the rear bearing outer race and carrier bore. On removable pinion retainer types, removing shims between the retainer and carrier will increase pinion depth.

Fig. 23-38 Checking ring gear backlash (Chrysler-Plymouth Division, Chrysler Corporation).

Pinion depth must be coordinated with ring gear backlash. Backlash is reduced by moving the ring gear closer to the drive pinion gear, and increased by moving it away from the pinion gear.

Tooth contact can be observed by coating the ring gear with red lead. Turning the ring gear with tension held against pinion turning will wipe the red lead so that the tooth contact pattern can be observed. Pinion bearing preload must be set when the proper tooth contact pattern is established. Pinions with a solid spacer plus shims between the bearings have their preload adjusted by removing shims to increase preload. Preload is checked with no oil seal, the case removed and the companion flange nut torqued. The drive pinion is then turned with an inch pound torque wrench. After shims are selected to provide the correct turning torque, the companion flange is again removed and a front oil seal is installed, the companion flange installed and the nut tightened to specified torque.

Preload on pinions using a compressed spacer between the bearings is adjusted by tightening the companion flange nut until the pinion turning torque is correct with the oil seal in place. New spacers are always used.

(c)

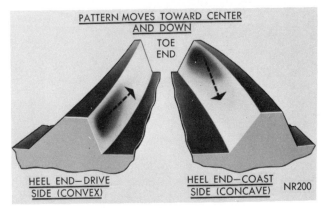

(d)

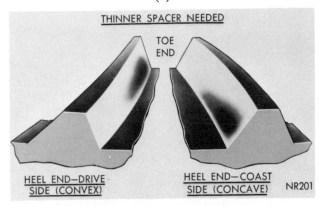

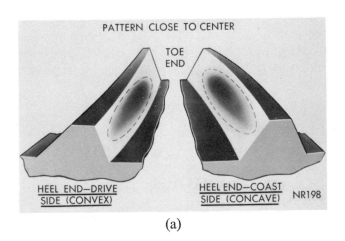

(a)

Fig. 23-39 Ring and pinion gear tooth pattern and corrections (Chrysler-Plymouth Division, Chrysler Corporation).

(b)

(e)

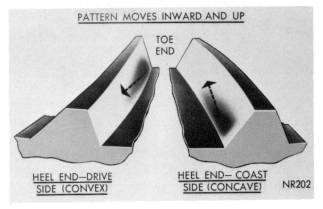

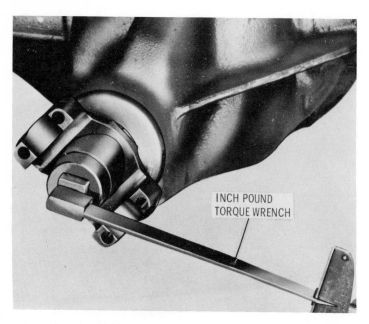

Fig. 23-40 Measuring pinion preload (Oldsmobile Division, General Motors Corporation).

Fig. 23-41 Measuring limited slip differential locking force.

Pinion preload is sufficient to eliminate any end play in the pinion shaft and still low enough to prevent bearing damage.

Differential side bearings must also be preloaded. This is done by tightening the adjusting nuts on the adjustable type or by installing the correct thickness shims in the shim adjust type.

After final adjustments are made, the ring and pinion tooth contact pattern should be rechecked to see that it is still correct. If it is not, it will be necessary to disassemble the entire assembly and install corrective spacers and shims.

When final adjustments are complete, the rear axle can be reassembled using new gaskets, then filled with new differential oil.

Limited slip differentials are adjusted in the same manner as standard differentials. The clutch will require additional service. It is working correctly when one wheel is blocked and the other wheel has a minimum turning torque, about 30 foot pounds.

Worn clutch disc and plates should be replaced. Wear may be determined by the space between the discs and plates measured with a feeler gauge blade. Weak or warped clutch springs should also be replaced. Some manufacturers of cone-type clutches recommend replacement of the cones and case as an assembly when they do not function properly.

Review Questions Chapter 23

1. How is driving and braking torque reaction absorbed by the chassis?

2. What determines propeller shaft minimum and maximum sizes?

3. What means are used to shorten the required propeller shaft length?

4. What is the purpose of front and of rear universal joints?

5. Describe the motion transfer through a cross and yoke universal joint operating at an angle.

6. Why does a double Cardan joint transfer uniform motion?

7. What methods are used to check universal joint working angles?

8. How are universal joint working angles adjusted?

9. Describe the procedures used to balance a propeller shaft on a vehicle.

10. Describe disassembly and reassembly of a cross and yoke universal joint.

11. What are the advantages of a hypoid-type ring and pinion gear?

12. What limits rear axle ratio extremes?

13. What causes the rear wheels to turn at different speeds?

14. What causes the carrier nose to raise on acceleration?

15. Describe differential action in a standard differential assembly.

16. Why does torque divide equally between the drive axles?

17. How is drive pinion depth and preload adjusted to specifications?

18. What is meant by overhung mounting when describing a bearing installation?

19. How are the drive pinion bearings lubricated?

20. How are banjo and Salisbury rear axle housings identified? What are their SAE names?

21. What loads are put on rear axle bearings?

22. What retains each axle, when using ball-type bearings, from sliding from the housing in a right turn?

23. What retains each axle, when using straight roller bearings, from sliding from the housing in a right turn?

24. What are the advantages and disadvantages of a limited slip differential?

25. Describe the principle that allows the limited slip differential to operate.

26. What forces are used to apply limited slip differential clutches?

27. What type of clutches are used in limited slip differentials?

28. What is the limited slip torque split between the inside and outside axle on a car while making a turn at low speed and at high speed?

29. Describe the methods used to remove rear axles.

30. What precautions should be taken when replacing axle bearings?

31. Describe differential carrier removal.

32. How can ring and pinion tooth contact pattern be changed?

33. Why is preload required?

Quiz 23

1. Propeller shafts for domestic automobiles use one, two, or three universal joints. At least two joints are required with a
   a. Torque tube type drive
   b. Hotchkiss type drive
   c. Cardan type drive
   d. Bendix-Weiss type drive.

2. The front universal joint is necessary to compensate for rear axle
   a. jounce and rebound
   b. housing twist
   c. torque absorption
   d. vibration insulation.

3. Some propeller shafts have a heavy ring installed near one end. This acts to
   a. improve inertia loads
   b. control velocity
   c. dampen whirl
   d. reduce vibration.

4. The mechanic can correct an unbalanced propeller shaft by
   a. bending
   b. adjusting the universal joints
   c. adding Wittek clamps
   d. repositioning the shaft angles.

5. Which of the following operating conditions makes the most use of a differential's operating characteristics?
   a. one wheel going over a bump
   b. acceleration at full throttle
   c. skidding on a turn
   d. crusing at turnpike speeds.

6. The differential gears
   a. split the torque equally to each drive wheel
   b. change the drive rotation 90°
   c. provide final speed reduction
   d. give the torque to each wheel.

7. Bearing preload is required in a rear axle assembly to
   a. provide maximum bearing and gear life
   b. maintain ring and pinion gear contact position
   c. minimize pinion gear backlash
   d. control ring gear run out.

8. Rear axle end play must be adjusted when the axle bearings are the
   a. ball type
   b. uncaged roller type
   c. caged roller type
   d. taper roller type.

9. Limited slip differential's have a clutch that lock
   a. the slipping axle
   b. the driving axle
   c. both axles to the case
   d. both axles to the housing.

10. Which of the following precautions should be observed when working on a limited slip differential?
    a. do not remove an axle until the differential cluth plates are released
    b. do not operate in gear with only one wheel jacked up
    c. do not take the "C" washer retainer from the differential until the clutch pressure is released
    d. do not allow oil to get on the clutch facings while assembling the differential.

chapter 24

Automotive Brake Systems

Automotive service brakes must be able to stop the car, prevent excess speed when coasting downhill and hold the vehicle in position when stopped on grades. They are designed so that braking effort can be changed and controlled by the driver to keep the vehicle under control.

To reduce the wheel's rotating speed and slow the automobile, the service brake has a friction lining which presses against a moving cast iron surface that rotates with the wheel. The lining force against the moving surface is controlled by the driver through the use of mechanical and hydraulic mechanisms. Friction of the sliding brake surfaces converts the moving energy of the automobile into heat energy, which is dissipated into the air surrounding the brake parts. Braking effort increases as the driver increases pressure to force the friction lining against the moving surface. Maximum braking effect occurs just before the wheel is stopped and the tire slides on the road. Maximum braking, therefore, depends upon good adhesion between the tire and the road surface. When the tire slides on the road, braking effort is reduced and vehicle directional control is lost.

24-1 BRAKE TYPES

Two types of mechanical devices are used in automotive service brakes. In one, a shoe with friction lining surface is expanded into the inside of a rotating drum. The other type of brake has friction pads that are pressed against each side of a rotating disc. The friction developed between the friction element and rotating element is converted to heat, which is concentrated primarily in the rotating element.

Drum Brakes. The major difference among the various drum designs is the shoe attachment or anchor location and the location of the actuating mechanism or *wheel cylinder*. The shoes are attached and supported by a backing plate which is, in turn, attached to the vehicle steering knuckle on the front brakes and to the axle housing on the rear brakes.

Location of the shoe anchor in relation to forward wheel rotation is used to describe the type of shoe and its parts. The anchor end of the brake shoe is called the *heel*. Actuating force is applied to the toe end of the shoe. When the brake drum rotates from the shoe toe and toward the shoe heel, it is called a *leading shoe*. If the rotation is from the heel toward the toe end of the shoe, it is called a *trailing shoe*. Brake assemblies have been designed to use both leading shoes, both trailing shoes, and one of each brake shoe type.

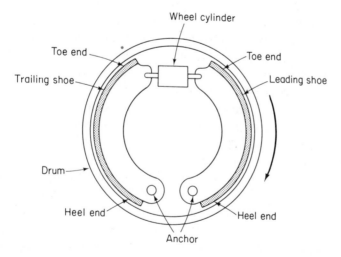

Fig. 24-1 Brake shoe type identification.

A leading shoe anchor allows the shoe to dig into the drum surface as it turns. This causes the shoe to *self-energize* and pull itself tighter into the drum, increasing friction and stopping the vehicle quicker with the same application effort. This action might be compared to a trailer that comes loose from a car and falls on its tongue. The tongue digs into the road surface rapidly stopping the loose trailer. This type of self-energizing action in brakes is called *servo action*.

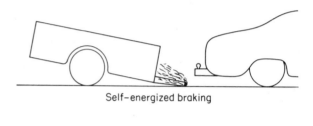

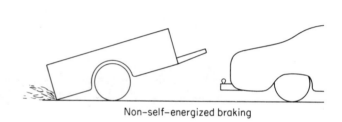

Fig. 24-2 Comparison of self-energizing and non self-energizing braking.

The trailing shoe with the drum turning away from the anchor does not self-energize. Action between the shoe and the drum tends to push the friction lining away. If the trailer, in the previous example, had fallen onto its back end with the tongue in the air, it would easily drag or bounce over bumps, stopping much more slowly. This action can be compared to the trailing brake shoe's non-servo action.

The drum brake on most modern automobiles uses a dual servo brake shoe arrangement with two forward acting shoes. One of these shoes is a *primary shoe* that transmits force to another shoe. The other shoe is a *secondary shoe* that receives force from the primary shoe. The primary shoe's heel end is attached through an adjustable link to the secondary shoe's toe end. The secondary shoe's heel fits against an anchor pin. In operation, the dual servo brake wheel cylinder actuates the brake by pushing the toe end of the primary shoe against the drum. The primary shoe has servo action because it is a self-energizing leading shoe. Its servo action pushes on the toe end of the secondary shoe with a force greater than that from the wheel cylinder alone. This, in turn, causes high self-energizing servo action of the secondary shoe. Dual servo action of both brake shoes may cause the secondary shoe to provide as much as 75% of the total braking effort. The dual servo brake was first patented by Bendix Corporation in 1928. They called it a Duo-Servo brake. The patents have expired and the basic Bendix design is now used almost exclusively for automobile drum brakes.

Disc Brakes. Disc brakes absorb vehicle energy with friction pads or shoes that are forced against a rotating disc. The shoes are held in a housing called a *caliper* that is supported on the steering knuckle or axle housing. The disc is attached to the wheel hub. Hydraulic pressure within the caliper cylinder pushes the shoe against the disc. Disc brakes have no servo action so they require 4 to 5 times more pressure than is required by the dual servo brake. Most American passenger cars, therefore use a power brake with disc brakes to provide this required extra pressure.

24-2 BRAKING REQUIREMENTS

The manufacturer's selection of the brake type is dependent upon the stopping force required, the kinds of friction material used, space available for the brakes, and the maximum driver effort desired.

It is desirable for a service technician to thoroughly understand brake system requirements to help him appreciate the physical demands on automobile brakes so that he will take proper care in making repairs. The brake requirements are more meaningful as a means of comparing automobile brake performance if the requirements are expressed in known values of time, pressure, distance, and energy. For this it is necessary to use several mathematical equations, just as the use of mathematical equations is needed when comparing engine performance. Mathematical expressions may be even more meaningful to a reader who wishes to build a modified vehicle to ensure satisfactory braking performance.

Horsepower is foot-pounds of work expended in a given period of time. The quicker a given number

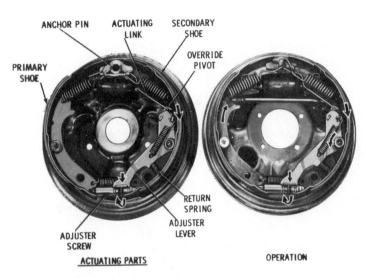

Fig. 24-3 Drum brake part nomenclature (Oldsmobile Division, General Motors Corporation).

of foot-pounds of work can be done, the more horsepower is produced. This holds true of both engines and brakes. A vehicle that could be accelerated from a dead start to 60 mph in nine seconds may be required to stop from 60 mph in three seconds. The brakes are required to absorb three times the amount of engine horsepower energy in its heat equivalent form. Brakes must be and are capable of decelerating a vehicle at a faster rate than the engine is able to accelerate it.

Kinetic Energy. Heat of combustion is conevrted into mechanical energy by the engine to drive the vehicle. One BTU per second will produce 1.44 hp. The more horsepower the engine is able to produce, the faster a car can be accelerated. With equal power, a lighter car can be accelerated faster than a heavy car. More horsepower is required to accelerate up to highway speeds than is required to maintain highway speed. Engine horsepower energy is converted to energy of motion, or *kinetic energy*, of the vehicle and is expressed in foot-pounds. Kinetic energy must be dissipated as heat by the brakes as the vehicle speed is reduced. This energy can be calculated using the following formula:

Vehicle Kinetic Energy $= .0334\,W\,[(V_1)^2 - (V_2)^2]$ ft-lb

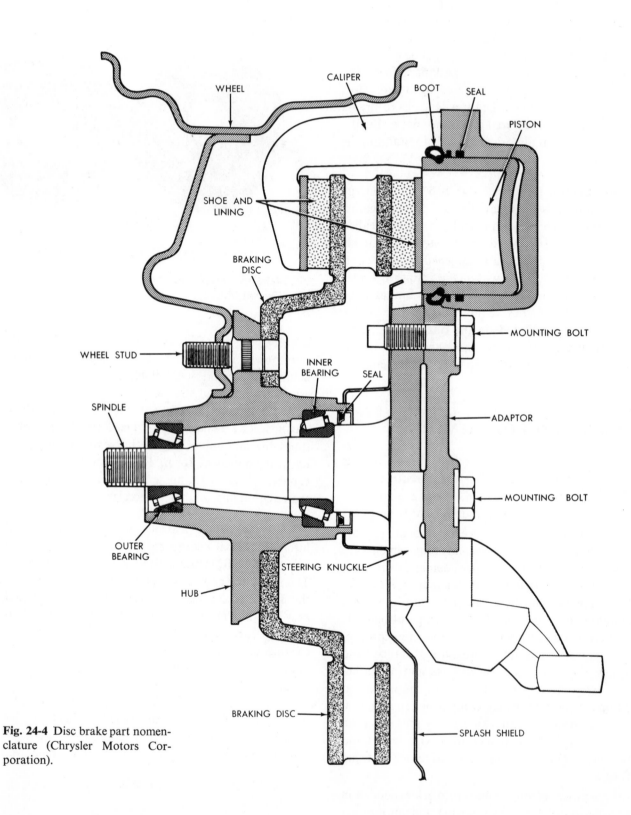

Fig. 24-4 Disc brake part nomenclature (Chrysler Motors Corporation).

Where: W = vehicle gross weight

        V_1 = initial velocity

        V_2 = terminal velocity

If a 4000 lb automobile (W) were brought from 60 mph (V_1) to a stop (V_2) the kinetic energy absorbed by the brakes would be 480,960 ft-lbs.

$$KE = .0334 \times 4000 (60^2 - 0^2) \text{ ft-lbs}$$
$$= .0334 \times 4000 \times 3600 = 480,960 \text{ ft-lbs}$$

Note that the kinetic energy doubles as the weight doubles, but it increases by four times as the speed is doubled.

Coefficient of Friction. Kinetic energy is the force that tends to keep the vehicle moving. Friction opposes this motion, consuming power and producing heat. Retarding friction can occur in the brakes or between a sliding tire and the road surface when the brakes lock wheel rotation. The vehicle's kinetic energy and its ability to stop is related to the coefficient of friction between the rubbing surfaces. The coefficient of friction is the force required to keep the vehicle moving at a constant velocity divided by the weight of the vehicle. Maximum usable coefficient of friction occurs between the tire and road surface, rather than at the brakes. The coefficient of friction, then, is dependent upon the type of materials that are sliding and not the weight. For example, if the weight of the vehicle is doubled, the force required to slide it is also doubled and the coefficient of friction remains the same. For dry concrete, the coefficient of friction is usually considered to be 0.6. Some specially compounded tires may have a coefficient of friction as high as 0.8 on dry concrete. If 600 lbs were required to keep a 1000-lb weight sliding on a one square inch surface at a constant speed, the coefficient of friction between these surfaces is 600/1000 or 0.6. This is the maximum available coefficient of friction under these conditions.

A free falling object accelerates at a rate of 32.2 feet per second per second (ft/sec^2). To stop at this same rate would require a coefficient of friction of 1.0. With a coefficient of friction of 0.6, the maximum braking deceleration without sliding the wheels is approximately 20 ft/sec^2 ($32.2 \times 0.6 = 19.3$). In actuality, this would be considered a panic stop. A 14 ft/sec^2 deceleration is a severe and un-

comfortable stopping rate. Under 8 ft/sec^2 is a comfortable stopping rate. Maximum deceleration rates for passenger cars run as high as 19 ft/sec^2.

The shoe force against the drum or disc replaces the vehicle weight when calculating brake coefficient of friction. Passenger car brakes have a 0.3 to 0.5 coefficient of friction. The amount of energy the brakes are able to absorb is dependent upon the coefficient of friction, their diameter, their surface area, shoe geometry, and the pressure used to actuate them. Stopping a car in a shorter period of time requires the vehicle motion energy to be converted into heat in a shorter period of time. This means that the total friction must be greater, resulting in high temperature.

Brake Balance. When the wheels are locked and skidding with the same tire and road conditions, the stopping distance is the same, regardless of the weight, number of wheels, or vehicle load. Maximum braking power occurs when the wheels are braked just below the locking point, or point of *impending skid*. Non-skid brake systems are designed to operate at or below this point.

Changes in load on a wheel will change the point of impending skid. The load changes can occur as the vehicle leans while rounding a curve and as a result of weight transfer between front and rear wheels during braking.

The effective braking force of a vehicle occurs at ground level. Vehicle weight and kinetic energy of the vehicle effectively act through the vehicle center of gravity that is above ground level. This causes the vehicle to tend to pitch forward as the brakes are applied. Pitching forward effectively transfers some of the vehicle weight from the rear wheels to the front wheels. The front brakes, therefore, must absorb more kinetic energy than the rear brakes. The maximum amount of weight transfer can be calculated by:

Weight transferred (lbs.)

$$= \frac{\text{Coefficient of friction} \times \text{Height of CG (inches)} \times \text{VGW*}}{\text{Wheel base (inches)}}$$

*Vehicle gross weight

407

This weight transfer is subtracted from the static weight on the rear wheels and added to the static weight of the front wheels. The front wheel static weight is normally 55% of the vehicle weight.

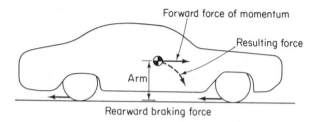

Fig. 24-5 Center of gravity arm causing forward weight transfer.

For example, what is the amount of weight transfer during braking, on a 4000 lb vehicle with a 120″ wheel base having a center of gravity 18″ above the road surface, when the coefficient of friction between the tire and road surface is .5?

$$\text{Weight Transfer} = \frac{.5 \times 18 \times 4000}{120} = 300 \text{ lbs}$$

If the normal conditions placed 55% of the weight on the front wheels they would carry 2200 lbs and the rear wheels would carry 1800 lbs. The weight transfer of 300 lbs during braking would reduce the braking rear wheel weight to 1500 lbs and increase the front wheel braking weight to 2500 lbs.

Front brakes are designed to absorb this extra brake effort by selecting shoe-drum or shoe-disc combination types, brake size, lining coefficient of friction, wheel cylinder size, and differential hydraulic actuating pressures.

It is desirable to have the rear brakes lock up slightly ahead of the front brakes. This allows the front wheels to steer, even if the rear wheels are skidding. This principle is especially true with trailers to avoid jack knifing.

Stopping Distance. Stopping distance is based on the deceleration rate. As shown, maximum deceleration occurs at approximately 20 ft/sec² or .6 times the force of gravity. Using this value as the deceleration rate (d ft/sec²) and the vehicle speed (V mph), the stopping distance (S ft) can be expressed as:

$$S = 1.074 \times V^2/d \text{ feet.}$$

If an automobile going 60 mph (V) stopped at a moderate deceleration rate (d) of 8 ft/sec² it would require 484 feet to stop from the time the brakes were applied.

$$S = 1.074 \times 60^2/8$$
$$= 1.074 \times 3600/8 = 484 \text{ ft}$$

The time (t sec) in seconds required to stop the vehicle from an initial speed (V mph) using the same deceleration rate (d ft/sec²) is expressed as:

$$t = 1.465 \frac{V}{d} \text{ seconds.}$$

It takes 11 seconds (t) to stop an automobile from 60 mph (V) at a deceleration rate of 8 ft/sec² (d):

$$t = 1.465 \times 60/8 = 11 \text{ sec}$$

The stopping distance is also affected by the tire deflection, air resistance, engine braking effects, and the inertia of the drive line. These additional stopping effects can be illustrated by a car traveling at 70 mph on a level road being placed in neutral without braking. At the end of a mile, the car will still be going about 15 mph. Going up hill will reduce speed faster, whereas going down a slight grade will reduce the speed more slowly.

Brake Fade. Brake fade occurs after a number of severe stops or after holding the brakes on a long downhill grade. The brakes convert vehicle kinetic energy into heat. Brake lining material is a poor conductor of heat, so most of the heat goes into the brake drum or disc. If the drum or disc is heated by friction faster than it is cooled by the surrounding air, it will reach high temperatures. Under severe use, brake drums may reach 600°F. The coefficient of friction between the drum and lining is much lower at these high temperatures, so braking will require additional pedal pressure. A point is eventually reached when the coefficient of friction drops so low that little braking effect is available. This is called brake fade.

Drum brakes are more susceptible to fade than disc brakes. In drum brakes, the lining covers a large portion of the internal drum surface, allowing little cooling space. Disc shoes, on the other hand, cover only a small portion of the disc, so there is a lot of cooling time as the disc rotates. As the vehicle moves, cooling air is directed around the drum and disc to remove brake heat.

Leading shoes are more susceptible to fade than trailing shoes. This occurs because the self-actuating servo action force decreases as the coefficient of friction becomes less. Trailing shoes do not use servo action for their operation.

Dual servo drum brakes have outstandingly high output compared to the pedal input effort. However, they show large variations in brake coefficient of friction from wheel to wheel and are adversely affected by brake fade. Not only does the forward acting primary shoe lose its force, but it cannot actuate the forward acting secondary shoe. This type of brake is the most susceptible of all types of brakes to fade.

Fade resistance brakes must limit brake shoe arc to 110° and the power absorption to 25 hp per square inch of lining. The horsepower absorbed by the brakes during a stop can be calculated by the formula:

$$Hp = \frac{KE \ (ft\text{-}lb)}{550 \ (ft\text{-}lb/sec/hp) \times t}$$

The horsepower absorbed when stopping a 4000 lb automobile in 11 seconds (t) can be calculated when using the kinetic energy of 480,960 ft lbs determined using an earlier equation. Placing these values in the equation for horse power above:

$$Hp = \frac{480,960}{550 \times 11} = 78.5$$

If 42.4 btu is the heat equivalant of one horsepower then in one stop of this automobile from 60 mph, the brakes are required to absorb 3871 btu of heat (78.5 × 42.4).

Brake Torque. When the brakes are applied, the drum or disc tries to twist the shoes or caliper anchors from their mountings. This twisting action is called *brake torque*. The amount of torque is determined by the effective axle height, which is the torque arm in feet, and the stopping force

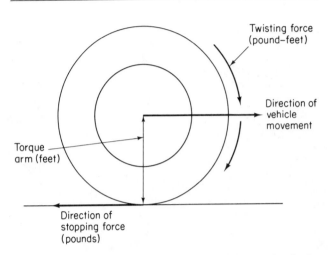

Fig. 24-6 Braking torque producing a twist on the brake anchor.

between the tire and road surface in pounds. Torque is expressed in pound-feet.

Brake torque is absorbed on the front wheels by the knuckle and suspension control arms. In the rear, it is absorbed by the axle housing and the leaf spring or control arms. Braking torque during a panic stop is much higher than accelerating torque at full throttle. Brake supporting and anchoring members must, therefore, have sufficient strength to withstand these high braking loads.

24-3 DUAL SERVO DRUM BRAKE DETAILS

The dual servo drum brake is supported by a backing plate which, in turn, is fastened to the steering knuckle or the axle housing. Brake torque is transferred from the linings and shoes through the anchor to the backing plate. The plate also serves as a dust and splash shield to keep contaminants from the brake. The upper end of the shoes are held against the anchor with retracting springs. A short spring holds the lower ends against a *star wheel* adjusting screw. Hold down pins, sometimes called nails, with springs and spring cups hold the shoes squarely against contact surfaces on the backing plate. Self-adjustment cables, levers, and springs are added to automatically turn the star wheel adjuster when

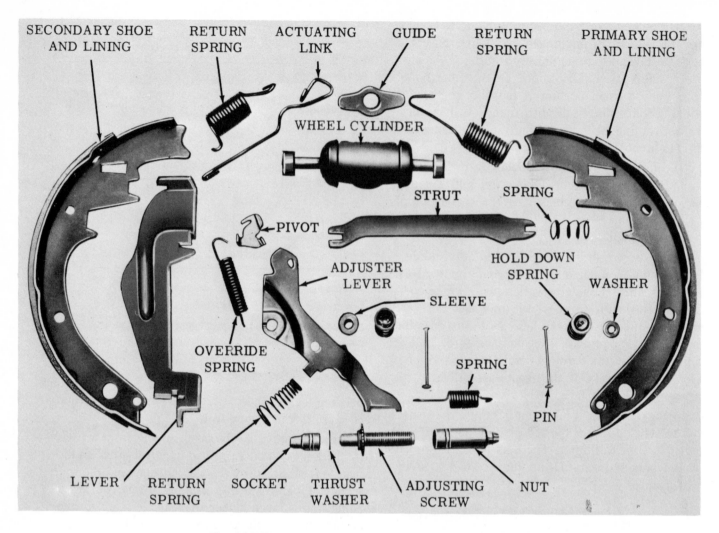

SECONDARY SHOE AND LINING   RETURN SPRING   ACTUATING LINK   GUIDE   RETURN SPRING   PRIMARY SHOE AND LINING

WHEEL CYLINDER

STRUT   SPRING

PIVOT

ADJUSTER LEVER   HOLD DOWN SPRING   WASHER

SLEEVE

OVERRIDE SPRING   SPRING

PIN

LEVER   RETURN SPRING   SOCKET   THRUST WASHER   ADJUSTING SCREW   NUT

Fig. 24-7 Drum brake part identification (Oldsmobile Division, General Motors Corporation).

shoe to drum clearance permits. Rear shoes are fitted with a cable operated parking brake lever and strut that can actuate the shoes. A wheel cylinder is located between the shoes directly under the anchor pin and guide. Wheel cylinder connecting links, sometimes called push rods or actuator pins, connect the wheel cylinder pistons to the brake shoes. This entire brake assembly is covered with a brake drum that is mounted on the axle.

Linings. Brake linings are made primarily from asbestos fibers, a material consisting chiefly of calcium and magnesium silicate. It is molded into the desired form with a high temperature synthetic bonding agent. Other materials such as lead, zinc, brass, copper, graphite, and ceramics are added to give the lining the desired coefficient of friction and

heat resistance properties. These linings can withstand temperatures as high as 600°. One stop from 60 mph may raise the brake temperature to 450°. Good quality brake linings maintain their friction characteristics at high temperatures and give long service life.

Sintered metal linings that can withstand higher temperatures without fade have been used where severe braking requirements are encountered. Sintered lining materials were dropped as a high performance material when disc brakes were adapted to these vehicles.

The secondary lining does about 75% of the braking. It is generally made longer than the primary lining, so the wear rate of the two linings will be nearly equal. Wear rate generally results from the

410

amount of work in stopping the vehicle. Wear rate also increases as the temperature increases. Passenger cars are provided with about one square inch of lining for each 25 pounds of vehicle gross weight. A 4000-lb. vehicle would use 160 square inches of lining.

Shoes. The linings are supported by brake shoes. Brake shoes form a metal backing for the lining and have a supporting web on which springs, actuators, and anchors attach. Linings are fastened to the shoes by rivets or a bonding cement. Riveted linings usually provide a soft quiet brake. The bonded linings lend themselves to high volume, production line techniques.

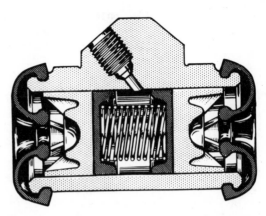

Fig. 24-9 Sectioned view of a wheel cylinder (The Bendix Corporation).

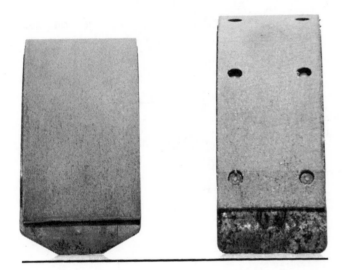

Fig. 24-8 Bonded brake lining (left) and riveted brake lining (right).

Brake shoe design and anchor location control the servo action that is developed by the shoe. Servo action increases as the anchor is moved toward the center of the brake. If the anchor were moved inward too far, the brake would lock like a Sprag one-way clutch. It would have to be turned backward to release the shoe. This, of course, would be unsatisfactory for service brakes. Service brake systems are designed so the wheel can be locked with no more than 100 pounds force on the brake pedal.

Wheel Cylinder. Brakes are actuated by hydraulic pressure in the wheel cylinder. The wheel cylinder has a piston on each end. Inside each piston are two lip-type rubber seals that retain the brake fluid.

Some wheel cylinders incorporate a spring between the brake cups. A rubber boot is fastened around the connecting link and over the cylinder end to keep contaminants out of the cylinder.

When sufficient pressure is developed in the cylinder, fluid pushes the pistons, connecting links, and shoes outward until they touch the drum. The linings in their release position are within .010 to .015″ of the drum so there is actually very little shoe movement.

Brake retracting springs pull the shoes back away from the drum and against the anchor when fluid pressure is released. The returning shoes also force the wheel cylinder pistons back to their original released position.

Drums. Brake drums are designed to have adequate strength with minimum weight. They must be able to rapidly absorb and dissipate the heat which comes from friction. The braking surface must have good wear properties. It must fit within the wheel space available and be designed for low cost mass production. These requirements are satisfactorily met on production automobiles.

The braking surface on brake drums is cast iron. Some brake drums are one-piece cast iron. Cast iron works very well as the drum friction surface, but cast iron tends to be too brittle for the drum back or disc. Composite drums were developed with stamped steel discs fastened to a cast iron hoop-shaped ring section braking surface. Another method

Fig. 24-10 Drum brake fitting within the wheel (Buick Motor Division, General Motors Corporation).

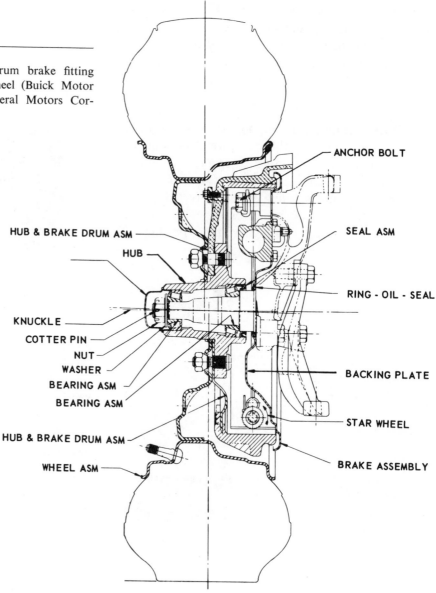

ANCHOR BOLT

HUB & BRAKE DRUM ASM

SEAL ASM

HUB

RING - OIL - SEAL

KNUCKLE

COTTER PIN

NUT

WASHER

BACKING PLATE

BEARING ASM

BEARING ASM

STAR WHEEL

HUB & BRAKE DRUM ASM

WHEEL ASM

BRAKE ASSEMBLY

Fig. 24-11 Drum construction. (a) Stamped disc with cast iron hoop braking surface, (b) steel drum with centrifugal cast iron braking surface.

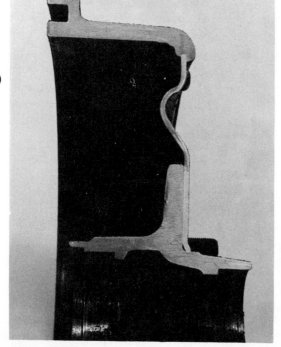

(a)

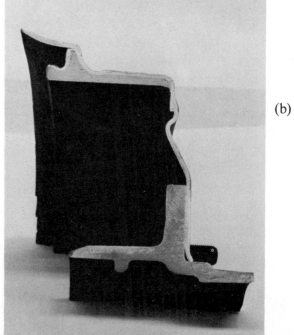

(b)

used to make brake drums is to centrifugally cast an iron braking surface into a stamped steel drum. Centrifugal cast iron is more dense than plain cast iron, which gives long service life. Sometimes, these drums use cast fins on their outer surface to aid in cooling which will reduce brake fade. The most advanced brake drums are a bimetallic-finned aluminum casting with a braking surface of centrifugal cast iron bonded to the inner drum surface.

Brake drum size is limited by the space allowed behind the vehicle wheel. In the early 1960's, vehicle wheel sizes were made smaller to give the vehicle a lower silhouette. This limited brake size, so brake performance became critical. By the late 1960's, the wheel size was increased and larger brakes improved braking performance.

Fig. 24-12 Typical brake disc (Kelsey-Hays Company).

24-4 DISC BRAKE DETAILS

High performance and heavy passenger cars have overtaxed drum brake capacity. Disc brake development has provided the needed high capacity, fade resistant brake. Disc brakes have been used for years on light-weight European cars and on aircraft. The European brakes were too small to be used directly on domestic passenger cars. Aircraft disc brakes had time to cool after stopping the airplane before being used again and, therefore, they did not have the capacity, considering their size, that was required for passenger car applications.

Discs. Most domestic passenger cars use a ventilated cast iron disc. The two solid outer disc surfaces are the braking surfaces. These are held apart in alignment with cast webs. Air flow through the disc cools it before fade can occur. Studies have shown that a solid disc would operate cooler on the first few stops because the added metal would act as a heat sink. The ventilated disc operates cooler after the first few stops.

The disc is attached to the hub wheel bolts. In some designs, the hub and disc are made in one piece. In each type, minimum lateral disc run-out must be maintained for smooth braking. The braking surfaces must be parallel to each other to minimize brake pedal pulsing effects.

Caliper. The first production disc brakes were of a fixed caliper, four-piston design. The caliper was fastened securely to the steering knuckle or axle

housing. In operation, two pistons on each side of the disc pushed the pads or shoes against the disc, thereby clamping the disc between the shoes. The cylinder fluid chambers were interconnected, so the pistons pushed with equal force. Friction between the shoes and disc converted the vehicle kinetic energy into heat.

One problem that developed in early disc brakes was boiling brake fluid. The heat from friction heated the caliper so hot that the fluid turned to a vapor, which could be compressed instead of having a solid fluid column, so the brakes would no longer hold. Heat insulators and a high boiling point brake fluid were developed for disc brake equipped

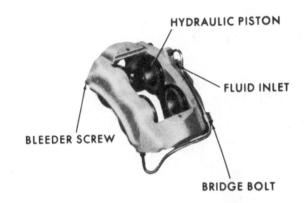

Fig. 24-13 Typical four-piston caliper assembly (Kelsey-Hays Company).

413

vehicles. Only high boiling point brake fluid is suitable for disc brakes in modern domestic passenger cars.

The four-piston fixed caliper required accurate centering so the shoes would not drag or the pistons come too far out of their bores. During overhaul, each caliper requires servicing all four cylinders. Interconnecting passages are subject to leaks and the caliper is expensive to manufacture.

A single-piston floating caliper has been developed for disc brakes. The inboard side of the caliper contains the piston and cylinder, and holds the inboard shoe. The outboard side holds the outboard shoe. When the cylinder is pressurized, the piston and shoe move against the disc. Pressure in the cylinder fluid chamber moves the caliper along

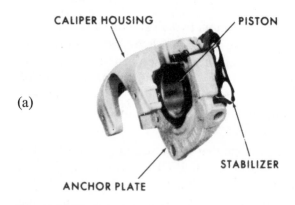

(a)

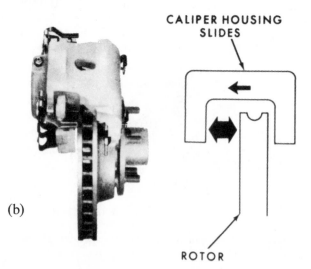

(b)

Fig. 24-14 Typical single-piston caliper assembly. (a) Assembly (Kelsey-Hays Company), (b) operation (Kelsey-Hays Company).

its anchor to force the outboard shoe against the disc. Single pistons are larger than any one of the pistons in a four-piston caliper, in order to do the same amount of work.

Disc brakes have no servo action. All of their force depends upon fluid pressure. Their shoes are much smaller than shoes used in drum brakes, so more pressure is required to get the same braking response. Compared to dual servo brakes, a disc brake requires from four to five times the cylinder area and twice the hydraulic pressure.

24-5 BRAKE ACTUATION PRINCIPLES

Hydraulic brakes are applied by the driver through an actuating system using hydraulic principles to multiply brake pedal force. The science of hydraulics is based on Pascal's principle which states that pressure applied to any area of an enclosed fluid is transmitted undiminished in all directions to every interior surface of the vessel. In brake actuating systems, the enclosed vessel is a master cylinder and wheel cylinder with connecting lines and hoses. Any pressure applied to the master cylinder is transmitted undiminished to each wheel cylinder.

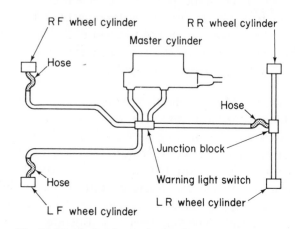

Fig. 24-15 Typical brake hydraulic system schematic.

Brake System Forces. Hydraulic pressure multiplied by the area on which it acts determines the force produced. For example, if 100 psi pressure were applied on a one square inch surface, the force would be 100 pounds. If, however, this same 100 psi pressure were applied against a $1\frac{1}{2}$ square inch surface, the total force would be 150 pounds. This principle can continue to any amount of pressure and surface area. The total force equals square inches of area times the pressure. This system can also work in reverse. If a mechanical force were pushing on an area, it would produce hydraulic pressure. The formula for this reaction is:

$$\text{Pressure} = \frac{\text{Force}}{\text{Area}}$$

If a mechanical force of 50 pounds pushed on an area of .75 square inches, the total pressure would be 66 psi (50 lb/.75 in²).

In a brake actuating system, the driver applies a force through a mechanical linkage to the master cylinder piston. The master cylinder piston applies pressure to the enclosed hydraulic brake fluid. This pressure, in turn, pressing on the wheel cylinder pistons, will push the linings against the brake drum or disc.

For example, the brake pedal force the driver applies is multiplied by the mechanical linkage ratio to apply force on the master cylinder piston. If the driver applies a 75-pound force through a 7:1 linkage ratio, the force applied to the master cylinder would be 525 pounds (75 × 7). This force divided by the master cylinder piston area will give the pressure in the hydraulic system. If the master cylinder bore diameter is one inch, its cross sectional area is .785 square inches [$\pi \times$ (diameter/2)²), or (.785 × diameter²)]. The hydraulic pressure, using the above mechanical force, is 670 psi (525 lb/.785 sq in). Very often, the front and rear wheel cylinders are different sizes. If the front wheel cylinders for this example had a 1.125 in diameter, their area would be .995 square inches (.785 × 1.125²). The force pushing the front lining against the brake drum would be 666 pounds (670 psi × .995 sq in).

If the rear brakes in the same example had a .875 inch bore diameter, their piston area would be .600 square inches (.785 × .875²). The force developed by the rear wheel cylinders would be 403 pounds (670 psi × .600 sq in).

If the vehicle in this example were equipped with front disc brakes instead of drum brakes, the wheel cylinders would be much larger. Using front wheel cylinder 2.5 inches in diameter, the cylinder area would be 4.90 square inches (.785 × 2.5²). The force produced using the same example would be 3290 pounds (670 psi × 4.9 sq in). Disc brakes require high forces such as this. Power boosters

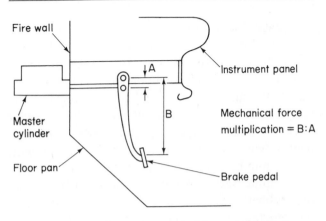

Fig. 24-16 Brake pedal mechanical force multiplication.

are required to produce adequate braking force on heavy vehicles equipped with disc brakes.

In the above example, the driver's 75-pound force on the brake pedal resulted in a 666-pound force on the front linings with drum brakes and a 403-pound force on the rear linings. A higher force is usually required on the front brakes, because they do a larger portion of the braking. Front disc brake force would be raised to 3290 pounds. The brake's hydraulic lines and hoses must be in good condition to withstand these pressures.

Force multiplication requires an equivalent increase in pedal travel. If the master cylinder had 1/2 the area of the wheel cylinder, the wheel cylinder output force would be twice the master cylinder input force, but the master cylinder piston travel would be twice as great as the wheel cylinder piston travel. Force is multiplied at the expense of pedal travel. This principle can be expressed as: output force × output travel = input force × input travel. This principle holds true only after the lining touches the drum or disc. The first part of the pedal travel is required to take up clearances in the linkage, cylinders, and lining-to-drum or lining-to-disc before pressure begins to be built up and is called pedal free travel. A high pedal indicates small clearances, while a low pedal indicates excess clearances. If the sum of the clearances becomes too large, the brakes will not apply on the first stroke, but will require "pumping" to get the shoes to touch the drum or disc. When the clearance is taken up, pressure can build up as described in the example above.

Brake Fluid. Water will transfer hydraulic force in an enclosed vessel. It would, however, be very unsatisfactory for brake fluid. Fluid used for brake systems is a specially compounded non-petroleum liquid. It must remain as a liquid throughout the temperature extremes encountered. Its viscosity or thickness must change very little between the temperature limits encountered. Brake hydraulic systems use a number of different metals and rubbers. Brake fluid must not corrode the metal or attack the rubber. It must also be able to lubricate the moving parts in the master and wheel cylinders.

The brake fluid's most critical characteristic is its boiling point. Friction heat from stopping the vehicle raises the fluid's temperature. If the fluid temperature reaches the boiling point, it will turn to vapor. The brake pedal action would then become spongy, like it does with air in the line. Required pressures could not be developed and the brakes would become ineffective.

The Society of Automotive Engineers have specified 374°F as the minimum brake fluid boiling point requirements in their handbook specification number J1703, which is a refinement of the older fluid specification 70R3. Most brake fluids exceed these minimum temperature specifications.

Most brake fluids are manufactured by large chemical companies. They sell bulk fluid to other companies who, in turn, package it for the consumer under their own label. To ensure use of the correct brake fluid, most automobile companies package the required quality fluid and sell it by number through their own parts departments.

The minimum boiling point specifications of heavy duty brake fluid must be at least 374°. Brake fluid is also available with boiling points of 400, 470, 500 and 550°. Disc brake fluid tends to get hotter than the drum brake fluid because the wheel cylinder is a bore in the caliper body. Much heat is absorbed by the caliper and this heats the fluid. One automobile company recommends only the use of 550° boiling point fluid which they market through their own parts departments. The 550° fluid should be used on all disc brake systems. Use of any other heavy duty brake fluid may allow the fluid to boil. For safety, the manufacturer's recommendations must be followed.

24-6 DETAILS OF BRAKE ACTUATION COMPONENTS

The mechanical linkages used to actuate the master cylinder will differ between the car models. The brake pedal is usually suspended from a channel bracketed between the steering column-to-dash attachment point and the fire wall. A push rod connects the pedal to the master cylinder piston. The location of the push rod pivot between the pedal pivot and foot pad determines the mechanical force multiplication.

Master Cylinder. The master cylinder is a cast iron body containing a cylinder bore, a fluid reservoir, and fluid passages. Holes or ports are drilled between the reservoir and the cylinder bore to allow make-up fluid to enter the system or to allow expanded fluid to return to the reservoir.

A single master cylinder will be used to simplify the description of master cylinder operations. The master cylinder piston is a long piston with two lip-type cup seals, one close to each end. The inner seal, called a *primary cup*, is used to build up hydraulic pressure in the system. The outer seal, called a *secondary cup*, keeps fluid from leaking out of the master cylinder. An inlet or breather port between the cups allows any fluid that gets past the primary cup to return to the reservoir. The only pressure against the secondary cup is caused by the weight of the fluid in the reservoir. A piston spring holds the piston against the push rod coming from the pedal linkage. When the brake pedal is released, the piston is moved to its rest position at the push rod end of the cylinder bore. In this position, a small hole, called a compensation port, on the spring side of the primary cup, is open between the cylinder bore and the reservoir. The lip of the primary piston must move across this compensating port before any fluid will be pushed into the lines or wheel cylinders. This movement or pedal free travel is part of the clearance or lash that must be taken up before brake pressure will build up.

Continued piston movement toward the outlet end of the cylinder opens a check valve that allows fluid to enter the brake lines. The lines and master

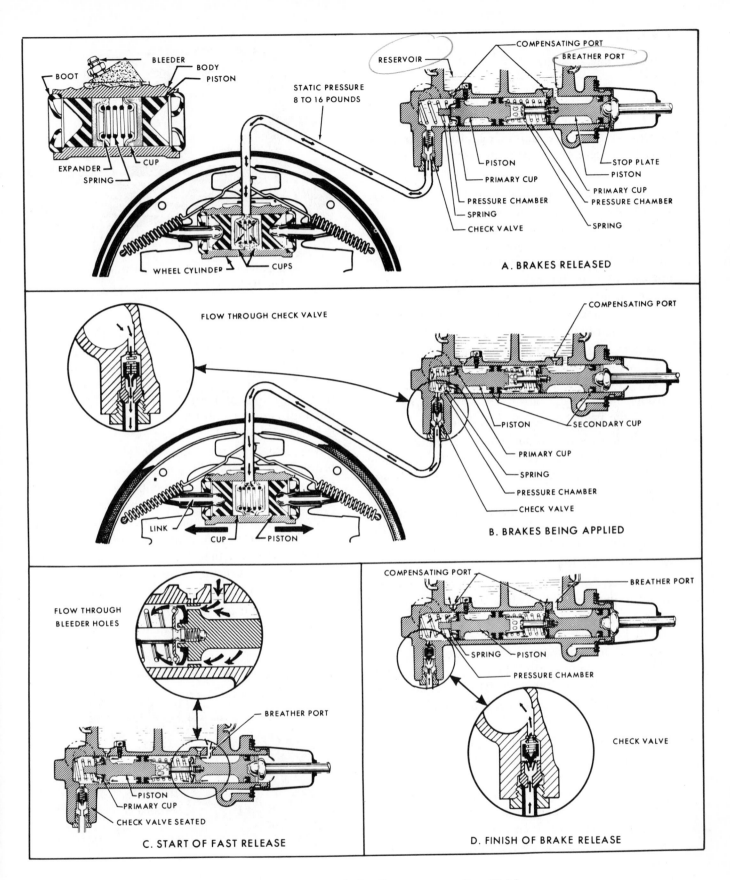

Fig. 24-17 Principle of brake hydraulic system operation (Buick Motor Division, General Motors Corporation).

cylinder are always full of fluid and free of air, so on application only sufficient fluid will enter the system to move the linings against the drum or disc. From here on, pressure increases with no fluid flow.

When the brake pedal is released, the brake retracting springs pull the linings from the drum. This forces retraction of the wheel cylinder pistons. In disc brakes, the seal action retracts the piston. In both types, the piston movement returns a small amount of fluid through the residual check valve to the master cylinder and the master cylinder piston is pushed back by the piston spring to its at-rest position. If the fluid is warm and expanded, excess fluid goes into the reservoir through the compensating port. When additional fluid is required in the system, fluid enters through the inlet port, goes through holes in the piston, then around the back side of the primary cup lip.

When used, the residual check valve holds from six to eighteen psi of pressure in the hydraulic system. This pressure holds the parts under a slight force to minimize clearances in the system. This slight system pressure also prevents air leakage into the system. It is a positive means of keeping the system full of fluid and ready to operate each time the pedal is applied.

Master cylinders have been divided for safety to form two separate hydraulic systems. Loss of pressure in one system does not cause complete loss of brakes as it does on single master cylinder systems. The two systems' pistons are in the same cylinder bore, one behind the other, so that pedal pressure is effective on both. This type of master cylinder is called a *dual* master cylinder or a *tandem* master cylinder.

Each section of the master cylinder operates the brakes on one axle, either front or rear. The piston closest to the push rod is called the primary piston and the piston furthest from the push rod is called the secondary piston. In some vehicles, the primary piston operates the rear wheel cylinders while in other systems, it will operate the front wheel cylinders.

Hydraulically, each portion of the dual tandem master cylinder acts in the same manner as a single

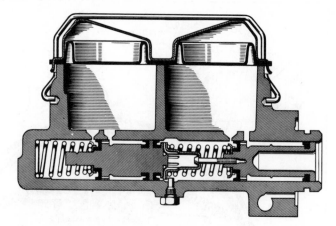

Fig. 24-18 Cross section of a typical drum brake master cylinder (The Bendix Corporation).

master cylinder. The difference is the way the secondary piston is moved. The primary piston is moved directly by the push rod. The pressure that is built up in the primary cylinder pushes on a reversed piston cup located on the primary end of the floating secondary piston. This force is transmitted through the secondary piston, sometimes called a slave piston, to the fluid behind the secondary piston. This method of moving the secondary piston equalizes the pressure in the two separate brake pressure systems. There is a piston spring between the pistons and a second spring behind the slave secondary piston. The primary spring between the pistons is stronger than the secondary spring. These springs help return the pistons to their at-rest position after brake pedal pressure is released.

Each piston has an extension on its lower end. If pressure is lost in the primary system, the pro-

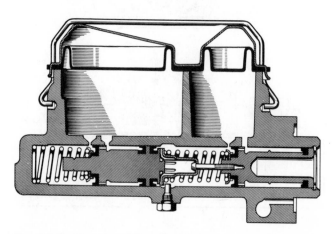

Fig. 24-19 Cross section of a typical disc brake master cylinder (The Bendix Corporation).

jection on the primary piston bottoms against the secondary piston, moving it mechanically. If pressure is lost in the secondary system, the projection on the end of the secondary piston bottoms on the end of the cylinder. This allows pressure to be built up between the primary piston cup and the inverted secondary piston cup to pressurize the primary system.

Tandem master cylinders used with disc brakes usually omit the residual pressure check valve from the portion of the cylinder connected to the disc brakes. Disc brake cylinders are larger than drum brake wheel cylinders, so the master cylinder usually has a larger reservoir for the front wheel portion.

Brake Warning Light or Distributor Switch. All cars that are provided with tandem brake master cylinders use a warning light to immediately indicate to the driver that one of the brake hydraulic systems is not functioning. The brake warning light switch usually takes the place of the tee fitting that would divide the flow of hydraulic fluid to the front and rear wheels. The switch consists of a small two-headed piston that is centered by springs. Pressure from the primary piston is impressed against one head of the piston and the secondary piston pressure against the other head. An insulated contact button is located between them. When one system fails, pressure in that system falls and the piston shifts toward the failed pressure, touching the insulated contact. This grounds to complete the electrical circuit of an instrument panel brake warning light. The centering springs are strong enough so slight variations in brake pressure will not actuate the warning light.

Lines and Hoses. Brake pressures may approach 1500 psi when a strong person makes a panic stop in a car equipped with power assisted brakes. Hydraulic brake pressure lines must have adequate strength to withstand these pressures. Manufacturers use steel tubing with double flared ends and inverted flare nut fittings. Some of the lines are even double walled steel. Special heavy duty copper lines can be used, but they are much more expensive and are only used where corrosion resistance is required. Common copper lines have thin walls that will burst under high hydraulic brake pressures.

Tubing is used from the master cylinder to the bottom of the vehicle frame structure. A loop is

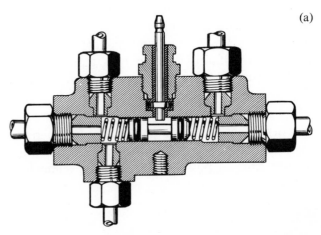

(a)

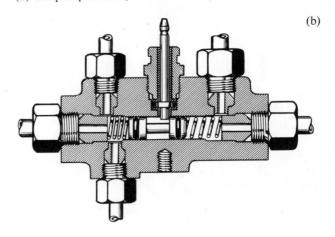

Fig. 24-20 Brake warning light switch. (a) Equal pressure, (b) unequal pressure (The Bendix Corporation).

(b)

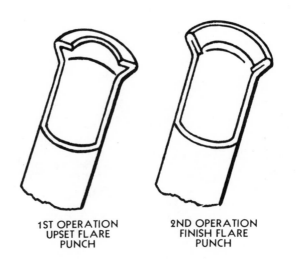

1ST OPERATION UPSET FLARE PUNCH

2ND OPERATION FINISH FLARE PUNCH

Fig. 24-21 Double flair end on brake tubing (Chevrolet Motor Division, General Motors Corporation).

419

provided between the master cylinder and frame to absorb any slight motion that might occur. One hose is used between the frame mounted tubing and the rear axle fitting. Tubing runs along the rear axle housing from the fitting to the wheel cylinders. One hose is used on each front brake between the frame mounted tubing to the wheel cylinder.

Brake hoses must be strong enough to retain the hydraulic pressures encountered. Generally, they are as short as possible, but still long enough to avoid being stretched. They are routed across the suspension so they will not interfere with suspension motion.

Drum Brake Wheel Cylinders. Cast iron wheel cylinders are attached to the backing plate for firm support. A sealing gasket may be used between them to help keep contaminants out of the brake assembly. The brake hose or tubing is attached to the wheel cylinder fitting on the back side of the backing plate. The cylinder is provided with a bleeder screw fitting leading from the top center of the wheel cylinder bore to allow removal of all of the air from the hydraulic system.

Wheel cylinders are fitted with two aluminum pistons with an anodized finish, one on each end of the cylinder bore. The outer end of the pistons have a seat for the shoe actuating push rod pin. The inboard end is flat to back up the wheel cylinder lip-type sealing cup. Some wheel cylinders have a light spring separating the cups to help keep lash from the brake system. A piston cup expander may be used on each end of the spring to hold the cup lip against the sides of the cylinder bore.

Dust boots are fitted over the cylinder end and around the push rod. This keeps the dust and moisture from the cylinder surface to help prevent sticking or corrosion.

The outer end of the push rods are slotted to fit into notches on the brake shoe web.

Disc Brake Wheel Cylinders. Disc brake wheel cylinders are located in the calipers. The first disc brakes used on domestic passenger cars had four pistons in each caliper, two on the inside of the disc and two on the outside of the disc. The caliper had to be designed for disassembly in two halves in order to manufacture and service the cylinder bores. The cylinder pressure areas of the two halves were interconnected with either internal passages or with external tubing to ensure equal pressure on the disc from all four pistons.

The pistons hold the linings close to the disc, so little lost motion is present to cause excess pedal travel. Some early designs encountered a phenomenon called *knock back* as the disc hit the shoes while rotating. This would knock the pistons back into the bore and thus cause excess pedal travel on the next brake application. To compensate for knock back, a spring was installed behind the alu-

Fig. 24-22 Brake line feeding the wheel cylinder and bleeder valve above.

Fig. 24-23 Disassembled wheel cylinder.

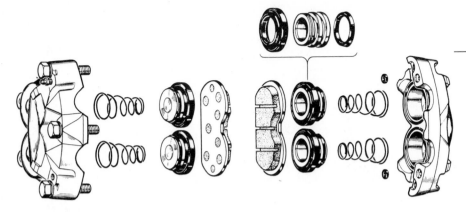

Fig. 24-24 Exploded view of a four-piston caliper (The Bendix Corporation).

minum piston to give it a slight push toward the disc while still minimizing shoe to disc drag. The drag effects of this system used .8 hp at 100 mph, which is insignificant. This slight drag did not cause excessive wear.

The early four-piston caliper disc brakes tended to transfer excessive heat to the brake fluid. This would cause the fluid to boil with a loss of pedal. Insulators were installed between the lining and pistons which minimize heat transfer to the fluid. High boiling point fluid eliminated the need for these insulators.

The four-piston type fixed caliper uses a cast iron body securely attached to the steering knuckle

Fig. 24-25 Caliper operation (Kelsey-Hays Company). (a) Four-piston caliper on rotor, (b) four-piston caliper operation, (c) single-piston caliper on rotor, (d) single piston caliper operation.

CALIPER ASSEMBLY

(a)

HUB AND ROTOR ASSEMBLY

CALIPER HOUSING STATIONARY

(b)

ROTOR

(c)

(d)

UNAPPLIED   APPLIED

421

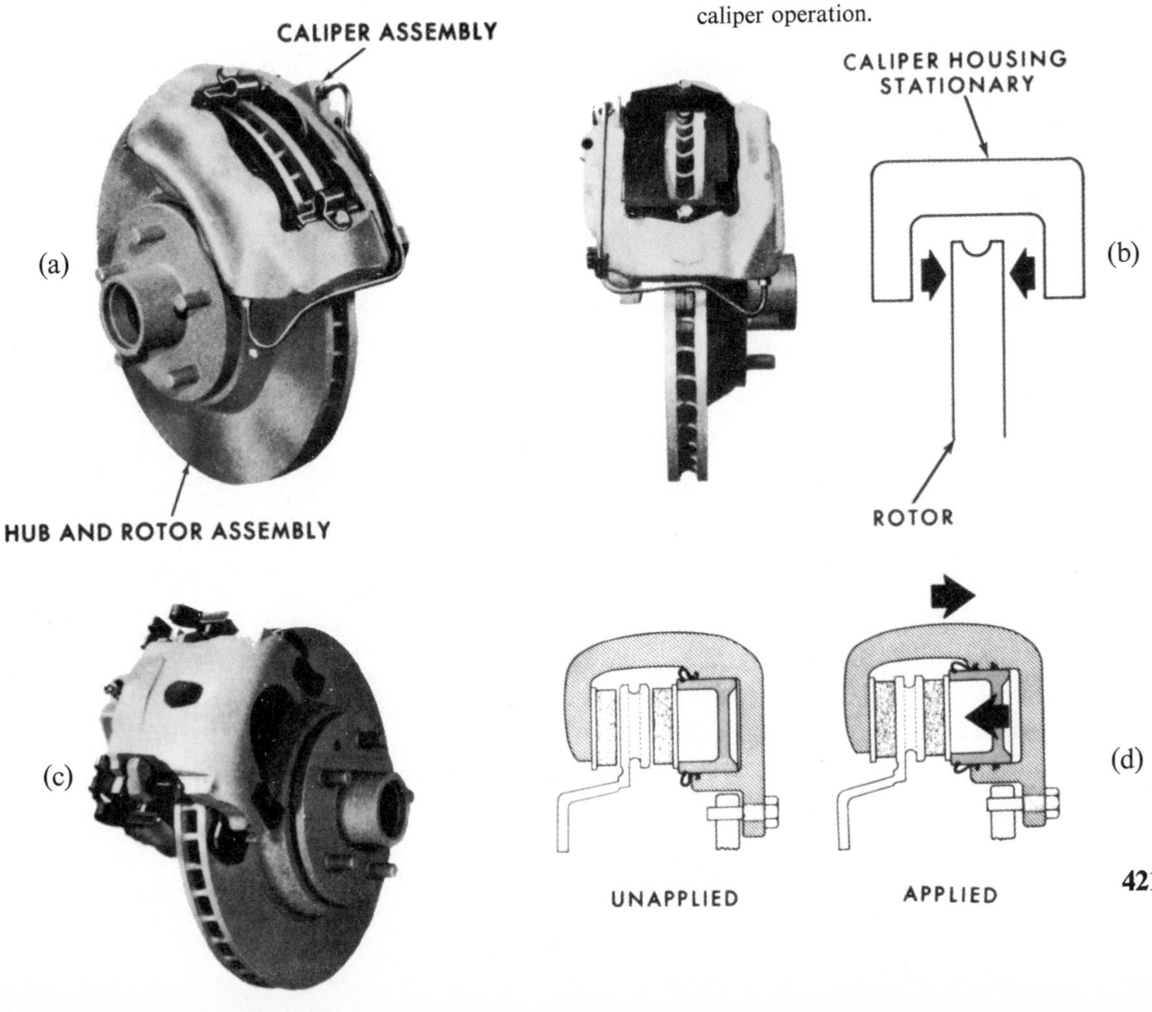

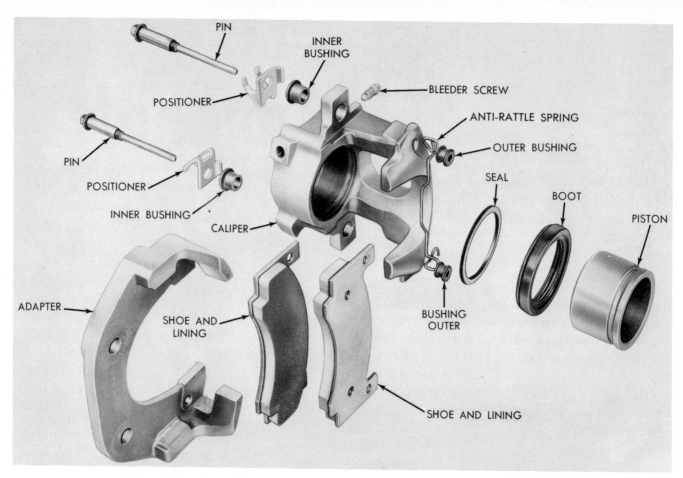

Fig. 24-26 Disassembled single piston caliper with part identification (Chrysler Motors Corporation).

through an adapter plate. Any variation in disc position or shoe wear is compensated for by the respective positions of the pistons in their wheel cylinder bore. The fixed caliper has been replaced by a single-piston floating cast iron caliper on the majority of passenger cars. The single-piston caliper is one piece, so it is more rigid. Machining one bore uses less assembly time and is more economical.

A single-piston floating caliper works like a small hydraulic press. The portion of the caliper outside of the disc is like the press table and the inside portion with the cylinder is like the press ram. If the press were turned on its side and supported on rods, it could move to center on the disc. The table would pull on one side as hard as the ram pushed on the other side.

The large single piston is an inverted cup formed of stamped steel, precision ground, and plated with nickel-chrome. The plating gives it a hard durable surface. A rectangular section seal fits into a groove in the wall of the cylinder and presses against the piston skirt. The open ends of the piston contact

the lining. This design minimizes heat transfer to the fluid. Hydraulic pressure on the piston head pushes the piston toward the inner surface of the disc and the pressure in the cylinder head pulls the caliper toward the outer disc surface, applying the brake.

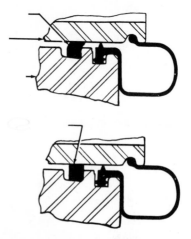

Fig. 24-27 Seal action to return caliper piston after application (The Bendix Corporation).

Movement of the piston and caliper distort the rectangular piston seal. When pressure is relieved, the seal returns to its normal position. This action pulls the piston back a slight distance into the cylinder. This, in turn, pulls the shoe back to keep it from dragging on the disc.

Proportioning Valves. In most applications where disc brakes are used, the front brakes are disc and the rear are dual servo brakes. Disc brakes require a higher pressure to get the same braking effort as the dual servo brakes, unless large cylinders are used with high coefficient of friction lining materials. Therefore, the front disc brakes and rear drum brakes require different pressures for proper braking. In a hard stop, the effective weight transfer increases the front disc brake requirements even more. If

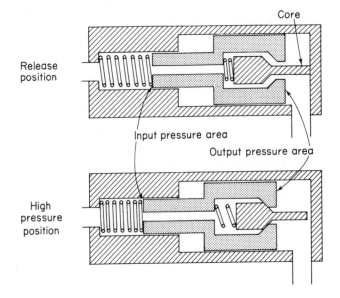

Fig. 24-28 Principle of the proportioning valve.

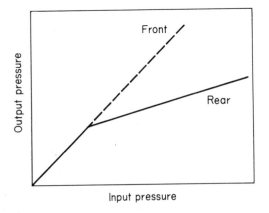

the brakes received equal pressure, the rear wheels would lock, causing rear end skid. A *proportioning valve* is used to provide a reduced pressure to the rear wheels in hard stops.

The proportioning valve, located in the rear brake line, has a sliding core. Under light braking pressure, the fluid passes freely through the valve. On heavy applications, a pressure area causes the core to shift in the direction of fluid flow, blocking the outlet to the rear wheels. The outlet side of the sliding core senses outlet pressure on a large surface area. This balances the input pressure on a small pressure area. The output pressure increases as a percentage of the input pressure in proportion to their balancing surface areas. Upon brake release, the input pressure drops, the proportioning valve opens, and the fluid freely returns to the master cylinder.

Metering Valve. On slippery or icy road conditions, light braking with the disc brakes may lock the front wheels. If this occurs, directional control is lost. Some vehicles install a metering valve in the front wheel brake line to prevent front brake application during light braking. At pressures above 100 psi, the front brakes receive full master cylinder pressure.

In the metering valve, a spring holds a seal against master cylinder pressure. When the pressure is sufficient to move the valve against the spring, much like a pressure relief valve, the valve opens to allow the pressure to go to the front wheel cylinders. Upon release, a second valve allows free return of fluid to the master cylinder.

The metering valve is equipped with an external push rod that can be used to open the internal relief valve. The release valve can be held open for bleeding air from the hydraulic system.

Some vehicles are equipped with both a proportioning valve and a metering valve. Other vehicles may have either one or the other of the valves. Still other vehicles may not require either of these valves.

Anti-Lock Braking. Maximum braking occurs while the wheel is still rotating just before it skids.

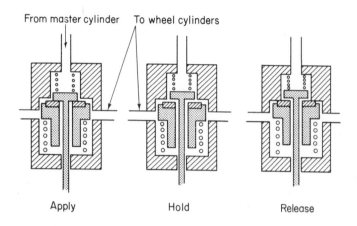

Apply   Hold   Release

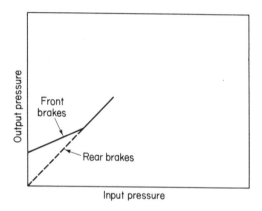

Fig. 24-29 Principle of the metering valve.

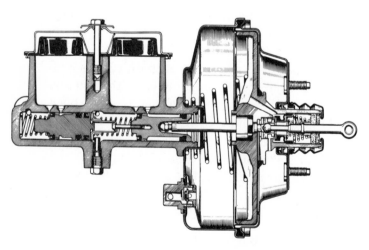

Fig. 24-30 Section view of a typical power brake unit (The Bendix Corporation).

Vehicle control is possible with a turning wheel. Anti-lock braking systems have been developed for use on vehicle rear wheels and on all four wheels. The rear anti-lock system will be used as an example. A sensor is located on each rear axle. The sensor consists of a toothed disc turning in a coil of wire. As it rotates, it produces an alternating current signal. The signal from each wheel is sent into a solid-state electronic control module. The signal to the control module will stop when the wheel stops turning. Sensing this, the control module slightly releases the power brake. As the wheel speeds up, the signal increases, so the control module increases brake application. This cycle occurs about three times each second.

Anti-lock braking has very little effect on braking distance. It prevents wheel lock up and, therefore, practically eliminates rear end skid, or *yaw*. It allows the driver to maintain vehicle control during braking, even on the most slippery surfaces.

24-7 POWER BRAKES

Power brakes have been mentioned several times in this chapter. Their function is to provide the required hydraulic pressure while requiring much lower pedal effort. In many cases, pedal travel has been reduced. This increases the power brake's force multiplication requirement.

Engine vacuum and atmospheric pressure are used as the power source to operate power brakes. Vacuum is applied to a chamber on one side of a diaphragm and atmospheric pressure to a chamber on the other side. This causes the diaphragm to tend to move toward the vacuum side. Diaphragm movement force is directed to the master cylinder piston through a push rod. The force on the master cylinder increases as the difference in pressure exists between the vacuum and atmospheric chambers increases.

In the at-rest position with the brake released, the pressure in both chambers is equal. When both chambers are under vacuum while at rest, the system is called a *vacuum suspended* power brake. If both chambers are under atmospheric pressure, it is called an *atmospheric suspended* power brake. For brake application, a control valve allows air to enter the back chamber of the vacuum suspended type unit. The valve in the atmospheric suspended

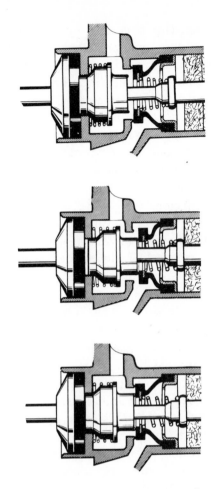

Fig. 24-31 Principle of the power brake control valve during apply, (atmospheric valve open), release (vacuum valve open) and hold (both valves closed).

unit allows vacuum to be applied to the front chamber during application. On application, both units have atmospheric pressure in the rear chamber and vacuum in the front chamber.

An actuating push rod connects the pedal linkage to the control valve. The control valve housing or body is located in the diaphragm center. When the brakes are applied, the control valve moves forward, opening the required passages to unbalance the diaphragm chambers. Unbalancing causes the diaphragm to move forward carrying the control valve housing forward with it. When the valve housing moves forward far enough, it catches up with the control valve, closing the valves so the diaphragm and valve body move forward to a new hold position. This type of action which adds power effort to the mechanical input effort is another form of servo action.

When the brake pedal is released, the control

valve moves to the back of the body, opening the at-rest valving, equalizing the pressures in the two diaphragm chambers. A spring in the front chamber pushes the diaphragm back to its at-rest position. This diaphragm movement allows the master cylinder piston to return to its at-rest position.

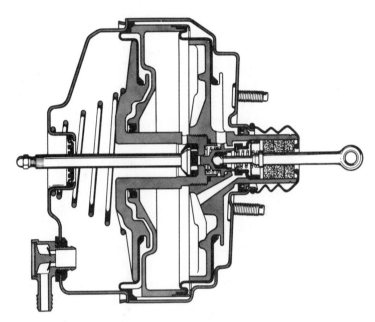

Fig. 24-32 Section view of a typical tandem diaphragm power brake booster (The Bendix Corporation).

Some power brakes require more assist than can be provided by a single diaphragm. These units use two diaphragms in tandem with a chamber dividing support plate between them. This provides two atmospheric chambers and two vacuum chambers to double the power boost effect in the same diameter power brake unit.

24-8 BRAKE SYSTEM SERVICE

Brakes are serviced in a routine manner when a brake problem exists. A routine maintenance inspection should be done every 10,000 miles or once each year with self-adjusting brakes. Brakes that require manual adjustment should be inspected each time they are adjusted. Brake problems usually consist of noise, low pedal, pulsing pedal, gradual loss of pedal height, brake fade, or brake pull. When a problem exists, the brakes should be inspected to identify the problem so it can be corrected.

Routine Maintenance. Brake fluid level is normally checked each time the engine oil is changed. Low brake fluid is usually an early sign of a brake problem. It could be a leak from the system or worn shoes that let the wheel cylinder pistons move out in their bores. This increases the wheel cylinder volume that must be filled from the master cylinder. Leaks may occur from the lines or hoses, from their end fittings, or around the wheel and master cylinder cups. Any leak must be repaired.

A visual inspection of the shoe's condition will indicate the service life remaining. If the lining is worn within 1/32″ of the rivet heads on riveted lining or 1/32″ of the backing on bonded lining, it should be replaced.

Brake inspection should include an examination of the drum or disc braking surface for excessive wear and scoring. Springs should be examined for indications of stretch or discoloration from heat. Wheel cylinders should be checked for signs of leakage. The adjuster mechanism should be free from binding.

Most drum brakes have self-adjusters, so they need no periodic mechanical adjustment. Some heavy duty drum brakes, however, do require adjustment. This is done using the star wheel adjuster to tighten the shoes against the drum, then backing them off a specific number of "clicks" (about 12).

Brake Problems. Brake problems may be characterized by the driver's pedal feel or the vehicle's response to the driver's pedal effort. The pedal may be low, indicating excess clearance must be taken up before the lining contacts the drum or disc. A spongy pedal occurs when air or vapors are present in the hydraulic system. These are removed by bleeding the hydraulic system. A high hard pedal results from minimum clearance and from an inoperative power brake unit.

Brake noise results from vibrating parts. During a stop, the lining may momentarily grab the drum,

then release. This cycle may occur at a relatively fast rate. If the vibration frequency is within the audible range, it can be noisy. Most drum brakes are fitted with dampening or anti-rattle springs and retainers to reduce brake noise. Drums often have a spring around their outer edge to dampen drum vibrations. Excessive brake noise may be the result of failure of one of these parts. It could also result from a hard or glazed brake lining and from drum hard spots.

Unsatisfactory vehicle braking response is the result of improper or unequal coefficient of friction between the lining and drums. If a brake on one side of the vehicle has a lower coefficient of friction than a drum on the other side, the vehicle will tend to pull in the direction of the brake with the greatest coefficient of friction when braking.

Brake coefficient of friction changes as the brake temperature increases. High temperature brake linings have a low coefficient of friction, causing *fade*. The high temperature expands the drum diameter, so the linings have to move further to contact the drum. This tends to increase brake pedal travel as fade occurs. Discs also increase in diameter as they get hot. With the linings pushing on the side of the disc, expansion has no effect on the brake pedal position.

Lining contamination will affect brake coefficient of friction. Contamination may come from handling the lining or drum with dirty hands, from wheel bearing grease being thrown off, from rear axle oil seal leakage, from brake wheel cylinder fluid leakage, from water, and from dust or dirt. Slight amounts of contaminants may increase the coefficient of friction while greater amounts of the same contaminant will reduce it. When the brake pull occurs, all of the brakes should be inspected to determine the exact cause. Contaminated linings should be replaced and the cause of contamination corrected.

Drum Brake Service Operation. With the drum removed, the brake shoes are removed by removing the shoe retainers, then unhooking the retracting springs from the anchor. The shoe assembly can be slightly spread to disengage the wheel cylinder push rod, then lifted from the backing plate. Overlapping the shoe anchor ends will release the spring tension so the parts can be completely disassembled. All springs should be checked for distortion and signs of overheating. If any abnormality exists, the spring should be replaced. The star wheel should have free running threads. Automatic adjuster linkages and cables should show no abnormal wear.

Brake drums can be reconditioned by resurfacing the braking surface. This is usually done by turning the drum surface on a special drum lathe. A damper is placed around the drum while turning to eliminate chatter marks on the surface. Maximum oversize turning is usually limited to .060″ increase in drum diameter. Occasionally, a small car is limited to .030″ oversize and some large cars allow as much as .080″. Manufacturer's specifications should be checked for each drum. If the drum surface does not clean up within the specified oversize limits, the drum should be replaced. This is necessary for safety, because excessive turning will weaken the drum hoop, allowing distortion or cracks.

Fig. 24-33 Brake drum turning.

New linings can be put on the shoes; however, it is standard procedure to exchange the used shoes for shoes that have been reconditioned. The linings are ground to fit the new diameter of the drum. Shoes with thicker or oversize linings should be used with turned drums. Linings are installed on both brakes of an axle at the same time to eliminate brake pull on brake application.

When wheel cylinders are to be reconditioned, the dust covers and push rods are removed and the cups pushed out of the wheel cylinder bores. The wheel cylinder bore can be reconditioned by honing.

If honing doesn't thoroughly clean the bore within a .005″ oversize, the wheel cylinder should be replaced. Many service technicians replace the wheel cylinder as a standard procedure when reconditioning brakes. All new rubber parts and springs for the wheel cylinders come in a repair kit. These are installed, using brake fluid or a special assembly lubricant. It is advisable to open the wheel cylinder bleeder screw to let the air escape as the new cups are installed.

Brake service procedures recommend the use of a thin coating of special high temperature brake lubricant on all metal-to-metal contact points within the brake assembly. Care should be exercised to avoid getting the lubricant on linings or drums. This lubricant helps to minimize brake noise when the brake is first assembled. It will usually evaporate after the brakes have become hot from several hard stops.

In assembly, the adjuster and adjuster spring are connected between the brake shoes. The assembly is lifted into place. The wheel cylinder push rods and parking brake linkages are guided to their proper seats on the brake shoe web. The shoe retainers are connected, the anchor plate installed, the automatic adjusting mechanism connected, and the retracting springs connected to the anchor. After assembly, the brake should be rechecked to see that all linkages and springs are correctly assembled and seated.

The drum is installed and the adjuster turned until the linings are tight in the drum, then backed off the specified amount. The adjuster lever is held away from the star wheel while it is manually adjusted. On rear drums, it is necessary to release the parking brake before adjustment.

Disc Brake Service Operations. Discs and shoes can be inspected by removing the wheel. Some disc brake shoes can be replaced without removing the caliper. This can be done by removing the retaining clips and forcing the pistons into their bores. It may be necessary to remove some brake fluid from the reservoir because the wheel cylinders have a larger fluid capacity than the master cylinder reservoir. New shoes are merely slipped into the caliper and

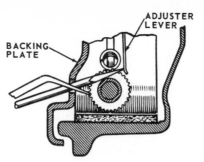

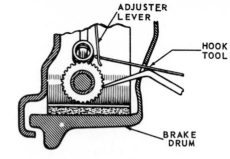

BACKING OFF ON ADJUSTING SCREW
(Access Slot In Backing Plate)

BACKING OFF ON ADJUSTING SCREW
(Access Slot in Brake Drum)

Fig. 24-34 Typical drum brake clearance adjustment methods (The Bendix Corporation).

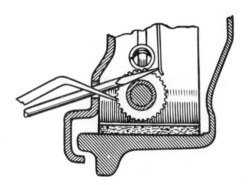

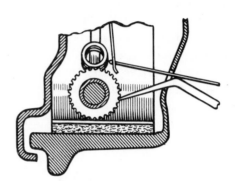

held with retaining pins. Other types of calipers require caliper removal before the shoes can be replaced.

A disc with a rusty edge outside the area wiped by the shoes should be cleaned before new shoes are installed. The best way to do this is to remove the disc and refinish it on a brake lathe with a disc grinder attachment.

The caliper has to be disassembled or removed from the adapter mounting to remove the wheel

hub and disc. To prevent damage to the hose, the caliper should be supported so it doesn't hang on the brake hose.

When new caliper piston seals are required, the caliper must be removed from the adapter plate, then the brake hose is removed to free the caliper. A four-piston caliper needs to be separated for cylinder service. The caliper can be supported in a vice, for service. Excessive clamping pressure that would distort the bore should be avoided.

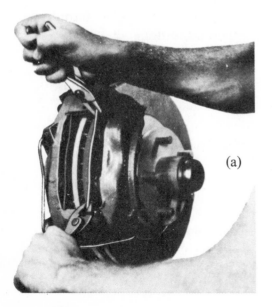

(a)

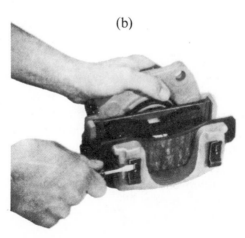

(b)

Fig. 24-35 Removing disc brake shoes (Kelsey-Hays Company). (a) Four-piston caliper type, (b) single-piston caliper type.

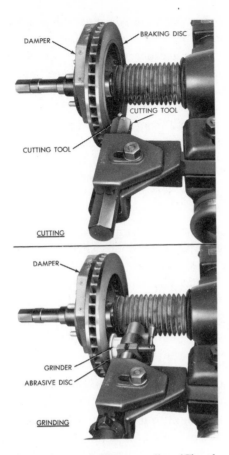

Fig. 24-36 Refinishing a disc (Chrysler Motors Corporation).

The dust boot is removed and then the piston can be removed. The piston is hollow on the open end so it requires an expanding tool that will lock into the open piston center for pulling. When the piston is seized so tight that it won't come out, it can be drilled with a tap drill, then threads tapped into the hole. A bolt screwed into these threads will jack the piston from the bore. If the piston is damaged or shows signs of corrosion or wear, it should be replaced. Remove all rubber parts.

The wheel cylinder bore is honed to remove any rust and minor pits. If they are not easily removed, the caliper will have to be replaced. New rubber parts are used during assembly. Brake fluid is used as a lubricant for assembly. An open bleeder screw will facilitate piston assembly.

The disc brake is assembled in the reverse order of its disassembly using new rubber parts and new linings. Care must be taken to avoid cocking or binding.

Master Cylinder Service. Fluid leakage at the master cylinder bore indicates that the master cylinder requires rebuilding. External leakage is easily visible. Internal leakage is indicated by a gradual loss of pedal height without loss of fluid as pressure is held on the brake pedal. The piston, springs and check valves are removed from the

Fig. 24-37 Removing a piston from a caliper (Kelsey-Hays Company).

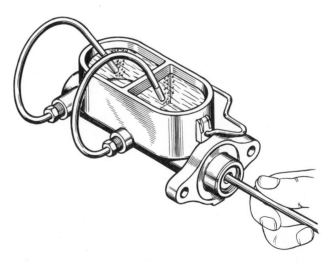

Fig. 24-38 Master cylinder bleeding method (The Bendix Corporation).

429

master cylinder body. The master cylinder body is thoroughly cleaned and the cylinder bore honed. All rubber parts and check valves are installed. New pistons and springs are used if they show any signs of abnormal wear.

Brake Bleeding. Brake system bleeding is a process of removing air from the hydraulic system. The master cylinder may be bled before it is installed to reduce bleeding time. Master reservoirs are filled and bleeding tubes are connected to the outlet fittings. The bleeder tube free ends are submerged back into the top of the reservoirs. Slow pumping will remove all of the air bubbles.

The master cylinder is installed and the brake lines connected. A pressure brake bleeder is installed on the master cylinder. This keeps the master cylinder full and under pressure. Bleeding is done by starting with the cylinder furthest from the master cylinder. A bleeder hose is attached to the wheel cylinder bleeder fitting. The free end of the bleeder hose is placed below the surface of hydraulic fluid in a glass jar, so air will not enter the hose free end. The bleeder is opened and fluid allowed to run until no further bubbles come from the end of the bleeder hose. This procedure is used at each wheel.

Bleeding can be done by manual bleeding. It is much slower than pressure bleeding. The master cylinder must be kept full as the bleeding is being done. Two people are required, one to operate the brake pedal and one to open and close the bleeder

Fig. 24-39 Pressure bleeding a hydraulic brake system (The Bendix Corporation).

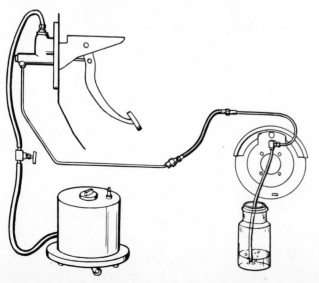

screw. A bleeder hose is connected to the cylinder bleeder and the free end submerged in brake fluid in a jar. The bleeder is opened and the pedal is slowly depressed. This forces fluid into the jar. When the pedal is fully depressed, the bleeder is closed, then the pedal is allowed to come up slowly. This brings fluid from the reservoir into the system. These cycles are repeated until no bubbles appear in the jar. Fluid will need to be put in the master cylinder as fluid enters the system. This procedure is used at each wheel cylinder to finish the bleeding job.

Brakes with metering valves have to have the metering valve held open when bleeding with a pressure bleeder. If time is available, the brakes will gravity bleed. The master cylinder must be kept full of fluid and the bleeder valve must be open until a solid stream of fluid drains from the bleeder hose. Service manuals should be checked for special instructions.

Power Brakes. Power brake units are faulty when they will not provide assist. This could be the result of faulty vacuum hoses, plugged breathers, faulty control valves, or chamber leaks. Hoses can be easily checked. If the problem is in the power unit, the unit will have to be disassembled to be repaired. Disassembly requires the use of special tools, so the unit is usually exchanged for a rebuilt unit. When tools are available, the booster housing is twisted to unlatch the housing sections. The booster is completely disassembled, cleaned, and inspected. Rubber diaphragm, valves, or seals are usually at fault and these are always replaced with new parts. Other faulty parts must be replaced. Special tools are also needed to reassemble the booster unit.

Parking Brake. Parking brake cables are adjusted after the service brakes are bled and adjusted. They are adjusted so they will fully apply and completely release. Parking brake adjustments are made on the parking brake cable. The cable must move freely in the flexible housings going through the rear brake backing plate.

The manufacturer's detailed instruction procedures and specifications should be followed. When properly serviced, brakes will provide safe vehicle stops. Only the best materials and workmanship are good enough for the brake system.

Review Questions
Chapter 24

1. Define the following brake terms: heel, toe, leading shoe, trailing shoe, servo action, primary shoe, and secondary shoe.

2. Describe the operation of the dual servo brake application.

3. How does a disc brake differ from a drum brake?

4. What determines the brake temperature after a stop?

5. Why is vehicle kinetic energy important to consider when studying brakes?

6. What is the advantage of braking at the impending skid point?

7. What causes weight transfer during braking?

8. What factors in addition to brakes will help stop a car?

9. What causes brake fade?

10. Why are dual servo brakes susceptible to fade?

11. Where is brake torque absorbed in the vehicle?

12. From what materials are linings made?

13. What are the advantages and disadvantages of bonded linings?

14. Name three types of construction used for brake drums.

15. Why are disc brakes replacing drum brakes?

16. Why are single-piston calipers replacing four-piston calipers on disc brakes?

17. Why is it critical to use the correct brake fluid?

18. Describe the operation of a master cylinder during apply and release.

19. Describe the operation of a tandem master cylinder with one-half inoperative.

20. How does a brake warning light operate?

21. How does a four-piston fixed caliper differ from a single-piston floating caliper?

22. Why are proportioning valves and metering valves used in disc brake applications?

23. How is wheel speed sensed in anti-lock braking?

24. What two types of power brake diaphragms are used?

25. Describe the servo action of a power brake valve unit during application, hold, and release.

26. What is meant by a tandem diaphragm power brake unit?

27. What is included in a routine brake inspection?

28. Why does a high temperature brake drum lower the pedal position while the disc brake pedal height is not affected by a high temperature disc?

29. List the service operations required to recondition drum brakes.

30. Describe the dual servo brake disassembly and reassembly procedure.

31. How is a brake disc removed from the vehicle?

32. How is the caliper reconditioned?

33. What are the indications of master cylinder problems?

34. How is a brake system bled?

35. What can go wrong with a power brake unit?

Quiz 24

1. Maximum braking of a vehicle is limited by the
   a. coefficient of friction between the lining and disc
   b. size of the brakes installed
   c. brake type installed
   d. tire adheasion to the road.

2. One of the main advantages of disc brakes over drum brakes is that the disc brake
   a. can stop a vehicle in a shorter distance
   b. is more fade resistant
   c. weighs less than drum brakes
   d. requires less pedal force to stop the vehicle.

3. Front wheel braking torque is absorbed by the
   a. spring
   b. disc
   c. spindle
   d. knuckle.

4. Brake servo action
   a. reduces required pedal pressure
   b. is noticable in disc brakes
   c. causes the primary lining to do most of the work
   d. is required on high performance and heavy vehicles.

5. Disc brake systems used on most domestic cars require
   a. frequent adjustments
   b. accurate caliper centering
   c. a brake booster
   d. long brake pedal travel to provide enough cylinder fluid.

6. The use of improper brake fluid may result in
   a. fluid vapors in the system
   b. plugged lines that prevent brake release
   c. improper hydraulic pressures
   d. excessive brake pedal travel.

7. Disc brake shoe return force is provided by
   a. especially designed return springs
   b. unequal hydraulic pressures
   c. master cylinder suction
   d. rectangular seal distortion.

8. Proportioning valves are required on some vehicles with front disc brakes because disc brakes
   a. are not effective during light braking
   b. have greater holding ability
   c. require higher pressures
   d. have larger wheel cylinder volumes.

9. The greatest advantage of anti-lock braking is that it will
   a. stop the car in a shorter distance on ice
   b. stop the car in a shorter distance on dry concrete
   c. allow directional control during maximum braking
   d. prevent panic stops that would throw the occupants against the dashboard.

10. Brake bleeding is a procedure to
    a. eliminate air from the hydraulic system
    b. remove excess fluid to reduce brake pressure
    b. remove excess fluid to reduce brake pressure
    c. filter contamination from the fluid
    d. make final brake shoe adjustments.

chapter 25

Tire Design and Operation

Vehicle control, acceleration, and braking occur through the tires and their footprint or contact patch on the road surface. Tire demands are low when the vehicle is operated at low speed and light loads on smooth, dry road surfaces. The requirements on them increase as speed, load, and handling demands increase.

Tires must be large enough and strong enough to support the load they are expected to carry. They must absorb or cushion, by deflecting, part of the shock from road irregularities. They must develop tractive forces for accelerating, cornering, and braking. While doing this, passenger car tires rotate approximately 800 revolutions for each mile traveled.

The force required to make the tire slip on its footprint, called traction, is the same in all directions while the tire tread is flat on the road surface, whether it is accelerating, cornering, braking, or any combination of these. The total available tractive force is not important until the vehicle is near the tractive limit, where sliding or skidding will occur. Tractive force to control the vehicle drops rapidly when a skid starts and vehicle control is lost.

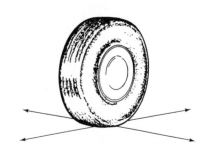

Fig. 25-1 Tractive force is equal in all directions.

25-1 TIRE CONSTRUCTION

A tire is made from rubberized fabric plys over a rubber liner. The edges of the plys are wrapped around a wire bead that holds the tire to the wheel rim. The fabric plys are covered with a rubber compound tread and a different rubber compound for the side walls. The tire is cured in a mold to vulcanize the parts into a single unit and form the tread design.

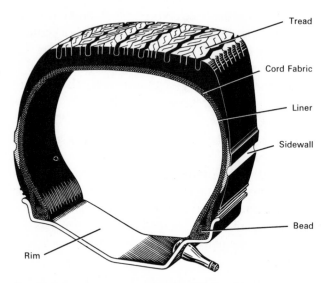

Fig. 25-2 Section of a tire showing parts (The Firestone Tire and Rubber Company).

Plys. Several types of fabric cord materials are used in tire plys. Tire manufacturers and fabric producers are continually striving to improve their materials and develop new materials that will better meet tire requirements.

Rayon was introduced as a tire cord material to replace cotton in 1938, just before World War II. It was much more durable, produced a soft ride, was more resilient, and less expensive than cotton. Rayon's tensile strength, or the pulling force required to break it, is 94,000 lb. per sq. inch. After World War II, rayon became the major tire cord material. Since its first introduction, it has had several modifications to improve its characteristics and reduce its cost.

Two forms of nylon, another synthetic material, were introduced as tire cord material in 1947, soon after World War II. Its 122,000 lb. per sq. in. tensile strength is about 30% greater than rayon, producing high impact strength. It is more heat resistant and water resistant than rayon. Nylon cord tires have less flexibility than rayon, and this feature helps to produce better vehicle handling. This same lack of flexibility, however, tends to produce a harsh ride. Nylon cord's major disadvantage is the characteristic that causes nylon cord tires to take a set while standing. This produces flat spots that produce a thump when the car first starts to roll. As the tires warm from rolling, the cords relax and the flat spot quickly disappears. Techniques have been developed to stretch and temper nylon cord before it is used in a tire, to reduce the flat spotting tendency. Nylon is expensive when purchased by the pound; however, smaller cord diameters, called *denier* in the English system and *tex* in the metric system, will be as strong as larger rayon cords. For this reason, the cost difference is not as great as the price per pound would indicate. Nylon cord has been improved over the years of use to enhance its characteristics for tires as well as to reduce its cost.

In 1962, polyester cord was introduced for use in passenger car tire fabrics. Its 104,000 lb. per sq. in. tensile strength is between rayon and nylon. It produces a soft ride with no tendency to flat spot. It is less heat resistant than nylon and more heat resistant than rayon. Polyester cord tires have increased their application as original equipment tires and appear to be becoming the dominant tire cord material.

Tire manufacturers give tire cord materials a trade name when the material is specially processed for their specific tire. Rayon has been called Dynacor and Tyrex. Nylon cord is usually followed by a number to designate the specific processing. Numbers 6 and 66 are the ones most often used for tire cords.

Polyester has been called Vitacord, Dacron, and Kodel.

Strands of fiberglass show superior strength, 407,000 lb. per sq. in. tensile strength, to other tire cord materials, but have a poor flexing resistance. In 1962, Owens-Corning perfected a technique to impregnate fiberglass yarn with a plastic material. This plastic separated the individual strands so they would not chafe against each other as they flexed. This breakthrough allowed fiberglass to be used as a specialty cord in tires. It cannot be used as a side wall cord because it has low flexibility strength. Fiberglass was initially used for a breaker ply or belt between the tire ply and tread in 1968 and provided a much longer tire life.

Steel cords are used for belts in some tires. They have high impact strength and are quite rigid.

Tires may use from two to ten plys of cord fabric. The cords in the plys may be large or small denier, and have two or three twisted strands. The number of plys, in itself, does not indicate tire strength so a load rating scale has been developed by the Tire and Rim Association to classify and rate tires.

Tire Rubber. Rubber used in tires is an elastomer compound that blends natural and synthetic rubbers with additions of chemicals and filler compounds to produce the desired characteristics. Tire tread stock must be able to resist wear and abrasion while providing traction. Large amounts of carbon black are added to the tread rubber to increase wear and abrasion resistance. Traction results from tread rubber hardness, compounding, and tread design. Hard compounds provide good wear and poor traction. Soft compounds give good traction and poor wear. The tread compound is a selected compromise to provide the properties required for each tire application.

Side wall and ply impregnation rubber is a more flexible rubber compound than tread rubber. It gives the tire its required flexibility and strength properties. The side wall must be flexible enough to deflect as it passes the tire footprint on each revolution. It must also flex to absorb any shock that is produced by irregularities in the road surface. The side wall must have sufficient strength to transfer all of the acceleration and braking torque between the wheel rim and tire tread. It also must withstand cornering forces that are applied to the vehicle.

Tire rubber deteriorates with temperature and age. Rubber compounds are, therefore, varied to provide the expected service life requirements of the tire. A tractor tire may be expected to last twenty years, a truck tire 50,000 miles, a passenger car tire 30,000 miles, and a racing tire 500 miles.

Manufacturing Tires. Tire manufacturing starts with raw materials being processed in supplier plants. Natural rubber comes from plantations while synthetic rubbers and the basic cord fiber materials come from the petrochemical industry. The cord material is made into a fabric in textile mills before it is sent to the tire manufacturer.

Tire fabric is primarily strands of tire cord running lengthwise in the fabric. Small cross strands are woven through the cords to hold them in place for handling and have no function in the final tire.

Additional fabric processing is done by the tire manufacturer. The fabric is stretched and heated to give it uniform mechanical properties, then coated with an adhesive. Adhesive is required as a bonding agent between the cord and rubber compound. The treated fabric then goes to large steel rollers, called *calendars*, that squeeze the uncured rubber into the cord fabric to produce a sheet. This rubberized sheet is cut into strips at an angle or *bias*, then reassembled into a long strip with the cords running at the required bias angle. The rubberized cord fabric is now ready to be used in tire construction.

Tread rubber and side wall rubber compounds are extruded into the required shape and cut to length at an angle to provide a long tapered joint.

Wire for the tire bead is rubber coated and rolled into the required size bundle or bead, two per tire.

The tire is made on an expandable drum. One bead is slid over the drum to be in position when needed. The drum rotates as the tire is built in layers. The first layer consists of a rubber sheet that takes the place of an innertube to seal the air. This is followed by two or more plys of rubberized cord fabric. The fabric is carefully cut to length parallel to its cords, then lapped over the other end of the ply with the required overlap joint, to produce an enclosed cylinder shape. Adjacent plys have their bias in alternate directions to give the tire strength, much like the grain in plywood. The plys are followed by belts or breakers when required. The beads are placed over the edges of the ply. The ply is then wrapped over the bead back onto itself, locking the bead bundle into place.

A tread and sidewall rubber strip is wrapped around the plys. White or colored rubber used for tire identification and trim is molded within the side wall strip. The entire assembly is pressed together by a process called stitching.

At this point, tire construction is completed. The tire looks like an open ended barrel. It is inspected and if deviations are noted, the tire can be repaired because it is still green or uncured rubber.

After the green tire passes inspection, it is sent to the mold to be cured. The green tire slides over a bladder that expands as the hot mold closes around the tire. This bladder forces the tread surface outward into the mold. The tread pattern and identification data for the tire are cut into the mold surface. Small holes in the mold allow air to escape as the rubber fills the mold. These holes also produce the small rubber projections often seen on new tires. The rubber composition determines the mold temperature, about 320°, and time needed for curing, around twenty minutes.

The tire is trimmed and inspected when it comes from the mold. Side walls are cut or ground to expose tire striping rubber. The tire is now ready to be packaged and sent to the customer.

25-2 TIRE DESIGN FEATURES

The greatest difference in appearance in tires the same size is in their tread design, trim stripes, and name or identification data. The greatest difference in tires, however, is in the cord material and the way it is put into the tire.

Tire Body. Most original equipment tires have the cord running at an angle or bias. This provides a cross-cord sidewall to give the required strength to transfer acceleration and braking torque. The cross bias cord angle runs from 30 to 40°.

Original equipment tires and the majority of replacement tires have gone from four-ply to two-ply construction. Two-ply tires run cooler, are more flexible to absorb shock from road irregularities, and apply greater self-aligning torque to the steering system after a turn. Two-ply tires are as strong as four-ply tires, because the tire cord denier

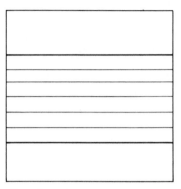

Normal tread ahead of contact patch

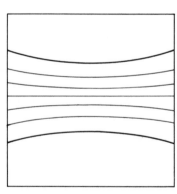

Contracted tread in contact patch

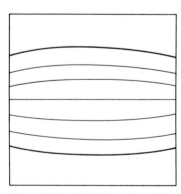

Expanded tread behind contact patch

Fig. 25-3 Tire flexing through the tire contact patch.

is larger than that used in four-ply tires. The strength of the ply is the result of the weight of the cord rather than the number of plys. Service experience has shown fewer failures with two-ply tires than with four-ply tires. This is primarily the result of lower temperature operation and their ability to flex over road hazards rather than resisting a hazard which would break the cord.

Bias-ply tires allow the tire to squirm as it goes through the tire footprint. The tread is pushed together as it goes into the footprint. This stores energy in the rubber. As it comes out of the footprint, the tire rapidly expands and goes beyond the neutral point into a stretched position. The tread then contracts, causing an oscillation. At high speeds, this tread squirm is evidenced as a standing wave on the back side of the tire as it comes up from the tire contact patch or footprint. Closing and opening of the tread as it goes through the contact patch is one of the major causes of normal tire wear.

Tread stability and reduction of squirm in belted tires results in up to 100% improvement in tire mileage compared to bias-ply tires. By holding the tread shape, belted tires run cooler, improve fuel mileage, improve traction, and double blowout resistance when compared to bias-ply tires.

Fig. 25-4 Belted tire on the left with minimum squirm. Bias tire on the right shows excessive squirm (The Goodyear Tire and Rubber Company).

Belted tires do not flex as easily as bias cord tires, so they transfer more road shock into the wheels and suspension system. Because of this, the wheel spindles, knuckles, and suspension system need to be stronger. Vehicle springing is modified to reduce road shock transfer to the passenger compartment when the vehicle is designed to use the bias belted tires.

Radial ply belted tires have been built in Europe for a number of years on special tire building equipment. The radial ply cord angles run from 88 to 90° and the belt cords run from 12 to 20°. The radial cord provides a soft side wall that will produce a softer ride than belted bias tires. The belt around the radial cords holds the tread shape through the contact patch or footprint. Radial belted tires provide more cornering power and less wear than bias belted tires as a result of a lower slip angle. Low slip angle helps the tire hold the road under nearly 10% higher side load forces. With the radial belted tires, loss of tire-to-road adhesion occurs suddenly, with little warning, especially on wet surfaces. Ultimate adhesion of belted tires is the same as the bias and bias belted tire. This sudden loss of adhesion may come too rapidly for the average driver to make a compensation adjustment and control will be lost. Radial belted tires produce a harsh ride at low speeds, require a high steering effort, especially when parking, and they are expensive.

Tire Tread. Tire tread design is not necessary for a tire running on dry pavement. The best example of this are the racing "slicks" that are designed to have maximum possible tire-to-road adhesion on dry hard surfaces. Tire tread design becomes important when the vehicle is operated on gravel, sand, snow, or wet surfaces. Tire treads that are satisfactory for a trailer may not be satisfactory for use on the steering wheels. Still another tread design may be better for the driving wheels. When the wheels are required to both drive and steer, the best tire design becomes more complex. Original equipment tire tread designs are a compromise among normal steering, driving, and braking requirements, modified by cost considerations. Premium

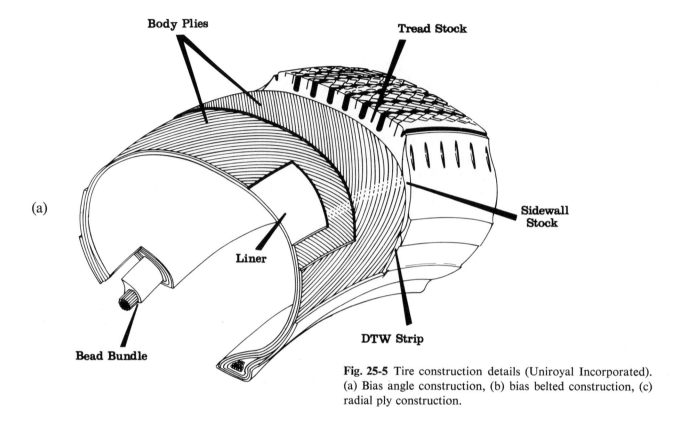

(a)

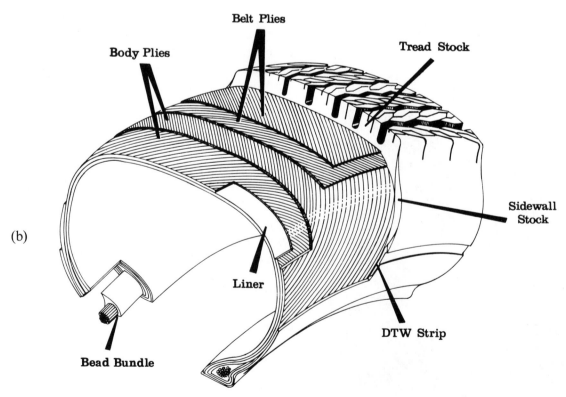

(b)

Fig. 25-5 Tire construction details (Uniroyal Incorporated). (a) Bias angle construction, (b) bias belted construction, (c) radial ply construction.

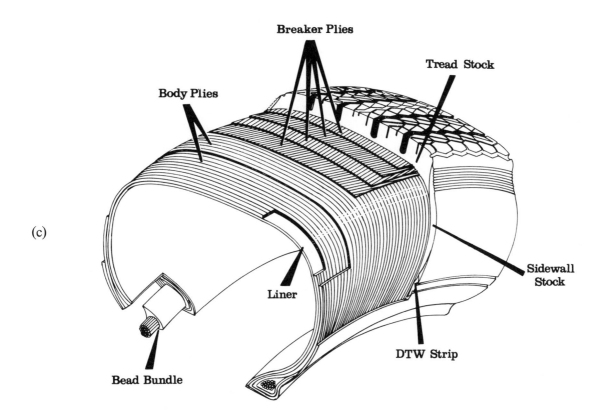

Breaker Plies

Tread Stock

Body Plies

(c)

Liner

Sidewall Stock

Bead Bundle

DTW Strip

tires have a much finer tread pattern than original equipment tires. Some of the premium tires have small cuts across the tread surface that are called *blades* or *sipes*. They act as many edges to grip the road surface and as fins to dissipate heat. The blades are cut in an unequal pattern to break up the harmonic noise that would result from equal spacing.

The average tread depth on new tires is 3/8″. Tread can be safely worn down to 1/16″. Tires have a *wear indicator* that shows as a flat streak across the tread when the tire tread is worn to 1/16″ deep. When the indicator appears, the tire should be replaced.

Economy tires have a coarse tread pattern compared to original equipment tires. Specialized tire treads for snow, rain, sand, etc., are available where special tire-to-road traction requirements exist.

Tire-to-road adhesion is much less when the road becomes wet. The water must squeeze from the contact patch on the road surface in order for the tire to contact the road surface to give adhesion. Water on the road surface is displaced by the tire as it rolls so the water must be moved. Water displacement can be seen by the splash from a tire

Fig. 25-6 Tire tread wear indicator (Chrysler-Plymouth Division, Chrysler Corporation).

439

traveling through water. It is also evident by the relatively dry tracks left behind a car traveling on a wet surface. The noticeable splash comes from the side of the tire; however, a large portion of the water will squirt endwise through the tread grooves and is not easily seen on a rolling tire. Grooves forming the tread design provide a place for the water to flow from the tire contact patch.

Water has mass and requires time to displace. A tire moving at high speeds through an 1/8″ of surface water may actually climb up on the top of the water and hydroplane. This occurs because the water cannot find a rapid path to escape the contact patch. A hydroplaning tire cannot drive, steer or brake, so it provides no vehicle control. Large straight tread grooves provide the best tire adhesion on a wet surface. As a tire wears, the groove depth reduces and its wet adhesion depreciates. A nearly smooth tire will have poor wet adhesion. "Slicks" will obviously have very poor adhesion on a wet surface. This is the reason that it is a good practice for a driver to slow down when driving on a wet road, especially with worn tires.

Tire Size. Tire sizes are based upon the size of wheel rim, the load range, the capacity, and the tire series.

Wheel diameter and width between rim flanges are measured at the wheel bead diameter. Larger wheel diameters require larger tires which, in turn, will support more weight. Under fender clearance limits the maximum tire size that can be used on a vehicle. Oversize tires on a vehicle may require wheels with wider rim widths, because the rim width must also match the tire size and tire design. Vehicle or tire manufacturer's specifications should be consulted.

Bias-ply tires use a number preceding the bead diameter to indicate tire width. This number is the approximate width of the inflated tire. Wider tires are capable of supporting more weight or have more capacity with their larger contact patch area.

Some bias-ply and all belted bias ply tires use a letter preceding a number to designate tire capacity. This would be similar to the number in the bias-ply tires described above. The letter is independent of the rim size or load range. As the letters advance from A, the capacity becomes greater.

Early tire specifications rated tires by the number of cord plys. As new cord fabrics were used, the ply as a rating was no longer meaningful so tire manufacturers listed both the actual number of plys and the ply rating as compared to the older construction methods. This led to confusion on the part of the customer, so the tire industry replaced the ply rating with a letter to indicate the load range. B load range is used in standard automotive applications. The D load range may be used on vehicles that carry heavy loads or tow trailers.

Series. The series number indicates the approximate ratio of the tire section height to the section width. If the height of the tire is 78% of the width,

Fig. 25-7 Selected sample of tire sizes and load limits.

78 Series	70 Series	60 Series	Load rating D ———→							Load rating C ———→		Load rating B ——→	
		psi	20	22	24	26	28	30	32	34	36	38	40
B78-14			870	910	960	1000	1050	1090	1130	1170	1200	1240	1280
C78-14			950	1000	1050	1100	1140	1190	1230	1270	1320	1360	1400
D78-14	D70-14		1010	1070	1120	1170	1220	1270	1320	1360	1410	1450	1490
E78-14 E78-15	E70-14 E70-15	E60-15	1070	1130	1190	1240	1300	1350	1400	1440	1490	1540	1580
F78-14 F78-15	F70-14 F70-15	F60-15	1160	1220	1280	1340	1400	1450	1500	1550	1610	1650	1700
G78-14 G78-15	G70-14 G70-15	G60-15	1250	1310	1380	1440	1500	1560	1620	1680	1730	1780	1830
H78-14 H78-15	H70-14 H70-15	H60-15	1360	1440	1510	1580	1650	1710	1770	1830	1890	1950	2010

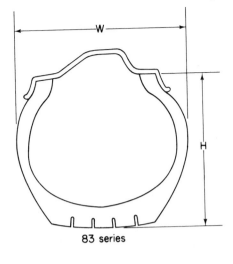

83 series

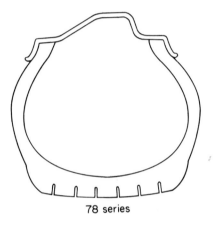

78 series

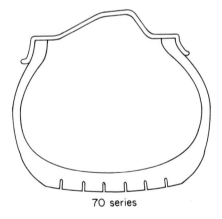

70 series

Fig. 25-8 Cross section of tire series.

as low as 35% to 45%. Tires above 80% have bias-ply construction. Below 80%, they may be bias; however, they are usually belted.

The trend is to use low profile tires with lower aspect ratios. These tires improve vehicle handling and give a performance styling look to the vehicle.

Tire Size Designation. The series number designation is placed on the tire directly behind the letter that indicates tire capacity. This, in turn, is followed by the rim diameter. The complete designation for the tire size is, for example: E78-14 or H70-15. Radial ply tires of 70 series place an R immediately after the capacity letter; for example: GR 70-14 or FR 70-15 to indicate the tire size and capacity. Most passenger car tire sizes are available in load ranges B, C, and D.

Tire size and type should not be mixed on vehicles. The slip angle of each tire type is different. Mixing tire types results in unpredictable control at highway speeds; thus the vehicle could be dangerous to drive.

25-3 TIRE OPERATION

Wheel rim widths used with tires are important. If the rim width nearly matches the tread width, the sidewall will be approximately straight up and down. This allows very little flexing and produces a harsh ride. Passenger car rims are narrower than the tread and the sidewall curves inward to produce a softer ride. Some racing wheel rims are wider than the tread, allowing the sidewall to lean outward. The tire is designed to match the rim to keep a tight air seal which keeps air pressure in the tire. This tire bead to rim match serves another function that is often overlooked. Engine acceleration torque tries to turn the rim inside of the tire. The only thing that keeps this from happening is the friction between the bead and rim. This type of force also occurs during braking, but in the reverse direction.

During a turn, the tire is deflected sidewise. This force tends to loosen the bead from the rim on one side of the tire. The tire bead must be secure enough to maintain rim contact.

the tire is a 78 series. If the tire section has the same height, but is wider, the ratio of height to width changes. For example, this wider tire's height could be 70% of the width to make a 70 series tire. This ratio of height to width is called tire *aspect ratio.* Passenger car tires' aspect ratios may run from 95% to 60%, the smaller number indicating a relatively wide tire. Racing tires may have an aspect ratio

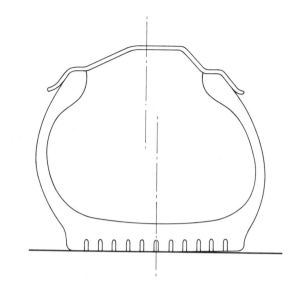

Fig. 25-9 Tire deflection caused by a side force.

At high vehicle speeds, centrifugal force increases the tire diameter. This force tries to throw the bead from the rim. The bead wire holds the bead diameter so it will remain in contact with the rim. Belted tires keep the tread from expanding at high speeds; thus stabilizing the tread and minimizing heat buildup.

Tires flex as they rotate while carrying vehicle load. This flexing distorts the tire, especially when the tire assumes a side load while going around a curve. Distortion is a natural reaction of a tire. It allows the tire to absorb road shock and to flex through the contact patch without skidding as the vehicle makes a turn.

Natural tire flexing causes heat buildup in the tire. Heat in a normal tire operated within its load range will stabilize at a safe temperature. Excessive heat is a tire's worst enemy. Temperatures above 250° result in the loss of tire strength, the rubber-to-cord bond separates and the air escapes, often as a blowout. In some cases, tires become so hot they start to burn.

Tire heat can be reduced by reducing the factors that produce heat. The simplest method is to slow the vehicle speed. This results in less flexing per minute and provides more cooling time between flexing. Excess heat can be the result of underinflation, which allows the sidewalls to flex excessively as they go past the tire contact patch. Proper inflation will eliminate this problem. Excessive weight on a tire causes the same type of flexing as underinfla-

tion. This problem can be corrected by reducing the weight being carried or by installing a larger capacity tire.

Abnormal wear results from improper tire pressure. Underinflation causes tread edge wear as well as excessive flexing, heat, and tire body damage. Excess flexing will also lead to improper vehicle handling that is noticeable at speeds as low as 35 miles per hour.

Tires that run underinflated or with too much weight are severely damaged before the air leaks out. Tires that are ruined when flat were most likely damaged well before the air pressure escaped.

Overinflation prevents flexing. It usually causes wear on the center of the tire tread. The reduction in flexing produces a harsh ride and the tire is vulnerable to impact that could puncture the tire rather than allowing the tire to flex over the obstacle.

25-4 TIRE SELECTION

Tire selection is based upon the wheel rim size and the kind of operation expected from the vehicle. Operating considerations include the type of driving, the type and condition of the road surface, the weight to be carried, the miles driven per year, and the length of time the vehicle is to be used.

Original equipment tires are called 100 level tires. Tires with less quality will cost less and tires with better quality will cost more. Each tire manufacturer has a large selection of tire brand names and styles in their inexpensive tires below the 100 level quality. These are usually competitively priced and are only satisfactory for low speed, lightly loaded service. Each manufacturer will usually have only one or two tire styles in their premium classification. Tire selection can be summarized as they relate to mileage, ride, and handling.

A stiffer tire will provide better handling and a harsh ride. Belted tires give more tire mileage, along with a ride more harsh than bias-ply tires. Wide treads have more style and are difficult to steer, especially while parking. Tires with hard rubber in their treads wear longer, but provide less tire-to-road adhesion. No one tire is best for all types of vehicle operation. Vehicle and tire manufacturer recommendations should be followed for the most satisfactory results.

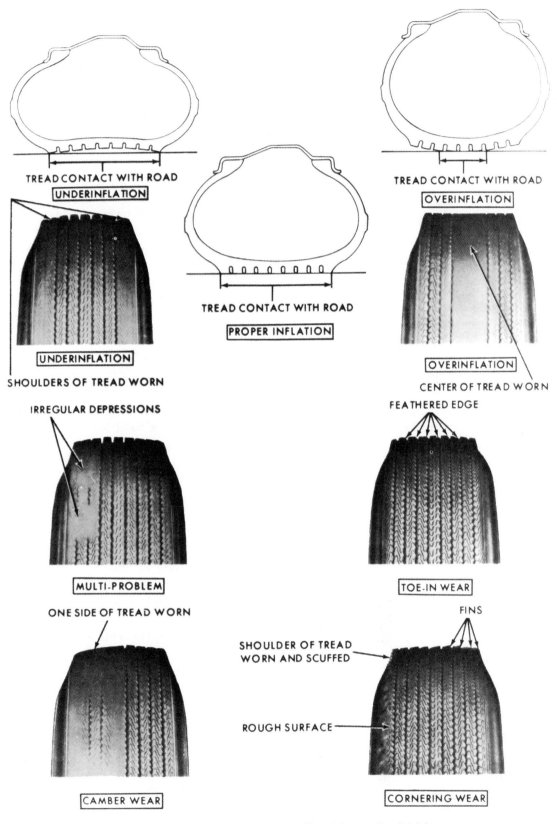

TREAD CONTACT WITH ROAD
UNDERINFLATION

UNDERINFLATION
SHOULDERS OF TREAD WORN

TREAD CONTACT WITH ROAD
PROPER INFLATION

TREAD CONTACT WITH ROAD
OVERINFLATION

OVERINFLATION
CENTER OF TREAD WORN

IRREGULAR DEPRESSIONS

MULTI-PROBLEM

FEATHERED EDGE

TOE-IN WEAR

ONE SIDE OF TREAD WORN

CAMBER WEAR

FINS
SHOULDER OF TREAD WORN AND SCUFFED

ROUGH SURFACE

CORNERING WEAR

Fig. 25-10 Tire wear indications (Cadillac Motor Car Division, General Motors Corporation).

25-5 TIRE SERVICE

Tire service starts with a visual inspection for abnormalities that may exist. Abnormal wear is the most obvious. Tread wear shows the result of abnormal inflation, abnormal suspension alignment or condition, and cornering wear. The tread rubber should be checked for cracks in the grooves and for cuts or tears from hitting objects. Side walls should be checked for abrasion and cuts from operating at low pressure or from hitting objects. Any bulges on the tire indicate separation of plys, tread rubber, or sidewall rubber. Internal damage may exist that does not show up on the outside of the tire. The tire should be removed from the rim for inspection any time the tire has gone flat or there is any reason to suspect possible tire body damage.

Punctures should be patched on the inside of the tire following approved plugging and patching techniques. Emergency repairs of small punctures may be made from the outside of the tire. These should be permanently repaired on the inside at the earliest possible opportunity.

Normal tire tread wear is rated at 60 miles per hour. Lower speeds improve tire mileage while higher speeds reduce it. Tire mileage on a set of tires may be extended by rotating the tire and wheel position each 5000 miles. Experience has shown that the most even wear will result when the

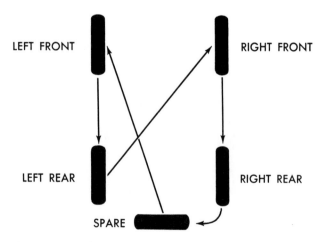

Fig. 25-11 Normal tire rotation sequence (Chrysler-Plymouth Division, Chrysler Corporation).

tires and wheels are rotated as shown in Figure 25-11. Some vehicles use different tire pressures on front and rear so the tire pressure should be checked and adjusted after tire rotation.

Wheel and tire balance is another of the service operations that will extend tire mileage and suspension life while producing a smooth riding vehicle. Wheel unbalance sets up vibrations in the suspension system that shake the vehicle.

To roll smoothly, the tire must not only be balanced, but must be round. Out of roundness can come from tire and wheel tolerance stack up. The wheel is centered on the attaching bolt holes. When mounted on the hub, the tire bead surface must not run out beyond the limit specification. These limits are approximately .035″ radial run-out and .045″ lateral run-out. The tire is also made with tolerances, but these are difficult to check when the tire is not mounted on a wheel. Total wheel-tire radial run-out is usually limited to .090″ and lateral run-out to .125″. Some manufacturers may recommend slightly different limits.

When tire-wheel run-out is excessive, it can be corrected by repositioning the tire on the wheel or by removing tread rubber from the high side on special tire truing equipment. Truing the tire along with balancing will give the tire smooth rolling operation and maximum mileage.

If an object were spun in space, all forces would tend to balance each other. Spinning action will be in a plane of rotation around the center of gravity, regardless of the object shape. If an odd-shaped object is thrown, it will spin in a plane of rotation around its center of gravity. A round solid ball has its center of gravity in the geometric center. Some plastic "funny balls" are made with heavy sides. When thrown, they appear to wobble, but they are actually spinning in a plane around their center of gravity and not their geometric center. A wheel and tire would react in the same way if allowed to spin free, but it is attached to a spindle. If the wheel and tire are in perfect balance, the spindle is located at the center of gravity and the tread centerline is on the plane of rotation, so the wheel will spin smoothly. If the wheel and tire assembly are unbalanced, the unbalance force will shake the spindle when the wheel is spun. The effect of this shake increases as the square of the speed, so it is much more noticeable at high speeds.

During tire construction, random assembly

(a)

(b)

Fig. 25-12 Tire run out (American Motors Corporation). (a) Radial run out, (b) lateral run out.

may place splice overlaps on one side of the tire causing a heavy spot. If this tire were placed on a free turning wheel, the heavy spot would swing to the bottom. On a bubble balancer, the heavy side would drop. This is called *static balance* because it will always stop at the same point with the heavy spot down. If the wheel and tire assembly were rotated, the heavy spot would develop a greater centrifugal force than the rest of the tire. This force tries to displace the tire and wheel assembly to a new center of rotation. The wheel spindle, bearings and wheel hub prevent this action, so the shaking force goes into the suspension system. The suspension is restrained from moving forward and backward, but has a degree of freedom to move up and down. As the wheel spins, the static unbalance heavy spot lifts and lowers the suspension, causing a vertical vibration or bounce that is often called *wheel tramp*. Static wheel unbalance can be counterbalanced with weights added to the wheel rim opposite the heavy point. A static balanced wheel will cause no tramp and will stay level on a bubble wheel balancer.

During tire manufacture, the ply splices may

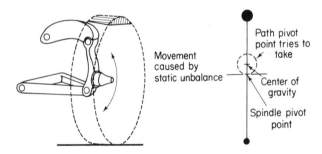

Fig. 25-13 Wheel static unbalance.

be concentrated on one edge of the tire tread or the tread rubber may be more dense on one side of the tread centerline than it is on the other. This tire could have perfect static balance, but when it is spun on a spindle, the tire force will try to establish a new plane of rotation. The top and bottom ends of the suspension knuckle are retained by the ball joints and front suspension, but the system has a degree of freedom to shake the front and rear of the tire-wheel assembly, turning the wheel inward and outward causing a *shimmy* condition. This type of unbalance can only be detected while the tire-

445

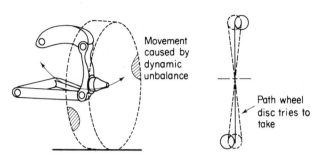

Fig. 25-14 Wheel dynamic unbalance.

Location of static balance weights at the tire light point

Location of dynamic balance weights to counter balance tire heavy section

Fig. 25-15 Location of balance weights.

wheel assembly is spinning. It is, therefore, called *dynamic balance*. Dynamic unbalance can be counter-balanced by placing two equal weights on the light portion of the wheel rim 180° apart and on opposite sides of the wheel. The use of two weights corrects dynamic unbalance, while maintaining static balance.

Many times, the correct placement of static balance weights can also be used to counter-balance dynamic unbalance. Balancing equipment instructions must be followed for satisfactory wheel balance.

Maximum tire mileage and maximum customer satisfaction occur when an accurately aligned vehicle in good condition is fitted with the correct tires, properly inflated and properly balanced. Tires should be rotated and inspected at recommended intervals.

Review Questions
Chapter 25

1. What are the tire requirements?

2. When does the total tire tractive force become important?

3. Describe tire construction.

4. What types of tire cord materials are used? What advantages and disadvantages does each have?

5. How does tire ply relate to load rating?

6. How do tire tread and side wall rubber compounds differ?

7. How do two- and four-ply tires differ? How are they the same?

8. How does squirm cause normal tire wear?

9. What are the advantages of the different types of tire body designs?

10. Why are different tire tread designs used?

11. How does road surface water affect tire adhesion?

12. What are the advantages and disadvantages of using oversized tires?

13. Describe tire designations.

14. Why should the mixing of tire types be avoided on one automobile?

15. Why is it important to have a good fit between the tire bead and rim?

16. What causes tire heat? How can it be reduced?

17. What is the result of over or under inflation?

Quiz 25

1. A tire's maximum tractive force is
a. greatest during acceleration
b. greatest during braking
c. greatest while making a turn
d. the same in all directions.

2. Belted tires give more tread life than non belted tires because
a. the belt holds the tire rigid
b. the belt keeps the tire from expanding at high speed
c. there is less tread squirm in the contact patch
d. they operate cooler.

3. Several flat streaks across the tire tread indicate
a. poor tire manufacturing control
b. uneven tire wear
c. tread depth is too shallow for safe operation
d. that the tire should be balanced.

4. One of the main reasons that few radial tires are built by domestic tire manufacturers is that
a. radial tires require different tire machines
b. automobile manufacturers prefer bias tires
c. the after market prefers low cost tires
d. radial tires have poor ride characteristics.

5. Maximum tire size that can be used on a vehicle is limited by

18. What is a 100 level tire?

19. What may be the advantage of using a tire level of less than or more than a 100 level?

20. What causes static unbalance and dynamic unbalance?

a. the maximum size available
b. rim and chassis clearance
c. wheel diameter
d. the maximum load that can be carried.

6. Overloading a tire will result in
a. excessive tire heating
b. high tire pressures
c. excessive center tread wear
d. uneven tire wear.

7. Wider tires give
a. more ultimate tractive force
b. a softer ride
c. more tire mileage
d. higher steering effort.

8. Excessive tire pressures may resilt in
a. more frequent punctures
b. difficult steering
c. rapid heat buildup
d. side wall cracking.

9. Tire rotation helps to
a. keep tires balanced
b. increase the mileage of the tire set
c. provide even tire wear
d. maintain wheel alignment.

10. Wheel vertical bounce or tramp can usually be corrected by
a. static wheel balancing
b. dynamic wheel balancing
c. replacing the tire
d. rotating the tire on the rim.

chapter 26

Vehicle Handling & Suspension

High production domestic passenger cars are designed for drivers who may be poorly equipped physically and mentally to drive, even though these drivers actually feel that they are very good drivers. Passenger car suspensions and steering are designed so that poorly equipped drivers will be able to sense impending loss of control in sufficient time to safely take corrective action. This slow driver handling response may be contrasted to a quick, sensitive handling response right up to the point that control is lost, that is found in race cars. The race driver must have trained senses to enable him to drive his race car at its maximum handling limit while he maintains control of the car.

Vehicle handling characteristics depend upon the chassis and suspension design. At one extreme is the suspension designed to give a soft boulevard ride of the type found on domestic luxury automobiles. At the other extreme is the suspension designed to give a stiff firm ride such as the suspension of a racing car. In between are the great majority of domestic automobiles that have suspensions which provide a ride that is a compromise between these extremes.

An improperly operating suspension is usually most noticeable to the driver as the vehicle handling characteristics change. These characteristics may change so slowly that he is not aware of the change until it has become dangerous. The suspension should be checked anytime there is any sign that the vehicle is handling improperly.

26-1 HANDLING REQUIREMENTS

All forces affecting automobile handling must pass through the interaction of the tire and road. Almost all automobile ride and handling characteristics are related directly to the properties of the tires being used. Changes in tire types, design, and condition will usually cause a drastic change in a vehicle's ride and handling reactions. Therefore, replacing the tires with new ones having the desired properties is often the best solution to a handling complaint.

Ride and handling are subjective values. They are terms that relate to the passenger and driver *feel*. No objective values have been devised that will satisfy everyone; however, passenger car manufacturers have run studies using large numbers of persons to determine driver feel characteristics that are acceptable to the majority of drivers for each vehicle type. For this reason, driver feel is different between a luxury passenger car, a sports car, and performance car.

Driver feel includes sensations created by changes in the vehicle direction, tire squeal, and body roll. Forces proportional to the road condition and the amount of tire slippage are felt in the steering wheel to warn the driver that the vehicle is approaching a skidding condition. A vehicle becomes uncontrollable in a skid.

The vehicle suspension, along with the tires and steering linkages, is designed to provide the driver with safe positive vehicle control and be free of irritating vibrations. Its design will produce minimum wear on the tires and other parts of the suspension system.

26-2 SUSPENSION REQUIREMENTS

Suspension systems may be designed to give a soft or firm ride. A soft ride, usually found on luxury passenger cars, results from large vehicle deflections using soft springs and mild shock absorber dampen-

ing that allows the deflection energy to be absorbed over a longer period of time. Sudden changes in the road, wind gusts, or steering positions will cause a sidewise body roll or fore and aft pitch. This, in turn, may produce difficult vehicle handling control. Conditions like this seldom occur on the modern highways. As the amount of vehicle deflection is reduced, ride becomes harsh and vehicle control improves. Vehicle suspension designs are a compromise between ride softness and handling ability, depending upon the manufacturer's design objective.

Maximum vehicle control exists when all four tires are in equal contact with the road surface. Control depends upon the friction between the tires and the road. The amount of friction that exists results from the type and surface condition of both tire and road, as well as from the weight on the tire. Acceleration forces, braking forces, and steering forces are *dynamic forces* that depend upon this friction. The vehicle suspension and weight distribution are designed to keep the wheels in maximum contact with the road to maintain desirable vehicle control. Control is lost on any wheel if the dynamic load exceeds the tire to road friction because the tire will slip or skid.

Tires encounter both large and small bumps as they roll over the road surface. Deflections from small bumps are absorbed by the tires. As the bumps become larger, the tires can no longer absorb the shock so the vertical deflection is sent through the wheels, drums, and bearings to the vehicle suspension system. Suspensions with large deflections can absorb these bumps and allow the vehicle body to ride smoothly. Suspensions with limited deflection bounce the vehicle body.

Bumps tend to bounce the tire from the road, thereby reducing tire to road friction when the effective weight becomes less at the high side of the bounce. Vehicle control is lost when the tire loses contact with the road. The suspension system must not only absorb shock, but it must keep the tire in contact with the road to ensure vehicle control.

Automotive suspension systems must support the vehicle weight while being flexible enough to absorb road shock. At the same time, the sus-

Einfedern (handwritten in margin)

Ausfedern (handwritten in margin)

pension must keep the tires in proper contact with the road surface. Vehicle load is supported by a flexible coil, leaf, or torsion spring. As a car goes over a bump, the spring is compressed. This motion is called *jounce*. Jounce stores energy in the spring. The stored energy forces the spring to return to its original shape. As it returns, it overruns the neutral position into the expanded or extended position. This motion is called *rebound*. The spring oscillates back and forth from jounce to rebound at a rate of 60 to 80 cycles per minute. Each cycle, jounce and rebound becomes smaller and smaller, due to friction of the spring's molecular structure and the suspension pivot joints. A shock absorber is added to each suspension to rapidly dampen and stop spring oscillation. Maximum jounce is limited by a rubber bumper and maximum rebound is limited by a bumper or the extended limit of the shock absorber.

Tire position is controlled during jounce by the spring itself or by linkages, levers, and arms. One

end of the linkage is connected to the movable portion of the suspension and the other end is attached to the vehicle structure. As the suspension moves into jounce or rebound, the movable end of the linkage swings in an arc. It is necessary to understand the characteristics of linkages swinging through an arc in order to understand the suspension reaction on an automobile.

The vertical and horizontal distances between the stationary end and the movable end of a link change as the link rotates through an arc. There is a variable distance between the vehicle structure when the hinge point of the suspension is on the stationary vehicle structure and the movable point is connected to the spindle, wheel and tire. This action forms the basis for suspension and steering geometry.

In Figure 26-2, the vertical distance (A) is called displacement when it is applied to automotive suspensions. For a given displacement, a long linkage (1) will give less horizontal change (B) than a short linkage (2). Linkage length and hinge points (P) are designed to maintain the best possible tire to road contact during all vehicle maneuvers while staying within the limits of lever length and available space in the vehicle.

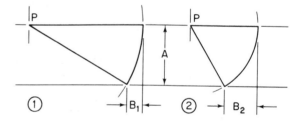

Fig. 26-2 Vertical and horizontal distance moved by an arc.

26-3 REAR SUSPENSION DESIGN

The simplest example of lever system principles on automobiles is the leaf-type rear spring suspension. The front portion of the leaf spring is attached to a spring hanger on the vehicle frame member. The rear axle housing is fastened near the middle of the spring. At rest in a static position or curb position, the section of the spring in front of the axle housing is nearly horizontal with the ground. During jounce and rebound, the axle will be at its maximum aft position when the spring hanger center and the axle center are the same distance above the ground.

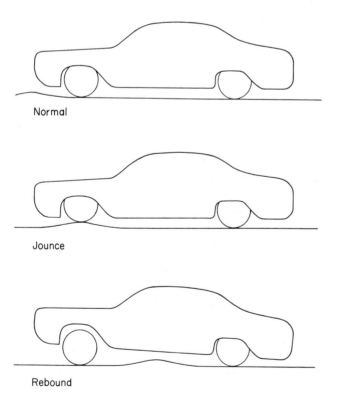

Fig. 26-1 Front wheel position in normal, jounce and rebound positions.

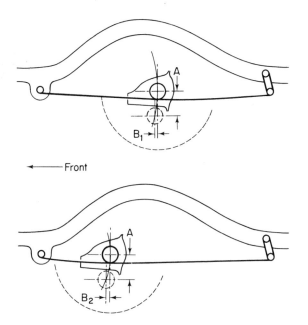

Fig. 26-3 Vertical distance, (a) compared to horizontal distance, (b) on different rear suspension geometry.

The axle will move forward from this position during all other positions of jounce and rebound. Forward movement increases with a short spring section in front of the axle when using the same spring deflection.

The leaf spring also serves as a lever to absorb rear axle torque that occurs during acceleration and braking. Torque tends to twist the axle housing which, in turn, attempts to twist the spring. This action is often called *wind-up*. The effect of wind-up is reduced with a short stiff forward spring section. Automotive leaf spring designs compromise the torque absorbing properties of the spring with the rear suspension geometry to produce the desired effects.

The rear portion of the leaf spring does not control torque, but merely helps to support vehicle weight and control *side sway* which occurs when the

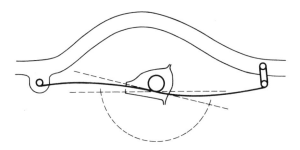

Fig. 26-4 Differential twist on acceleration.

rear of the car moves sideways. Spring shackles are attached between the rear end of the spring and vehicle frame. The shackle provides a flexible link that will compensate for spring length changes as the spring flexes. The spring shortens as it curves and lengthens when it straightens. The weight in pounds necessary to deflect the spring one inch is called *spring rate*. The higher the spring rate, the stiffer the spring will be and the heavier load it can support. The rear suspension spring rate is about 120% of the front suspension spring rate. Increasing spring rate will decrease spring flexibility and increase ride harshness. Shock absorbers are added to dampen oscillation, and they are often placed at an angle to help control side sway.

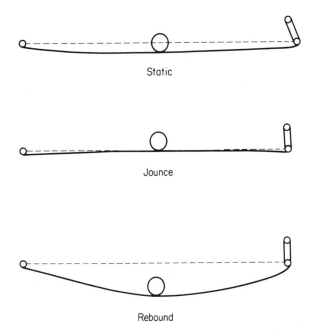

Fig. 26-5 Spring shackle movement as the leaf spring arc changes.

Coil springs can support weight. They require linkages to maintain tire-to-road alignment and to transfer braking torque and acceleration torque to the frame. One or two links near each end of the rear axle housing hold the axle in the correct fore and aft position. These links are also used to transfer braking and acceleration torque to the frame. Side sway is controlled by linkages near the center of

451

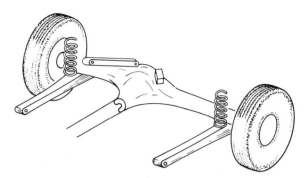

Fig. 26-6 Typical rear suspension using coil springs.

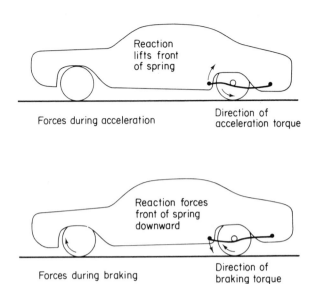

Fig. 26-7 Rear wheel torque forces on the vehicle.

the axle. The axle end of each of these links swings through an arc. This changes the relative position of the body and tires during jounce and rebound.

Ideally, the tires should contact the ground squarely and should roll without any sidewise force or side thrust. This, of course, is not possible on a moving automobile encountering road irregularities, wind gusts, required directional control, changes in weight, acceleration, braking, and having movable suspension systems to absorb shock.

Rear wheel torque, produced by the engine, pushes the forward part of the driving tires downward. This, in turn, lifts the front of the driving axle housing and is called rearward weight transfer. The upward force on the axle housing is transferred to the chassis through the rear suspension. This tends to lift the vehicle front tires from the ground, reducing front tire to road friction, which will reduce steering control. Some specialized drag racing cars have so much torque delivered to the rear wheels that the front tires leave the ground and steering control is completely lost. Rearward weight transfer moves the rear suspension into jounce and the front suspension into rebound. On vehicles with a straight rear axle, the tire remains straight while the front tire changes its angularity in relation to the road surface as a result of front suspension geometry.

During braking, the axles are forced in the direction that the wheels are turning. The rear suspension absorbs this torque and transfers it into the frame and body. Braking torque will force the front suspension into jounce as it accepts greater effective weight when the rear suspension goes into the rebound position. This action produces a

forward weight transfer that reduces rear brake effect while increasing the load on the front brakes.

The drive wheels must push against the suspension to accelerate the vehicle mass and braking action will hold back against the suspension member to slow the vehicle mass. This fact is often overlooked when discussing vehicle suspension.

26-4 VEHICLE DYNAMICS

A side load is put on the suspension system any time the vehicle is steered from straight ahead. When the front wheels are slightly turned, they move in a track that is at an angle to the direction

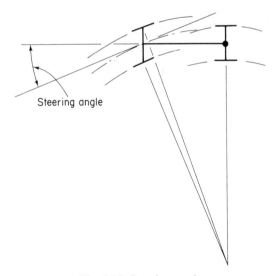

Fig. 26-8 Steering angle.

that the vehicle is traveling. This angle is called the *steering angle*. Turned wheels produce a side load on the front suspension that moves the front of the vehicle in the direction the wheels are pointing. If the driver holds the wheels at this angle, the relative angle between the tire and the car is constant so the car will continue to turn in an arc and the tire centerline will be tangent to that arc. If this angle is reduced, the arc diameter is increased. If the steering angle is increased, the turning arc is reduced.

A vehicle holding a constant steering angle will only follow in the direction in which the front wheels are pointing when the vehicle is moving at very low speeds. As vehicle speed increases, centrifugal action on the vehicle mass will tend to cause the vehicle to roll outward.

The centrifugal force acts through the vehicle center of gravity. The center of gravity is the point that has an equal amount of weight on every side of it. The center of gravity in automobiles is always above ground and the tire-to-road friction always occurs at ground level. This causes the centrifugal force to tend to tip or roll the vehicle body toward the outside of the turning arc. Body roll causes a sidewise weight transfer that forces the outside suspension to go into jounce and the inside suspension to go into rebound. Sidewise weight transfer places a great deal of weight on the outside wheel and lightens the load on the inside wheels.

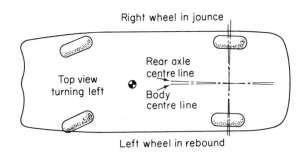

Fig. 26-10 Result of roll steering.

During body roll, the rear suspension geometry will make one wheel move further ahead than the other wheel. This causes the straight rear axle housing to twist in relation to the body center line producing a steering tendency. This is called *roll steer*. Roll steer may steer into the turn or out of the turn, depending upon the suspension linkage length and pivot position.

In addition to body roll, centrifugal force in a turn will cause the tires to deflect or twist so the actual path or angle that the vehicle follows is somewhat less than the steering angle. The difference in these two angles is called *slip angle*, even though the tire is only deformed within the tire-to-road contact patch area.

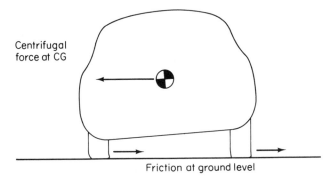

Fig. 26-9 Forces producing body roll.

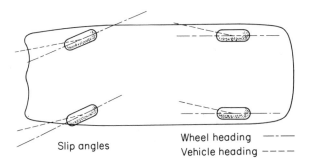

Fig. 26-11 Slip angle caused by centrifugal force.

Loss of tire to road friction on the lightly loaded inside driving wheel resulting from body roll often shows up as a car leaves a stop sign, accelerating as it turns onto a busy street. The inside rear wheel will lose adhesion and squeal, even though the vehicle is only mildly accelerated.

Centrifugal force increases as the vehicle speed increases in a turn, while a constant steering angle is held. When the centrifugal force exceeds the force of tire-to-road friction, the tires begin to slide and the vehicle skids, resulting in loss of vehicle control.

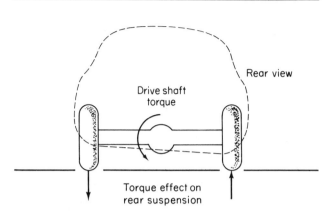

Fig. 26-12 Engine torque effect on the rear suspension tire loading.

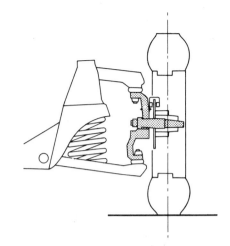

Fig. 26-13 Typical front suspension configuration.

Engine torque is applied down the driveshaft, twisting it in a counterclockwise direction as viewed from the driver position. During heavy acceleration, this driveshaft torque pushes downward on the left rear wheel and lifts the right wheel. This causes the left rear suspension to go into rebound and the right suspension to go into jounce, which produces a roll steer effect. It also reduces the effective weight on the right rear tire so it loses its tire-to-road friction before the more highly loaded left wheel does; therefore, the right wheel will spin free before the left wheel when the vehicle is under high acceleration.

26-5 FRONT SUSPENSION DESIGN

Front suspension geometry is much more complex than rear suspension geometry. Each side of the front suspension of modern passenger cars has independent springing. It must provide a method for steering the front tires while controlling deflection loads, side loads, and braking loads.

Two types of springs are used in automobile vehicle front suspensions; coil springs and torsion bars. If one were to study a one-inch section of each of these springs during jounce and rebound, it would be obvious that each section would be twisted in the same manner. A torsion bar is basically a stretched out or unwound coil spring. To say it another way, a coil spring is a coiled torsion bar. Their main difference lies in the method of attaching

one end to the frame and the other end to the suspension linkage system.

The front wheel hub or drum is placed on bearings that are supported by a spindle which is part of the steering knuckle. A brake backing plate or caliper is bolted to the knuckle behind the wheel drum or disc. The inboard end of the wheel knuckle has two attachment points with ball joints used to support the spindle while allowing rotation for steering.

The upper and lower ball joints are held to the vehicle frame with control arms. The length of these arms and the placement of the inner pivot points controls tire position during jounce and rebound. The upper control arm is shorter than the lower

Fig. 26-14 Typical front suspension geometry change produced by repositioning the support arms.

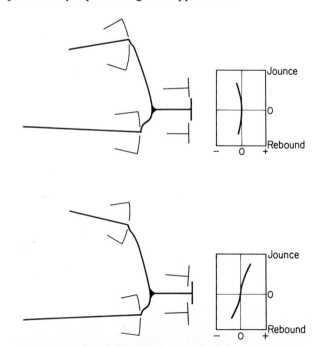

control arm. With a given suspension deflection in jounce, the upper arm goes through a larger portion of its arc than the lower arm. If the arms were parallel while in the static position, the change during jounce would cause the upper ball joint to move inward a greater amount than the lower joint. This, in turn, would move the top of the tire inward more than the bottom. This produces a tire angle called *negative camber*.

If the control arm pivot points were widely separated so the control arms moved in a different portion of the arc, the top of the tire could move outward during jounce. This tire angle is called *positive camber*.

The upper control arm is a stamped steel triangularly shaped member. The upper ball joint is

attached to one point of the triangle. The other two points of the triangle are attached to the vehicle frame through rubber insulation bushings.

Two types of lower control arms are used. The one that has been used for the longest time is similar to the upper control arm, being a stamped, riveted or welded steel triangular member with the lower ball joint at one point, the other two points being connected to the frame through insulation bushings. The second type of lower control arm is made of two pieces. The main arm is a stamped steel channel with the lower ball joint at the out-

Fig. 26-15 Typical support arm designs (Monroe Auto Equipment Company). (a) One-piece triangular lower arm, (b) single lower arm and strut, (c) torsion bar, arm, and strut.

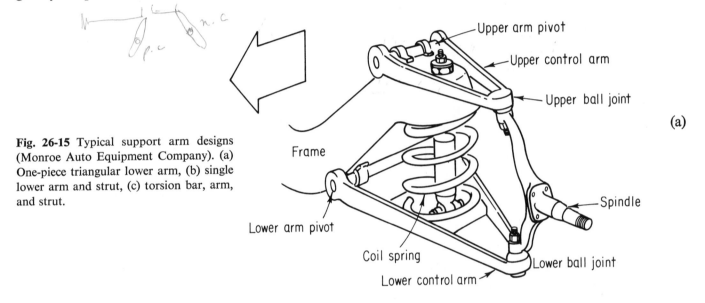

(a)

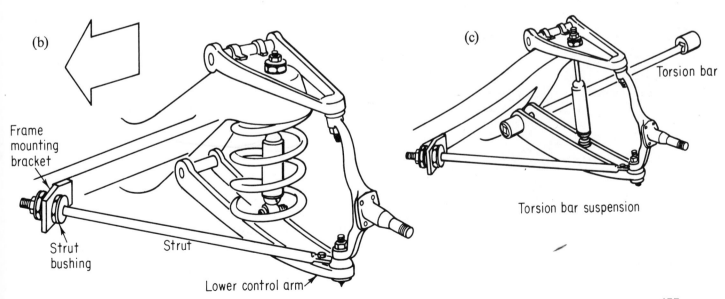

455

board end and an insulation bushing at the inboard end. A rod or strut extends forward from a point just inboard of the ball joint to a point on the front section of the frame. This second lower control arm

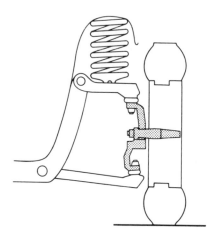

Fig. 26-16 Front suspension with the spring above the upper arm.

Fig. 26-17 Torsion bar attachment points.

type allows more space for engine and brakes, as well as reducing tooling costs when compared to the one-piece type of lower control arm.

The hub of the front wheel and spindle are located near the bottom of the knuckle, so the fore-and-aft road shock is transmitted primarily to the lower control arm. The inboard portion of the lower control arm is, therefore, widely spaced. Wide spacing gives the insulating bushings and supporting members the large leverage that is necessary to reduce the forces they must retain. The upper control arm stabilizes the upper end of the knuckle; thus, front suspension geometry is controlled by the position of the control arms.

Front coil springs may be located either between the center of the lower control arm and the frame or between the center of the upper control arm and a frame spring tower under the front fender. In each case, the vehicle weight is supported through the spring, control arm, knuckle, spindle, drum, wheel, and tire.

The front suspension of vehicles equipped with front torsion bars absorbs the load through their lower control arms. The torsion bar is usually connected from the inboard end of the lower control arm pivot to the vehicle frame at a point parallel with the rear engine mount.

The ball joint on either the upper or lower end of the spring loaded control arm is called the *weight carrying* ball joint. When this ball joint fastens to the knuckle above the control arm, it is called a *tension ball joint* because the vehicle weight tends to pull the ball joint from the knuckle. When the control arm is located above the ball joint, it pushes the ball joint into the spindle and is, therefore, called a *compression ball joint*.

The ball within the ball joint that is located on the unloaded control arm is not held in its socket by vehicle weight so it is preloaded with an elastomer disc or metal spring. It is, therefore, called a *preloaded ball joint*, a *friction ball joint*, or a *follower ball joint*. The preload must be sufficient to keep the ball seated during various vehicle loads, road irregularities, cornering, and panic brake stops.

The inboard pivot point axis of the upper control arm is angled upward at the front to minimize vehicle brake dive, that is, the front of the vehicle lowering during braking as a result of forward weight transfer. During braking, the brake tries to

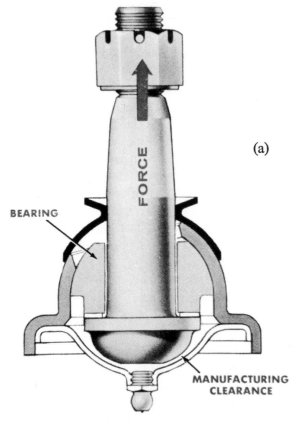

(a)

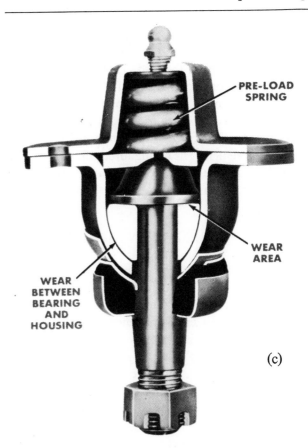

(c)

Fig. 26-18 Typical ball joint types (TRW Replacement Division). (a) Tension-type ball joint, (b) compression-type ball joint, (c) preloaded ball joint.

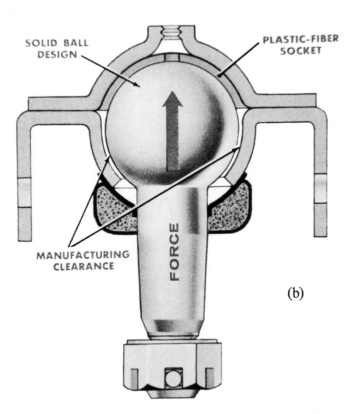

(b)

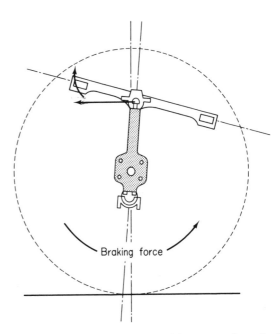

Fig. 26-19 Upper control arm position to reduce brake dive.

457

force the spindle to rotate in the direction the wheels are rotating. This means that the upper part of the spindle tries to move forward. This forces the outer end of this upper control arm forward. The outer end of this control arm is below the front inner pivot so the forward force tries to go under the front pivot point. This force then attempts to lift the front of the vehicle. The diving force will be balanced by the lifting force when the pivot point axis has the correct upward angle.

26-6 SUSPENSION CONTROL DEVICES

Rubber bushings are used between the control arms, hangers, and shackles to help absorb road shock, provide deflection, and reduce the transmission of noise to the passenger compartment. Bushing rubber type and hardness is carefully selected to provide correct physical and durability properties required for each application. The use of rubber bushings has also minimized the number of lubrication points and has allowed for slight assembly misalignment, both of which reduce vehicle cost by allowing larger manufacturing tolerances and, at the same time, provide a better suspension system.

Rubber bushings are often constructed with a metal outer shell and a metal inner bushing. During assembly, the bushing is pressed or screwed into a sized hole in the control arm or spring eye and then fastened to the frame bracket with a bolt. The bracket is tightened against the inner bushing. All movement occurs within the rubber deflections and the metal-to-metal contact does not move. This type of bushing, therefore, has no need of lubrication, not even rubber lube. It is important

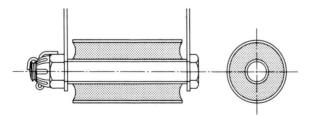

Fig. 26-20 Cross section of a typical rubber suspension bushing.

during suspension assembly that the vehicle be in the neutral position before the bushing bracket bolt is tightened. This prevents preloading the bushing rubber in a position that would lead to unnatural loads and short bushing life.

A sway bar or stabilizer bar is used on the front suspension of some vehicles. It is a "U" shaped rod whose center is attached to the frame through rubber insulators with one end attached to each lower control arm. As both wheels go into jounce, the stabilizer bar merely rotates in its rubber frame insulators. This will not affect a soft ride. It is a different matter when one wheel goes into jounce. The stabilizer bar twists, just like a torsion bar to lift the frame and the opposite suspension. This action reduces the vehicle roll tendency. Excessively heavy stabilizer bars usually cause the vehicle to wander by overcorrecting.

The vehicle weight resting on a spring will oscillate up and down when its static equilibrium is disturbed, such as by driving over a bump. The amplitude of the oscillations is gradually diminished by friction in the suspension system. Suspension system friction is in the pivot bushings and in the spring molecular structure. Coil springs, single leaf springs, and torsion bars develop very little friction. Multileaf springs develop friction as the leaves rub together on insulating spacers and so they dampen or stop the oscillation more rapidly.

An oscillating vehicle would be very difficult to control and would become dangerous as the effective weight on the tires kept changing. This type of oscillation could allow the tires to bounce clear of the road so all control would be lost. It would also allow the body to roll steer, making directional control difficult. Shock absorbers are installed on a suspension system to rapidly dampen the natural vehicle spring oscillation and thus improve ride, vehicle controlability, and vehicle handling.

The spring supports the weight and the shock absorber controls the spring oscillation. Contrary to many people's ideas, the shock absorbers do not support weight. Some shock absorbers have accessories added to them to absorb weight, such as external springs or a compressed air chamber. New standard shock absorbers cannot lift a sagging suspension system.

A shock absorber is basically a cylinder with a piston moving in it. Both sides of the piston are

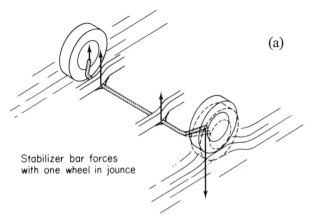

(a)

Stabilizer bar forces
with one wheel in jounce

Fig. 26-21 (a) Forces produced by a deflected stabilizer bar, (b) typical stabilizer bar installation.

(b)

fitted with valves and sized openings or orifices that allow fluid to flow through the piston at controlled rates as the piston moves back and forth in the cylinder. The cylinder is surrounded by a fluid reservoir tube. A valve between the cylinder and reservoir chamber controls the flow of fluid between them. The bottom of the shock absorber housing is mounted to the suspension through rubber bushings. A rod extending from the piston is connected to

the vehicle frame through rubber bushings. The piston is forced downward in the cylinder during jounce and upward in the cylinder during rebound. Different valve and orifice designs control resistance to piston movement.

The energy absorbed by the shock absorber is converted into heat. The heat warms the fluid and dissipates it through the housing into the surrounding air. When the shock absorber is larger, it can absorb more heat and can, therefore, absorb more energy than small diameter shock absorbers.

Rear axle shock absorbers are connected between the spring seat on the rear axle housing and the frame. The shock absorber may be mounted vertically or canted inward in a "sea leg" type mounting, and slightly forward to add control to body roll, handling, and roadability.

Front shock absorbers are mounted inside the spring when coil springs are used. This location provides good mounting attachments, uses otherwise wasted space and provides protection from damage. The shock absorber is mounted in the same location between the lower control arm and frame when using torsion bar springs as it is when using a coil spring mounted on the lower control arm.

Many shock absorbers look identical. Their difference lies in their internal valving, which is designed to match the vehicle suspension dynamics. Correct part number shock absorbers must be

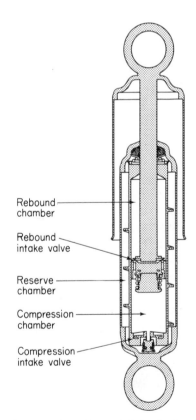

Rebound
chamber

Rebound
intake valve

Reserve
chamber

Compression
chamber

Compression
intake valve

Fig. 26-22 Cross section of a typical shock absorber (Monroe Auto Equipment Company).

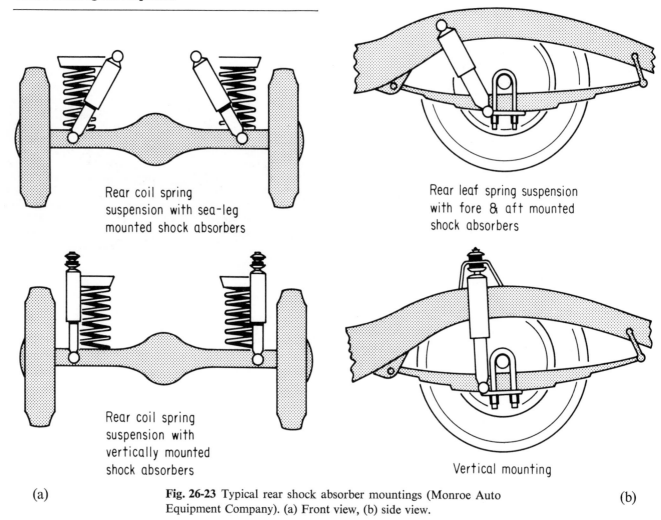

(a)

Fig. 26-23 Typical rear shock absorber mountings (Monroe Auto Equipment Company). (a) Front view, (b) side view.

(b)

installed to produce satisfactory ride and handling performance.

Shock absorbers are designed to rapidly dampen suspension oscillation. Standard passenger car shock absorbers are usually designed to provide greater control on extension as the vehicle rebounds than it is on compression during jounce. These shock absorbers would be specified such as 20-80 (20% control during compression to 80% control during rebound), 30-70, etc., as percentages of the shock absorber's full control capacity. The ratio is entirely dependent upon the vehicle design, ride requirements, handling needs, and driving conditions. In general, racing cars have heavier control than passenger cars, but they also have a harsh ride, reduced driver comfort and less vehicle durability.

During shock absorber extension, the oil trapped above the piston in the rebound chamber meters through the piston to the lower compression chamber below the piston. The piston rod displaces fluid in the upper rebound chamber and there is no rod in the lower compression chamber. Because of this, during extension, some fluid must also flow from the reservoir into the lower compression chamber to make up for the fluid displaced by the piston rod. During rebound, fluid is, therefore, flowing through both piston valves and reservoir valves. During compression, a reverse fluid flow occurs to both chambers.

Fluid control during compression and extension uses metered holes and flutter valves. Flutter valves are discs held with light springs. Oil flow in one direction seats the disc to restrict flow. Oil flow in the reverse direction lifts the flutter valve from its seat and allows free flow. Because these valves are flow valves, rather than pressure valves, shock absorber control forces change as the shock absorber stroke rate is changed. In general, the faster the shock absorber is stroked, the more control force it applies. This allows the vehicle to have a soft, easy ride and, at the same time, provides heavy control over sudden severe jounce or rebound. The valve design also controls the rate at which control build-up occurs. Rapid build-up gives a solid and somewhat harsh ride while a gradual build-up gives a soft ride. As a result of this valve action, it is not possible to determine shock absorber control or condition by hand operation.

26-7 SUSPENSION SERVICE

Vehicle suspension must be at the correct height and all of the pivot points must be secure but not binding, if the vehicle is to give satisfactory ride with good handling characteristics. Suspension service is preceded by a thorough visual inspection of all structural parts and of the insulator bushings. This is followed by supporting the suspension against the spring with a jack, or support wedge positioned between the frame and upper control arm on suspensions having the spring above the upper control arm, so that the suspension joints are free to be moved. In this way, any looseness can be detected. During this inspection, some movement should always be detected in the load carrying ball joint. The extent of this movement should be compared to the vehicle specifications before condemning a joint as faulty. One may also detect a slight but normal movement in the wheel bearings. Any excessively loose pivot or ball joint will need to be replaced if the vehicle is to regain its normal ride and handling characteristics.

Spring sag is another source of suspension problems. Vehicle manufacturers recommend replacing weak coil and leaf springs; however, some parts replacement companies produce items that are designed to readjust spring height, using metal or rubber spacers that are placed between the spring coils. These repair items will return the vehicle to its correct height, but they limit spring flexibility and travel. Their use is a patch job repair method that will lead to poor handling and spring breakage.

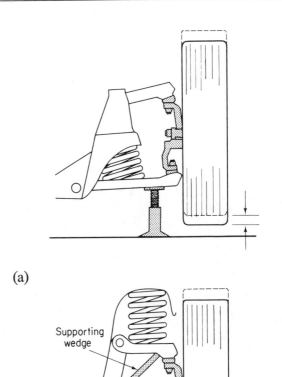

(a)

Supporting wedge

Axial movement

Fig. 26-24 Checking ball joint looseness. (a) Jacking method, (b) indicator position (Chrysler-Plymouth Division, Chrysler Corporation).

(b)

Booster springs placed around the shock absorbers, inflatable air chambers built into shock absorbers, auxiliary booster springs, and inflatable air bags will provide extra suspension support without upsetting normal spring operation. They are an added expense item that will, in most cases, provide satisfactory repair.

Fig. 26-25 Measuring vehicle height at the front suspension (Chrysler Motors Corporation).

Torsion bar equipped front suspensions have an adjustment on one end of the torsion bar that enables the vehicle height to be set without replacement or addition of height adjustment items.

Shock absorber condition is usually checked for leaks, physical damage and secure mountings by a visual inspection. This is followed by rapidly pushing the end of the vehicle up and down. Upon release, the vehicle oscillation should completely stop in one or two cycles. If excessive shock absorber leakage occurs or the bouncing is not dampened, the shock absorbers should be replaced. Some shock absorber manufacturers recommend shock absorber replacement every 25,000 miles, regardless of how they appear. They claim that shock absorbers deteriorate so they will not provide proper control beyond this mileage.

Chassis suspension condition should be checked whenever the vehicle body sags at one end, at a corner, or at a side. It should also be checked whenever the vehicle does not handle correctly or the tires show signs of abnormal wear. The suspension check is usually followed by an alignment check to see that the front suspension geometry is correct. This process is called checking wheel alignment.

Review Questions
Chapter 26

1. What is meant by driver feel?

2. List the suspension requirements.

3. What causes spring oscillation?

4. What is the purpose of shock absorbers used in suspension systems?

5. How does lever arm length affect horizontal movement with a given deflection?

6. What limits maximum jounce and maximum rebound?

7. Describe rear suspension system function and parts.

8. What causes rear suspension wind up?

9. What is spring rate?

10. What causes weight transfer between axles?

11. How does steering angle differ from slip angle?

12. What is meant by roll steering?

13. In what way are coil springs and torsion bars similar?

14. What causes negative or positive camber?

15. Describe the front suspension types.

16. What stabilizes the steering knuckle?

17. Why are the different types of ball joints used?

18. How is brake dive counteracted?

19. Why is rubber lubricant not desirable for use on rubber bushings?

20. How do shock absorbers affect spring sag?

21. How is excessive ball joint looseness detected?

22. How should spring sag be corrected?

23. How should shock absorbers be checked for continued service?

Quiz 26

1. Vehicle control depends upon
   a. the driver's ability to sense impending skid
   b. shock absorbers and wheel balance
   c. spring rate and suspension geometry
   d. friction between the tire and road.

2. Passenger car suspensions with large suspension deflection will generally
   a. give a rough ride
   b. give a soft ride
   c. carry heavy loads
   d. provide good control on rough roads.

3. Suspension systems are designed to support the gross vehicle weight. They also are designed to
   a. limit jounce
   b. limit rebound
   c. keep the tire in contact with the road
   d. minimize any friction in the suspension.

4. On a rear suspension using a leaf spring, braking torque is absorbed by the
   a. links
   b. struts
   c. torque rods
   d. springs.

5. Spring shackles are required on leaf springs to
   a. connect the spring to the frame
   b. compensate for spring length changes
   c. dampen vibration and noise
   d. provide suspension flexibility.

6. Dynamic loads on the vehicle produce weight transfer. Wheels on which the weight is reduced will
   a. have less vehicle control
   b. normally rotate faster
   c. show signs of excessive wear from slipping
   d. provide improved vehicle handling.

7. When driver effort is required to hold a vehicle in a turn, the vehicle is said to have
   a. understeer
   b. oversteer
   c. neutral steer
   d. roll steer.

8. High slip angles that are equal on all tires cause the vehicle to
   a. understeer
   b. oversteer
   c. neutral steer
   d. roll steer.

9. A preloaded ball joint may also be called a
   a. follower ball joint
   b. weight carrying ball joint
   c. tension ball joint
   d. compression ball joint.

10. A standard shock absorber is designed to
   a. support part of the vehicle weight
   b. absorb suspension deflections
   c. dampen suspension oscillations
   d. reduce suspension road shock.

chapter 27

Steering and Wheel Alignment

The paramount requirement of the automotive steering system is *safety*. Parts are made from special alloy steels, often being heat-treated to develop the strength properties required. The entire suspension system and steering geometry are designed with a neutral directional sense so the automobile will naturally go straight ahead. They are also designed to allow the driver to safely guide the vehicle on a selected path with minimum effort. While doing this, the vehicle should have minimum tire wear.

Maximum tire mileage and maximum tire-to-road friction for control occurs when the tire is rolling straight in an upright position. The wheel-tire position is maintained by the vehicle suspension and steering linkage design. Adjustment devices that are provided within the suspension system are used to compensate for manufacturing tolerances and for service wear conditions.

The specifications for alignment may not position the tire upright or straight ahead when the vehicle is standing at a curb or on an alignment rack. In operation, the suspension system is under dyna-

464

mic forces. These forces take up linkage slack and slightly deflect the suspension system members. The alignment angle specifications used to set the vehicle while stationary on the alignment rack are positioned so the tires will run straight most of the time the vehicle is moving with dynamic forces acting on them.

Dynamic forces and their reactions on suspension and steering are interrelated to produce the required ride and handling characteristics. When discussing the effects of suspension geometry, it is necessary to discuss each suspension property and its effect on the function of the entire suspension system.

27-1 CAMBER

Camber is the angle measured in degrees between the tire tread centerline and a line perpendicular to the road surface. If the top of the tire leans slightly outward, the suspension has *positive camber*. If the top of the tire leans slightly inward, the sus-

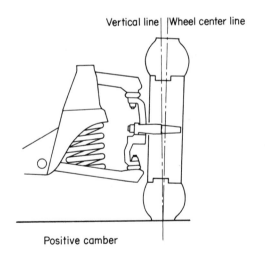

Positive camber

Fig. 27-1 Camber illustrated.

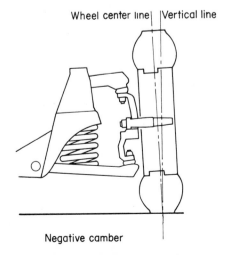

Negative camber

pension has *negative camber*. Suspension linkages cause the camber to change as the suspension goes to jounce or to rebound.

Some vehicle suspensions are designed to have negative camber during both jounce and rebound in order to keep the tire tread centerline following a straight path down the road. Other vehicle suspensions are designed to have positive camber during jounce and negative camber during rebound. This will keep the tire tread surface flat on the road when going over bumps and dips that cause vehicle body roll. During a turn high negative camber on the outside tire helps provide cornering power as the tire deflects under the high side loads that result from the vehicle centrifugal force. This same high negative camber will also cause rapid tire wear. The final suspension camber is a compromise of these factors to produce the desired vehicle handling results. Normal camber on automobiles is small, usually within $+1°$ to $-1°$ with a tolerance of $\pm\frac{1}{2}°$ with the automobile standing.

Camber used on any vehicle is the result of the vehicle designer's objectives and of the front end geometry. Incorrect camber usually is noted by abnormal tire wear along one half of the tread.

Camber is adjustable by changing the position of one end of the steering knuckle. Some vehicles provide adjustments at the upper control arm pivots and others provide adjustments at the upper ball joint. Still others adjust the lower control arm pivot. Each method provides a means to move the knuckle end inward or outward to adjust camber.

27-2 STEERING AXIS INCLINATION

The steering axis is an extension of the ball joint pivot centerline to the road surface when looking at the front of the vehicle. The steering axis is inclined outward at the bottom and inward at the top. The angle of the axis to a line perpendicular to the road surface is measured in degrees, and is called the *steering axis inclination* (SAI).

If the steering axis centerline is extended to the road surface it would contact the road surface near the tire tread centerline. The distance between these

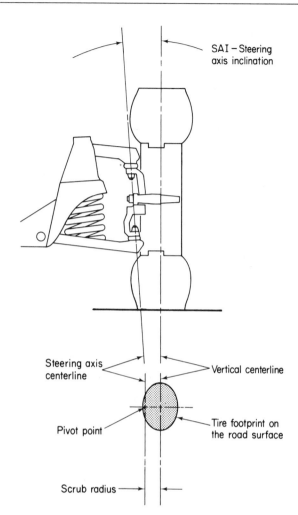

Fig. 27-2 Steering axis inclination.

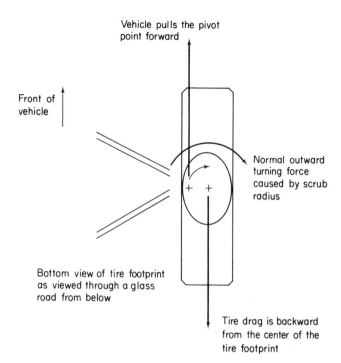

Fig. 27-3 Forces in the tire footprint producing a scrub radius.

two lines at the point they intersect the road surface is called the *scrub radius*. A small scrub radius is desirable because it minimizes steering wheel shock from road irregularities and reduces steering effort.

Dynamic forces on the front tire tend to push the tire backward. These forces tend to concentrate at the tire tread centerline. If the steering axis centerline contacts the road surface inside the tire tread centerline, the natural tendency of the scrub radius will cause the tire to be turned outward while running down the road. The scrub radius in this example would be positive. The turning tendency would be inward if the steering axis centerline contact point is designed to contact the road surface outside the tire centerline. In this case, the scrub radius is negative.

The effect of unequal brake force on the front wheels increases when the scrub radius is large. This would contribute to poor vehicle control by making the vehicle pull sidewise as the brakes are applied. The wheel with the highest braking force will pull outward on a suspension with a positive scrub radius.

Air pressure in the tire also affects vehicle directional pull. A vehicle with a positive scrub radius tends to pull outward or toward the side which has a tire with low pressure. The scrub radius is designed into the knuckle and spindle. It will remain correct as long as the knuckle is not bent. If the knuckle is damaged so the scrub radius is incorrect, the knuckle must be replaced. This damage can be detected by measuring both camber and steering axis inclination. If steering axis inclination does not fall within specifications when camber is correct, the knuckle is bent.

Reverse-type wheels that move the wheel rim outward in respect to the wheel center disc greatly increase the scrub radius, causing a great increase in the outward turning tendency, hard steering, and steering wheel shock. The stated purpose of reverse wheels is to provide widely spaced tires that make a wide wheel tread for stability and

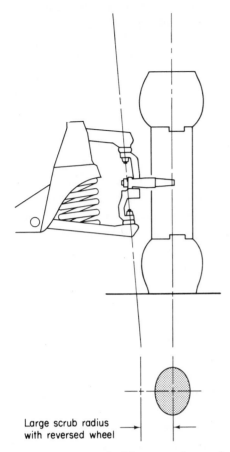

Fig. 27-4 Reverse-type wheel increases the scrub radius.

are turned in either direction, the tip of the spindle tries to move downward; however, it cannot move downward because the spindle is in the center of the wheel and the wheel is in contact with the ground. Therefore, as the spindle pivots in the ball joints, it must lift the vehicle. The weight of the vehicle will, therefore, produce a strong tendency to return the wheels to a straight ahead position after the turn has been completed. This force is great enough to provide excellent directional stability so the vehicle has a natural tendency to run straight ahead.

The steering axis inclination angle is selected to compromise steering effort, neutral returning force, and wheel pull sensitivity. In passenger cars, it is inclined from four to eight degrees. The final steering axis inclination is dictated by vehicle design and handling requirements.

good appearance. Its purpose is not to improve steering or handling. The location of the tire centerline of these wheels is out beyond the spindle so there are large overhung loads on the wheel bearings that overload the outer small bearings and reduce bearing life.

When the vehicle wheels are in the straight ahead position, steering axis inclination positions the vehicle body as low as possible. As the wheels

27-3 CASTER

Caster is the tendency of a steerable wheel to follow the lead of the point where an extension of the pivot axis contacts the road surface. The weight of the vehicle causes the tire to flatten slightly to form a contact patch where it contacts the road surface. The effective weight of the vehicle can be considered to be concentrated at the contact patch center point, directly under the center of the spindle. This contact patch center point tends to follow the pivot axis center point. The pivot point always moves in the direction that the vehicle is moving.

This is most familiar on the front wheel of a bicycle. The extension of the fork pivot centerline contacts the road ahead of the tire contact patch center. This gives the bicycle a natural tendency to steer straight ahead, the contact patch center following the pivot center point. This caster tendency allows the bicycle rider to ride without holding onto the handle bars.

Backward tilt of the pivot axis tends to aid directional steering. The angle produced by the axis tilt with respect to vertical is called the *caster angle*. The caster angle is *positive* when the top tilts backward and *negative* when the top tilts forward. No steering force is exerted when the pivot

Fig. 27-5 Vehicle lift produced by steering axis inclination during a turn.

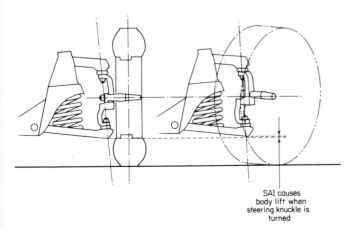

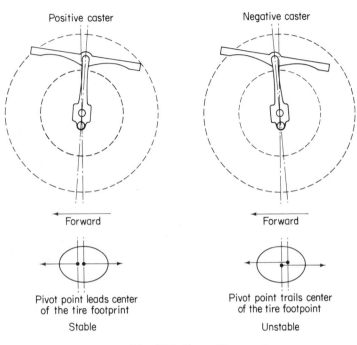

Fig. 27-6 Caster illustrated.

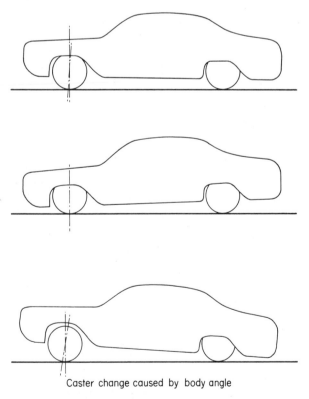

Fig. 27-7 Caster change with improper body angle.

point axis extension contacts the center of the tire patch. Positive directional steering force occurs when the pivot point is in front of the contact patch center, leaving a large portion of the contact patch behind the pivot point. This causes the tire to swing behind the pivot point to produce a positive caster effect. If the pivot point is behind the center of the contact patch, the large portion of tire contact patch is ahead of the pivot point. The normal tendency of the large area is to move around behind the pivot point. When the large area is in front, it results in a continual force to turn from the straight ahead position, producing a negative caster effect.

Vehicle sag from weak springs or overloading will affect caster because steering axis changes with vehicle body angle. A low rear body tends to increase caster directional stability and steering effort. A high vehicle rear end reduces caster and reduces directional stability resulting in a poor vehicle control. It is important for the vehicle to have correct spring height and body angle for proper vehicle handling and control.

Caster angle can be designed to add to or subtract from the tendency of the front wheels to return to the straight ahead position resulting from steering axis inclination. Normal caster on passenger cars falls between $+2°$ to $-2\frac{1}{2}°$ with a tolerance range of $\pm1°$.

Caster, like steering axis inclination, tends to change vehicle height when it is not set at zero. The weight of the vehicle having positive caster

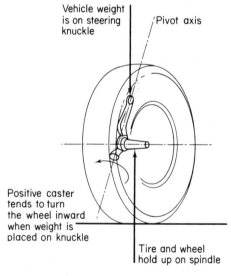

Fig. 27-8 Inward turning tendency caused by caster.

tends to turn a wheel inward to allow the body to lower. Negative caster causes an outward turning effect. The greater the caster angle, the greater the turning effect on the vehicle. Caster angle is adjustable and, therefore, may be changed to correct for directional pull or drift tendencies of the vehicle.

Caster adjustments can be made on most vehicles by repositioning the inner pivots of the upper control arm to move the upper ball joint forward or backward. Some vehicles move the lower ball joint forward or backward by adjusting the lower control arm strut at the vehicle frame attaching pivot.

27-4 TOE

Zero toe exists when the tires are running parallel. If they are closer together at the front than at the rear, they have *toe-in*. Toe-in causes the tires to slide or scuff sidewise, from the outside. *Toe-out* occurs when the wheels are further apart at the front than at the rear. This results in a scuff across the tread from the inside.

The wheels are set with a slight amount of toe-in while at rest on an alignment rack. Static toe-in specifications on passenger cars run from 0 to 5/16″. Toe-in returns to zero as the dynamic forces develop while moving down the road to deflect steering linkages and take up slight clearances. Excessive steering linkage looseness will, of course,

allow the wheels to toe-out under dynamic loads.

Toe-in and toe-out cause excessive tire wear. Toe wears the edge of the tire grooves to a sharp edge or feather on their insides with toe-in and on the outside with toe-out. Toe-out also may contribute to road wander as the wheels deflect back and forth when the tire hits road irregularities, compressing and releasing the steering linkages.

Toe is adjusted with threaded sleeves on linkage members called *tie rods*. Both sides must be adjusted to keep the steering wheel centered as the vehicle goes straight down the road. This is required because the steering gear mechanism has a high spot or tight spot in the center to reduce steering mechanism looseness. Steering mechanism tightness is not required in a turn, because all of the dynamic loads are in one direction and tend to return the wheel to the center position.

27-5 STEERING LINKAGES

Steering linkages are designed not only to hold the front wheels parallel while going straight down the road, but they must also turn the wheels the correct

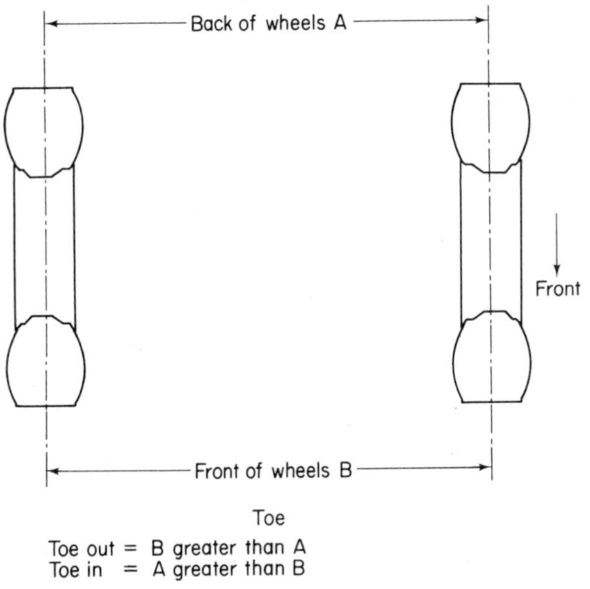

Back of wheels A

Front

Front of wheels B

Toe

Toe out = B greater than A
Toe in = A greater than B

Fig. 27-9 Toe illustrated.

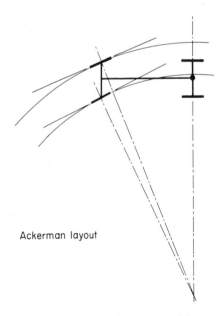

Ackerman layout

Fig. 27-10 Ackerman steering layout requiring toe out on turns.

amount while moving the vehicle smoothly through a turn. The rear wheels are on the same axle so their tires' centerlines remain parallel during a turn. The front wheels are on independent spindles. During a turn, the inside wheel turns in a smaller radius arc than the outside wheel. Each tire tread centerline is tangent to the arc of the turn and the spindle is on the radius of the arc. The steering angle of either wheel in a steady turn is equal to the wheel base of the vehicle divided by the radius of the turn. A steering linkage that allows the wheels to track correctly through the turn is also known as the *Ackerman* layout.

The Ackerman layout uses the previously discussed principle of levers moving through different portions of an arc to produce the required reaction. Steering arms attached to the spindles angle inward in the general direction of the rear axle

midpoint. In a turn, the linkages push the outside wheel steering arm through the portion of an arc that produces little angular rotation. This same linkage travel moves the inside wheel steering arm through the portion of an arc that creates large angular rotation. The angularity difference makes the wheels *toe-out on turns* to follow the correct path for each wheel. The length and direction of the steering arms are made to match the vehicle tread and wheelbase.

Parallelogram-type steering linkage is used on domestic passenger cars. A straight center link connects between the steering gear lever, or Pitman arm on the left, and an idler arm mounted on the right frame member. A short tie rod connects each steering arm to the center link at a point near the lower suspension control arm pivots. This minimizes toe changes or roll steering effects during suspension jounce and rebound. Steering linkages are not altogether geometrically perfect, but are compromises made necessary by other vehicle features and by the dynamic action of the steering linkages, suspension, and vehicle mass.

27-6 SLIP ANGLE

Centrifugal force applies more side load to the tires as the speed through a turn increases or as the turn sharpens. This force causes both front and rear tires to deflect. First, the tire tends to roll inward. Second, the contact patch or footprint twists. If the tire contact patch could be viewed from the bottom through a glass road, it would be seen to twist in relation to the rest of the tire. This twist allows the vehicle to actually travel at a slightly different angle than the tires are headed. The angle between the heading and the actual direction of travel is really an *apparent* slip angle, but it is called

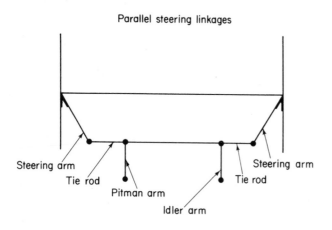

Parallel steering linkages

Steering arm

Tie rod

Pitman arm

Idler arm

Steering arm

Tie rod

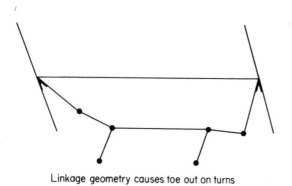

Linkage geometry causes toe out on turns

Fig. 27-11 Typical domestic passenger car parallel steering linkages.

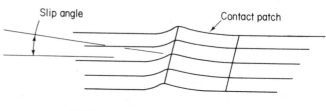

Slip angle

Contact patch

Twist in tire contact patch

Fig. 27-12 Tire twist in the tire patch to match the slip angle.

470

slip angle, even though the tire is distorting rather than slipping.

Equally loaded tires on a vehicle develop greater cornering ability at a given slip angle than unequally loaded tires. Tire size and stiffness will affect the slip angle. Overloading decreases cornering ability and increases slip angle. As ultimate cornering force is approached, the slip angle rapidly increases with little additional lateral load. The driver can sense this change and make corrections before the tires start to slide, causing loss of control. Ninety per cent of all handling considerations involve cornering loads and vertical loads resulting from weight.

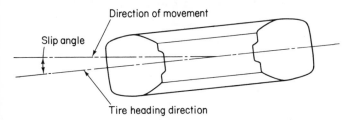

Fig. 27-13 Slip angle compared to tire heading.

If the cornering load produces equal slip angles at the front and rear tires, the vehicle will follow a turning arc at an angle to the original heading. This reaction is called neutral steer. If the slip angle is greater on the front tires than on the rear, the front tends to reduce its turning arc, producing *understeer*. If the rear tires' slip angle is greater than the front tires', the rear end of the vehicle tends to increase the turning arc as the back end slips outward. This turns the vehicle into the corner by *oversteering*.

Vehicles with large amounts of weight on the front tires generally tend to understeer while vehicles with large amounts of weight on the rear tires tend

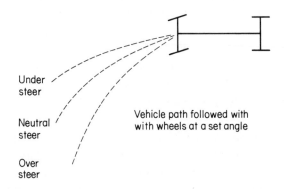

Fig. 27-14 Understeer is less than neutral and oversteer is greater than neutral.

to oversteer. Understeer is indicated when larger steering wheel turning angles are needed at highway speeds as compared to the turning angle required at near zero speed. Low tire pressure and heavy weights will increase the slip angle. The front and rear slip angle, not weight distribution, determine how a vehicle can negotiate a corner.

An understeering vehicle is a directionally stable vehicle. It is necessary to hold the steering wheel into the turn to continue the turn. Upon release of the steering wheel, the vehicle will tend to go straight. Understeer reduces vehicle responsiveness and is good for the average driver. An oversteering vehicle is unstable. It will negotiate a turn with small steering wheel angles and, in some cases, will require reverse steering wheel position. An oversteering vehicle is very responsive, but will spin out if pushed too hard into turns.

A strong crosswind has an effect on slip angle. As the wind blows against the side of the car, all of the side force can be considered to react through the center of pressure, the point around which all of the air pressure forces are balanced. The center of pressure is usually behind the center of gravity. Slip angle caused by the wind is compounded by the understeer tendency to correct the line of vehicle travel. The worst possible condition would exist in a cross wind with a normally oversteering, heavily loaded station wagon or van. Wind gusts on the large rear section would exaggerate the oversteer condition, resulting in rapid loss of control.

Roll steer characteristics, as discussed in chapter 26, are useful in designing a stable car. With properly designed suspension and steering linkages, body roll will move the wheels to compensate for slip angles by changing camber and toe. Generally, a large rear roll steer increases understeer and stability.

27-7 WHEEL ALIGNMENT

The suspension and steering linkage alignment is usually checked when abnormal tire wear exists, when the vehicle handles improperly, when the suspension has been repaired or when making a normal

CONDITION	RAPID WEAR AT SHOULDERS	RAPID WEAR AT CENTER	CRACKED TREADS	WEAR ON ONE SIDE	FEATHERED EDGE	BALD SPOTS
CAUSE	UNDER INFLATION	OVER INFLATION	UNDER-INFLATION OR EXCESSIVE SPEED	EXCESSIVE CAMBER	INCORRECT TOE	WHEEL UNBALANCED
CORRECTION	ADJUST PRESSURE TO SPECIFICATIONS WHEN TIRES ARE COOL			ADJUST CAMBER TO SPECIFICATIONS	ADJUST FOR TOE-IN 1/8 INCH	DYNAMIC OR STATIC BALANCE WHEELS

Fig. 27-15 Typical tire wear patterns (Chrysler-Plymouth Division, Chrysler Corporation).

(a)

Fig. 27-16 Wheel alignment machines. (a) Portable, (b) permanent installation.

(b)

preventative maintenance check. It is helpful for the technician to know the reason the vehicle needs an alignment so abnormalities can be carefully examined.

A number of preliminary checks must be made before aligning the front suspension and steering systems. The suspension pivots and ball joints must be in good condition, the spring height must be correct, the shock absorbers should be in good condition and the tires inflated to the correct pressure. Faulty parts should be replaced to ensure satisfactory operation after alignment is completed.

Tires should be "read" to see if they indicate any specific alignment problem. Tire wear on one side of the tread usually indicates improper camber on that wheel. Smooth tire wear on both sides of both front tires suggests excessive slippage when negotiating corners at high speeds. Wear on the edges of only one tire usually indicates underinflation of that tire. Wear of the center portion of the tire tread suggests tire overinflation. Feather edge tread indicates improper toe. Cupping around the tire edge may be caused by underinflation or suspension mechanical irregularities.

Alignment machines may be either portable or permanent installations. Some of the alignment adjustments are made from under the car as the car rests on its wheels so some means must be provided to allow the technician to get under the vehicle to make these adjustments. Portable wheel stands are usually used with portable alignment heads. Alignment racks are either above the floor or extended over a pit in which the technician can work. In all cases, the alignment rack or set of wheel stands must be level so that alignment angles can be compared to vertical lines. Turn tables are located under the front tires to allow the wheels to be turned any desired degree.

Alignment gauges use some method of sensing a vertical position. One form uses a bubble level to set the gauges and read the angles. Other gauges use a swing weight to sense the vertical position. The position of the swinging weight may be amplified or expanded with electricity or a light beam and displayed on a visual screen for easy reading.

Instrument heads are attached to the front wheels or to the spindle end. If they are attached to the wheel rim, it is necessary to check the adaptor run-out so that wheel and adaptor clamping variations do not affect the readings. Direct readings may be made from the adapters attached directly to the spindle.

Camber is read directly from the instrument head or screen after the instrument head has been leveled.

Caster is measured as it affects camber angle during a turn. Basically, the change in camber of the wheel that exists as the wheel is turned from

Fig. 27-17 Alignment readout. (a) Bubble, (b) screen.

(a)

Fig. 27-18 Instrument attachments. (a) Spindle adapter, (b) clamp on.

(b)

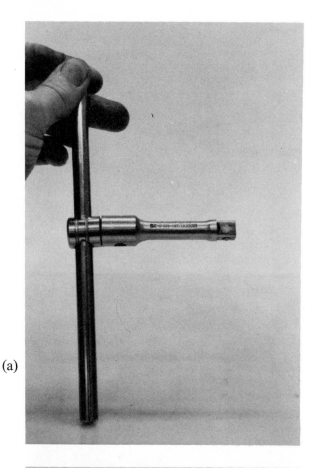

(a)

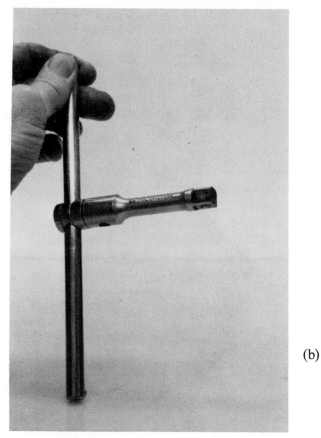

(b)

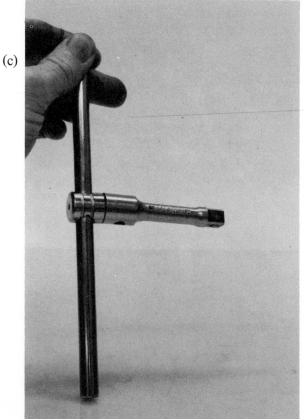

(c)

Fig. 27-19 Example of how positive caster is measured. A level would be attached to the socket extension. (a) Level straight ahead, (b) raised when turned inward, (c) lowered when turned outward.

20° inward to 20° outward, with the brake applied, will indicate caster. If caster is zero, there is no change in camber. Camber change as the wheel turns 40° will increase as caster increases. Caster is read on a special scale that converts camber change into a caster reading.

Steering axis inclination is measured in a manner similar to caster. However, it uses a change in caster during the same 40° wheel turn instead of camber. This requires the use of a repositioned scale or a different scale for readout.

Toe is checked by measuring the difference in distance between the front tires at their rear and at their front. This can be done by rotating the wheel to scribe a line on the surface of the tire. Some alignment equipment measures between the wheel rim at the front, then the car is rolled forward to

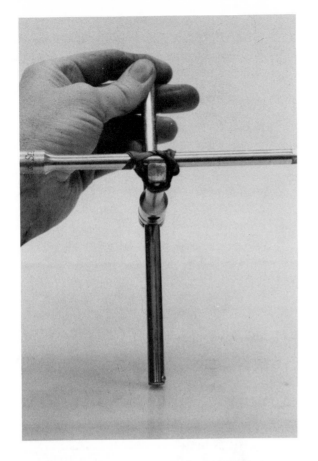

(a)

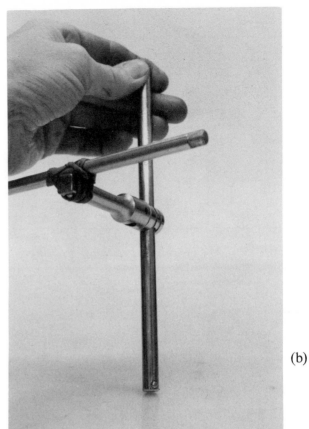

(b)

Fig. 27-20 Example of how steering axis inclination is measured. A level would be attached to the socket extension. (a) Level straight ahead, (b) tipped forward when turned inward, (c) tipped backward when turned outward.

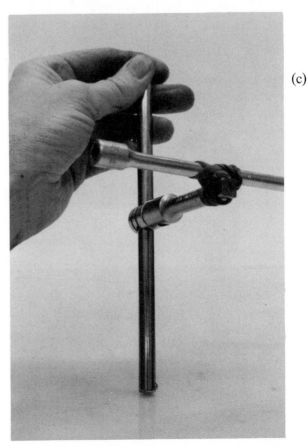

(c)

remeasure the wheel at the same point when it is in the rear. Some alignment equipment racks have reference points built onto them so that toe can be read directly. Others use a light beam for toe adjustment.

Detailed instructions describing specific alignment procedures are supplied with each wheel alignment unit. These instructions must be followed for correct alignment angle readout.

Alignment readings are compared to the specifications that apply. If the readings fall within specifications on a routine maintenance inspection and the vehicle drives properly, no further work is needed. Tire wear or handling complaints may be corrected by adjusting the suspension geometry within the specification range.

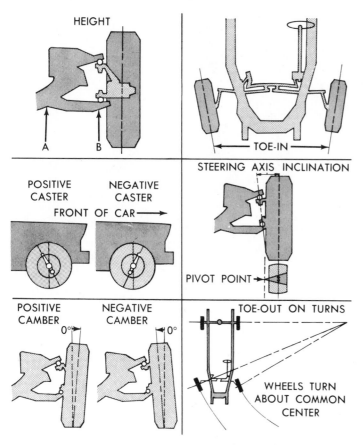

Fig. 27-21 Alignment items to be checked (Chrysler-Plymouth Division, Chrysler Corporation).

27-8 ALIGNMENT ADJUSTMENT

Means are provided on the front suspension to adjust camber and caster. Many vehicles use the same adjustment devices to adjust both camber and caster. Some vehicles provide separate adjustment means.

The majority of vehicles provide a means to adjust both upper control arm pivot points. This may be by shims, cams, or slots. Both pivots are moved outward or inward the same amount to adjust camber. One is moved outward and the other inward by the same amount to change caster. If both caster and camber need to be changed, it may be possible to make the entire correction at only one of the pivot points.

Some vehicles provide an eccentric adjustment around the upper ball joint to adjust camber. Others use a cam at the lower control arm pivot. Both methods control camber by changing the relative position of the steering knuckle, spindle, wheel, and tire.

Some models adjust caster by lengthening or shortening the lower control arm strut. Adjustment nuts are provided at the front strut-to-frame attachment. This moves the lower end of the knuckle forward or backward to change caster.

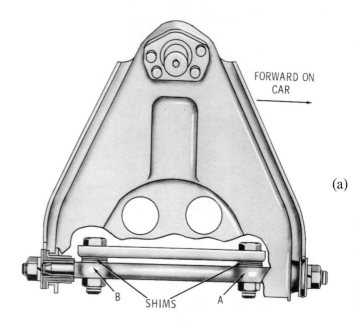

(a)

TO DECREASE POSITIVE CASTER: ADD SHIM AT "A".

TO DECREASE NEGATIVE CASTER: REMOVE SHIM AT "A".

° TO INCREASE CAMBER: REMOVE SHIMS AT BOTH "A" AND "B".

° TO DECREASE CAMBER: ADD SHIMS AT BOTH "A" AND "B".

° BY ADDING OR SUBTRACTING AN EQUAL AMOUNT OF SHIMS FROM "A" AND "B", CAMBER WILL CHANGE WITHOUT AFFECTING CASTER ADJUSTMENT.

(b)

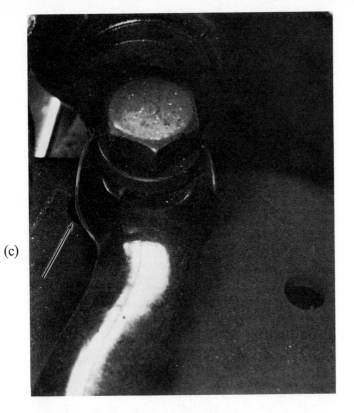

(c)

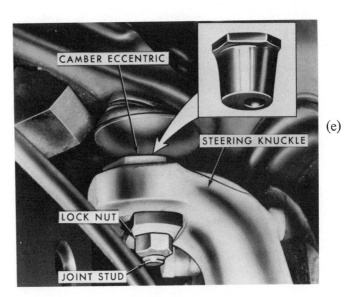

(e)

Fig. 27-22 Typical caster-camber adjustment methods. (a) Shims (Oldsmobile Division, General Motors Corporation), (b) cam adjust, (c) slot adjust, (d) strut adjustment (Cadillac Motor Car Division, General Motors Corporation), (e) eccentric adjustment (Cadillac Motor Car Division, General Motors Corporation).

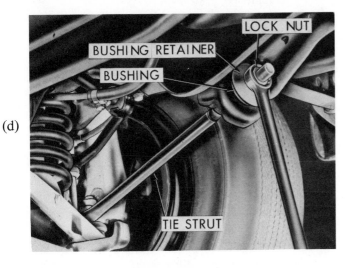

(d)

Toe is always adjusted by adjusting sleeves on the tie rods. One end of the sleeve has left-hand threads, the other end has right-hand threads. Turning the sleeve will lengthen or shorten the tie rod to obtain correct toe. It is usually necessary to adjust both the tie rods to keep the steering wheel centered.

Fig. 27-23 Typical tie rod adjuster for setting toe.

Steering axis inclination cannot be adjusted separately from camber but is only used to check for a bent steering knuckle. When both camber and steering axis inclination do not fall into their respective specification range, the knuckle is bent.

Alignment adjustments should always be followed by a road test to see that the car tracks straight and handles properly. Slight changes in caster, within the specification range, will usually correct tracking problems if the suspension is in normal condition.

Review Questions
Chapter 27

1. Why do the specifications give angles even though tires should roll straight and upright with zero angle?

2. What is camber?

3. How is camber adjusted?

4. How does scrub radius relate to steering axis inclination?

5. How does scrub radius relate to braking and tire pressure?

6. What are the advantages and disadvantages of reverse-type wheels?

7. How does steering axis inclination help directional control?

8. How does caster affect directional stability?

9. How does front or rear spring sag affect directional stability?

10. How does caster adjustment affect vehicle directonal control?

11. Define toe as it is used in wheel alignment.

12. How is toe adjusted?

13. What are the characteristics of an Ackerman steering linkage layout?

14. Why is toe-out on turns required?

15. Describe slip angle.

16. Define neutral steer, understeer, and oversteer.

17. What makes a vehicle directionally stable?

18. How does a cross wind affect directional stability?

19. How does roll steer affect directional stability?

20. Under what conditions are the wheels aligned?

21. What parts should be checked before aligning the wheels?

22. Why must the vehicle be level when the wheels are being aligned?

23. How is camber measured?

24. How is caster measured?

25. How does the measurement of steering axis inclination differ from caster measurement?

26. How is toe measured?

27. How can handling complaints be corrected if the alignment is already within specifications?

28. What means are provided to make changes in wheel alignment on passenger cars?

29. Why is steering axis inclination checked but never adjusted?

Quiz 27

1. Maximum tire mileage occurs when the rolling tire
   a. has slight toe-in
   b. has slight positive camber
   c. has camber to compensate for toe
   d. is perpendicular with zero toe.

2. Incorrect camber results in
   a. abnormal tire wear
   b. vehicle pull when braking
   c. pronounced vehicle directional drift
   d. wheel shimmy.

3. On a vehicle in normal condition, changes in steering axis inclination result in
   a. camber change
   b. caster change
   c. toe change
   d. scrub radius change.

4. Installing reverse wheels will
   a. reduce steering effort
   b. minimize steering wheel shock
   c. increase scrub radius
   d. improved tire-to-road adhesion.

5. During a turn, the steering geometry slightly lifts the vehicle as a result of
   a. roll steer
   b. steering axis inclination
   c. positive camber settings
   d. toe-in.

6. Heavy loads in the rear of the vehicle will produce
   a. increase in camber
   b. decrease in camber
   c. increase in caster
   d. decrease in caster.

7. The Ackerman steering layout causes the
   a. outside wheel to turn more
   b. outside wheel to turn less
   c. both wheels to turn the same amount
   d. wheels to toe-in on turns.

8. Slip angle usually results from
   a. sliding rear tires
   b. sliding front tires
   c. sliding front and rear tires
   d. tire twist in the contact patch.

9. A vehicle with large rear roll steer will generally
   a. be stable
   b. tend to oversteer
   c. cause loss of control
   d. also have large front roll steer.

10. Caster and camber are often adjusted by
    a. making a slight bend in the knuckle
    b. turning adjusting sleeves on the tie rods
    c. moving the position of the upper ball joint
    d. placing shims between the knuckle and spindle.

chapter 28

Steering Gear and Columns

The driver controls the direction of the front wheels of the automobile with the steering gear. The modern steering gear is made up of two major units, a gear unit and a steering column. The gear unit multiplies the driver's steering effort to provide adequate force for steering control. The steering column is primarily a supported shaft that connects the driver's steering wheel to the gear unit.

The power steering gear is similar to the standard steering gear but it has surfaces upon which hydraulic pressure is applied to aid the driver's control of the front wheels. Power for the steering gear is provided by an engine driven pump. The pump forces fluid through a system controlled by a valve that is sensitive to the driver's steering effort to put fluid pressure against the pressure surfaces to assist the driver.

The steering column in the modern automobile is a complex mechanism. It is designed to collapse in a collision to protect the driver. In some installations it may be tilted and telescoped to place it at a convenient angle for the driver. To reduce the chance of theft, it contains steering gear and transmission locks. Because it is easily accessible to the driver the steering column carries the transmission shift control, turn signal switch, and flasher switch. It must, therefore, be thoroughly understood so that it can be properly serviced.

28-1 STANDARD STEERING GEAR

The steering gear unit consists of two gears, a worm gear and a section or sector of a spur gear. It is normally designed to swing the front wheels through a 60° arc, from lock to lock. Turning effort on the steering wheel is multiplied through the steering gears to turn the front wheels, even when the vehicle is not moving. If a steering wheel requires five full turns from lock to lock to swing the wheels 60°, the steering ratio is 30:1. This is because each full turn of the steering wheel is 360°. In five turns, the steering wheel turns 1800°. Eighteen hundred degrees of steering wheel turn divided by 60° wheel steering turn equals the 30:1 steering ratio.

Steering gears are based on the action between a worm gear and a spur gear section to give the required mechanical advantage. Therefore, the driver can easily control the front wheels and the front wheel road shock will not twist the steering wheel from his hands.

Friction between the worm and sector is usually quite large. This friction was reduced as steering gear designs improved by replacing the sector with a roller and then further reduced by placing a nut with exterior teeth over the worm. The threads between the nut and worm are modified into grooves that will take ball bearings. Selective fit balls, very close to the same size, are placed between the nut and worm so the turning action is as free rolling as a ball bearing. The ball groove may be cut for either right- or left-hand thread directions.

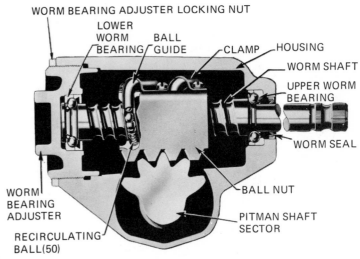

Fig. 28-2 Typical worm and recirculating ball nut type steering gear (Buick Motor Division, General Motors Corporation).

The balls are fed into what is the equivalent of two separate ball races. These races are on an angle so the balls move endwise as the worm turns. The balls are redirected by a guide from the end of each slot back to the entrance across the outside of the nut.

The ball nut gear teeth engage with the sector that, in turn, is part of the cross or Pitman shaft. This whole assembly is enclosed in a case that can be attached to the chassis frame. A *Pitman arm* connects the Pitman shaft to the steering linkage.

Each end of the worm is supported in ball bearings. A worm lash adjustment provides a bearing preload that holds the worm securely in position.

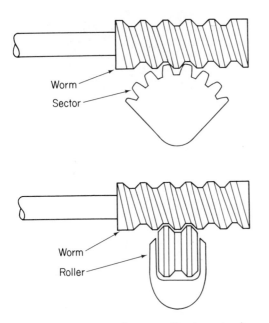

Fig. 28-1 Worm-sector and worm-roller type steering gears.

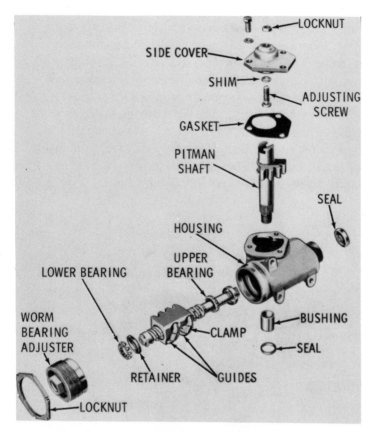

Fig. 28-3 Exploded view of a typical worm-ball nut steering gear (Oldsmobile Division, General Motors Corporation).

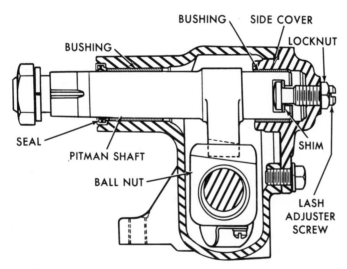

Fig. 28-4 Cross section of a typical worm-ball nut type steering gear showing angled teeth that allow lash adjustment (Chevrolet Motor Division, General Motors Corporation).

On some vehicles, the worm shaft bearing preload adjustment is on the lower end of the gear case, while others have the adjustment on the upper end of the case.

Needle bearings or bushings support the Pitman shaft. Both may be located on the Pitman arm side of the sector or one may be on each side of the sector. The ball nut gear teeth and the sector teeth are cut at an angle. Moving the sector gear into close mesh with the ball nut teeth reduces backlash. This adjustment is made in the cover on the upper end of the cross shaft.

The steering gear teeth are cut to provide a closer fit at the center teeth than at the end teeth. This reduces gear backlash at the center position where most of the driving occurs and, at the same time, allows sufficient cost reducing gear tolerance at the off-center positions where the close fits are not needed. Sector backlash adjustments must be made at the normally tight center position.

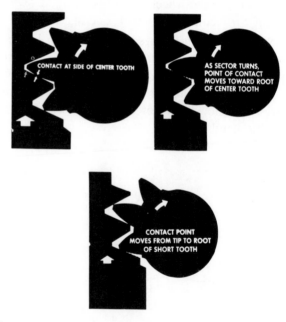

Fig. 28-5 Typical steering gear sector-to-ball nut tooth contact (Buick Division, General Motors Corporation).

The standard steering gear case is partly filled with a specified lubricant, usually the same lubricant that is used in the differential. An oil seal is installed at the lower end of the Pitman shaft to keep the oil from leaking out the bottom of the gear case. In most steering gears, there is no seal on the upper end of the worm shaft because it is usually above the lubricant level, where only a dust seal is required.

A power steering gear is basically a power assisted standard steering gear. The driver supplies part of the steering effort and the power assist portion of the unit supplies the remaining effort required. This reduction in driver steering effort allows the power steering gear ratio to be about 2/3 of the standard steering ratio. Power steering, therefore, provides much faster steering response than standard steering.

The power steering system consists of an engine-driven oil pump with reservoir, a control valve, and pressure surfaces that are used to assist steering effort. The pump is usually belt driven and located on the front of the engine. In some applications it is mounted at the front of the crankshaft. Pressure surfaces in most power steering systems are located in the steering gear case. This type of power steering gear is called an *integral type*. A few power steering pressure surfaces are located in an exterior power cylinder connected between the steering linkages and vehicle frame. These are called *link-type* power steering gears.

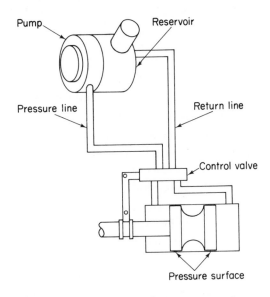

Fig. 28-6 Schematic of a typical power steering gear.

Control Valve. All the time the engine is running, power steering fluid keeps flowing through the system from the pump to the control valve then back to the reservoir, with both pressure surfaces exposed to the same system pressure. When the wheels are straight ahead, the fluid flows freely through this circuit. When steering effort is applied

to the steering wheel, the control valve shifts. This directs fluid to one pressure surface and increases the return passage opening from the opposite pressure surface back to the reservoir. The amount of valve shift is proportional to the effort applied to the steering wheel and the amount of control valve shift will provide the proportional amount of pressure to give power assist.

The power steering control valve is either located inside or is attached to the exterior of the integral-type power steering gear. The link-type power steering may have the control valve built into the end of the power cylinder or it may be a separate unit, depending upon its design.

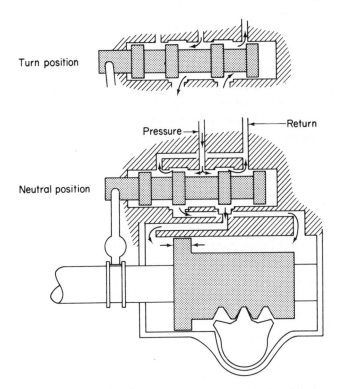

Fig. 28-7 Principle of a power steering control valve in neutral and during a turn.

The control valve is balanced between the mechanical input force applied by the steering wheel, and the mechanical-hydraulic resistive force of the steering linkage and tires on the road. As the steering wheel is turned, its mechanical input force moves the control valve toward the linkage resistive force.

In this position, the control valve restricts the pressure area outlet flow to cause a pressure buildup on the pressure surface in a direction that assists the steering wheel input force to move against the steering linkage resistance. During steering wheel movement, the input force always leads by first moving the control valve. The hydraulic assist force is always trying to catch up with the control valve position by helping to move the steering linkage. When the steering wheel arrives at the desired position, it is held steady and the linkage finally catches up, centering the control valve to terminate assist.

The control valve is provided with some type of natural centering device, usually springs. When no effort is being applied to the system, the centering springs center the spool position to balance pressures on both pressure surfaces, holding the steering linkage in place.

If the steering wheel is held in position when the front tires hit an object that tries to deflect them, the control valve directs pressure to the pressure surface that opposes the upsetting force. This allows the driver to maintain vehicle control.

Two types of control valves are used, sliding spools and rotating spools. The sliding spool valve may be located between the Pitman arm and steering linkage in the link-type units, mounted concentric with the worm shaft or placed parallel in a housing outside the steering gear case in integral types. When a rotary spool-type valve is used, it is always mounted concentric with the worm shaft. In any of these types of power steering gears, control action is the same.

The sliding spool valve in the integral steering gear is controlled by either of two actuating methods. One movement is actuated by a slight endwise movement of the worm shaft or steering linkage. The front wheels and steering linkages hold the sector so it resists movement. The worm shaft is pushed endwise against one of its bearings as the ball nut tries to move the sector. This slight movement is transmitted to the parallel spool valve with a pivot lever.

The concentric spool valve endwise movement is actuated by a torsion bar. The worm shaft is turned through a torsion bar, so the upper end turns slightly more than the lower end. The maximum amount of torsion bar flex is limited by a loose fitting spline between the input shaft and worm shaft. A short length helical spline around the input shaft engages an actuator. The other end of the actuator is splined to the worm shaft.

The steering wheel input effort twists the torsion bar. This twist changes the relative position of the worm shaft actuator assembly in relation to the input shaft position to move the actuator endwise on the helical splines.

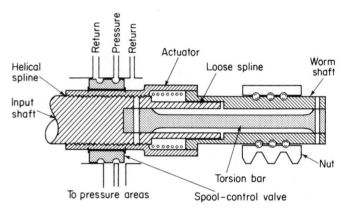

Fig. 28-8 Section view of a torsion bar actuated sliding control valve.

The spool valve is held in position on the actuator with snap rings so any actuator endwise movement also moves the spool valve endwise.

Endwise movement of the spool valve fully opens the fluid return from one pressure surface. At the same time, pressure is built up on the other pressure surface to provide steering effort assist.

The rotary spool control valve is also operated with a torsion bar. The spool valve body surrounds the control valve. It is attached to the worm shaft. The valve spool is attached to the input shaft. Steering effort on the input shaft twists the torsion bar. This makes a relative difference between the valve body attached to the worm shaft and the valve spool attached to the input shaft. Repositioning the valve spool within the valve body opens a return passage to one of the pressure areas and directs fluid under pressure to the opposite pressure area.

Reaction Control. Power steering gears are designed to give the driver some feel of the amount

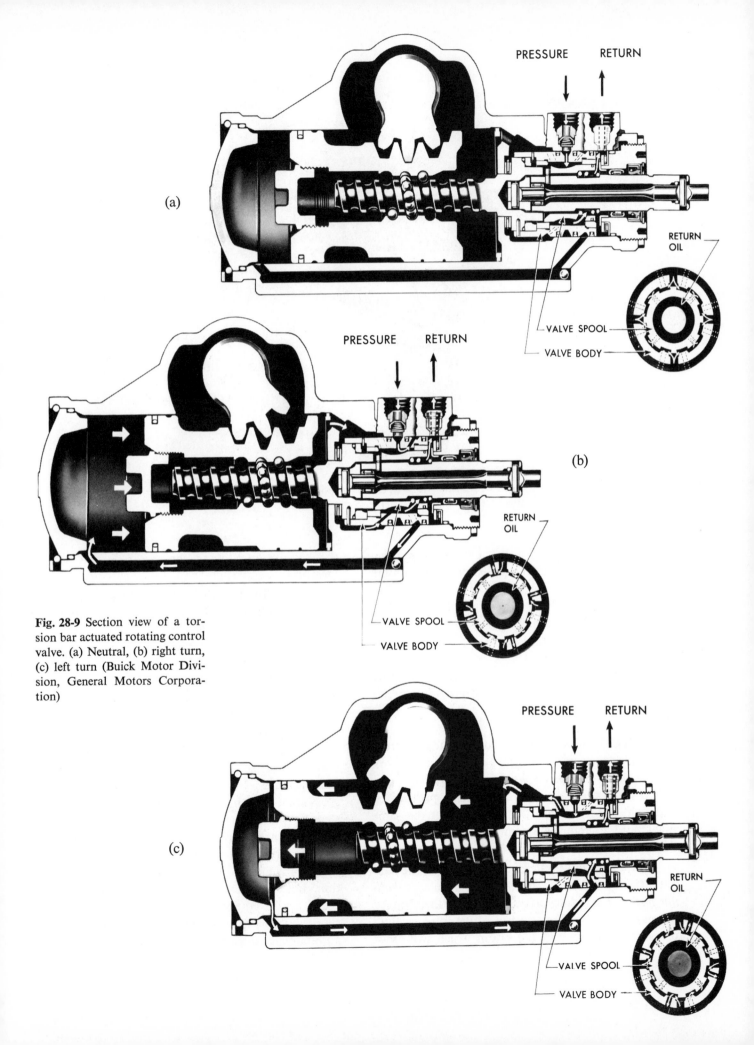

PRESSURE RETURN

(a)

RETURN OIL

VALVE SPOOL

VALVE BODY

PRESSURE RETURN

(b)

RETURN OIL

VALVE SPOOL

VALVE BODY

Fig. 28-9 Section view of a torsion bar actuated rotating control valve. (a) Neutral, (b) right turn, (c) left turn (Buick Motor Division, General Motors Corporation)

PRESSURE RETURN

(c)

RETURN OIL

VALVE SPOOL

VALVE BODY

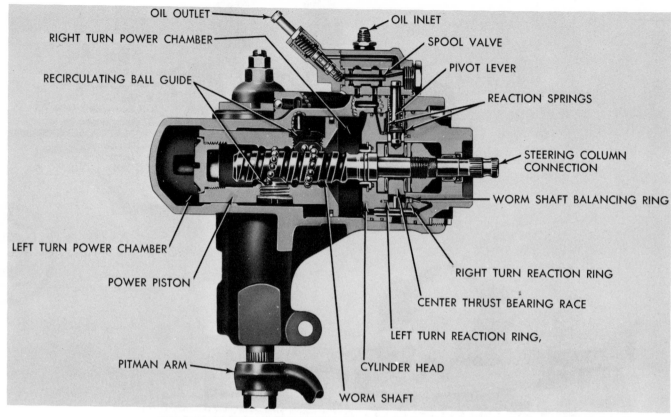

Fig. 28-10 Section view of a sliding spool control valve (Chrysler-Plymouth Division, Chrysler Corporation).

of effort he is putting into the steering system. This driver feel is called reaction control. The torsion bars provide driver feel when they are used. The pivot lever actuated type of control valve gives driver feel with centering springs and with fluid pressure developed on reaction rings while assist is occurring. The link-type power unit may have a reaction valve that is proportional to the pressure developed in the steering system to provide a driver feel.

Power Chambers. The pressure surfaces or areas of the link-type power steering are the surfaces on either side of the piston within the power cylinder. As pressure rises, the chamber fluid is pressurized and fluid is forced into the chamber. At the same time, fluid is returned from the opposite side of the piston.

In integral power steering gear designs, the ball-nut exterior acts as a piston and is called a *ball-nut piston*. Each side of this piston is, therefore, a power chamber. The control valve directs fluid pressure to the side of the piston which will assist

the ball-nut in moving the sector in the desired direction.

The ball-nut piston seal ring may be above or below the rack teeth. In either case, the oil pressure can go between the worm shaft and ball-nut to pressurize the interior when the ball-nut is assisting in the downward direction. Pressure is applied to the ball-nut end and piston flange when assisting in the upward direction. Reaction areas may be used to balance the worm shaft and control valve in some power steering applications.

The ball-nut piston has a rack of gear teeth that rotate a sector in the same way the standard steering does. Steering ratios for power steering gears are usually numerically lower than the standard steering gears, so they have a quicker response to steering wheel movement. A very fast response is not desirable in the straight ahead position where slight movements would make too much correction, but it is desirable in a turn. Power steering gears are a compromise when using a constant ratio. Variable ratio steering gears are used in some automobiles to give a slow ratio when steering in the straight ahead position and a fast ratio on turns. This is done primarily by the way the sector teeth are cut.

28-3 POWER STEERING PUMPS

Three types of power steering pumps are in common usage, the vane type, the slipper type, and the roller type. Their principles of operation and design are very similar. A power steering pump consists of a belt driven rotor that is turned within an eliptically shaped cam insert ring. Vanes, slippers, or rollers are installed in the rotor slots, grooves, or cavities. Pressure thrust plates on each side of the rotor and cam seal the pump. This assembly is placed in a housing that contains rotor bearings and oil passages. The pump housing is usually surrounded by an oil reservoir. The pump and reservoir are sealed with "O" rings for easily assembled oil tight joints.

In operation, the rotor spins, causing centrifugal force to throw the vanes, slippers, or rollers outward so their outer surface maintains contact

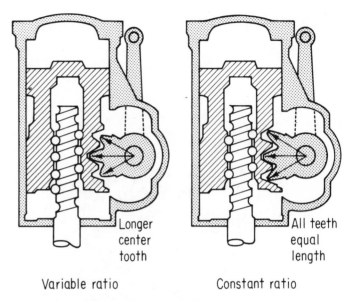

Variable ratio   Constant ratio

Fig. 28-11 Constant steering ratio compared to a variable ratio steering gear (Buick Motors Division, General Motors Corporation).

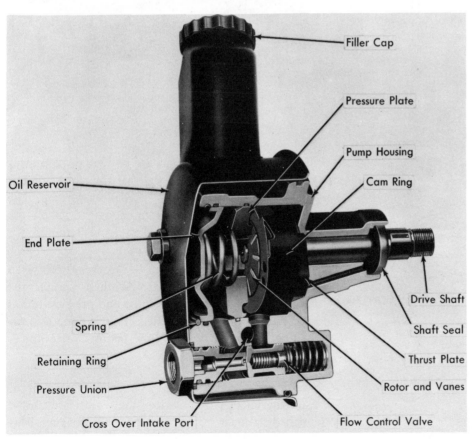

Fig. 28-12 Section view of a typical vane type power steering pump and valves (Cadillac Motor Car Division, General Motors Corporation).

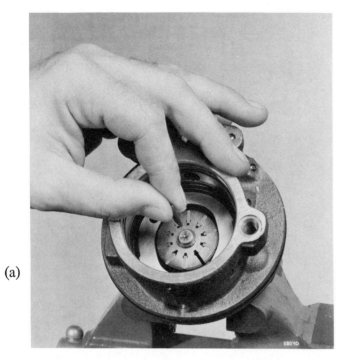

(a)

Fig. 28-13 Power steering pump types. (a) Vane (American Motors Corporation), (b) slipper (Chrysler-Plymouth Division, Chrysler Corporation), (c) roller (American Motors Corporation).

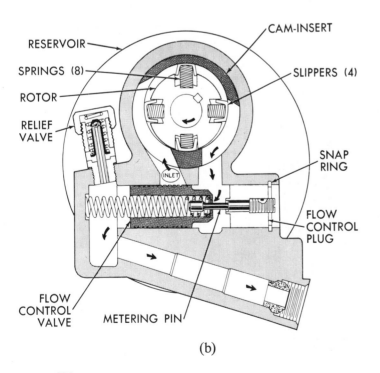

(b)

with the cam. Slippers usually have a backup spring to aid in maintaining cam contact.

The cam fits the rotor closely at one or two opposing locations. The spaces between the vanes, slippers, or rollers gradually move outward as the rotor turns them past the close fitting point. This portion of the pump is connected to the inlet passage from the reservoir so pump fluid will flow from the reservoir into these expanding spaces. As the vanes, slippers, or rollers reach the widest part of the cam insert, they pass the inlet passage from the reservoir and contact the pressure passage. Continued turning now decreases the volume between the vane, slippers, or rollers, forcing the pump fluid into the pump pressure outlet passage.

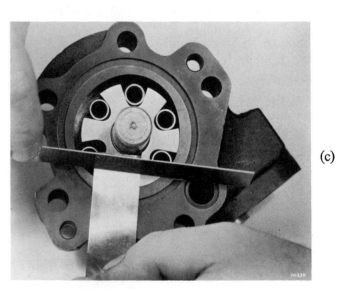

(c)

Power steering pumps are positive displacement pumps. Each revolution delivers the same amount of fluid, no matter what speed it is turning. The pump capacity must be large enough to supply the required fluid volume and pressure required for parking while the engine is idling.

Power assist requirements are very low when driving at highway speeds. At these speeds, the pump will produce high volume and pressure unless the pump output is modified. This is done by providing the pump with a flow control valve and a pressure relief valve.

Flow Control Valve. The greatest amount of steering effort is required as the wheels are turned with the vehicle not moving or while parking. This is the operating condition that requires most assist. Unfortunately, the engine is idling during this time, so the engine driven power steering assist pump is also running slowly. Pump speeds are fast at highway speeds, when little or no power assist is required. To compensate for high pump volumes at cruising speeds, a flow control valve is used.

The flow control valve is operated by small differences in pressure along with a calibrated spring. The passage from the pump outlet contains a restricting orifice. Pressure is greater on the upstream end of the orifice than it is on the downstream end. The pressure drop difference across the orifice increases when the oil flow increases.

High oil pressure from the upstream side of the orifice is directed at one end of the flow control valve. Low oil pressure from the downstream side of the orifice is directed at the other end of the flow control valve. A calibrated spring also is located on the low pressure side of the flow control valve.

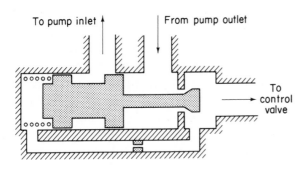

Fig. 28-14 Flow valve principle.

Flow Control Valve Operation. As the engine speed increases from idle, the pump flow and pressure increases, causing a pressure drop across the orifice. When flow increases to the maximum required flow, the flow control valve moves toward its low pressure end. This movement opens a passage between the pump outlet and pump inlet, bypassing a portion of the fluid back to the pump inlet. The opening gets larger as the pump speed increases, thus keeping the flow at the maximum required rate. Recirculating the oil back through the pump reduces pump power requirement and keeps the oil temperature low. Some control valves have a tapered metering pin that moves in the orifice to provide a variable orifice which reduces the effective orifice size at high pump speeds. Another type of flow control valve does this by restricting

a passage that parallels the orifice. These both provide close flow control operation.

Pressure Relief Valve. The flow control valve just described operates when there is little restriction in the power steering system. Flow is restricted by the control valve when it sends fluid to one of the power chambers causing the pressure to rise. If the driver turns the wheels against the turning stops and continues to hold the steering wheel in the full turn position, pressure will build to a maximum. Pressure must be limited to a safe value to avoid damage to the power steering unit seals and hoses. The pressure relief valve limits this pressure by opening a passage between the pump outlet chamber and the pump inlet or the pump reservoir. In some power steering pumps, the pressure regulator is a separate valve, while in others, it is built into the flow control valve and acts as a pilot valve. When pressure on the low pressure side of the flow control valve reaches a predetermined point, the pressure relief valve opens to allow oil to flow from the low pressure side of the flow control valve to the pump inlet. This drops the pressure in the low pressure side of the flow control valve so the flow control valve will snap open to allow the pump output to flow freely into the inlet, thus lowering the pressure. Pressure will balance the valve at the pressure for which it is set.

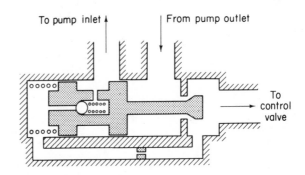

Fig. 28-15 Pressure regulator principle.

The power steering pump is connected to the power steering gear control valve with one high pressure hose and one low pressure return hose. The high pressure hose is frequently made in two sizes that will dampen oil pulsations to reduce noise.

The ends have screw-type tubing fittings to hold the high pressure. The low pressure hose, on the other hand, is attached to the steering gear and reservoir with less expensive hose clamps.

28-4 POWER STEERING SERVICE

Power steering problems are either external fluid leaks or operating problems. External fluid leaks are the result of damaged oil seals, damaged "O" rings, cracked hoses, or cracks in the metal parts. These can be readily seen and corrected by replacing the damaged items.

The first thing to do in any power steering test is to see that there is adequate fluid in the reservoir and that the drive belt has correct tension. Operational problems involving hard steering or lack of assist will either involve the pump assembly, the steering gear assembly, or the steering linkage. The steering linkage should be checked for binding before accusing the pump or steering gear of being at fault. A pump pressure test will indicate the problem location. The pressure test unit consists of a valve with a gauge on the high pressure side. This unit is installed between the pump and the steering gear high pressure hose. The pressure should rise

Fig. 28-16 Power steering test valve and gauge (Cadillac Motor Car Division, General Motors Corporation).

when the steering gear is turned to the extreme position. If it doesn't, the valve is closed. If the pressure does increase then, the pump is functioning satisfactorily, so the problem is in the steering gear. If, on the other hand, the pressure still doesn't rise when the valve is closed, the pump is causing the problem.

The most likely cause of pump failure is either the flow control or the pressure valve sticking open. These can be removed, cleaned, and polished with crocus cloth. Care must be taken to avoid rounding the edges of these valves.

Self-steering or unequal assist is another problem encountered. This usually results from an improperly centering control valve. Self-steering of the parallel sliding type control valve housing can usually be corrected from the outside by adjustment. Gears using the concentric-type control valve will have to be disassembled and inspected to correct the problem. Unequal assist may also result from internal fluid leaks in the steering gear. The steering gear will have to be disassembled to make either of these repairs.

Before disassembly, be sure to have the service manual that applies to the gear being serviced. Usually, special tools are required for alignment and installing seals without damage. These are required for satisfactory servicing. To avoid damage, the disassembly instructions must be carefully followed and all precautions observed.

The gear should be thoroughly cleaned externally to avoid contaminating the interior during disassembly. Fluid is drained and the gear is carefully disassembled, noting the condition of parts, and making the required checks as the parts are removed. The parts should be thoroughly cleaned after disassembly, then inspected for looseness, binding, scoring, wear, etc., as described in the applicable service manual.

After making any required repairs and obtaining replacement parts, including all new seals, the parts are lubricated with power steering fluid or other specific lubricant as they are assembled. All domestic passenger car manufacturers specify a special power steering fluid for use in their automobiles. This fluid is essentially a clear fluid with properties similar to automatic transmission fluid. Some manufacturers even package their fluid as power steering and automatic transmission fluid. Assembly instructions must be followed carefully to be sure that all parts are put in their proper place with the correct adjustments. After assembly, the steering gear unit should be tested before installation in the vehicle by connecting it to the power steering hoses. With fluid in the system and the engine running, the gear may be operated throughout its range to purge air from the system. Details for each gear type are given in the applicable service manual.

Power steering gear worm preload is set as part of the assembly procedure. The Pitman shaft adjustment is done in the same way as it is done on standard steering gears.

28-5 STEERING COLUMN

Automobile safety engineering brought a focus on the steering wheel and steering column as a potential safety hazard. Engineers have concentrated a lot of effort on steering column design to make it collapse as it absorbs impact energy in collisions. In 1956, the first deep dish steering wheel designs were installed on cars to move the actual column away from the driver. In 1967, a collapsible column was designed that would crush on impact. In 1969, a steering column that increased protection from theft was introduced. The ignition switch located on the column locked the steering wheel position and locked the transmission shift linkage in park when the switch was turned off.

Braking a vehicle to a stop absorbs the vehicle energy by converting it to heat in the brakes. In a panic stop, the brakes lock and the energy is absorbed by sliding the tires on the road surface, stopping at about 20 ft/sec² rate. A panic stop will slow the vehicle at the maximum deceleration rate of 20 ft/sec² (d) as discussed in Chapter 24. Using the given equation: $t = 1.465 \, V/d$, the required time to stop a vehicle from 20 mph (V) is 1.5 seconds [$t = (1.465 \times 20)/20$ sec]. This panic stop tends to lift the passengers from their seats. If the car stopped in a still shorter time period, it would stop faster than the driver and passengers within the car. The driver and passengers' energy would carry them into the front of the passenger compartment, unless they were secured with seat and shoulder belts.

In a head-on collision, two collisions actually occur. The first is the vehicle's collision with the object and the second is the occupants' collision with the instrument panel and windshield in the

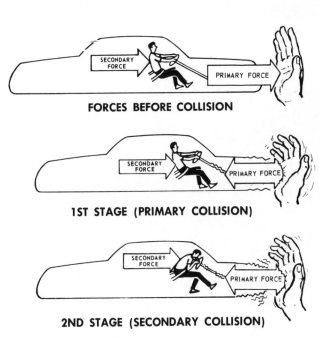

Fig. 28-17 Stages of vehicle crash forces (Chevrolet Motor Division, General Motors Corporation).

front of the passenger compartment. The modern passenger car front end is designed to crush approximately 1"/mph on collision, in order to decelerate the passenger compartment in the longest possible time period and, thereby, reduce the severity of the secondary collision of the occupants.

In a head-on collision, the driver is thrown against the steering wheel about one-hundredth of a second after the front of the vehicle begins to crush. The old style steering column was often pushed into the driver as the front of the vehicle collapsed. Impact absorbing steering columns are designed to have their lower section collapse, rather than having it pushed back into the driver. The upper end of these columns is also designed to absorb the secondary impact of the driver hitting the wheel by collapsing as the driver is thrown into it. As an extra precaution wedges located at the upper attaching point cause the column to be pushed downward while absorbing impact loads.

The steering column must be strong enough and rigid enough to support normal driving loads and yet collapse at a controllable rate when collision loads are applied. Extreme care must be taken when

(a)

(b)

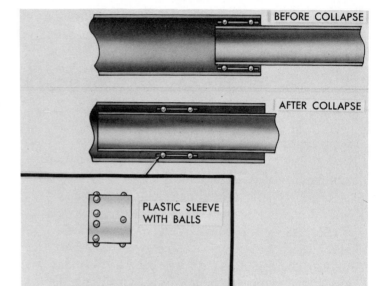

(c)

(d)

Fig. 28-18 Collapsible steering gear jacket types. (a) Diamond-shaped jacket perforation type, (b) steel balls between jacket sections type (Chevrolet Motor Division, General Motors Corporation), (c) bellows jacket type, (d) corrugated can type.

removing or installing the column so the collapsing components are not damaged. It should not be hammered in any way to remove or assemble parts. Instead, special puller tools should be used. The column must be carefully aligned and fastened through break-away attachments with the correct length bolts properly torqued. Carelessness or abuse will cause permanent failure or improper crushing action in case of impact collision. If the column is damaged, it must be entirely replaced. It is not repairable.

Column Construction Features. The steering column consists of three major components, a steering shaft, a shift tube, and a column or mast jacket. The steering shaft connects the steering wheel through a universal joint type coupling to the steering gear unit. In some of the old steering gears, the steering shaft was an extension of the steering gear worm shaft. A shift tube surrounds the steering shaft. The upper end is connected to the shift selector lever and the lower end has a bell crank that attaches to the shift linkages. The shift tube is enclosed in the mast jacket that provides the supporting shaft bearings, the mounting brackets and column trim.

The mast jacket is held in the vehicle by a floor plate retainer at the lower end and a break-away bracket just below the instrument panel. Attachments are designed to allow the column to move downward in a collision and prevent any upward movement.

The first impact absorbing mast jackets had a section with diamond perforation cutouts. In a collision, these perforation sections bulge outward, allowing the jacket to shorten. The perforation folds collapse quite easily after they start to fold. A second generation impact absorbing mast jacket is made of two tubes. The upper tube section is sized to just slip over the lower section. Steel balls in an injected plastic sleeve are wedged between the two tubes, jamming them together to make a secure mast jacket. Upon impact collision, the two sections of the mast jacket telescope together. The steel balls extrude grooves in the tubes as they are forced together and, thus, gradually slow the secondary driver impact at a controlled rate.

Another collapsible design uses a large diameter crushable can just below the steering wheel. The secondary collision will collapse the can to minimize personal injury.

An adapter is placed in each end of the mast jacket to either serve as a bearing or bearing support for the shift tube and steering shaft.

The shift tube is made of two or three short pieces of tubing, one fitted inside the other. Rectangular and round holes are cut in the tubes at the joints. These joints are then injected with plastic to hold their position. In a collision, the plastic inserts in the holes will shear, allowing the shift tubes to telescope together. The shift tube is in all steering columns to provide rigidity, even though the vehicle may be equipped with a floor mounted gear shift lever.

The steering shaft has a solid rod upper section that fits into a hollow lower section. Two external flats on the upper section mate with internal flats in the lower section to transmit steering effort. Plastic inserts are injected into holes in the lower section and around grooves in the upper section just under the holes. This injected plastic locks the two steering shafts together. An impact will shear the plastic to allow the steering shaft to telescope and become shorter.

The upper end of the steering column has become quite complex on the modern automobile. There are a number of items in addition to the upper steering shaft bearing and steering wheel that are installed on the upper end of the steering column. These items include the transmission selector lever, turn signal switch, emergency flasher switch, ignition switch, shift and steering lock mechanisms,

speed control selector, steering wheel tilt mechanism, and a means to allow the wheel to travel in and out. It is very important to follow the manufacturer's service manual when working on these units to make sure the great number of pieces are removed, installed, and adjusted in the correct order, using the correct special tools.

The transmission selector lever is connected to the shift tube. It has a gate that restricts shifter movement between neutral and drive unless the shift lever is lifted as it is moved. This prevents accidental movement into a lower gear, reverse, or park, which could cause transmission damage. Standard transmission gates are designed so the shift linkage goes through neutral before a new gear can be selected. The selector lever fits through a housing or hub that trims the upper end of the steering column.

The turn signal switch is located directly under the steering wheel. A protrusion on the bottom of the steering wheel cancels the signal switch after a turn is completed.

A horn contact touches a slip ring on the steering wheel. When the horn is actuated, contact is made between the slip ring and the steering column metal. This completes the horn circuit to ground, blowing the horn.

Tilting and telescope traveling steering columns have a much more complex upper steering column end. The upper end of the steering shaft is fitted with a yoke that is part of a universal joint. A short upper shaft is also fitted with a yoke. The universal joint is completed with a plastic sphere that fits between the two yokes. The yoke and upper shaft are enclosed in a support housing and end cover. The upper shaft support swivels up and down in the housing, locking in a number of positions. Position locking shoes are released with a lever when the driver wishes to tilt the steering wheel to a new position.

The hollow upper shaft slides into the hollow upper yoke to allow the steering wheel to travel in and out. It is held in place with a cam-type wedge locking into a keyway in the yoke. The wedge is locked by tightening a locking ring on the steering wheel. This pushes a rod located in the hollow upper

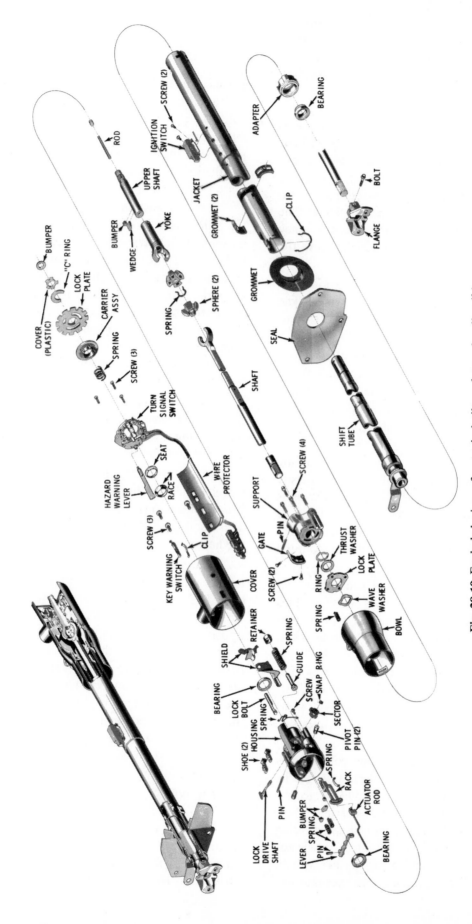

Fig. 28-19 Exploded view of a typical tilt and travel collapsible steering column (Oldsmobile Division, General Motors Corporation).

494

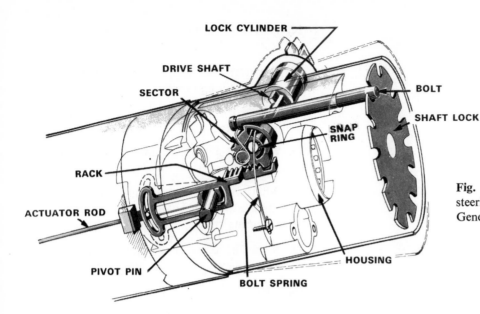

LOCK CYLINDER

DRIVE SHAFT

SECTOR

BOLT

SHAFT LOCK

SNAP RING

RACK

ACTUATOR ROD

PIVOT PIN

BOLT SPRING

HOUSING

Fig. 28-20 Details of a typical locking steering column (Oldsmobile Division, General Motors Corporation).

shaft against the wedge which, in turn, locks the sliding action.

A rod extends from the back side of the steering column mounted ignition switch to actuate the steering and shifting locks. A plastic sector is mounted on the inner end of this rod. When the ignition key is turned, the sector pulls a rack that releases the shift actuator. At the same time, the other side of the sector pulls a bolt from the steering lock plate, releasing the steering system. When the ignition switch is turned off, the transmission shaft actuator and steering lock bolt are returned to their lock position.

28-6 STEERING COLUMN SERVICE

Barring accidents, most of the steering column service involves work on the upper end of the steering column. Much of this can be done with the steering column remaining in the car. Care must be exercised to follow the applicable shop manuals and use the required special tools.

Almost any work on the steering column is begun by the removal of the steering wheel. The upper trim, often a horn button, bar or ring must be removed before the steering wheel can be removed. It may have a press fit cover, a twist lock cover, or the cover may be fastened by screws from the bottom of the steering wheel. Removal of the upper trim exposes the steering wheel nut.

The steering wheel must be pulled from a set of splines on the steering shaft after the nut is

removed. Pullers are usually attached to screws in the steering wheel hub or they have padded hooks that loop around the steering wheel spokes. The position of the master spline should be checked so the wheel can be properly reinstalled. Removal of the steering wheel exposes the turn signal switch mechanism.

With the wheel removed, any of the upper steering column mechanisms may be disassembled to make needed repairs. The mechanisms should be handled very carefully because they can be damaged if they are hit or forced during disassembly or reassembly.

Review Questions
Chapter 28

1. What changes in steering gear design have reduced friction and steering effort?

2. How is steering ratio determined?

3. In what way is a power steering gear the same as a standard steering gear?

4. Describe the power steering oil flow when operating straight ahead at highway speeds.

5. Describe the power steering oil flow when the vehicle is turning a corner.

6. How does power steering help to oppose road shock?

7. Describe the operation of sliding spool and rotary spool valves.

8. Why is reaction control desirable?

9. Describe constant ratio and variable ratio steering gears.

10. Describe the operation of a power steering pump.

11. Why is a flow valve needed in a power steering pump?

Quiz 28

1. Most modern standard steering gears on domestic cars use a steering gear that is called a
   a. worm and sector
   b. worm and roller
   c. ball-nut and sector
   d. rack and pinion.

2. In a power steering gear, the oil pressure is forced to increase by
   a. increasing the regulator valve pressure
   b. closing a return passage
   c. increasing engine speed
   d. opening a pressure apply passage.

3. A torsion bar in a power steering gear
   a. provides driver feel
   b. limits the turning force that can be applied
   c. absorbs road shock
   d. acts as a reactor device.

4. A flow control valve is needed
   a. during parking
   b. while driving in city traffic
   c. during turnpike driving
   d. when maximum assist is required.

5. What is the problem with a power steering system that self-steers?
   a. higher maximum pressure in one direction than the other
   b. inoperative flow valve
   c. broken torsion bar
   d. control valve is not centered.

6. A secondary collision causes the
   a. upper part of the steering column to collapse

12. How does a flow control valve differ from a pressure relief valve?

13. How can a test gauge help to pinpoint a power steering problem?

14. What are the chief causes of power steering failures?

15. Why are steering columns designed to crush?

16. What servicing precautions should be observed when working on impact absorbing steering columns?

17. Name the parts of the steering column that collapse during an impact collison.

18. What mechanisms are located at the upper end of the steering column?

   b. lower part of the steering column to collapse
   c. vehicle to rapidly decelerate
   d. rear of the vehicle to collapse.

7. Steering columns that have been only slightly collapsed should be
   a. removed for repair
   b. repaired in the vehicle
   c. continued in service if it isn't too bad
   d. replaced.

8. Some steering columns contain a shift lever gate. Its purpose is to
   a. lock the shift lever in park
   b. allow shifting at low speeds
   c. prevent accidental shifting into park
   d. allow the engine to be started in neutral.

9. When adjusting the cross shaft, the steering gear should be
   a. set straight ahead
   b. turned either right or left
   c. under a turning load
   d. moved right and left to check for binding.

10. While an improperly operating integral power steering system was being checked with a pressure gauge, the pressure came up as the valve was closed. The problem is in the
    a. pump
    b. flow valve
    c. pressure valve
    d. steering gear.

chapter 29

Instruments and Accessories

Light, instrument, and accessory systems are often neglected in a study of the automobile. This is most evident in automobile repair shops where technicians often find it difficult to pinpoint the cause of malfunctions in these areas. Service manuals have trouble shooting charts and give specific test procedures that should be followed. In new car dealerships, these charts are accompanied by service bulletins. The technician often overlooks this valuable information as he changes parts until the system will function properly. Even though each car type and model is different, they all have a number of common elements. An understanding of these elements will be a great aid in helping a technician follow specific servicing procedures provided by the manufacturer.

To properly service electrical accessories the technician must have an understanding of the principles upon which the accessories operate and he needs to develop a systematic testing procedure so that he can pinpoint the cause of any accessory malfunction. When both of these are accomplished the technician will be able to rapidly diagnose, repair, and adjust lights, instruments and accessories.

29-1 ELECTRICAL CIRCUITS

Wiring diagrams of a vehicle's electrical system are very confusing at first glance. They are different for each type of car line and differ among models and body styles. When the variety of electrical accessories available are added to the wiring diagram, it is not surprising to see why the technician ignores them!

Wiring Diagram. Wiring diagrams are not difficult when one understands the basic automobile electrical circuit requirements and the symbols used to identify individual parts.

Electricity and electrical circuits required for engine operation have already been covered in Chapters 14 through 17. The rest of the automobile electrical system connects into the engine system to make use of the electrical energy from the battery and charging system. Electricity is conducted through wires and switches to the operating units, and through *the vehicle body metal* to complete the circuit with the battery and charging systems.

Electrical units must have a complete circuit supplying them with adequate current. Wiring diagrams use lines to show the insulated circuit connections. In general terms using electron theory,

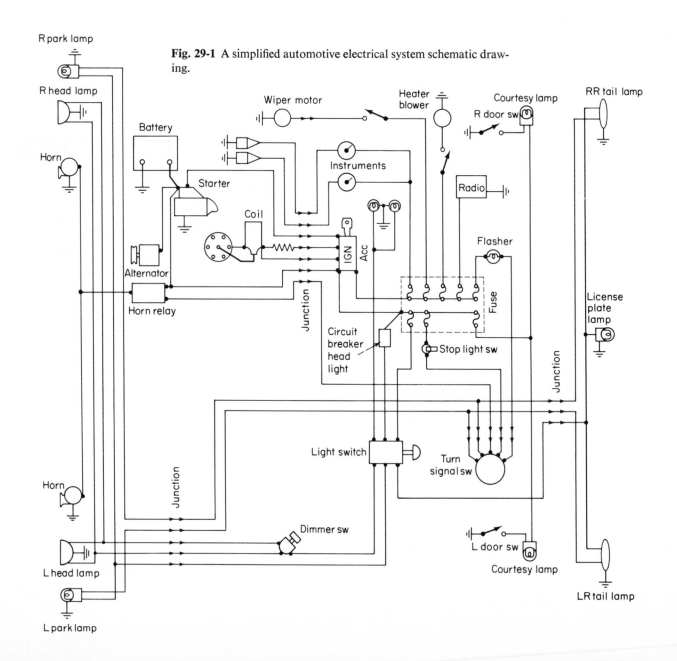

Fig. 29-1 A simplified automotive electrical system schematic drawing.

electrical power flows from the negative battery post to the body sheet metal. Current goes through operating units and into the insulated circuit. The circuit is connected through a switch to a fuse block that is part of a junction block where many circuits combine. The current completes its circuit to the positive battery post from the junction block.

Each operating unit on the wiring diagram is represented by a symbol, either a simple line drawing picture or an electrical schematic drawing. The wiring diagram is essentially a road map between two or more of these electrical units. It includes a means to identify each wire, each junction, each switch and each safety device. A simple means of avoiding confusion while following one circuit is to lay a thin paper over the wiring diagram, then trace the desired circuit on the paper. Some service manuals have separate circuit drawings as individual illustrations.

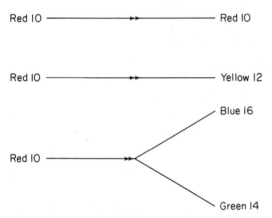

Fig. 29-2 Typical connector arrangement.

All lines on the wiring diagram that represent wires are given a color code. In general, the color follows from the fuse to the operating unit; however, in some cases, it will change color from one side of a junction to the other side. There are even cases where two different colored wires come from the far side of a junction. The color codes used in the diagram are the same colors as those used on the vehicle's wires. This makes it easy to follow the circuit in the wiring diagram and then to find the same circuit wire in the vehicle.

Vehicle wiring is made of several wiring harnesses. One end of each harness is connected to a junction block or connector block. The major junction blocks are located at the fire wall. The other

end of the harness wire is attached to the operating units. The junction block end of the wire has a terminal that snaps into the block. This allows the terminals to make electrical contact when the two halves of the junction block are assembled. The terminal must be partly compressed to remove it from the block. Many types are used so the service manual should be consulted for the specific terminal removal method when removal is necessary. The front end horn and lighting harness is routed along the fire wall and front fenders. The body wiring usually runs from behind the dash along the left lower sill to the rear of the car with branches running to interior lights. A number of smaller harness assemblies are usually attached to the main harness.

Wiring Requirements. The engineer designs vehicle wiring to provide safe and efficient operation at a minimum cost. It is installed in the vehicle so that it is accessible for assembly and for service. In most cases, the junction connectors are designed in a manner that prevents accidental incorrect connection.

Wires must be large enough to carry the current required with minimum voltage loss. If resistance is high, the wire temperature will increase. Wire and connector temperature rise must be less than 225° above the surrounding air temperature. If the wires are larger than necessary, they will increase vehicle weight, take additional space and increase vehicle cost. Generally, Number 16 is the smallest size used in body wiring and Number 10 is the largest. Most wire sizes fall between these two extremes.

Wiring used for automobile lights, instruments, and accessories is called primary wiring. The wire is covered with a molded plastic insulation. Different colors are used as a means to identify the circuit. Many types of plastic compounds are used. Their main differences are in their insulating properties and their melting point. The one that will meet the operational requirements at least cost is the one that is used.

Terminals are attached to the ends of the wires to connect to an operating unit or junction. Many of the original equipment terminals are attached to the wire, then covered with molded plastic insula-

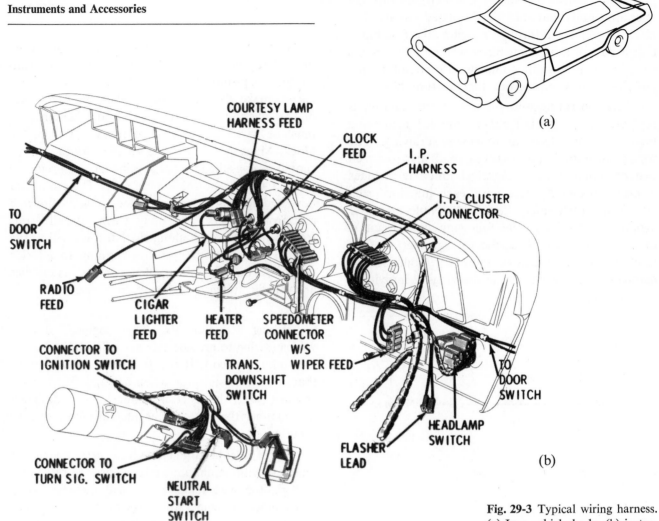

COURTESY LAMP
HARNESS FEED

CLOCK
FEED

I.P.
HARNESS

I. P. CLUSTER
CONNECTOR

TO
DOOR
SWITCH

RADIO
FEED

CIGAR
LIGHTER
FEED

HEATER
FEED

SPEEDOMETER
CONNECTOR
W/S
WIPER FEED

TO
DOOR
SWITCH

CONNECTOR TO
IGNITION SWITCH

TRANS.
DOWNSHIFT
SWITCH

HEADLAMP
SWITCH

FLASHER
LEAD

CONNECTOR TO
TURN SIG. SWITCH

NEUTRAL
START
SWITCH

(a)

(b)

Fig. 29-3 Typical wiring harness. (a) In a vehicle body, (b) instrument panel (Oldsmobile Division, General Motors Corporation).

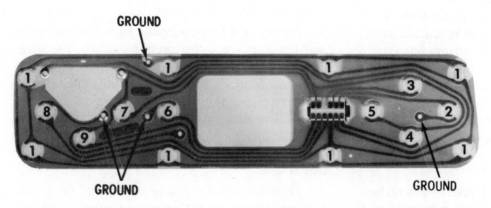

GROUND

GROUND

GROUND

Fig. 29-4 Typical printed instrument panel circuit (Oldsmobile Division, General Motors Corporation).

1. ILLUMINATION LAMPS
2. LEFT TURN SIGNAL
3. HOT LAMP
4. BRAKE LAMP
5. COLD LAMP
6. CENTER LAMP
7. AMP LAMP
8. RIGHT TURN SIGNAL
9. OIL LAMP

tion. Other terminals are attached by crimping, swaging, welding, or soldering. All of these methods are satisfactory if they make a good electrical bond that is mechanically strong. Each wire terminal is exposed even though a number of wires are held together with a fabric braid or plastic tape to form a wiring harness. In some cases, a soldered joint may be located inside a harness.

Instrument panels use printed circuits. These consist of thin conductor ribbons on an insulator. If the printed circuit is damaged, the entire circuit board will require replacement.

Wiring Service. When an operating unit fails to function, the unit should be checked. If there is no apparent problem with the unit, the wiring may be at fault. Wiring can break to cause an open, two wires can contact each other to cause a short, or a wire can contact the frame, causing a ground. Each of these can be partial or intermittent which increases the difficulty in locating the problem point.

When a malfunction exists in a circuit, the first thing to do is to see that voltage is available at the operating end. These checks can be made with a test light or a voltmeter. The test light usually has a pointed prod to get into the circuits. It will draw some current and is easy to use. A voltmeter will show if adequate voltage is available. Each method has its own advantage.

If voltage is available to the circuit but it doesn't arrive at the operating unit, the circuit is open and its section must be checked to pinpoint the problem. The connectors at the fuses, junction blocks, and switch terminals make convenient points to check for voltage. Move the insulated voltmeter lead from terminal to terminal down the circuit until the specific wire causing the problem is identified. This part of the harness should be loosened from its attachments and thoroughly inspected. If the problem point is not visible, the harness will have to be opened at intervals and the test prod forced through the insulation of the problem wire until it touches the metal. Several prods are made until the exact problem point is located. It can usually be repaired by soldering the wire with rosin core solder, then taping the repair and all other prod openings.

Grounds allow current to bleed to the vehicle sheet metal. They will usually draw enough current to open one of the safety devices that are installed in the circuit to protect the wiring from overheating.

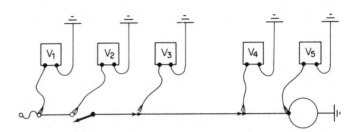

Fig. 29-5 Voltage tests to determine system opens.

Junctions should be disconnected to locate the specific wire that is grounded. Grounds may be located by lifting the harness away from the sheet metal and giving it a thorough inspection. Ground and short finders are available. They consist of a circuit breaker that can be installed in place of the circuit's safety device. These allow current to flow, then break before the circuit wiring is overheated. When the breaker cools, it again closes the circuit. This provides the circuit with a pulsing direct current. When current flows, it induces a surrounding magnetism which can be sensed with a magnetism indicator. The indicator is moved along the conductor. When it reaches the short, it will no longer indicate a magnetic field. This can be used to quickly pinpoint the ground or a short.

Shorts between wires usually put electrical power into adjacent circuits. For example, a short between filaments in a tail light bulb could cause the instrument panel lights to flash as the turn signal flashes. Shorts are difficult to locate. The best procedure is to follow both circuits on the wiring diagram to see where they might possibly be shorted together. The system should be separated at the junctions to locate the specific wires that are shorting. The actual short can usually be seen.

When electrical circuit problems are encountered, the technician should check the safety device, the operating unit, and the wiring diagram. Consider the possible cause of the problem and then proceed with a systematic check of the system causing the problem.

Safety Devices. All electrical circuits, other than engine circuits, are protected with safety devices. The safety device opens the circuit when high cur-

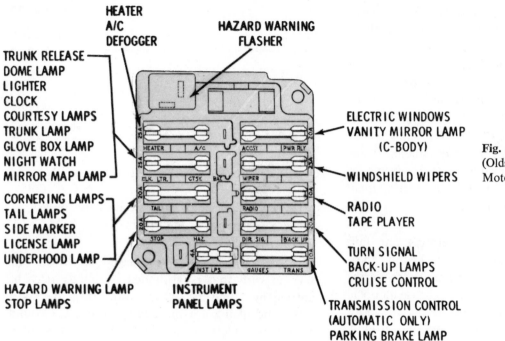

HEATER
A/C
DEFOGGER

HAZARD WARNING
FLASHER

TRUNK RELEASE
DOME LAMP
LIGHTER
CLOCK
COURTESY LAMPS
TRUNK LAMP
GLOVE BOX LAMP
NIGHT WATCH
MIRROR MAP LAMP

CORNERING LAMPS
TAIL LAMPS
SIDE MARKER
LICENSE LAMP
UNDERHOOD LAMP

HAZARD WARNING LAMP
STOP LAMPS

INSTRUMENT
PANEL LAMPS

ELECTRIC WINDOWS
VANITY MIRROR LAMP
(C-BODY)

WINDSHIELD WIPERS

RADIO
TAPE PLAYER

TURN SIGNAL
BACK-UP LAMPS
CRUISE CONTROL

TRANSMISSION CONTROL
(AUTOMATIC ONLY)
PARKING BRAKE LAMP

Fig. 29-6 Typical fuse block (Oldsmobile Division, General Motors Corporation).

rent flows so the wiring, insulation, or surrounding structure is not damaged. Safety devices used in automobiles take three forms: fuses, circuit breakers, and fusable links.

A fuse is a small metal strip in a glass tube that burns out to break the circuit when high current flows. Fuses are usually grouped together in a fuse block under the dash. Sometimes, they are mounted separately in a circuit. A fuse will carry a 10% overload and will burn out immediately with a 35% overload. This protects the wiring and operating units. Fuses are used in low amperage light and accessory circuits. Circuits that draw high current usually use circuit breakers.

A circuit breaker is a set of contact points mounted on a bimetal arm. As excess current flows, the bimetal arm heats. Heat causes the arm to bend, breaking the point contact which stops current flow in the circuit. When the arm cools, the points close to re-establish a complete circuit. Circuit breakers are used as a safety feature in the headlight circuit. In case of a short, the lights do not stay out, but will flash on and off to give the driver a chance to safely stop the vehicle. Circuit breakers are also used on high current drawing units like power windows, and power seats. The breaker may be located under the dash or adjacent to the operating unit.

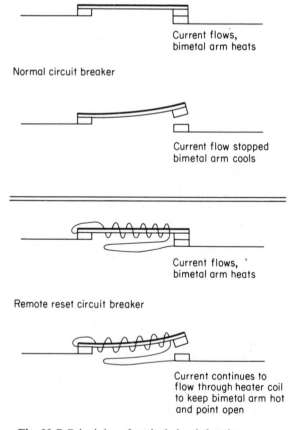

Current flows, bimetal arm heats

Normal circuit breaker

Current flow stopped bimetal arm cools

Current flows, bimetal arm heats

Remote reset circuit breaker

Current continues to flow through heater coil to keep bimetal arm hot and point open

Fig. 29-7 Principles of typical circuit breakers.

Some circuit breakers do not automatically reset, so the circuit remains open until repairs are made. They may be reset manually after being tripped. A remote reset breaker has been developed to reset the breaker at will. It has a resistance wire wrapped around the bimetal spring and connected across the points. When the points are closed, no current will flow through the coil. When excess current causes the bimetal spring points to open, current flows through the coil and the coil gets hot. Coil heat holds the points open. The circuit breaker will close when the switch is turned off or the battery disconnected.

Many circuits are further protected with a fusable link, even though they have a fuse or a circuit breaker. Fusable links will protect the circuit if someone accidentally shorts out one of the other safety devices. A fusable link is a short piece of wire four sizes smaller than the circuit wire it is designed to protect. For example, the #10 wire in the charging circuit is protected by a #14 fusable link and a #16 light wire is protected by a #20 fusable link. The fusable link is covered with thick Hypalon plastic insulation that will not burn. Its exterior size suggests that is a large wire. When the link fails, the grounded point that caused the failure must be repaired before a new link is installed. In some cases, the link is connected with terminals and in other cases, it is soldered in the circuit as an integral part.

29-2 LIGHTS

Exterior lights are a safety factor anytime visibility is poor. Under these conditions, many states require their use. Lights inside the vehicle are a convenience that helps to reduce driver strain and, thus, lead to safety. Anytime a light does not function, it becomes a factor contributing to an unsafe vehicle.

In most cases, light failure results from a burned out filament in the bulb and is easily corrected by bulb replacement. When a whole set of lights fail, it is often caused by an open system safety device. The failure could also be caused by the wiring, terminals, or bulb socket.

The light bulb must be the correct type. It must have a base to match the bulb socket and it must have the correct filament. Filament size and design controls bulb brightness. The bulb must be bright enough to give the necessary light, but not so bright that it uses excess current or is blinding bright.

Headlights. The most critical lights on the automobile are the headlights. They must be bright enough so the driver can see the road ahead but not so bright that they will blind the oncoming driver. Many state laws have limited the headlight brightness to a maximum of 75,000 candle power.

With candle power limited, headlight engineers have designed headlights so they will concentrate the available light onto the road and avoid blinding the oncoming driver. This is done by making prisms and asymmetric left flutes in the bulb lens interior to widen the beam and minimize glare. Careful filament placement and a tilted reflector aims the light beam to the road.

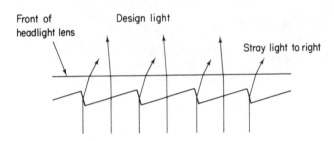

Fig. 29-8 Headlight lens design.

Automobiles are equipped with a high beam and a low beam. Most of the driving in cities and on busy highways is done using low beam. High beam is only used when there is no oncoming traffic.

Two types of headlights are used to meet driving needs. Type 1 headlights have one filament aimed to give maximum light on the road. They are used as the inboard or lower lights in the four headlight system. Type 2 headlights have two filaments. The main filament is located to provide maximum light on low beam. These were brought onto the market as more cars made traffic heavier, so that more of the driving was being done with low beam than with high beam. The second filament in Type 2 bulbs provides high beam light. Type 2 lights are used for the outboard or upper bulbs in the four headlight system and for all two headlight systems. Headlight bulbs used in the four headlight system are $5\frac{3}{4}''$ in diameter and the two headlight system bulbs are $7''$ in diameter. The type number is embossed on the lens face for easy identification. In addition, the mounting lugs are offset at different angles so they will not fit in the improper location.

Fig. 29-9 Headlight bulb number.

Headlights can be designed and manufactured correctly, but they will function correctly only when they are properly aimed. Headlight aiming is the largest single item found to be faulty in safety check lane inspections. Headlights can be easily adjusted with a minimum of equipment.

The headlight bulb is fastened in a metal adjuster ring. The adjuster ring has one screw that controls horizontal movement and another that controls vertical movement. These are used to place the light beam hot spot in the correct position so it will provide the driver with maximum road lighting.

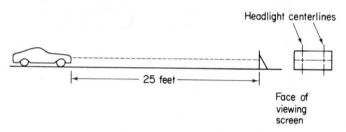

Fig. 29-11 Headlight aiming principle.

Headlight aiming is based on a distance of 25 feet between the front of the headlight bulb and a viewing screen, which may be a wall. The center of the vertical lines should be directly in front of the vehicle headlights and the horizontal line should

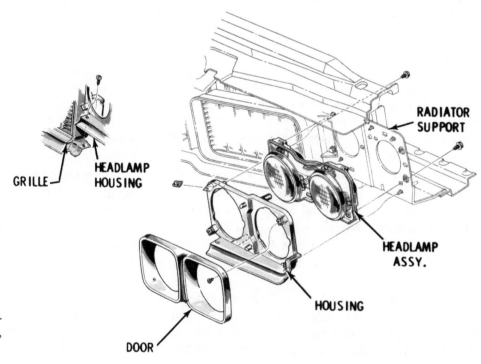

Fig. 29-10 Headlight housing assembly (Oldsmobile Division, General Motors Corporation).

be at the same height as the center of the headlight bulbs. Before aiming the headlights, the vehicle should have a full tank of fuel, the spare tire in its normal location, all tires inflated correctly, and any other regularly carried materials should be loaded. The hot spot should be located as shown in Figure 29-12. Adjusting screws are used to correctly position the hot spot. Type 1 bulbs are aimed with high beam turned on, while Type 2 bulbs are aimed with low beam turned on.

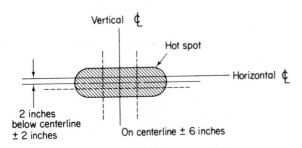

Type 1 headlight

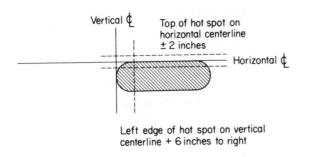

Type 2 headlight

Fig. 29-12 Viewing screen patterns of the headlight hot spot aiming area.

Light beam aiming requires a relatively dark area. Mechanical aimers have been devised for use in full daylight. They are built with mathematical corrections to aim the light bulbs as accurately as aiming by the light beam method. Mechanical aimers are seated against three reference locating lugs provided on the bulb. Specific operating details differ between aimers. In general, they use spirit levels, strings, and reflecting mirrors with split images to align headlight pairs. Some aimers used in daylight use the headlight with optics so the pattern in the aimer appears the same as it would on the viewing screen.

(a)

Fig. 29-13 Headlight aimers. (a) Mechanical, (b) light beam.

(b)

No matter what method is used, headlights should be accurately aimed for proper night visibility. At today's driving speeds, any light less than the maximum possible does not give the driver sufficient reaction time in case there is an unexpected change in the road ahead.

29-3 INSTRUMENTS

Instruments are used to indicate many vehicle operating conditions. All vehicles are equipped with a speedometer to show vehicle speed and distance. Some means is provided to indicate engine low oil pressure, high temperature, and battery discharge. A fuel gauge is provided to show the amount of fuel remaining in the tank. Each vehicle has an indicator to show the operation of high beam headlights and turn signals.

In addition to these basic instruments, many vehicles have additional instruments to give the driver more information about the operation of the vehicle. These would include instruments such as a tachometer, clock, and compass.

Indicator Lights. Many operating conditions are shown by indicator lights. These are frequently referred to as "idiot lights" by those who do not recognize their great value. A driver's attention is immediately called to a light signal that indicates a problem even though he is concentrating on driving the vehicle. It is interesting to note that the aerospace industry uses lights to indicate abnormal operating conditions to alert the pilot to the problem. He may also have a gauge to check the actual operating value.

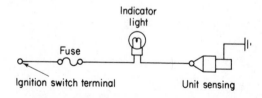

Fig. 29-14 Typical indicator light circuit.

Indicator lights pick up their power at the engine or tank unit. The circuit goes through to the indicator light bulb, then on to the ignition switch, where it is attached to a junction block to complete the circuit. It should be noted that these indicator bulbs are some of the few in the vehicle that are not grounded at the bulb. The engine and tank units are electrical switches that connect the circuit to ground to turn the indicator light on.

A diaphragm in the oil pressure unit opens the points when sufficient oil pressure exists. When the pressure drops dangerously low, the points close to turn on the indicator light. Points on a bimetal arm are used in the temperature unit. When engine temperature is excessive, the heat bends the bimetal arm in the engine unit so the points close to complete the circuit and turn on the warning light. In some cases, the temperature unit is equipped with a second set of points to indicate low temperature. These points are normally closed to keep the cold light on. As the engine warms, the bimetal arm bends enough to separate the points which turn out the cold signal light.

Charging system discharge lights operate in a different manner. They use a light relay, usually located within the regulator. When the generator is charging, the relay is energized to open the points. When the system is not charging, the points close, completing the indicator circuit and the warning light comes on.

A number of other warning lights may be used, such as parking brake signal, low fuel level, seat belt fastening, door ajar, etc. Each helps to improve safety and convenience, while adding to the original and maintenance costs.

A relatively new indicating method makes use of fiber optic conductors, consisting of a bundle of plastic filaments that transmit light. They are used to show the driver if lights are on or off. One end of the bundle is at the light source and the other is visible to the driver.

Gauges. Instrument gauges are used where it is important to know values, such as vehicle speed and remaining fuel. Oil pressure, engine temperature, and charging rate values are also used to recognize impending failure before it occurs. Gauges are generally more expensive than indicating lights and the majority of drivers would not notice or recognize an incorrect reading anyway, so lights are usually used. Gauges are standard equipment on certain sport and performance model cars and optional equipment on many other cars.

The speedometer is a mechanical device, making use of induction between a rotating magnet and a cup. The cup position is retained by a hair spring. As the magnet rotates, it pulls the cup against the hair spring an amount proportional to the magnet's rotating speed. The cup is connected to an indicator needle to show speed. The rotating magnet is driven by a flexible shaft which, in turn, is driven by a gear in the transmission output shaft or by a gear on the left front wheel.

Most of the other gauges are electrically operated. All but the ammeter operate on the same basic principle. A coil of resistance wire is wound around a bimetal arm. The more current that flows through the coil, the more it heats and bends the bimetal arm. The movable end of the arm is connected by a linkage to an indicator needle. Different scale panels are placed behind the needle to show the correct value.

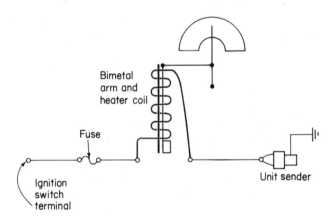

Fig. 29-15 Typical instrument circuit.

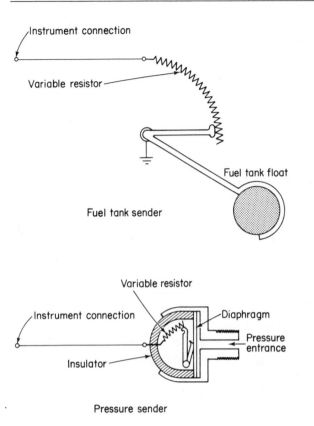

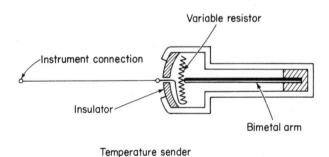

Fig. 29-16 Typical instrument tank and engine unit principles.

Because this type gauge mechanism is sensitive to current flow, it is important to have a constant voltage source for accuracy. In most cases, these instruments are supplied from a vibrating point voltage regulator that keeps the voltage at a constant value, usually five volts. The regulator may be a separate unit or part of the fuel level gauge.

The gauge sender, which is a tank or engine unit, actually connects the system to ground where it indirectly connects to the negative side of the battery to complete the circuit. A variable resistance rheostat is connected to the hinged tank float. When the fuel level is high, the gauge circuit connects directly to ground, allowing full current to flow through the instrument coil. This moves the instrument needle to the top of the scale. As fuel is used, the float drops. This causes the instrument circuit current to flow through part of the variable resistance, adding resistance that reduces current flow reducing instrument coil temperature so the gauge reading lowers. The gauge reading is, therefore, proportional to the tank fuel level.

Electric oil pressure and temperature gauges work in a similar manner. Design of the engine unit is their only difference. Oil pressure gauges have a spring loaded diaphragm. Diaphragm movement caused by the oil pushing the diaphragm toward the spring changes the instrument circuit resistance proportional to the diaphragm movement. Resistance is low when oil pressure is high, giving a high instrument reading. The temperature gauge has a bimetal spring that changes resistance proportional to engine heat. The free end of the bimetal spring is attached to a variable resistance so the instrument circuit resistance is changed proportional to the engine temperature. When the engine is hot, the engine unit resistance is low, which will give a high instrument reading.

If the sending unit end of the wire is grounded, the normal reading will always be high. If no current flows, the reading will always be zero. Some service manuals give resistance values that can be temporarily inserted in the circuit to check gauge accuracy. They are also helpful in troubleshooting a gauge problem.

The ammeter is connected in the part of the charging circuit that leads to the battery. Its purpose is to indicate the amount of current being put into or taken from the battery. It does not indicate generator output. Ammeter wiring circuits are, therefore, made from large wire sizes. The ammeter itself must also have heavy construction to carry high current. Several ammeter movement types are used. All basically use an application of induction. As current flows, it forms a magnetic field that is deflected by a permanent magnet in the instrument. High current flow causes high magnetic field deflection. The moving portion of the gauge is connected to an indicator needle. The needle's normal position is upright. The needle would move to the right when the current is flowing to charge the battery and to the left when discharging current flows from the battery.

Troubleshooting becomes routine when the technician understands the basic operation principles of these instruments and when the service manual instructions are followed. The biggest problem encountered in instrument troubleshooting in some vehicle models is to get to the instrument leads to check them, especially in a car equipped with air conditioning and a center console.

29-4 ACCESSORIES

Accessories are items added to the basic vehicle for additional safety, comfort, or appearance. Vehicle operation is not impaired if they fail; however, their failure is a great source of annoyance to the driver or his passengers.

Radio. A radio is one of the most common accessories. It may be merely an AM radio or a complex AM/FM stereo with a tape deck. The automotive technician's only responsibility is to properly install or remove it, see that it is supplied with electrical power, trim the antenna, and adjust the push buttons. If additional service is required, the radio will have to be removed and repaired by a specialist.

In most cases, the radio is connected to the ignition accessory terminal and is fused in the connecting wire. In some cases, the fuse is built into the radio chassis.

Trimming the antenna is a means of balancing the radio and antenna with a trimmer screw located on the back or bottom of the radio chassis. The radio is tuned to a weak station around 1600 KC and the trimmer screw adjusted to get the strongest signal.

Push buttons are pulled outward to release them. The station is tuned in with the dial. When the push button is pushed in, it will lock the station to the button. In most cases, the driver will adjust the push buttons to the station himself.

Motors. Many accessories operate with small electric motors. In some cases, they are reversible motors. Electric motors used for accessories make use of the same motor principles as starters, described in Chapter 15. The motor has a rotating armature within a field. Current is transferred to the armature through commutator brushes. The armature is supported in bearings within the housing.

Reversible motors are equipped with two fields. One field is used when the motor runs clockwise and the other field is used when the motor runs counterclockwise.

Motors are used as fan drives in the heater, air conditioner, and defogger. They are used for power to operate power windows, power seats, power antennas, hydraulic pumps for power tops, windshield wipers, windshield washers, electric fuel pumps, and many other units.

If a motor does not operate, the first thing to do is check to see that electrical power is available at the motor lead. If it isn't, the circuit should be checked as previously described. If power is available, the motor should be removed for service. Many of these motors are low cost, high production units that are not repairable, but must be replaced. Motors that are repairable should be disassembled.

Motor repair follows the same procedures used for servicing starters. The parts are wiped clean, then inspected for grounds or opens. The commutator can be turned and new brushes installed. Bearings and gear housings should be properly lubricated as the motor is assembled. After assembly, it should be checked for correct operation before installing it in the vehicle.

Buzzer. Buzzers are used to call the driver's attention to an unusual condition, such as the key left in the ignition when the door is opened. The buzzer principle is also used for vehicle horns. In horns, the vibrating armature is connected to a metal diaphragm that is vibrated to produce the sound.

In the buzzer, current flows through a coil, then on to spring loaded, normally closed points. Coil magnetism pulls the armature to open the points, which breaks the coil's current, so the coil loses its magnetism. The spring will then close the points and the cycle repeats. Cycling speed or frequency is based on the balance between the spring force, coil strength, air gap, and armature weight. Different cycling frequencies produce different horn pitches. Most horns have an adjusting screw to change spring tension for tuning the horn pitch.

Solenoid. A solenoid provides a pull force. Solenoid details in Chapter 15 explain its use to engage the starter drive. It is also used as a remote control to operate items such as door locking, trunk opening, and applying the air conditioning compressor clutch. A movable core is attached to the mechanism. When current flows through a coil, the core is pulled toward the coil center to operate the mechanism.

Relay. A relay is a remote switch. It is usually used where heavy current is required and voltage losses would be too great if the entire circuit ran to the driver's control switch. A horn relay or a starter relay are examples of this requirement. The normally open relay points on the relay armature are heavy enough to carry the required current. One end of a fine wire coil is connected to the relay

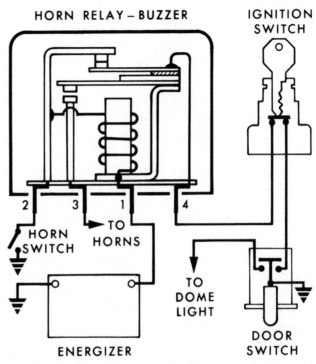

Fig. 29-17 Typical horn and safety buzzer circuit (Chevrolet Motor Division, General Motors Corporation).

power input and the other end lead is connected to a switch on the dash. When the driver closes the switch, current flows through the coil to close the relay points. This supplies current to the required units. When the driver releases the switch, the relay opens to break the current.

Vacuum Controls. Some accessories are vacuum operated, rather than electric. Engine manifold vacuum is the vacuum source. Small vacuum hoses and valves are connected together in a manner very similar to the electrical wiring to connect the vacuum source to the operating unit.

Vacuum is used for a pull motion. It is usually used to position heater, air conditioning, and ventilation doors. It may be used in the some applications in the place of solenoids on door locks, trunk locks, and headlight covers.

Vacuum actuators may also be called vacuum motors. They consist of a rod extending from a diaphragm. Vacuum on the far side of the diaphragm moves the diaphragm to pull the rod.

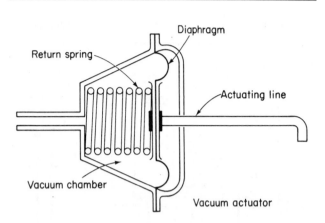

Fig. 29-18 Section view of a typical vacuum actuator.

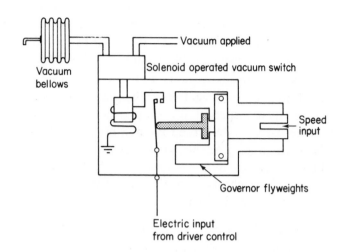

Fig. 29-19 Schematic of a typical speed control.

Troubleshooting vacuum systems is similar to electrical troubleshooting. The line may be plugged (like an electrical open) or the hose may have a leak (like an electrical ground). Valves or vacuum switches may be faulty and the vacuum actuator diaphragm may be perforated. Vacuum systems may be equipped with a reservoir to provide a limited vacuum source when the engine is not operating.

Speed Control. A speed control is a relatively new accessory to reduce driver fatigue. The driver can lock it at almost any desired speed. It will hold the vehicle speed constant within the engine power range. The driver can override the control with the throttle and release it with a slight touch of the brake pedal.

Speed is sensed by a regulator. The regulator is a mechanical governor driven by the speedometer cable. The governor opens and closes contact points. Electrical current is sent across the points when the driver energizes the system. This current flows through an electrical solenoid that controls a vacuum valve. A vacuum bellows assembly is used to position the throttle. Opening and closing governor points controls the average position of the bellows vacuum valve so that the bellows position will match the control speed. Underspeed opens the throttle and overspeed closes it.

Many other accessories are used and many new ones will be developed. If the technician can master the basic concepts, he can easily adapt to the new and varied units as he has occasion to work on them.

Review Questions
Chapter 29

1. Why is it important to have operating units properly grounded?

2. Why are wiring diagrams color coded?

3. Describe typical wiring harness routing through the automobile body.

4. What is the basis for selecting the vehicle's wire size?

5. What type of wiring is used for lights, instruments, and accessories?

6. What are the advantages and disadvantages of using a test light and a voltmeter?

7. What general procedures should be followed to pinpoint an open wire? A grounded wire? A shorted wire?

8. What are the advantages and disadvantages of the different types of safety devices in the electrical circuits?

9. What is the usual cause of light failures?

10. How do the headlight types differ? How can they be identified?

11. Describe headlight aiming with the light beam and viewing screen method.

12. Describe headlight aiming with a mechanical aimer.

13. What are the advantages of indicator lights?

14. How do the oil pressure and coolant temperature engine units differ?

15. List as many indicator lights as possible that can be found on domestic automobiles.

16. How are fiber optics used as indicators?

17. How does the operation of oil and temperature instruments differ from the operation of indicator lights?

18. Why is a voltage regulator used for an instrument voltage source?

19. What does the instrument sending unit do in the system?

20. How can known resistances be helpful in troubleshooting gauge problems?

21. What is the purpose of the ammeter?

22. What service may be done on accessory motors?

23. What service is performed by the technician on a radio?

24. Where are buzzers used in automobiles?

25. When is a relay used rather than a mechanically operated switch?

26. How do vacuum circuits compare to electrical circuits?

Quiz 29

1. Different colored wires are used to
   a. indicate wire size
   b. indicate which switch is used
   c. identify different circuits
   d. identify operating units.

2. The smallest size wire that can be used in body wiring is limited by
   a. the wire length
   b. temperature
   c. the number of circuits in use
   d. vehicle voltage.

3. A short in the body wiring will generally
   a. cause the insulation to overheat
   b. act like an open switch
   c. burn out a light bulb
   d. blow a fuse.

4. When one circuit is turned on and another also comes on, the cause is a
   a. short circuit
   b. open circuit
   c. grounded circuit
   d. insulated circuit.

5. When a safety device is found to be open, the correct procedure is to
   a. connect a voltmeter at the operating unit to check for current
   b. reset the breaker or install a new fuse
   c. check the circuits for opens
   d. check the circuits for grounds.

6. If the engine unit is open, an instrument will
   a. give a full scale reading
   b. not produce a reading
   c. give either a high or a low reading
   d. be damaged so it will have to be replaced.

7. A safety device could be blown when
   a. all of the interior lights fail at one time
   b. one instrument panel light fails
   c. a turn signal wire is found to be open
   d. the turn signal fails to operate in one direction.

8. Headlights are aimed so the top center of the light beam hot spot is
   a. centered ahead of the vehicle and level
   b. level and slightly to the right
   c. centered ahead of the vehicle and slightly down
   d. slightly down and to the right.

9. A service technician should be able to
   a. rebuild a speedometer
   b. rebuild a vacuum actuator
   c. trim the radio antenna
   d. repair a relay.

10. When a vehicle ammeter is used, it is connected in the electrical system between the
    a. alternator and the rest of the system
    b. fuse block and the rest of the system
    c. battery and the rest of the system
    d. alternator regulator and the rest of the system.

chapter 30

Automotive Air Conditioning

Air conditioning has become a very important optional accessory in Northern United States and a necessity in the South. The air conditioner, operating in conjunction with the heater, provides control of the passenger compartment temperature, humidity, and air cleanliness to provide a quiet, clean, comfortable environment for the vehicle occupants. Safety is improved because the driver does not become fatigued as quickly as he does without air conditioning.

Air is conditioned by directing an air flow across a cool metal surface called an evaporator. This cools the air and causes moisture in the air to condense, much as the moisture will condense on the outside of a glass that contains a cool drink. Condensed moisture traps dust and pollen to clean the air. The dirty condensed water is then drained from the system.

Automobile air conditioning is divided into two distinct systems—the air distribution system and the refrigeration system. Both must function correctly to provide adequate air conditioning.

30-1 AIR DISTRIBUTION SYSTEM

The air distribution system consists of blower fans to move the air, ducts to carry the air and valves to control the air flow direction. Electric motors drive the fans and air valves are positioned by vacuum adjusters or mechanical controls.

Air distribution systems differ among vehicle manufacturers, vehicle models, and air conditioner types. Their details are described in the applicable service manual; however, they fall into three basic system types.

The simplest type is the self-contained air conditioner. Its air distribution system is completely separate from the vehicle heater system. Air flow is controlled by fan speed and by louvers that control the air flow direction.

Most factory installed air conditioners are built to combine their air distribution system with the heater air distribution system. All of the air to be cooled flows across the evaporator. If this cools too much, some or all of the cool air is then directed across the heater core to be reheated to the desired temperature. A combination of cooling, which removes moisture and dirt, followed by sufficient reheating, provides ideal air conditioning.

The most complex factory installed air conditioning systems have fully automatic air distribution controls. The driver can set the temperature desired and the controls will cool or heat the air as necessary to maintain that temperature within maximum cooling to maximum heating limits.

The air distribution system is basically a mechanical system. Its service involves mechanical adjustments that move air distribution valves in the position required for each range selected. If a valve doesn't operate, it may be the result of an inoperative vacuum control or binding valve mechanism. Specific test procedures as described in the service manual may be required to locate the cause of problems in automatic control type systems.

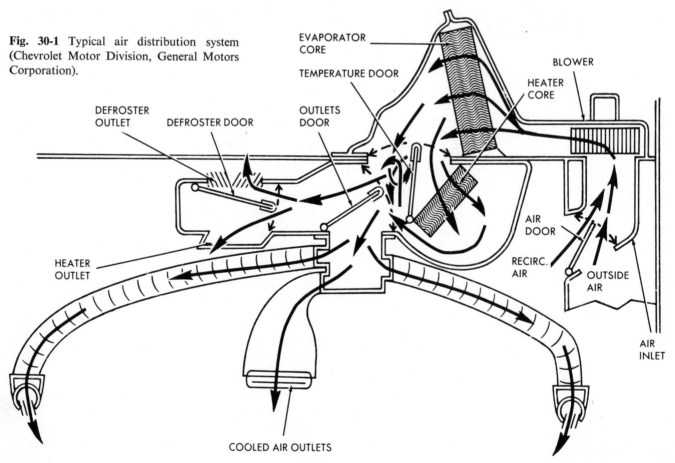

Fig. 30-1 Typical air distribution system (Chevrolet Motor Division, General Motors Corporation).

30-2 REFRIGERATION SYSTEM

In simplified terms, the air conditioner refrigeration system is similar to an engine cooling system. The engine coolant is forced to circulate by a pump. It picks up engine heat and carries it to the radiator, where the heat is transferred to the outside air. Heat is always transferred from the highest temperature to the lowest temperature. The coolant then recirculates back through the engine to remove more heat.

In the air conditioner's refrigeration system, refrigerant picks up heat from the passenger compartment and is pumped to the condenser where it gives up its heat to the outside air. The refrigerant then flows back through the system to pick up more heat. Refrigerant is recycled in a closed system like engine coolant.

Freon 12 is used as the heat transfer medium in automotive air conditioner refrigeration systems and is usually called Refrigerant 12, F-12, or R-12. It provides good heat transfer in the required temperature range and does not deteriorate system components.

In operation, the refrigerant continually changes from a liquid to a gas, then back to a liquid again. A great amount of heat is required to boil the refrigerant in the evaporator while turning it into a vapor. Heat to boil the refrigerant is taken from the passenger compartment air, thus cooling the air.

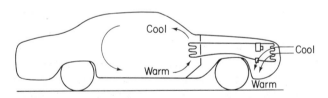

Fig. 30-2 Heat movement from the passenger compartment through the refrigeration system to the outside air.

The refrigerant boiling point is dependent upon its pressure just as the engine cooling system boiling point can be changed by means of a pressure cap. High pressure raises the boiling point and low pressure reduces it. Refrigerant in the closed system is allowed to evaporate or boil in the evaporator under controlled pressures, which, in turn, controls evaporator temperature.

It is a well known fact that it requires a great deal more heat to change a liquid to a gas at the same temperature than it does to raise the temperature of a liquid. The refrigeration cycle makes use of this principle. Refrigerant liquid enters the evaporator at a controlled rate. Heat from the passenger compartment air warms the refrigerant in the evaporator and thus cools the air. This heat causes the refrigerant to boil as it changes from a liquid to a vapor. The vapor is then pumped from the evaporator by the compressor, compressing the vapors to increase pressure in the same way a compressor would compress air. These high pressure, high temperature vapors are run through a condenser where they are cooled with outside air. Cooling at high pressure causes the vapors to condense back to the liquid state to be reused in the evaporator. This forms a continuous cycle to carry heat from the evaporator in the passenger compartment to the condenser where it is given up to outside air.

30-3 AIR CONDITIONING REQUIREMENTS

Vehicle air conditioning requirements are based upon a number of factors. Heat comes into the vehicle from the temperature of outside air, from the sun radiation heat, from engine heat that filters in and from vehicle occupants' body heat. The amount of heat absorbed is modified by the vehicle insulation, position and intensity of the sun, variations of light and shadow, vehicle color, tinted glass, vehicle speed, and wind direction and velocity. An automobile air conditioner must be capable of removing all the heat input in addition to reducing the temperature of a vehicle that has been standing in the sun.

Heat load on the air conditioner may be as high as 15,000 BTU per hour. This is equivalent to 1.5 tons of air conditioning. About half of this heat is conducted through the vehicle metal and glass. The remainder comes from air leaks, warm parts within the vehicle, and occupants' body heat. The air conditioner can only reject about one third of this heat at engine idle, so full cooling cannot occur until engine speed increases.

Temperature is only one comfort factor. Humidity, in many cases, is an even more important factor. Removing excess humidity, therefore, is one of the most important air conditioning requirements. This is especially true in the humid climates which include areas in the north that have satisfactory temperatures, but high humidity. The factory installed air conditioner can be adjusted by the operator to remove humidity without lowering temperature to provide occupant comfort in these climates.

Condensed moisture that accumulates on the evaporator core will fall to a drip pan to be drained from the vehicle. When the air conditioner is not used for some time, a fungus may form on these wet surfaces and produce a stale odor when the air conditioner is restarted.

30-4 REFRIGERATION CONTROLS

Refrigeration controls use the principle that the refrigerant boiling temperature depends upon its pressure. An *expansion valve* is used to control the refrigerant flow into the evaporator.

Expansion Valve. Maximum cooling occurs when all of the liquid refrigerant is turned to a vapor as it rises through the evaporator. If insufficient refrigerant is allowed to flow into the evaporator, the system will be starved. No cooling occurs after the liquid has vaporized. When too much liquid refrigerant is allowed to enter the evaporator, there is not enough room for vapor to form, so the system is inefficient. The expansion valve controls this refrigerant quantity. It is controlled by temperature and pressure at the evaporator outlet. At idle, the temperature will be about 55°, while at highway speed, the temperature will go down to about 35° and sometimes slightly lower.

The expansion valve changes the medium-temperature, high-pressure liquid refrigerant from the condenser to a low-temperature, low-pressure liquid to feed the evaporator. The temperature control portion of the expansion valve opens the valve when the evaporator outlet temperature rises 10 to 15° above the refrigerant boiling point and closes the valve when the temperature lowers to 10 to 15° below the refrigerant boiling point.

Temp °F	PSI
0	9.2
5	11.7
10	14.6
15	17.7
20	21.0
25	24.6
30	28.5
35	32.6
40	37.0
45	41.7
50	46.7
55	52.5
60	57.7
65	63.8
70	70.2
75	77.0
80	84.2
85	91.8
90	99.8
95	108.3
100	117.2
105	126.6
110	136.4
115	146.8
120	157.7
125	169.1
130	181.0

Fig. 30-3 Table of Freon 12 pressure at a range of temperatures.

The amount of heat picked up by the evaporator will control the evaporator temperature. When the heat load is greatest, a large quantity of refrigerant is converted to vapor. When the vehicle cools and the heat load is less, it will vaporize less refrigerant, so the expansion valve reduces refrigerant flow, keeping the evaporator outlet temperature nearly constant.

Freeze-Up Control. The expansion control does not satisfactorily control minimum temperature throughout the wide speed range of engine driven compressors found on automobiles. Additional control is required to keep the temperature as low as possible, but still above the freezing point. If evaporator temperature goes below freezing, the condensed moisture would freeze, plugging the air flow passage. This blockage would prevent air flow, so the air would not be cooled.

Self-contained air conditioners and some factory installed units use a thermostatic switch that senses evaporator temperature. When the temperature approaches freezing, the thermostatic switch disengages the compressor clutch to stop the refrigerant cycle. When evaporator temperatures increase, the compressor is again engaged to start the cycle.

It is normal to have rapid compressor clutch cycling when the system is under a high heat load. In some of these units, the thermostatic switch is manually adjustable, so it can be used to control air conditioning temperature above minimum temperature. This system is the least expensive type of automotive air conditioning and is usually used in add-on units. It does produce temperature variations as it cycles and is reported to be hard on compressor drive belts in some installations.

A second method of preventing freeze-up is to keep evaporator pressure above 28.5 psi. At this pressure, refrigerant 12 boils at 30° which is slightly below the freezing point. The rate at which heat is removed from the air keeps the evaporator from freezing with the refrigerant at this temperature. Minimum evaporator pressure is maintained with a valve located between the evaporator and compressor. It will be located either on the evaporator outlet or within the compressor inlet. It goes under names such as: suction throttling valve (STV), pressure operated absolute (POA), and evaporative pressure regulator (EPR). It is open wide under high heat loads and automatically reduces the opening as the heat load reduces.

The suction throttling valve may be adjusted to control evaporator temperature and, thus, control the amount of air conditioned cooling. When used in this way, it has a thermal element to sense temperature. The temperature is converted into an electrical or vacuum signal to adjust the valve. In some cases, the valve is moved mechanically to give the operator direct control of the desired cooling temperature.

Valves used with the reheat air distribution system are completely automatic. They are factory set for maximum cooling. If the evaporator gives too much cooling, part of the air is passed through the heater core to provide an air mixture of the desired temperature.

A receiver drier is located in the system between the condenser and expansion valve. It serves as a refrigerant reservoir with an element for absorbing small amounts of moisture that may have become trapped in the closed refrigeration system. A sight glass is usually located on or adjacent to the receiver drier outlet. Its purpose is to allow the service technician to observe refrigerant flow. Flow should be in a liquid form. Bubbles or foam in the sight glass usually indicates a loss of refrigerant.

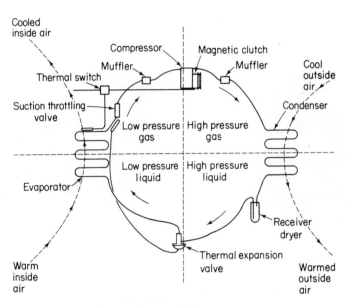

Fig. 30-4 Schematic composite diagram of an automotive air conditioning refrigeration system.

30-5 COMPRESSOR

Three types of compressors are used in automotive air conditioners. One is a two-cylinder in-line unit. A second is a 90° vee design. Both operate with typical piston, connecting rod, crankshaft combinations. The third type is an axial compressor. It has three double ended pistons lying parallel to the drive shaft. A wobble plate on the drive shaft produces piston endwise movement to pump refrigerant.

The entire compressor, including the crankcase, is sealed into the closed refrigeration system. Some of the compressor lubricant oil will flow with the refrigerant, but it is not lost because it returns with the refrigerant as it completes the cycle. In some cases, oil return lines and passages are provided from pockets where the oil can separate from the refrigerant.

Compressors are belt driven through an electromagnetic clutch. Magnetism formed by an electric current engages the clutch. When not operating, the drive pulley rotates freely on bearings. When the clutch magnet is energized, it pulls the clutch into engagement to drive the compressor. Clutch drive wear is a direct function of the number of clutch

517

applications. This is especially critical on the systems that engage and disengage the clutch to control evaporator temperature. Many systems are fitted with inlet and outlet mufflers to reduce compressor noise.

30-6 SERVICE

Air conditioner service is only required when the system does not function properly. As with any unit, the first thing to do when trouble exists is to give the system a thorough inspection to determine the exact problem. If it involves the compressor drive or the air distribution system, the problem can be corrected by standard mechanical service procedures. Special techniques are required to service the refrigeration system.

The closed refrigeration system is always under pressure. Its pressure is determined by the system temperature. If the air conditioning has not been run for some time, the pressure equalizes throughout the system. If it has been operated, the pressure will be higher on the condenser side and lower on the evaporator side.

Repair and replacement of any refrigeration part requires that the system be bled down to remove the pressure, then evacuated and recharged to check the operation. This requires time and the recharging

Fig. 30-5 Air conditioning compressors. Left, two cylinder inline, right, two cylinder V, lower, three cylinder axial.

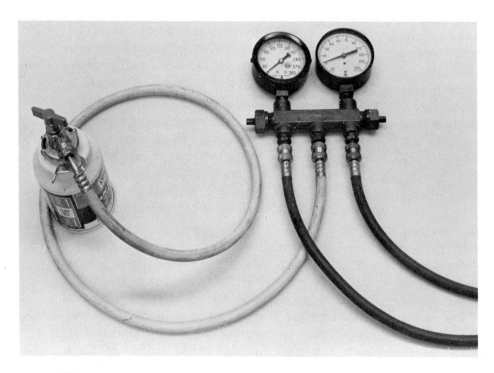

Fig. 30-6 Typical air conditioning gauge set and refrigerant can.

refrigerant is expensive, so it is very important to make very careful tests to pinpoint the problem before the system is drained.

A gauge set is used to measure the compressor outlet pressure, the evaporator outlet pressure and, in some cases, the compressor inlet pressure. Temperature gauges may also be required. Using these gauges and following the service manual test sequence will identify the malfunctioning unit. Refrigerant that is released to the atmosphere chills very rapidly. Therefore, one should be protected with safety glasses and gloves.

The refrigerant system must be free of dirt, water and air. It is, therefore, important to bleed air from the gauge lines before flowing refrigerant through them into the system. If the system has been completely open, it must be purged with a vacuum pump before recharging.

System overcharging and incorrect belt tension are the most common air conditioning problems that occur after service, because systems are filled and belts tightened by rule-of-thumb rather than by specification. Refrigerant quantity can only be determined by weight and belt tension with a special belt tension gauge.

Review Questions
Chapter 30

1. What type of air distribution systems are used?

2. In what way is a refrigeration system similar to an engine cooling system?

3. How does boiling the refrigerant increase the heat transfer capacity?

4. Describe the refrigeration cycle.

5. What must an air conditioner be able to do?

6. What happens when too little liquid is allowed to enter the evaporator? What if too much enters?

7. When is the correct amount of liquid entering the evaporator?

8. What type of freeze-up controls are used?

9. What do bubbles or foam in the sight glass usually indicate?

10. How are compressor bearings lubricated?

11. What precautions should be taken when working on the refrigeration system?

Quiz 30

1. The first thing to check when an air conditioner fails to cool a vehicle is the
   a. air distributor system
   b. compressor sealing
   c. condenser freezing
   d. expansion valve operation.

2. The air conditioning system absorbs heat by
   a. boiling liquid refrigerant
   b. cooling with refrigerant vapors
   c. cooling with refrigerant liquid
   d. circulating cold refrigerant.

3. If the evaporator temperature reaches 20°F, the
   a. condenser will freeze
   b. system will cool too much
   c. refrigerant will freeze
   d. evaporator will restrict air flow.

4. The highest pressure in the refrigeration cycle is between the
   a. expansion valve and evaporator
   b. evaporator and throttling valve
   c. throttling valve and compressor
   d. compressor and condenser.

5. For maximum heat transfer, all of the refrigerant leaving the
   a. condenser will be vapor
   b. evaporator will be vapor
   c. expansion valve will be vapor
   d. receiver will be vapor.

6. Bubbles in the sight gauge indicate
   a. normal operation
   b. low compressor pressure
   c. low refrigerant
   d. worn out refrigerant.

7. A suction throttling valve is used in some air conditioners to
   a. prevent evaporator freeze-up
   b. control the expansion valve
   c. maintain low condenser pressure
   d. control compressor cycling.

8. The refrigerant supply in the system is stored in the
   a. condenser
   b. evaporator
   c. compressor
   d. receiver.

9. Compressor operation is controlled by the
   a. magnetic clutch
   b. mechanical clutch
   c. centrifugal clutch
   d. free wheeling clutch.

10. One of the most common air conditioning servicing faults is
    a. improper filter installation
    b. use of the wrong type of refrigerant
    c. overadjusting the expansion valve
    d. overcharging.

Glossary

A

ACCELERATION: A change in speed in a given period of time such as one second or one minute.

ACKERMAN: Steering geometry that turns the inner and outer wheels at different angles to minimize scuff during a turn.

ADDITIVE: A product added to a material that will improve a certain characteristic of the material.

ADHESION: The characteristic that causes one material to stick to or cling to another material.

AEROSOL: Very small particles that float in the air.

AFTERBURNER: A device attached in place of the exhaust manifold that holds the exhaust gases at high temperature to aid in oxidizing unburned hydrocarbons.

AFTERBURNING: Luminous products remaining in the gases after combustion.

AFTERMARKET: The sales market designed for the consumer after he purchases a product from the dealer.

AIR/FUEL RATIO: A mixture of air and fuel by weight. Pounds of air per pound of fuel.

521

ALTERNATOR: The name given to a diode-rectified automotive generator.

AMBIENT: The temperature of the surrounding air.

AMMETER: An instrument connected in series in an electrical circuit to measure current flow.

AMPERE: A measure of the rate of electrical current flow.

AMPLITUDE: The extent or size limits of vibrating motion.

ANCHOR: The stationary terminal at one end of a brake shoe or band.

ANNULUS: An outer ring.

ANODIZE: An electrochemical process that hardens the surface of aluminum.

ANTI-PERCOLATOR: A device used in carburetors to vent fuel vapors from the manifold when the engine is not running.

API: American Petroleum Institute.

ARMATURE: A rotating conductor within a magnetic field.

AROMATIC: A hydrocarbon with a benzene ring form that has a natural high octane number.

ASYMMETRIC: Unequal surfaces or sizes.

ASPECT RATIO: The ratio of width to length, also the ratio of tire cross section width to cross section height.

ATOMIZATION: Breaking into very fine particles, such as fuel delivery by a discharge nozzle.

AVAILABLE VOLTAGE: Maximum voltage an ignition system is capable of producing.

AXIAL: Having the same direction or being parallel to the axis of rotation.

B

BACK FLUSH: A procedure used to clean a system by forcing reverse flow from an external source.

BALANCE: Having equal weight on each side of a supporting point. No change in the position of the center of gravity when a part is in motion.

BALL JOINT: A suspension attachment connecting the knuckle to the control arms allowing movement upward and downward as well as rotation.

BALL NUT: A casting with internal threads used in a steering gear. Ball bearings roll in the threads to move the casting along the worm to rotate a sector which in turn moves a Pitman arm.

BALL AND TRUNION JOINT: A universal joint with pivoting spherical rollers that transfer motion between a pin and a housing that has partial cylindrical bores.

BAND: A strip of metal with friction lining that is used as a brake to stop and hold drum rotation in an automatic transmission.

BANK: The portion of a V-8 block containing four inline cylinders.

BDC: Bottom dead center. The lowest position of the piston.

BARREL: The opening in a carburetor through which air/fuel mixture enters the manifold.

BASE CIRCLE: The part of the cam with the smallest diameter from the camshaft center.

BEAD: A reinforcing ridge. The wire reinforcing around a tire opening where it fits the wheel rim.

BEARING: The surface that supports a load. In vehicles it supports a moving load with minimum drag.

BEARING TANG: A notch or lip on a bearing shell used to correctly locate the bearing during assembly.

BELL CRANK: A moving arm that pivots near the middle. It is used to change the direction of motion.

BENDIX-WEISS JOINT: One type of constant velocity universal joint using two yokes to drive through inter-meshed balls.

BEST AIR/FUEL RATIO: The air/fuel ratio that will produce the most engine power.

BEST TIMING: Ignition timing that produces the highest engine torque at the running speed.

BEVEL: Angled. Usually gears cut on an angle to change the direction of rotation.

BIAS: Lines running at an angle. Refers to the cord angle in tire plys.

BI-METALIC SPRING: A coil spring made of a double strip of two different metals. When it is heated it will either wind tighter or unwind, depending on the metals and spring design.

BLADES: Sharp edges, often used to describe windshield wiper edges and the edges of tire grooves.

BLOCKING RING: A ring that blocks tooth engagement until equal speeds are reached.

BLOW-BY: Combustion chamber gases that slip past the piston and rings to get into the crankcase.

BLOW-DOWN: Release of combustion pressure immediately after the exhaust valve opens.

BOG: An expression used to describe an engine misfiring condition that may occur as the throttle is opened, and which causes engine power to drop rather than increase.

BORDERLINE LUBRICATION: A term that may be used in place of boundary lubrication. Minimum lubrication that occurs when the oil film can't quite support the load and high spots touch.

BORDERLINE: The line between satisfactory operation and failure.

BORE: (1) A process of enlarging a hole with a cutting tool. (2) The diameter of a hole, especially the cylinder.

BOSS: A heavy cast section that is used for support, such as the heavy section around a bearing.

BOUNDARY: The line between normal and unsatisfactory operation. For example, boundary lubrication that occurs when the oil film breaks down and the parts start to contact.

BMEP: Brake mean effective pressure. The average pressure within a cylinder during the power stroke that would produce the horsepower determined on a dynamometer.

BRAKE: A device used to slow, stop or hold a moving member.

BRAKE DIVE: The tendency of the front of the vehicle to lower during braking as a result of forward weight transfer.

BRAKE FADE: The loss of braking power due to excess heat from previous brake applications.

BREAKER POINTS: Cam-operated contacts in the distributor that connect and separate the primary circuit.

BREATHING: Air flow into an engine during operation.

BRIDGING: A build-up of current carrying crystals through the battery separator.

BROACH: A machining operation that is completed in one pass of a tool having a large number of cutting edges.

BULKHEAD: A strengthening partition separating compartments, such as the firewall or engine main bearing webs.

BUSHING: A spacing device, usually a sleeve. In engine applications it often has a bearing surface on its inside surface.

BURNISHING: A sizing process that pushes metal to size by pressure.

BUTT: Square ends used on a piston ring.

BYPASS: Go around some restriction such as a valve, switch, circuit, etc.

C

CAM ANGLE: The number of degrees of cam rotation while the breaker points are closed between each cam lobe.

CAMBER: The angle of the vertical wheel center line to absolute vertical.

CAM FOLLOWER: A device that follows the cam contour as it rotates, usually a lifter or tappet.

CAMSHAFT: A long shaft on which lobes and bearing journals are located. It is usually used to open the valves.

CANISTER: A container filled with activated charcoal to absorb evaporative emissions.

CANTED: Angled away from another object or from vertical.

CAPACITIVE DISCHARGE: An ignition system that stores a high voltage charge in a condenser. When the distributor is in position the charge is released through the sparkplug to ignite the mixture.

CAPACITOR: A device consisting of two metal plates in close proximity to each other with an insulator between. Electrons readily collect at one plate and holes collect at the other.

CARBON PILE: A variable resistance made of carbon discs or plates that can carry high currents.

CARBURETOR: A device that mixes air and fuel in the correct proportions for engine operating conditions.

CARBURETOR THROAT: The portion of a carburetor between the venturi and intake manifold where the throttle plate is located.

CARDAN JOINT: A cross and yoke universal joint. Also called a Hooke joint.

CARRIER: A part that carries other parts. Usually referring to the part of a differential or a planetary gear set that carries the pinions.

CAST: A part made by pouring melted metal into a mold where it cools to the shape of the mold.

CASTER: The tendency of a wheel to line up in the direction of its pivot point movement.

CASTING: The process of making a cast part.

CATALYST: A product that increases the speed of a reaction but does not enter into the reaction.

CATALYTIC CONVERTER: A chamber in the exhaust system that contains a catalyst which aids in oxidizing exhaust gases to reduce the amount of unburned hydrocarbons in the exhaust gases.

CAVITATION: A space created at the center of a rotating pump when it does not fill as fast as the fluid is pumped out.

CEMF: Counter electromotive force. Electrical pressure within a device that opposes external electrical pressure.

CENTER OF GRAVITY: A point around which all weights balance.

CENTER OF PRESSURE: A point around which all pressures balance.

CENTRIFUGAL: A force in a direction away from the turning center of an object moving in a curved path.

CHAMFER: An angle cut across the corner of an otherwise sharp edge.

CHARGE: A process of replacing the material in an

expended container. For example, charge a battery to store electrical energy or charge an air conditioner system so it has sufficient refrigerant to operate.

CHASSIS: The vehicle frame, suspension and running gear.

CHECK VALVE: A valve that will allow flow in one direction and will stop flow in the opposite direction.

CHOKE: A variable restriction in the carburetor air inlet to produce a rich mixture for starting.

CHOKE STOVE: A pocket or tube that heats choke air by the exhaust heat so the choke's bi-metallic spring can sense engine temperature.

CIRCUIT BREAKER: An electrical device that protects the circuit from overload by opening the circuit. It can be reset to again close the circuit.

CLUSTER GEAR: A group of gears made on a common casting. Used in a standard transmission to connect the clutch shaft to the first, second, and reverse idler gears.

CLUTCH: A device to connect and disconnect members that are rotating at different speeds.

CLUTCH SHAFT: The shaft coming out of the front of the transmission that goes through the center of the clutch.

COEFFICIENT OF FRICTION: An expression that relates the force to move an object to the weight or load produced by the object. Coefficient of friction = force/load.

COLOR CODE: Color marking on lines and wires to identify the circuit.

COMBUSTIBLE MIXTURE: A mixture of air and gasoline vapors in a ratio that will burn.

COMBUSTION: A rapid chemical reaction between air and fuel that releases heat.

COMPENSATION SYSTEM: A portion of the carburetor circuit that prevents overenriching the air/fuel ratio as air velocities increase.

COMPRESSION IGNITION: A term applied to the diesel engine operating principle. Heat to initiate combustion is produced by compression.

COMPRESSION RATIO: A ratio between the volume above the piston when it is at bottom center to the volume above the piston when it is at top center.

COMMUTATOR: A number of bars connected to armature windings that transfers current to the brushes and rectifies the current.

COMPRESSION TEST: A test using a pressure gauge to measure maximum pressure in the cylinder while cranking the engine with the starter.

CONCENTRIC: Located evenly around a common center.

CONDUCTOR: A material that will carry electrical current.

CONE CLUTCH: A clutch made of an inner and outer cone. When the outer cone is forced over the inner cone a wedging action occurs that locks them together while they remain under the force.

CONTACT PATCH: The part of the tire that contacts the road surface.

CONTROL ARM: A suspension member mounted nearly horizontal with one end attached to the frame and the other end to the knuckle or axle housing.

CORE: The central portion, usually a part used in casting to form an opening in the finished part when the core is removed after casting.

CORROSION: A combination of a metal and oxygen or water that causes the surface of the metal to disappear.

COUNTER BORE: A concentric machined surface around a hole opening.

COUNTER GEAR: A gear that rotates backward. The cluster gear in a standard transmission.

CRANK ANGLE: The number of degrees the crankshaft has turned past top center.

CRANK PIN: The portion of the crankshaft upon which the connecting rod fastens.

CRANKSHAFT: The part of an engine that changes the reciprocating motion of the pistons into rotating motion.

CROCUS CLOTH: An extremely fine abrasive cloth that is used for polishing.

CROSS OVER: An opening through the intake manifold below the carburetor that connects the two exhaust manifolds.

CRUSH: A slight distortion of the bearing shell that holds it in place as the engine operates.

CUBIC INCH DISPLACEMENT: The volume displaced by all of the pistons as the crankshaft makes one revolution.

CYCLE: A complete circle back to the beginning. In engines, a series of events; intake, compression, power and exhaust.

D

DAMPEN: To slow or reduce oscillations or movement.

DASHPOT: A variable displacement chamber that has a restriction. It is used to slow or dampen movement.

DEAD CENTER: Refers to the maximum upper or lower piston position when all movement in one direction stops before it reverses direction.

DECARBONIZING: The process of removing carbon from parts during overhaul.

DECK: The flat upper surface of the engine block where the head mounts.

DEFLECTION: Bending or moving to a new position as the result of an external force.

DEGREASING: The process of removing grease from parts.

DEGREE WHEEL: A disc divided in 360 equal parts that can be attached to a shaft to measure angle of rotation.

DENIER: The size of a strand that makes up tire cord.

DETONATION: Engine knock produced by rapid chemical reaction of the gases ahead of the combustion flame front.

DIAPHRAGM: A flexible membrane on one side of an enclosed chamber.

DIECAST: A casting process for light metals using permanent forms and pressure to accurately form a part.

DIESEL: A fuel-injected charge ignited by temperature resulting from high compression.

DIFFERENTIAL: The part of a rear axle that allows the rear wheels to rotate at different speeds.

DIFFERENTIAL PRESSURE: Differences in pressure that cause flow from the highest pressure to the lowest pressure.

DIODE: A solid-state electrical check valve.

DISC: The plate shaped part of the brake or clutch that rotates as the vehicle moves.

DISC BRAKE: A brake type having a disc plate that rotates with the wheel. Pads or shoes press against the disc to slow or stop the vehicle.

DISH: A depression in the top of a piston.

DISPLACEMENT: The volume displaced by the pistons during one crankshaft revolution.

DISTILLATE: A low volatility fuel used in diesel and turbine engines.

DISTILLATION: The process of separating hydrocarbons by their boiling temperatures.

DIVERGENT ANGLES: Lines that are further apart at one end than at the other end.

DOWN SHIFTING: Shifting to a higher numerical ratio that is usually associated with lower speed, high torque operation.

DRAW FILE: Smoothing a surface with a file moved sidewise.

DRIFT: A gradual random movement.

DRIVE LINE: The power carrying part of a vehicle from the engine to the drive wheels.

DRIVE LUGS: Projections on a plate or disc that interlock in slots on a hub or in a drum.

DRUM: A hoop shape with a web or plate across one side of the opening.

DRUM BRAKE: A ring-shaped drum surface that rotates with the wheel. Brake shoes slow and stop rotation by pressure against the inside of the drum.

DWELL: The number of degrees the cam turns while the breaker points are closed between cam lobes.

DYNAMIC: Moving parts.

DYNAMOMETER: A device that is used to measure loads, engine torque and driving forces.

E

ECCENTRIC: Two or more circles, one surrounding the other and each having a different center.

ECONOMY: The lowest cost for the same result.

EDDY CURRENT: Localized induced currents in parts that are rotating in a magnetic field. These currents produce heat and absorb power.

EFFECTIVE PRESSURE: The pressure that does work. Usually the mean or average pressure in the combustion chamber during the power stroke.

EFFICIENCY: Obtaining the highest possible output for a given input.

ELASTOMER: A rubber-like plastic or synthetic material.

ELECTROLYTE: The acid solution in battery cell.

ELECTRON: The smallest, negative charged particle. It is part of an atom. Its movement to adjacent atoms forms electricity.

ELECTRO-CHEMICAL: A reaction between chemicals that produces a current or a current that produces a chemical reaction.

ELEMENT: The smallest distinct variety of matter. Also the combined plates and separators of a battery cell.

END GASES: The combustion gases ahead of the flame front after ignition.

ENERGIZED: Charged or full of energy. Ready to be operated.

ENGINE: A prime power source.

ENGINE LOAD: The vehicle resistance applied to the engine crankshaft.

ENGINE SPEED: Crankshaft revolutions per minute.

ERODE: Wear away by high velocity abrasive particles.

EXPANSION PLUGS: Hole plugs that can be expanded to securely close a hole.

F

FADE: Loss of braking effect when brakes get hot.

FATIGUE: A breakdown of material through a large

number of loading and unloading cycles. The first signs are cracks followed shortly by breaks.

FIELD: The area of magnetic force surrouding a magnet, either permanent or electromagnet.

FIELD STRENGTH: A measurement of the effective size of a magnetic field.

FILAMENT: A wire in a light bulb that glows when current passes through it to produce light.

FILLET: A rounded joint between two surfaces.

FILLER: Material added to produce bulk. It may add special properties to the product.

FIN: A thin metal surface usually used to transfer heat between metal and air.

FIRE WALL: The metal surface separating the passenger compartment from the engine compartment.

FLANGE: A small surface at an angle to the major surface used to position, reinforce or fasten the major surface in place.

FLANK CIRCLE: The part of a cam that has constant diameter. No lift is produced from the flank circle.

FLOAT: (1) Device supported by fluid, as a carburetor float, to sense fluid levels. (2) Float can occur when the valve train is tossed from the cam and the parts float on air until control is regained.

FLOAT BOWL: The carburetor compartment that houses the float.

FLOOR PAN: The metal surface that forms the base of the passenger compartment.

FLUTE: Angular grooves in the face of a headlight bulb used to deflect light.

FLUTTER VALVE: A spring-loaded valve that moves to allow flow in only one direction.

FLUX: The force of magnetism. Also a substance applied during soldering or welding to free oxides.

FLYWHEEL: A weighted disc on a crankshaft that provides inertia to carry the crankshaft between power pulses.

FOOT PAD: A surface on a pedal upon which to push with one's foot to produce pedal movement.

FOOT PRINT: The area on the road in contact with the tire.

FORGED: A part made by forging.

FORGING: A process of hammering or compressing a red hot metal part to form it into the desired shape.

FOUR STROKE CYCLE: An engine cycle consisting of a downward intake stroke, an upward compression stroke, a downward power stroke and an upward exhaust stroke. The cycle then repeats on the next four strokes.

FRAME: The base structure upon which the rest of the structure is mounted or attached.

FREE PLAY: Looseness in a linkage between the start of application and the actual movement of the device.

FREQUENCY: The number of cycles or vibrations per second.

FRICTION: The resistance to slipping or skidding.

FULCRUM: The hinge point of a lever.

FUEL DROP OUT: Liquid gasoline separating from an air/fuel mixture.

FUEL MIXTURE: A mixture of air and gasoline. The gasoline must be in a vapor state to burn.

FUSE: A soft wire in a holding device that melts when a circuit is overloaded.

FUSABLE LINK: A small diameter wire section of a circuit that will melt before any of the rest of the circuit is damaged by overheating.

G

GALLERY: A large passage in the engine block that forms a reservoir for engine oil pressure.

GASSING: Formation of bubbles in the battery electrolyte during charging.

GENERATOR: An electromechanical device to supply electrical power by changing mechanical energy to electrical energy.

GRADABILITY: The ability of a vehicle to climb slopes.

GROUND: To connect an electric circuit to the vehicle frame or structure.

GROUP: A number of battery plates welded to a connector.

H

HEAVY DUTY: Applications more severe than passenger car service.

HEEL: The anchor end of a brake shoe.

HELICAL GEARS: Gears cut on an angle so that at least two pairs of gear teeth are in contact at all times.

HELIX ANGLE: The angle produced by a spiral form around a round part.

HOOK JOINT: A universal joint formed by a cross and two trunions.

HORSEPOWER: A value calculated from engine torque and rotating speed. One horsepower equals 33,000 ft-lbs per min.

HOT SOAK: A part warming to the surrounding temperature.

HYDRAULICS: A study of fluids.

HYDROCARBONS: Molecules made from hydrogen and carbon atoms.

HYDRODYNAMIC: A study of fluid in motion.

HYDRODYNAMIC LUBRICATION: A lubricating film generated in a fluid by relative motion between two surfaces.

HYDROMETER: A floating device that measures specific gravity of a fluid by the depth the float sinks into the fluid.

I

IDLE: Running freely with no power or load being transferred.

IDLING GEARS: Rotating gears that are not transferring a load.

IMPENDING SKID: The tire traction point at which any increase in load will produce a tire skid.

IMPINGE: Hit against the surface.

IMEP: Indicated mean effective pressure. The average indicated pressure in the combustion chamber during the power stroke as measured on a pressure-volume indicator card graph.

IMPELLER: A rotating part that increases the moving speed or velocity of a fluid.

INDUCTANCE: The process of an electromagnetic force being produced in a conductor located in a moving magnetic field.

INERTIA: The tendency of a body at rest to stay at rest or when moving to keep moving.

INERTIA TORQUE: Twisting force produced by the inertia of a rotating body.

INTEGRAL: Part of or contained within a larger major part.

INSULATOR: A material that will not conduct. It may not conduct heat or electricity.

INLINE ENGINE: Cylinders located one next to the other with parallel bore centerlines.

INVOLUTE: A curve traced by a point on a thread as it is wound on a drum.

ION: An atom having excess electrons (negative ion) or lacking electrons (positive ion).

J

JET: A carefully sized opening in a carburetor passage to measure the flow of either gasoline or air.

JOUNCE: The condition of the suspension which will cause spring compression.

JOURNAL: The surface on which a bearing operates.

JUNCTION: An electrical connection.

K

KEEPER: The split lock that holds the valve spring retainer in position on the valve stem.

KEYED: Prevented from rotating with a small metal device called a key.

KICK DOWN: A forced downshift on an automatic transmission.

KNOCK: The sound produced in the combustion chamber as a result of abnormal combustion, usually detonation.

KNUCKLE: The part of the front suspension that connects to the control arms and supports the wheel spindle.

KNURL: A roughened surface caused by a sharp wheel that displaces metal outward as its sharp edges push into the metal surface.

L

LAMINAR FLOW: Flowing in smooth layers, not turbulent.

LANDS: The large diameter portions between piston ring grooves.

LASH: Looseness in linkages that must be absorbed before movement can begin.

LEACH: To desolve one material out of another.

LEADING SHOE: A brake shoe that has the drum rotate from the toe toward the heel.

LIFTER: The part that rides against the cam to transfer motion to the rest of the valve train.

LIFTER VALLEY: The chamber between the cylinder bores on a V-block engine.

LOAD: The part of the system that absorbs energy.

LOCK: A device to easily connect or disconnect two parts.

LUG: To operate an engine with high loads at low speeds.

LUGS: Heavy fastening flanges on parts.

M

MAGNETIC LINES OF FORCE: Lines that form when iron filings are sprinkled on a surface over a magnet.

MAGNITUDE: Size.

MANIFOLD: Cast passages that connect openings from each cylinder to a common opening.

MANIFOLD RUNNERS: A single passage in a manifold from one cylinder to the major manifold opening.

MASS: The amount of material in a part. Often equated to weight for easy understanding.

MASTER CYLINDER: The cylinder in a brake system that converts mechanical force to hydraulic force.

MEAN EFFECTIVE PRESSURE: The calculated average pressure in the combustion chamber during the power stroke.

MEAN RADIUS: A radius that has equal surfaces on each side.

MECHANICAL EFFICIENCY: Calculated as brake horsepower divided by indicated horsepower.

MENISCUS: The curved upper surface of a liquid in a chamber.

MIDSHIP: An engine location immediately ahead of the rear axle.

MODULE: A small compact complete unit. The whole unit can be replaced as a unit, but not in parts.

N

NAILS: A common name given to brake shoe hold-down pins.

NEUTRON: A neutral charged particle that makes up part of most atom nuclei.

NODE: A point in a vibrating body that is relatively free of movement.

NOMINAL: Normal position, size or operating condition.

NOSE CIRCLE: The high curved portion of a cam that produces maximum lift.

NUCLEUS: The central part of an atom that contains most of the atom's weight.

O

OCTANE NUMBER: A number that indicates a gasoline's resistance to detonation knock.

OCTANE REQUIREMENT: The lowest octane number fuel on which an engine can operate knock free.

OHM: A unit of electrical resistance.

OHM'S LAW: A constant relationship between resistance (R), voltage (E), and current (I). $R = E/I$.

OIL SEAL: A device to keep oil from leaking out of a compartment. It usually refers to a dynamic seal around a rotating shaft.

OLEFIN: An unsaturated hydrocarbon molecule with a double carbon bond.

ONE WAY CLUTCH: A clutch that will allow free rotation in one direction but locks when reversed.

OPEN: In an electrical circuit the circuit is broken so a gap exists and no current can flow.

ORIFICE: A carefully sized opening that controls a fluid flow.

OSCILLATION: A vibration back and forth or up and down.

OSCILLOSCOPE: A device that displays a trace on the face of a picture tube proportional to input voltages.

OVERHUNG: A load outside of a bearing.

OVER RUNNING CLUTCH: A clutch that will run freely in one direction but locks when turned in the opposite direction.

OXIDIZE: A combination with oxygen causing a change in the molecule. Generally it reduces the value of the oxidized material.

P

PAD: Flat surfaces on castings upon which parts are mounted.

PANIC STOP: A stop with maximum brake pedal pressure, usually locking the wheels and causing the tires to skid.

PARALLEL: Straight lines that are the same distance apart from end to end.

PARAMETER: The maximum limit in a direction.

PEAK PRESSURE: The highest pressure in the combustion chamber that occurs during the early part of the power stroke.

PEENED: Upset surfaces by pounding.

PERFORMANCE: Effectively operating at the maximum designed specification.

PHOTOCHEMICAL: A process requiring light and a chemical.

PIEZOELECTRIC CRYSTAL: A crystal that produces a voltage proportional to the pressure applied to the crystal.

PILOT BEARING: The bearing in the back of the crankshaft that supports the front of the clutch shaft.

PINION GEAR: A gear that rotates with a carrier to transfer loads between the carrier and two intermeshing gears.

PISTON HEAD: The top or crown of a piston.

PISTON SLAP: A sound made by a piston with excess skirt clearance as the crankshaft goes across top center.

PITMAN ARM: The arm that connects the steering gear to the steering linkages.

PIVOT: A point around which an item turns.

PLANETARY: A type of gear train having pinion gears rotating around a central gear.

PLASTIC: A material capable of being deformed without rupturing. Generally a synthetic material.

PLASTIGAUGE: A small sized plastic thread for measuring clearances. It is smashed as parts are assembled, then disassembled to check the width of the smashed gauge.

PLATE: A thin flat surface.

PLOTTING: Locating points on a graph.

PLYS: Layers assembled together. Usually the grain direction is alternated between adjacent layers.

POLE SHOES: Extended core material of an electromagnet.

PONTOON: A container or block that will float on a liquid to support an object.

POPPET VALVE: A valve that rises perpendicularly to and from its seat.

POP UP: A raised portion of a piston head.

PORT: An opening through which liquids or gases flow.

PORTING: A process of enlarging the intake and exhaust passages of the head.

PREFLAME REACTION: Chemical reactions that occur in the gases before the flame front reaches them.

PREIGNITION: Ignition of the combustion charge before the spark forms across the sparkplug electrodes.

PREVENTATIVE MAINTENANCE: Service procedures that are done before a malfunction occurs to prevent failure.

PRELOAD: Mechanically loading bearings to prevent end play.

PRESSURE DEPRESSION: A term describing less than atmospheric pressure or vacuum.

PRESSURE HEAD: The height of a column of fluid that produces pressure by the weight of the fluid.

PRESSURE PLATE: A heavy plate with back up springs or hydraulic pressure to lock it against a clutch disc.

PRIMARY SHOE: A brake shoe actuated by a wheel cylinder.

PROPAGATION: Self sustaining and spreading or expanding.

PROPELLER SHAFT: The shaft that connects the transmission to the rear axle to propel or drive the vehicle.

PROPRIETARY: A product sold to the public with a formula owned by the manufacturer.

PROTON: A positively charged particle of an atom nucleus containing most of the atom's weight.

P-T CURVE: Pressure-time curve that shows the change in pressure in the combustion chamber as combustion progresses.

PUMP GRADES: Gasoline available at service stations.

PUMPING LOSS: Engine power required to move the piston during the intake, compression, and exhaust strokes.

PUSH ROD: The rod between the lifter and rocker arm that pushes the rocker arm to open the valve.

P-V CURVE: Pressure-volume curve, that shows the pressure in the combustion chamber at each piston position.

Q

QUENCH: Cool to the temperature at which the flame will go out.

R

RACE: The part of a bearing on which the rollers or balls roll.

RADIAL: Moving straight out from the center.

RADIATOR: A thin metal heat transfer device that lowers the temperature of the engine coolant by air flow.

RAM: Air pressure produced by air velocity.

RAMP: A gradual slope or incline on a cam to take up clearance of lash.

RANKIN: An absolute temperature scale that uses the same temperature divisions as Fahrenheit. $°R = 459.6 + °F$

REACH: The length of the threaded portion of a spark plug.

REACTION: The result of an action.

REACTOR: A device that acts to produce a reaction, such as a stator in a torque converter.

REAM: Size a hole to exact dimensions with a cutting tool called a reamer.

REAR AXLE: The drive between the differential side gear and the wheel.

REBOUND: An expansion of a suspension spring after it has been compressed as the result of jounce.

RECIPROCATE: Move back and forth.

RECTIFY: To straighten out. To convert an A-C current to a D-C current.

RELAY: A remote control switch that carries a large current.

RELIEVING: Grinding restrictions from around valves and seats.

REQUIRED VOLTAGE: Ignition voltage high enough to form an arc across the spark plug electrodes.

RESISTOR: A unit installed in an electrical circuit to provide the required resistance.

RETAINER: A device to hold parts together.

REVERTED GEAR TRAIN: A gear train that drives to the side then returns to the original centerline.

RHEOSTAT: A device to provide variable resistance. It is sometimes called a pot.

RIDE: The characteristic feel as one rides in a vehicle.

RING GEAR: A hollow gear that has a ring shape.

ROCKER ARM: A lever that converts the upward movement of the push rod to the downward movement required to open a valve.

ROLL: Movement around the center of gravity.

ROLL STEER: The steering effect as a result of body lean during a turn.

ROTOR: A rotating drive mechanism.

RUMBLE: A characteristic low frequency vibration that results from surface ignition.

RUN OUT: The amount a shaft rotates out of true.

S

SAE: Society of Automotive Engineers

SADDLE: The upper main bearing seat.

SADDLE MOUNTING: A bearing on each side of a gear.

SAG: Engine power loss during acceleration as the result of improper air/fuel ratios.

SAYBOLT: An obsolete method used to measure oil viscosity.

SCAVENGE: Clean out or remove either exhaust gas or sump oil.

SCROLL: A curved passage that gets larger and has a larger radius toward the outer edge.

SCRUB RADIUS: The distance on the road surface under the front tire between an extension of the pivot point and the center of weight.

SCUFFING: Sliding a tire on the road surface.

SEALS–DYNAMIC: An item that prevents leakage around a rotating shaft.

SEALS–STATIC: An item that prevents leakage between two stationary parts. It is usually called a gasket.

SECONDARY SHOE: A brake shoe that is actuated by a primary shoe.

SECTOR: A section of a gear.

SEMICONDUCTOR: An electronic component that allows current to flow under special conditions.

SEPARATION: A porous insulator sheet between battery plates.

SERIES: A single path through a number of items, one after the other.

SERVICE MARKET: The people who need service work done on their cars.

SERVO: A device that can control a large force by being remotely operated with a small force.

SERVO ACTION: A large action that results from a small input action.

SET: Repositioning of a spring as the result of loading for long periods of time.

SHEDDING: Active material loosening from battery plates.

SHIMMY: A violent front wheel shake caused by over corrective action.

SHOE: The brake part that supports the lining.

SHORT: An electrical path that goes back to the battery without going through the complete circuit.

SHROUD: A cover between the edges of the radiator and fan tip used to increase the fan's efficiency.

SHUNT: An electrical device connected in parallel to bypass some of the current.

SIAMESED PORTS: An intake or exhaust port that serves two cylinders.

SIDE SWAY: A force causing a lean one way then the other.

SIGNALS: Changing pressures in a carburetor or automatic transmission that controls fluid flow.

SINTER: A process of pressing and heating powdered metal which will fuse to form the desired part.

SIPES: Slits in the tire tread to produce more blade surface for traction.

SKID: A tire sliding on the road surface.

SLINGER: A ring on a shaft that throws oil from the shaft before it gets to the oil seal.

SLIP ANGLE: The angle between the tire heading and the actual direction of movement.

SLIPPER SKIRT: A piston with a lower surface on the thrust surfaces only.

SOFT PLUGS: Expandable plugs used to securely close machined holes in metal parts.

SOLENOID: A remote controlled electrical device that produces mechanical movement.

SPARK IGNITED: The combustion started by an arc across the spark plug electrodes.

SPARK PLUG: An electrical unit with two electrodes and an air gap between them that fits into the head. A spark across the gap ignites the combustion charge.

SPEED: Distance or revolutions in a given period of time.

SPENT GASES: Hot gases remaining in the combustion chamber after combustion.

SPIDER: A name often given to the cross in a universal joint.

SPINDLE: The part of the front suspension that supports the wheel bearings.

SPLINED: Sized grooves on a shaft and in a hole that match to prevent torque slippage.

SPRAG: A special form of over running clutch that has smooth races and cam shaped segments between them.

SPREAD: Wider than normal.

SPRING: An elastic part that recovers its original shape after being distorted and released.

SPRING RATE: The weight required to deform a spring one inch.

SPUR: A pointed projecting part.

SPUR GEAR: The simplest form of toothed wheel with radial teeth parallel to its axis.

SQUIRM: The twist of the tire rubber in the foot print.

SQUISH AREA: An area in the combustion chamber where the piston approaches very close to the head.

STALL: Operating the engine at full throttle on a torque converter equipped car placed in gear while the car is held with the brakes.

STAMPING: A process of forming sheetmetal by forcing it between shaped dies.

STANDING WAVE: A wave in a flexible body that continues to stay when the vibrating frequencies match the wave frequencies.

STAR WHEEL: An adjustable link between a primary and secondary brake shoe.

STATIC: Stationary.

STATOR: A part of a torque converter that stands still as torque is being multiplied, then rotates as the turbine approaches the impeller speed.

STEADY STATE: Constant conditions with no variation.

STEERING: A means to control the direction of a vehicle.

STEERING AXIS INCLINATION: The inward tilt of the front wheel pivot axis.

STITCHING: A method of pressing the green tire parts tightly together before curing.

STOICHIOMETRIC: A chemically balanced air/fuel mixture.

STOVE: A pocket or passage where heat is picked up to send to the choke bi-metal spring.

STROBOSCOPIC LIGHT: A high-intensity, short duration light that has a controlled flash time.

STROKE: Piston movement in one direction, from one extreme to the other.

STUB FRAME: A short frame on the front of a unitized body that carries the engine, front suspension and front sheet metal.

SULPHATION: Hardening of the sulfur crystals in the battery plates while the battery has a low state of charge.

SUMP: The lowest part of the oil pan.

SUN GEAR: The central gear in a planetary gear set.

SURFACE TO VOLUME RATIO: The ratio of all of the combustion chamber surfaces to its contained volume.

The surface to volume ratio reduces as the shape approaches a sphere.

SUPERCHARGER: Device which forces the charge into the combustion chamber with a pressure greater than atmospheric pressure.

SURFACE IGNITION: Ignition caused by some hot spot other than the arc across the sparkplug electrodes.

SURGE: Increasing and decreasing engine speed while holding a steady throttle position.

SUSPENSION: The springs, shock absorbers and linkages that support the vehicle.

SYNCHRONIZER: A device in a standard transmission that gets two parts operating at the same speed before engagement.

SYNCHRONIZER HUB: The part of the synchronizer attached to the shaft.

SYNCHRONIZER SLEEVE: The engaging part of the synchronizer that slides on the outside of the hub.

SYPHON: A means to allow liquid to flow to a lower level over an intermediate elevation.

T

TANG: A lip on the end of a plain bearing used to align the bearing during assembly.

TANDEM: One directly in front of the other and working together.

TAPPET: Transfers the cam position to the push rod. Usually referred to as a lifter.

TAPPET VALLEY: The chamber in the block that contains tappets or lifters.

TDC: Top dead center. The highest a piston can move.

THERMAL EFFICIENCY: The equivalent heat energy of the brake horsepower produced divided by the total heat energy in the fuel used.

THERMOSTATIC VALVE: A valve that is controlled by heat.

THERMODYNAMICS: A study of heat transfer in gases.

TEX: The same as denier but in the metric system.

THROATING: Removing metal from the narrowest part of the valve seat with a high angle stone to raise the seat.

THROW ANGLES: The angle in degrees between crankshaft throws.

THROW-OUT BEARING: The bearing between the clutch fork and the pressure plate release fingers.

THRUST WASHERS: Washers with bearing surfaces that are designed to retain end thrust.

TIMING: An event occurring in relation to the angle of crankshaft rotation.

TOE: (1) The leading edge of a brake shoe. (2) The angle between the center lines of the front tires.

TOPPING: Removing metal from the widest part of the valve seat with a low angle stone to lower the seat.

TORQUE: The twisting force on a shaft in lb-ft.

TORQUE ARM: The length of the turning arm from the center.

TORQUE CAPACITY: The maximum twisting force a clutch or brake can hold before slipping or breaking.

TORQUE CONVERTER: A hydromechanical device to multiply torque through a fluid.

TORQUE MULTIPLICATION FACTOR: The total torque multiplication of a standard transmission.

TORSIONAL MOTION: Motion around the turning center.

TORSIONAL VIBRATION: Back and forth motion around the turning center.

TRACE: A line appearing on the face of an oscilloscope.

TRAILING SHOE: A brake shoe with the anchor at the toe end.

TRANSISTOR: A semiconductor used as a solid-state electrical switch.

TRANSMISSION: A device to multiply torque and to provide reverse gearing.

TREEING: A build up of current carrying crystals through the battery separator.

TURBINE: A finned disc that is made to rotate by the force of a high velocity fluid stream.

TURBINE WHEEL: A wheel-shaped turbine.

U

UMBRELLA: An oil deflector placed near the valve tip to throw oil from the valve stem area.

UNDERCUT: A machined groove below the normal surface.

UNITIZED FRAME: A chassis frame built as an integral part of the body.

UNIVERSAL GAS CONSTANT: A gas pressure times its volume divided by its temperature will always equal the same number for a given gas when absolute values are used. This number is its universal gas constant.

UNIVERSAL JOINT: A coupling that allows power to be transferred through an angle.

UPSET: Bent over.

V

VACUUM: Less than atmospheric pressure, approaching zero pressure.

VALVE: A device that will open or seal an opening.

VALVE CLEARANCE: Looseness designed into the valve train so the valve will positively seat.

VALVE FLOAT: A valve train that cannot keep up with the cam so excess clearance is temporarily allowed to occur.

VALVE GUIDE: A sized hole in the head to hold the valve in position.

VALVE LIFT: The maximum distance a poppet valve will open.

VALVE LOCK: A device that connects the valve spring retainer to the valve stem.

VALVE OVERLAP: The number of crankshaft degrees the exhaust valve opens before the intake valve closes.

VALVE SEAT: The surface of the head on which the valve rests when the port is closed off.

VALVE SPRING SURGE: A natural vibration in a valve spring that may allow a valve to open at the wrong time.

VAPOR: The gaseous form of a liquid.

VAPOR LOCK: Vapors forming on the inlet side of the fuel pump that stops fuel flow.

VAPOR PRESSURE: Pressure produced by the volatile portion of the fluid evaporating.

VARIABLE DISPLACEMENT: A chamber whose effective volume changes as it operates.

VEHICLE: A self-propelled controllable conveyance.

VELOCITY: The distance traveled in a given time.

VENTURI: A smooth flowing restriction in the carburetor that increases air velocity to lower its pressure.

VIBRATION: A very rapid back and forth movement.

VISCOSITY: The thickness or fluid body of a fluid.

VISCOSITY INDEX: A comparison of the change in a fluid's viscosity, as temperature changes, with a standard fluid.

VOLATILITY: The tendency to evaporate.

VOLT: A measurement of electrical pressure.

VOLUMETRIC EFFICIENCY: The actual air consumed by an engine compared to the cubic displacement of the engine.

VULCANIZE: The process of bonding and curing rubber with heat and pressure.

W

WEB: A supporting structure across a cavity.

WELL: A deep chamber.

WHEEL CYLINDER: A device in the brake that converts hydraulic force to mechanical force to apply the brakes.

WHIRL: Rapid rotation of a shaft with slight bend in it.

WILD PING: An occasional knock in an engine caused by deposit ignition. When the deposit is consumed the ping stops.

WINDAGE: Air movement around a spinning object.

WORM GEAR: A gear built with a spiral thread.

Y

YAW: Move or turn sidewise.

YOKE: A link connecting two driving points to produce movement at a center connection.

Z

ZENER: A diode that will allow reverse current flow at the designed voltage.

Air Conditioning p. 516

Index

A

Acceleration, 164
Acceleration, bog, 209
Acceleration pump, 210
    check valve, 196, 210
    overflow return, 212
Acceleration, sag, 209
Acceleration, vehicle, 336
Accumulator, 368
Acid in lubricant, 96
Ackerman layout, 470
Adhesion, 192
Aiming, headlight, 504
Air bleed, 192
Air preheat, 26
Air valve dampening, 209
Alternator, 247
    heat sink, 255
    output, 256, 257
    rectification, 253
    rotor, 247
    stator, 247, 249
    tests, 256

Ambient temperature, 97
Ampere, 225, 230, 235
Amplitude, 168
Antenna trimming, 508
Anti-lock braking, 423
Anti-percolator, 192
Aspect ratio, tire, 441
API classification, 112
Atom, 224
Atomized fuel, 188
Automatic transmission:
   disassembly, 370
   fluid, 372
      Dexron, 372
      type F, 372
   inspection, 369
   problem areas, 371
   removal, 370
Axle shaft:
   bearings, 388
   features, 388
   flange-type, 390
   taper-type, 390

B

Back flush, cooling system, 105
Balance, tire, 444
   dynamic, 446
   static, 445
Ball joint, 454, 456
   compression, 456
   follower, 456
   friction, 456
   pre-loaded, 456
   tension, 456
   weight carrying, 456
Ball-nut piston, 486
Bands, automatic transmission, 357
Battery:
   charging rate, 230
   cycling, 232
   discharge, 226
   fast charge, 232
   gassing, 227
   group, 228
   electrolite, 225
   element, 225, 228
   state of charge, 227, 230
Battery capacity, 231

Battery cell, 228
   chemical reactions, 226
   connectors, 228
   construction, 225
Battery plate, 225, 228
   lead peroxide, 225
   shedding, 228
   sponge lead, 226
   sulphation, 227
Battery rating:
   acceptance rate, 230
   ampere-hour, **231**
   cell voltage, 231
   twenty-hour rate, 231
Battery separator, 225
   bridging, 227
   treeing, 227
Bearing:
   anti-friction, 76
   condition, 150
   crush, 80
   design, 79
   manufacture, 79
   oil bleed holes, 64, 79
   overlay, 79
   overplate, 79
   rear axle, 396
   requirements, 76
   spit hole, 64, 79
   spread, 80
   tang, 80
Bearing, cam journal, 73
Bearing characteristics:
   conformability, 78
   corrosion resistance, 78
   embedability, 78
   performance, 77
   score resistance, 78
Bearing load, 77
Bearing materials, 78
   aluminum, 78
   babbitt, 78
   copper-lead, 78
Bell housing, 92
Block deck, 85
Block, line bore, 156
Blocking ring, synchronizer, 340
Blue printing, engine, 157
Body, 3
Body roll, 449, 453
Boyle's Law, 177
Brake balance, 407
Brake bleeding, 430
Brake caliper, 413

Brake coefficient of friction, 407
Brake, disc, 405, 413
  caliper, 405
  service operations, 427
Brake distributor switch, 419
Brake dive, 456
Brake drum, 404, 411
  service operations, 426
Brake fade, 408
Brake fluid, 415
Brake lining, 410
Brake horsepower, 409
Brake hose, 419
Brake kinetic energy, 405
Brake knock-back, 420
Brake lines, 419
Brake master cylinder, 416
  compensation port, 416
  dual, 418
  primary cup, 416
  secondary cup, 416
  service, 429
  tandem, 418
Brake mean effective pressure, 180
Brake metering valve, 423
Brake, parking, 430
Brake, power:
  atmospheric suspended, 424
  service, 430
  servo action, 425
  vacuum suspended, 424
Brake problems, 426
Brake proportioning valve, 423
Brake routine maintenance, 426
Brake shoe, 411
  heel, 404
  leading, 404
  primary, 404
  secondary, 404
  self adjusting, 404
  servo action, 404
  toe, 404
  trailing, 404
Brake star wheel, 409
Brake system force, 414
Brake torque, 409
Brake warning light, 419
Brake wheel cylinder, 411
  disc, 420
  drum, 420
Breaker plate, 285
Breaker points, 284
Breaker point resistance, 293
Broach, 89

Bushing, suspension, 458
Buzzer, 509
Bypass, cooling system, 100

C

Cam:
  base circle, 171
  lobe, 70
  flank circle, 171
  nose circle, 171
  ramp, 46, 171
Camshaft:
  bearing service, 156
  design features, 73
  condition, 136
  location, 12
  materials, 72
  requirements, 70
Camber:
  negative, 455, 465
  positive, 455, 465
Carburetor:
  acceleration pump, 189
  air valve, 209
  barrel, 21, 189
  choke, 189, 196
  compensation, 192
  float, 191, 200
  fuel level, 189, 198, 205
  main well, 202
  metering rods, 205
  metering signal, 187, 190
  power valve, 206
  secondary barrels, 207
  step-up rods, 205
  velocity valve, 209
  venturi, 191, 203
Carburetor details:
  acceleration circuit, 209
  automatic choke circuit, 212
  float and needle valve, 198
  idle system, 200
  main and compensation system, 202
  power circuit, 203
Carburetor float pontoon, 200
Carburetor icing, 212
Carburetor materials, 198
Carburetor principles:
  acceleration system, 195

Carburetor principles (*Contd*)
    choke circuit, 196
    idle system, 193
    simple main system, 191
    power system, 195
    return check, 197
Carrier, differential, 386, 387
Carrier features, 387
Caster angle, 467
Casting cores, 86, 187
Cathode ray oscilloscope, 276
Charles' law, 177
Charging circuit, voltage drop test, 261
Check valve, ball, 206
Check valve, poppet, 206
Choke bi-metalic spring, 212
Choke cross-over link, 212
Choke heat, 26
Choke stove, 26, 212
Choke well, 26
Circuit board, 501
Circuit breaker, 502
Clutch, automatic transmission:
    free wheeling, 354
    multiple disc, 355
    release spring, 356
Clutch disc, 331
    torsion damper springs, 331
Clutch coefficient of friction, 331
Clutch inertia, 326
Clutch, one way, 358
Clutch plate:
    Belleville spring, 329
    diaphragm spring, 329
    Hook's law, 329
    spring deflection, 329
Clutch pilot bearing, 327
Clutch pressure plate, 327
Clutch shaft, 337, 338
Clutch throw out bearing, 330
Clutch torque capacity, 326
Coefficient of friction, bearing, 108
Collision, 491
Color code, 499
Combustion, 7
    chamber, 7
    end gases, 181
    external, 7
    internal, 7
    quench, 96

Combustion (*Contd*)
    preflame reactions, 180
    smoothness, 32
Combustion, abnormal, 181
    deposit ignition, 183
    knock, 181
    preignition, 183
    rumble, 183
    run-on, 183
    surface ignition, 181, 182
    wild ping, 183
Combustion chamber, 7
    blow down, 169
    gas pressure, 172
    hemispherical, 33
    non-turbulent, 33
    quench area, 33
    squish area, 33
    turbulent, 33
    wedge, 33
Companion flange, 381
Compression ratio, 14
Compression test, 304
Compressor, air conditioning, 515
Condenser capacity, 280
Condenser plates, 280
Conductor, 225
Connecting rod offset, 62
Control arms, 455
Controls, automatic transmission:
    causative controls, 365
    smoothness controls, 368
Controls, power steering, 484
Converter operation, 350
Coolant flow, 99
Coolant type, 97
Cooling:
    air, 97
    high temperature requirement, 96
    liquid, 97
    low temperature requirement, 96
    methods, 10
    normal temperature, 96
Cooling system:
    antifreeze, 97
    air, 11
    automatic transmission, 351
    bypass, 100
    coolant flow, 99
    heat rejection, 104
    liquid, 10
    pump cavitation, 103
    radiator, 101
    radiator core, 101

Cooling system (*Contd*)
  pump scroll, 99
  service, 105
  shroud, 102, 103
  thermostat, 100
Cooperative Research Council, 185
Corona, 281
Cost reduction, 3
Counter electromotive force:
  battery, 232
  starter, 240
Cover service, 157
Crankshaft:
  bearing journal, 49
  condition, 148
  crank pin, 49
  deflection, 67
  design features, 68
  materials, 67
  manufacturing, 67
  requirements, 67
  throw, 49
  torsional dampeners, 67
Critical speed, valve train, 173
Critical speed, propeller shaft, 376
Cut-out, 266
Cycles:
  actual, 178
  California seven-mode, 312
  four stroke, 9
  ideal, 178
  operating, 10
  thermodynamic, 178
  two stroke, 9
Cylinder:
  boring, 155
  burnishing, 153
  hone, 155
  out-of-round, 131
  ridge, 125
  run-out, 131
  skirt, 85
Cylinder leakage test, 304
Cylinder head assembly, 141
Cylinder head service, 137
Cylinder wall service, 147, 155

D

Dashpot, anti-stall, 197
Dead center, 169
Deck, block, 85
Design objective, 1
Design parameter, 2

Detent, 367
Detonation, 181
Detonation reduction, 182
Dew point, 213
Differential, 4, 384
  assembly, 397
  carrier, 386, 387
  pressure, 190, 191
  hypoid, 383
Diode, 247, 250
  forward bias, 252
  reverse bias, 252
  Zener, 253
Displacement, 14
Dowel pins, 92
Draft tube, 119
Drive axle, 386
Drive line, 4
Drive pinion, 383, 386
Dwell, 291
Dynamometer:
  eddy-current, 301
  direct current, 301
  water brake, 301
Ward–Lenard, 300

E

Efficiency, mechanical, 16
Efficiency, thermal, 16
Efficiency, volumetric, 16
Economizer, 195
Electricity, 225
Electrical circuit:
  grounds, 258
  opens, 258
  parallel, 236
  series, 236
  shorts, 257
  voltage drop, 235
Electrical current, 225
  alternating, 250
  direct, 250
  eddy, 239
  sine wave, 250
  three phase, 250
Electrical resistance, 235
Electro-chemical reaction, 225
Electromatic induction, 240
Electromotive force, 225

Electron, 224
Electron drift, 224
EMF, 225
Emission:
    carbon monoxide, 310
    crankcase, 309
    engine operation factors, 311
    evaporative, 312
    exhaust, 310
    hydrocarbons, 310
    nitric oxides, 311
Emission control, 316
    crankcase emissions, 316
    evaporative emissions, 320
Emission reduction:
    control of charge, 313
    control of combustion, 314
    modifying exhaust gases, 314
Engine, 4
    configuration, 11
    lubrication relief valve, 115
    mount, 93
    rotating, 12
    surge, 310
Energy wave, 225
Evaporator, air conditioning, 513, 515
Expansion valve, air conditioning, 516
Exhaust cross-over, 23

F

Fan, 103
Fast idle cam, 189, 197
Fiber optic, 506
Firewall, 4
Flame ionization detector, 316
Floor pan, 4
Footprint, tire, 5
Force:
    acceleration, 164
    centrifugal, 164
Frame, 3
Freeze up control, 516
Frequency, 165, 168
    radio, 287
    television, 287
Fuel:
    antiknock quality, 184
    octane number, 184
    octane rating, 184

Fuel (*Contd*)
    sensitivity, 185
    volatility, 184
Fuel, primary reference, 184
    isooctane, 184
    n-heptane, 184
Fuel pump, 190
Fuel pump eccentric, 74
Fuel ratio requirements, 188
Fusable link, 503
Fuse, 502

G

Gasket binder, 90
Gasket characteristics:
    conformability, 90
    impermeability, 90
    resiliency, 90
    resistancy, 90
Gasket, fire ring, 91
Gasket materials, 90
Gasket requirements, 90
Gauges, 506
Gauge, sender, 507
Gear:
    counter, 337, 338
    idling, 342
    ratio, 337
    helical, 343
Governor, automatic transmission, 366

H

Head disassembly, 124
Headlight, 503
Headlight aiming, 504
Heat load, extra, 104
Heat riser, 23
Heptane, 184
Hole, electrical, 251
Horsepower:
    brake, 15
    friction, 16
    indicated, 15
Hot idle compensation, 202
Housing, differential:
    banjo, 388
    carrier-tube, 388
    Salisbury, 388
    separable carrier, 388
    unitized carrier, 388
Hydrometer, 230
Hypalon insulation, 503

I

Idle air bleed, 193
Idle tube, 193
Ignition:
    available voltage, 279, 281
    ballast, 281
    capacitor discharge, 282
    coil, 275, 277
    required voltage, 272, 273
    voltage available, 275
Ignition advance, 393
Ignition pattern:
    primary, 291
    secondary, 289
Ignition reserve, 275, 291
Ignition service:
    breaker points, 294
    spark plugs, 294
Ignition suppression, 287
Ignition, transistor, 282
Ignition types, 10
Indicated mean effective pressure, 180
Indicator diagram, 180
Indicator lights, 506
Inductance, 265, 278
Insulation, Hypalon, 503
Insulator, 225
Intake manifold runner, 21
    log, 22
    H-pattern, 22
    tuned, 22, 29
Intake porting, 36
Ion, 225, 316
Iso-octane, 184

J

Jet, 190
Jounce, 450

K

Kick down, 367
Knock, combustion, 181
Knuckle, 454

L

Lifter, 45
    condition, 136
    pump-up, 46, 173
    roller, 173
Load, electrical, 237

Lubricant contamination, 96
Lubrication:
    boundary, 108
    cam, 110
    hydrodynamic, 108
    laminar flow, 79
Lubrication system:
    .oil pump, 115
    pressure regulator, 115
    scavenger pump, 114
    sump, 114
    lugging, 152

M

Magnetic field, 237, 239
Magnetism:
    ampere turns, 239
    flux lines, 237
    left hand rule, 237
    lines of force, 237
Magniflux, 133
Main bearing service, 156
Mass, reciprocating, 162, 165
Mass, rotating, 164
Matter, 224
Mean best timing, 314
Mean effective pressure, 180
Metering valve, brake, 423
Microfarad, 280
Micrometer, 131
Mole, 178
Motors, 508
Motor-generator, 301
Manifold:
    closed, 26, 27
    disassembly, 124
    heat, 23
    open, 26, 27
    runners, 21
Mounting lugs, 83
Mounting pads, 83

N

Neutrons, 224
Node, vibration, 93
Non-dispersive infra-red, 315
Nucleus, 224

O

Octane, iso-, 184
Octane number, 184
Octane number requirement, 185
Ohm, 235
Ohm's law, 235
Oil:
    consumption, 120, 121
    contamination, 113, 119
    fire point, 112
    flash point, 112
    pour point, 112
Oil drain periods, 120
Oil filter, 116
Oil gallery, 117
Oil pan, 118
Oil passages, 117
Oil pressure, 114
Oil pump, 115
    automatic transmission, 263
    service, 157
Oil seal design, 75
Oil seal requirements, 75
Oil slinger, 76
Oil viscometer, 110, 111
Oil viscosity, 110
    centipoise, 111
    centistoke, 111
    index, 110
    kinematic, 111
    SAE, 111, 112
    saybolt, 110
Oscilloscope, 179, 276
Oversteer, 471
Oxides of nitrogen, 311

P

Pan, oil, 125
Piston acceleration, 164
Piston assembly, 174
Piston balance, 55
Piston damage:
    corrosion, 143
    heat, 141
    mechanical, 143
Piston disassembly, 125
Piston expansion control, 53
Piston finish, 55

Piston head, 51
    dish, 51
    pop-up, 51
Piston pin:
    fits, 57
    offset, 57
    retaining methods, 57
Piston position, 162
Piston service:
    pins, 147
    ring grooves, 144
    skirt, 144
Piston skirt, 53
    cam drop, 54
    cam ground, 53
    slotted, 53
    slipper, 55
Piston slap, 53, 57
Piston velocity, 163, 164
Piston ventilating, 53
Piston ring:
    blow-by, 58
    gap, 59
    groves, 52
    static pressure, 58
Pitch, 449
Pitman, 481
Planetary gear train:
    annulus gear, 351
    calculating ratios, 352, 355
    carrier, 351
    internal gear, 351
    Ravingeau gear train, 355
    ring gear, 351
    simple gear set, 351
    Simpson gear train, 353
    sun gear, 351
Plastigauge, 133
Points, breaker, 284
Point resistance, 293
Port, 35
    transfer, 194
    siamesed, 35
Pollution, 307, 308
Power, 15
Power steering gear, 483
Preignition, 183
Pre-load, 400
Pressure cap, 102
Pressure depression, 190
Pressure, line, 364
Pressure, modulated, 364
Pressure operated absolute, 517
Pressures, carburetor, 189

Pressure-time curve, 180
Pressure-volume curve, 179, 180
Preventative maintenance, 5
Primary wire, 499
Propeller shaft, 376
   critical speed, 376
   hotchkiss, 376
   torque tube, 376
   whirl, 376
Proportioning valve, brake, 423
Proprietary additives, 114
Protons, 224
PSIA, 177
PSIG, 177
Pushrod, 45
Pushrod condition, 136
Pump, internal-external, 363

Q

Quench area, combustion chamber, 33
Quenching, combustion chamber, 310

R

Radiator, 101
Radiator cap, 102
Radio, 508
Rankin degrees, 177
Receiver drier, 517
Regulator, electrical:
   battery, 263
   current, 265
   field relay, 262
   mechanical voltage, 263
   solid state, 266
   voltage, 261
Regulator, evaporative pressure, 517
Regulator valve, automatic transmission, 364
Relay, 509
Required voltage, 272, 273
Resonator, 29
Reverse current, 266
Reverted gear train, 338
Ring gear, 383
Rocker arm, 43
   ball stud, 45
   condition, 136
   pivot bar, 45
Roll steer, 453
Rotating combustion chamber, 12
Running gear, 5

S

Safety devices, electrical, 501

SAI, 465
Scavenger pump, 114
Scrub radius, 466
Sector, 481
Seals, automatic transmission, 371
Seals, rear axle, 396
Service considerations, 157
Service, wiring, 501
Shaft removal, 126
Shift, automatic transmission, 362
Shift quality, 362
Shifting yoke, 338
Shimmy, 445
Shock absorber, 458
Short finder, 501
Slip angle, 453, 470, 471
Slip joint, 378
Soft plugs, 86
Solenoid, 509
Spark plug reach, 286
Speed control, 510
Spider, 379
Spit hole, bearing, 79
Splines, 378
Springs, chassis, 5
   hanger, 450
   jounce, 450
   rate, 451
   rebound, 450
   shackle, 451
   wind-up, 451
Squish area, combustion chamber, 33
Stabilizer bar, 458
Stack-up, tolerance, 359
Standard transmission, shifting, 338
   direct drive, 342
   first gear, 341
   reverse gear, 342
   second gear, 342
   synchronizer, 339
Star wheel, brake, 409
Starter draw, 243
Starter overrunning clutch, 240
Starter parts:
   armature, 239
   brush, 239
   commutator bars, 239
   end frame, 241
   field frame, 241

Index

Starter solenoid, 240
   hold-in winding, 241
   pull-in winding, 241
Starter stall test, 244
Steady state, 189
Steering angle, 453
Steering axis inclination, 465
Steering column, 492
Stoichiometric mixture, 188, 310
Stopping distance, 408
Stopping energy, 405
Stopping time, 408
Stumble, 195
Sub assemblies, engine, 127
Suction throttling valve, 517
Sump, 114
Surface ignition, 182
Surface tension, 192
Surge, engine, 310
Sway bar, 458
Synchronizer blocking ring, 340
Synchronizer operation, 339
Syphon breaker, 193

T

Tappets, 45
Throttle valve, 366
Throw out bearing, clutch, 330
Thrust bearing, 361
Tie rod, 469
Timing:
   advance, 273, 284
   basic, 284
   mean best, 314
   valve, 169
Timing cover, 92
Tire, 436
   aspect ratio, 441
   cord, 435
      denier, 434
      fiberglass, 435
      nylon, 434
      polyester, 434
      rayon, 434
      tex, 434
Tire load range, 440, 442
Tire manufacturing, 435
Tire plys, 434, 435
   bias, 437

Tire plys (*Contd*)
   radial, 437
Tire repair, 444
Tire rubber, 435
Tire run-out, 444
Tire series, 440
Tire side wall, 435
Tire size, 440, 441
Tire tread, 435, 437
   blades, 439
   sipes, 439
Tire wear indicator, 439
Toe-in, 469
Toe-out, 469
Toe-out on turns, 470
Torque, 15, 299
Torque arm, 300
Torque converter, 349
   cavitation, 349
   coupling point, 350
   impeller, 349
   reactor, 349
   stall speed, 350
   turbine, 349
   torque multiplication factor, 337
Trace, 179
Transmission main shaft, 340
Transistor construction, 266
   base, 267
   collector, 267
   emitter, 267
Transistor operation, 267
Transistor regulation, 268
Tune-up, mechanical condition, 303
Tune-up test sequence, 304
Turbine engine, 12
TVRS cable, 288

U

Understeer, 471
Unloader, 196
Unitized body, 3
Universal gas constant, 178
Universal joint, 377
   ball and trunion, 370, 377, 380
   Bendix-Weiss, 377, 379
   Cardan, 377
   constant velocity, 378
   Hooke, 377

V

Vacuum controls, 509

Valve arrangement, 11
Valve clearance, 45
Valve design, 38
Valve duration, 170
Valve expansion, 516
Valve face, 40, 41
Valve float, 46, 171
Valve flutter, 460
Valve guide, 41, 42
Valve interference angle, 139
Valve keeper, 42
Valve lash, 45, 171
Valve locks, 42
Valve lock condition, 137
Valve materials, 40
Valve motion, 170
Valve oil seals, 43
Valve overlap, 169
Valve necking, 135
Valve ports, 11
Valve problems, 135
   excessive temperature, 135
   high mileage, 136
   high velocity seating, 135
   misaligned valve seats, 135
Valve relieving, 36
Valve retainer condition, 137
Valve seat, 41, 133
   recessing, 125
   throating, 139
   topping, 139
Valve service, 139
Valve spring, 42
Valve spring condition, 137
Valve spring shim, 140
Valve spring surge, 172
Valve, suction throttling, 517
Valve, power steering:
   control valve, 483
   flow control, 488, 489
   pressure relief valve, 489
   spool valve, 484

Valve train critical speed, 173
Valve type:
   elastic, 40
   poppet, 38
   rigid, 40
Vibrations:
   cyclic, 161
   harmonic, 165
   primary, 165
   secondary, 166
   torsional, 162
Viscometer, 110, 111
Viscosity, 108, 110
Viscosity, fuel, 192
Volatility, 183
Voltage, 225, 235
Voltage available, 279, 281
Voltage drop, 261
Voltage required, 272, 273

W

Weight transfer forward, 452
Weight transfer rearward, 452
Windage, 302
Wiring diagram, 498
Wiring requirements, 499
Windage tray, 118

Y

Yaw, 424

Z

Zyglo, 133